Foreign and Commonwealth Office, Whitehall, London SW1

(Photograph, Courtesy of Central Office of Information, London)

Teaching Ethics

Volume One:
Government Ethics

Cambridge Conference
Proceedings
1989 – 1995

Edited by Rosamund M. Thomas
Ph.D., M.Soc.Sc., M.A. (Cantab.)

Centre for Business and Public Sector Ethics,
Cambridge, England

Volume One:
Government Ethics

     LONDON: HMSO

Published by HMSO in association with
Ethics International Press Ltd., Cambridge

First hardback edition published by
Centre for Business and Public Sector Ethics International Press Ltd., 1993

for the

Centre for Business and Public Sector Ethics,
Lilac Place, Champney's Walk, Cambridge CB3 9AW, England.

Revised edition published by HMSO in association with
Ethics International Press Ltd., 1996.

GLOUCESTERSHIRE

CLASS

COUNTY LIBRARY

ISBN 0 11 702053 2

Printed in the United Kingdom for HMSO

Contents

Foreword by Sir Robin Butler GCB, CVO   i

Introduction by Dr Rosamund M. Thomas   iii

Acknowledgements   ix

Part I: **GOVERNMENT ETHICS:**
         GENERAL

Chapter
1   Standards of Conduct in the Foreign and   1
         Commonwealth Office and the Diplomatic
         Service
         Sir Mark Russell, recently Deputy Under Secre-
         tary of State – Chief Clerk, Foreign and Com-
         monwealth Office of the United Kingdom

2   Government Accounting, Standards and   20
         Ethics: The British Experience
         Sir John Bourn KCB, Comptroller and Auditor
         General, the National Audit Office of the
         United Kingdom

3   The Professional Ethic of the Home Civil   48
         Service of the United Kingdom
         Hayden Phillips, CB, recently Deputy
         Secretary, Her Majesty's Treasury

4   Military Ethics   67
         James Stuart-Smith, CB, QC, recently the
         Judge Advocate General of the Forces
         (Army and Royal Air Force)

5   Government, Ethics and the Media: the   101
         United Kingdom Defence, Press and Broad-
         casting Committee and its D Notice System
         Rear Admiral D. M. Pulvertaft, CB, Secretary
         of the D Notice Committee

Part II: **GOVERNMENT ETHICS:**
CONFLICT OF INTEREST

Chapter

6   Conflict of Interest as Part of Political   105
         Ethics: The Canadian Federal Government
         Experience
         Jean-Pierre Kingsley, recently Assistant Deputy
         Registrar General of Canada

7   Public Sector Conflict of Interest at the   121
         Federal Level in Canada and the United States:
         Differences in Understanding and Approach
         Andrew Stark, Assistant Professor, Faculty of
         Management, University of Toronto,
         Canada

8   To Serve with Honor: Report of the United   148
         States' President's Commission on Federal
         Ethics Law Reform (1989)
         Chairman: the Honourable Malcolm R. Wilkey

9   Second Biennial Report to Congress: United   167
         States' Office of Government Ethics,
         (March 1992)

Part III: **GOVERNMENT ETHICS:**
SECRECY, ACCESS TO INFORMATION
AND PRIVACY

Chapter

10   Public Sector Ethics, with Specific Reference   203
         to Secrecy in Government from the Perspec-
         tive of the Experience of India
         Professor R. B. Jain, Head of the Department
         of Political Science, University of Delhi,
         India

Chapter

11   Information Law, Policy and Ethics: The   230
      Canadian Federal Government Experience
      Robert Peter Gillis, Director, Information
      Management Practices, Treasury Board of
      Canada

12   The Official Secrets Acts of the United   256
      Kingdom 1911-1989
      His Honour Judge David H. D. Selwood (Direc-
      tor Army Legal Services (UK) 1990-1992)

13   Confidentiality of Information   261
      Discussion by A. J. MacDonald, Deputy Under
      Secretary, Ministry of Defence, British
      Civil Service

14   Export Controls: The 'Super Gun' Affair   264
      John Meadway, Under Secretary, Department
      of Trade and Industry, British Civil Service

15   Confidentiality and Security in the British   270
      Nuclear Fuels Industry: some Special
      Problems
      Dr W. L. Wilkinson, recently Deputy Chief
      Executive, British Nuclear Fuels plc

16   Confidentiality of Information   274
      Discussion by John Mayne, recently Principal
      Finance and Personnel Officer, Department
      of Health, British Civil Service

17   What are the Proper Limits to which People   277
      in Official Positions should be able to go to
      communicate with each other, Parliament,
      and the Media?
      David E. R. Faulkner, CB, recently Deputy
      Secretary, Home Office, British Civil
      Service

Chapter

18   Privilege, Proceedings and Information given   292
to Parliament
Robert Rogers, a Deputy Principal Clerk, House
of Commons, Westminster

19   Free Speech – Prince of Rights?   303
The Honourable Sir John Laws, Justice of the
High Court, Queen's Bench Division, for-
merly Treasury Devil

20   Free Speech – Prince of Rights?   308
Reply by Sir John Bourn, KCB, Comptroller and
Auditor General, the National Audit Office
of the United Kingdom

Part IV: **GOVERNMENT ETHICS:
CONCEPTS, EDUCATION AND
TRAINING**

Chapter

21   Ethics in Governance: the United Kingdom   315
1979-1990
Andrew Dunsire, Emeritus Professor of Politics,
University of York, England

22   The Concept of Trust   335
Discussion by Andrew Dunsire, Emeritus
Professor of Politics, University of York

23   Ethics for Public Sector Administrators: 339
Education and Training
Professor O. P. Dwivedi, Department of Politi-
cal Studies, University of Guelph, Canada

24   The Teaching of Ethics in American   354
Government Classes
Professor Leicester R. Moise, Department of
Political Science, University of Louisville,
United States

Appendices

Appendix Part I   381

Appendix Part II   469

Appendix Part III   597

Appendix Part IV   651

Addendum   681

Bibliography   693

Index   711

Foreword

by Sir Robin Butler, GCB, CVO,
The Secretary of the Cabinet and
Head of the Home Civil Service
of the United Kingdom

I am pleased, as Secretary of the Cabinet and Head of the United Kingdom Home Civil Service, to provide a foreword for this compilation of Conference papers on the subject of government ethics. Since the 19th century, the British Civil Service has attached considerable importance to maintaining the proprieties of its relationships with Parliament, with Ministers, with the media, and of course with the general public. That sort of continuous self-examination is not unique to the public sector. But it is something that must play a part in the ethos of any organisation whose primary business is not business at all, but service. It is of particular importance in the public sector where the providers of services must constantly strive to maintain standards of behaviour that reflect their duty to the public.

It is for that reason that I particularly welcome the publication of the papers initiated by Dr Rosamund Thomas, which are assembled in this Volume 'Teaching Ethics: Government Ethics'. Some of the papers deal with bodies and situations which I know well, and I am pleased to see contributions from a number of colleagues and ex-colleagues of mine. Others are less familiar, and one of the most interesting aspects of Dr Thomas's work is the international perspective here presented. It is true that I have never believed, in any sphere, that we can crudely lift administrative practices and arrangements from one country and transplant them to another. Different plants grow in different soils. But what we can and should do is to learn from each other and contribute to the development of a broader debate on public sector ethics in the democratic world. Problems arise at different times and demand different responses, depending on the country and system, but there will always be lessons to be learned in the diversity of responses in different places at different times.

For a variety of reasons the role of the public sector in this country, as in others, is being examined, redefined, and challenged with more insistence than ever before. The re-examination has produced benefits both for the public services and for the citizens they serve. In large part, the experience has been a positive one because our Civil Service has a solid bedrock of tried and tested ethical principles. At the same time, governmental systems in the Western world are being studied by countries which have tried and discarded alternatives. Our methods are being criticised and extolled, modified and imitated, all at the same time.

Against that background, I know that I am not alone in thinking that time spent on looking at the ethics of Government is time very well spent. The papers here are snapshots of a fascinating debate in progress and I welcome their publication.

Sir Robin Butler, GCB, CVO
Whitehall, London SW1
2 April 1993

Since I wrote the foreword to the first edition of this Volume three years ago, the debate on Government ethics in the United Kingdom has moved formally into the political and public mainstreams.

In response to public anxiety in the United Kingdom, the Prime Minister set up the Committee on Standards in Public Life in October 1994. Its terms of reference are:

> 'To examine current concerns about standards of conduct of all holders of public office, including arrangements relating to financial and commercial activities, and make recommendations as to any changes in present arrangements which might be required to ensure the highest standards of propriety in public life.'

In its first report, published by the Prime Minister on 11 May 1995, the Committee concentrated on three subjects, namely Members of Parliament, Ministers and civil servants, and non-departmental and NHS bodies. Most of the recommendations have been implemented already. Parliament has established a new Select Committee on Standards and Privileges, and appointed as Parliamentary Commissioner for Standards, Sir Gordon Downey. Guidelines on the acceptance of appointments outside Government by former Ministers of the Crown took effect from the start of the current session of Parliament, last November. Sir Leonard Peach has been appointed the Commissioner for Public Appointments. And, from 1 January 1996, a Civil Service Code was introduced which summarises the constitutional framework within which civil servants work and the values they are expected to hold. These further developments in the United

Kingdom are covered in the *Supplement to Volume One* Government Ethics, published separately.

The Committee's second report on local spending bodies, such as further and higher education bodies, grant maintained schools, training and enterprise councils and local enterprise companies, and registered housing associations, was published in May of this year. The Committee has begun work on its third study, into local government.

I know that colleagues in other countries, like the United States and Canada, have been dealing with similar issues, as we see in this *Volume One: Government Ethics*. Developments in Australia, Spain and Ireland are discussed in the separate *Supplement to Government Ethics*.

Sir Robin Butler, GCB, CVO
Whitehall, London SW1
8 July 1996

Dedication

It was the *De Rerum Natura* of Lucretius that fascinated me most... The Lines at the beginning of the Second Book still remain in my memory, and I often repeat them to myself when alone:

> 'Sed nil dulcius est, bene quam munita tenere
> Edita doctrinâ sapientum templa serena,
> Despicere unde queas alios passimque videre
> Errare atque viam palantis quaerere vitae,
> Certare ingenio, contendere nobilitate,
> Noctes atque dies niti praestante labore,
> Ad summas emergere opes rerumque potiri.'

Translated from Lucretius, ii.7. Munro's Translation (adapted) as:

> 'But sweeter far to dwell remote, aloof
> In some high mansion, built on Wisdom's hill:
> Thence watch the errant crowd go to and fro,
> Matching their wits, striving for precedence,
> Toiling and moiling, hurrying night and day,
> To rise to fortune and possess the world.'

'it has... been (my creed)'.

Richard Burdon Haldane, (1856–1928), British Minister of the Crown, philosopher, lawyer and educational reformer, from his *Autobiography*.

Dr. Rosamund M. Thomas
Director of the Centre for Business and Public Sector Ethics, Cambridge

Introduction

by Dr Rosamund M. Thomas, Director
Centre for Business and Public Sector Ethics, Cambridge

Volume I: *Government Ethics* is the first in a new series of three main Volumes being published under the title TEACHING ETHICS. The term TEACHING ETHICS is one selected as early as 1989 by the Centre for Business and Public Sector Ethics, Cambridge, for this series of books to encapsulate the Centre's innovative approach to the re-emerging subject of ethics, both as an academic field of study and as 'best practice' in modern government, business, and professional institutions internationally.

1. The Cambridge Conferences on Ethics 1989-1995

In the fast-moving, complex and international subject of ethics, no one sector of modern society holds the key to unlock the knowledge: the Centre for Business and Public Sector Ethics, Cambridge, decided in 1989 to unite, through Conferences, leaders in government, business, the professions and academia at home and abroad. Six international Conferences have been held in Cambridge, England between 1989-1995 on aspects of ethics in Government, Business and the Professions. The Centre's Inaugural Conference was held from 13-15 July 1989, with the three days being devoted as follows to: Day 1 – 13 July 1989 – *Government Ethics;* Day 2 – 14 July 1989 – *Business Ethics* (including 'Corporate Responsibility for the Environment'); and Day 3 – 15 July 1989 – *Teaching Ethics* in academic institutions. Again, in 1991 the Centre held three separate one-day Conferences specialising in 'Confidentiality of Information', Secrecy, and Personnel and Physical Security issues. The national press was invited to the third of these one-day Conferences on this topic held in Cambridge in November 1991. Then, on the Centre's Fifth Anniversary in March 1993, a Conference was held from 3-4 March, taking further the subject of 'Corporate Responsibility for the Environment', or *Environmental Ethics.* On 2 March 1995, the Centre's Sixth International Conference took place.

The programmes for the Centre's six Conferences 1989-1995 were taken from the Classification Schema on Ethics, referred to later in this Introduction, to which the Centre has access, and Conference papers were requested – in a balanced ratio – from business, government, professional and academic participants invited to attend each of the Conferences. The Centre announced during preparations for the Inaugural Conference in 1989, that these original Conference papers would be published subsequently under the title TEACHING ETHICS. In arranging the six international Conferences, close collaboration and direction was maintained by the Centre with each of the paper-givers, so that the contents of the Conference programmes would reflect the proper balance between the subjects of (1) Law; (2) Management/Administration; and (3) Morality; and between the countries invited to take part.

2. Volume I: Government Ethics and Supplement

As Director of the Centre for Business and Public Sector Ethics, my first task was to reorganise all the Conference papers delivered in Cambridge, England, under the Centre's auspices between 1989-1995, into those relating primarily to *(1) Government Ethics; (2) Business Ethics; and (3) Environmental Ethics*. This Volume I: *Government Ethics* and the separate *Supplement* represent the finished task in regard to the papers on government. Conference papers given in Cambridge as early as 1989 have been updated, where relevant, by their exponents and divided by me, as Editor, into four parts in this Volume I:

Part I	:	Government Ethics: General
Part II	:	Conflict of Interest
Part III	:	Secrecy, Access to Information, and Privacy
Part IV	:	Concepts, Education and Training

To augment the *original* papers delivered at the Cambridge Conferences between 1989-1995, which appear in the main body of the book Parts I-IV), additional papers have been included by me, as Editor, in four separate Appendices (I-IV) to this Volume I: *Government Ethics*. These additional papers are not original to the Centre, but have been included on the grounds that they enrich the main Parts I-IV of the book.

Unlike the original Conference papers in Parts 1-IV [1] of this Volume I: *Government Ethics*, the materials in the Appendices of this book have been published elsewhere first, but are arranged and reprinted here in the same subject divisions as the original papers:

---

1 Conference papers in Parts I-IV of this Volume I are *original*, having been prepared expressly in conjunction with the Centre for Business and Public Sector Ethics and not having been published elsewhere, with the exceptions of Chapters 6, 7 and 8. The latter Chapters are fundamental to the subject of *Government Ethics* and therefore are located in the main Parts I-IV of this book, rather than in the Appendices with the other materials which have been published previously.

Appendix Part I   :   Government Ethics: General
Appendix Part II :   Conflict of Interest
Appendix Part III :   Secrecy, Access to Information and Privacy
Appendix Part IV :   Concepts, Education and Training

The United Kingdom has tended hitherto to legislate less than North America in the fields of standards of conduct and ethical behaviour and, instead, relies more on *non-statutory,* self-regulatory codes and practices. This difference of approach can be seen in this Volume I: *Government Ethics.* Part I: Government Ethics: General contains mainly United Kingdom papers, while Part II: Conflict of Interest denotes the legislative history and present developments in both the United States and Canada towards the modern phenomenon of conflict of interest. Until now this narrower field of financial conflict of interest has not been the over-riding concern in the United Kingdom, about ethics. In Britain professionals, like Chartered Accountants, and government officials, have been more concerned, as Part III demonstrates, with actual and potential breaches of trust, and leakages of information, and how to deal with them. A new Official Secrets Act of the United Kingdom was enacted in 1989 (replacing the old section 2 of the Official Secrets Act, 1911) but, at the time of first writing this Introduction in April 1993, Britain has no national Freedom of Information Act nor a general right to Privacy enshrined in statute. Given our Constitution and traditional ethos and methods of public administration, some argue that the British Civil Service- remains one of the most highly regarded in the European Community. In any event, law alone cannot ensure that standards of conduct are upheld. Motivation of staff, training and education are also important. Part IV of this Volume I: *Government Ethics* introduces approaches to teaching ethics in academic institutions in Canada and the United States. In the British Civil Service, education and training in ethics is not given in the same way in which it is part of the programme of the United States' Federal Office of Government Ethics. Nor, at the time in 1989 that the Centre's Inaugural Conference papers were requested, was the subject of ethics, on the whole, being taught in United Kingdom universities. Since then, however, the teaching of ethics is being introduced widely in academic institutions throughout the world and sometimes is a compulsory subject. Volume I: *Government Ethics* and the separate *Supplement* are intended to be a basis for teaching courses on ethics both in-house in government, business companies, and the professions, as well as in academic institutions. What this Volume I: *Government Ethics* and the *Supplement* attempt to provide is a clear pathway through the ethics maze. They avoid unnecessary abstract language and seek to substitute an approach, without technical jargon, to the subject. Volume II: *Business*

Ethics and Volume III: *Environmental Ethics* will be published later in 1996 and 1997 to serve the same purposes.

Supplement to Government Ethics

The *Supplement to Government Ethics*, to be published separately as a companion volume to *Government Ethics*, covers the Nolan Committee. The independent committee on 'Standards in Public Life', under the Chairmanship of the Rt. Hon. The Lord Nolan, was set up by the Prime Minister in October 1994 and reported in May 1995.

The Director of the Centre for Business and Public Sector Ethics, Cambridge, Dr Rosamund Thomas, gave detailed written evidence to the Nolan Committee during late 1994 and early 1995, and the Centre's Sixth International Conference held in March 1995 was entitled 'Ethics in Government: Before and After Nolan.' The Centre's evidence to the Nolan Committee, and further developments, are to be published separately in the *Supplement to Government Ethics*.

3. What does 'Ethics' mean?

From the outset the Centre for Business and Public Sector Ethics has maintained that ethics can be taught, and the three major volumes in this series TEACHING ETHICS provide at least some parts of the curriculum for teaching. The Centre's approach, by uniting intellectual ideas with best practice, does not use the term 'Applied Ethics'. Instead, a *unification* of theory and practice is provided, rather than an artificial separation of (1) Academic theories and (2) Applied Ethics.

Ethics is used as a term in this Volume I mainly in relation to the issues or *dilemmas* in complex, modern, international life.

However, Volume I: *Government Ethics* does not cover every modern ethical issue or dilemma. Dilemmas remain at both the macro- and micro-levels in public services and in governments generally. In the United Kingdom, for example, the issue of privatisation and the extent to which it is advisable to reduce the Civil Service is a topic on the Centre's agenda but is given only passing reference in this Volume. Ethical issues like allegations of misleading Parliament and Ministers are touched upon but, in practice, in Britain bodies like the House of Commons Treasury and Civil Service Committee have been investigating the relationship between civil servants and Ministers and related issues. Certain new high profile cases relevant to Government Ethics have arisen recently in the United Kingdom and other countries, like the eventual resignation of David Mellor, a Govern-ment Minister. The issue, *inter alia,* of Government representatives accepting foreign holidays from 'so-called' friends, and others, is still at large. Furthermore, the Conservative Government has been in power in Britain since 1979 which has changed some traditional theories and practices associated with Cabinet Government.

In the West, we have now a 'consumer-led' society: a new set of Citizen's Charters in the United Kingdom and more clearly enunciated citizen's rights to inform the people of their entitlements. At the same time, Government responsibilities are being reduced and the role of the State (having increased during the Twentieth Century) is being cut back. There is an inherent contradiction in this symbiotic development: of more citizen's rights and entitlements and fewer public services and benefits. These and other developments, nationally and internationally, are all leading to fresh ethical dilemmas. In addition, fast moving events in Central and Eastern Europe increase both the complexity and the issues. A systematic approach to their study and a real commitment to ethics is needed.

Some academics have pursued the 'Applied Ethics' route through the maze [2] and others the 'Ethics Code' route. A Code may have a role to play in promoting standards of conduct. But, as this Volume I: *Government Ethics* portrays, the understanding of ethics requires more than the compilation of Codes.

4. The History and Background of the Centre for Business and Public Sector Ethics, Cambridge

The Centre for Business and Public Sector Ethics, Cambridge, was established in 1988, having as the Director myself and thereby making a link between my own research background in the subject of ethics over the past fifteen to twenty years and the work of the Centre of Expertise. As Director of the Centre, I have been able to draw on my earlier book, THE BRITISH PHILOSOPHY OF ADMINISTRATION: A COMPARISON OF BRITISH AND AMERICAN IDEAS 1900-1939, first published by Longman in 1978, and republished in 1996 by HMSO in association with Ethics International Press Limited, Cambridge. THE BRITISH PHILOSOPHY OF ADMINISTRATION contains a founding chapter on 'Ethical Ideals' for the period 1900—1939 and is a useful introduction to the subject of ethics.

In 1977–78 I held a one-year Postdoctoral Research Fellowship at Harvard University, sponsored by the American Association of University

---

2 The front covers on both the Canadian Federal Government publication *Conflict of Interest in Canada, 1992: A Federal, Provincial and Territorial Perspective* (1992) and the *Harvard Business School Bulletin 1992* (1992) depict an ethics maze.

women, to research and develop ethics in government and business, and during that year, I cross-read, adopting a research plan I had devised, in the Harvard Professional Schools of Government, Business and Law. My earlier year at Harvard undertaking Ph.D. research as a Fulbright Scholar (1972-73) was based in the academic Department of Government, Faculty of Arts and Sciences, and that year coincided with the Watergate affair in the United States when I witnessed history in the making by sitting in on the Senate (Congressional) Hearings investigating Watergate, which were held in Washington, D.C. in 1973. In 1978 I returned to the United Kingdom to take up a Lectureship at the London School of Economics and Political Science, while still continuing to develop the modern *comparative* research which now underlies the work of the Centre for Business and Public Sector Ethics, Cambridge.

By 1983 the research into ethics, on which I have been engaged without interruption since the 1970s, had reached proportions where I welcomed the opportunity to research full-time, in order to cover fully and properly this complex, fast-moving, comparative subject. Therefore, in 1983 I took the opportunity then offered to me to move to Cambridge to develop the work generally and to bring forward for particular research those aspects relating to information law and practice. The specific research on information law and practice culminated in my second book ESPIONAGE AND SECRECY: THE OFFICIAL SECRETS ACTS 1911-1989 OF THE UNITED KINGDOM (first published by London, Routledge and being republished in 1996/7 by HMSO in association with Ethics International Press Limited, Cambridge).

From 1977 onwards I deemed it necessary to draw up a comprehensive Classification Schema for classifying ethical issues relevant to the United Kingdom, but also *comparative:* between government, the professions and academia; comparative between countries; and comparative across academic subjects. The Schema embraces the *general* level of Law, Management, organisational behaviour, culture, values, and standards of conduct, as well as *particular* case-studies and ethical issues. This Schema has been developed in a logical, structured, methodical – yet exciting – manner from 1977 to the present.

The Centre for Business and Public Sector Ethics, Cambridge, has access to this Classification Schema on Ethical Issues which gives the Centre a sense of purpose, and the ability to draw up programmes for international Conferences and Seminars, to assist in Curriculum Development on ethics, to direct research projects involving a range of complex ethical issues which unite both theory and practice, and the potential to lead small task forces globally. Indeed, the scope for the use of this knowledge, built up systematically from 1977 to 1996, is unlimited.

5. The Future and the United Kingdom Nolan Committee (1994–)

Now more scholars in the University of Cambridge and elsewhere, as well as leading practitioners, are interested in developing the subject of ethics. Sponsorship of, and joint collaborative work with, the Centre is invited from interested parties to progress further this important work on a global/international basis.

In October 1994, the Nolan Committee on 'Standards in Public Life' was set up, as referred to earlier in this *Introduction*. This United Kingdom development, together with other world developments, are to be published in the separate *Supplement to Government Ethics,* which is intended to be read with this Volume: *Government Ethics.*

Rosamund M. Thomas,
Ph.D., M.Soc.Sc., M.A. (Cantab.),
Lilac Place, Champney's Walk,
Cambridge CB3 9AW
July 1996

Acknowledgements

As Editor of this Volume 1: *Government Ethics* I extend my sincere thanks to all those from the United Kingdom and overseas, named in this book, who prepared and delivered papers at the Cambridge Conferences 1989-1993 of the Centre for Business and Public Sector Ethics. In the case of civil servants I thank them for arranging clearance of their papers for publication in this Volume. Such co-operation includes, in the United Kingdom, the Secretary of the Defence, Press and Broadcasting Committee; the Office of the Judge Advocate General; the Ministry of Defence, and the Ministry of Defence (Directorate of Army Legal Services); the Department of Trade and Industry; the Department of Health; the Home Office; and the Cabinet Office. I should like to thank especially the Head of the Home Civil Service and Secretary of the Cabinet, Sir Robin Butler, GCB, CVO, for writing the *Foreword* to this Volume. Also, I should like to thank Sir Clifford Boulton, KCB, and Clerks of the House of Commons, particularly Robert Rogers, for their co-operation. I thank, too, British Nuclear Fuels Plc for their contribution.

Overseas, I should like to show my appreciation to all those participants in these Cambridge Conferences 1989-1993, especially Jean-Pierre Kingsley and Robert Peter Gillis of the Canadian Federal Government, Ottawa, as well as the many others who attended these Cambridge Conferences and contributed to the deliberations.

The staff of the Centre for Business and Public Sector Ethics, Cambridge, who helped me with these Conferences are acknowledged herewith, together with those persons who undertook the typing and computerisation of the Conference papers for publication, including Chris Poulter, my computer operator; and the services of the University of Cambridge Computer Laboratory and the Squire Law Library, University of Cambridge (Andrea Semark in particular). Dave and Alison Harrison are thanked for preparing the index to this Volume. Staff at Piggott Printers, Cambridge, are thanked for the typesetting and at Profile of Burwell, Cambridgeshire, for the artwork designs, in conjunction with the Centre for Business and Public Sector Ethics Press.

Finally, I should like to thank my extended family for their patience and support during the proof stages, and before, of this Volume 1: *Government Ethics.*

We are grateful to the following in the United Kingdom for permission to reproduce copyright material: Editor and Her Majesty's Stationery Office (HMSO) for the text of (1) the *Civil Service Management Code – Personnel Management* Volume: *4. Conduct and Discipline* (February 1993), which includes 'The Armstrong Memorandum' of 1987; the *Diplomatic Service Regulation (DSR) 13A Official Secrets Acts and the Duty of Confidentiality* (April 1992); (3) the *Diplomatic Service Order 1991* (5 February 1991); (4) extracts from the *Queen's Regulations;* (5) extracts from the House of Commons, Trade and Industry Committee, Second Report, *Exports to Iraq; Project Babylon and Long Range Guns* (HC 86, Session 1991-92); and (6) extracts from the House of Commons, Select Committee on Members' Interests, First Report, *Registration and Declaration of Members' Financial Interests* (HC 326, Session 1991-92 4 March 1992).

The Editor and the Office of the Civil Service Commissioners for the text of *The Role of the Office of the Civil Service Commissioners in Recruitment to the Civil Service: a Note for Visitors* (February 1993). The Editor and the Central Office of Information (COI) for the photograph of the Foreign and Commonwealth Office, London, SW1; the Editor and British Central Government Departments, including the Cabinet Office, for the text of the *Memorandum of Guidance for Officials appearing before Select Committees* (the Osmotherly Rules, March 1988); the Editor and the National Audit Office for the text of the National Audit Office Standards and other Guidelines; the Editor and the Press Complaints Commission for the *Code of Practice* published in full in its Report No. 1 (January-June 1991); the Editor and the Council of Civil Service Unions for extracts from the text of the 1989 FDA Commemorative Lecture given by Peter Hennessy entitled 'The Ethic of the Profession' from the July 1989 edition of *The Bulletin;* the Editor and the Industrial Relations Services, Eclipse Group, 18-20 Highbury Place, London, N5 1QP for the text of the legal case *Lord Chancellor's Department ex parte Nangle*, published in their *Industrial Relations Law Reports* [1991] p. 343. The Editor and Sweet and Maxwell Ltd., publishers, for the text of the article 'Analysis: Judicial Review and Civil Servants: Contracts of Employment Declared to Exist' by Sandra Fredman and Gillian Morris *Public Law* [1991] pp. 485-490; and 'Disclosure of Financial Interests by MP's' by Michael Ryle *Public Law* [1990] pp. 311-322. The Editor and the Police Staff College, Bramshill for reproducing the essay 'A Plea for Applied Ethics' by Neil Richards, first published in *Contemporary Policing: An Examination of Society in the 1980s* ed. by J. R. Thackrall (Sphere Reference Books). The aforementioned authors are also thanked.

We are grateful to the following in countries overseas for permission to reproduce copyright material: the Editor and the Canadian Federal Government for the text of the paper by Georges Tsaï '*Conflict of Interest Issues in Canada: the 1991 Review*', Office of the Assistant Deputy Registrar General of

Canada, Consumer and Corporate Affairs, Canada, reproduced with the permission of the Minister of Supply and Services Canada, 1992 and also the paper by George Tsaï 'Conflict of Interest in Canada, 1992: A Federal, Provincial and Territorial Perspective', reproduced as above. The Editor and the Canadian Federal Government (Privy Council Office) for extracts from *Commission of Inquiry into the Facts of Allegations of Conflict of Interest concerning the Honourable Sinclair M. Stevens, 1987*, Chapters 1, 26 and 27 and the Preface, reproduced with the permission of the Minister of Supply and Services Canada, 1993. The Editor and the Royal Canadian Mounted Police for a photographic image of Canadian Mounted Police (reference number RCMP-GRC/89-798) on the dustjacket of this Volume 1: *Government Ethics*. The Editor and the Institute of Public Administration of Canada for the article by Jean-Pierre Kingsley published in *Canadian Public Administration*, Vol. 29 Winter 1986 pp. 585-94.

The Editor and the Honourable Malcolm R. Wilkey for extracts from the *Report of the United States' President's Commission on Ethics Law Reform* (March 1989); the Editor and the United States (Federal) Office of Government Ethics for extracts from that Office's *Second Biennial Report to Congress* (March 1992) and for additional data supplied by the Director of the Office of Govenment Ethics, Mr Stephen D. Potts and his staff; the American Society for Public Administration for an article by Andrew Stark based on material published in the journal *Public Administration Review* September/October 1992 under the title 'Public Sector Conflict of Interest at the Federal Level in Canada and the United States: Differences in Understanding and Approach'; the Editor and M. E. Sharp, publishers, for the similar essay under the same title published in the book *Ethics and Public Administration* (1993) ed. by Professor H. George Frederickson. The Editor and Little Brown & Co., publishers, Boston, Mass., U.S.A. for the text of Chapter IV 'The Public Interest' by Walter Lippmann in his book *The Public Philosophy* (1955).

The Editor and Robert K. Todd for the text of both his Lecture and Commentary on 'Independent Review of Administrative Decisions on the Merits – Successes and Strains in the Australian Experience' presented at the Eleventh Lawasia Conference in Hong Kong on 18 September 1989. The Editor and the Government of India for the text of the Official Secrets Act, 1923 of India. The Editor and the International Institute of Administrative Sciences for the text of the article by Rosamund M. Thomas entitled 'The Duties and Responsibilities of Civil Servants and Ministers: a Challenge within British Cabinet Government' in the *International Review of Administrative Sciences* (December 1986) pp. 511-538.

VOLUME I   GOVERNMENT ETHICS

PART I

Government Ethics:

General

Standards of Conduct in the Foreign and Commonwealth Office and the Diplomatic Service

by Sir Mark Russell, recently Deputy Under Secretary of State – Chief Clerk, Foreign and Commonwealth Office of the United Kingdom

Introduction

I welcome the opportunity which the Centre for Business and Public Sector Ethics, Cambridge, has kindly given me to participate in this Conference [1] and to put some thoughts to you from the perspective of the Foreign and Commonwealth Office and the Diplomatic Service. We are only a part of the public service in the United Kingdom. But we share fully the principles and ethics which have guided the British public service at home, in the former Empire and overseas since the last century.

When we are talking of 'ethics' some may think of Aristotle and Plato. But much more practically we are thinking about the way people run their lives: the codes (written and unwritten) by which they live and work. Insofar as institutions survive and contribute to national good, it is probably because they develop such codes. Without them, the law of the jungle applies. In that sense ethics are equally important in the public and the private sector. Standards of conduct are needed in business and finance. But I would say that they are vitally important in the public sector, where officials are working to promote 'public good' or 'national interest' rather than their own gain or that of their shareholders; and where they are accountable to Parliament and the public. For the Diplomatic Service there is an added dimension. Overseas we represent not only Her Majesty's Government, but the United Kingdom. We are in a very real sense the shop-window of our country, not by any means the only one, but an important one.

1. History

I have to say at once that the history of the Foreign Office does not always

---

1 The Inaugural Conference of the Centre for Business and Public Sector Ethics held in Cambridge 13 July 1989.

provide evidence of high moral tone. The beginning was promising enough with the appointment of the first permanent English Ambassador to the Vatican in 1479. But during the hundred year pay freeze of the British Diplomatic Service between 1689 and 1789, the going got a lot tougher. After two years as Minister in Vienna, Sir Robert Keith found himself 'unavoidably verging into beggary', which is seldom the best background for incorruptible behaviour. The beggared diplomat of those days in any case could secure some useful pickings: for example, the 1763 Treaty of Paris, which may have brought Britain Canada, also brought the Duchess of Bedford the magnificent Sèvres service now at Woburn.

In the Victorian era it was observed that 'it was only with difficulty that the clerks (at the Foreign Office) were induced to appear by noon', and when they did, they apparently used red tape to haul up baskets of strawberries from street vendors. A fitting use you might say of red tape, but not quite what it was intended for. One John Bidwell, left in charge of the French Section of the Foreign Office for a few hours in 1850, dressed himself up as a Choctaw Indian, with a hearthrug as his only covering, a circle of quill pens round his head and his face dotted with red wafers – when the French Ambassador was suddenly announced! Good clean fun, but hardly the tone we expect from the Foreign Office today.

But Victorian England, with the Northcote-Trevelyan Report of 1854 and the founding of the Indian Civil Service after the Indian Mutiny, also saw the start of the era in which the Civil Service became open to all talents and in which morality, high ethical standards and probity became cardinal features of the British public service. The Foreign Office was perhaps rather slower to follow the 'open to all talents principle' though not, I hasten to add, the features of morality and probity. It was not until the Eden reforms of 1943 that the way was opened for candidates without private means to enter the post-War Foreign Service. Lecturing to new entrants to the new Service through the first reconstruction competition in 1945, Harold Nicholson cited *reliability* as the most valued quality in the diplomat. He also listed as the main components of that reliability truthfulness, precision, loyalty, modesty and a sense of proportion. Many of his phrases bear repetition today: 'There exists a current theory, or suspicion that the successful diplomatist is a man steeped in cunning and adept at the art of deception. This is a false theory. Any study of diplomatic history should convince one that cunning or ingenious diplomacy is always unsuccessful in the end; and that common sense or decent diplomacy, although it may at the moment lose a trick or two, eventually wins the rubber ... The quality of truthfulness is the most important quality which any member of a foreign service can possess. And the reason is obvious. Negotiation between sovereign States not only secures the interchange of immediate mutual advantage, but implies the expectation of further profitable exchanges to come. That expectation can only be founded upon confidence; and, as in a sound business proposition, confidence can only be created and maintained by scrupulous truthfulness'.

But Nicholson set high standards not only in the context of truthfulness and honesty. How many of us could follow his advice (under his strictures concerning the cultivation of modesty) about how to acquire the art of suffering fools gladly. When in charge in Berlin, he tells us: 'I forced myself to invite two bores to luncheon every day ... having completed this little daily duty I felt I could spend my evenings as I liked'.

There is a not altogether pleasant air of effortless superiority behind those remarks aimed at fast stream entrants and very much orientated towards political work, the traditional 'Chancery' or 'Diplomatic' function. Neither the fast stream entrants nor political work are preponderant in the Foreign and Commonwealth Office today. Commercial work, consular work, entry clearance work, secretarial, communications, clerical and security duties, occupy the majority of staff in the Service today. But all staff from the most senior to the most junior may find themselves handling papers of great sensitivity and working in foreign environments where the temptation to breach the rules of conduct and discipline may be strong. A high requirement is placed on the integrity of every member of the Diplomatic Service today. Members of the Foreign and Commonwealth Office are subject to all the temptations to which normal flesh and blood is heir; and occasionally to some which other people do not usually experience. We rightly expect them to resist those temptations, so that the image of the United Kingdom is not sullied and the interests of the United Kingdom are not placed in jeopardy. I am glad to say that generally speaking the standard of behaviour of Foreign and Commonwealth Office staff is very high. We expect high standards and I think we get them.

2. Recruitment

The first step in ensuring high ethical standards comes at the recruitment stage. Our methods of recruitment, along with those of the Home Civil Service, ensure that there is no corruption, nepotism, or similar risk, at that early stage. Nobody can find his or her way into the corridors of power eased by a bribe or by the influence of those in positions of power. It may sound extreme to talk in these terms, but it is worth remembering that at the bottom line all our 'free and fair' competition rules are aimed at keeping out corruption.

Some Civil Service recruitment is done by the Civil Service Commission, [2] some by Departments themselves. But all career recruitment jobs are filled

---

2 Now known as the Recruitment and Assessment Services, see Note 2 to the paper by Mr Hayden Phillips in this Volume, pp. 63-66.

solely on merit, through fair, impartial and open competition. This means that:

i. The qualities, experience and qualifications required by candidates are always decided before recruitment begins;

ii. *All* who are eligible, whatever their sex; marital status or race, must have an opportunity to apply. So vacancies are thoroughly advertised;

iii. All candidates are given equal consideration at every stage of the selection process;

iv. Sifting and selection is always carried out by a Board of at least two (usually more) assessors. And the Chairman, at least, has always been trained for his task.

Our rigorous recruitment procedures are designed to eliminate the risk of favouritism. Once in the Service, however, career progression is less open to public scrutiny. Therefore, we have devised internal procedures to ensure that favouritism or patronage (by the managers or Ministers) does not influence appointments or promotion unduly. We do this through:

i. A strong central Personnel Department which manages every officer's career;

ii. Submission of Personnel Department's recommendations for appointments and promotions in .all grades to selection boards.

iii. Further submission or review of decisions by the various boards by senior members of the Service, including at the top, the Secretary of State.

3. Conduct and Discipline

All those in the Foreign and Commonwealth Office and the Diplomatic Service obviously remain subject to the United Kingdom law. Various statutory provisions can bring the conduct of Crown servants abroad within the jurisdiction of the courts of the United Kingdom. Certain laws, such as the old and the new Official Secrets Acts, [3] are obviously of particular relevance to us. Our own Diplomatic Service Regulations are legally binding in that the Secretary of State's power to make such regulations flows from the Diplomatic Service Order in Council of 1964 which established the Diplomatic Service as a separate Service under the Crown. [4] In addition,

---

3 For a brief explanation of the old section 2 of the Official Secrets Act 1911, and the new Official Secrets Act of 1989 which replaces it, see Note 2 to this paper. See also this paper, footnote 6.

4 A new Diplomatic Service Order in Council came into effect in 1991, see Note 1 to this paper.

whenever we have reason to believe that a member of the Foreign and Commonwealth Office may have committed a criminal offence, the case is reported to the Crown Prosecution Service, who decide whether or not to prosecute. But whether or not they do decide to prosecute, the Foreign and Commonwealth Office may pursue their own disciplinary proceedings. These proceedings and the basic rules which Diplomatic Service officers are expected to follow are set out in Diplomatic Service Regulations (DSRs), a set of which is issued to every officer when he or she joins.

The message of those regulations is spelt out in training. It is made clear on induction courses that DSRs constitute an essential portion of our conditions of service and that they must be read thoroughly and taken properly into account. For the more junior new entrants, each section is explained fully at that early stage; their attention is also drawn to guidance on the Duties and Responsibilities of Civil Servants issued in 1987 by Sir Robert Armstrong, (later Lord), then Head of the Civil Service. The importance of DSRs and of maintaining high standards of behaviour is stressed again at the point when staff go abroad on their first posting – usually some two years after they join the Service.

DSRs try to offer both *general guidance* about the sort of behaviour we expect of members of the Foreign and Commonwealth Office and the Diplomatic Service, and *specific guidance*: for example, in areas such as political activities.

The general principles of conduct listed are as follows:

a. You must give your undivided allegiance to the State on all occasions when the State has a claim on your services;

b. You must not subordinate your duty to your private interests, nor put yourself in a position where your duty and your private interests conflict;

c. You must not use your official position to further your private interests, nor act so as to create a reasonable suspicion that you have done so;

d. You must not engage in heavy gambling or speculation;

e. You must not engage in private financial transaction in connection with any matter on which as a member of the Diplomatic Service you might be suspected of having access to information which could be turned to private gain;

f. You must not engage in any occupation or undertaking which might conflict with the interests of the Diplomatic Service or be inconsistent with your position as a member of that Service;

g. You must not fall short of the professional standards expected of members of the Diplomatic Service or act in a way which might bring discredit on the Service.

Of these, I would emphasise particularly the last. It suggests both our awareness that one cannot define ethical standards too tightly; and the need, all the same, to give a very clear general idea of what we expect.

Subsequent individual regulations go into specific areas in more detail. Our aim is common sense; flexibility (more rigorous rules for more senior officers) and no unnecessary restriction. The following are important examples:

i. *DSR 9: Acceptance of Gifts and Advantages*
The basis is that no official should be (or might be held to be) compromised by acceptance of a gift. The rules we adopt are Whitehall-wide. Officials may keep inexpensive gifts. Otherwise gifts must be surrendered. If an officer wishes to retain one, he may buy it at the United Kingdom retail price less a nominal sum.

ii. *DSR 10: Acceptance of Decorations from other Governments*
Diplomatic Service officers and spouses are not allowed to accept Orders and Decorations from other Governments without The Queen's specific permission.

iii. *DSR 11: Political Activities*
Its general statement reads as follows: 'Diplomatic Service officers are required to discharge loyally the duty assigned to them by the Government-of-the-day of whatever political persuasion. For the Diplomatic Service to service successive Governments of different political complexions, it is essential that Ministers and the public should have confidence that officers' personal views do not cut across the discharge of their official duties'. The Regulation goes on to lay down rules about the extent to which a Diplomatic Service officer may take part in political activities without forfeiting that confidence. These activities will vary according to the seniority of the officer. Junior officers are allowed to engage in a wide range of political activities. Middle ranking officers may engage in some national or local political activities, provided they have obtained permission beforehand, but no candidature for Parliament or the European Assembly. But at these levels permission to undertake such activities will vary with individuals. Staff working in Ministerial private offices or in News Departments as the Foreign Office's spokesman would not normally be granted permission. More senior officers (above First Secretary) are barred from national political activities, but may seek permission to take part in local politics.

iv. *DSR 13: Publications, Contacts with the Media, Speeches and Conferences: Use of Official Information or Experience*

This is obviously an important and difficult area. DSR 13 states: 'The basic principle is that Ministers expound policy in the United Kingdom; that it may often be appropriate for officials to expound it abroad; and that contributions by officials to public debate in the United Kingdom which fall short of exposition of policy should be such as will not prejudice national security, create the possibility of embarrassment to the Government in the conduct of its policies, or bring into question the good name and impartiality of the Diplomatic Service'.

Once again the Regulation aims to be flexible and useable in the real world. It recognises that there may be occasions when members of the Diplomatic Service both at home and abroad can and should make a contribution to public knowledge on the basis of information and experience obtained in the course of their official duties. It is designed to set ground rules so that an individual can judge when he may go ahead on his own authority and when he must seek permission from higher up. It puts the burden on the individual to know the ground rules and to seek permission as necessary. [5]

v. *DSR 14: Private Occupations*
Again this Regulation is flexible and pragmatic. We do not have a blanket rule barring all members of the Diplomatic Service from taking jobs or sitting on Boards. But we do aim to avoid —conflict of interest—. DSR 14 states that a request to take up a private occupation will normally be granted provided, for example, that the appointment does not place the official in conflict with the general principles of DSRs; require the use of official information or experience; carry security risks; encroach on official time; contravene the Vienna Convention on Diplomatic Relations or on Consular Relations, for those serving overseas.

The immediately following DSR 15 states that, if an individual has an interest in a company which is involved in contracts with Government, he or she is required to disclose in full, details of that to the Foreign and Commonwealth Office's Administration. We also expect an individual who becomes bankrupt or insolvent, or who is charged with a criminal offence, to inform the Administration of that fact. That knowledge is important, partly for general reasons of good conduct and discipline; but also because, more than in many areas of government, security considerations loom very large for the Foreign

---

5 A recent amendment to DSR 13 has added the following: 'Members of the Diplomatic Service must not seek to frustrate the policies or decisions of Ministers by the use or disclosure outside the Government of any information to which they have had access by virtue of their position'.

and Commonwealth Office and the Diplomatic Service. Hostile intelligence agencies are only too ready to exploit individual weaknesses and to use knowledge of guilty secrets for blackmail purposes.

vi. *DSR 21: Outside Appointments after Retirement or Resignation*
The demands for probity and irreproachable conduct do not stop with departure from the Service. Our Regulations cover activities after retirement or resignation. Again it is a question of balance. DSR 21 recognises that: 'It is in the public interest that people with experience of public administration should be able to move into business or other bodies'. But it also recognises that: 'It is also no less important whenever a Diplomatic Service officer accepts a particular outside appointment that there should be no cause for any suspicion of impropriety'.

Therefore DSR 21 sets out rules requiring Diplomatic Service senior officers in particular (less stringent rules apply to more junior officers) to seek permission before taking a job within a two-year period after their retirement. In certain circumstances an officer may be refused permission (though that is very rare) or, more likely, asked to wait for a cooling off period between leaving the Service and starting work in some outside appointment.

4. How is such Conduct Accomplished?

Officers entering the Diplomatic Service become quickly aware, if they did not know it already, that they are entering an organisation in which high standards of conduct and probity are the tradition, and the norm. But the content and basic message of DSRs is also conveyed through training courses. People grasp quickly the parameters within which they should conduct themselves. It is also the responsibility of line managers to ensure that in cases of doubt staff receive proper and timely guidance about the interpretation and application of the Regulations. It is for management to ensure that standards are maintained. Both line management and the Administration are well placed to monitor conduct through annual staff reports, accounts, checks and so.

5. Are there Particular Problems?

On the whole I do not think that DSRs generally cause members of the Service serious problems. Most of what they lay down is common sense. But, as I have said earlier, members of the Diplomatic Service, are no more immune than anyone else from temptation. Lapses of conduct such as black marketeering, illicit sales of consumer goods, and so on, do occasionally occur. Where they are found out, they are jumped on. But that sort of issue is comparatively clearcut compared with the conflicts of interest and issues of public morality which on occasion can arise. On that Harold Nicholson was forthright. He said: 'You will find, when you have been working for some time in the Foreign Service, that atrocious conflicts of loyalty are bound to arise. You must therefore make quite clear in your own mind as to which of your many loyalties must be given priority. You will find sometimes that a clash arises between loyalty to your own Government, loyalty to what you believe to be your principles, loyalty to your own staff, loyalty to the Government to which you are accredited. Obviously, and without question and in all circumstances, the loyalty which matters most, the one which must have precedence over all other loyalties, is the loyalty to the Foreign Secretary . . .' He went on to say: 'The man who resigns, because of his principles, at a moment of crisis, does not command my respect. It is the man who carries out his instructions with undeviating loyalty, although he hates and loathes those instructions, and who resigns when all is over, who can claim the title of a good public servant.'

Others have argued in recent years in the United Kingdom in a different sense, namely that there are matters of conscience which may transcend the need for a hundred percent loyalty to the Government or Ministers-of-the-day. Debate on that issue led Sir Robert Armstrong, then Head of the Civil Service, to issue in 1987 his Memorandum on 'The Duties and Responsibilities of Civil Servants in Relation to Ministers'. This Memorandum was sent at the time to all Foreign Office posts and Departments endorsed by the Permanent Under-Secretary at the Foreign and Commonwealth Office, who is also the Head of the Diplomatic Service. Sir Robert, later Lord, Armstrong laid down the message of our own DSRs: namely, that civil servants are servants of the Crown, which for all intents and purposes means the Government-of-the-day; and that the duty of the individual civil servant is first and foremost to the Minister of the Crown who is in charge of the Department in which he or she is serving.[6] He went on to state: 'A civil servant should not be required to do anything unlawful. In the very unlikely event of a civil servant being asked to do something which he or she believes would put him or her in clear breach of the law, the matter should be reported to a senior officer or to the Principal Establishment Officer (of the Department) who should if necessary seek the advice of the legal adviser to the Department. If legal advice confirms that the action would be unlawful, the matter should be reported in writing to the permanent Head of the Department'.

But Sir Robert Armstrong noted that there could be exceptions. On that

---

6 The 'Armstrong Memorandum' is appended as a separate Note to Chapter 3 in this book by Mr Hayden Phillips, pp. 58-62. The duty of members of the Diplomatic Service of confidentiality and loyalty to the Crown is expressed now in a new DSR (DSR 13A) dated April 1992. The latter DSR incorporates specific guidance on the new Official Secrets Act 1989, which replaces the old section 2 of the 1911 Act.

he said: 'There may exceptionally be circumstances in which a civil servant considers that he or she is being asked to act in a manner which appears to him or her to be improper, unethical, or in breach of constitutional conventions, or to involve possible mal-administration, or to be otherwise inconsistent with the standards of conduct prescribed in this Memorandum and in the relevant Civil Service codes and guides. In such an event the matter should be reported to a senior officer and if appropriate to the permanent Head of the Department.'

This last procedure is now explicitly built into the Foreign and Commonwealth Office's own Diplomatic Service Regulations.

All that said, Diplomatic Service staff, particularly abroad, can face complex dilemmas between their responsibility to uphold the national interest, against perfectly presentable sectional interests. They can come under pressure to support causes, commercial, humanitarian or even religious, which it might not be in the national interest, as defined by the Government-of-the-day, to promote. In these circumstances they must use their judgement; and if in doubt ask their superior.

One cannot legislate in advance for every eventuality. What would most of us have done if faced by the war Fiat issued by the Emperor Haile Selassie in 1935? It read as follows:

a. When this order is received, all men and boys able to carry a spear will go to Addis Ababa.

b. Every married man will bring his wife to cook and wash for him.

c. Every unmarried man will bring any unmarried woman he can find to cook and wash for him.

d. Women with babies, the blind, and those too aged and infirm to carry a spear, are excused.

e. Anyone found at home after receiving this order will be killed.

One can see a few conflict of interest possibilities there, not to mention problems with the equal opportunities legislation!

But, seriously, at the end of the day, however many rules and regulations there are, they can provide only part of the answer. It is the feeling of belonging to an organisation which places, and rightly places, enormous emphasis on probity and high moral values, which will cause its members to react instinctively in the right way when faced with temptation or conflicts of interest. It is what Peter Hennessy described in a recent article as the 'genetic code' [7] of example and shared experience handed on from

---

7 Peter Hennessy's 'genetic code' is reproduced in Appendix 1 to this Volume, pp. 409-15.

generation to generation which is the greatest safeguard of incorruptibility in our public life. The image of the smooth and slippery diplomat will always die hard. The following lines, adapted, I think, from G. K. Chesterton, illustrate that:

> 'You cannot hope to bribe or twist,
> thank God, The Queen's diplomatist.
> But seeing what the man will do,
> unbribed, there's not occasion to!'

But the truth is that we in the Diplomatic Service share very much in Peter Hennessy's genetic code. As someone who is about to retire from that Service after thirty-five years [8] I hope I have done my part in passing on that code to my successors.

---

8 Sir Mark Russell retired from the Foreign and Commonwealth Service on 2 September 1989.

NOTE 1

Diplomatic Service Order 1991

At the Court at Buckingham Palace

THE 5th DAY OF FEBRUARY 1991

PRESENT,

THE QUEEN'S MOST EXCELLENT MAJESTY
IN COUNCIL

WHEREAS by the Diplomatic Service Orders 1964 to 1982 (hereinafter referred to as "the principal Order") provision was made relating to the appointment of persons to situations in Her Majesty's Diplomatic Service and for regulating the conditions of service therein:

AND WHEREAS it is expedient to make further and separate provision for Her Majesty's Diplomatic Service in relation to the matter aforesaid:

NOW, THEREFORE, Her Majesty is pleased, by and with the advice of Her Privy Council, to order, and it is hereby ordered as follows:—

Definitions

1. In this Order, except where otherwise expressly provided,

"The Commissioners" means the persons for the time being appointed by Her Majesty in Council to be Her Majesty's Civil Service Commissioners for the purposes of this Order;

"grade" includes post and special appointment, and "special appointment" means an appointment for which the remuneration or pension arrangements are individually determined;

"the Head of the Service" means the Permanent Under Secretary of State and Head of the Diplomatic Service or such person authorised to act on his behalf for the purposes of this Order;

"the Secretary of State" means Her Majesty's Principal Secretary of State for Foreign and Commonwealth Affairs;

"Scheduled grade" means any grade for the time being listed in Schedule 1 to this Order;

"the Service" means Her Majesty's Diplomatic Service.

Selection on Merit

2.—(1) Except as otherwise expressly provided by this Order, no person shall be appointed to a situation in the Service unless

    (*a*) the selection for appointment is made on merit on the basis of fair and open competition, and

(b) the person appointed satisfies such qualifications as may be prescribed pursuant to article 5(2)(b).

(2) Article 2(1)(a) shall not apply to appointment to any situation listed in paragraph 2 of Schedule 2 to this Order, and paragraph 3 of that Schedule shall have effect with respect to appointment to such of the situations so listed as are therein specified.

(3) Notwithstanding article 2(1)(b), a person may be appointed where it appears to the Head of the Service that it is necessary that the appointment be made before appropriate enquiries are completed, and there is no prima facie doubt whether that person satisfies all the prescribed qualifications and is otherwise suitable for appointment.

Appointments to Scheduled Grades

3.—(1) No appointment (except to a situation listed in paragraphs 2(a) to (e) of Schedule 2) shall be made to any situation in a Scheduled grade without the written approval of the Commissioners, whose decision shall be final.

(2) Such approval may be conditional upon the person proposed for appointment satisfying such of the prescribed qualifications as the Commissioners may specify.

(3) The Secretary of State, after consultation with the Commissioners, by direction

(a) may change the title of any grade listed in Schedule 1, and may remove any grade so listed where the requirement for the performance of the duties of that grade has permanently ceased;

(b) shall add to the grades so listed any new grade the duties of which are the same as or are substantially similar to those of one or more of the grades so listed at the date this Order comes into force; and

(c) may add any other grade to the grades so listed.

Functions of the Commissioners and the Secretary of State

4. Without prejudice to any other function of the Commissioners under this Order, the Commissioners

(a) may make rules relating to the selection of persons for appointment to any situation in the Service in a Scheduled grade;

(b) shall advise the Secretary of State concerning such rules made or to be made by him pursuant to article 5(2)(c) as relate to selection on merit on the basis of fair and open competition; and

(c) shall monitor the application of such rules and, if it appears to the Commissioners to be necessary or appropriate, make recommendations to the Secretary of State.

5.—(1) The Secretary of State shall from time to time make regulations for the Service.

(2) The said regulations may in particular provide for all or any of the following matters:

(a) the division of the Service into grades;

(b) the qualifications for appointment of new members to situations in the Service;

(c) the selection of persons for appointment to any situation in the Service except a situation in a Scheduled grade;

(d) the conditions of service of members of the Service, including matters relating to conduct and discipline;

(e) the salaries for the grades of the Service;

(f) the conditions of promotion in the Service;

(g) in conformity with any Act or Acts of Parliament which may be applicable, the conditions of retirement and pension of members of the Service.

(3) The said regulations, in so far as they specify salaries, allowances, travelling allowances, or conditions of retirement and pension, shall not be made without the concurrence of the Treasury.

Mobility requirement for members of the Service

6.—(1) Members of the Service may be employed in any appropriate post of the Service in the United Kingdom or overseas as required in the public interest.

(2) A member of the Service may be seconded for special duties outside that Service or may be transferred to a branch of Her Majesty's Home Civil Service.

Exercise of the Commissioners' powers and duties

7.—(1) Any power or duty of the Commissioners under this Order may be exercised by

(a) the First Civil Service Commissioner or any Commissioner authorised for that purpose by him; or

(b) any officer of the Commissioners authorised for that purpose by the Commissioners.

(2) The Commissioners may from time to time and to such extent as they think fit authorise any person to perform any of their functions relating to the selection and recruitment of persons prior to the exercise by them of their power of approval under article 3(1).

Citation etc

8.—(1) This Order may be cited as the Diplomatic Service Order 1991, and shall come into force on the first day of April 1991.

(2) The principal Order is hereby revoked.

(3) Without prejudice to paragraph (4) below, nothing in the said revocation shall affect any instrument or other thing whatsoever made or done or having effect as if made or done under the principal Order, and every such instrument or thing shall continue in force and so far as it could have been made or done under this Order shall have effect as if made or done under this Order.

(4) The Interpretation Act 1978(a) shall apply for the interpretation of this Order and of any regulations or orders made under this Order as it applies for the interpretation of an Act of Parliament, and as if for the purposes of section 16(1) of that Act this Order were an Act of Parliament and the principal Order were an Act of Parliament thereby repealed.

G. I. de Deney

(a) 1978 c.30.

SCHEDULE 1 Article 3(1)

SCHEDULED GRADES

Diplomatic Service Grade 8
Diplomatic Service Grade 7D
Diplomatic Service Grade 5
Diplomatic Service Grade 5S
Diplomatic Service Grade 4
Diplomatic Service Senior Grade

Legal Grades

Assistant Legal Adviser
Senior Assistant Legal Adviser
Legal Counsellor
Deputy Legal Adviser
Second Legal Adviser
Legal Adviser

Research Grades

Senior Principal Research Officer
Principal Research Officer

SCHEDULE 2   Article 2(2)

EXCEPTIONS TO SELECTION ON MERIT
ON THE BASIS OF FAIR AND OPEN COMPETITION

1. In this Schedule

"appointed on secondment" means appointed to a situation in the Service under an arrangement pursuant to which the person appointed performs duties for and on behalf of the Service and is, for the period of the appointment released from all or some of his obligations under any other employment, service or office (including any employment, service or office under the Crown), or under a partnership agreement;

"public service" means any civil service of the State (other than the Service), and such public authority, or non-governmental body or institution discharging public functions, as the Treasury shall from time to time determine to be a public service for the purposes of this Schedule.

2. The appointments referred to in article 2(2) are appointments to any situation or office

(a) where the holder is appointed directly by the Crown;

(b) as High Commissioner where the appointment does not fall under sub-paragraph (a) above;

(c) where the holder is appointed by a Minister of the Crown for the purpose only of providing advice to any Minister, and under which the period for which the situation is to be held terminates at the end of an Administration;

(d) under which the total period of service (continuous or otherwise) when added to any period of service (continuous or otherwise) in any situation in the Service held immediately before appointment, does not exceed twelve months;

(e) not exceeding five years in length, and for the duration of which the holder is required to work for no more than a total of six months in any period of 12 consecutive months;

(f) under which the total period of service (continuous or otherwise) is between one and five years and the Head of Service or, if the situation is in a Scheduled grade, the Commissioners, are satisfied exceptionally that the proposed appointment is justified for reasons relating to the needs of the Service;

(g) where the Head of the Service or, if the situation is in a Scheduled grade, the Commissioners, are satisfied that it is desirable to make the appointment and the person proposed for appointment is a person who

   (i) would be appointed on secondment, and is qualified effectively to discharge the duties of the situation effectively; or

   (ii) is, or has recently been, employed on functions which have been or are being transferred to the Crown, and whose appointment is justified by the needs of the Service and his proven ability (provided that no such appointment shall be made from a date earlier than the date of transfer); or

   (iii) already holds a situation in a public service, (provided the appointment is justified by the needs of the Service and the proven ability of the person); or

(iv) has reached an appropriate standard in a competition for another situation without securing appointment (provided that it is desirable also to make the appointment by reason of a shortage of qualified candidates);

(*h*) where it appears to the Head of the Service or, if the situation is in a scheduled grade, the Commissioners, that the person proposed for appointment satisfies the standard for entry or promotion into the grade, and that

(i) immediately before appointment the person is the holder of a situation to which he was appointed on secondment, or under which the total period of service (continuous or otherwise) does not exceed five years, and the appointment would be on an exceptional basis; or

(ii) the person has previously held a situation in the Service in any other public service to which appointment was made on merit on the basis of fair and open competition, and is seeking reinstatement or re-employment; or

(iii) the person has previously held a situation in a public service to which appointment was made on merit on the basis of fair and open competition.

(*i*) where the Head of the Service, or if the situation is in a scheduled grade, the Commissioners, are satisfied that the appointment of the person proposed for appointment is justified for exceptional reasons relating to the needs of the Service and the proven distinction of the person proposed for appointment.

3. If in exceptional circumstances it appears appropriate to the Head of the Service, or, in the case of a situation in a Scheduled grade, to the Commissioners, that the terms of an appointment made—

(*a*) by virtue of paragraph 2(*d*) should be varied so that the total period of service (continuous or otherwise) under the appointment, when added to any period of service (continuous or otherwise) in any situation in the Service held immediately before the appointment, would exceed 12 months but be not more than 2 years, or

(*b*) by virtue of paragraph 2(*c*) should be varied so that the total period of work in any consecutive period of 12 months would exceed six months but be not more than nine months,

then any appointment so varied shall be treated as properly made under paragraphs 2(*d*) or 2(*e*), as the case may be.

EXPLANATORY NOTE

(This note is not part of the Order)

This Order revokes and re-enacts with substantial amendments the Diplomatic Service Orders 1964 to 1982.

The principal provisions are:—

(*a*) Article 2 provides that, except as otherwise provided in the Order, selection for appointment to the Service will be on merit on the basis of fair and open competition, and the person appointed must satisfy such qualifications as are prescribed. Schedule 2 lists the situations to which there may be appointment otherwise than on merit on the basis of fair and open competition.

(*b*) Article 3 provides that no one shall be appointed to a grade listed in Schedule 1 (a "Scheduled grade") without the approval of the Civil Service Commissioners. A grade may be added to or removed from the Schedule, and may have its name changed; new grades the duties of which are substantially similar to those listed when the Order comes into force are to be added to the Schedule.

(*c*) Article 4 provides for rules to be made by the Commissioners relating to the selection of persons for appointment to Scheduled grades, the Commissioners have a new duty to advise concerning the rules made by the Secretary of State (under article 5(2)(*c*)) relating to selection on merit on the basis of fair and open competition, and to monitor the application of such rules.

(*d*) Article 5 provides for the Secretary of State to make regulations for the Service, the qualifications for appointment and the conditions of service of persons employed therein, as well as regulations for the selection of persons for appointment to grades other than Scheduled grades.

(*e*) Article 6 provides for members of the Service to be employed in any appropriate post in the United Kingdom or overseas as required in the public interest or to be seconded for special duties outside the Service or transferred to another branch of the Civil Service.

(*f*) Article 7 empowers a Commissioner acting alone to exercise any power or duty of the Commissioners under the Order, and allows the delegation of any such power or duty to any officer of the Commissioners. The Commissioners may also authorise others to carry out selection and recruitment work prior to the exercise by them of their power of approval under article 3(1).

NOTE 2

DSR 13A: OFFICIAL SECRETS ACTS AND THE DUTY OF CONFIDENTIALITY

1   As a member of the Diplomatic Service, you, in common with all other Crown Servants, owe duties of confidentiality and loyalty to the Crown. Constitutionally, the Crown acts on the advice of Ministers who are answerable for their Departments in Parliament. These duties are therefore owed, for all practical purposes, to the Government of the day. The scope of these duties is set out below. If you are in any doubt about them, you should always consult a senior officer.

DUTIES AND OBLIGATIONS

2   Crown Servants and former Crown Servants, including members of the Diplomatic Service, are bound by the provisions of the criminal law which protect certain categories of information. You should, in particular, be aware of, and acquaint yourself with, the provisions of the Official Secrets Acts 1911 – 1989. These Acts apply not only during your employment, but also apply when you have left the Service, either on retirement or for other reasons. The main provisions of the Official Secrets Act 1989, which replaces Section 2 of the 1911 Act and which came into force on 1 March 1990, are summarised in the Annexes to Chapter 1 of DSP Security Volumes 1 and 2. Section 1 of the 1911 Act, which sets out the penalties for spying, remains unchanged.

3   There are also many other Acts of Parliament which create criminal sanctions for the disclosure of certain kinds of official information. Many of these relate to information received or gathered under a statutory framework for official purposes. You should consult Security Department if you have any doubts about specific information which you receive in the course of your duties.

4   You also owe to the Crown, as your employer, a duty of confidentiality. Whether or not the criminal law applies, it is your duty to protect official information which is held in confidence, either because it has been communicated in confidence within the Government, or because it has been received in confidence from others, and no decision has been taken to lift the restriction. This duty of confidentiality continues after you have left Crown employment.

April 1992

2

Government Accounting, Standards and Ethics: The British Experience [1]

by Sir John Bourn KCB, Comptroller and Auditor General, the National Audit Office of the United Kingdom

Introduction

'... when complicated questions and doubtful points arise, the King's assessors are amongst the greatest and most prudent in the realm. For the highest skill at the Exchequer does not lie in calculations, but in judgements of all kinds'.

Richard Fitz Nigel was writing in 1180 about the challenge posed by the management and stewardship of public funds. And he was right to identify the importance of judgement in selecting correct and appropriate behaviour. But judgement implies principles and choice.

What principles should govern the behaviour of those responsible for the expenditure, receipt, recording and audit of public monies?

Three sets of principles or considerations come to mind. [2] First, that such behaviour should be in accordance with the relevant rules; here, for example, the rules laid down in the voluminous pages of Government Accounting. Secondly, that the behaviour should be immediately fitting to the situation in which it is performed; for example, an auditor should take 'reasonable care' in carrying out his or her work. What is to count as 'reasonable' standard of care cannot be deduced from the rules alone; judgement is required. Thirdly, that the behaviour should tend to produce good consequences. Thus behaviour might accord with the rules, be immediately fitting to the situation, and yet produce bad consequences. For example, an official of a certain

---

1 My paper, prepared on this topic at the invitation of the Centre for Business and Public Sector Ethics, was delivered in Cambridge at the Centre's Inaugural Conference on 13 July 1989. This paper has been revised subsequently for publication.

2 I was helped in the preparation of this scheme by C. D. Broad's *Five Types of Ethical Theory* (Routledge 1930) and by his 'Outline of the Relevant General Principles of Ethics' included in his 'War Thoughts in Peace Time', the Earl Grey Lecture at King's College, Newcastle upon Tyne, 1931, reprinted in C. D. Broad *Religion, Philosophy and Psychical Research* (Routledge 1953) pp. 247-281.

rank might have the right to order goods for his Department under the rules; his requisition would be seen by colleagues as the correct way to restock a needy area; yet his personal gain through the purchase of shoddy goods, if he were corrupt, might have disastrous practical and financial consequences for the public authority concerned.

I recognise that this enumeration of separate sets of principles will sound pedantic and artificial. In everyday life we do not usually determine our actions by analysing them in this way; very often we act by 'feel', or by repetition of past actions. But if we are to do justice to the subject of this paper some such disaggregation of considerations will be helpful; and whilst the scheme that I have suggested is not the only one that could be proposed, I think that it should serve for present purposes. [3]

Indeed, this scheme is especially helpful for evaluating British experience. The reason is that, broadly speaking, three periods can be distinguished, and in each of them a different set of considerations were of particular significance, though not, of course, uniquely so.

The first period, which dates from, say, the Exchequer and Audit Act of 1866 to the First World War, I call the period of 'rules', whereby special emphasis was given to the development – indeed proliferation – of rules relating to government accounting and auditing. I illustrate this reliance on 'rules' with several examples from the period.

The second period, from, say, 1914 to the Fulton Report of 1968, I call the period of 'ethos and tradition', where a sense of fitting conduct, not laid down in rules or a code, was of special significance. I illustrate this era from recent work concerning the approaches of two Heads of the Civil Service in that period, Sir Warren Fisher and Lord Bridges.

The third period from, say, 1968 to the present day, I call the period of 'calculation', where special emphasis is laid on setting objectives; determining the 'best' mode of their achievement; and evaluating the economy, efficiency and effectiveness with which they are achieved. I illustrate this concern with 'calculation' by reference to the Government's Financial Management Initiative of 1982; and the 'Next Steps' Initiative of 1988; to HM Treasury's publications on the 'Central Government: Financial Accounting and Reporting Framework' and on 'Policy Evaluation' also of 1988; and to some studies of the National Audit Office under the National Audit Act 1983 which gave specific statutory responsibilities to the Office to supplement its

---

3 For example, another possible scheme is that proposed in R. M. Hare *Moral Thinking* (Oxford University Press 1981) where two levels of moral thinking are proposed; the 'right opinions' or intuitions of morally educated persons, and utilitarian calculation to deal at a higher level with cases where 'right opinions' conflict. And a concern with utilitarianism is evident in David Flint's *The Philosophy and Principles of Auditing* (Macmillan 1988) where he argues that an audit should be designed to produce an economic or social benefit.

traditional certification work by 'value for money' investigations of the implementation of government policy.

Some of these studies illustrate the interdependence of the three sets of principles that I have outlined here. And this interdependence, indeed, is the general conclusion of this paper: namely, that the behaviour of those responsible for the expenditure, receipt, recording and audit of public expenditure cannot have regard to rules alone; or to a sense of what is 'fitting' in all the circumstances; or even to the results of a latter day Benthamite felicific calculus. Instead, those concerned with responsibilities in the area of government accounting must be cognisant of all three sets of principles or considerations; and must then, as in the rest of life, make and stand by their individual judgements.

1. The Period of 'Rules'

I would like to illustrate my thesis first by describing some examples from the period of 'rules'; that is, the second half of the Victorian age and up to the beginning of the Great War. Then, as now, the Comptroller and Auditor General reported to Parliament and his findings were considered by the Committee of Public Accounts. The record of their deliberations shows again and again how the problems of poor financial control within the Civil Service were resolved by the creation of rules. Sometimes they were new and original regulations but, more often than not, they represented a development or sophistication of existing controls.

For instance, during his audit of the Navy Appropriation Account in 1880, the Comptroller and Auditor General found that there were far more seamen and boys in the Navy than Parliament had provided funds for. One explanation given by the Department was that an extra large number of ships were in commission 'because of the uncertainty of foreign affairs in 1878'. The Public Accounts Committee recommended, and the Government accepted that, in future, if the Navy needed to put extra men on the payroll, it should first obtain the consent of Parliament. [4]

Only a year later, the Committee felt it necessary to provide guidance on the payment of ransom money. The Foreign Office had paid the curiously exact sum of £10,787 2s 9d to recover a Colonel Synge who had been kidnapped by brigands in Turkey. The Department wanted him to pay at least part of it back by instalments. As a result of the Committee's enquiry, the Treasury subsequently issued a circular announcing that Her Majesty's Government would no longer 'make pecuniary advances' for private British subjects who were kidnapped. [5]

---

4 *Epitome of the Public Accounts Committee Reports 1857 to 1937* p. 103.

5 Ibid p. 107.

Another area of uncertainty was cleared up in 1891 after the War Office found that they were liable for a bale of cloth which had been rejected and subsequently lost while still on Army premises. The Committee recommended and the Government accepted that, in future, notice should be given to a contractor as soon as his goods had been rejected that he should remove them within a certain time, after which the War Department was no longer responsible. [6]

But perhaps the best example of the way in which rules proliferated to cover increasing numbers of contingencies can be found in the records of 1902. The Committee discovered that a war widow's pension had been increased from that of a major to a lieutenant-colonel. The increase was due to the fact that the deceased major had been promoted to the higher rank twelve months after his death. As a result of this case, the Committee recommended that, with regard to pensions, existing rules needed supplementation and that any posthumous grant of a rank must 'not only have earned, but determined upon independently of his death, and at a time when he was at least supposed to be living'. [7] This recommendation was accepted by the Government.

Thus rules were developed, one into another, or supplemented by further guidance.

2. The Period of 'Ethos and Tradition'

The earlier period of general reliance on the regulatory approach was to be modified in the administrative maelstrom of the First World War. The scale and scope of the conflict, encompassing not only all the great nations of the world, but civilians as well as fighting men, illustrated only too clearly that rules were not enough. The system had been unable to cope and the war had produced a new frame of mind, characterised by initiative, will and force. But initiative and will could not be allowed, it was thought then, to roam freely through government accounting and Civil Service work generally: co-ordination under governing principles was needed to give direction and focus. Such principles were not set down: hence I have chosen to call it the period of 'ethos and tradition'. It is exhibited in the behaviour of Sir Warren Fisher and Lord Bridges, both of whom served as Permanent Secretary to HM Treasury during this period. Their careers are discussed in a book by Richard Chapman [8] on whose account of the case of Sir Christopher Bullock I rely upon to illustrate this concept.

Bullock was born in 1891. He was educated at Rugby and Trinity College,

---

6 Ibid p. 274.

7 Ibid p. 446.

8 Richard A. Chapman *Ethics in the British Civil Service* (Routledge 1988).

Cambridge; was placed in the first division of the first class of the classical tripos in 1913; was offered a Fellowship at Trinity; took first place in the open competition for the Home and Indian Civil Services in 1914; served as an infantry officer in the trenches and was seconded to the Royal Flying Corps, gaining his wings as observer and pilot. In 1930, at the age of 38, he became Permanent Secretary at the Air Ministry. He had worked there since 1919 and was chosen for his outstanding ability, and his capacity for hard work, as well as his understanding of his Department. However, the qualities that had facilitated his progress did not make him universally popular. In particular, his strong personality and commitment to the Ministry seem to have antagonised Sir Warren Fisher, Head of the Civil Service from 1919 to 1939. Nevertheless, Bullock successfully helped to build up the Royal Air Force in the 1920s and to win political support for strengthening it in the 1930s during the rise of Nazi Germany.

Bullock's career came to an end sharply in 1936 when, after a Board of Inquiry appointed by the Prime Minister, he was dismissed. It was found that his conduct had been at variance with the tenor and spirit of a Treasury Circular issued in 1928 which, in effect, served as a Civil Service Code of conduct. But Bullock had not broken any specific rules. Possibly, this is a unique case of a Permanent Secretary being dismissed and serves to illustrate the values of the 1930s and 1940s.

There were several factors involved in the civil servant's case. He had on three occasions over two years sounded Sir Eric Geddes, Chairman of Imperial Airways, over whether he, Bullock, might become a Government Director of Imperial Airways. He was interested also in succeeding Geddes as Chairman or serving under him as Deputy Chairman. This scenario does not have quite the implications it might if this had been an ordinary firm with which the Government had regular contractual relationships. Imperial Airways was a semi-public company; the Air Ministry had a direct shareholding in it and the right to appoint two Directors to its Board. As a result, the relationship between the top managements in the Air Ministry and the company were very close. Furthermore, Bullock had a genuine commitment to, and enthusiasm for, civil aviation. He felt he could make a positive contribution to Imperial Airways in the future and made no secret of this ambition.

There were two other factors involved. One was the negotiations going on at the time between the two parties; the other was the offer Bullock made to Geddes concerning a further honour.

From mid-1934 the Air Ministry was negotiating with Imperial Airways for an Empire Mail Service. There was deadlock over the contract which was broken only by Bullock's suggestion of a sliding scale of payments. This proposal constituted a very hard bargain for the company but Bullock pursued it vigorously, especially, perhaps, as he knew no futher money was available to fund the scheme.

The possibility of an additional honour for Geddes was the other element in the case. Bullock thought it would be an appropriate gesture if Geddes were to receive an honour. After putting aside the idea of an hereditary honour, Geddes eventually agreed to a GCMG, though this was a lower honour than Geddes already had. Against the background of discussions about the Empire Air Mail, however, he began to worry that the honour might be seen as a bribe for accepting the hard-fought contract, and changed his mind about accepting.

All these matters came to a head in June 1936 when papers outlining the situation were sent to the Chancellor, Mr Neville Chamberlain, following discussions between Geddes and Sir Warren Fisher, on the one hand, and Lord Swinton, Secretary of State for Air on the other. Because of the suspicion of a conflict of public and private interests, Bullock was suspended. Fisher played a significant role in deciding the nature of the Board's inquiry and its membership. The Board concluded:

> 'We do not say that he consciously used his official position to further his interests ... but ... the whole course of these proceedings shows ... a lack of that instinct and perception from which is derived that sure guide by which the conduct of a Civil Servant should be regulated'. [9]

There was, then, agreement that no corruption was involved. Bullock himself felt that he had been unjudicious but not improper.

The importance of the case, however, was illustrated by the reaction of Sir Warren Fisher. He wrote that just because Bullock has not committed a criminal offence, 'it is quite unjustifiable to say that [it] ... is any less serious'. [10] In Fisher's view, Bullock's instinctive perception and appreciation had been insufficient in a situation which had gone beyond those envisaged in specific rules and guidelines for financial and other conduct in the Civil Service but where, Fisher believed, a civil servant should have been able to draw upon his knowledge of what behaviour was appropriate in the discharge of his duties and act accordingly.

Bullock campaigned over the years for his reputation to be restored and in 1947 came into contact with Sir Edward (later Lord) Bridges who had taken over as Head of the Civil Service in 1945. He felt that Bullock's dismissal had been harsh but that his conduct had been indiscreet and not that of a Permanent Secretary. Nevertheless, Bridges began an initiative to clear Bullock's name, but without Ministerial support it was doomed to failure. In the final analysis, Bullock was not guilty of breaking any financial rules. His crime was

---

9 Ibid p. 147.
10 Ibid p. 157.

to infringe the ethos of his colleagues and his time; indeed, it is interesting to speculate that a man of Bullock's energy and drive might have fitted better into the Civil Service of the 1980s, with its emphasis on management considerations and clear statements of purposes, than that of the 1930s, with its greater reliance upon unwritten conventions of conduct.

These unwritten conventions have been recognised and expanded upon by Peter Hennessy. In a recent article [11] he wrote of a Civil Service ethic 'transmitted from one generation to the next, as if it were a genetic code, by example and shared experience among a small group of men and women in the senior Civil Service who work in close proximity for 30 years or more'.

Hennessy identifies several elements in the code. He cites first probity; and then a care with evidence and a respect for reason. He also emphasises a willingness to speak the truth to political masters and a readiness to carry out instructions to the contrary if overruled. Closely linked to this attribute is an appreciation of the wider public interest in the sense that the prospects of all of us can be harmed if Central Government policy is made without due care and attention. Finally, he recognises an equity and fairness in the treatment of the public across the country. [12]

To Hennessy these qualities are the essence of the decency and duty he identifies with civil servants. In addition he sees three further crucial objects of concern; the law, Parliament and democracy. These values, which Hennessy describes as 'the ethic of the profession' were certainly felt by many civil servants and those outside this profession to be important governors of their conduct so that, as in the Bullock case, civil servants could be condemned for not following them, even though they were not comprehensively set out and such condemnations, as with Sir Christopher Bullock's, were inevitably seen by many then, as today, to be problematic and in some senses arbitrary and unfair.

3. The Period of 'Calculation'

In many ways the era of 'ethos and tradition' might be interpreted as one regulated by the values of a certain group or even class. But by the mid-1960s some aspects of these values were seen as insufficient for tackling the problems of the modern State. This change was signalled by the Fulton

---

11 Peter Hennessy 'Genetic code of conduct inherited by mandarins' *The Independent* 5 June 1989. See also Appendix 1 in this Volume, pp. 409-15.

12 Josiah Stamp and other civil servants writing in this period of 'Ethos and Tradition' drew attention earlier to these aspects of the wider public interest, such as equity and fairness, see Rosamund M. Thomas *The British Philosophy of Administration: A Comparison of British and American Ideas 1900-1939* (Cambridge, Centre for Business and Public Sector Ethics, 1989), pp. 222-23.

Committee Report of 1968, [13] some of whose members saw a senior Civil Service guided by specific rules and this traditional ethos as no more than gifted amateurs.

But the debate following the Fulton Report did not see the 'ethos and tradition' approach as merely amateurism. Many critics of the Service also characterised it as a disguise for a middle class preference for preserving the *status quo* in the face of possible radical change. They detected a prejudice against business and commerce as representing philistine and second order values; and saw some civil servants accepting with quiet resignation that Britain was doomed to be a fourth rate power, slipping futher behind the living standards first of Germany, then of France and next Italy.

The Fulton Report therefore provided a growing concern for the outcome of actions. It was no longer sufficient to 'do the right thing'. Performance, impact, results and their calculation and measurement; these were to become among the overriding concerns of the British Civil Service and no more so than in the planning and control of its finances.

Improved financial management took a step forward with the Rayner Scrutinies [14] in the early 1980s, followed by MINIS [15] (Management Information Systems for Ministers), which identified resources consumed on specific activities by organisational units. The Financial Management Initiative (FMI) was launched by the Prime Minister (then Mrs Thatcher) in 1982 as part of the Government's reply to the Treasury and Civil Service Committee's report on 'Efficiency and Effectiveness in the Civil Service'. [16]

---

13 *The Civil Service Report of the Committee 1966-68* (Chairman: Lord Fulton), Cmnd. 3638.

14 Sir Derek (later Lord) Rayner was appointed by the then Prime Minister, Mrs Thatcher, in 1979 to establish and run an efficiency unit. Rayner instituted a programme of scrutinies that looked at the implementation of policies by examining in great detail particular aspects of Civil Service work. In the first six years of the programme, three hundred scrutinies and multi-Departmental reviews were carried out – mainly by small teams of bright young officials, reporting to the Efficiency Unit and then to the Prime Minister on the one hand, and to the relevant Secretary of State on the other. By 1986 cumulative savings of £950 million had been made. Examples of scrutinies are: peaking of work in Unemployment Benefit Offices, Forensic Science Service, and winter road maintenance by the Department of Transport.

15 MINIS resulted from a Rayner Scrutiny in the Department of the Environment (DOE) initiated by the then Secretary of State, Mr Michael Heseltine. MINIS was set up in the DOE in 1980 to collect information about the Department's activities and costs which focussed on designated managerial units and which could be used to ensure that resources were allocated according to priorities and targets and performance measures set accordingly. The Treasury and Civil Service Committee report on 'Efficiency and Effectiveness in the Civil Service' in 1982 recommended the introduction of MINIS-type systems in all Government Departments. For an analysis, see Rosamund M. Thomas 'The Politics of Efficiency and Effectiveness in the British Civil Service' *International Review of Administrative Sciences* Vol. L No. 3 Autumn 1984, pp. 239-51.

16 *Efficiency and Effectiveness in the Civil Service: Government Observations on the Third Report from the Treasury and Civil Service Committee Session 1981/82*, HCP 236. Cmnd. 8616.

The Initiative recommended:

i. A clear view of objectives and performance/output measures;

ii. Responsibility for making the best use of resources;

iii. Information, training and expert advice to do this properly.

The initiative was an attempt to alter the way that decisions were made about public expenditure through the creation of line management responsibility. This decentralisation into 'cost centres' made managers more aware of the costs they incurred and the results they achieved.

A natural progression of the Financial Management Initiative was to the Next Steps Initiative launched in February 1988 through the Ibbs report, 'Improving Management in Government: The Next Steps'. [17]

The report proposed the creation of executive agencies, headed by Chief Executives. They were to be responsible for their own targets, budgets and results based on a framework of policy and resources set by the parent Department. The essence of the 'Next Steps' Initiative is that it emphasises a concern for the *delivery* of government services more efficiently and effectively. Several agencies, such as the Social Security Benefits Agency and the Forensic Science Service, have been set up and a firm programme lies ahead. Furthermore, the 'Next Steps' agencies give a structure to the Government's previous financial initiatives and build on the idea of objectives and achievement. [18]

The Citizen's Charter, [19] launched by the Prime Minister, John Major, in July 1991, exemplified the Government's desire to make public services answer better to the wishes of their users and to raise their quality overall. The Charter highlights the importance of quality, choice, standards and value in public sector services. All this emphasis demands a further evolution in the way public services are managed, and in the way public servants think and act.

The Charter encourages the citizen to expect standards, openness, information, choice, non-discrimination and accessibility. Better redress is promised when things go wrong. The paper outlines how the programme is to be implemented in areas as diverse as transport, where one hundred percent of

---

17 Efficiency Unit *Improving Management in Government: The Next Steps*. Report to the Prime Minister. HMSO, 1988.

18 Eighth Report of the Treasury and Civil Service Committee 1987-88: *Civil Service Management Reform: The Next Steps* HC 494. HMSO, 1988. [*Editor:* See also 'Next Steps: The Pace Falters' *[Public Law]* 1990 pp. 322-29 and 'Next Steps – the IPPR Report' *The Bulletin of the Council of Civil Service Unions* Vol. 11 No. 10 November 1991 pp. 147-51.]

19 *The Citizens Charter* (London, HMSO Cm. 1599 July 1991). See also *The Citizens Charter First Report 1992* (London, HMSO Cm. 2101 November 1992).

trains should be cleared each day, to education, where parents are promised regular and independent inspection of all schools with reported results.

The Prime Minister wants the Citizen's Charter to be 'one of the central themes of public life in the 1990s'. The range of mechanisms include more privatisation, wider competition, further contracting-out, more performance-related pay, published performance targets and tougher and more independent inspectorates.

The Government's concern for improving public services is underlined further in the White Paper 'Competing for Quality', [20] published in November 1991. The latter describes how competition is to be expanded in the public sector and represents a key part of the Citizen's Charter programme. The White Paper emphasises the role of public sector managers in buying services on behalf of the public either from the private sector or within the public sector. It gives public sector staff 'the opportunity to compare the services they provide in fair and open competition with the best of the private sector'.

The introduction reads, 'The potential benefits of competition are great, but delivering them requires imagination, realism, commitment and skill on the part of the purchaser. Managers in Central and Local Government, and in the National Health Service, have to account for their performance against financial and quality targets. This responsibility requires them to look for the best deal for the users of their services, whether the task is done in-house or bought in from outside. These managers have come a long way since 1979. The best of public sector management now ranks alongside the best of private sector management. And like all good managers, they welcome the stimulus of competition'. All these changes enable managers to focus on buying the best standards of service achievable within a given budget.

The Efficiency Unit situated in the Management and Personnel Office within the British Civil Service has asked each Department to set out what it has achieved already and what it now plans to do. This data will lead to the setting of specific targets for market testing.

Much of the philosophy behind this guidance is based on the three measures of value for money: economy, efficiency and effectiveness. It is in this area of financial accountability that the National Audit Office has become a leading exponent. The National Audit Office was created by the National Audit Act of 1983, having originally been known as the Exchequer

---

20 HM Treasury *Competing for Quality* (London, HMSO Cm. 1730 November 1991). [*Editor*: This 1991 White Paper *Competing for Quality*, in fact, seeks to capture the benefits of competition by promoting the possible transfer of work through 'contracting out', privatisation, or 'hiving off' of a Central Government function to another public sector organisation. See also *The Bulletin of Council of Civil Service Unions* Vol. 12 No. 1 January 1992.]

and Audit Department. The Act specifically gave the Comptroller and Auditor General the power to conduct studies into the economy, efficiency and effectiveness of Central Government spending. The scope of this value for money audit covers cash flows of about £450 billion and assets of much greater value so the challenges and opportunies are immense. The National Audit Office currently publishes about fifty studies each year but two examples will illustrate clearly the interdependence of the three principles discussed above.

The National Audit Office's study on the quality of service in war pensions and various allowances was published in 1992. [21] The Department of Social Security and the Benefits Agency aim to provide a good, customer-orientated service to two million disabled people and their carers.

But our report found that:

a. A significant number of disabled people and their carers did not know about the allowances to which they were entitled;

b. Only 7% had found out about the schemes from the Department;

c. 23% found it difficult to complete the forms without help;

d. 38% had had to wait more than three months to hear the result of their claim;

e. 10% of war pension claims took more than sixty-six weeks to clear.

By reflecting on the considerations outlined above, three points emerge in an analysis of this study. Rules exist on the eligibility for these pensions and allowances, for example. There was a helpful, friendly and professional ethos governing the standards of the Departmental staff. But these two positive factors had still led to poor consequences: the allowances were not being administered efficiently.

A similar lesson was learnt from the National Audit Office's study into prices paid for spare parts by the Ministry of Defence. [22] The Ministry spend about £2 billion a year on spare parts and hold over 2.7 million different items in their spares inventory. An internal report in 1987 identified potential savings of at least £75 million a year by improving spares procurement. But our 1992 report revealed that the proportion of spares contracts subject to tender was still only 25%, compared with 66% of spares procured by the United States' Department of Defence.

Again in analysing the problem it is clear that sufficient rules existed. The

---

21 National Audit Office *Quality of Service: War Pensions; Mobility Allowance; Attendance Allowance; Invalid Care Allowance* HC. 24. HMSO, 1992.

22 National Audit Office *Ministry of Defence Prices paid for Spare Parts* HC 34. HMSO, 1992.

purpose and objectives of moves towards competitive tendering within Ministry of Defence were clear. And the ethos of the Department was strong: a number of initiatives were underway in the conduct of spares procurement. But ultimately the Ministry of Defence was failing to meet its objectives and therefore giving poor value for money.

Calculation, then, might appear to be the final answer, complementing and suprevening over rules and traditions, systems and people, and placing them all within a clear regard for measurable consequences. But this does not always happen: concepts and their interdependence can dissolve under analysis.

The definitions of economy and efficiency are reasonably clear and therefore tend to be the objects of most attention and measurement. The National Audit Office defines these [23] as follows:

> *Economy* is concerned with minimising the cost of resources acquired or used, having regard to appropriate quality.

> (in short, spending less)

> *Efficiency* is concerned with the relationship between the output of goods, services or other results and the resources used to produce them. How far is maximum output achieved for a given input, or minimum input used for a given output?

> (in short, spending less)

But perhaps effectiveness, the most abstract criterion in evaluating government spending, is the most important measure and the one which should be tested before anything else. The National Audit Office says:

> *Effectiveness* is concerned with the relationship between the intended results and the actual results of projects, programmes or other activities. How successfully do outputs of goods, services or other results achieve policy objectives, operational goals and other intended effects?

> (in short, spending wisely)

This definition of effectiveness raises problems. For instance, in considering a youth training programme we might wish to measure output (places taken up), impact (newly skilled people) and adequacy (whether the increased skilled labour force is adequate to reduce unemployment). These concepts demand different standards and measures of performance. As auditors the Office has to assess how relevant and reliable they are. The National Audit Office currently concentrates on highlighting Departments' relative lack of clear objectives and means of measuring output; they are

---

23 National Audit Office *A Framework for Value for Money Audits*.

obvious omissions and are still prevalent. Ultimately, however, as Departments begin to respond to internal and external pressures to become more
economic and efficient, the Office will have to look closely at its definition
of effectiveness because this evaluation will become the true test. It could be
argued that effectiveness measures should be given priority now. An assessment of a programme's effectiveness might make measures of its economy
and efficiency unnecessary if it appeared that the programme had failed to
have the desired effects. If a gun cannot fire shells that hit the target, it matters little that the materials to make it were purchased economically, and that
the factory that manufactured it was organised efficiently.

There is a final point to make. To ensure an ethical approach in the context of government, rules, conventions and calculation in themselves may be
insufficient: understanding and application depend on proper communication. Accountancy in the public and private sectors produces documents
which are difficult to understand. There exists a specialised vocabulary in
many professions to express the meaning of particular concepts, but if its
link with ordinary language weakens, the possibilities of ethical conduct
within professions is reduced.

Recent developments have acknowledged these dangers. They have been
recognised notably by Professor Geoffrey Whittington,[24] academic adviser
to the Accounting Standards Board (ASB) and by David Tweedie,[25] the
Chairman of the Board.

Whittington recognises that financial reporting is an important vehicle for
communicating information to a broad range of interested parties. But both
he and Tweedie have identified problems of recognition and measurement
which are impairing this process. To give some examples: the financial
activities of a 'subsidiary' may or may not be included in the group accounts,
depending on its definition; the 'repackaging' of acquisition transactions
which allows them to be treated in accounting terms as mergers; and the true
meaning of 'value' and 'profit' (Whittington questions whether there can be
such a thing as a 'bottom line' profit figure).

Whittington and Tweedie both argue that if financial reporting is to be
efficient and cost-effective, it must be given a common language. And the
path is more likely to be through regulation rather than legislation, which
would be too inflexible, or through evolution which requires a collective will
notably absent in this age of creative accounting in a highly competitive
market place. The Accounting Standards Board has been given the authority

---

24 Geoffrey Whittington 'Financial Reporting: Current Problems and Future Direction' (London: Institute of Chartered Accountants in England and Wales) 1990.

25 David Tweedie and Geoffrey Whittington 'Financial Reporting: Current Problems and their
   Implications for Systematic Reform' *Accounting and Business Research*, 1990, Vol. 21, No. 81,
   pp. 87-102.

to set such standards which are intended to be timely, flexible and have enough support to be authoritative. Only by narrowing the variety of reporting practices can we make financial reporting an effective communication tool. This is as true for the public as for the private sector.

Conclusion

Ethical conduct in the handling and accounting and auditing of public money [26] therefore requires an attention to three sets of considerations:

- the relevant rules;
- the appropriate behaviour in the relevant professional setting;
- an attention to the consequences of actions and their evaluation.

No one set of considerations is definitive; no automatic ranking of their constituent parts yields generally accepted answers to problems. Thought and discussion must precede timely action.

---

26 A recent case concerns the legal expenses incurred by Norman Lamont, the Chancellor of the Exchequer, in dealing with adverse publicity relating to a prostitute who rented the Minister's London house, while he and his wife moved to 11 Downing Street. The payment from public funds of certain of these legal expenses was investigated by Sir John Bourn. See Memoranda by the Comptroller and Auditor General to the Committee of Public Accounts (London, HMSO HC 386-i, Session 1992-93, 13 January 1993).

NOTE 1

National Audit Office Auditing Standards

1. Auditing standards for the National Audit Office, approved by the Comptroller and Auditor General, are at Notes 1A and 1B. They are intentionally brief, concentrating on essential audit objectives.

2. The standards have been written as applying to male staff but they are equally applicable to female staff. It is important that the standards are understood and applied by staff at each stage of the audit. In the event of any formal dispute concerning the adequacy of the NAO's performance it can be expected that reference will be made to the degree to which the standards have been observed.

3. Detailed guidance is provided in the Audit Manual on the procedures which the auditor should apply in order to meet the standards. However, it is not practicable to produce a code of rules sufficiently elaborate to cater for all situations which the auditor may encounter. There may be occasions when it is appropriate to depart from the guidance given; this will be a matter of judgement for the auditor acting under delegated authority and with the circumstances of departure properly documented and considered.

APC Standards and Guidelines

4. The Auditing Practices Committee (APC) of the Consultative Committee of Accountancy Bodies has developed auditing standards and guidelines for use by the accountancy profession. The NAO's own standards and the Audit Manual take precedence over all external material. They therefore replace the APC standards. However, it is NAO policy that auditors should comply with APC guidelines where they are relevant to the work of the Office. A list of existing APC guidelines showing their applicability to the NAO is at Note 1C; this follows closely their guideline on the applicability to the public sector of auditing standards and guidelines.

5. APC guidelines should always be read in conjunction with NAO guidance and any cases of doubt about applicability should be referred to AG Division for advice. Staff will be notified of any new guidelines that are issued, indicating their relevance to the work of the NAO. Where necessary, detailed guidance on their application will be issued and incorporated in the Audit Manual.

6. Prior to the promulgation of auditing guidelines the APC issues material

in the form of Exposure Drafts (EDs). The auditor is not necessarily expected to apply the principles underlying these documents but, where the subject is particularly relevant to an audit, should be aware of the material as evidence of current thinking in the profession. Staff will be informed of important developments which are under consideration.

NOTE 1A

National Audit Office Operational Standard

1. Part 1 of this auditing standard applies to all audits carried out by the NAO including examinations of economy, efficiency and effectiveness. Part 2 applies to audits carried out in support of the certification of financial statements or the statutory reports on revenue and store accounts.

Part 1

Planning, controlling and recording

2. The auditor should adequately plan, control and record his work.

Audit evidence

3. The auditor should obtain relevant and reliable audit evidence sufficient to enable him to draw reasonable conclusions therefrom.

Part 2

Accounting systems

4. The auditor should ascertain the audited body's system of recording and processing transactions and assess its adequacy as a basis for the preparation of financial statements.

Internal controls

5. If the auditor wishes to place reliance on any internal controls, he should ascertain and evaluate those controls and perform compliance tests on their operation.

Review of financial statements

6. The auditor should carry out such a review of the financial statements as is sufficient, in conjunction with the conclusions drawn from the audit evidence obtained, to give him a reasonable basis for his opinion on the financial statements.

NOTE 1B

National Audit Office Reporting Standard

1. Part 1 of this auditing standard applies to all audits carried out in support of the certification of financial statements and, under sections 2 and 4 of the Exchequer and Audit Departments Act 1921, in support of the annual reports made on revenue and store accounts. Part 2 applies to all examinations of economy, efficiency and effectiveness.

Part 1 : Certification Audit
Certification of Financial Statements

2. On conclusion of the audit of financial statements the auditor shall provide a certificate giving his opinion on those statements. The certificate should state expressly:

a. the financial statements to which it relates;

b. that the audit has been carried out in accordance with relevant statutory or other authority and with the auditing standards of the National Audit Office; and

c. the auditor's opinion as to whether, in the case of:

 i. *Appropriation accounts*, the sums expended have been applied for the purposes authorised by Parliament and the account properly presents the expenditure and receipts of the relevant Vote for the year to which the certificate relates;

 ii. *Other cash accounts*, the account properly presents the receipts and payments of the audited body for the relevant financial period;

 iii. *Accounts prepared on an accruals basis*, the financial statements give a true and fair view of the state of affairs as at the end of the relevant financial period and of the financial results and, where applicable, the source and application of funds for the period then ended.

3. The auditor should qualify his certificate where he is unable to satisfy himself in all material respects that:

 i. no limitations have been placed on the scope and conduct of the audit;

 ii. the sums expended have been applied to the purposes intended and the expenditure conforms to the authority which governs it;

iii. the financial statements properly present the transactions of the body concerned or give a true and fair view of its state of affairs;

iv. all accounting and reporting requirements, statutory or otherwise, have been observed.

The auditor should briefly summarise the reasons for the qualification in his audit certificate and, where relevant and practicable, quantify the effect on the financial statements. The auditor should supplement his certificate by a separate report on the circumstances and reasons for qualification.

Revenue Accounts

4. The auditor shall present an annual report on the results of his examination of revenue accounts to the House of Commons.

Stock and Store Accounts

5. The auditor shall present an annual report on the results of his examination of stock and store accounts to the House of Commons.

Part 2: Examinations of Economy, Efficiency and Effectiveness

6. The auditor shall at his discretion present to the House of Commons reports which result from examinations he carries out under sections 6 and 7 of the National Audit Act 1983 into the economy, efficiency and effectiveness with which bodies to which those sections apply have used their resources in discharging their functions.

7. The auditor shall at his discretion present to the appropriate authority reports which result from examination he carries out into the economy, efficiency and effectiveness with which other audited bodies have used their resources in discharging their functions.

NOTE 1C

Applicability of APC Auditing Guidelines to the NAO

	All NAO work	All Certification Audits	Certification Audits of Accruals Accounts only	Audits Undertaken by Agreement only	Notes
Planning, controlling and recording		X			1
Accounting systems		X			
Audit evidence		X			1
Internal control		X			
Review of financial statements		X			
Bank reports for audit purposes		X			
Amount derived from preceding financial statements		X			
Auditing in a computer environment		X			
Reliance on internal audit		X			
Financial information issued with audited financial statements		X			
Events after the balance sheet date			X		
Representations by management			X		
Attendance at stocktaking			X		2
The auditor's consideration in respect of going concern			X		
Auditors' reports and SSAP 16 'Current Cost Accounting'			X		3
Engagement letters				X	4
Quality Control	X				
Reliance on other specialists		X			
Reports to management		X			1
Group financial statements-reliance on the work of other auditors		X			
Applicability to the public sector of Auditing Standards and Guidelines		X			
The impact of regulations on public sector audits		X			

In addition Industry Guidelines are applicable to NAO certification audits of bodies of similar or equivalent status. Those to which the guidelines are most likely to have relevance are 'Charities' and 'Housing Associations'.

Notes
(1) Also generally applicable to examination of economy, efficiency and effectiveness
(2) Also applies to stores audits under s. 4 of the Exchequer and Audit Act of 1921
(3) Where the Treasury have directed SSAP 16 to be applied
(4) Including, where appropriate, reference to examination of economy, efficiency and effectiveness.

NOTE 2

Professional and Ethical Standards for National Audit Office Staff

NAO Professional and Ethical Standards

Attaining satisfactory standards for the conduct of the audit is in practice closely linked with, and even dependent upon, the personal conduct and approach of NAO staff. The professional and ethical standards at Note 4 therefore set out the principles applying to personal professional conduct within the Office. They are amplified in the Administration Manual and may be supplemented by official notices dealing with specific issues in greater detail.

The NAO's professional and ethical standards take precedence over formal codes of conduct or ethical guidelines issued by professional bodies of which staff may be members. In the event of any conflict or potential conflict staff should consult D/PA.

General

1. All members of staff have a duty to behave in accordance with these standards and to aim for the highest standards of proficiency in their work.

Propriety and Integrity

2. Staff should maintain a high standard of professional and personal conduct in performing their work and in their relationships with staff of audited bodies.

Independence

3. Staff should be independent of the audited body and maintain an independent attitude.

Objectivity

4. Staff should carry out their work impartially and objectively.

Constructiveness

5. Staff should adopt a constructive and positive approach to their work and relationships.

STANDARDS: NATIONAL AUDIT OFFICE

Proficiency

6. Staff are expected to maintain and develop their professional competence and expertise.

Reasonable Care

7. Staff should take all reasonable care in planning and carrying out their audit work, in gathering and evaluating evidence, and in reporting findings.

Confidentiality

8. Staff must respect the confidentiality of information obtained in the course of their work.

Economy, Efficiency and Effectiveness of Operations

9. Staff should seek to improve the economy, efficiency and effectiveness with which the Office uses its own resources in carrying out its work.

NOTE 2A

Explanatory Notes:
Professional and Ethical Standards

Propriety and Integrity

1. In order to sustain the confidence of Parliament, audited bodies and all others with whom NAO staff come into contact in their work, the Office and its staff must be above suspicion and beyond reproach. Improper conduct reflects badly on the integrity of the individual and the quality of his work. In addition, it casts doubts on the reliability and competence of the Office as a whole. Staff should therefore maintain the highest standards of personal conduct.

2. The Office is concerned only with any private and personal activities of its staff which impinge on the performance of their duties or risk bringing discredit to the Office. Particular difficulties may arise in the following areas, either in the course of undertaking official duties or outside the Office:

    a. staff should not make financial commitments beyond their means and should avoid heavy gambling or speculation which may put them in financial difficulties;

    b. staff should take care not to discriminate on the grounds of sex, marital status, race or religion;

    c. staff should adopt high standards of personal discipline, appearance and punctuality, and avoid any forms of over-indulgence or addiction which may adversely affect their conduct or impair the performance of their official duties;

    d. sexual harassment at work will not be tolerated and staff should be careful in their personal relationships not to cause embarrassment for the Office, the audited body or their colleagues;

    e. staff should be reticent in matters of public and political controversy so that their audit impartiality is not in doubt (see also paragraph 4);

    f. staff should seek to prevent any conflicts arising between their duties and private interests, and must not make use of their official position to further their private interests.

Independence

3. Independence implies impartiality and freedom from, or rejection of, improper influences in conducting the work and in reaching judgements and conclusions. Staff must not only be independent but be seen to be so. The basic independence of the C&AG is guaranteed by statute and in a number of other ways. Staff must ensure that this independence is reinforced by their own independence of approach and attitude.

4. Independence may be impaired in the following ways:

   a. restriction of access to sources of information;

   b. actions or persuasion designed to influence the conduct or scope of an audit or the content of an audit report;

   c. previous employment by the body being audited or association with its executive decisions;

   d. relationships which might cause the auditor to fail to carry out his duties to the full;

   e. preconceived ideas towards individuals or audited bodies or their projects or programmes;

   f. financial interest by the auditor, or close associate, in the audited body or its activities.

Objectivity

5. The validity of the Office's work and the confidence placed in it by audited bodies and Parliament depend on the objectivity that is brought to bear. Audit opinions and reports should be influenced only by the evidence obtained and assembled in accordance with the NAO's auditing standards. This standard requires that staff should not pre-judge an issue.

Constructiveness

6. This standard encourages staff to adopt a constructive rather than a negative attitude in their audit work. Although the NAO should avoid compromising their independence through acting as a consultant, staff should aim to reach helpful conclusions. Criticism is not an end in itself; its purpose is to point the way to necessary improvement.

Proficiency

7. Staff are expected to demonstrate their professionalism by carrying out their duties with competence and expertise. They should seek the highest levels of proficiency and have a professional responsibility for self-improvement and development.

Reasonable care

8. This standard requires professional performance of a quality appropriate to the audit being undertaken. Exercising reasonable care means evaluating the nature and risks involved in the audit and taking appropriate steps to obtain and evaluate necessary evidence and to prepare audit reports. Reasonable care is necessary in planning and in carrying out the work.

Confidentiality

9. Information obtained from an audited body must not be disclosed to a third party without the body's knowledge and consent. In particular, all members of staff must have regard to their obligations under the Official Secrets Acts 1911, 1920 and 1989. No official information may be disclosed to an unauthorised person unless official permission has been received or the information has already been made public officially.

10. All staff should exercise care and discretion in discussing work in which they are engaged or other audits being undertaken in the Office with colleagues and more importantly with friends, relatives and others outside the Office. The appropriate security and confidentiality of all information, in whatever form it may be held, must be ensured at all times.

Economy, Efficiency and Effectiveness of Operations

11. Just as the Office advocates and attempts to stimulate economy, efficiency and effectiveness in audited bodies this standard sets the staff an obligation to pursue the same ends in their own work.

NOTE 3

Aims and Objectives of 'Value for Money' (VFM) Audit

The NAO's work is predominantly concerned with accountability to Parliament. The primary objective of its VFM audits is therefore to provide Parliament with independent information, assurance and advice about economy, efficiency and effectiveness in major fields of revenue, expenditure and the management of resources. Limitations on NAO's own resources are involved and where value for money is judged to be most at risk.

NAO's approach involves examination and evaluation of arrangements within bodies receiving public funds for securing *good value for money*, as well as exposing serious waste, extravagance or other examples of *bad value for money*. The C&AG may also bring to notice the consequences of legislation or policy decisions which he believes Parliament would wish to know about or to review.

A secondary objective of VFM audit is to identify ways of improving value for money and to encourage and assist audited bodies to take the necessary action to improve systems and controls.

Responsibility for securing good value for money rests with management. The auditor's role is to provide an independent examination of how far and how well that responsibility is discharged. He does not intervene in the formation of policy, although considering and acting upon his findings may involve policy changes. He must be careful not to erode or undermine management's responsibility, nor to use hindsight to second-guess their decisions.

The constraints on NAO examinations involving the merits of policy objectives affect particularly, though not exclusively, examinations of effectiveness. In this area the NAO's VFM audits are concerned with such matters as:

- the accuracy, reliability and completeness of the information provided for determining policy objectives and deciding on the means of pursuing them;

- the clarity with which policy objectives have been defined and communicated to those responsible for implementing them;

- the appropriateness and consistency of lower level operational aims, targets and priorities;

- the management information systems and other arrangements for monitoring results and achievement against objectives, and taking any necessary action;

- directly assessing the economy, efficiency and effectiveness with which objectives are being pursued and achieved, including unforeseen side effects;

- significant evidence about economy, efficiency and effectiveness in the implementation of policy objectives which would not otherwise be reported to Parliament.

In some areas of activity and for some subjects the definition and limits of 'policy objectives' can be difficult to establish. And the boundaries between the merits of policy objectives (off limits area) and the implementation of policy (legitimate area) can be vague and uncertain. Particular care and judgement are therefore needed in pursuing relevant investigations.

The difficulties involved are not confined to matters of definition. In many areas assessing effectiveness involves the use of a range of performance measures and indicators – of either intermediate outputs or ultimate impacts and results. Considerable judgement is required in determining the relevance and reliability of available yardsticks of this kind.

For example, the direct output of a health service training programme may reasonably be judged by resulting increases in the number of well-qualified nurses, and this may be regarded as one measure of performance or effectiveness. But ultimate effectiveness depends on the impact of the additional nurses on patient treatment and on health, and this will almost certainly be much more difficult to measure or assess. A housing programme may be judged in simple terms by the number of houses provided, but a more fundamental test is the extent of social and other benefits which in practice flow from the relief of overcrowding (offset perhaps by adverse effects in terms of the break up of communities, etc). In many cases effectiveness can be judged only by taking into account a variety of different measures and assessments; there is rarely a single, simple yardstick. And often the auditor is dealing with 'soft' measurements rather than clear, quantified data.

NOTE 3A

Types of 'Value for Money' (VFM) Investigations

The NAO divides its VFM investigations into four broad categories:

- Selective investigations of signs of possible serious waste, extravagance, inefficiency, ineffectiveness or weaknesses in control. These are largely confined to examining whether criticism is justified, examining causes and considering action taken or needed to introduce improvements. For example, finding out why a weapon system overran its costs or time-table or failed to meet the requirements for which it was designed and developed; and how far the lessons learnt are being applied to future projects.

- Major broad-based investigations of a whole audited body or of impor-tant activities, projects or programmes. These are designed to lead to reports giving assurance in major areas where arrangements are found to be satisfactory and no criticism is justified, as well as drawing atten-tion to material weaknesses in control or achievement and their conse-quences. For example, investigating the implementation and results of the various schemes which form the Government's programme for reducing or alleviating unemployment.

- Major reviews of standard managerial operations which tend to follow common patterns or procedures or established good practice. Areas for such 'good housekeeping' examinations include stores procurement, maintenance of buildings or equipment, operation of transport fleets, etc.

- Smaller-scale investigations. These are not normally expected to lead to a report to Parliament but are directed towards producing useful improvements in value for money, strengthening systems and fostering cost-consciousness. They are often undertaken as project work for pro-fessional trainees.

The general aim is to secure a 'mixed diet' of investigations and reports, covering each of the first three categories above. Some examinations pursue matters within a single Department which 'across the board' studies follow up a particular subject or function – for example investment appraisal on control of building maintenance – across a number of different Departments.

3

The Professional Ethic of the
Home Civil Service of the United Kingdom

*by Hayden Phillips, CB, recently Deputy Secretary,
Her Majesty's Treasury* [1]

Introduction

Almost any generalisations about the corporate ethos of an organisation as large and diverse as the modern United Kingdom Civil Service are apt to be misleading. The non-industrial Civil Service has declined steadily over the past fifteen years from its 1976 peak of 748,000, but still numbers some 498,735 [2] people. Their range of duties is enormous. It runs from working closely with Ministers on the formulation of Central Government policies to the control of passengers and goods at ports and airports, and from the frontiers of scientific research in Government establishments to the delivery of social security benefits at local offices. The great majority of civil servants are employed on general administrative duties (which nevertheless may call for a high degree of expertise within specialised areas), but significant numbers exercise specific professional skills as lawyers, economists, statisticians, accountants, engineers and so on. The span of grading, ability, educational qualifications, and pay is similarly extremely wide; and, contrary to the popular stereotype of the Whitehall man or woman, less than fifteen per cent of non-industrial civil servants work in inner London. Of the latter, only a very small proportion are recognisably engaged in the kind of activities embodied in the popular imagination by 'Yes Minister'. [3]

1. The Ethos of the Home Civil Service

Although this paper seeks to identify some of the general duties and attitudes common to all civil servants, it is important to recognise that these general attitudes are underpinned for particular groups by a network of more immediate loyalties, notably to professional standards, to individual

---

1 This paper was delivered at the Second Conference of the Centre for Business and Public Sector Ethics, Cambridge, held on 14 May 1991, and the paper has been revised subsequently. Mr Hayden Phillips is now Permanent Secretary, Department of National Heritage.

2 October 1991 Civil Service Staff in post.

3 'Yes Minister' refers to the popular British television programme by that name.

Departments, to the local management unit, and to client interests. It is from the balance between these demands on the commitment of the Civil Service, constantly changing over time, that the wider ethos of the Service is formed, as much as from any formal code of conduct. It would be easy, if unconvincing, to give the impression that all civil servants are motivated solely by a desire to serve the Government-of-the-day, and through them, the nation as a whole. Undoubtedly considerations of this kind play a large part in the day-to-day work of most public servants. They provide individuals at all levels with the satisfaction of knowing that they are making a contribution to the important activity of good government. Civil servants, like all other employees in both the private and the public sectors, are driven also by more personal imperatives in the shape of acceptable levels of remuneration, career prospects, job satisfaction, and security of employment. The art of successful personnel management is to integrate the aspirations of the individual with the needs of the organisation in a mutually supportive way. This operation is not, of course, peculiar to the management of the public service, but, unlike similar activities in commerce and industry, it is one which has to be carried out to the satisfaction of a wider constituency, including Parliament, the media, a multitude of pressure groups, and the public at large.

2. The Civil Service in the Constitution

All civil servants are employed by the Crown at pleasure, though a recent Divisional Court ruling in the case of *Nangle* [4] has overturned an earlier decision that civil servants had no legally enforceable contracts of employment. The regulation of the Civil Service is provided for by the prerogative Civil Service Order in Council 1991, which delegates to the Minister for the Civil Service (the Prime Minister) and the Treasury powers to issue instructions in specified areas of management. These powers in turn are currently exercised by the publication of the detailed and prescriptive Civil Service Pay and Conditions of Service Code, and by the issue of supplementary instructions from time to time. With one or two exceptions, other Departments of State have no independent powers of management, though the trend in recent years has been to set the central instructions in terms wide enough to give Departments a good deal of scope for adapting their management arrangements to the needs of their own businesses. This trend is being taken a stage further by the preparation of a new series of Codes on individual subjects which will keep the mandatory requirements to a minimum, and replace much of the existing

---

4 *R. v. Lord Chancellor's Department ex parte Nangle* [1991] I.R.L.R. 343. See also *Public Law* [1991] p. 485. Both these references are reproduced in Appendix Part I of this Volume, pp. 416-34 and 435-40 respectively.

prescriptive material with discretionary authority and guidance.

It follows that all civil servants owe the Crown and, by extension, Ministers of the Crown, an undivided duty of loyalty, including a life long duty of confidentiality. A full description of the duties and obligations of civil servants to Ministers was given by the former Head of the Home Civil Service in a note published in December 1987 (The 'Armstrong Memorandum'), a copy of which is attached as Note 1 to this paper; and it is from those duties and obligations that the core Code provisions governing the conduct of civil servants (covering such matters as involvement of political activities and the use of official information) stem. Civil servants have a right, and indeed an obligation, to advise the Government-of-the-day impartially, but, except in the minority of cases where officials are given direct statutory authority (notably in the legislation governing the two Revenue Departments), they have no power to act other than on the directions of Ministers. As a matter of constitutional convention, most civil servants have no identity distinct from that of their Ministers. Similarly, Ministers in charge of Departments are assumed to be directly responsible for all the actions of their civil servants, and are answerable for them to Parliament.

In practice, the growth and decentralisation of the functions of Central Government since the Second World War have led to some dilution of the pure doctrine of Ministerial responsibility. Most of the executive powers of Departmental Ministers are necessarily delegated to officials, many of them remote both geographically and in terms of the chain of command from the centre of the Department. No-one in modern conditions seriously expects a Minister to resign because of the misdemeanour or misjudgements of one of his civil servants unless, of course, the official concerned was acting on the Minister's direct instructions, the Minister had failed to take proper corrective action when he became aware of the difficulty, or the problem was due to organisational weaknesses of which the Minister was or should have been aware. Conversely, the individual civil servant may be operating under powers delegated in terms which leave him a wide margin for the exercise of his own judgement. In such circumstances, the constitutional identity with the Minister can apply only in a general way; the individual's actions must be consistent with the known overall approach of the Government, but he cannot be expected to know how the Minister would wish him to act in every conceivable situation. Therefore, he will seek to make his own decisions in a rational and defensible way within the framework set by the Minister. In doing so, he will be aware that he may well have a direct legal liability for his actions, even where these are in strict accordance with Ministerial directions. [5]

---

5 On 17 December 1992 the Civil Service (Management Functions) Act 1992 (Ch. 61) received the Royal Assent. This Act empowers a Minister of the Crown to delegate further management functions invested in him, or transferred to him by another Minister, to the Home Civil

(Footnote 5 →)

This interplay between constitutional convention and the exigencies of practical administration mean that the character of public administration is determined both by the policy of the Government-of-the-day, and by the cumulative effect of the decisions taken on a day-to-day basis by thousands of individual civil servants. The aim of effective machinery of government arrangements is to ensure that the two strands converge to the maximum possible extent.

3. Parliament and Propriety

At the heart of the relationship between Parliament and the Executive is Parliament's control over the granting of Supply – in other words, its control over the flow of money from the Consolidated Fund to individual Departments for expenditure on defined purposes. Observing the principles of propriety, in the sense of not spending public money for any purpose other than that for which it was voted by Parliament, runs very deep in the culture of the Civil Service, and these principles are coming to condition the thinking of individuals as well as of Departments as budgetary and management responsibilities are delegated to lower levels of management. The responsibility for ensuring that money is spent economically, efficiently, and for the right purpose rests not on the Departmental Minister, but on the Accounting Officer, usually the Permanent Secretary, but sometimes another senior official, including the Chief Executive in the case of one of the 'Next Steps' agencies discussed later in this paper. The Accounting Officer is directly answerable to Parliament for his stewardship of the Department's finances, and there are formal mechanisms for recording any disagreement between him and his Minister about the propriety of particular kinds of expenditure. It is interesting to note that this is one of the very few occasions when a civil servant has the right, and indeed the obligation, to expose publicly the advice which he has given to a Minister.

The budgetary relationship between Parliament and individual Departments does not have, of course, a direct impact on those engaged in the delivery of services of various kinds at lower levels, but they will operate also within a hierarchy of budget and performance targets deriving ultimately from the Departmental Vote. Performance against targets is linked closely to the assessment and remuneration of the individual, and in this way each civil servant has an incentive to carry out his job as efficiently as possible in support of the Department's functions as determined by Parliament. To the extent that improving efficiency increasingly implies exploiting the initiative and creative flair of the individual, there is a continuing need to be aware of

→ Service. In other words, the Act extends by delegated legislation management powers and functions to civil servants. The new Code for British civil servants, dated February 1993, on the subject of 'Conduct and Discipline' which gives greater discretionary authority and guidance to Central Government Departments, is reprinted in Appendix Part 1 of this Volume, pp. 441-67.

the position of the dividing line between propriety and uninhibited enthusiasm for enhanced performance. This balancing is another of the basic skills of the public service manager, and can at different times be the source of much frustration as well as of considerable job satisfaction.

4. Information

The collection and analysis of information is classically one of the most important tasks of almost all civil servants. To the extent that the democratic process in a modern State is heavily dependent on the informed consent of the electorate, there is clearly a strong argument for saying that it is in the public interest that official information should be made available as freely as possible, subject only to the overriding needs of national security. But it is also in the public interest that Governments of all complexions should feel able to work with the permanent administrators in conditions of complete confidence, that there should not be premature disclosure of proposals which have yet to be fully thought through, and that those providing information to Government, whether compulsorily or voluntarily, should not be inhibited by the prospect of its publication against their will. Although Whitehall often is represented as uniquely secretive, these considerations of confidentiality are really no more than the kind which would motivate the safeguarding of information by any sizeable commercial undertaking. In both the public and the private sector, the objective has to be to present policy proposals in an orderly fashion with sufficient supporting information to enable the intended audience (whether the public at large, Parliament, or shareholders) to come to a properly considered view, without necessarily revealing the processes in Cabinet or board room which went into their formulation. In this context, the timing of the release of information is often as important as its substance.

Civil servants are bound therefore by the provisions of the criminal law which protects certain categories of information. That law includes the Official Secrets Act 1989,[6] but also numerous other legislative provisions – many relating to information received or gathered under a statutory framework for official purposes, where the purpose of the legislation is to protect organisations outside the Government who are required to provide information for official use. In addition it is regarded as a potentially serious disciplinary offence under the Civil Service Pay and Conditions of Service Code for a civil servant to disclose information which it is his duty to hold in confidence – for any of the reasons given in the above paragraph, for example. Such disclosures are corrosive of the trust that must exist between Ministers and civil servants if the British system of government is to function effectively. None of these constraints need imply any undue secrecy

---

6 See Rosamund M. Thomas *Espionage and Secrecy: The Official Secrets Acts 1911-1989 of the United Kingdom* (Routledge, 1991).

over the whole field of government information; they merely recognise the reality that official information is a valuable and sensitive resource, and that the control of its release is properly a matter for political rather than bureaucratic decision.

5. The Legal Dimension

Although all public and private sector businesses operate within a legal framework, the civil servant is probably more conscious of the fact than his counterparts in the private sector. The reason is that, at the risk of oversimplifying, the private sector is free to do anything not prohibited by law, while the public service can act only in accordance with specific legal authority. Nearly all civil servants operate within a field circumscribed by statute, regulations, and case law and much of the image of the Civil Service as an excessively cautious 'paper and precedent dominated' organisation stems from its consciousness of its vulnerability to legal challenge, with potentially embarrassing political consequences, if it went too far in emulating the methods of the entrepreneurial risk takers who are sometimes held up as role models. Even when very extensive statutory powers are provided – as, for example, in some areas of tax enforcement – the balance between what is legally permissible and politically and publicly acceptable has to be weighted carefully. Any real or supposed erosion of the rights and freedoms of the individual has to be proportionate to the overall benefit to the public interest which it is designed to achieve.

In addition to legal challenge based on an alleged exceeding of legal powers, there has been an increasing tendency in recent years for aggrieved citizens to resort to the public law remedy of judicial review, under which the Courts can be invited to set aside official decisions on the grounds that, although they were not unlawful in themselves, they were arrived at without proper consideration of all the facts, or in some other unreasonable or unjust way. The development of this supervisory jurisdiction does not transfer the substance of decision making from the government machine to the Courts, but this development does imply the need for a wider public interest test of what is acceptable than simple adherence to the letter of the law and the wishes of the Government. In that sense, it links in with the growing interest within Government in the development of the concept of customer service.

6. Customer Service

Civil servants who deal directly with members of the public have always had a sense, if not necessarily a very clearly formulated one, of the importance of maintaining acceptable levels of service. Put at its most basic, the task of carrying out the various duties laid upon the Service is facilitated greatly if those at the receiving end can be persuaded to co-operate, and that calls for courtesy and patience on the part of officials, clear and simple explanations of what is required, and a prompt dealing with enquiries. Quality of service has tended, however, to be regarded in the past as the icing on the administrative cake, and something that inevitably suffered when the Service was subject to a tightening of resource constraints, or an expansion of its functions. Now it is accepted that quality of service should have a much higher profile in determining the conduct of official business; a theme which has been endorsed repeatedly by the present Prime Minister, [7] from his time as Chief Secretary. [8]

Customer service is an area where the Civil Service can learn much from the private sector. The criteria are, however, not identical. When a bank or an airline improves its reception areas, it does so in order to maintain or increase its share of the market, and normally will expect the enhancement to be self-financing. The cost of improvements in the quality of most Government services has to be born ultimately by the taxpayer, and their extent has to be determined by what is socially and politically acceptable, rather than by straightforward balance sheet considerations. Squalid public offices are no longer acceptable either to staff or to clients conditioned to regard the standard of services provided elsewhere in a consumer society as the norm. It is not difficult to defend the provision of clean, bright public offices as a minimum, but where the line is drawn beyond that is a matter of judgement. Some changes can be shown to yield direct benefits in terms of improved efficiency; others may have less tangible benefits in terms of enhanced customer satisfaction. The most important point is, perhaps, that both civil servants and the public should know what is expected for particular services. Particularly with the development of 'Next Steps' agencies, the publication of clear service targets is becoming much more common, and that in turn provides a closer integration between the needs of the organisation, the personal aspirations of civil servants, and the public interest.

The 'Next Steps' Initiative was launched by Mrs Thatcher in 1988, as Sir John Bourn noted in his preceding paper, following a report by the Efficiency Unit on ways of further improving management in Government. The Unit had argued that a major factor inhibiting the further development of the programme of improved efficiency stemming from the earlier Financial Management Initiative [9] was the confusion of the policy and executive

---

7 Mr John Major.

8 The result of this emphasis was the publication of the White Paper 'The Citizen's Charter' (London, HMSO Cm. 1599) in July 1991. See also The Citizens Charter First Report: 1992 (London, HMSO Cm. 2101 November 1992).

9 The 'Next Steps' Initiative was a development following the earlier Financial Management Initiatives launched under Mrs Thatcher's Administrations. For further details of the FMI Initiatives, see, for example, Rosamund M. Thomas, 'The Politics of Efficiency and Effectiveness in the British Civil Service' International Review of Administrative Sciences Vol. L No. 3 1984 pp. 239-51.

roles of Government. It maintained that the system put too much emphasis on the roles of civil servants as policy advisers, while Ministers, instead of concentrating on the main strategic issues, were wasting far too much of their energies on day-to-day management matters. The solution proposed by the Unit, and subsequently accepted by the Government, was that to the maximum extent practicable the purely executive functions of Government should be made the business of Executive Agencies within the Civil Service, each headed by a Chief Executive and working within a policy and resources framework set by the responsible Minister in consultation with the Treasury and the Cabinet Office. Once the framework had been set, the Chief Executive would have a wide degree of freedom to decide how best to deliver the results required by it, without routine intervention by the Minister or the senior management of the Department concerned. By giving civil servants at all levels in the agencies a greater sense of ownership, coupled with wider personal responsibility and scope for initiative, it was hoped to release managerial energies. [10]

In the succeeding three years, some fifty agencies have been set up, and many more are in the pipeline. [11] They range in size from the National Weights and Measures Laboratory, employing fifty people, to the Social Security Benefits Agency, with 68,000 staff. By the end of 1992, some 285,000 civil servants will be working either in Next Steps Agencies or (mainly in the case of the two Revenue Departments) in Departments organised into accountable executive units on Next Steps lines. By the turn of the century, probably over three-quarters of the non-industrial Civil Service will be organised in this way. Furthermore, the agencies have exended responsibility for recruitment of staff under two new Orders in Council of 1991, (see Note 2 to this paper).

All members of the agencies, whether they are career civil servants or recruited from outside on period contracts, are subject to basic Civil Service terms and conditions of employment, and are expected to abide by the recognised Code of conduct. Subject to these conditions, the early indications are that already there has been a shift in attitude on the part of those employed in agencies from looking inwards to their Departments and upwards to their Minister to looking outwards towards the customer interests, whether these are within or outside Government. The clarification of objectives and the setting of firm, published targets is already changing the outlook of many civil servants. One of the most interesting questions for

---

10 See also 'Improving Efficiency in Government: the Next Steps' (HMSO 1987); 'Making the Most of Next Steps: the Management of Ministers' Departments and their Executive Agencies' (HMSO 1991); and J. F. Garner 'Next Steps: The Pace Falters' *Public Law* 1990 pp. 322-37.

11 By 1992 the latest tally of Executive Agencies amounts to seventy-two, with a further twenty-seven candidates announced.

the immediate future is how that change in outlook will affect the role of those civil servants who remain in the core Departments working on policy issues, and on how they, their Minister, and their agencies will conduct their relationships with Parliament.

7. The European Community

Finally, it may be relevant to say something about how the United Kingdom's membership of the European Community has affected the role of the Civil Service.

The duty of civil servants engaged in negotiation with the Community institutions and the other Member States is clear – it is to advance the interests of the United Kingdom in accordance with Government policy. Whatever their personal inclinations may be, British civil servants have no official loyalty to the Community over and above their undivided commitment to the Crown. At the same time, it has to be recognised that the legal and bureaucratic framework within which United Kingdom administrators have to work is set increasingly by the Community. That change means that the European dimension inevitably has conditioned the ways of thought and action of the United Kingdom Civil Service (just as the attitudes of other Member States and the European Community institutions have been changed by contact with the Anglo-Saxon approach). This development is less a matter of dramatic constitutional change than a steady and evolutionary process of adaptation to working within a wider European context.

The loyalties of British civil servants transferred or seconded to the Community institutions is more complex. In theory, their allegiance shifts on their appointment from the United Kingdom to the employing institution. In practice, it is tacitly accepted that all Community civil servants will retain a leaning towards their parent country, if only because of their previous training. Member States have no qualms about maintaining links with their own nationals in the institutions, from the Commissioners themselves downwards, and this link forms one more element in the complex balancing of loyalties which has to be performed by all national and international civil servants.

Conclusion

This paper has tried to identify for discussion some of the pressures which go to shape the attitudes and conduct of United Kingdom civil servants. Although the Civil Service Pay and Conditions of Service Code sets out the basic standards of conduct required, civil servants are motivated less by a set of hard-and-fast rules than by a complex network of legal, political, and practical considerations which determine what is acceptable in particular situations at particular times. The selection, training, and development of civil servants is designed to produce managers who are simultaneously capable of exercising individual initiative and flair, and of acquiring an intuitive grasp of the wider context within which they have to operate. The modern trend towards setting out much more clearly and publicly the targets to be achieved by each management unit is an indispensable part of improving the efficiency of the Service; but it cannot be substituted for the corporate ethos of integrity and public service which has developed over the last one hundred and fifty years. [12] It will be apparent from this paper that this ethos is an organic and adaptable one; its essential principles do not change, but the ethos accommodates itself to movements in the society of which the Civil Service is a part. In a country without a written constitution, it is particularly important that the Government and the electorate should continue to have faith in the underlying good sense of its public service. That faith has always been the British tradition, and it is one which we must continue to foster through the radical changes which lie ahead as we move towards the next century.

---

12 [*Editor:* In Spring 1990 the Permanent Head of the Home Civil Service, Sir Robin Butler, emphasised that British civil servants pick up a sense of right and wrong in public administration through the traditional way of 'apprenticeship from their seniors'. Sir Robin is reported as regarding this method as 'still adequate' and saw no need 'for special courses in ethics, say, at the Civil Service College'. See *The Times*, 19 March 1990. His viewpoint contrasts with those in North America where, for example, the United States Office of Government Ethics incorporates education and training on ethics and standards of conduct matters into its programmes. See *Part II* on Conflict of Interest in this Volume, pp. 167-98, which reproduces extracts from the Second Biennial Report to Congress of the U.S. Office of Government Ethics, March 1992].

NOTE 1

'The Armstrong Memorandum: The Duties and Responsibilities of Civil Servants in relation to Ministers'

by the then Head of the Home Civil Service,
Sir (later Lord) Robert Armstrong [1]

1. In February 1985, with the consent of the Prime Minister, I issued a note of guidance restating the general duties and responsibilities of civil servants in relation to Ministers.[2] That note was reproduced in a Written Answer by the Prime Minister to a Parliamentary Question on 26 February 1985 (OR 26 February 1985, cols *130* to *132*). In the light of subsequent discussion, including observations of the Treasury and Civil Service Select Committee and the Defence Committee of the House of Commons and comments from the Council of Civil Service Unions, I have expanded the note of guidance, and a revised version is now issued. As previously, the note is issued after consultation with Permanent Secretaries in charge of Departments and with their agreement. As with the earlier version, this revised version is issued with the consent of the Prime Minister, and will be reported by her to the House of Commons.

2. This note is concerned with the duties and responsibilities of civil servants in relation to Ministers. It should be read in the wider context of Ministers' own responsibilities, which were set out in the Government's reply to the Seventh Report from the Treasury and Civil Service Committee (Cmnd 9841):

> *'The Government believes that Ministers are well aware of the principles that should govern their duties and responsibilities in relation to Parliament and in*

---

1 The Armstrong Memorandum of 1987 continues to be the principal statement of the duties and obligations of civil servants in relation to Ministers. It is reprinted here as Note 1 to this paper but, in fact, The Armstrong Memorandum forms Annex A to the new Code for United Kingdom civil servants, dated February 1993, on the subject of 'Conduct and Discipline'. The new Code is reproduced in full (except Annex A above) in Appendix Part I of this Volume 1: *Government Ethics*, pp. 441-67.

2 For a detailed analysis, see the paper reproduced in the Appendix to this book, pp. 383-408, by Rosamund M. Thomas 'The Duties and Responsibilities of Civil Servants and Ministers: a Challenge within British Cabinet Government'. An earlier version of this paper was first published in *International Review of Administrative Sciences* Vol. 52 No. 4 December 1986 pp. 511-38.

relation to civil servants. It goes without saying that these include the obligations of integrity. They include the duty to give Parliament and the public as full information as possible about the policies, decisions and actions of the Government, and not to deceive or mislead Parliament or the public. In relation to civil servants, they include the duty to give fair consideration and due weight to informed and impartial advice from civil servants, as well as to other considerations and advice, in reaching policy decisions; the duty to refrain from asking or instructing civil servants to do things which they should not do; the duty to ensure that influence over appointments is not abused for partisan purposes; and the duty to observe the obligations of a good employer with regard to terms and conditions of service and the treatment of those who serve them.'

3. Civil servants are servants of the Crown. For all practical purposes the Crown in this context means and is represented by the Government-of-the-day. There are special cases in which certain functions are conferred by law upon particular members or groups of members of the public service; but in general the executive powers of the Crown are exercised by and on the advice of Her Majesty's Ministers, who are in turn answerable to Parliament. The Civil Service as such has no constitutional personality or responsibility separate from the duly constituted Government-of-the-day. It is there to provide the Government-of-the-day with advice on the formulation of the policies of the Government, to assist in carrying out the decisions of the Government, and to manage and deliver the services for which the Government is responsible. Some civil servants are also involved, as a proper part of their duties, in the processes of presentation of Government policies and decisions.

4. The Civil Service serves the Government-of-the-day as a whole, that is to say Her Majesty's Ministers collectively, and the Prime Minister is the Minister for the Civil Service. The duty of the individual civil servant is first and foremost to the Minister of the Crown who is in charge of the Department in which he or she is serving. The basic principles of accountability of Ministers and civil servants are as set out in the Government's response (Cmnd– 9916) to the Defence Committee's Fourth Report of 1985-86:

- Each Minister is responsible to Parliament for the conduct of his Department, and for the actions carried out by his Department in pursuit of Government policies or in the discharge of responsibilities laid upon him as a Minister.

- A Minister is accountable to Parliament, in the sense that he has a duty to explain in Parliament the exercise of his powers and duties and to give an account to Parliament of what is done by him in his capacity as a Minister or by his Department.

- Civil servants are responsible to their Ministers for their actions and conduct.

5. It is the duty of civil servants to serve their Ministers with integrity and to the best of their ability. In their dealings with the public, civil servants should always bear in mind that people have a right to expect that their affairs will be dealt with sympathetically, efficiently and promptly.

6. The British Civil Service is a non-political and professional career service subject to a code of rules and disciplines. Civil servants are required to serve the duly constituted Government-of-the-day, of whatever political complexion. It is of the first importance that civil servants should conduct themselves in such a way as to deserve and retain the confidence of Ministers, and to be able to establish the same relationship with those whom they may be required to serve in some future Administration. That confidence is the indispensable foundation of a good relationship between Ministers and civil servants. The conduct of civil servants should at all times be such that Ministers and potential future Ministers can be sure that that confidence can be freely given, and that the Civil Service will at all times conscientiously fulfil its duties and obligations to, and impartially assist, advise and carry out the policies of, the duly constituted Government-of-the-day.

7. The determination of policy is the responsibility of the Minister (within the convention of collective responsibility of the whole Government for the decisions and actions of every member of it). In the determination of policy the civil servant has no constitutional responsibility of role distinct from that of the Minister. Subject to the conventions limiting the access of Ministers to papers of previous Administrations, it is the duty of the civil servant to make available to the Minister all the information and experience at his or her disposal which may have a bearing on the policy decisions to which the Minister is committed or which he is preparing to make, and to give to the Minister honest and impartial advice, without fear or favour, and whether the advice accords with the Minister's view or not. Civil servants are in breach of their duty, and damage their integrity as servants of the Crown, if they deliberately withhold relevant information from their Minister, or if they give their Minister other advice than the best they believe they can give, or if they seek to obstruct or delay a decision simply because they do not agree with it. When, having been given all the relevant information and advice, the Minister has taken a decision, it is the duty of civil servants loyally to carry out that decision with precisely the same energy and good will, whether they agree with it or not.

8. Civil servants are under an obligation to keep the confidences to which they become privy in the course of their work; not only the maintenance of the trust between Ministers and civil sevants but also the efficiency of government depends on their doing so. There is and must be a general duty upon every civil servant, serving or retired, not without authority to make disclosures which breach that obligation. This duty applies to any document

or information or knowledge of the course of business, which has come to a civil servant in confidence in the course of duty. Any such unauthorised disclosures, whether for political or personal motives, or for pecuniary gain, and quite apart from liability to prosecution under the Official Secrets Acts, result in the civil servant concerned forfeiting the trust that is put in him or her as an employee and making him or her liable to disciplinary action including the possibility of dismissal, or to civil law proceedings. He or she also undermines the confidence that ought to subsist between Ministers and civil servants and thus damages colleagues and the Service as well as him or herself.

9. Civil servants often find themselves in situations where they are required or expected to give information to a Parliamentary Select Committee, to the media, or to individuals. In doing so they should be guided by the policy of the Government on evidence to Select Committees, as set out in memoranda of guidance issued from time to time, and on the disclosure of information, by any specifically departmental policies in relation to departmental information, and by the requirements of security and confidentiality. In this respect, however, as in other respects, the civil servant's first duty is to his or her Minister. Thus, when a civil servant gives evidence to a Select Committee on the policies or actions of his or her Department, he or she does so as the representative of the Minister in charge of the Department and subject to the Minister's instructions,[3] and is accountable to the Minister for the evidence which he or she gives. As explained in paragraph 2, the ultimate responsibility lies with Ministers, and not with civil servants, to decide what information should be made available, and how and when it should be released, whether it is to Parliament, to Select Committees, to the media or to individuals. It is not acceptable for a serving or former civil servant to seek to frustrate policies or decisions of Ministers by the disclosure outside the Government of information to which he or she has had access as a civil servant.

10. The previous paragraphs have set out the basic principles which govern the relations between Ministers and civil servants. The rest of this Note deals with particular aspects of conduct which derive from them, where it may be felt that more detailed guidance would be helpful.

11. A civil servant should not be required to do anything unlawful. In the very unlikely event of a civil servant being asked to do something which he or she believes would put him or her in clear breach of the law, the matter

---

3 A Permanent Head of a Department giving evidence to the Committee of Public Accounts does so by virtue of his duties and responsibilities as an Accounting Officer as defined in the Treasury memorandum on *The Responsibilities of an Accounting Officer*: but this is without prejudice to the Minister's responsibility and accountability to Parliament in respect of the policies, actions and conduct of his Department.

should be reported to a senior officer or to the Principal Establishment Officer, who should if necessary seek the advice of the Legal Adviser to the Department. If legal advice confirms that the action would be likely to be held to be unlawful, the matter should be reported in writing to the Permanent Head of the Department.

12. There may exceptionally be circumstances in which a civil servant considers that he or she is being asked to act in a manner which appears to him or her to be improper, unethical or in breach of constitutional conventions, or to involve possible maladministration, or to be otherwise inconsistent with the standards of conduct prescribed in this memorandum and in the relevant Civil Service codes and guides. In such an event the matter should be reported to a senior officer, and if appropriate to the Permanent Head of the Department.

13. Civil servants should always recall that it is Ministers, and not they, who bear political responsibility. A civil servant should not decline to take, or abstain from taking, an action because to do so would conflict with his or her personal opinions on matters of political choice or judgement between alternative or competing objectives and benefits; he or she should consider the possibility of declining only if taking or abstaining from the action in question is felt to be directly contrary to deeply held personal conviction on a fundamental issue of conscience.

14. A civil servant who feels that to act or to abstain from acting in a particular way, or to acquiesce in a particular decision or course of action, would raise for him or her a fundamental issue of conscience, or is so profoundly opposed to a policy as to feel unable conscientiously to adminster it in accordance with the standards described in this Note, should consult a senior officer. If necessary, and if the problem cannot be resolved by any other means, the civil servant may take the matter up with the Permanent Head of the Department and also has a right, in the last resort, to have the matter referred to the Head of the Home Civil Service through the Permanent Head of the Department; detailed provisions for such appeals are included in the Civil Service Pay and Conditions of Service Code. If the matter still cannot be resolved on a basis which the civil servant concerned is able to accept, he or she must either carry out his or her instructions or resign from the public service – though even after resignation he or she will still be bound to keep the confidences to which he or she has become privy as a civil servant.

NOTE 2 [1]

The Role of the Office of the Civil Service Commissioners in Recruitment to the Civil Service: a Note for Visitors

The Civil Service Commissioners

1. There are 6 Civil Service Commissioners. At present two are full-time civil servants. Since 1978 other Commissioners have been drawn from outside the Civil Service in order to provide experience of good personnel management practice in the private sector; they serve part-time, normally for periods of three or four years each.

The Commissioners' Functions

2. The Commissioners are appointed under the Royal Prerogative, not under Statute, as part of the Executive. They derive their powers from the Civil Service, and Diplomatic Service, Orders in Council, 1991. The Orders promulgate the government's general policy in respect of entry to the two Services – no appointments may be made unless selection has been carried out 'on merit on the basis of fair and open competition'. All appointments are made by Ministers or on their behalf. In respect of certain defined grades the Orders provide that the Commissioners' approval is a precondition of appointment; the Commissioners base their approval on the knowledge that in each case selection has been conducted in accordance with the policy. The Commissioners act independently of Ministers when giving or withholding approval in individual cases, and are personally answerable for the decisions they reach. The Commissioners report annually on their work to the Queen, not to Parliament, and their report is published.

3. The Orders set out the scope of the Commissioners' responsibilities broadly as follows:

- approval of candidates before senior appointments (Grade 7 level and above) and appointments to the fast-stream feeder entries can be made;

- rules in respect of selection to those appointments;

---

1 This Note reprints in full the text of a 'Note for Visitors' to the Office of the Civil Service Commissioners.

- advice to the Minister for the Civil Service and the Foreign Secretary on the formal Rules, made by the two Ministers, to govern the selection procedures to be followed by departments and agencies when making appointments at grade levels below those controlled by the Commissioners;

- monitoring the way departments and agencies apply the Minister's Rules.

The Commissioners' powers do not extend beyond the Home Civil Service and Diplomatic Service to the Northern Ireland Civil Service or to any other part of the public service, and involve no Service-wide personnel management functions other than selection for first appointment.

4. The First Commissioner, as a senior official in the Cabinet Office (Office of Public Service and Science) also has administrative responsibility for central liaison with the careers services of schools, and universities, and for advising the Minister for the Civil Service on nationality rules and character standards for entry to the Civil Service.

The Office of the Civil Service Commissioners (OCSC)

5. The Commissioners have a staff of 21 people based at Basingstoke (45 miles South West of London). The First Commissioner has an office of two people in London. Staff in the Office oversee the selection arrangements for the Commissioners' area of recruitment responsibility; advise on the legal framework for recruitment and on the Minister's Rules; monitor departments' and agencies' compliance with these Rules; and promote awareness of job opportunities in the Civil Service by maintaining links with the careers services of academic institutions. They also, as officials of the Office of the Minister for the Civil Service, advise on nationality rules and character standards for entry to the Civil Service.

A Brief History

6. The 19th Century reform movement criticised the then current system of patronage, purchase and favour, under which either the Minister of the department or the Patronage Secretary of the Treasury nominated candidates for appointment to posts in the Civil Service. In 1854 the Northcote-Trevelyan Report identified patronage as one of the main reasons for the Service's endemic inefficiency and public disrepute. It recommended open competitive examination to test merit. In the following year the first Civil Service Commissioners were appointed to run the examinations and to give approval for the appointment of those duly qualified.

7. The Commissioners quickly set up an office – the Civil Service Commis-

sion – and recruited the necessary staff. The years 1870 to 1920 saw the steady extension of the Commissioners' powers to cover virtually all appointments. Until the 1939-45 War, selection was mainly by specially prepared written examinations. Thereafter methods such as interview of those possessing appropriate academic qualifications, psychometric testing, and assessment centres were introduced to supplement or replace the traditional examination.

8. The Civil Service Commission retained its independent existence as a government department until 1968 when, on the recommendation of the Fulton Committee Report on the Civil Service, it was merged with the personnel management divisions of the Treasury to form the Civil Service Department (which was subsequently incorporated into the Cabinet Office). The Office of the Civil Service Commissioners forms part of the Office of Public Service and Science. The Commissioners' independence in individual selection decisions has been preserved throughout these changes.

9. In 1982 the Civil Service Order in Council was changed so as to divide responsibility for selection between the Civil Service Commissioners on one hand and Ministers on the other. The Commissioners retained responsibility for the selection of middle and senior level staff – about 15% of the Civil Service. On behalf of their Ministers departments assumed full responsibility for selection at junior levels, constituting the majority of recruitment, subject to central regulation by the Minister for the Civil Service in support of the policy of selection on merit on the basis of fair and open competition.

10. In 1991 two new orders in Council were made (one for the Home Civil Service and one for the Diplomatic Service with parallel provisions as appropriate). These extended departments' and agencies' area of responsibility to over 95% of recruitment to the Service. At the same time the Civil Service Commission was replaced by two discrete organisations:

- an office of the Civil Service Commissioners (OCSC – see paragraph 5); and

- Recruitment and Assessment Services (RAS), an Agency set up under the Next Steps initiative to provide, on full repayment, recruitment and related services for government departments, executive agencies, the Civil Service Commissioners and other statutory and public bodies. RAS is located in Basingstoke (in the same building as OCSC), and in London (24 Whitehall). The Chief Executive of RAS is a Commissioner. The other Commissioners have no responsibility for the Agency.

The order gives the Commissioners discretion to delegate to others the authority to undertake on their behalf the practical administration of the selection process. Where the Commissioners use RAS or any other recruitment specialists as their agent, the relationship is that of customer (the Commissioners) and contractor (RAS/other recruitment specialists).

Current Allocation of Other Recruitment Responsibilities
Minister for the Civil Service

11. The Minister for the Civil Service is the Prime Minister, who has given day-to-day responsibility to the Minister of State, Privy Council Office. The Minister settles selection policy ('selection on merit on the basis of fair and open competition') and any selection Rules for departmental and agency recruitment needed to support the policy. The Civil Service Commissioners have a duty to advise the Minister on these Rules and to monitor their application by departments and agencies (paragraph 3). The Minister also settles some other central requirements in respect of recruitment relating to health, character, nationality and other matters (such as security).

Treasury

12. Treasury has responsibility for recruitment policy (grading of posts and the levels to which direct recruitment may take place) and for ensuring that departments and agencies derive maximum value for money from their recruitment. Treasury also settle some other central requirements in respect of recruitment such as age (though age limits were abolished for Service-wide grades in August 1990), educational qualifications, professional attainment, experience, aptitude or potential.

Department and Agencies

13. On behalf of their Ministers departments and agencies are responsible for selection for junior and middle level appointments (i.e. all those not the responsibility of the Civil Service Commissioners). They can choose whether to

- undertake the recruitment themselves;
- employ the Recruitment and Assessment Services (see paragraph 10); or
- use some other recruitment agency,

subject to observance of the Minister's Rules on selection and to any other centrally laid down requirements.

14. The allocation of responsibilities is also set out in the Civil Service Order in Council 1991.

Office of the Civil Service Commissioners
February 1993.

4

Military Ethics

by James Stuart-Smith CB, QC,
recently the Judge Advocate General of the Forces
(Army and Royal Air Force) [1]

1. The Legislative Framework

Members of the British Armed Forces are subject either to the Army Act
1955, the Air Force Act 1955 or the Naval Discipline Act 1957, according to
their service. Though the Army and Air Force Acts also deal with such
matters as enlistment, pay, conditions of service, billeting powers and many
other things, each of these Acts contains the disciplinary code of the Service
to which it applies, defining in a series of sections the offences for which the
soldier, sailor or airman is punishable, the maximum punishments for them,
and prescribing the legal machinery for their trial. Many of the offences are
purely disciplinary, having no counterpart in the criminal law, for example,
unauthorised absence without leave, desertion, malingering, using insubor-
dinate language to superiors, ill-treatment of inferiors, misapplying or waste-
fully expending the employer's (that is, public or service) property.

Each of the Acts also includes a section which makes the commission of 'a
civil offence' (by a person subject to them) an offence under that Act. A
'civil offence' is defined for this purpose as 'Any act or omission punishable
by the law of England or which, if committed in England, would be punishable by that law'. The effect is to enable the trial under the Act of any person subject to it (which, as far as this particular provision is concerned,
includes British civilians accompanying our forces overseas) for any *criminal*
offence alleged to have been committed by them. Servicemen, to whom the
Acts apply at all times, are thus liable when in the United Kingdom to a dual
jurisdiction in respect of criminal offences, the civil jurisdiction and the
military jurisdiction, (though a *proviso* to the section excludes from the service jurisdiction murder, manslaughter, treason and rape where the offence
was committed in the United Kingdom); for offences which are only offences against service law, they of course can only be tried by service courts,
under the Service Acts. In the United Kingdom, primary jurisdiction over all
criminal offences rests with the civil authority and it is for the civil authority

---

1 This paper was presented at the Inaugural Conference of the Centre for Business and Public
Sector Ethics held in Cambridge on 13 July 1989. See also footnote 6, p. 70.

to say whether they are prepared to allow the matter to be dealt with by the services. In practice, offences committed on service property, or involving only members of the services, are usually left to the services to deal with. [2] Overseas there is similarly a dual jurisdiction, [3] the serviceman (and the civilians accompanying the force) being subject both to the law of the country in which they are serving and, by virtue of the Service Acts, the English criminal law as well. The question of which jurisdiction shall predominate, or which shall operate in the particular case, is likely to be the subject of treaty or other agreement. In Germany, for example, offences committed by soldiers on duty would fall *prima facie* within the military jurisdiction, but offences by off-duty soldiers against German civilians would fall to the German law. [4] In practice, however, the Germans are content to leave even murders and rapes of German citizens to be tried by our own courts-martial processes, in which, over the past forty years, they have gained complete confidence. It is relatively seldom that offences by soldiers or civilians, other than motoring offences, are claimed by the German courts.

Some of the disciplinary offences call for special mention in the context of our present study. Section 36 of the Army/Air Force Acts 1955 makes it an offence for a person subject to them (which, in relation to this section too, includes a civilian member of the military community abroad) to disobey 'standing orders'. Standing orders are orders permanently in force, published by a responsible commander for the governance of those under or within his command. For example, in Germany the issue of driving licences to British servicemen and associated civilians, and the registration of their private cars, is, by the Status of Forces Agreement, a function of the service authority. It is standing orders which lay down the conditions on which licences and registrations are to be applied for and granted and which prescribe that it shall be an offence against them to drive unlicensed, unregistered or uninsured. There are many other departments of day-to-day life in which standing orders fill the part played in the United Kingdom by national or local legislation (which does not, of course, have effect outside these shores). A commander's power to issue orders is limited, however, to orders which are not contrary to English or international law and *which are justified in the military interest by some valid military purpose*. This latter condition would, of course, be sufficiently satisfied if the order in question could be seen as aimed at maintaining the good order, health, welfare or efficiency of the fighting force under his command. It could not be justified merely by his personal view

---

2 See Queen's Regulations J7.001 to 7.007 (Copies of all Queen's Regulations referred to in footnotes are attached to this paper).

3 See generally Part 1 of Chapter 7 of Queen's Regulations.

4 See Status of Forces Agreement: Annex A(J) to Chapter 7 of Queen's Regulations in Note 3 attached.

that what he was ordering was desirable in itself and, as a matter of general principle, the military order would be justified only if the justification for it outweighed the very strong presumption in favour of the liberty of the subject. Thus, whilst it is perhaps arguable that a commander could lawfully order soldiers who were being trained to undertake a military venture for which supreme physical fitness was essential temporarily to give up smoking, he would not be entitled arbitrarily to order the civilians under his command to do so, on the basis of his opinion, however strongly held, that everybody would be better for not smoking.

Section 60 of the Act makes it a specific military offence to disclose information to an enemy.

Section 64 provides that, 'Every officer who behaves in a scandalous manner unbecoming the character of an officer shall, on conviction by a court-martial, be liable to dismissal from Her Majesty's service with or without disgrace'. The court itself can pass for this offence no punishment less than dismissal. The historic rationale for a mandatory sentence of expulsion of the officer corps for an officer convicted of this particular offence is that it would be inconsistent for the court, having found their fellow officer guilty of conduct unbecoming the character of an officer, to do less than remove him from that status. (There is, however, power in higher authorities, subsequently reviewing the case, as an act of mercy, to commute this extreme sentence to one which will permit the offender to remain in the services, the court having already made clear the opinion of his brother officers of his standards of conduct.) None-the-less in 1992 at least two Officers were dismissed from the Army for behaviour 'unbecoming the character of an officer'.

Section 66 provides for the offence of 'Disgraceful Conduct of an Indecent Kind', which is employed mainly to deal with homosexual acts between servicemen. The Sexual Offences Acts of 1956 and 1967 expressly preserved the right of the services to charge servicemen under this section in respect of homosexual activity which had taken place in circumstances in which it would not have constituted an offence against the Sexual Offences Acts themselves (for example between consenting adults in private). [5]

The courts-martial which try charges under the Army or Air Force Acts are composed of officers (not less than five for a General Court-Martial, or three for a District Court-Martial, which has more limited powers) and if the

---

5 This legal position is currently under review. Though the legal position was not disturbed by the Armed Forces Act 1991, the report of the Select Committee which examined the state of military law in the preparation of that Act included a recommendation that consideration be given to excluding from the ambit of section 66 homosexual acts between servicemen in circumstances in which the act would not be criminal under the Sexual Offences Acts. See also p. 76.

accused is a civilian member of the service community abroad, the composition of the court can include, in place of service officers, a proportion of civilian Crown Servants. A General Court-Martial and the more serious District Courts-Martial will have a Judge Advocate sitting with them, whose functions during the trial are similar to those of a Judge sitting with a jury in an English Criminal Court. The maximum punishments available to courts-martial are similar to those of a Crown Court (that is, imprisonment for those who have attained their majority and a form of youth custody for those under the age of twenty-one years). Below these there are for servicemen a range of specifically military punishments and for civilians a range of punishments similar to those available to the civil courts.

2. The Judge Advocate General

The Office of Judge Advocate General dates from 1666 and, at the time of preparing this paper, the writer was its fiftieth holder in direct succession. [6] He and the lawyers who form his judicial staff are civilian barristers. His counterpart for the Royal Naval is the Judge Advocate of the Fleet. Originally JAG's responsibility was for the Army alone, but since 1919 he has also been responsible for the Royal Air Force. Nowadays he and the judicial staff appointed to assist him (who must be barristers, of a minimum of five years' standing) come under the Lord Chancellor and his responsibilities with regard to courts-martial and military discipline are confined to their judicial aspects, that is, providing the Judge Advocates who officiate at courts-martial and advising the service authorities after the trial upon its legal validity and, if asked, the sentence. (Before 1948 he was jointly responsible to the Secretaries of State for War and Air and the responsibilities of his Office included the conduct of prosecutions at courts-martial. These prosecutions were in practice dealt with exclusively by military and air force departments within his office, composed of legally qualified officers of those services. In that year all responsibility for prosecution was removed from JAG, his military and air force departments becoming Legal Directorates of their respective services, who are now responsible for prosecution and the giving of other legal advice within their service). JAG remains the primary advisory authority to the Secretary of State for Defence and the Service authorities, on legal and legislative questions concerned with the administration of service law.

3. The Administrative Framework

The overall powers of command over, and administration of, the armed

---

6 James Stuart-Smith Esq., CB., QC retired recently from the Office of Judge Advocate General. His successor, the fifty-first holder of this Office in direct succession, is Judge J. W. Rant, QC.

services are vested (by the Defence (Transfer of Functions) Act 1964) in the Defence Council. That Act also established the Admiralty Board, the Army Board and the Air Force Board, which were charged under the Defence Council with the administration of matters relating to their respective services. The many legal functions with which the Defence Council is vested by the Service Acts and other enactments (for example the Courts-Martial (Appeals) Act 1968) are exercisable by the individual service boards, who have also been delegated by the Defence Council to have command over the officers and soldiers of their respective services. The Secretary of State for Defence and the Ministers and Parliamentary Under Secretaries of State for the Armed Forces and for defence procurement serve on the Defence Council and also on each of the service boards, the Secretary of State for Defence being chairman of all of them. The service element of the Defence Council consists of the Chief and Vice Chief of Defence Staff and the Heads of each of the individual service staffs, and the military component of the Army Board (for example) consists of the Chief and Vice Chief of the (Armies) General Staff and the military heads of the major departments, personnel, logistics and material. It is these bodies who determine the policy of the services, both generally as to each individual service, and, in particular these service officers who set the standards that members of their service are expected to follow.

The guidance of the Defence Council and the Service Boards over the whole wide spectrum of the life, professional activities, administration, conduct and ethics of the three services is conveyed by means of Queen's Regulations, which are Regulations approved by Her Majesty but issued under the aegis of the Defence Council, and by instructions issued in a variety of forms. The Army, for example, publishes volumes of 'Army General Administrative Instructions' and letters of guidance on particular subjects which may from time to time issue from Heads of Staff. (Neither Queen's Regulations, nor AGAIs, nor these policy letters are 'standing orders' and failure to comply with them does not of itself constitute a punishable offence under section 36 of the 1955 Acts, to which I have referred above). Queen's Regulations and these other Instructions provide a clear and detailed body of ethical and administrative guidance and it is to them that one must look first in trying to ascertain the ethical standards at which the services are aiming.

I must make clear at once my own inadequacies as a spokesman for service ethics or, in particular, to compare them with those in civil life. I am not part of the services and cannot claim personal involvement in their own very special ethos. I have worked with servicemen, though, for the past thirty-four years and spent eleven of those years living amongst them abroad so that I have had ample opportunity to observe them. I am very conscious, however, that I am handicapped in my present task by a complete lack of any first-hand knowledge or experience of business, industry, and their ethics, or the standards of ethics obtaining in any department of civilian life outside the law, so that I have to tread very cautiously indeed in that area. So far as the services are concerned, I have indicated already that the Navy is outside my scope and though of course I know them well, and that their standards of honour and ethics are of the very highest, it would not be appropriate for me to speak of them. I can try to speak only of what I know of the Army and the Royal Air Force, and I propose to base what I have to say mainly on the Army. The standards and attitudes of the Royal Air Force are, however, no different.

4. The Standards of Conduct

The British Army accepts that its declared standards, although they are constantly under review in the light of changing social mores, do not necessarily reflect attitudes fashionable in civil life, especially in the standards it expects of its officers. A relatively recent (1989) policy letter stated that:

> 'The Army Board's view is that it is not sufficient to abide by standards of social behaviour acceptable in civilian life. On the contrary, acceptance of the Queen's commission carries with it a duty to uphold the highest standards, often more stringent than those accepted by society as a whole. While officers may not be immune from the pressures and temptations which arise in personal relationships within the community at large, they are nevertheless required to set and maintain standards (in both their private and professional lives) consistent with the demands of the service'.

5. Queen's Regulations and Other Instructions [7] Business Relations – Civil Offences – Divorce

Queen's Regulations lay down clear rules for many ethical situations, for example the conduct of service personnel whose jobs require them to deal with civilian contractors or other business people and the acceptance of business appointments on retirement. [8] Instructions of this kind are, of course, common to all Government Departments, in the civil as well as the armed services. Nor are the armed services unique in requiring their members to report to a superior any involvement with the criminal

---

7 Queen's Regulations are published by Her Majesty's Stationery Office (HMSO) and can be purchased without restriction. Army General Administrative Instructions are classified as 'Restricted' and Letters of Policy Guidance normally are classified 'In Confidence'. Copies of the relevant paragraphs and annexes to Queen's Regulations to which reference is made in this paper are attached as Notes. It will be appreciated that it is not possible to provide copies of classified publications or documents in the same way, but references have been made to them in the text.

8 Queen's Regulations J5.075 to 5.080.

law, (minor traffic offences excepted). [9] With an officer whose offence involves indecency, the misuse of drugs, fraud, drink/driving offences or a breach of the peace, the report has to go as high as the Army Board. Though each case, of course, is, examined on its merits, the public would hardly expect the services to be prepared to retain as an officer anybody who had been convicted of indecency, fraud, or involvement with drugs. Nor would any civilian firm or organisation, which regarded such a conviction as clearly incompatible with the position in which the offender was employed by them, retain such an employee. There are, however, a number of situations in civil life, which could be regarded as a minor conviction (a minor ticket fraud, an act of petty shoplifting or being caught importuning another man in a public lavatory) which would not necessarily spell the end of a career. The most marked difference is probably in the attitude to drink/driving. It may be questionable whether very many commercial firms would look particularly gravely upon a competent middle-manager's conviction for drink/driving (unless his consequent disqualification from driving affected his ability to do his job). Conversely, an officer convicted of drink/driving is likely to receive at least a formal notice of the Army Board's displeasure (which would affect his promotion prospects) and a really bad offence, capable of bringing discredit on the service to which he belongs, could lead to his compulsory retirement. In ranks below this, a Warrant Officer or non-commissioned officer convicted of drink/driving could find his suitability for the rank he holds being considered administratively.

An officer of either sex who is involved as a respondent or co-respondent in divorce proceedings is required by Queen's Regulations to inform the commanding officer. [10] Whether the report need go beyond the commanding officer, or is likely to lead to any action being taken, will depend on the circumstances of the case. In most instances, most probably not. But if there has been adultery with the wife of someone *subordinate* to the officer, especially with the wife of an ordinary soldier under his command, this could well be regarded as unbecoming an officer. Whether the affair has broken up somebody else's marriage is another factor likely to be taken into consideration. Another consideration is, whether there has been public scandal, capable of lowering officers generally in the public estimation. Most cogent of all, probably, is whether discipline and the officer's credibility has been affected, especially where the parties involved are all serving in the same unit or on the same station. There are some, no doubt, who would see this concern of the Army Board in the private lives of its officers as interference and reflecting out-dated moral attitudes. Others, perhaps, getting a little closer to the reality, could see in it touches of hypocrisy ('Has there been public

---

9 Queen's Regulation 5.062.
10 Queen's Regulation 5.063.

scandal?'). What is clear is that the Army, even of the 1990s, is pre-eminently concerned for its own good name and reputation and that it should not be sullied by publicly unacceptable behaviour by those who hold the Queen's commission. Beyond that, it is also concerned to maintain *within its own ranks* the concept of an officer as an honourable man, particularly towards those under him, and entitled to their respect. It may be seen by some as clinging to standards that, in the eyes of the sophisticated man of today, are outmoded; the Army themselves would see it as necessary to maintain the fabric of leadership and discipline.

Through firm leadership from the top, and making clear what is expected, the services have succeeded in imposing and maintaining these standards. There are, of course, those servicemen who fall below the standards of conduct, and the evident surprise of some of them that their own conduct should even have been called into question, make it apparent that they have failed to comprehend that practices which pass as acceptable in some walks of civil life are not acceptable in the services or in accord with what a very senior officer has called 'the rules of the club'. The members of the club generally (of all ranks), accept them, make no complaint of them and conduct themselves according to them.

6. 'Expense Account Fiddling'

Few, if any, of those serving in the armed forces have an 'expense account'. They are entitled, however, within strictly prescribed regulations to claim various fixed rate allowances for overnight subsistence and travelling. These include a mileage allowance where a private car is used either for a journey on duty, or to travel to a leave destination within the United Kingdom (in lieu of claiming the railway warrant to which servicemen going on leave traditionally are entitled). One of the commonest criminal offences tried under the Service Acts is obtaining money by deception by means of a false claim, either to have travelled to a duty destination in the claimant's own car, when in fact he had been given a lift by a colleague, or by pretending to have gone on leave to a destination far more distant than the place where the leave had in fact been spent (if, indeed, the fraudulent claimant had gone away from home at all). It must be said in fairness to more scrupulous members of the forces that in an average year less than two in ten thousand of the strength of the armed forces come to trial charged with offences of this kind, but it would be unrealistic not to assume that for every case of fraud detected and punished a number of others succeed. The amounts involved are small, often no more than between £10 and £40 – far less than the cost of an expense account lunch – but the punishments service courts' award for dishonesty of this kind often includes dismissal from the service (particularly for officers, warrant officers or non-commissioned officers, who are normally entitled to a high measure of trust) and sometimes custodial sentences in addition. The services recognise no unwritten right to perks on the side, nor are they prepared to listen to the excuse that the offender was trying only to recover within the rules his expenditure for the benefit of the service on something for which the rules did not provide. In their old-fashioned eyes, lies are lies and dishonest when used to obtain something to which the claimant knew perfectly well he was not lawfully entitled.

7. Violence and Bullying

In the ethics of physical violence, the attitudes of the leadership and the ethics of the barrack room have to be distinguished. The attitude of the leadership is the attitude of the law, that violence of any kind cannot be tolerated. The ethics of barrack room are those of any community of young males, that a man is expected to stand up for himself physically in the last resort. There are two rather worrying trends in this 'grass roots' world. One is the steady escalation over the past thirty years in the nature and degree of violence regarded as acceptable. Soldiers, like schoolboys, have also been prone from time to time to come to blows. It is a constant theme in Kipling and countless other books of regimental life. Until comparatively recently, though, they fought with their fists (occasionally, in group battles, with their belts) and kicking was frowned upon; the technique of head-butting was unknown fifty years ago (except perhaps to a few sophisticates from Glasgow) and the use of knives or broken glass as a weapon would have been unthinkable to the British soldier (or the British civilian; judges in those days frequently stigmatised the use of a knife as 'un-English'). Today, kicking a fallen opponent has become the normal and expected thing. As a number of young soldier witnesses were at pains to explain in a murder trial a few years ago, when a soldier had been kicked to death in an inter-regimental fight in a German street, 'Of course you have to kick him to put him out of action. Otherwise, he just gets up and goes on fighting'. The use of a weapon, either a knife or broken glass or bottle has become all too common. These are not, of course, peculiarly military attitudes; they simply reflect the conventions of violence in the society from which young servicemen mostly come. The other disturbing trend is towards 'Initiation Ceremonies' for those joining a particular unit which, in one or two (already well-publicised) cases which have come to light, involve the infliction on the victim of torments and indignities which could only be described as horrific. Of course the service establishment does not tolerate or close its eyes to this sort of behaviour. It is most severely discountenanced and some of the ringleaders have gone to prison for a long time. What is worrying though is what may be called the public opinion of the barrack room which would appear to tolerate some of the barbarities that have occurred, and even to join in them. The ill-treatment of recruits and young soldiers by their instructors has come much under the public spotlight in recent years. It has always been strictly forbidden officially, but young soldiers nowadays may be more aware of their rights and ready to complain than those in the more distant past. Where ill treatment occurs, it often represents a conflict of ethical values. The training, Non-Commissioned Officer's zeal and devotion to the ethics of military perfection, can tempt him to forget his own self-discipline and the truer ethics of the service to which he belongs.

8. Homosexuality

I have mentioned that section 66 of the Army/Air Force Acts 1955 effectively renders servicemen liable to trial for homosexual activity, even where it took place in circumstances in which it would no longer amount to an offence against the criminal law of England. [11] The services adopt no *moral* stance towards homosexuality, male or female. They do regard, however, homosexual practices amongst young servicemen as unacceptable for a number of reasons. In the close male community of service life, where young men are required to live together and work as a team, it could be subversive of the discipline both of the couples who had formed a physical and emotional relationship between them and of other young servicemen, not themselves of that orientation, who are liable to find such activity distasteful and give disorderly expression to their disapproval. The fear of Aids, whether or not ill-founded, is likely nowadays to lend added heat to their antipathy to the presence of known homosexuals amongst them.

9. Aids

What are the ethics of compulsory testing for Aids? There are conflicting schools of medical thought. One, broadly, holds the view that if the illness were to reach sufficiently epidemic proportions there would, in the public interest, be a strong case for universal testing. The opposing view appears to be that the consequences of a positive result upon almost every aspect of the victim's life are so destructive that no man (or woman) should be compelled to undertake the risk of being labelled with the disease unless he himself has chosen voluntarily to do so. What of the soldier? Should he be differently treated from others? Not only does he live day-to-day in the most intimate proximity with his fellows, eating and sleeping cheek by jowl with them, the soldier's occupation is in its nature rough and hazardous. Soldiers bleed and can bleed on one another. Indeed, in action, there are techniques for giving a direct blood transfusion from one to another. If the medical services were to

---

11 But see footnote 5, p. 69. The suggested change in the law, if it were to go through, would not imply, of course, the services' acceptance of homosexual activity in their ranks. For the reasons given in the text, they might well take the view that men who had shown themselves to be practising homosexuals should be discharged. And such conduct between two servicemen in some circumstances could disclose other grounds for disciplinary action.

advise that the risk of infection was in these circumstances of a sufficiently high order, would it be proper to require *every* soldier to submit to testing for the HIV virus? Or those about to be sent on active service? Or to make an Aids test part of the medical examination for any candidate for enlistment? If so, should the patient be warned that the test to which he is consenting will include testing for Aids? And must he be told the result if it is positive? For their own part, the attitude of the Services themselves is that they would be most reluctant to treat their members any differently from the general public and that as far as their present medical advice goes there is no need to do so; though obviously different considerations could arise if it were necessary to send a force into battle.

10. Drugs

The stance of the Armed Forces towards drug abuse is firm, unequivocal and Draconian. Remembering the purposes for which armed forces exist and the demands they make upon the reliability and personal resources, both physical and mental, of their members, from their own point of view, it is also purely practical. The experience in combat – and out of it – of other armies has taught how drug taking can spread in an armed force, especially one under the intense strains of war, and how it can rot morale and fighting effectiveness.

It is this aim to prevent the spread of drug taking, not any idiosyncratically puritan outlook on the intrinsic moralities or wickedness of illegal drug indulgence, that accounts for the generally greater severity of service sentences on individual drug offenders, compared with the penalties imposed by magistrates' courts. The civilian caught with a relatively small quantity of cannabis for his own use ordinarily will be punished by the magistrates with a quite modest fine. If his offence had been committed in his own time, away from work, it's unlikely that his employer would regard an isolated instance as grounds for terminating his employment, or, if he did take so stern a view, that an Appeal Tribunal would agree with him. The serviceman, however, caught similarly, would face a custodial sentence of some substance, albeit of military detention rather than imprisonment, combined with dismissal from the service, for those found guilty of supplying illicit drugs to others, even by offering them a puff of a 'joint', the punishment will be even more severe, and, as in the criminal courts, the use or supply of more sophisticated drugs – LSD, 'crack', heroin – will attract correspondingly severer penalties.

Though it would be impossible to eradicate indulgence in drugs altogether amongst young men and women who come from a society in which they are commonplace (and who are called on to serve in places where they are even more readily on offer than in this country), the services' strong – and constantly publicised and enforced – official disapproval of drug usage does seem to have created in their ranks a climate of general reluctance in the majority to have anything to do with them, and of disapproval of their use by others.

There has been no change in the overall attitude of the services towards homosexuality. For the reasons given earlier in my text they are still not prepared to permit known homosexuals to serve in their ranks, despite strenuous endeavours by 'gay' pressure groups to have them compelled to do so. However, the Select Committee of the House of Commons which sat to examine service law in preparation for the Armed Forces Act 1991 recommended that consideration should be given to removing from the ambit of section 66 of the Army/Air Force Acts, 1955 homosexual activity between service men committed in circumstances in which it would not amount to an offence against the Sexual Offences Acts. The effect of this recommendation, if it were to be adopted, would be that the act itself would no longer constitute an offence under section 66, as 'disgraceful conduct of an indecent kind'. It could, however, in some circumstances, still amount to a breach of good order and service discipline in other repects and be chargeable as such; for example if there was an abuse of rank involved (such as an officer seducing a young soldier). And, even if there was no offence any longer under the Service Acts, the parties could, and almost certainly would, be removed from the service administratively.

11. Official Secrets

I have mentioned already that the Service Acts embody a specific Service offence of 'Unauthorised Disclosure of Information Likely to be Useful to an Enemy' and servicemen are, of course, also liable to prosecution under the Official Secrets Acts. I am attaching extracts from Chapter 12 of Queen's Regulations, from which the serviceman has to take his guidance on the wider aspects of official discretion. So far as his ethical considerations are concerned, the serviceman is in no different position from any other public servant. Some could be confronted no doubt with the same ethical dilemmas which some civil servants professed to have faced. Thinking back to the 1930s, one is reminded of the deeply patriotic service officers who, at the risk of their careers, kept Winston Churchill fed with information to which, out of office, he was not entitled. I shall listen with the keenest interest to the views of others in the public service on this topic, and the ethical considerations involved and any general views that may be expressed as to what the law should be. However, whatever one's personal view may be, as the law stands there can, in most cases, be only one *lawful* answer.

12. Superior Orders

The soldier is obliged to obey any lawful command given him and the penalty for failure, whether wilful or through neglect, is imprisonment. [12] To be lawful the command must, '. . . not be contrary to English or International Law'. A note in the Manual of Military Law, [13] advises that, 'If a command is manifestly illegal, the person to whom it is given would be justified in questioning and even refusing to execute it'. But what if the soldier is not sure, or has no time to think about it, let alone question it? For example, the soldier in the Belfast streets, with a fleeing civilian in the sights of his rifle, his corporal's urgent voice ordering him to shoot, and doubts in his own mind whether his target is anything more than a terrified bystander? It is not an easy problem, even for the lawyers, considering it at leisure let alone the unfortunate soldier. The Manual of Military Law itself suggests [14] as a general proposition that whilst, 'It has been suggested that if . . . the act ordered is not manifestly illegal, a person who obeys it will not incur criminal responsibility by doing so, especially if he had little opportunity to consider the order before carrying it out, '. . . *The better view* appears to be . . . that an order . . . whether the act or omission is manifestly illegal or not, can never of itself excuse the recipient if he carries it out . . .' (and it turns out in the event to have been unlawful). The example offered depicts a situation which is particularly acute for the (by no means imaginary) soldier. In others he may have more time to make a choice, but be in no better position to assess the true legalities of what he is being ordered to do. In either situation he is impaled on the dilemma of being punished if he disobeys the order or, possibly being even more severely punished for having obeyed it. As Ian Brownlee has remarked in a recent article in the *Criminal Law Review*, 'This dilemma is likely to arise increasingly where military forces are deployed not on conventional battlefields but rather in support of the civil power'. [15] Though the arguments about how the soldier's responsibility ought to be determined, for practical reasons, must be in terms of the law which governs his position before the courts, they rest upon what are essentially ethical questions, namely the potential conflict between the soldier's duty of obedience to his superiors and his personal responsibilities to his fellow human beings.

13. The Ethics of War – Its Laws and Customs [16]

By the end of the Middle Ages it had begun already to be generally accepted

---

12 See section 34 of the Army/Air Force Acts 1955.

13 Note 3(a) to section 64 on p. 296.

14 Para. 23 of Chapter VI at pp. 156A/157.

15 *Crim. L. R.* [1989] p. 396.

16 My observations in this section owe much to Ingrid Detter de Lupis's recently published 'The Law of War', (LSE Monograph in International Studies: published by Cambridge University Press), the index to which, under the heading 'Ethics of Warfare' has led me to a number of helpful passages in its text and reference sources.

that warfare, at least between Christian nations, should be conducted according to certain ethical rules, falling broadly into two main groups, one concerned with honour and the other with humanity. From these beginnings have grown our present body of the laws and customs of war.

The first of these concepts has demanded fairplay between the combatants. Treacherous onslaughts upon another State, delivered suddenly and without warning from an apparently clear political sky, were regarded as plainly wrongful. Soldiers were expected to identify themselves by wearing the uniform of their own side (and the un-uniformed spy was, if caught, liable to forfeit his life) and to fight under their own flag (though, perhaps rather curiously, the use of a false flag has always been accepted as a legitimate ruse de guerre in naval warfare, the true battle flag being run up immediately before engaging). It was, in their early days, suggested that the use of submarines was 'perfidious' and they ought to be banned. Nowadays, there is an elaborate body of such conventions, most of them well accepted, but the essential ethic behind them all is that of honourable conduct and the avoidance of treachery.

There have been calls in the name of humanity ever since the Middle Ages for the limitation of weapons seen contemporarily as capable of inflicting injuries unnecessarily severe. There were strong voices against the crossbow. Detter de Lupis mentions a medieval restriction on the use of cannon, limiting them to knocking down the walls of cities and prohibiting using them in field battle against human targets. [17] Coming to more modern times, the St. Peterburg's Convention of 1868 (which banned explosive bullets) stated the underlying principle as being that since, to defeat an enemy, '. . . it is sufficient to disable the greatest possible number of men', it is not permitted to use, 'arms which uselessly aggravate the suffering of disabled men or render their death inevitable'; the 1907 Hague Conventions, re-affirming that, 'The right of belligerents to adopt means of injuring an enemy is not unlimited', introduced a complete prohibition of, 'Arms, projectiles or material calculated to cause unnecessary suffering'. Countless other international conferences and agreements have confirmed, of course, and enlarged upon these principles since then.

Certain methods of warfare are specifically prohibited. For example the starvation of civilians by besieging a city, once a recognised means of bringing pressure to bear on the enemy, has recently been prohibited by the Geneva Conventions. [18] Foodstuff for the civilian population are also protected from attack, and so are civil defence and personnel buildings. [19] It has long been held that an order to give no water is impermissible and this too is

---

17 Ibid. See footnote 96 on pp. 134-35.

18 Protocol 1 of 1977.

19 Ibid.

now expressly stated in the Geneva Protocols. [20] The main protection for the helpless, sick or wounded combatant, prisoners of war or civilians derive from the Geneva Conventions of 1949, which have been ratified or acceded to by most nations of the world and which are designed to ensure the humane treatment of all who have fallen into the hands of their enemy.

The ethics of warfare, indeed, could be said to have given rise to one of the most important and oldest areas of international co-operation and of international law.

---

20 Ibid.

NOTE 1

Queen's Regulations: Chapter Five [1]
General
Part 2 – Personal Conduct and Efficiency

Character and Conduct

J5.062. An individual who has been charged before a civil court with a criminal offence, or who has received a formal caution from the civil police in respect of a criminal offence as an alternative to prosecution, is at once to report the circumstances to his commanding officer. In the case of an officer the commanding officer is to decide whether the circumstances justify suspension from duty (*see* para **6.015**). This paragraph does not apply to minor road traffic offences.

5.063. Whenever an officer is involved in divorce proceedings as a respondent or co-respondent he is to report the circumstances to the Ministry of Defence (PS 2(Army)) through his commanding officer and formation or district headquarters. Each forwarding authority will record his comments.

Relationship with non Service Business

J5.075.

a. Serving personnel must at all times guard against being placed in such a position as may leave them open to the suspicion of being influenced in the discharge of their duty by other than purely public considerations. They must be scrupulously careful in their relationships and in any private dealings with Government contractors and their agents or employees. They are forbidden to furnish testimonials to any company, firm or person in respect of the quality of commodities supplied for Service purposes.

b. If a member of the regular forces has, in the course of his duty, to come into contact with any matter concerning a business organisation in which he has an interest he is to disclose that interest to his superior officer and ask that some other person may deal with the

---

1 The *relevant* Queen's Regulations: Chapter Five only are reproduced here and *not* the entire Chapter.

case. He should not be permitted to deal with the case without the approval of the Ministry of Defence.

Acceptance of Business Appointments

J5.076. A member of the regular forces may not, without authority, accept any continuous employment of profit during his full time service. Subject to para **J5.078** or any separate instructions, he may not without Ministry of Defence (PS 2a(Army)) approval:

a. carry on any profession, engage in trade or accept any profitable employment;

b. be a member of a governing body of any corporation, company or undertaking, or of any partnership engaged in any trade or carrying on any profession;

c. assist, advise or act directly or indirectly as agent for any corporation, company, partnership, undertaking, or individual which or who is carrying on any profession or is engaged in trade or is profitably employed.

J5.077. An application for special approval under para **J5.076** must contain an undertaking that:

a. The applicant's private business will in no way interfere with his Service duties.

b. He will take no part in activities connected with the firm which could give rise to suspicion that he has used or could use his Service knowledge to further his own business interests or those of his firm.

c. He will take no part in transactions between the firm and the Services or any Departments or branches of the Government or any semi-public organisation brought into being by the Government. The applicant must also confirm that he understands that no special facilities such as leave of absence will be granted to him and that approval will not debar his being required to serve, whether afloat or ashore, at home or abroad.

Acceptance of Business Appointments after leaving the Services

J5.080.

a. The principles governing the acceptance of business appointments by officers of the Crown Services after leaving the Services are laid down in Command Paper 5517, an extract of which is reproduced at Annex C to this Chapter.

b. Before accepting, within two years of leaving the Service, an offer of employment of the type set out in Annex C to this chapter, an officer of or above the rank of rear admiral, major general or air vice-marshal and any other officer who has been, before leaving the Service, in any special relationship either with a business firm of the type set out in Annex C to this chapter or with its direct competitors must obtain the approval of the Ministry of Defence (CM(IR)5) AL13.

NOTE 2

Queen's Regulations: Chapter Seven [1]
General Legal Matters
Part 1 – Jurisdiction

General

J7.001. Jurisdiction in respect of offences by members of the armed forces may lie either with the Service authorities under the Service Acts or with the civil authorities under the ordinary law, or it may lie with both; in the last case, the issue is subject to rules which differ at home and abroad. Before charges are brought it is necessary to consider carefully, according to the circumstances, where jurisdiction lies as to the offence and the place in which and the time at which it was committed. Attention is drawn to the Manual of Military Law, and the texts of the relevant Acts and the regulations made under them.

J7.002. In general, jurisdiction lies as follows:

a. *In the United Kingdom*

1. Wholly with the Service authorities where the offence is against Service law only, e.g. disobedience of a lawful command, or desertion.

2. Wholly with the civil authorities where the offence is treason, murder, manslaughter, treason-felony, rape, genocide or aiding, abetting, counselling or procuring suicide.

3. With both the Service authorities and the civil authorities where the offence is not one to which (1) or (2) applies; for the rules which determine in a particular case which authorities shall exercise jurisdiction *see* para **J7.003**.

b. *Abroad*

1. Wholly with the Service authorities where the offence is against Service law only but subject, in a foreign country or independent country within the Commonwealth, to the law of that country or

---

1 The *relevant* Queen's Regulations: Chapter Seven are reproduced here and *not* the entire Chapter.

the terms of a treaty or agreement permitting the Service authorities to exercise such jurisdiction.

2. Wholly with the civil authorities where the offence is an offence solely under the local law.

3. With both the Service authorities and the civil authorities where the offence is an offence against both Service law and the law of the country or colony concerned; subject, in a foreign country or independent country within the Commonwealth, to the law of that country or the terms of any treaty or agreement permitting the Service authorities to exercise jurisdiction; in such circumstances it will be the local law or the terms of the treaty or agreement which will decide in a particular case which authorities shall exercise jurisdiction.

4. In the case of a force which is forming part of a United Nations force occupying former enemy territory, jurisdiction generally lies exclusively with the authorities of the force.

Jurisdiction in the United Kingdom

J7.003. In the United Kingdom a person subject to Service discipline may be tried for certain civil offences by either the Service or the civil authorities (*see* para **J7.002a(3)**). The following paragraphs indicate how such cases are to be proceeded with.

J7.004. In most cases where it is necessary to involve the civilian authorities, a commanding officer should report the circumstances to the chief officer of police for that area. However, where a Ministry of Defence employee or his property is involved, the matter may be left to the Ministry of Defence police, if available; if they are not readily available, a commanding officer should report to the police force for that area.

J7.004A. In addition to reporting those cases excluded from Service jurisdiction under para **J7.002a(2)**, a commanding officer is to report to the chief officer of police for that area, at the earliest possible moment, the following cases where the offence is alleged to have been committed by a member of the forces:

a. Any case of death or serious injury likely to lead to death, which may justify a charge of murder or manslaughter.

b. Any serious sexual assault which may afford grounds for a charge of rape.

c. Any other case where civilians are involved and Ministry of Defence Police are not *in situ* or readily available.

d. Any traffic offence which occurs on roads to which the public has access or in public places where these roads or places are:

   1. Outside the boundaries of Ministry of Defence property; or

   2. Inside the boundaries of Ministry of Defence property but at a place where Ministry of Defence police are not in situ or readily available.

e. Any other offence which may require to be dealt with by the civil authorities, for example, because it is one of a category of offence of importance to the community either locally or nationally, or because the case falls within the requirements of para J7.007e.

J7.005. Where jurisdiction lies with either the Service or the civil authorities, (including cases which come to the notice of the police direct as well as those reported to them under para J7.004):

a. In cases reported to the police for that area it is for the chief officer of police to decide (normally after consultation with the commanding officer), whether the alleged offender is to be tried by the civil court or is to be dealt with by the authorities of the Service concerned.

b. Although the decision whether an offender is to be tried by a civil court or under Service law always rests with the civil authorities, in cases referred to the Ministry of Defence Police, the decision will normally be taken on their behalf by an officer of the Ministry of Defence Police, not below the rank of inspector, in consultation with the commanding officer. No proceedings by courts-martial are, in any event, to be undertaken in the United Kingdom in respect of an offence under the Official Secrets Acts 1911 to 1989 or under the Race Relations Act 1976 without prior authority from the Ministry of Defence (PS 2(Army)).

J7.006. In making his decision, the chief officer of the police for that area or the Ministry of Defence Police officer, in consultation with the commanding officer, will take into account the general principle that an offence, whether committed on Ministry of Defence property or premises or not, which affects the person or property of civilians should normally be dealt with by a civil court but that an offence which involves only Service personnel, their property or Service property should, unless specifically excluded from Service jurisdiction, normally be dealt with by the authorities of the Service concerned.

J7.007. The chief officer of police will, however, also take into account the following qualifications:

a. If the alleged offence is committed by a member of the forces who is about to be sent overseas, the police will normally hand the man over to the Service authorities unless it is a serious offence or one specifically excluded from the jurisdiction of the Service authorities or the circumstances are otherwise exceptional.

b. If the alleged offender was on duty at the time and the offence constituted a breach of that duty, the police will normally hand him over to the Service authorities even though the offence may affect the property of a civilian. This would not apply to a charge such as dangerous driving which involves risk to the general public.

c. The Service authorities will generally deal with an offence committed by a member of the forces on Service premises, if it can be dealt with summarily, and was either a minor assault on a civilian or a minor offence against the property of a civilian.

d. If a Service offender has a civilian accomplice, proceedings against both will normally be taken in a civil court.

e. If the alleged offender is already the subject of a suspended sentence ('deferred sentence' in Scotland), a probation order, an order for conditional discharge or some other form of binding over by a civil court, any further offence will be required to be brought to the notice of the civil authorities notwithstanding that it would otherwise normally be dealt with by the Service authorities.

NOTE 3

Queen's Regulations:
Annex A(J) to Chapter Seven
(Referred to in Para. J.7014)

Agreement Regarding the Status of Forces of Parties to the North Atlantic Treaty (Cmd. 9363)

Article VII

1. Subject to the provision of this Article,

   a. the military authorities of the sending State shall have the right to exercise within the receiving State all criminal and disciplinary jurisdiction conferred on them by the law of the sending State over all persons subject to the military law of that State;

   b. the authorities of the receiving State shall have jurisdiction over the members of a force or civilian component and their dependants with respect to offences committed within the territory of the receiving State and punishable by the law of that State.

2. a. The military authorities of the sending State shall have the right to exercise exclusive jurisdiction over persons subject to the military law of that State with respect to offences, including offences relating to its security, punishable by the law of the sending State, but not by the law of the receiving State.

   b. The authorities of the receiving State shall have the right to exercise exclusive jurisdiction over members of a force or civilian component and their dependants with respect to offences, including offences relating to the security of that State, punishable by its law but not by the law of the sending State.

   c. For the purposes of this paragraph and of paragraph 3 of this Article a security offence against a State shall include:

      1. treason against the State;

2. sabotage, espionage or violation of any law relating to official secrets of that State, or secrets relating to the national defence of that State.

3. In cases where the right to exercise jurisdiction is concurrent the following rules shall apply:

   a. The military authorities of the sending State shall have the primary right to exercise jurisdiction over a member of a force or of a civilian component in relation to:

      1. offences solely against the property or security of that State, or offences solely against the person or property of another member of force or civilian component of that State or of a dependant;

      2. offences arising out of any act or omission done in the performance of official duty.

   b. In the case of any other offence the authorities of the receiving State shall have the primary right to exercise jurisdiction.

   c. If the State having the primary right decides not to exercise jurisdiction, it shall notify the authorities of the other State as soon as practicable. The authorities of the State having the primary right shall give sympathetic consideration to a request from the authorities of the other State for a waiver of its right in cases where that other State considers such waiver to be of particular importance.

4. The foregoing provisions of this Article shall not imply any right for the military authorities of the sending State to exercise jurisdiction over persons who are nationals of or ordinarily resident in the receiving State, unless they are members of the force of the sending State.

5. a. The authorities of the receiving and sending States shall assist each other in the arrest of members of a force or civilian component or their dependants in the territory of the receiving State and in handing them over to the authority which is to exercise jurisdiction in accordance with the above provisions.

   b. The authorities of the receiving State shall notify promptly the military authorities of the sending State of the arrest of any member of a force or civilian component or a dependant.

   c. The custody of an accused member of a force or civilian component over whom the receiving State is to exercise jurisdiction shall, if he is in the hands of the sending State, remain with that State until he is charged by the receiving State.

6. a. The authorities of the receiving and sending State shall assist each other in the carrying out of all necessary investigations into offences, and in the collection and production of evidence, including the seizure and, in proper cases, the handing over of objects connected with an offence. The handing over of such objects may, however, be made subject to their return within the time specified by the authority delivering them.

   b. The authorities of the Contracting Parties shall notify one another of the disposition of all cases in which there are concurrent rights to exercise jurisdiction.

7. a. A death sentence shall not be carried out in the receiving State by the authorities of the sending State if the legislation of the receiving State does not provide for such punishment in a similar case.

   b. The authorities of the receiving State shall give sympathetic consideration to a request from the authorities of the sending State for assistance in carrying out a sentence of imprisonment pronounced by the authorities of the sending State under the provision of this Article within the territory of the receiving State.

8. Where an accused has been tried in accordance with the provisions of this Article by the authorities of one Contracting Party and has been acquitted, or has been convicted and is serving, or has served, his sentence or has been pardoned, he may not be tried again for the same offence within the same territory by the authorities of another Contracting Party. However, nothing in this paragraph shall prevent the military authorities of the sending State from trying a member of its force for any violation of rules of discipline arising from an act or omission which constituted an offence for which he was tried by the authorities of another Contracting Party.

9. Whenever a member of a force or civilian component or a dependant is prosecuted under the jurisdiction of a receiving State he shall be entitled –

   a. to a prompt and speedy trial;

   b. to be informed, in advance of trial, of the specific charge or charges made against him;

   c. to be confronted with the witnesses against him;

   d. to have compulsory process for obtaining witnesses in his favour, if they are within the jurisdiction of the receiving State;

e. to have legal representation of his own choice for his defence or to have free or assisted legal representation under the conditions prevailing for the time being in the receiving State;

f. if he considers it necessary, to have the services of a competent interpreter; and;

g. to communicate with a representative of the Government of the sending State and, when the rules of the court permit, to have such a representative present at his trial.

10. a. Regularly constituted military units or formations of a force shall have the right to police any camps, establishments or other premises which they occupy as the result of an agreement with the receiving State. The military police of the force may take all appropriate measures to ensure the maintenance of order and security on such premises.

b. Outside these premises, such military police shall be employed only subject to arrangements with the authorities of the receiving State and in liaison with those authorities, and in so far as such employment is necessary to maintain discipline and order among the members of the force.

11. Each Contracting Party shall seek such legislation as it deems necessary to ensure the adequate security and protection within its territory of installations, equipment, property, records and official information of other Contracting Parties, and the punishment of persons who may contravene laws enacted for that purpose.

NOTE 4

Queen's Regulations: Chapter Twelve [1]

Official Information and Public Relations
Part 1 – General

Disclosure of Official Information

J12.003. It is an offence against the Official Secrets Acts for a person to divulge, whether during or after a period of service with the armed forces, official information acquired by him during such service unless expressly authorised to do so. All personnel are forbidden to communicate any official information, including information about to be made public, to any person other than one to whom they are authorised to communicate it or one to whom it is their official duty to communicate it. The use of such information for personal controversy or for any private purpose during or after completion of service without due authority is a breach of the Official Secrets Acts. Information acquired in an official capacity by any one seconded for service with another Government Department is not to be disclosed without the express permission of that Department.

J12.004. Any information of a professional or technical nature that a member of the armed forces may acquire in the performance of his duty, or in the course of his official studies, is the property of the Crown and is not to be published in any form without the prior approval of the Ministry of Defence.

Restrictions on Use of Official Documents

J12.005. Official reports, correspondence and documents of whatever description, whether classified or not, are the property of the Crown. The only legitimate use which personnel may make of official documents, or information derived from them, is for the furtherance of the public service in the performance of their duty.

---

1 The *relevant* Queen's Regulations: Chapter Twelve are reproduced here and *not* the entire Chapter.

Part 2 – Activities Involving the Use of Official Information or Experience

General Considerations

J12.015. Greater openness in the work of Government requires:

a. The fullest possible exposition to Parliament and to the public of the reasons for Government policies and decisions when those policies and decisions have been formulated and are announced.

b. The creation of a better public understanding about the way in which the processes of Government work and about the factual or technical background to Government policies and decisions.

The development of openness in this sense does not imply a licence to Service personnel to discuss with unauthorised persons Government policies and decisions which are in the process of being formulated before announcements are made. Nor does it cover participation by Service personnel in the public discussions of politically controversial topics, whether the issues are important or relatively trivial. (A politically controversial issue is one which is, has been, or is clearly about to be, a matter of controversy between political parties in this country.) The exposition of Government policies and decisions is the responsibility of Ministers. It would therefore be improper for individual members of the Services to be personally identified in public with any line in conflict with declared Government policy. There will, from time to time, be opportunities for personnel to help in creating a better understanding of the way in which the processes of Government work and, in some instances, about the factual or technical background to Government policies or decisions. There will also be occasions when personnel can and should make a contribution to knowledge on the basis of specialised information and experience obtained in the course of their official duties; in particular, professional, scientific and engineering personnel are encouraged to participate in discussion with learned bodies so long as policy, defence and commercial interests are protected. Any such participation in public discussion or contribution to knowledge of this kind must, however, be such as will neither prejudice national security; create the possibility of embarrassment to the Government in the conduct of its policies; nor bring into question the impartiality of Her Majesty's forces. Although these principles apply primarily to the disclosure of information and for the discussion of political issues, they apply with equal force to the public expression, in the press or elsewhere, of opinions which are, or could be, embarrassing to the Government when given by individuals who are identified, or are readily identifiable, as Service personnel. It is essential therefore that control over what is made public should rest with the appropriate authorities of the Ministry of Defence.

Personnel who have left the Service

J12.018. Personnel who, after leaving Her Majesty's forces, wish to publish any information which they have acquired or to which they have had access as a result of their official position or service, and which is covered by the Official Secrets Acts, should seek the official sanction of the Ministry of Defence before publication, as required by the Declaration which is signed on termination of service (MOD Form 135).

Principles

J12.019. The general principles which apply to outside activities involving the use of official information or experience are:

   a. There must be no disclosure of classified 'In confidence' information.

   b. There should be no discussion of issues which are sensitive, politically or otherwise (see para J12.015).

   c. The relations between Service personnel and Ministers, or the confidential advice given to Ministers, should not be disclosed.

   d. There should be no comment on individuals or organisations in terms which the Ministry of Defence would regard as objectionable.

   e. The activity should not conflict with the interests of the Services or the Ministry of Defence, or bring their good name, or that of the Civil Service generally, into disrepute.

   f. The commercial and parent interests of the Ministry of Defence, of other Government Departments, and of organisations and contractors collaborating with them, should be fully protected. It is the responsibility of those proposing to take part in an outside activity to seek advice if these commercial interest might be jeopardised in any way, and in particular if the activity relates to work under departmental contracts. It should be noted that disclosure, even under conditions of confidence, to whole sections of industry may in some circumstances constitute publication for patent purposes and might make it impossible to secure valid patent protection for the subject matter disclosed.

   g. The security or other national interests of collaborating countries should be fully protected in discussions about international collaborative projects or agreements to which Her Majesty's Government is a party, even where United Kingdom interests are not directly affected.

h. Permission should be obtained to republish any material covered by copyright, whether the copyright owner is the Crown or not. Particular care is necessary where it is proposed to use material the origin of which is obscure.

Press Announcements
J12.020.

a. Official communications to the press will normally be made by Public Relations staffs. They may, however, be made by other duly authorised personnel in British commands, ships, units and establishments, e.g. the commanding officer or his representative, when the information given is factual and relates solely to the command, ship, unit or establishment concerned and when this is in accordance with any separate instructions. They must avoid comment on issues of a politically controversial nature.

b. Where casualties have occurred, the names of persons killed or injured are not in any circumstances to be divulged until it is definitely known that the next of kin have been informed.

Broadcasts and Press Interviews
J12.021.

a. Invitations for Service personnel to take part in a radio or television programme are usually made by the broadcasting authorities through official channels, but a direct approach may sometimes be made. If an individual is approached direct he should immediately report the matter as in para 1 of Annex A to this Chapter. Invitations to cooperate in the production of programmes or for help in providing briefing and background information for a programme should be reported similarly.

b. Public justification of Government policy is a function if Ministers not of Service personnel. Members of Her Majesty's forces should not therefore take part in a broadcast discussion or press interview on the merits of a policy which is, or may become, a matter of controversy between the political parties. As even a factual statement on such a subject may be open to misconstruction, it is preferable that personnel should not speak in public on any politically controversial issue (see para J12.015 above). An unrehearsed interview or discussion on a non controversial subject can easily move into an area of political controversy and the position of Service personnel on controversial matters must therefore be made quite clear to the commentator or interviewer beforehand. So as to reduce the possibility of subsequent misinterpretation a public relations or other officer is to be in attendance at all press interviews and radio or television appearances.

Payments for Broadcasting, Lecturing or Writing for Publication

J12.022. Broadcasts by serving personnel acting as official spokesmen and speeches and lectures on official subjects will normally be undertaken as part of their official duty and, as such, covered by their Service pay; no question of extra payment to individuals will therefore arise. If, however, all or part of the preparatory work and delivery of the broadcast, speech or lecture is done during the individual's off duty time he may retain the whole or part of any fees payable, as appropriate. This provision also governs the retention of any fees payable for the writing of books or articles on official matters or involving material or experience. Details of any payments should be sent to the appropriate Public Relations or Publication Clearance authority (see Annex A to this chapter) to consider what proportion should be credited to public funds.

Outside Seminars and Study Conferences

J12.023.

    a. Members of Her Majesty's forces in their official capacity should not, in the absence of specific permission, accept invitations to conferences convened by, or under aegis of, party political organisations. They may, in their official capacity, attend or take part in non-governmental conferences, seminars etc., which are not conducted under the aegis of a party political organisation provided that the Ministry of Defence is satisfied as to the character of the conference and the advantages likely to accrue.

    b. Personnel who receive an invitation from a non governmental and non political body to participate in a study conference, seminar or discussion are, before accepting:

        1. If serving in Ministry of Defence headquarters to seek prior authority through the appropriate DPR.

        2. If serving outside Ministry of Defence headquarters, to seek the prior authority of the CinC or head of establishment, or other officer, official or authority to whom his responsibility has been delegated.

In any case of doubt the Secretary of the Defence Studies Steering Group (Head of the Sec Pol Studies, Ministry of Defence) should be consulted. Texts should be submitted for clearance in advance under the procedure set out in Annex A to this chapter.

    c. Service personnel are free to join the International Institute for Strategic Studies (IISS), the Royal Institute of International Affairs

(RIIA) or the Royal United Services Institute (RUSI) for Defence Studies and may actively participate in the proceedings of those bodies, subject to the general consideration set out in subparas *e* and *f*, without seeking prior approval as in subpara *b*. They are, however, required to seek guidance if they are in doubt about the propriety of their participation on any particular occasion.

d. Individuals who are nominated by the Ministry of Defence to take part in a study conference or seminar may make oral or written contributions to the discussions, but if they are doubtful about any point they should consult the Secretary, Defence Studies Steering Group.

e. Personnel who join the IISS, the RHA or the RUSI, or who are nominated to take part in study conferences or seminars of defence problems, are encouraged to make as useful a contribution to the discussion as possible; but they must be discreet in what they say, bearing in mind the nature of their subject and their audience and the risk that their remarks may be reported even if publicity is not expected. They may discuss, in non-committal and professional terms, possible alternative policies or courses of action and the advantages or disadvantages which might be claimed for them; but it would be improper for them to appear to be personally identified with any line in conflict with Government policy. If it is impossible to avoid commenting on politically controversial quesions they should confine themselves to statements of Government policy on the questions involved and should avoid expressing personal views. They may intervene to correct gross errors of fact where silence might be interpreted as acquiescence.

f. Classified or commercially significant information must not be revealed. Personnel are advised to consult their security organisation if they think it possible that security problems may arise during a seminar or study conference.

Members of Parliament, Foreign Countries, Committees and Contractors

J12.025. Instructions are contained in the relevant Security Manuals about the disclosure of information to:

a. Members of Parliament (see also para J5.013).

b. Foreign countries and foreign nationals.

c. Committee members, consultants and defence lectures.

d. Contractors.

J12.026. Defence Press and Broadcasting Committee (DPBC). 'D' Notices are addressed to national and provincial newspaper editors, to radio and television organisations, and to some publishers of periodicals and books on defence and related subjects. ('D' Notices are issued and amended on the authority of the DPBC.) The Secretary of DPBC is available at all times to advise on questions that arise as to the application of a D Notice to some particular set of circumstances. Any advice requested by the press as a whole on the publication of items of information which appear to come within the scope of a D Notice should be referred to the Secretary DPBC whose address may be obtained through the Defence Public Relations Staff.

Part 3 – Public Relations

Public Relations – General

J12.030. While observing the need for security and the confidentiality of many Service transactions, members of the armed forces have a responsibility for maintaining good relations with the public and the press. The regulations in this chapter are supplemented by the Army Manual of Public Relations 1967 (Code No. 70430). By press is meant not only newspapers and periodicals but also other publications, radio and television, films and news-reels, i.e. all information media.

Visits by Press Representatives

J12.031. Commanding officers must ensure that instructions governing the admission of press representatives to Service units and establishments and the facilities to be granted in connection with such visits are carefully observed.

Incidents Liable to Cause Parliamentary or Press Comment

J12.032. In general the preceding regulations deal with the control of information and the release of it to the press. It is equally important, however, that CinCs and senior officers and, as appropriate, officers in command of detached units should provide the Ministry of Defence (Defence Press Office) with the earliest possible official information of any incidents or occurrences in which the Royal Navy, the Army or the Royal Air Force is involved and which may be liable to form the subject of comment in Parliament or in the press as defined in para **J12.030**.

J12.033. When it is impossible for a full account of any incident to be rendered before the facts have been thoroughly examined, an incomplete account should be sent at the earliest moment, followed in due course by any detailed report considered necessary.

J12.034. Where such an incident occurs in a detached unit the commanding officer is to inform the Ministry of Defence direct by immediate signal, as well as the CinC and such other authorities as may be laid down in local orders.

5

Government, Ethics and the Media:
The United Kingdom Defence, Press and
Broadcasting Committee and its D Notice System

*by Rear Admiral D. M. Pulvertaft, CB, Secretary of
the D Notice Committee* [1]

Guidance aimed at preventing the publication of information damaging to national security is made available to editors, publishers and producers by the Defence, Press and Broadcasting Committee and its D Notice system, which provides a voluntary advisory service.

The Committee, which came into being in 1912, is a semi-official body composed of about a dozen editors and executives from the various parts of the media and four senior civil servants from the Ministry of Defence, Home Office and Foreign and Commonwealth Office.

The Committee has approved the issue of eight unclassified standing D Notices (listed below) covering general areas where the publication of information might endanger national security. These sets of D Notices are held by editors, publishers and producers who are asked to seek advice before publishing information in the various areas described in the D Notices. Advice on particular cases is given to editors on a day-to-day basis by the Secretary of the Committee who acts as an honest broker between the media and the officials and ensures that the system is not used as a means of avoiding political embarrassment.

The system is voluntary and there are no statutory powers of enforcement. Editors are obliged neither to seek advice nor to accept it if offered and the final decision on whether or not to publish rests firmly with the editor. Nor is there any link between the D Notice system and the Official Secrets Acts which must be a matter for consideration by the editor's lawyers, if necessary, in consultation with those of the Government.

---

1 This statement on 'D Notices' is made available in the United Kingdom to editors and others. An earlier version of this statement was given to the Centre for Business and Public Sector Ethics, Cambridge, by the then Secretary of the D Notice Committee, Rear Admiral W. A. Higgins, CB, CBE, (Retd.), in November 1991 during his discussion at the Centre's Fourth Conference on 'Confidentiality of Information' in November 1991. This amended statement has been provided by the new Secretary of the D Notice Committee, Rear Admiral D. M. Pulvertaft, CB.

Compliance with D Notice advice does not guarantee immunity from prosecution under the Official Secrets Act any more than failure to seek or accept advice automatically implies prosecution. Action under the Official Secrets Act depends upon the availability of evidence that an offence has been committed under the provisions of that Act and would be entirely a matter for the prosecution authorities.

Editors, defence correspondents, journalists, authors, publishers and television producers frequently consult the Secretary of the Committee if they have any doubts whether publication of a particular piece of information might prejudice national security. In those cases where there are national security implications it is seldom necessary for a whole story to have to be abandoned as minor amendments usually allow the story to run without causing damage.

Discussions between editors and the Secretary of the Committee are regarded as taking place in confidence and are not revealed to other parts of the media. [2]

CURRENT D NOTICES

No. 1   Defence Plans, Operational Capability, State of Readiness and Training

No. 2   Defence Equipment

No. 3   Nuclear Weapons and Equipment

No. 4   Electronic Equipments and Electro-Magnetic Transmissions

No. 5   Cyphers and Communications

No. 6   British Security and Intelligence Services

No. 7   War Precautions and Civil Defence

No. 8   Photography, etc. of Defence Establishments and Installations.

---

2 See this book Part III 'Government Ethics: Secrecy, Access to Information and Privacy' for detailed chapters on this subject. In particular see pages 287-291 for the non-statutory code of conduct enforced by the Press Complaints Commission of the United Kingdom, in respect of publication by the media of information (other than information likely to damage national security which is dealt with under this D Notice System). However, it should be pointed out that in recent years editors have not observed D Notices with the observance of the past.

VOLUME I   GOVERNMENT ETHICS

PART II

Government Ethics:

Conflict of Interest

6

Conflict of Interest as Part of Political Ethics: The Canadian Federal Government Experience

by Jean-Pierre Kingsley, recently
Assistant Deputy Registrar General of Canada[1]

Introduction

On September 9, 1985, Prime Minister Brian Mulroney introduced in the Canadian House of Commons a comprehensive package of initiatives related to ethics which included:

- a new Conflict of Interest and Post-Employment Code for Public Office Holders;

- a programme of Parliamentary scrutiny of Governor in Council appointments;

- the registration of consultants more commonly called 'lobbyists' (since implemented through Bill C-82);

- advice to Crown corporations not to employ lobbyists as intermediaries in dealings with the Government;

- a review of the judicial appointments process;

- an instruction to Ministers imposing strict limitations on the hiring of family members;

- a request to Members of Parliament and Senators to examine their rules of conduct.

In his open letter to Members of Parliament concerning these initiatives Mr. Mulroney wrote: 'It is a great principle of public administration – I could even say an "imperative" – that to function effectively the government and the public service of a democracy must have the trust and confidence of the public they serve. In order to reinforce that trust, the government must

---

1 This paper was delivered at the Inaugural Conference of the Centre for Business and Public Sector Ethics held in Cambridge, England on 13 July 1989. Mr Jean-Pierre Kingsley is now Chief Electoral Officer of Canada. Mr Georges Tsaï is the current Assistant Deputy Registrar General of Canada.

be able to provide competent management and, above all, to be guided by the highest standards of conduct.'

I believe it is not an exaggeration to state that the people's trust in government is fundamental to our democratic system. Basic to that trust is the people's belief that its political leaders and its public servants are acting in the public interest, 'guided by the highest standards of conduct', in the execution of their public responsibilities and authorities (and are *not* benefitting personally from their public office.)

As is indicated by the title of this presentation, I intend to dwell principally on the Canadian experience in dealing with conflict of interest as a *part* of political ethics. For purposes of this paper, I should clarify that *political* ethics is defined to apply to elected public office holders and to appointed ones: the public servants who are answerable to them in the execution of their duties. The paper presents my views of the important events in respect of the evolution of the régimes governing conflicts of interest and is not meant to be an exhaustive history in this respect.

1. Overview of Other Parts of Political Ethics

I would be remiss, however, if I did not touch briefly on other areas or parts of political ethics.

Favouritism in appointments based on considerations other than merit, has been curtailed significantly through a number of measures:

i. The Civil Service Amendment Act of 1908 and the Civil Service Act of 1918 replaced party affiliation with the merit principle as the basis of employment practices in the Canadian Federal public service. These Acts were updated through the Public Service Act of 1967.

ii. The process of appointments to the judiciary has been modified over time; it now requires consultation with the Attorneys General of the Provinces, the Ministers of Justice, the judiciary, the legal profession and interested groups and organisations.

iii. The Government has introduced and developed review procedures for Governor-in-Council appointees in 1985. Standing Committees of the House of Commons have the authority to review all non-judicial appointments and do so on a selective basis. Although a Committee cannot veto an appointment, it can report concerns for consideration by the House of Commons and the Government.

In another area, lobbying legislation was passed in 1988 requiring all paid lobbyists to register and identify their clients. This initiative has allowed the public to be aware of the activities of those former public office holders who have moved from public to private life in this field of endeavour and of others who may be viewed as having close connections with the party in power.

Contracting rules have been tightened also over time and an elaborate system now exists with separate authorities to *sign* for a good or service, to *approve* such a purchase, and to *commit* funds. In addition, there are rules on the authority to let contracts, stratified in dollar amounts by Department and central agency and stipulating whether a contract is by competitive tender, by standing offer, or by sole source. The latter is an exception, and special rules exist.

Legislation has been implemented since Confederation to regulate ethical conduct in public life in Canada:

a. The *Canadian Criminal Code*, recently amended, has contained for some time prohibitions on certain forms of conduct so clearly unacceptable from public office holders that they are criminalised: for example bribery, fraud, breach of trust, and sale or purchase of appointments to public office.

b. *The Parliament of Canada Act* prevents elected members of the House of Commons and Senators from using their offices for private gain. They are forbidden to receive rewards or advantages for services rendered in their public capacity. A person is ineligible to sit as a Member of the House of Commons if he or she holds financial contracts or agreements with the Government of Canada. Moreover, Members of the House of Commons are not entitled to vote upon any question in which they have a direct pecuniary interest.

c. *The Canada Elections Act* places limits on party and candidate expenses during election campaigns and most contributions over $100 to parties or candidates must be declared to the Chief Electoral Officer. 'Corrupt inducement of voters' is also an indictable offence. If I may open a parenthesis here, election and party financing and utilisation of funds present legislators with a particular challenge, in that they must attempt through legislation to meet ever increasing public demands for transparency and the real need that they perceive for funds for campaign purposes. Party financing is clearly a part of political ethics which must be covered in its detail by a text of law, and not one that lends itself easily to resolution of difficult cases under a Code of conduct.

2. Conflict of Interest

We now come to the main theme of this paper. Preoccupation with conflicts of interest, compared to what we have covered so far, is a relatively recent phenomenon in Canada. It was only twenty-five years ago that the Government first set up rules of conduct in an attempt to resolve difficulties in this area.

Conflict of interest rules are the concrete application of the ethical principles enunciated by Prime Minister Mulroney and his predecessors with the object of separating public office holders' public interest from their other interests; they attempt to deal with perception, as well as the fact of a conflict or the potential for one.

A number of factors have influenced approaches to conflict of interest issues over time. The expansion of the public sector has meant that there are more public office holders having personal interests which are affected by decisions in which they take part in their official capacity. Moreover, the complexity of issues Governments face requires expertise from those who have knowledge and usually concomitant private interests in those areas.

Further, with the daily inundation of live and direct communications, Canadian society is informed better now than ever. Indeed, the influence of the media in Canada, as in other countries, has had a major influence on the evolution of conflict of interest rules in Canada. Here, as elsewhere, the investigative approach in journalism has had a major impact. Journalists have been assisted in their work by Access to Information legislation concerning government files and just generally easier access to business information such as directorships and shareholders of major public companies.

Approaches to the subject of conflict of interest were usually incremental and were developed largely in response to allegations and facts that caused the general public to question and doubt the moral conduct of public office holders.

The general trend has shown progressively wider coverage of officials – first Ministers, then their staffs and Governor-in-Council appointees, public servants, Lieutenant Governors, and finally Parliamentary Secretaries and appointees to quasi-judicial boards and commissions.

To date, one aspect has remained constant – rules have been established by the Prime Minister-of-the-day and were added to public office holders' terms and conditions of office and to their oaths of office.

3. Conflict of Interest – Developments from 1964-1985
Prime Minister Pearson (1964-1968)

In 1964, a major scandal arose involving a former fundraiser for the Liberal Party of Canada, charged in the United States with smuggling heroin, who faced extradition hearings in a Canadian court. It was alleged, during the course of the trial, that his friends and various aides to Cabinet Ministers tried to persuade Counsel for the United States' Government not to oppose bail application. A Commission of Inquiry (the Dorion Commission) discovered evidence that friends who made representations on the former fundraiser's behalf to ministerial staff were guilty under Criminal Code provisions of attempts to obstruct justice. However, the same findings of a criminal nature did not apply to the ministerial staff. The Commissioner noted the obvious absence of rules governing the activities of Executive Assistants to the Crown. On November 30, 1964 Prime Minister Lester Pearson used the occasion of what is known as the Rivard Affair to issue a letter to Ministers on the proper conduct of people in government service.

The letter itself stands as the basis of all subsequent conflict of interest régimes in the Government of Canada. It was directed specifically to ministerial staff, but the Prime Minister made reference to Ministers and civil servants.

First, the same 'high code of conduct' expected of Ministers of the Crown should apply to a Minister's staff. He went on to say that '... members of Ministers' staffs, equally with Ministers, must not place themselves in a position where they are under obligation to any person who might profit from special consideration or favour on their part, or seek in any way to gain special treatment from them. Equally, a staff member, like a Minister, must not have a pecuniary interest that could even remotely conflict with the discharge of his public duty'.

The onus was clearly on the individual public office holder; the right to privacy of the public office holder was also clearly recognised as an important element of this admittedly modest régime.

4. Prime Minister Pierre Trudeau (1968-1979)

Shortly after the Right Honourable Pierre Elliott Trudeau took Office, new directions and programmes were implemented and as a result the Federal Government expanded. In 1969, the Government passed a major Government Reorganisation Act realigning government programmes and creating new Departments.

When the question of staffing key positions in these new organisations arose, the decision was made to look beyond the public service, and to recruit from the business community. Previously, most senior officials had entered the public service at lower levels and worked their way up in the 'mandarin' tradition.

Overnight the problem of potential conflicts of interest arose. The outside experts who had been recruited had worked their way to the top in the business, industrial, and manufacturing sectors, owned shares, stock options and other assets which could be influenced by Government decisions in which they would be taking part.

A quick review of the conflict of interest situation at the time revealed only two avenues of recourse to prevent conflicts of interest from arising: one through the sale of assets and the second through recusal or the avoidance of defined activities.

Accordingly, the President of the Privy Council was assigned responsibility for reviewing the issue of conflict of interest. Two research papers were prepared on this subject. The first, presented to the Privy Council Office in September 1969 by Professor Jeremy Williams of the University of Alberta, despaired of any specific régime to govern instances of conflicts of interest. It set out 'cardinal rules' designed to prevent obvious and objectionable forms of conflicts and outlined enforcement remedies, with a Tribunal to determine if indeed a conflict had occurred. The second, written by Professor Yvon Marcoux of Laval University and presented to the Privy Council Office in June 1970, discussed various approaches to the subject of conflict of interest and recommended that special committees of both Houses be appointed to draft Codes of ethics and rules specific to each House respecting disclosures of Members' financial interests.

These two papers became working documents for an Interdepartmental Committee established in April 1970 at the request of Mr Gordon Robertson, then Clerk of the Privy Council. The Committee was instructed to develop a conflict of interest régime for public servants. The main recommendation was the acknowledgment and observance of a clear imperative: if a public servant's personal interests conflict with his or her public responsibilities, the public interest must take precedence. This principle was to be applied through an honours system, not legislation.

Events in the United States triggered further Government action. Kenneth Kernaghan, in his book *Ethical Conduct: Guidelines for Government Employees*, wrote that the extensive coverage of the 'Watergate Affair' created a 'widespread climate of opinion in several countries, including Canada, against unethical conduct in government.' [2]

On July 17, 1973 a Green (discussion) Paper entitled the *Members of Parliament and Conflict of Interest*, was tabled in the House of Commons by the then President of the Privy Council, Allan J. MacEachen. It included a draft 'Independence of Parliament Act' which was intended to regulate the conduct of Members of the House of Commons and the Senate. The Green paper was subsequently re-tabled in the House of Commons in November 1974 and in the Senate in April 1975. Ensuing reports were never debated. On July 18, 1973, Prime Minister Trudeau announced in the House a set of Conflict of Interest guidelines for Ministers, followed on December 18, 1973 by guidelines for Governor-in-Council appointees and public servants. They were considered the first so called 'Conflict of Interest Guidelines'. Cabinet approved further guidelines for Governor-in-Council appointees in November 1974. Heads of posts were added to the list in 1978 and Ministers' exempt staff members in 1979. Lieutenant Governors were asked to adhere to basic principles of conduct in 1975; and Parliamentary Secretaries were

---

2 Kenneth Kernaghan *Ethical Conduct: Guidelines for Government Employees* (Toronto: Institute of Public Administration of Canada 1975) p. 3.

subjected to post-employment principles in 1980.

Mr Trudeau rejected legislation to enforce compliance with a conflict of interest régime. He took the approach that they were part of a Prime Minister's 'conditions of employment' on public office holders and that successive Prime Ministers should be able to change these rules to fit their situation. General guidelines would allow the Government to respond quickly and effectively to conflicts as they arose. The Prime Minister preferred political reprimands including the ultimate sanction of removal from office rather than what he viewed as cumbersome judicial remedies for ethical transgressions of a public office holder's duties.

His letter of December 1973 and subsequent guidelines followed the general principles articulated in Prime Minister Pearson's letter of 1964. The arrangements of personal affairs remained a matter of personal responsibility. Ministers were required to divest of assets which could be affected by their decisions as Members of Cabinet and they were not to participate in outside professional, commercial or financial activities.

Assets that were not exempt, that is, that were not for personal or recreational use, were either publicly declarable or subject to divestment by sale, or by placing them in either a blind or frozen trust. Trustees of frozen trusts were to maintain the holdings as they were at the time of deposit while trustees of blind trusts were to make all business decisions affecting the holdings without any information being exchanged between the settlor and the trustee.

Conflict of interest guidelines for Public Service Employees were issued under Order-in-Council in 1973. They outlined rules to be observed by public servants in conflict of interest situations.

The Prime Minister asked employees not only to obey the law governing their conduct, but to act in a manner so scrupulous that it would bear the closest public scrutiny, an echo from Mr Pearson's 1964 letter. Public servants were prohibited from accepting government contracts or using confidential information to aid themselves or their friends while in office. The guidelines stipulated that public servants arrange their private interests, including outside employment, accordingly upon assumption of office. They were to notify superiors of situations where private interest affected their public duties.

In May 1974, Prime Minister Trudeau established the Office of the Assistant Deputy Registrar General (ADRG) to assist Ministers, their exempt staff members and Governor-in-Council appointees in their efforts to comply with these new guidelines. The Office was set up within the Department of Consumer and Corporate Affairs, and made responsible to the Prime Minister through the Clerk of the Privy Council for the administration of conflict of interest arrangements with public office holders. Its basic mandate has remained essentially the same and to this date it has not been mandated formally to undertake investigations or inquiries. Through experience, the Office has defined sub-categories of disclosable assets, liabilities and outside activities and established precedents governing gifts, hospitality and economic benefits. Interpretations have also been provided concerning post-employment requirements for individual cases.

This conflict of interest régime remained intact until the next public controversy arose in March and April of 1976. Two Deputy Ministers retired early to establish together a public consulting firm. The firm was perceived to be lobbying the Government directly and giving advice to others to enable them to approach the Government to pursue their particular interests. The ensuing public outcry of possible conflict between the Deputy Ministers' former responsibilities to the Crown and their new ones in the private sector persuaded the Government to formulate a policy on post-employment practices for public office holders.

The Federal Cabinet reviewed two Memoranda on the subject of post-employment practices in the immediate aftermath of what became known as the Reisman-Grandy Affair. The first, dated 23 June 1976, urged the Government to legislate the practices appropriate to former public servants. Such a statute would provide for an independent advisory body to interpret the guidelines therein. This proposal was not accepted: such conflicts were problems to be solved by politicians, not judges. The second Memorandum to Cabinet outlined the actual guidelines to govern post-employment practices of former public office holders (Ministers, Parliamentary Secretaries, Governor-in-Council appointees, senior public servants, and Ministers' exempt staff members). This proposal was accepted, and the first post-employment guidelines were tabled in the House of Commons on 17 December 1976, to be effective on January 1, 1978.

Guidelines were adopted to limit former public office holders, for defined periods, from:

a. accepting employment to a board of directors with firms with which they have had a special working relationship;

b. changing sides with respect to matters with which they dealt while employed by the government; and

c. lobbying Departments and government agencies with which they were employed or had a close working relationship.

Ministers, senior ministerial exempt staff members, Governor-in-Council appointees, Parliamentary Secretaries and public servants were subject to similar conditions.

Provision was made for special advisory committees to administer the post-employment régime and they were given the authority to recommend exemptions from the guidelines in special circumstances; few were established.

5. Prime Minister Joe Clark (1979-1980)

In the 1979 general election, under the leadership of Mr Clark, the Progressive Conservative Party won a plurality of seats to form a minority Government. Being the prerogative of the Prime Minister, changes to the previous conflict of interest guidelines were made by the Right Honourable Joe Clark.

Two general principles were outlined: Ministers were required not only to perform, but to *appear* to perform their duties and arrange their private interests 'in a manner that will conserve and enhance public confidence'. Second, Ministers were not to use their influence as servants of the Crown for private gain. Again, the onus for proper conduct fell on the shoulders of the Minister. Prime Minister Clark chose to follow Mr Pearson and Mr Trudeau's approach that compulsion to honour the guidelines was moral and the remedy for abuses rested in his hands.

For the first time gifts or benefits received with a value of more than $100, except those from family, friends or official gifts from foreign countries, were to be disclosed within thirty days for inclusion into the Public Registry.

Another initiative to the effect that Ministers' spouses and minor or dependant children be subject to the same requirements as for Ministers in respect of assets, liabilities, and gifts or other benefits, created controversy. The requirement held throughout his term in office.

6. Prime Minister Pierre Trudeau (1980-1984)

The defeat of the minority Conservative Government and return of the Liberal Party led once again by Mr Trudeau brought changes to the conflict of interest guidelines on April 28, 1980. The principles were nearly identical to those that were implemented under the Clark Government. However, Mr Trudeau held fast to his 1973 statement on spouses and dependants disclosure: he had previously said in the House of Commons on 18 July 1973, 'Ministers' spouses and their families are not being required to follow the strict rules that are being set out for Ministers themselves. This is simply not practical and may not even be just'. He removed that requirement, all the while reminding Ministers to be vigilant in respect of it. A few additions were made to the exempt assets category, the guidelines established Retention Trusts for family holding companies established for estate planning purposes; and the floor for disclosable gifts was raised to $200. Finally, it was decided that the public purse should reimburse certain trust costs on the basis that compliance with the conflict of interest guidelines was a condition of appointment, once approved by the ADRG.

A scandal soon arose over an alleged breach of the post-employment guidelines by a former Minister of Energy, Mines and Resources. He had left public life and had established a consortium to promote research and development in new fuels, at a time of high energy costs. The consortium had sought a grant from his former Department to promote development of technology to convert coal to oil. The former Minister then wrote to the Deputy Minister of Energy, Mines and Resources, his former subordinate from 1975 to 1979, on the status of the loan request.

The intensive media scrutiny of the affair known as the 'Gillespie Affair' rekindled public and Parliamentary debate about acceptable moral conduct of present and past public office holders. As a result, Prime Minister Trudeau appointed two Privy Councillors, the Honourable Mitchell Sharp, a former Liberal Minister in Prime Ministers' Pearson and Trudeau's Cabinets, and the Honourable Michael Starr, a former Conservative Minister in Prime Minister Diefenbaker's Cabinet, to head a Task Force into ethical conduct in the public sector. The Task Force tabled its report in May 1984, after Mr Trudeau had announced his decision to resign. He would leave any decision concerning this matter to his successor.

7. Prime Minister John A. Turner (1984)

Mr Turner, who shortly after assuming office called a general election, did not have the time to consider the Task Force's recommendations; as an interim measure, he continued with the guidelines then in force.

The Report of the Task Force on Conflict of Interest, entitled 'Ethical Conduct in the Public Sector' constitutes the most comprehensive examination of conflict of interest régimes in Canada and their history, to say nothing of its succinct analysis of ethical régimes in the public sectors of other countries. Its approach attempted to balance the need to maintain high standards of ethical conduct in the public service without unduly inhibiting people of high quality and profile in the private sector from assuming public office. The Report lamented the piecemeal fashion in which past guidelines were established and suggested three simple 'touchstones' for the formulation of future guidelines: simplicity, fairness, and reasonableness.

These 'touchstones' informed the Report's final recommendations, including a proposal to legislate a model 'Code of Ethical Conduct' applicable to all public office holders to replace previous guidelines. The Report suggested a legislative approach to implement the Code, while maintaining at the same time that the principle of individual responsibility for one's conduct in any conflict of interest régime should be maintained: no mean feat! Another recommendation was that the Office of the Assistant Deputy Registrar General should be made into an Office of Public Sector Ethics headed by an 'Ethics Counsellor'. He or she would be given a mandate to advise, investigate, educate, administer an ethical code as well as perform the duties previously under the direction of the Assistant Deputy Registrar General. The Commission concurred with Mr Trudeau that the inclusion of spouses and children would not be warranted.

8. Recent Events
Prime Minister Brian Mulroney (1984-   )

Two weeks after the 1984 election, Prime Minister Brian Mulroney asked the Honourable Eric Nielsen, Deputy Prime Minister and President of the Privy Council, to pursue three major governmental initiatives including Conflict of Interest and Post-Employment Guidelines. The Starr-Sharp Report and the Nielsen Task Force bore upon the philosophy and contents of the next conflict of interest initiative.

On 9 September 1985, as part of the package of major initiatives on public sector ethics referred to at the outset of this paper, Prime Minister Mulroney tabled in the House of Commons *The Conflict of Interest and Post-Employment Code for Public Office Holders*. It *codified* in one document the rules governing all public office holders in the Government of Canada. The word 'code' replaced the word 'guideline' thus reinforcing the requirement for its application, and nine principles reflect the intent, if not the actual words, of the proposed code in the Sharp-Starr Report. Although the Ethics Counsellor did not replace the Assistant Deputy Registrar General, the latter, along with the Secretary to the Treasury Board, was given the responsibility to educate public office holders on the requirements of the new Code.

Prime Minister Mulroney adhered to past practice in his approach. His Code attempts to balance the need to enhance public confidence in the integrity of government with the desire to attract competent people into public office. This goal is achieved by a Code of conduct that requires public office holders to arrange their personal interests in order to avoid situations of conflict of interest in their official duties. Moreover, the Code does not unduly breach the privacy of the individual. Public office holders are to observe the Code as a condition of holding office. The Prime Minister expressed the belief that 'the success of the régime will depend upon the goodwill and the sense of public service of public office holders.' Onus for compliance rests primarily on the public office holder and judgement on his or her ethical conduct remains the responsibility of the Prime Minister.

There were slight alterations to the requirements applicable under the 1980 guidelines. As with the guidelines, the Code is comprised of general statements dealing with the standards of conduct required of public office holders as well as particular and technical compliance measures designed to minimise the risk of conflict of interest from arising.

The Code emphasises the obligation of public office holders not to accord preferential treatment and to avoid being placed or the appearance of being placed under an obligation to a third party.

The compliance measures are broken down into two categories. The more stringent requirements apply to Ministers, Parliamentary Secretaries, senior members of a Minister's staff, and all full-time Governor-in-Council appointees. The less demanding requirements apply to members of a Minister's staff who are not considered senior staff and to public servants. Public office holders are required to make a confidential report of assets that are not exempt, of direct and contingent liabilities, and of outside activities (current and past) including involvement as trustee, executor or under power of attorney.

If a public office holder has non-exempt assets, he or she must report them to the Office of the Assistant Deputy Registar General and subsequently either make a public declaration of them in a written statement available in a Public Registry maintained in that Office or divest of them by sale at arm's length or through the establishment of a blind trust agreement, as agreed by the Assistant Deputy Registrar General. With respect to activities, offices, and directorships in for profit companies, the practise of a profession, and holding office in a union are prohibited and must be resigned. For those which are permissible, a public declaration is required for positions of office and directorships. All gifts, hospitality or other benefits received of a value of $200 or more (except those from family members or close friends) must also be declared when determined acceptable under the Code. Others must be declined.

When the methods of observation specified in the Code are not suitable as compliance arrangements in respect of the public office holder's personal situation, the Assistant Deputy Registrar General may establish the most appropriate measures while ensuring that proper 'Chinese Walls' are built in order to prevent any real, potential, or apparent conflict of interest situation from arising. 'Chinese Walls' refer to the measures common in the securities industry to prevent insider trading; they are designed to prevent specified information from reaching certain parties within the organisation and the possibility of involvement in the consideration of certain matters on the part of persons who possess the information and who could benefit from it.

Public office holders are also subject to post-employment compliance measures which are intended to minimise the risk of their taking improper advantage of their previous public office. The post-employment measures provided for a prohibition on switching sides in respect of a specific ongoing proceeding, transaction, negotiation or case to which the Government is a party and in respect of which the public office holder advised the Government. The measures also provide a limitation period or 'cooling-off' period of one year (two years for Ministers) concerning appointment to a board of directors or employment with an entity with which they had significant official dealings, making representations to government Departments or agencies and giving counsel concerning the programmes or policies of the Department with which they were employed, or with which they had a direct and substantial relationship. The provisions also provide for a reduction of the limitation period, if determined to be in the public interest, on application by the former public office holder.

In May 1986, the media and Opposition parties alleged that the Minister of Regional Industrial Expansion had used his position in attempts to deal with financial matters associated with private interests placed in his blind trust. After a period of controversy, Prime Minister Mulroney established a Commission of Inquiry, an action similar to Prime Minister Pearson's response to the Rivard Affair. Mr Chief Justice William D. Parker of the Ontario Supreme Court was appointed as Chairperson.

The Commission of Enquiry into the Facts and Allegations of Conflict of Interest Concerning the Honourable Sinclair Stevens held televised hearings and deliberated from July 1986 to February 1987. In his Report, tabled on December 3, 1987, [3] Justice Parker attempted to give precise definition to the expression 'conflict of interest' on the basis of the 1980 guidelines and the 1985 Code: neither provided a specific definition of 'conflict of interest'. He defined conflict of interest as 'a situation in which a Minister of the Crown has knowledge of a private economic interest that is sufficient to influence the exercise of his or her public duties and responsibilities'. Apparent conflict of interest 'exists when there is a reasonable apprehension, which reasonably well-informed persons could properly have, that a conflict of interest exists.' Accordingly, Judge Parker found the Honourable Sinclair Stevens to be in conflict in fourteen instances.

Justice Parker found that the Minister's blind trust was not really blind. Mr Stevens had placed in his blind trust his private company which in turn controlled a public company. Neither could be sold, so therefore the trust was not blind. Further, on the basis of circumstantial evidence, the judge argued that the Minister had knowledge of his financial affairs on a fairly regular basis while a Member of Cabinet, and much of that information came to him from his wife, a lawyer who held offices and directorships in the group of companies in which the Minister held ownership interest. Consequently, Justice Parker urged the Government of Canada to adopt full disclosure of the assets of spouses and dependants of Ministers, and added that if the spouse had a career, he or she should be required to disclose those activities of a commercial nature associated with his or her position. Finally, a new 'Conflict of Interest Office', endowed with investigatory powers and the

---

3 Canada, *Commission of Inquiry into the Facts and Allegations of Conflict of Interest Concerning the Honourable Sinclair M. Stevens* (Commissioner: Justice W. D. Parker, Ottawa: Supply and Services Canada, 1987). To read an extract from this Commission of Inquiry Report, see Appendix III of this Volume, pp. 451-88.

authority to make rulings on matters of compliance, should replace the Office of the Assistant Deputy Registrar General. On the matter of blind trusts, the Commission recommended their abolishment.

The events and recommendations of the Parker Inquiry, and the public demand for governmental action to prevent further transgressions of the Conflict of Interest Code, undoubtedly had a significant impact on the formulation of Bill C-114, 'An Act to provide greater certainty in the reconciliation of the personal interests and duties of office of Members of the Senate and House of Commons, to establish a Conflict of Interest Commission and to make consequential amendments to other Acts'. This proposed legislation was tabled in the House of Commons on 24 February 1988, several weeks after another Minister, the Honourable Michel Cote, was asked by the Prime Minister to resign from the Cabinet for having failed to report a significant personal liability to a friend. The Bill died on the order paper at Second Reading before the 1988 General Election.

The Bill sought to extend many of the provisions in the 1985 Code to all Members of Parliament both of the House of Commons and of the Senate, instead of Ministers and Parliamentary Secretaries only. The centre-piece of the Bill was the establishment of a three member independent Commission to administer it. It was believed that the establishment of an independent Commission would lend greater credibility to the Federal conflict of interest régime. The Governor-in-Council would appoint the Chief Commissioner after consultation by the Prime Minister with the Leader of the Opposition and leaders of other parties. One of the two other commissioners would be appointed from persons approved by the Leader of the Opposition and leaders of other parties. The third member would be appointed without consultation.

The Bill further defined that a conflict of interest would exist 'when the member, the member's spouse or a dependant in relation to the member has significant private interests, other than permitted private interests, that afford the opportunity for the member to benefit, whether directly or indirectly, as a result of the execution of, or the failure to execute, any office of the member.'

All Members of Parliament and Senators would be required to disclose and regularly update to the Commission their assets, their liabilities, their outside activities and gifts, hospitality and economic benefits. Also they would also be required to provide this information on behalf of their spouses and dependants and the Commission would decide on the measures required of the member to be in compliance and on the information to be made public in a Public Registry.

The Commission would assume the responsibilities currently carried out by the Assistant Deputy Registrar General with respect to Ministers and Parliamentary Secretaries. It would be given the power of investigation, as well as that of inquiry under the Inquiries Act. The Prime Minister, the House of Commons or the Senate (by resolution), and the Commission itself could instigate an investigation. The Commission may reach one of the following conclusions:

a. 'the member has not failed, or has failed, with reasonable justification, to fulfil a duty or an obligation under the Act; in which case it so certifies, without explanation, to the member' (copy to the instigator); the member may then seek a written explanation from the Commission for use as the member sees fit;

b. 'the member failed, without reasonable justification, to fulfil a duty or an obligation under the Act' ... In the latter case, the Commission's report 'shall contain such information as will enable the person or persons to whom it is made to determine, what, if any, further action is warranted'. The Committee of the House or the Senate will consider the report, afford the Member the right of representation, and when it agrees with the Commission's report, recommend:

   a. a reprimand;
   b. a fine not to exceed $20,000;
   c. payment of compensation to an aggrieved third party;
   d. for a Member of Parliament, the Member's seat be vacated;
   e. for a Senator, the Member be requested to resign.

The Commission was to assume also the responsibilities of the advisory committees on post-employment practices, with the additional authority of reducing the requirements when it serves the public interest.

Moreover, the post-employment requirements for Ministers and Parliamentary Secretaries would be cut back to one year, as opposed to two years.

In effect, for the first time in respect of conflict of interest in Canada, the Prime Minister would be the sole custodian of the Federal conflict of interest régime no longer. Furthermore, the Commission would be required to ensure that its procedures with regard to due process and the evidence in respect of its findings would meet the vigorous test of law, in case of court challenges.

The Bill also foresaw the reimbursement of reasonable professional fees incurred in respect of it.

9. The Future

The Government was returned to office with a majority in the general election of November 1988, and in a Throne Speech to the new Parliament, the reintroduction of conflict of interest legislation was announced as a priority.

In answer to recent Opposition queries as to timing of the first reading of this important legislation, triggered by new reports of the police investigating several House Members for possible criminal offences, the Prime Minister replied that he expected it for the Fall of 1989.

As of April 1992, Bill C-46 (re-named Bill C-43), which in essence is identical to Bill C-114, was introduced during the current session of Parliament and was considered by a Joint Committee of the House of Commons and the Senate. The Special Joint Committee of the Senate and House of Commons of Canada on Bill C-43 tabled its report in June 1992. Instead of a separate conflict of interest law for Parliamentarians, it proposed consolidating conflict of interest rules into a separate part of *The Parliament of Canada Act*. It also proposed a draft Bill to that effect. The Government is considering now its course of action. Therefore, Bill C-43 may never become law, and if new clauses are enacted, they might be quite different from what is proposed in Bill C-43.

7

Public Sector Conflict of Interest at the Federal Level in Canada and the United States: Differences in Understanding and Approach

by Andrew Stark, Assistant Professor, Faculty of Management, University of Toronto, Canada

Introduction

Over the course of the past twenty years, and at the Federal level, Canadian and American responses to public-sector conflict of interest have shared a rough chronology. In 1973, the Trudeau Government tabled the *Green Paper on Members of Parliament and Conflict of Interest*, and in so doing became the first in Canadian history to propose taking a legislated approach to certain problems of public-sector conflict at the Federal level. The *Green Paper's* statutory proposals were eventually embodied in two Bills, C-61 and C-6, which died on the order paper in 1978. In the United States, 1973 was the penultimate year of Watergate, an ordeal which set off an intense five-year debate in Congress over Government ethics culminating in the Ethics in Government Act of 1978. Both Parliament and Congress further considered the problem of conflict of interest throughout the early and mid-eighties, and then in 1988 – responding to a rash of conflict-of-interest Code violations by Cabinet Ministers – the Mulroney Government introduced Bill C-114, an 'Act to Provide for Greater Certainty in the Reconciliation of the Personal Interests and Duties of Office of Members of the Senate and House of Commons.' C-114 died on the order paper in the fall of 1988. It was then reintroduced as Bill C-46 in November 1989, and, after again dying on the order paper, was reintroduced yet again as C-43 in November 1991 (C-43 has been reviewed recently by a Parliamentary Committee). Meanwhile – also in November 1989, and in response to a rash of conflict-of-interest transgressions by Administration and Congressional office-holders – the United States' Congress passed the Ethics Reform Act, a series of amendments to the 1978 legislation. On either side of the border, then, serious governmental discussion .of public-sector conflict of interest recurred regularly throughout much of the 1970s and 1980s. More generally – as one prominent scholar of Government ethics has noted – by the early 1970s, there had emerged already within the political culture of both countries a broad level of agreement as to the nature and harmfulness of a variety of Government-ethics problems. This consensus, Kenneth Kernaghan observes, arose in no small part as a result of the international publicity accorded the Watergate affair. [1]

Notwithstanding the historical and cultural commonalities between the two countries' recent experiences with public-sector conflict of interest, however, important differences remain. In many other areas of administration and policy – from public-service morale to health-care – scholars continue to explore the ways in which structural differences between the two forms of government have led to divergences in understanding and approach. [2] In what follows, I shall examine the ways in which differences in the structural confiduration of the two governments has issued forth in different cross-border understandings of, and approaches to, public-sector conflict of interest at the Federal level. Several of these government-structure-induced differences persist, even as, at the political-cultural level, a convergence in the substance and extent of public and media concern may have occurred.

Specifically, I will discuss initially four areas in which the structural differences between the Canadian and American systems of government have led to divergences in the two countries' approaches to public-sector conflict of interest: (a) the circumstances under which each government has attempted to use statutory as against non-statutory conflict régimes; (b) their differing understandings of the post-employment questions raised by the activity of former Cabinet Members; (c) disparities between the two countries' approaches to remedies and penalties for conflict; and (d) the divergent fashion in which the two countries handle representations which legislators make before the Executive on behalf of paying clients. I will then discuss a fifth, more historical and – one might say – philosophical difference between Canadian and American approaches to public-sector conflict of interest, one which is attributable also to the structural differences between the two countries' governments. This particular difference, it should be noted, has to a large degree been neutralised by the recent cultural convergence that has taken place in the two countries' attitudes toward conflict of interest. And, in fact, it represents less a structural difference between the American and Canadian governments *per se*, than one between the United States' Presidential system and the British Parliamentary system.

---

1 This paper takes into account the earlier paper by Mr Jean-Pierre Kingsley delivered at the Inaugural Conference of the Centre for Business and Public Sector Ethics, Cambridge, England, 13 July 1989 and reproduced as Chapter 6 of this Volume. See also Kenneth Kernaghan 'Codes of Ethics and Public Administration: Progress, Problems and Prospects' *Canadian Public Administration* Vol. 58 (1980) pp. 208; 213.

2 See, for example, Bert A. Rockman and R. Kent Weaver, eds. *Do Institutions Matter?* (Washington: Brookings, forthcoming).

Nevertheless, since this difference has not been addressed explicitly in analyses of public-sector conflict of interest in Britain, and since to my knowledge it has never been explored in the case of Canada, I examine it in general terms in the paper's final section.

1. Statutory versus Non-Statutory Conflict-of-Interest Régimes

1.1 Statutory Régimes

One of the most critical, thorny and recurrent issues faced by both governments in the area of conflict-of-interest regulation has been raised by the need, at any given juncture, to decide whether to embody the substance of proposed conflict-of-interest régimes in statutory or non-statutory form. Two questions in particular have been key: How extensive should statutory regulation be? And to whom should it apply? At the most general level, the disposition of these questions in the United States has been determined by two strutural features of the Presidential system: because the Executive and Legislative branches are constitutionally separate, Congress historically has had a considerable degree of relatively independent control over the content and disposition of statute law. And because the two branches share the power of appointment, Congress participates, through confirmation as well as oversight, in determining the make-up of, and imposing operating requirements on, several layers of senior Executive-branch office-holders. As a result of both its independent power to legislate, and its prerogatives of confirmation and oversight, Congress has been able to impose upon Cabinet and sub-Cabinet-level Executive-branch office-holders significant *statutory* strictures in the areas of post-employment, divestiture, recusal, gifts and hospitality, without having had to encumber itself in the same fashion.

In Canada, by contrast, the Executive and Legislative branches overlap – Cabinet sits in Parliament, controlling and disposing of the legislative agenda – but the two do not significantly share the power of appointment and oversight: these powers belong essentially to the Executive, and to the Prime Minister in particular. As one senior Canadian civil servant succinctly put this latter point, 'the essence of Parliamentary government is that it depends for its effectiveness on those constitutionally responsible for the exercise of delegated authority, rather than detailed Parliamentary control of the Executive.' [3] Two important considerations regarding the disposition of statutory

---

3 Gordon Osbaldeston 'The Public Servant and Politics' *Policy Options* January 1987 p. 6. It should be noted that a minority school of thought within Canadian politics and political science has, for the past fifteen years, pushed for greater direct Parliamentary control over the Executive. For a decisive critique of this doctrine, see S. L. Sutherland 'Responsible Government and Ministerial Responsibility: Every Reform Is Its Own Problem' *Canadian Journal of Political Science* Vol. 24 (1991) pp. 91-120.

conflict-of-interest régimes in Canada follow from the fact that Cabinet sits in Parliament, providing the only medium for legislative monitoring of the sub-Cabinet Executive, and itself controlling the legislative agenda: first, Parliament has never been asked, and likely never will be asked, to consider conflict-of-interest legislation that applies to the sub-Cabinet Executive – meaning that any direct conflict-of-interest strictures on the sub-Cabinet Executive will remain non-statutory. [4] Second, Parliament is unlikely ever to be given the opportunity to consider conflict-of-interest legislation (whether stringent or relaxed) which treats Members of Cabinet significantly more severely than it treats Members of Parliament – at least by comparison with the statutory disparity between legislative and Cabinet-level strictures which has prevailed in the United States. [5] In other words, this difference in structure between the two Federal governments means that Canadian attempts at statutory conflict-of-interest régimes have excluded the public service, while

---

4 See, for example, the remarks of the Hon. Gerald Regan, in Canada, *House of Commons Debates* March 21, 1983 p. 23951. See also Kenneth Kernaghan 'The Ethical Conduct of Canadian Public Servants' *Optimum* 4 (1973) p. 16. Kernaghan has additionally made this point more broadly about Canadian Provincial governments; see Kernaghan 'Codes of Ethics and Administrative Responsibility' *Canadian Public Administration* Vol. 17 (1974) p. 529; and Kernaghan 'Codes of Ethics and Public Administration: Progress, Problems and Prospects' *Public Administration* Vol. 58 (1980) p. 210. More recently, as Kernaghan and Langford note in their book on ethics for Canadian public servants, 'rather than resort to legislation, most Canadian governments have been inclined to write down rules for responsible administrative behaviour in the form of guidelines, directives . . . or codes of conduct.' See Kenneth Kernaghan and John W. Langford *The Responsible Public Servant* (Halifax: Institute for Research on Public Policy, 1990) p. 184; see also, generally, *Conflict of Interest in Canada: A Federal, Provincial, and Territorial Perspective* (Ottawa: Office of the Assistant Deputy Registrar General, 1992) and reproduced in Appendix Part II to this Volume, pp. 500-29.

   None of this is to say, of course, that the Civil Service in Canada – both Federal and Provincial – is not subject to some statutory controls on ethical behaviour: the Canadian Criminal Code covers bribery, fraud, breach of trust, and influence-peddling among public servants, and the Public Service Act governs issues of political neutrality. Yet most scholars of the subject recognise that these statutes deal with problems other than those which conventionally fall under the rubric 'conflict of interest' — for which there has never been a statute proposed which would apply to Federal public servants. See, for example, Kernaghan and Langford *The Responsible Public Servant* p. 84, also p. 139. See also, generally, Kernaghan 'Codes of Ethics and Public Administration' pp. 209-211 *passim*; Michael M. Atkinson and Maureen Mancuso 'Do We Need a Code of Conduct for Politicians? The Search for Elite Political Culture of Corruption in Canada' *Canadian Journal of Political Science* Vol. 18 (1985) p. 461; and Jean-Pierre Kingsley 'Conflict of Interest as a Part of Political Ethics: The Canadian Federal Government Experience' Chapter 6 of this Volume p. 105-20

5 Ian Greene, for example, has observed generally of Canadian statutory strictures – both Federal and Provincial – that 'when legislation came, it was inevitably drafted so as to cover both Ministers and other legislators, with little apparent recognition that the apropriate standards of impartiality for these two groups might be different.' See Ian Greene 'Conflict of Interest and the Canadian Constitution,' *Canadian Journal of Political Science* Vol. 23 (1990) p. 251.

minimising (without necessarily entirely eliminating) any differences in the treatment accorded Cabinet Ministers and Members of Parliament. And it means that United States' statutory régimes have embraced the Civil Service, while maintaining a wider differential in the burden placed on Cabinet Secretaries, and the Executive branch broadly, as against Congressmen.

Consider the two occasions on which Canadian Governments have introduced statutory régimes: the *Green Paper on Members of Parliament and Conflict of Interest* in 1973 (which led to the introduction of Bills C-62 and C-6 in 1978), and Bill C-114 in 1988 (which was re-introduced without substantive changes as Bill C-46 in 1989). Both, to the extent possible – but in very different ways given the different climates of the times – confined themselves (in the one case completely, in the other, notably) to strictures the violation of which their drafters saw as equally objectionable, whether committed by a Cabinet Minister or an ordinary Member. The 1973 *Green Paper* took a minimalist approach, containing as it did only two statutory proposals: that Members and Ministers not be allowed to hold contracts with the government, and that they not be permitted to hold 'incompatible offices,' that is, offices in the Federal, Provincial and Municipal government. Any further strictures which one might have thought ought to apply to Cabinet but not to ordinary Members because of the great differential in their power, did not see the light of day – and did not see the light of day precisely because of the great differential in their power: Cabinet simply refused to introduce or accept them in the form of amendments.

In fact, both in the House and in Committee, Government Members advanced a doctrinal sub-structure for the equal statutory treatment the *Green Paper* proposed to accord Members of Parliament and Ministers, denying as they did that Ministers, by virtue of their office, display a greater tendency or capacity for conflict than do ordinary Members. One Government Member, for example, argued that 'Members of the Opposition have a[n even] greater capacity to put themselves into conflict of interest than [does] a Minister, whose time tends to be taken up with day-to-day administration.' [6] Another government Member of Parliament claimed that it is contrary to moral reasoning to draw distinctions between the harm posed by ministerial conflict and that posed by ordinary-member conflict – turpitude is turpitude, after all – and urged his colleagues in the House 'to first look at ourselves, every single one of us, and stop talking as if the situation is serious if it is big, and not too serious if it is small . . . It is darned nigh time that we started discussing the activities of Members of this House before we start worrying about Ministers of the Crown.' [7] (Not surprisingly, Opposition Members

---

6 *Minutes of Proceedings and Evidence of the Standing Committee on Privileges and Elections of the House of Commons.* First Session, Thirtieth Parliament, 1974-5 No. 12, pp. 10, 13; and No. 13, p. 7.

7 Canada, *House of Commons Debates,* December 10, 1974, pp. 2123-4. See also *Minutes and*

(Footnote 7 →)

responded to this attempted minimisation of the pertinent differences between Members and Ministers by declaring that the Government was patently
starting 'at the wrong end of the power structure by beginning with Members of Parliament'. [8])

The statutory recommendations of the 1973 Green Paper, though
embodied in Bills C-62 and C-6 (1978), never became law; they died on the
order paper at session's end. The only other occasion on which a Canadian
Government has introduced a statutory conflict-of-interest régime was with
Bill C-114/C-46 in February 1988 (re-introduced with minor modifications
as Bill C-46 in November 1989). Without descending to the 'lowest common
denominator' doctrine adopted by its predecessors, C-114/C-46 nevertheless
represents an approach in which the differences in the statutory treatment to
be accorded Members of the Legislature and the Cabinet – while by no
means non-existent – are notably smaller than they are in the American case.
Before exploring how this is so in particular, it must be noted that, in a
sense, the United States' Ethics Reform Act – itself passed in November,
1989 – did introduce some long sought-after parity into the regulatory treatment accorded the United States' Executive and Legislative branches.
Officers and employees of both branches, for example, are now subject to
equivalent post-employment, disclosure, and gift-receipt régimes. Yet Title
X of the Ethics Reform Act stipulates that all provisions of the Act applicable to Congressmen and their employees result from an exercise of the
rulemaking, as distinct from the legislative, power of the two Houses. As
such, these provisions can at any time be altered – insofar as they apply to
each House – by either House in the same manner as each changes its rules, a
process which is a far cry from the procedure necessary to amend legislation.
For all intents and purposes, then, although the Ethics Reform Act did bring
greater substantive parity to ethics treatment of the two branches, it
nevertheless brought (which is of greater interest here) no formal – that is,
statutory – parity. The differences between the statutory strictures governing
the Executive branch, and those governing the Legislative branch, remain in
essence as great as they were before.

Even if the disclosure, post-employment and gift provisions of the Ethics
Reform Act were to have applied as statute to the Congress as they do to the
Cabinet and the rest of the Executive branch, still – by comparison –
Canada's Bill C-46 would bring Legislators and Cabinet Members yet an even
more crucial step closer in terms of common statutory governance or parity.
As Robert N. Roberts suggests in *White House Ethics*, the heart of conflict-of-

---

→   *Proceedings* No. 21 p. 5. Similar sentiments were expressed by Ministers and Government
Members in the Debate of March 1983; see Canada, *House of Commons Debate* March 21 1983,
pp. 23949, 23955.

8 *House of Commons Debates*, December 10, 1974 p. 2117.

interest regulation lies neither in disclosure nor in post-employment strictures, but in the prohibition of contemporaneous conflicts between public duties and private interests. [9] And here, the Canadian Bill would provide equal statutory treatment for Cabinet Members and Legislators in a way that would be difficult to imagine happening in the United States. The Canadian Bill defines conflict of interest as occurring whenever a Member (including a Minister), or the Member's spouse or dependant, has 'significant private interests . . . that afford the opportunity for the Member to benefit, whether directly or indirectly, as a result of the execution of, or the failure to execute, any office of the Member.' The Bill then requires both Ministers *and* Members to 'arrange [their] private affairs' so as to avoid 'conflicts of interest,' as previously defined, 'from arising.' Or, more precisely, the Bill empowers an independent three-person Conflict of Interest Commission to 'advise' Ministers and Members of 'any action that the Commission considers to be required . . . to ensure that' the Minister or Member does not find him- or herself in a conflict of interest as the Bill defines it. For example, 'without limiting' the Commission's capacity to recommend other remedies, the Bill specifically empowers the Commission to 'recommend the establishment of a trust on such terms, and subject to such conditions, as it considers appropriate' for the interests of Ministers- and Members-in-conflict. As Ian Greene has noted, the Commission 'could also recommend the divestment of certain assets' by ordinary Members as well as Ministers. [10] Elsewhere, the Commission is given the power to certify that a particular Minister's – or Member's – 'private interest' is 'permitted . . . for the purposes of this Act.'

In other words, Bill C-46 would subject Members of the Canadian Legislature to statutory provisions which capture the spirit of 18 U.S.C. 208, the central United States' conflict-of-interest law which applies only to members of the Executive. While Congress has been willing to impose upon itself statutory disclosure, post-employment and gift provisions (and even then, as noted above, those statutes are in reality rules), it has never – and likely will never – impose upon itself statutory requirements for recusal or divestiture, that is, legally-required remedies for contemporaneous conflicts between private interests and public duties. As numerous Congressmen have declared in debate over the years, if legislators were required to recuse themselves in conflict situations, they would disenfranchise their constituents – an intolerable evil, and one which does not, of course, apply when Executive branch members are required to recuse. And again unlike Executive-branch employees, whose specialised public activities in most cases impinge only on a

---

9 Robert N. Roberts *White House Ethics: A History of the Politics of Conflict of Interest Regulation* (New York: Greenwood, 1988) p. 162.

10 Greene 'Conflict of Interest and the Canadian Constitution' p. 249.

select class of private interests, the public acts of legislators can, over time, affect every conceivable private interest. To require statutorily divestiture of legislators, it is argued, is thus a far more draconian proposition than requiring it of most Executive-branch employees, including Cabinet Members.[11] Such arguments suggest that *statutory* requirements dealing with conflict-of-interest *per se* will continue to apply to United States' Cabinet Members, while Members of the Congress will persist in remaining free of them. The Canadian legislation, by contrast, would subject both Cabinet Members *and* ordinary Members to statutory prohibitions on conflict of interest *per se* – a proposal which is testimony to the relative lack of independence of the Legislature under the Canadian Parliamentary system, and to Cabinet's power to pass on to Members many of the strictures which the public, at any given time, seems to require of Ministers.[12]

One might have reasonably expected that in Canada, the inequity in power between the Cabinet and the Legislature, over time, would have justified placing significantly heavier conflict-of-interest strictures on the former. Yet Canada's brief history of experimentation with proposed statutory conflict-of-interest régimes suggests that precisely because of that inequity – precisely because Cabinet sits in the Legislature, controlling the content of legislation (while itself necessarily remaining subject to any Bill covering legislators) – the differential in statutory strictures attempted, by comparison with United States' law, has been relatively modest. Conversely, the formal equity – or rather balance – in power between the United States' Legislature and Executive has suggested to many observers that there should be no substantial differential between most of the conflict-of-interest strictures placed on the two branches.[13] Yet it is precisely because of the particular structure of that interbranch balance of power, that Congress has been able to impose a more significant burden of statutory strictures on the Executive while in affect exempting itself.

---

11 See, for example, the arguments against including Congressmen under the ambit of 18 U.S.C. 208 in The President's Commission on Ethics Law Reform, *To Serve With Honor; Report and Recommendations to the President* (Washington, D.C.: U.S. Department of Justice, 1989) pp. 14-15 and reproduced in this Volume on pp. 148-99.

12 It should be noted, though, that in one respect the Canadian Bill would place on Cabinet Members statutory requirements more onerous than those imposed on Members of the Legislature: Cabinet Members, as distinct from ordinary Members, would not be allowed to engage in outside employment, carry on businesses, or hold directorships in other than charitable organisations, social clubs, religious organisations, or political parties.

13 See, for example, Association of the Bar of the City of New York, *Conflict of Interest and the Federal Service* (Cambridge, Mass. 1960), p. 13, and U.S. Senate, Committee on Governmental Affairs, *Post-Employment Lobbying Restriction* (100th Congress, 1st Session) 1987, pp. 113-15.

1.2 Non-Statutory Régimes

Though there is a discernible tendency toward *relatively* equal statutory treatment of Legislators and Cabinet Members in Canada, when it comes to non-statutory régimes, there is a marked inequality between the progress made by the two branches. And this is the case simply because, in the non-statutory instance, the inequity in power between Cabinet and Parliament has worked the other way: that is, it is precisely because the Canadian Executive is relatively untrammeled in its power and responsibilities, that a recognised need for extensive self-regulation has arisen. Thus, the last twenty years have seen the development of detailed non-statutory codes of conduct and bodies of precedent covering all Executive office-holders, from Cabinet Ministers down to the lowest ranks of the public service. Non-statutory controls in the Canadian Legislative branch, by contrast – while by no means non-existent – are nonetheless comparatively scanty. That Parliament has escaped such controls, and has not been subjected to any great pressure to introduce them, is largely attributable to the relatively circumscribed power of the average Member, and the virtually non-existent power of Parliamentary staff. Thus, the Canadian House of Commons' *Conflict of Interest Rules* volume is only eleven pages long, and much of it deals not with the private interests of Members, but with the ways in which a Member may be compromised by holding other public offices, or contracts with public entities. In the United States, by contrast, the relative balance in power between the two branches explains in part why both have developed comparably extensive non-statutory rules, regulations and bodies of opinions. The Senate Ethics Committee's *Interpretive Rulings*, for example, is a 275-page volume of detailed rulings; the House *Ethics Manual* is 264 pages in length; and both deal largely with conflict-of-interest questions. And, over the past ten years, the Office of Government Ethics has built up a correspondingly detailed body of advisory opinions to cover the United States' Executive branch – opinions which augment the detailed regulations which have been promulgated government-wide and for each Department and agency.

In sum, then, and as a general rule, in the United States, statutory régimes have tended to result in an inequity between the Legislature and the Executive to the Legislature's 'advantage,' while a rougher relative parity has been reached between the two branches in the extensiveness of their non-statutory régimes. In Canada, by contrast, statutory régimes have always pushed in the direction of equal treatment of Legislators and Ministers – whether that treatment is light, as it was with C-62 and C-6, or heavy, as it is with C-114/C-46. Conversely, non-statutory régimes – rules, regulations, codes and guidelines – show (certainly by comparison with the American case) a relative inequity between the two branches, also to the Legislature's 'advantage.' And this particular pattern of statutory/non-statutory approaches reflects, in turn, underlying configurations in the relative powers of the Executive and the Legislature in each country.

2. Post-Employment Provisions

In the area of the regulation of office-holders' post-employment activities, the most fruitful points of contrast between the two countries' approaches are to be found not in the post-employment situations of former Members of the Legislature, on the one hand, nor those of former sub-Cabinet Members of the Executive on the other, but rather in the post-employment situations faced by former Cabinet Members. For while, on the one hand, there is a far greater turnover in legislative membership in Canada after each Federal election than there is in the United States, on the other, there is a far greater turnover of senior sub-Cabinet Executive branch personnel in the United States after each election (especially where the Administration changes) than there is in Canada, where the Civil Service is permanent and non-partisan. Thus, because of the relatively lower level of legislative turnover in the United States, and of senior sub-Cabinet Executive-branch personnel in Canada, the class of office-holder for which the extent of turnover in the two countries is most nearly (though by no means exactly) proximate – and hence the best case study for comparative purposes – is that of ex-Cabinet members. And yet, although both Canadian and United States' Cabinets experience a relatively comparable measure of turnover over time, the post-employment circumstances surrounding the two types of turnover – and hence the post-employment strictures which govern them in C-46 and the Ethics in Government/Ethics Reform Acts respectively – differ markedly, and instructively.

Generally speaking, in Canada, Cabinet Ministers, drawn as they are from among the membership of a Parliamentary Legislature, are career politicians with uncertain tenure – in contrast to their United States counterparts, who are drawn largely from the private sector, and are called upon to serve a fixed term. In the Canadian – as opposed to the American – debate over conflict of interest, the fact that Cabinet Members are not preponderantly drawn from an immediate private-sector background has given rise to fewer suspicions that they would be likely to exercise certain kinds of favouritism while in office (that is, toward a former employer or industry), and to a common acceptance that they are less readily marketable upon leaving office. [14] And the fact that Canadian Cabinet Ministers face an uncertain tenure – the fact that they often depart the ministry after a govemment-wide political defeat at a juncture which they cannot predict beforehand – has come to signify that they are both more financially vulnerable while in office, and less likely to be able to exercise political influence upon departing, than

---

14 See, for example, Brenda Zosky Proulx, 'Life in the Slow Lane,' *Montreal Gazette (October 26, 1985)*, a report on the subsequent job problems faced by five Cabinet Ministers who were not re-elected in the 1984 general election. One ex-Cabinet Minister told Proulx: 'Finding work can be a problem for an ex-Cabinet Minister. The myth is that . . . the job offers run after you. That's not the way it works.'

are their American counterparts. In the words of *Ethical Conduct in the Public Sector*, a 1984 task-force report prepared at the request of Prime Minister Trudeau by two former Cabinet Ministers, Mitchell Sharp and Michael Starr, 'former Ministers... seldom resign voluntarily in order to take private employment; a high proportion of them, in one way or another, are forced out of office and have to look for a job.' Moreover, 'the ability of a former Minister to influence government decisions to his or her advantage depends upon which party is then in office'; if, as is likely the case, the former Minister finds himself in a post-employment situation in the first place because his 'party has been defeated, he is not likely to receive preferred treatment and [permanent] officials are likely to be very circumspect in dealing with him.' [15]

Broadly speaking, in none of these respects have United States' Cabinet Members been deemed to be in an analagous situation. By comparison with their Canadian counterparts, they are – in American public debate – commonly treated as if they are both more capable of surviving under a stricter post-employment régime, and more deserving of one. Since they are more often drawn from the private sector, ex-United States' Cabinet Members are, by comparison with their Canadian counterparts, generally seen to be more vulnerable to certain kinds of influence while in office (particularly that exerted by previous employers and clients), and more marketable on leaving it. And, because of the greater degree of knowledge and control which they possess concerning the timing of their departure, ex-Cabinet Members in the United States are generally deemed to be more protected from sudden job loss while in office, and more capable of exercising 'influence' with their former colleagues and subordinates upon departing.

These differing structurally-rooted career contexts of United States and Canadian Cabinet officers, along with the relevance of those career situations for the purposes of conflict-of-interest regulation, was neatly brought to the fore during a 1983 Canadian Parliamentary debate on the post-employment activities of Cabinet Ministers: In the United States, one of the main evils which critics associate with an overly-severe post-employment régime, is its tendency to deter competent private-sector individuals from becoming Cabinet Secretaries. In the 1983 Canadian debate, by contrast, the main evil which critics associated with the idea of an overly-severe post-employment régime, was its perceived tendency to cause Cabinet Ministers to cling 'inordinate[ly]' to office. [16] The fact that American Cabinet Secretaries are drawn primarily from business backgrounds has thus led some observers to conclude that, in all likelihood, the main casualty of a more stringent United

---

15 Michael Starr and Mitchell Sharp, *Ethical Conduct in the Public Sector: Report of the Task Force on Conflict of Interest* (Ottawa: 1984) p. 224.

16 *House of Commons Debates*, March 21, 1983 p. 23981.

States' post-employment régime would be the quality of Cabinet-level knowledge and skill, and in particular, Cabinet's accessibility to private-sector insights and aptitudes. The fact that Canadian Cabinet Ministers are drawn primarily from political backgrounds, by contrast, evidently suggests that the main casualty of a stringent post-employment régime would be the quality of Cabinet-level courage and political independence, and in particular, Cabinet's willingness to take the sorts of unpopular or impolitic action which could hasten their leaving office.

These differences in perceived post-employment situations – that is, the relatively greater economic vulnerability and diminished political clout which is said to characterise the situation of the former Canadian Cabinet Minister as distinct from his or her American counterpart – are reflected in dissimilarities between the post-employment provisions in C-114/C-46 and the Ethics in Government/Ethics Reform Acts. To be sure, ex-Canadian Cabinet Ministers under C-114/C-46 would be subjected to certain restraints which do not fall on ex-United States' Cabinet Secretaries. For example, for a period of one year after leaving office, ex-Canadian Cabinet Ministers would not be able to counsel companies which deal with their former Departments, and, again for a period of one year after leaving office, ex-Ministers would not be permitted to take employment with any entity with which they dealt while in Government. Ex-Cabinet Secretaries in the United States, by contrast, are not subject to such strictures. Yet notwithstanding – indeed, trumping – these other provisions, another section of the Canadian Bill would empower the three-person Conflict of Interest Commission (where the United States' Ethics in Government Act does not similarly empower the Office of Government Ethics) to waive any or all post-employment strictures, in situations in which 'the public interest in ensuring reasonable employment for former Ministers outweighs the public interest in prohibiting contacts between the ex-Minister and the government.' Moreover, should the Commission find that these two conceptions of the public interest are in implacable tension, it would be free to grant the ex-Minister a 'hardship allowance.' Specifically, beyond the six months' severance to which the ex-Minister is normally entitled, the Commission would have the capacity to authorise payment of another six months' salary to bring the ex-Minister to the end of the year-long cooling-off period. Neither such a waiver, nor the hardship allowance, is available to the former United States Cabinet Secretary. The possibility of the waiver – and also the justification for it – reflect the relatively less significant nefarious political influence which the Canadian ex-Cabinet Member is seen to be capable of exercising – at least by comparison with his or her United States counterpart. Similarly, the hardship allowance reflects the ex-Minister's arguably more significant economic vulnerability.

The Starr-Sharp report – which for all intents and purposes has become the Talmud of public-sector conflict-of-interest regulation in Canada – provides the rationale for yet another difference in the post-employment provisions mandated under the Canadian and United States' Acts. On those occasions on which 'rules regarding contacts between former [Cabinet Ministers] and the Government' are 'breach[ed].' Starr and Sharp ask, who should be 'responsible' – the ex-Cabinet Minister, or those public servants whom the ex-Cabinet Member contacts?' The United States' Ethics in Government Act is clear in its answer to this question: The responsibility for obeying the law and the penalty for breaching it fall exclusively on the ex-Cabinet Member. In the case of Canada, though, Starr and Sharp write:

> ... 'it may be quite unfair to place the primary responsibility upon the former [Minister]. He or she is bound to be at a disadvantage when allegations are made about the impropriety of his or her contacts with the Government. Every contact made, however innocent, becomes suspect and he or she cannot defend himself or herself when charges are made in the House of Commons. The [current] Minister [by contrast] can answer for himself or herself and his or her officials.
>
> The rules pertaining to post-employment activities should [therefore] not be drawn up in such a way that the onus is on the former Minister to prove that he or she did not break them. We believe that former Cabinet Ministers in Canada are entitled to the benefit of the doubt in terms of questions of ethical conduct. To put it any other way is an invidious basis on which to establish public policy.' [17]

The courtesies here extended to the ex-Cabinet Member-lobbyist would sound strange to American ears. For Starr and Sharp, the ex-Minister who comes under a cloud is apparently defenseless politically if not legally. Moreover, the ex-Minister is entitled not to be judged according to the higher moral standards of public life, but rather is to be extended the latitude which traditionally accompanies more mainstream standards of legal justice: he or she must always be given the benefit of the doubt. Starr and Sharp thus conclude that the onus for any wrongful contact between an ex-Minister and his or her former officials should lie on those former officials, who operate with less political vulnerability and labour under a greater public obligation: 'We believe,' Starr and Sharp write:

> 'that the only effective means of dealing with this problem of representations made to Government is to lay the responsibility on current office holders to avoid giving preferential treatment to former public office holders ... The fact that a former public office holder makes representations to the Department of which he had been Minister ... is not per se abhorrent. What matters is

---

17 Starr and Sharp *Ethical Conduct* pp. 224-25.

whether he or she receives treatment more favourable than might be accorded anyone else in similar circumstances.' [18]

In this passage, Starr and Sharp provide the rationale for one other important distinction between C-114/C-46 and the Ethics in Government/Ethics Reform Acts. To be sure, the Canadian Bill does not go so far as do Starr and Sharp in relieving the ex-Minister of any post-employment culpability. As does United States' law, it would place an affirmative requirement on the ex-Cabinet Member to observe the post-employment rules, and criminal penalties would attach to him or her for violation. But – unlike the United States' Act and along the lines of Starr and Sharp – the Canadian Bill also places a positive statutory onus on any current officer or employee not to grant contracts or benefits to any ex-Cabinet Member under circumstances in which the ex-Cabinet Member would be violating his or her own post-employment restrictions. The implication clearly is that the current Executive-branch employee – no matter how junior – is still more powerful and protected than is his or her ex-Ministerial boss, and should thus be considered capable of, and held responsible for, resisting the ex-Minister's blandishments. [19] Such a doctrine has no analogue in the United States' Ethics in Government/Ethics Reform Acts, nor in the debates surrounding them, which often explicitly assume an inability on the part of the former Secretary's inferiors to be indifferent to his influence or to the nature of their previous relationship. [20] In sum, the ex-Minister in Canada is seen to be less politically powerful and more politically vulnerable, not only than his or her counterparts in the United States' Cabinet, but also than his or her former subordinates in the Canadian Executive branch – and the post-employment provisions of C-114/C-46 reflect these relative differentials in perceived power and vulnerability.

3. Remedies and Penalties

Another notable set of structurally-induced differences between the Canadian Bill and American law lies in the area of remedies and penalties for legislative and Cabinet-level conflict of interest. Consider first remedies, that is, measures such as disclosure, divestiture, trust arrangements and recusal: Under the United States' Ethics in Government Act and other statutes, some remedies are made to rely for their effectiveness on direct democratic

---

18 Starr and Sharp *Ethical Conduct* p. 230.

19 This notion of placing a smaller relative onus on ex-Ministers – and a greater relative responsibility on incumbent officialdom – for ex-Ministerial transgressions, appears elsewhere in Canadian discussion. See, for example, *House of Commons Debates* March 21, 1983 pp. 23947 and 23980.

20 See, generally, U.S. Senate, *Post-Employment Lobbying Restrictions* (100th Congress, 1st Session) 1987.

sanction (in particular, full public disclosure for Congressmen and senior Executive-branch office-holders) or on indirect democratic sanction (as when various divestiture or recusal arrangements are imposed on senior Executive-branch employees by the people's representatives in the Senate). Other remedies – stipulations, regarding the use of the trust instrument for Executive-branch office-holders, for example, and certain requirements regarding recusal or divestitute – are to be found in the Act itself, or in organic Departmental and agency statutes and pursuant regulations.

Under the Canadian Bill, by contrast, remedies are more exclusively an administrative matter. The extent to which – and the detail in which – the Member's or Minister's disclosure would be made public is left to the discretion of a Registrar appointed by the three-person Commission, and arrangements for divestiture, trusts, and recusal are questions left to the discretion of the Commission itself. In the United States, in other words, remedies for legislative and Cabinet-level conflict fall to some considerable extent within the province of democratic politics, and Cabinet-level conflict is additionally governed by statute law and regulations. Under the Canadian Bill, by contrast, remedies for legislative and Cabinet-level conflict fall largely under the administrative discretion of an independent body.

Penalties, as well, fall under the rubric of different types of institutions in the two countries. In the United States, if a putative contravention of the applicable conflict-of-interest, disclosure or post-employment statutes is sufficiently serious, it falls for prosecution to a branch of Government independent of that which houses the alleged offender. Thus, while each House of Congress is responsible within bounds for policing the provisions of the law as they apply to its own Members, criminal breaches committed by Members of Congress fall to the Executive branch (specifically, the Attorney-General) to prosecute, and to the courts of judge. And while the Office of Government Ethics and the Attorney General are initially responsible for following up any putative contraventions of the conflict-of-interest statutes by fellow employees of the Executive branch, serious alleged criminal infringements by senior Executive-branch personnel are referred for prosecution outside the Executive branch, to a judicially-appointed independent counsel, and again, to the courts for judgement.

The Canadian Bill, by contrast, expressly states – with the one exception noted below – that 'failure to comply with any provision of this Act does not constitute an offence punishable . . . under the criminal code.' Instead – upon its receipt from the Commission of an adverse report regarding a Member's or a Minister's activities – it is only the Parliamentary Chamber in which the Member or Minister holds his seat which is empowered to apply a penalty: reprimand, fine, the payment of compensation, or permanent removal/request for resignation from the Chamber. Thus, while under the United States' Act, the adjudication of offences and the application of penalties of a certain severity are taken out of the hands of the Legislature and the Executive as the case may be, and given to independent branches to apply, in the Canadian Bill, they are ultimately levied by the Legislature, which means (assuming a majority Government) that they are levied by the Executive in part if not in whole. (The only exception here is the penalty for the post-employment provisions applying to former Cabinet Ministers, and these are left to the Executive-branch – that is, to a current Cabinet Minister, the Attorney-General – to prosecute, because the alleged offender is necessarily no longer a Member of the Legislature.)

In sum, under the Canadian Bill – as distinct from United States' law – remedies for legislative and Cabinet-level conflict of interest would fall more under the rubric of a discreet, discretionary and independent body, and less under the direct strictures of statute law or democratic politics. This difference likely reflects the great weight which Canadian governance places on the independent tradition and embodied wisdom of permanent public service bodies, and the great weight which American governance places on the ideals of popular sovereignty and a government of 'laws, not men.' And under United States' law, penalties for serious Legislative and Executive-branch conflicts of interest fall more under the auspices of bodies independent of the Legislature and the Executive, while under the Canadian Bill, they would fall ultimately under the responsibility of the Legislature and hence (normally) the Executive. This difference is straightforwardly reflective of the doctrine of separation of powers in the United States, and the constitutional supremacy of Parliament in Canada.

4. Rules Governing Legislative-Executive Interaction and Conflict of Interest

Another major point of difference between the two countries' understandings of public-sector conflict of interest concerns the permissibility of a Member of the Legislature's representing a paying client before an Executive agency or Department. United States' statute law proscribes the receipt of compensation by Members of Congress for advocatory services rendered on behalf of clients before Federal agencies or Departments in matters in which the United States is interested. According to the first Justice Harlan, the 'main object' of such a law 'is to secure the integrity of Executive action against undue influence' exerted by 'Members of [the Legislative] branch . . . whose favour may have much to do with the appointment to, or retention in, public position of those [Executive-branch office-holders] whose official action it is sought to control or direct.' [21] Others have argued that the quality of Executive-branch decision-making could be compromised

---

21 *Burton v. United States* 202 U.S. 344 [1906] p. 368.

whenever a Congressman – who by virtue of his office may possess some considerable control over a given Department's or agency's budget – makes representations, whether for a paying client 'or a nonpaying constituent, before that Department or agency.[22] In sum, because senior Executive-branch office-holders come under official political and financial control by Congress as a whole, they must – to avoid their being placed in conflicts of interest – be protected for any unofficial *ex parte* and pecuniarily-motivated representations made by individual Congressmen.

In Canada, by contrast, there is no equivalent law. Nor does the United States' rationale for one apply with equal force: Parliament has no independent control over Executive appointments, and – assuming a majority Government – no independent power of the purse. This is not to say that Canadian Legislators have been entirely sanguine about Members of Parliament representing paying clients before Executive agencies and Departments. Rather, the evil such interventions have been seen to portend is less in the manner of an impairment on the impartial judgement of the Executive officer being lobbied, than an encumbrance on the representational capacity of the legislator doing the lobbying. The *Green Paper*, for example, did include a non-statutory proposal to prohibit any member from 'advocating any matter or cause related to his personal, private or professional interests ... before any Government boards or tribunals for a fee or reward.'[23] Those few members who saw merit in the proposal, though, generally qualified their support along lines which make clear that they were concerned not to preserve untainted Executive-branch judgement, but rather to protect unhindered legislative-branch advocacy. One Member of Parliament claimed that a prohibition against a Member's representing a paying client before the Executive should apply only when the client is also a constituent – because a constituent has the right to his Member's representational talents *gratis* – but not if the Member is representing someone other than a constituent, who has no such similar right.[24] Another Member of Parliament argued that as long as the cause a given Parliamentarian is representing for a paying client is compatible with the interests of his constituents, he is entitled to charge a fee for advocacy before government tribunals.[25] And still another argued that a Legislator should be allowed to charge a fee for representation even to a constituent, as long as no

---

22 See Erwin G. Krasnow and Richard E. Lankford, 'Congressional Conflicts of Interest: Who Watches the Watchers?' 24 *Federal Bar Journal* [1964] p. 272. See also 'Communications with Administrative Agencies,' in *Ethics Manual for Members, Officers and Employees of the U.S. House of Representatives.* 100th Congress, 1st Session, (Washington: 1987) pp. 165-178.

23 President of the Privy Council, 'Members of Parliament and Conflict of Interest' (Ottawa: 1973) p. 28.

24 *Minutes and Proceedings* No.13, p. 16.

25 *Minutes and Proceedings* No.13, p. 21.

other constituent has a competing interest. [26] None of these Canadian Parliamentarians, in their ruminations on the propriety of paid legislative representation before the Executive, is concerned with protecting 'the integrity of Executive action,' as Justice Harlan put it, but rather with preserving the integrity of Legislative representation (and even so, just barely). In any case, the *Green Paper* proposal was never acted upon, and to this day, there are no restrictions on a Canadian Member of Parliament (or Senator) representing a paying client before an Executive Department or agency. (The Parliament of Canada Act, though, does prohibit a Member or Senator from receiving compensation for services rendered in the attempt to influence other Members of his or her particular Chamber.)

5. Independent Political Judgement: An Historical Example of Structurally-Induced Canadian:American Differences in Approaches to Conflict-of-Interest

One final structurally-induced difference between the two countries' approaches to public-sector conflict of interest is worthy of mention and explication – a difference which, in three respects, is 'of a slightly different key than the others discussed above. In the first place, this particular difference – by comparison with those discussed above – is perhaps somewhat more philosophical than legal in nature – that is, one finds evidence of it as much in debates and discourse as in laws and codes. And, finally, this particular difference is certainly more historical than contemporary in nature, although many signs of it still survive.

In essence, this final difference can be described in the following terms: in the United States, a Congressman's possession of private interests is generally regarded as an encumbrance on his or her capacity to exercise unfettered political judgement, while the only widely accepted argument in favour of significant public emolument for Legislators, is that a large enough public salary might free them from having to rely on what are seen as more compromising means of private support. [27] Because of the relatively greater power exercised by the Executive over the Legislature in Parliamentary systems, by contrast, the conception of conflict of interest prevalent in both the Canadian and British traditions has, historically, been skewed – certainly by comparison with the American conception just outlined – toward the idea that Legislators who rely on income from private interests are relatively

---

26 *Minutes and Proceedings* No. 13, p. 22; see also p. 16.

27 See, for example, U.S. House of Representatives *Presidential Pay Recommendations:* Hearings Before the Ad Hoc Subcommittee on Presidential Pay Proposals of the Committee on Post Office and Civil Service (95th Congress, 1st Session) 1977, p. 196; *Congressional Record* (95th Congress, 1st Session) February 9, 1977, p. 4004, and *Debates and Proceedings in the Congress of the United States* (15th Congress, 1st Session) December, 1816, p. 318.

more likely to retain independence of mind and integrity of judgement – that is, relatively more likely to serve their constituents and the public interest in a faithful and unencumbered way. And as something of a corollary, those Legislators in Canada and Britain who receive their remuneration solely from the public treasury have, historically, been thought more likely to find their judgement compromised in some fashion – whether by a debt to the Crown, the Prime Minister, the party in power, or the Executive broadly construed.

Consider the corollary first: even on the eve of the British House of Commons' first vote in favour of paying salaries to Members of Parliament in 1911, there still were many Members of Parliament who 'defended' their unsalaried 'status ... as a sign of their disinterestedness.' [28] Indeed for the previous century and a half, according to one observer, 'independence [of political judgement in Britain had] ... mean[t] only independence from the Crown,' [29] that is, independence of Executive patronage and royal pensions, not independence of private interests or personal retainers. And as recently as the late 1970s, British Members of Parliament, in debating new proposals to raise Members' salaries, expressed the view that Members' pay should not be so substantial as to make them feel beholden to the Government-of the-day (with its power of dissolution) for their livelihood, nor that ministerial pay be such that Ministers would feel financially inhibited from resigning on a matter of principle. As one Member urged, 'the genuine and individual, independent judgement that is so vital to the successful working of the House ... would be jeopardised to some extent if being an honourable Member represented a person's only livelihood.' [30] While such a line of argument can be found from time to time in the American debate, it is relatively muted. Certainly, the dominant chord governing the recent United States' proposals for Congressional pay increases had it that a Member's independence of judgement would be jeopardised *unless* his being a Congressman came to represent his only (earned) livelihood.

---

28 Barry McGill, 'Conflict of Interest: English Experience 1782-1941' *Western Political Quarterly* 12 (1959) p. 809.

29 McGill 'Conflict of Interest,' p. 809; see also pp. 808, 826, and Alan Doig *Corruption and Misconduct in Contemporary British Politics* (New York, N.Y.: Penguin, 1984) pp. 43-5, 95, 229. And see, for example, United Kingdom, *Parliamentary Debates* (August 10, 1911), 1414; *Parliamentary Debates* (March 24, 1893), 1113; and *Parliamentary Debates* (August 10, 1911) 1464.

30 See United Kingdom, *Parliamentary Debates* (July 28, 1978), 2107-8 and more generally 2083-2145. 'If we think of independence,' one Member argued, 'there is no one so independent of Government and the Whips as an unpaid Member.' 'Independence' here is simply and naturally equated with financial independence of the public treasury, not with financial independence of private interests. See also *Parliamentary Debates* (July 21, 1980) p. 175, and *The Daily Telegraph* August 16, 1983 (editorial): 'it is not desirable that MPs should become wholly dependent on their Parliamentary salaries [for] Parliamentarians wholly beholden to their parties may lose some independence.'

In the case of Canada, one can also find examples (some historic and some contemporary) of this particular structurally-rooted Parliamentary under-standing of conflict of interest – according to which the Legislator's receipt of a *public* salary is seen as posing the greater threat to his or her ability to exercise unencumbered judgement while in office. In Canada, up until the first few decades of this century, statute law held that any Member of Parlia-ment appointed to the Cabinet, and thereby made liable to receive a salary from the Crown, had to resign his seat and seek again in a by-election the approval of his constituents. This idea – which followed a British Parliamen-tary tradition of long standing – had its origins in the need of constituents 'to guard against Members being brought under sinister Executive control' by virtue of their receipt of public emolument as Cabinet Members. [31] Notably, the only two types of conflicts-of-interest which the Canadian *Green Paper* and Bills C-62/C-6 sought to prohibit were those posed by a Member's receipt of public, not private, sources of income: namely, other government offices and Federal Government contracts. [32] A latter-day variation on this strand of Parliamentary doctrine lay behind the recent decision of one of Canada's former Environment Ministers to recuse himself from his minis-terial responsibilities in all decisions respecting the environmental impact of a proposed crossing to be built between his island constituency and the Canadian mainland (as the local Member of Parliament, the Minister vigorously supported the link). The Minister termed his situation a 'conflict of interest'; but it is important to note that the conflict in question was not the generic sort that arises in representative democracy between the Legislator's twin roles as a delegate for his constituents and a trustee for the broader national interest. Rather, it was of a more specific type that arises in a Parliamentary democracy between a Minister's twin roles as a representative in the legislature – whether delegate or trustee (in both respects the Minister supported the crossing) – and a Member of the Executive (with Departmen-tal imperatives). The Minister argued that there was an encumbrance placed

---

31 R. MacGregor Dawson *The Government of Canada* 5th edition (Toronto: University of Toronto, 1970) pp. 329-31. Even to this day in Britain – although not in Canada – when Members became Ministers, and consequently begin to draw salaries for their Executive position, their Parliamentary pay is reduced, and for their services as Members, they receive less pay than do non-Ministerial members, i.e., backbenchers. This practice represents a ves-tige of the idea that the Member's capacity to be a representative – to be both a delegate-spokesperson for the views of his or her constituency, and a trustee espousing his or her own independent view of the public interest – is to some degree impaired when he or she becomes financially beholden to the pleasure of the Government and the Crown, by becoming a Mem-ber of the Executive.

32 See also the discussion in Canada, Library of Parliament Research Branch *Conflicts of Interest and Parliamentarians* October 15, 1968. In addition, as noted above, the Canadian House of Commons *Conflict of Interest Rules* are concerned preponderantly not with the conflicts which may arise when Members hold various private interests, but with those which arise when Members hold other public offices, or contracts with the Crown.

on his ability to act and to exercise his judgement as an independent Member of Parliament, not by virtue of any private employment he held, but by virtue of his public employment as a Member of the Cabinet. The Minister believed that his first obligation was to function as a representative, and in order to fulfil that obligation unencumbered, he felt compelled to free himself from the obligations under which he laboured as a Member of the Executive. [33] For his trouble, the Minister lost his seat in the subsequent general election.

Historically, then, Parliamentary tradition displays a strand of argument on which a seat in Cabinet, and public remuneration more generally, can place the Legislator in conflict. Conversely, it also displays a strand according to which independent pursuits, private interests, and private sources are all deemed fundamental to ensuring the Legislator's uncompromised political judgement. In the early 1980s, the British House of Commons debated the question of whether sitting Members should be permitted to retain outside interests and employment. A survey taken of Members at the time revealed that the minority who were in favour of some form of prohibition on outside private interests, were generally concerned less with abating conflict of interest than with diminishing encroachments on Members' time – that is, if private interests were seen to post a threat at all, it was a threat to Members' undivided attention, not to their unencumbered judgement. [34] Conversely,

---

33 The Prime Minister, it should be noted, refused the Minister's offer of recusal, and he did so, according to the Minister, because the Prime Minister 'thought the interests of Islanders would not be advanced by a diminution of my status as Minister of the Environment.' In other words, the Prime Minister's first concern appeared to lie with reassuring the Minister's constituents that his representational capacities would not be harmed (indeed, that they would be helped) were he to continue to serve as a Member of the Executive on this matter. The Prime Minister notably did not attempt to reassure environmental groups that his Environment Minister's Executive decision-making capacities would not be compromised by his continuing representational responsibilities (see *Charlottetown Guardian*, January 28, 1988).

34 See Sandra Williams *Conflict of Interest: the Ethical Dilemma in Politics* (Aldershot: Gower, 1984) p. 33. That the concern that private interests would encroach on a Member's time holds primacy over the concern that they might impede the Member's judgement, is evinced at various points in the history of the British debate. See, generally, D. C. M. Platt 'The Commercial and Industrial Interests of Ministers of the Crown,' *Political Studies* 9 (1961) pp. 279, 280, 284; and Doig *Corruption*, p. 97. When, in 1971, the Review Body on Top Salaries considered banning honoraria for U.K. Commons Committee chairmen, it did so because the events giving rise to such honoraria impinged on the time chairmen should be devoting to committee work, not because the honoraria themselves were thought to compromise their judgement (see *Review Body on Top Salaries, First Report: Ministers and Members of Parliament* (London, 1971), p. 10). By contrast, the need to avoid conflicts of interest is quite explicitly elevated over the need to avoid encroachments on time in U.S. Congressional argumentation in favour of restricting outside earned income and honoraria. See, for example, U.S. House of Representatives *Presidential Pay Recommendations* pp. 233-5, and *Congressional Record* October 28, 1981, pp. H7817, H7829.

the majority of Members of Parliament who had some difficulty with pro-hibitions against Members' holding outside interests, felt that such pro-hibitions would not only serve to deprive the House of 'valuable experience and expertise,' but that they would actually 'erode the independence of MPs.' [35]

It is worth noting in passing that this particular strand in Parliamentary doctrine on conflict-of-interest – according to which private interests and income are seen as less troublesome, and public emolument more – has sur-faced in Canada in connection with Executive-branch employees as well as Legislators. For example, there was no enduring controversy in Canada, com-parable to that in the United States, over the use of dollar-a-year men – Government Executives whose salaries were paid by private sector companies – during World War II. [36] More generally, in the United States, 18 U.S.C. 109 criminalises private supplementation of the salaries of Executive-branch employees (other than special government employees). In Canada, by con-trast, neither the current non-statutory code governing Executive-branch employees, nor (except in the case of Cabinet Ministers) the proposed Cana-dian legislation, prohibit Executive-branch employees, full-time as well as part-time, from accepting privately-sourced salaries for their work as public officials. Conversely, in Canada, there is no positive legal requirement, as

---

35 Williams *Conflict of Interest*, p. 34. In a recent study, Michael M. Atkinson and Maureen Man-cuso offer another explanation for the British Parliamentary system's greater tolerance for Legislators who hold private interests and sources of income. Specifically, Atkinson and Mancuso argue that the British Parliament enshrines a 'Burkean' philosophy of representa-tion on which Members are explicitly meant to represent pure interests. The U.S. Congress, by contrast, embodies a more classically liberal philosophy, on which 'representation has always been of persons [and therefore of constituencies]; the representation of interests has been viewed as an inevitable evil, to be tamed by a well-constructed Government.' Because their institutional culture thus impels them (or at least allows them) to represent broad interests – agricultural interests, banking interests, labour interests – British Members of Parliament have much greater latitude to engage in consultancies and receive retainers for 'promoting interests that are not attached to [their] constituencies or to persons as such.'

This is a useful set of observations, and it helps explain why British Legislators' retention of private interests is seen to be compatible with their being *effective representatives*: British MPs are simply viewed as being advocates for – or representative of – more than just a con-stituency. Answering the question of why British Legislators' retention of private interests should also be seen to promote their capacity to exercise *independent legislative judgement*, however, requires us to look at a different strand in the Parliamentary tradition – the one in which a Member's private interests, whether shared with or contrary to those of his con-stituents, help him retain his independence of the Crown, the Executive and the party. See Michael M. Atkinson and Maureen Mancuso 'Conflict of Interest in Britain and the U.S.: An Institutional Approach,' *Legislative Studies Quarterly* 16 (1991) pp. 481, 483.

36 Starr and Sharp *Ethical Conduct* p. 77, describe a 'period of quiet' in conflict of interest activity at the Federal level between the 1930s and 1951. By contrast see, generally, Michael Reagan, *Serving Two Masters: Problems in the Employment of Dollar-a-Year and Without-Compensation Men* unpublished Ph.D. dissertation, Princeton University 1959.

there is in the United States, that Executive-branch employees receive remuneration for their official services from the public treasury. The United States' Anti-Deficiency Act, which enjoins the Executive from engaging the services of personnel for whom Congress has not voted public remuneration, is at once a method of protecting against the conflicts which may arise when Executive employees rely on sources other than the government for their salaries, and a means of preserving Congress' constitutional ability to control the Executive through its power of the purse. As such, it rests on a principle significantly different from that which has operated historically within the Parliamentary system, in which the conflict of interest more to be guarded against is the one which arises when public officials come to rely on the public treasury for their salary, thereby coming under the compromising control of the Executive, which – in a Parliamentary system – controls the purse. Hence, in Canada, there is no Anti-Deficiency Act requiring that Executive-branch officials receive public remuneration for their official services, just as there is no 18 U.S.C. 209 prohibiting them from receiving private remuneration for their public services. Of course in practice, Executive-branch employees in both countries remain substantially on the public payroll; the pertinent difference being that in Canada, there is no legal tradition requiring that they be.

In sum, it is perhaps not surprising – as a study of 'Conflicts of Interest in England' found fifteen years ago – that none of the century's four British Royal Commissions on the Civil Service had given any significant attention to the conflicts of interest posed by public-officials holding private interests and pursuing outside activities. [37] Nor is it surprising that – as Starr and Sharp note in their report – 'conflict of interest guidelines [to say nothing of legislation] were not addressed in Canada until the late 1960s, and were only reflected in actual orders in council in the early and mid-nineteen seventies.' [38] In the United States, by contrast, legislation dates back to the nineteenth century. More recently, though – and as a result of the convergence in concern with conflict of interest which, as Kenneth Kernaghan has noted, has arisen in the political culture of all three countries – this particular structurally-induced Parliamentary/Presidential difference has grown muted. In Canada, the recent public consternation over Federal Cabinet Ministers who continued to pursue conflicting private interests while in office – as well as comparable offences at the Provincial level – suggest that this strand of Parliamentary doctrine has largely lapsed into history. In Britain, the recent case of John Browne, M.P. – in which Browne was found guilty by a House committee of failing to declare his interests under House

---

37 See Geoffrey Wilson, 'Conflicts of Interest in Public Law ... in England' *Proceedings of the Sixth International Symposium on Comparative Law* (Ottawa: University of Ottawa Press, 1969), p. 328.

38 Starr and Sharp *Ethical Conduct* p. 75.

rules – suggest that the forces of cultural convergence may also be making some headway in the United Kingdom. Still, as one scholarly observer of the British scene observes, notwithstanding the Browne affair, many of the issues which raise concern in the United States still 'are not seen as ethical or moral problems' in the United Kindom; indeed, 'the House of Commons still debates now and again whether the Register of Interests should become compulsory, which is perhaps an indication of how unserious a problem [conflict of interest] is' – or is seen to be – in Britain.[39]

There is a certain irony to this last, somewhat more historical and philosophical distinction between the Parliamentary and Presidential conflict-of-interest traditions. For decades, comparative political scientists have argued that Canadians and Britons live in nations built by big government and sustained by the welfare State, and that their political cultures place a premium on the reliability and trust that comes from being able to depend on the Crown and the public purse. Americans, by contrast, are said to live in a land built by individual enterprise; they are depicted as partisans of the independence of spirit that comes from relying on private means and wherewithal. [40] This distinction may very well be true, at least to some extent, of Canadian, British and American political culture as a whole. Yet when it comes to the ways in which citizens living under the Parliamentary and Presidential systems – again historically – like to see their office-holders behave, more the reverse seems to have been the case: in a variety of ways, Canadians and Britons have displayed a relative tendency to prefer (or at least to remain unbothered by) officials who, while in office, embody the independence which comes from relying on private means and wherewithal. Americans, by contrast, seem to feel more comfortable with officials who are

---

39 Letter to the author from Andrew Dunsire, Professor of Political Science Emeritus, the University of York, England, February 23, 1990. In a recent study of the considerable extent to which Parliamentary conflict of interest is now a concern in the United Kingdom, Malcolm Shaw notes several practices still operative in Parliament, which would not be permitted for U.S. Congressmen. For example, British 'Members may work for, or even form, a public relations or political consultancy firm which has clients with a stake in public policy outcomes.' See Malcolm Shaw, 'Members of Parliament,' in Michael Rush, ed. *Parliament and Pressure Politics* (Oxford: Clarendon, 1990) pp. 85-116, and especially p. 89.

It is also noteworthy that Anthony King, in his seminal 'The Rise of the Career Politician in Britain – and Its Consequences' *(British Journal of Political Science* 11 (1981) pp. 249-85), explicitly states that even the typical British 'career politician' he analyses may well 'live "for" politics . . . But he does not necessarily live off politics. He may have a large private income; he may earn substantial sums, possibly more than his Parliamentary salary, by writing for newspapers or practising at the bar . . .' (p. 250). In the United States, such an individual would not be considered a 'career politician.'

For details of the case of John Browne, M.P. and the UK House of Commons' Register of Members' Interests, see this Volume, Appendix Part III, pp. 559-68.

40 See, most recently, Seymour Martin Lipset, *Continental Divide: The Values and Institutions of the United States and Canada* (New York and London: Routledge, 1990) p. xiii.7.

dependent solely on the public purse. Given the reported tendency of the political culture of citizenship to tack in the opposite direction within the three countries, this particular Parliamentary-Presidential difference should be taken as testimony to the importance of governmental structure, and to its role in shaping traditional understandings of official morality.

Conclusion

In summary, differences in governmental structure have led Canada's recent conflict-of-interest tradition to differ in important respects from the American. In the first place, three factors have given rise to very different histories of the attempts to use both statutory and non-statutory régimes in the two countries. These factors are (a) the dual status of the Cabinet Member as a Minister and a Legislator in Canada (which means that in Canada – as distinct from the United States – the attempt is made to subject Legislators to many of the statutory controls proposed for Cabinet Members); (b) the relative isolation of the Canadian sub-Cabinet Executive branch from legislative control (which means that in Canada – as distinct from the United States – the sub-Cabinet Executive is not subject to statutory controls); and (c) the comparably limited powers possessed by the individual Canadian Legislator (which means that in Canada – as distinct from the United States – Legislators are not subject to particularly extensive non-statutory controls). In the second place, the Canadian ex-Minister's relative vulnerability and eclipsed power have given rise to a more liberal proposed post-employment régime for former Cabinet Members in Canada than obtains in the United States. Thirdly, the independence of Canadian public-service bodies, and the supremacy of the Executive-in-Parliament, mean that under the proposed Canadian conflict-of-interest régime, remedies and penalties respectively rest rather more in those two institutions than they do in their counterparts in the United States. Instead, in the United States, democratic forums and legal strictures are more relied upon for remedies, and branches independent of the Legislature and the Executive are more readily called upon for penalties. Fourth, because the Canadian Legislator commands a relatively circumscribed degree of control over the Executive, unofficial paid legislative representations before government agencies and Departments are not prohibited in Canada, while they are in the United States. (And, to the extent that they are found objectionable in Canada, they are deemed to be so for different reasons.) Finally, and more historically, because of the greater power exercised by the Executive over the Legislature in British Parliamentary systems, Canadian political history shows various signs of a more marked 'British' lack of concern over office-holders who have private interests and incomes, and a worry about office-holders dependent on the public treasury – a mentality largely foreign to United States' debate.

The two countries' comparative experiences in dealing with public-sector conflict usefully expand upon O. P. Dwivedi's suggestion that the idea of Government ethics (indeed, the very term itself) embodies a certain tension. For while ethics is often supposed to partake of – evince the character of – a timeless and universal 'higher law' or set of 'broad principles,' governments themselves 'assess complex social and political issues less according to the fundamental truths they proclaim [than] from the standpoint of changing directions and evolving public agenda. For is it not self-evident that some of yesterday's morally accepted 'issues have become today's immoral acts?' [41] If over the course of historical time, as Dwivedi suggests, evolving government agendas issue forth in different understandings of administrative rights and wrongs, then – so the Canadian and American experiences with public-sector conflict suggest – across geographical space, varying government structures can also issue forth in different understandings of administrative rights and wrongs: as we have seen, (a) the same types of officials (Legislators, Cabinet Members, public servants) are seen, in the two countries' approaches, to be amenable to very different types of regulatory schema; (b) the same situations are regarded as giving rise to very different divisions of responsibility among participants for regulatory transgressions (as between ex-Cabinet Members and the public servants they approach); (c) the same institutions (the public service, the Legislature, and the Executive-branch) are seen to possess very different degrees of competence in the ability to prevent or judge wrongdoing; (d) the same types of activities (paid legislative representations before the Executive) are for very different reasons classified as wrongdoing; and (e) more historically, an office-holder's possession of the same types of interests and income are seen to have very different consequences for the creation of conflict. These are all differences in ethics – in conceptions of moral responsibility, moral competence, moral right and wrong – and yet they are all directly attributable to differences in governmental structure. If Government ethics is often agenda-driven, as Dwivedi suggests, then it is also – notwithstanding the evident effect of broader cultural forces – structurally determined.

NOTES

A.   An earlier version of this paper was presented at the Conference on the Study of Government Ethics, Park City, Utah, June 1991, organised by the American Society for Public Administration Section on Public Administration Research. The author is grateful to several conference participants for helpful comments. As well, the author wishes to express his thanks to Ralph Clark Chandler, Stephane Dion,

41 O. P. Dwivedi 'Moral Dimensions of Statecraft: a Plea for an Administrative Theology' in *Canadian Journal of Political Science* 20 (1987) pp. 12, 13.

H. George Frederickson, J. Patrick Dobel, Andrew Dunsire, Stuart Gilman, Jean-Pierre Kingsley, John Langford, Mary Ann McCoy, John A. Rohr, David Rosenbloom, and Iris M. Young for reading a previous version of the paper and offering important suggestions.

B. *[Editor]* The Special Joint Committee of the Senate and House of Commons of Canada on Bill C-43 tabled its report in June 1992. Instead of a separate conflict of interest law for Parliamentarians, it proposed consolidating conflict of interest rules into a separate part of *The Parliament of Canada Act*. It also proposed a draft Bill to that effect. The Government is considering now its course of action. Therefore, Bill C-43 may never become law, and if new clauses are enacted, they might be quite different from what is proposed in Bill C-43.

8

To Serve with Honor:
Report of the United States'
President's Commission on Federal Ethics
Law Reform (1989)[1]

under the Chairmanship of the Honourable Malcolm R. Wilkey

1. Introduction

We have approached the President's request to evaluate existing ethics rules with twin objectives: to obtain the best public servants, and to obtain the best from our public servants.

Ethical government means much more than laws. It is a spirit, an imbued code of conduct, an ethos. It is a climate in which, from the highest to the lowest ranks of policy and decision-making officials, some conduct is instinctively sensed as correct and other conduct as being beyond acceptance.

Laws and rules can never be fully descriptive of what an ethical person should do. They can simply establish minimal standards of conduct. Possible variations in conduct are infinite, virtually impossible to describe and proscribe by statute. Compulsion by law is the most expensive way to make people behave.

The futility of relying solely or principally on compulsion to produce virtue becomes even more apparent when one considers that there is an obligation in a public official to be sure his [2] actions appear ethical as well as to be ethical. The duty is to conduct one's office not only with honor but with perceived honor.

We must start with a *will* at the top to set, follow, and enforce ethical standards. President Bush [3] has given this Commission his first Executive

---

1 The above is an extract from the Report of March 1989 to the then Republican President of the United States, Mr George Bush, by his Federal Ethics Law Reform Commission, under the Chairmanship of the Honourable Malcolm R. Wilkey. These extracts are taken from pp. 1-11 and 114-117 respectively. The Report was printed by the US Government Printing Office: 1989 0 231-642: QL 3.

2 Masculine or feminine pronouns appearing in this report refer to both genders unless the context indicates another use.

3 In November 1992, the press announced that the new Democratic President-Elect of the United States, Mr Bill Clinton, is expected to introduce shortly new stricter ethics rules to

(Footnote 3➜)

Order, by which he has set initially the ethical tone he expects to pervade his Administration.

That order and this report are but a beginning. Each cabinet officer, head of an agency, subordinate official with supervisory authority – each must lead by example, by training and educating coworkers, by fair, just and persistent enforcement of the laws. This necessity of leadership applies with equal force to the legislature. What the Framers rightly considered the most powerful branch bids fair to be the least accountable branch. That is a dangerous combination, recognized by thoughtful Members themselves. We do not exclude the judiciary, although more rigorous and easily understood standards have obviated many problems there.

We believe that public officials want to follow ethical rules, and that they will do so if the laws are clearly delineated, equitable, uniform across the board, and justly administered. As Napoleon said: 'There is no such thing as a bad soldier; there are only poor officers'.

Ethical rules and statutes rest on moral standards. They are supposed to carry a certain moral authority, as are most laws. When the lawmakers prescribe laws for others but not for themselves, in the eyes of the public the essential moral authority is diminished. This is why it is essential to create ethical rules for the legislative branch as closely similar to those of the judiciary and the executive as is possible, given their differing functions. Instead of statutes applying to only one branch or two, standards should be applicable to all. No part of the Federal Government should be satisfied with a standard of less than absolute honesty in the conduct of public officials.

While our analysis is based on certain fundamental functions which conflict of interest restrictions are intended to serve, our analysis also incorporates the four key principles noted by the President when he signed Executive Order 12668 [4] creating this Commission. One, ethical standards for public servants must be exacting enough to ensure that the officials act with the utmost integrity and live up to the public's confidence in them. Two, standards must be fair, they must be objective and consistent with common sense. Three, the standards must be equitable all across the three branches of the Federal Government. Finally, we cannot afford to have unreasonably restrictive requirements that discourage able citizens from entering public service.

Our recommendations are set out in such a way as to define the issues at

---

→ apply to top Federal public service political appointments in respect of lobbying and other activities in which appointees may engage after they leave office. These new ethics rules, it is reported, 'would precede the announcement of any of the nominations to serve in his Cabinet'. See *Financial Times* 12 November 1992.

4 Executive Order 12668 was dated 25 January 1989, see Note 2 attached.

stake in each instance, the alternatives considered in arriving at our conclusions, and to provide insight into the deliberative process adopted with respect to each issue. In each instance, a 'Black-Letter' statement of the recommendation will be followed by a discussion of the present law, the important considerations, including in some instances a further elaboration of our recommendations, and the alternatives which were considered by the Commission.

After this introduction, our report is divided into five major sections. First, we take up ethics issues which arise on the recruitment of the Government employee and during employment. Next, we treat post-employment restrictions. Financial disclosure deserves a section by itself, as does the structure of federal ethics regulation. We conclude with a discussion of new enforcement mechanisms.

We begin by recommending that the conflicts of interest statute forbidding decision by an executive branch official on a 'particular matter' in which he has a financial interest be extended to non-Member officers and employees of Congress and the judiciary, thus striving to achieve (at least in part) the level playing field desired in the ethics law. Judges are already covered by very strict statutory standards, but there are difficult problems in applying a statutory standard to Members of Congress.

We favor centralizing the issuance of interpretive regulations for the executive branch in the Office or Government Ethics, and we suggest the creation of a similar centralized ethics authority within the legislative branch.

As the newcomer prepares to enter Government service, he or she must fill out various forms disclosing assets and income. This frequently leads to the realization that the prospective official has assets and sources of income which, if retained, would create a recurring conflict of interest with governmental duties. While this conflict can be accommodated by recusal from decision-making or a waiver where the interest appears so small as to have no influence on the official's conduct, yet our strong recommendation is that the prospective official be encouraged to divest these troublesome assets at the very outset. If the official could do that by postponing the tax liabilities by a rollover of the troublesome assets into neutral holdings such as Treasury bills, municipal bonds, or bank certificates of deposit, then many more officials would do so. A divestiture of troublesome assets and reinvestment in neutral holdings is the single most important device we have encountered to eliminate completely or at least to mitigate greatly subsequent conflicts of interest. Many of the problems we discuss would never be problems at all, if such a change of holdings had occurred at the outset of the official's public service.

Since not all conflict problems can be erased by divestiture, we recommend that the Office of Government Ethics exercise a rulemaking authority to deal with *de minimis* issues, pension plans, mutual funds, the investments of charitable organizations, and the industry-wide effects of some rulings on individual companies. With executive branch-wide standardized positions promulgated by the Office of Government Ethics, the compliance of individual public servants with the rules will be much simpler and easier, and the general public as a whole will have a vastly better understanding of exactly what holdings are permissible, and the nature of those retained by public officials filing annual disclosure reports.

This whole process should encourage seeking advice. One principle which helps to avoid a conflict of interest, and even an appearance of such conflict, is the age-old principle which should permeate the whole governmental ethical compliance system, *i.e.*: 'No one shall be a judge in his own case'. The possibility of a conflict of interest can be put to rest by submission to an impartial ethics authority, and following the advice received.

We have made specific and uniform recommendations in regard to the thorny problems of augmentation of Government income by private sources, a cap (with the exact percentage yet to be determined) on outside earned income of senior officials of all three branches, a ban on honoraria, and on outside boards and directorships. We believe there must be some cap on most types of outside income earned by the public servant, otherwise many public servants would slowly edge into private activity as a disproportionate source of income, to the detriment of their expected public service. This danger is enhanced every year that governmental salaries lag further and further behind those which can be obtained by the same individuals in private enterprise. We would propose, however, that the President be authorized to exempt from the cap any category of income he determines to be generated by a type of activity which did not pose ethical issues or detract from full performance of official duties.

The disgracefully low compensation for public service affects also the increasingly notorious problem of honoraria. Executive branch rules now prohibit executive branch officials from receiving honoraria for any speeches, writings, or other actions undertaken in their official capacity. In stark contrast, in the legislative branch honoraria for speeches, writings, public appearances at industry meetings, or even at breakfast with a small group, have become a staple and relied-upon source of income up to, in some cases, the limit of thirty or forty percent of the Member's salary. Some Members earn several times their governmental salary by honoraria, and give the excess to charities of their choice. This practice, which some Members of the legislative branch defend as · both inevitable and proper in an era of recognized meager and unfair compensation, obviously produces several evils: first, the Member is diverted with increasing frequency from the performance of official duties; and second, the honoraria all too frequently come from those private interests desirous of obtaining some special influence with the Member. While we believe that no position of a Member of the legislative branch could be changed by a $2,000 honorarium, the honorarium is often perceived to guarantee or imply special access to the particular Member by the granting organization.

In the judicial branch, the apparent evil is simply the diversion of time from judicial duties. The groups before whom judges appear are usually professional groups who are genuinely interested in the judge's views on legal problems, and whose members have no expectation whatsoever of any special influence with a court. Individual lawyers or members of the public do not feel free to pick up the phone and talk to them; contact between bench and bar is in the decorum of a public courtroom.

Outside boards and directorships represent another diversion of a public official's time and energy. Sometimes they produce actual conflicts of interest, many times they create an appearance of a conflict of interest. Our recommendation is that senior public officials not serve on the boards of commercial enterprises, and that participation by such individuals in the management responsibilities of charitable organizations be carefully guarded, particularly if there is a danger of abuse of the public official's name for fund-raising purposes.

Gifts, travel, entertainment, and simple meals have caused ethical problems for years. We encountered the most amazing diversity of interpretation within the executive branch and a stark disparity between the three branches. Our recommendation is a uniform and, we hope, reasonable policy in all branches as to what may be accepted without creating an appearance of impropriety.

Negotiation for future employment while the public official is still serving has always created a disruptive effect on the work of the agency involved, and frequently real problems of a conflict of interest. Our recommendation is designed to make clearer and brighter the lines of what may be done and not done, and to minimize any disruptive effect.

Post-employment restrictions center on the question of the period of time during which former employees should be barred from contacting certain parts of the Federal Government with which they were previously associated. At the present time there is no statutory bar in the legislative and judicial branches, but there are four separate bars in the executive branch. Our recommendations attempt to equalize and simplify these post-employment restrictions. We recommend the extension of the one-year cooling-off period now applicable to senior employees of the executive branch to comparable positions in the legislative and judicial branches. Separate inconsistent and duplicative post-employment restrictions should be considered for repeal. The existing lifetime bar in the executive branch regarding representation on particular matters handled personally and substantially by the former employee should be extended to the judiciary. To thwart the former employee who wants to 'switch sides', there should be a two-year ban on using or transmitting certain types of carefully defined non-public information.

We think compartmentalization in each branch in applying these restrictions has its place, but it should not be abused. We recognize compartmentalization in limiting the ban for the legislative branch to one House only, and for the judicial to the specific court with which the former employee was affiliated. In the executive, we make no recommendation changing the responsibility of the Office of Government Ethics to prescribe compartmentalization in large departments, where a person working in one of numerous large sub-agencies would have little contact or influence with other agencies, but we do recommend that compartmentalization within the Executive Office of the President be abolished, as not consonant with the standards and objectives of this device.

We have carefully studied the question of whether the validity of the actions of the former employee, in making representations on behalf of others to the part of the branch with which he was previously affiliated, should depend on whether the employee receives compensation for such representational activity. We find that the injection of the element of compensation would vitiate the worthwhile objectives of the prohibition itself, and that there is no logical or constitutional justification for it. As a practical matter, requiring the element of compensation to make the representation improper would create a large loophole, which would inevitably be exploited to the Government's detriment. If representation of another person is improper, it is improper whether compensation is involved or not. We believe, however, that there should be no restriction whatsoever on a former employee's right to present his views on policy issues in any form – testimony, press articles, speeches, interviews – and indeed personally to represent his own interests anywhere.

Financial disclosure has been variously described as the linchpin of the ethical enforcement system, as the disinfectant sunlight which makes possible the cleaning up of abusive practices. We have made three basic recommendations on financial disclosure, two to strengthen it, the other to simplify it. To strengthen financial disclosure, to make it more meaningful, we would raise the highest limit describing assets to '$1,000,000 and over', and the highest limit describing income to '$250,000 or over'. We believe the present intermediate bands of assets and income are so close together as to be somewhat meaningless, and would leave to the Office of Government Ethics the responsibility of recommending the number and size of the categories between the $1,000 and $1,000,000 or $1,000 and $250,000 marks. To strengthen disclosure for political appointees we would eliminate the home mortgage and family debt exceptions, because in our view the existence of heavy obligations, no matter what the laudable purpose of assuming those obligations may be, is something about which the public should be informed. We are also recommending a simplification and increased uniformity to the extent possible of the disclosure forms required by the Senate committees, the White House, and the FBI, and propose that a coordinating committee with representatives from all three branches be convened to address this task.

We now turn to the structure of federal ethics regulation. In the executive branch we recommend the strengthening of the Office of Government Ethics for its advice, consultation, and rulemaking function. We would continue the principal investigative, enforcement and compliance responsibility in the individual departments and agencies for several reasons. We think there should be one overall set of government regulations interpreting the ethics statutes, promulgated by the Office of Government Ethics. Variations from these uniform regulations should be permitted only on a showing by the individual department or agency that such is necessary for its particular mission, and on the approval of the Office of Government Ethics. Likewise, the final authoritative interpretation of the regulations should rest with that office, to prevent the divergent standards and interpretations now current. The Office of Government Ethics should promote uniformity by an enlarged and strengthened training mission for the ethics officers in the individual agencies, and for an annual review of their plans and programs.

In contrast to the rulemaking centered in the Office of Government Ethics, we recommend that the investigative enforcement and compliance function remain principally the responsibility of the individual departments and agencies. The Cabinet secretary or the head of an independent agency is the person whom the President should hold responsible for ethical standards in his agency. He must therefore have the responsibility for investigation, enforcement, and producing compliance with the overall executive branch standards within his department. Furthermore, the agency inspectors general and ethics officers are closer to the facts of any violation, and would probably do a better job of investigation. Likewise, training and education within the department or agency is the responsibility of that agency, although assisted, reviewed, and checked by the Office of Government Ethics.

In the legislative branch we recommend the establishment of a joint ethics officer with an adequate investigative staff to investigate alleged offenses and bring the results of the investigation and recommendation for enforcement to the appropriate Congressional ethics committee.

The Commission recommends additional enforcement mechanisms. In this area we are especially indebted to the work already done by the Congress and embodied in the legislation introduced in the last Congress and in current proposed legislation. These new enforcement measures were singled out for praise by President Reagan in his message vetoing the legislation for other reasons. We believe that in addition to continuing the felony level penalties, there should also be misdemeanor penalties to give some flexibility in enforcement. Likewise, there should be civil penalties, which can be in some instances more persuasive and better tailored to the offense than criminal penalties. The Attorney General should have authority to seek injunctions to restrain conduct violative of ethical standards. We pass no judgement on the wisdom of the independent counsel device for investigating and prosecuting ethical violations, but we do urge that if the independent counsel device is retained, it apply to both the executive and legislative branches. If the device is retained, we also urge that it be strictly limited to the very highest officials in each branch, as this is the only area in which there may be justification for it.

In closing, we would emphasize that in addition to serving specific functions, our recommendations are also offered to stimulate the continuing development of the ethics system within the government. We believe that the implementation of these recommendations will serve both the public interest in protecting the integrity of the government, and the federal employee's interest in preserving an individual sense of pride and honor in serving the public good.

We now offer our recommendations.

2. Summary of Recommendations [5]

Recommendation 1:   The Commission recommends that the conflict-of-interest statute, 18 U.S.C. § 208, be extended to non-Member officers and employees of the judiciary and Congress, but not to Members of Congress themselves.

Recommendation 2:   The Commission recommends (1) that the Office of Government Ethics, in collaboration with the Department of Justice, issue interpretive regulations relating to financial conflicts of interest under 18 U.S.C. § 208; and (2) that legislation be enacted granting the Office of Government Ethics the authority to issue rules providing for general waivers under § 208(b)(2).

Recommendation 3:   The Commission recommends (1) that agencies granting waivers under § 208(b) be required to consult with the Office of Government Ethics in

---

5 In the Report of the then President's Ethics Law Reform Commission, this Summary of Recommendations is numbered II.

advance and provide that office with a copy of any waiver granted; (2) that further consideration be given to the mechanism for granting waivers for employees of the legislative branch; and (3) that legislation be enacted granting the President authority to waive the provisions of § 208(a) in situations where the national interest so requires.

Recommendation 4: The Commission recommends that legislation be enacted to grant tax relief to persons who are required to divest assets in order to avoid conflicts of interest.

Recommendation 5: To respond to certain unique circumstances that pose unusual conflict of interest issues, the Commission recommends (1) the enactment of legislation authorizing waivers from 18 U.S.C. § 208(a) for advisory committee members where the appointing authority determines, after review of financial disclosure forms, that the need for a member's expertise outweighs the potential for conflict of interest; and (2) that limitations on the activities of partners of federal employees (18 U.S.C. § 207(g)) apply only when the government employee and the partner are general partners, not when the government employee is a limited partner.

Recommendation 6: The Commission recommends (1) that federal employees in all three branches be prohibited from receiving honoraria, (2) that existing criminal prohibitions against supplementing government salaries apply to all three branches, and (3) that senior employees in all three branches be covered by a uniform percentage gap on outside earned income, but that the President have authority to exempt categories of earned income from the cap that do not present significant issues of ethical propriety or interfere with the full performance of job duties.

Recommendation 7: The Commission recommends that senior federal employees in all three branches of government be prohibited from serving on the boards of directors of for-profit commercial enterprises (whether or not compensated) and that requests by such employees to serve on the boards of directors of non-profit organizations be subject to review on a case-by-case basis.

Recommendation 8: The Commission recommends the following changes in the laws and regulations governing acceptance of gifts: (1) enactment of uniform gift acceptance authority government-wide; (2) enactment of a uniform maximum value for gifts to individuals; and (3) enactment of revisions to the current statutory bar on gifts to supervisors.

Recommendation 9: The Commission recommends that restrictions in 18 U.S.C. § 208 on negotiation for employment be amended to extend to Members and employees of the legislative and judicial branches. We further recommend that Congress reconsider the necessity of retaining statutes applying special restrictions to specified categories of employees. To the extent that Congress feels that such supplementary restrictions are necessary, those prohibitions should be consolidated into § 208.

Recommendation 10: The Commission recommends that the one-year cooling-off period presently applicable to Senior Employees of the executive branch be extended to the legislative and judicial branches and their senior staff. As to all three branches, the bar should permit self-representation by the former employee on particular matters involving the former employee specifically.

Recommendation 11: The Commission recommends that Congress enact legislation that adds a new provision to 18 U.S.C. § 207 creating a two-year post-employment bar, for executive and legislative branch personnel, against the use or disclosure of certain specifically defined, non-public information in connection with representing a party to the government or in connection with aiding or advising a party in such a representation. Such legislation should include: (1) a provision that includes non-public procurement-related proprietary or source selection information within the scope of the restriction; and (2) is specifically defineable, a provision that includes non-public information as to the government's

157

position and strategy in international trade, disarmament, and finance negotiations.

Recommendation 12: The Commission recommends amending the 18 U.S.C. § 207(b)(i) two-year official responsibility bar to add a knowledge requirement.

Recommendation 13: The Commission recommends repeal of the 18 U.S.C. § 207(b)(ii) two-year prohibition against Senior Employees assisting in a representational effort by personal presence.

Recommendation 14: The Commission recommends that the Executive Office of the President be treated as one agency for the purpose of the one-year cooling off period.

Recommendation 15: The Commission recommends that the receipt of compensation not be included as an essential element of any post-employment restriction.

Recommendation 16: The Commission recommends that the public financial disclosure reporting system mandated by the Ethics in Government Act of 1978 be continued, but the floors of the highest categories of value for reporting of income and assets should be raised, there should be broader ranges of values within the categories, and specified statutory reporting requirements should be replaced by general requirements, with an authorization for the Office of Government Ethics to impose detailed reporting requirements by regulation. In addition, for non-career appointees, the reporting requirements for liabilities should be expanded to include mortgages on personal residence and loans from specified relatives.

Recommendation 17: The Commission recommends that financial reporting requirements and review be made more uniform across the three branches of government.

Recommendation 18: The Commission recommends that a coordinating committee composed of ethics officials of the three branches of Government study ways to simplify the Presidential appointment process by reducing the number and complexity of forms to be completed by potential appointees.

Recommendation 19: The Commission recommends revision, updating and reissuance of Executive Ordere 11222 to emphasize the President's commitment to the highest ethical standards for executive branch employees.

Recommendation 20: The Commission recommends that the Office of Government Ethics be directed by executive order to consolidate all executive branch standards of conduct regulations into a single set of regulations. Individual agencies could supplement these regulations with stricter standards with the approval of the Office of Government Ethics. The Office of Government Ethics should also issue a comprehensive ethics manual.

Recommendation 21: The Commission recommends that executive branch agencies should be responsible for training their employees concerning ethics requirements, but an agency should obtain the Office of Government Ethics approval of its annual plan for training and awareness activities.

Recommendation 22: The Commission recommends that Congress appoint an independent ethics official, to be confirmed by both houses, who would head a permanent ethics office that would investigate allegations of misconduct, report findings publicly to the ethics committee of the appropriate house, and recommend appropriate sanctions.

Recommendation 23: The Commission believes that a White House Ethics Council or similar body could be helpful in preserving high ethical standards in the executive branch.

Recommendation 24: The Commission recommends the addition of misdemeanor and civil penalties as sanctions for violations of 18 U.S.C. § § 203-209 but recommends that willful violations of these laws should continue to be punishable as felonies.

Recommendation 25: The Commission recommends that Chapter 11 of title 18 of the United States Code be amended to allow the Attorney General to seek injunctive relief for all violations of 18 U.S.C. § § 203-209.

Recommendation 26: The Commission recommends the strengthening of administrative debarment procedures for former government employees who violate the post-employment restrictions in 18 U.S.C. § 207.

Recommendation 27: Assuming the continued use of an Independent Counsel mechanism, the Commission recommends that Congress enact legislation to extend the scope of the Independent Counsel statute to cover the legislative branch. [6]

3. Conclusion [7]

We conclude as we began. Laws do not in themselves create virtue, but clearly defined laws can give a standard to which honest citizens can repair. Laws can be persuasive and effective, but only in an atmosphere created by emphatic leadership at the top, leadership which asserts norms as the universal standard of conduct across the Government, leadership that is replicated at every echelon of Government.

Leadership at the top and at each subordinate level can create the desired atmosphere in which ethical standards will flourish and violations will be clearly seen as exceptional and intolerable conduct. We believe that these ethical standards should apply to and permeate the three branches of our Government, so that each branch will deserve and enjoy the equal respect of our citizens.

We note that the individual employee has the most critical role to play in the maintenance of government integrity. Our nation is possessed of freedom, and exults in the power of the individual citizen to choose his own course of conduct. In this respect, a free society such as ours must rest in good measure upon the personal conscience of the men and women who serve the public good.

The government, in turn, is responsible for nurturing each employee's sense of personal responsibility and accountability, by providing definitive standards of conduct. These guidelines serve as the foundation of the public servant's work ethic, and as such must be continually reviewed for consistency, fairness and viability.

To these ends, a truly effective program must reach unobtrusively into every aspect of government operations. The Commission hopes that the implementation of the recommendations contained here will facilitate that effort.

---

6 For the extent to which in December 1992 these 27 recommendations have been implemented, see Addendum to this Volume 1: *Government Ethics*, p. 692.

7 In the President's Report, this Conclusion is numbered VIII.

NOTE 1 [1]

Recommendations for
Technical Amendments

In addition to the major substantive recommendations contained in the body of our report, the Commission is including in this final section our views on a number of other matters discussed during our deliberations.

1. Dual Compensation Restrictions Affecting Retired Military Officers.

Although the question of limiting dual compensation for retired regular military officers is not a true 'ethics' problem, the Commission considered whether retired regular military officers should continue to be subject to this restriction. At present, 5 U.S.C. § 5532 reduces the retired pay of a retired regular officer of the uniformed services who holds a civilian office or position, appointive or elective, in the executive, legislative, or judicial branches of the government. The present dual compensation statutes evolved from the Dual Office Act of 1894, in an effort to place reasonable dollar limits on persons holding two positions. Retired military were considered to continue to hold a government position.

In our view, the existing restrictions may deter highly qualified retired officers from entering into civilian federal service. Although the dual compensation limitations may realize a dollar savings for the country, the government may thereby be foregoing the services of many talented retired military officers. Further, the public's perception of the equitable application of such federal statutes would be enhanced by taking action to achieve a better balance in this area.

Accordingly, we recommend that consideration be given to repealing 5 U.S.C. § 5532 as it applies to retired military officers, or, in the alternative, if the provision is necessary, then consideration should be given to expanding its coverage to include all federal retirees.

2. Separation of the District of Columbia and the Federal Government from 18 U.S.C. § § 203 and 205.

The Commission recommends that 18 U.S.C. § § 203 and 205 be amended

---

1 In the Report of the then President's Ethics Law Reform Commission, this Note 1 is entitled Appendix 1. However, this Volume of *Teaching Ethics* has adopted the term Note for appending materials.

so that they (1) no longer preclude employees of the District of Columbia government from appearing before federal agencies and courts, (2) no longer preclude most federal employees from appearing before District of Columbia agencies, and (3) no longer prohibit law students employed by District or federal agencies from participating in clinical legal programs sponsored by their law schools.

As presently written, 18 U.S.C. § § 203 and 205 prohibit all officers and employees of the federal government and the District of Columbia government from appearing before federal courts and agencies and entities of the District government. The theory behind § § 203 and 205 is that an employee should serve only one master and should not represent another entity against his primary employer. The laws do not reflect the current separate statutory status of the District government, however, and have the effect of precluding federal government employees from participating in outside charitable activities such as providing pro bono legal services to the poor in local courts. Another unfortunate effect is that law students who work as paralegals or clerks in federal or District government agencies are often precluded from participating in clinical legal programs sponsored by their law schools.

The Commission notes that the Office of Government Ethics has suggested that if there is to be any coverage of District of Columbia employees, these sections be amended so that federal employees are prohibited only from appearing before federal agencies and courts, and District of Columbia employees are prohibited only from appearing before District agencies and courts. The Commission agrees with the suggestion and also with the Office of Government Ethics' recommendation that there be an exception for the United States Attorney's Office because of its unique role in prosecuting cases in both the United States District Court and the District of Columbia Superior Court. Employees of the United States Attorney's Office should continue to be barred from appearing before entities of the District government except in accordance with their official duties.

3. Consistent Treatment of the Interior Department under § 208.

The Commission recommends the repeal of § 319 of Interior Department Appropriations, FY 1988, Pub. L. No. 100-446, 102 Stat. 1774, a provision that changed the application of 18 U.S.C. § 208 for all officers and employees of the Interior Department and of the Indian Health Service to only particular matters involving specific parties. As described earlier in this report, there has been uncertainty throughout the executive branch about the scope of the prohibition in § 208 against employees participating in a 'particular matter' in which the employee or persons closely associated with him have a financial interest, unless the employee obtains a waiver in accordance with the statute. In § 319 of the most recent Interior Department Appropriations Act, Congress narrowed the coverage of this section for employees of the Interior Department and of the Indian Health Service by providing that, as to them, the term 'particular matter' meant only a 'particular matter involving specific parties'. This provision was originally enacted as § 318, Department of the Interior and Related Agencies Appropriations Act, 1988, Pub. L. No. 100-202, 101 Stat. 1329, 1329-214, 1329-255.

The provision seems to have been enacted to deal with the special problems of American Indians who are government employees and may have birthrights in interests of their tribes which can be affected by actions of the government, particularly the Interior Department. The Office of Government Ethics has recommended repeal of this provision on the ground that this type of conflict can adequately be handled through the waiver process and that the special treatment afforded all employees of the Interior Department – many of whom have nothing to do with Indian affairs – is inequitable in comparison to the rest of the executive branch. The commission agrees with the Office of Government Ethics and recommends that this provision be repealed in the interests of establishing uniform and consistent ethical standards.

4. Restatement of Fine Amounts.

The Commission recommends that 18 U.S.C. § § 204-205 and § § 207-209 should be revised to eliminate the reference to a specific dollar amount of fines and refer instead to 'a fine in accordance with this title'. With the exception of § 209 and the partner provision in 18 U.S.C. § § 207(g), which are misdemeanor offenses, violations of the criminal conflict statutes are all felonies and all state the fine portion of the penalty as 'not more than $10,000'. Regardless of the fine stated in a substantive criminal provision, 18 U.S.C. § 3571 provides that the fine for a felony committed by an individual is the greatest of the amount stated in the offense, double the defendant's gain, or $250,000. Section 3571 also provides that the maximum fine for the type of misdemeanors set out in § § 2107(g) and 209 is the greatest of the amount set out in the offense, double the defendant's gain, or $100,000. The conventional language used in new sections of title 18 to refer to the fine provisions is 'fined under this title', or 'fined in accordance with this title'. Accordingly, in the interest of clarity, the Commission recommends this technical change (which has no substantive effect).

5. Fine-Tuning of Section 204.

Section 204, 18 U.S.C., probably the least used of any of the conflict-of-interest statutes, prohibits Members of Congress, Members-elect, the Delegate from the District of Columbia, and the Delegate-elect from practicing before the United States Claims Court and the United States Court of Appeal for the Federal Circuit. It does not preclude such practice by Delegates to Congress or Delegates-elect from Guam, American Samoa, or the Virgin Islands, although these persons stand on an equal footing with the Delegate from the District of Columbia.

The Commission notes that the Office of Government Ethics has recommended that if 18 U.S.C. § 204 is retained, it should be amended to include the Delegates from the three above-mentioned Territories. The Commission agrees that all Delegates and Delegates-elect should be treated the same.

NOTE 2 [1]

Presidential Documents
Executive Order 12668

President's Commission on Federal Ethics Law Reform

By the authority vested in me as President by the Constitution and laws of the United States of America, and in order to establish, in accordance with the provisions of the Federal Advisory Committee Act, as amended (5 U.S.C. App. 2), an advisory committee on reform of the Federal ethics laws, it is hereby ordered as follows:

Section 1. *Establishment.* (a) There is established the President's Commission on Federal Ethics Law Reform. The Commission shall be composed of not more than eight members appointed by the President. These members shall be distinguished individuals with broad experience in ethics and public service.

(b) The President shall designate a Chairman and Vice-Chairman from among the members of the Commission.

Sec. 2. *Functions.* (a) The Commission shall review Federal ethics laws, Executive orders, and policies and shall make recommendations to the President for legislative, administrative and other reforms needed to ensure full public confidence in the integrity of all Federal public officials and employees.

(b) The Commission shall report to the President by March 9, 1989, and shall provide a copy of its report to the Attorney General. [2]

Sec. 3. *Administration.* (a) The heads of Executive agencies and the Director of the Office of Government Ethics, to the extent permitted by law, shall provide the Commission such information, advice, and assistance as it may require for purposes of carrying out its functions.

(b) Members of the Commission shall serve without compensation for their work on the Commission. However, while engaged in the work of the Commission, members may be allowed travel expenses, including per diem in

---

1 In the President's Report, this Note 2 is entitled Appendix 2.

2 The extracts reproduced in this Volume *Teaching Ethics Vol. I: Government Ethics* are from this Report, which was submitted to the US Attorney General in March 1989, in accordance with his Executive Order 12668.

lieu of subsistence, as authorized by law (including 5 U.S.C. 5701-5707), to the extent funds are available therefor.

(c) The Attorney General, to the extent permitted by law and subject to the availability of appropriations, shall provide the Commision with such administrative services, funds, facilities, staff, and other support services as may be necessary for the performance of its functions.

Sec. 4. *Counsel to the President.* Following the submission of the Commission's report, the Counsel to the President shall provide the President with periodic reports regarding the implementation of reforms to Federal ethics laws, Executive orders, and policies.

Sec. 5. *General.* (a) Notwithstanding any other Executive order, the functions of the President under the Federal Advisory Committee Act, as amended, except that of reporting to the Congress, which are applicable to the Commission, shall be performed by the Attorney General, in accordance with guidelines and procedures established by the Administrator of General Services.

(b) The Commission shall terminate 30 days after its report, unless sooner extended.

Gy Bush

THE WHITE HOUSE,
January 25, 1989.

9

Second Biennial Report to Congress: United States' Office of Government Ethics (March 1992)

1. Introduction

1.1 Scope of Report

By Public Law 100-598 of November 3, 1988, the Office of Government Ethics (OGE) was reauthorized for a period of six years. As amended thereby, the Ethics in Government Act of 1978 (Act) now requires, at 5 U.S.C. App. § 408, that the Director 'shall, no later than March 31 of each year in which the second session of a Congress begins, submit to the Congress a report containing (1) a summary of the actions taken by the Director during a 2-year period ending on December 31 of the preceding year in order to carry out the Director's functions and responsibilities under this title; and (2) such other information as the Director may consider appropriate'.

This report includes data and information collected from staff members of the Office, as well as from each executive agency for calendar years 1990 and 1991. Agency data reported to this Office annually under § 402 of the Act has been synthesized so as to evaluate the strengths and accomplishments of agency ethics programs generally.

1.2 Mission

The Office of Government Ethics was established by the Act to provide 'overall direction of executive branch policies related to preventing conflicts of interest on the part of officers and employees of any executive agency'. Specific responsibilities, as outlined in the Act (5 U.S.C. App. § 402), fall into six general areas:

- Regulatory Authority – develop, recommend and review rules and regulations pertaining to conflicts of interest, post-employment restrictions, standards of conduct, and public and confidential financial disclosure in the executive branch.

- Financial Disclosure – review executive branch public financial disclosure reports of certain Presidential appointees to determine possible violations of applicable laws or regulations and recommend appropriate corrective action; administer executive blind trusts.

- Education and Training – implement statutory responsibility of 'providing information on and promoting understanding of ethical standards in executive agencies'.

- Guidance and Interpretation – prepare formal advisory opinions, informal letter opinions and policy memoranda on how to interpret and comply with requirements on conflict of interest, post-employment, standards of conduct, and financial disclosure in the executive branch; consult with agency ethics officials in individual cases.

- Enforcement – monitor agency ethics programs and review compliance, including financial disclosure systems; refer possible violations of conflict of interest laws to the Department of Justice, and advise them on prosecutions and appeals; investigate possible ethics violations and order corrective action or recommend disciplinary action.

- Evaluation – evaluate the effectiveness of conflict of interest laws and recommend appropriate amendments.

Responsibilities in these six areas expanded in 1989 by additional specific requirements of Executive Order 12674 and the Ethics Reform Act (Public Laws 101-194 and 101-280).

Executive Order 12674 requires that OGE:

- promulgate regulations establishing a single, comprehensive and clear set of executive branch standards of conduct;

- develop, disseminate and update an ethics reference manual for executive branch employees, describing the relevant statutes, regulations, decisions, and policies;

- promulgate regulations interpreting the general conflict of interest statute (18 U.S.C. § 208);

- promulgate regulations interpreting the statute prohibiting the supplementation of salaries (18 U.S.C. § 209);

- promulgate regulations establishing a revised system of confidential financial disclosure for executive branch employees, to complement the public disclosure system;

- review all implementing regulations issued by agencies in furtherance of the above-described OGE regulations, to insure consistency;

- coordinate the development of annual agency ethics training plans and require mandatory annual briefings for certain executive branch employees; and

- serve in a consulting capacity for all agencies in the granting of exemptions from the conflict of interest statute, pursuant to 18 U.S.C. § 208(b).

The Ethics Reform Act requires that OGE:

- issue new regulations implementing the revised post-employment restrictions at 18 U.S.C. § 207;

- promulgate new regulations implementing the revised public financial disclosure requirements;

- issue regulations implementing 5 U.S.C. § 7351 on gifts to superiors and review regulations to implement 5 U.S.C. § 7353 on gifts to employees from outside sources;

- consult with the General Services Administration on regulations to implement new 31 U.S.C. § 1353 on agency acceptance of travel reimbursement;

- collect semiannual agency reports of travel payments exceeding $250 accepted under 31 U.S.C. § 1353, and make them available to the public;

- issue regulations under 18 U.S.C. § 208(b), to define financial interests generally exempt from the § 208(a) conflict provisions as being too remote or inconsequential to affect the integrity of services, and to provide guidance to agencies for issuance of individual § 208(b) waivers;

- collect copies of all agency waivers under 18 U.S.C. § 208(b)(1) or (b)(3);

- issue regulations regarding tax relief for certain OGE-certified asset divestitures, and review all requests for divestiture certificates; and

- issue regulations implementing new statutory provisions on outside earned income, honoraria, and outside employment.

OGE began implementing each of these responsibilities in 1989 and, as noted in our first biennial report, many of these responsibilities require a long-term commitment. Thus, OGE has continued to take actions in these areas during 1990 and 1991.

1.3 History

OGE was created as part of the Office of Personnel Management, where it operated until becoming a separate agency on October 1, 1989, pursuant to Public Law 100-598.

OGE's current and past directors are:

08/90-present	Mr Stephen D. Potts
11/89-07/90	Mr Donald E. Campbell (acting)
12/87-10/89	Judge Frank Q. Nebeker
08/87-12/87	Mr Donald E. Campbell (acting)
08/83-08/87	Mr David H. Martin
08/82-08/83	Mr David R. Scott (acting)
10/79-08/82	Mr J. Jackson Walter
01/79-10/79	Mr Bernard Wruble (interim)

1.4 Organization

The OGE staff organization chart is illustrated in Graph 1. Functions of the various offices are as follows:

Office of the Director –

The Director provides overall direction of executive branch policies related to standards of ethical conduct and is responsible for OGE's fulfilling its Congressional and Presidential mandates.

Office of General Counsel and Legal Policy –

The Office of General Counsel and Legal Policy is responsible for establishing and maintaining a uniform legal framework of Government ethics for executive branch employees, and for assisting agencies in its implementation.

Office of Education –

The Office of Education is responsible for insuring that quality ethics education programs are provided to executive branch employees and materials are made available to facilitate these programs.

Office of Program Assistance and Review –

The Office of Program Assistance and Review serves as the overseer for executive branch agency ethics programs. Ethics specialists in the

Program Assistance Division assist agencies in development, maintenance and improvement of their ethics programs. Management analysts in the Program Review Division monitor agency and employee compliance with executive branch ethics laws and regulations through a series of ethics program reviews conducted according to an annual program plan.

Office of Administration –

The Office of Administration is responsible for providing and co-ordinating essential intra-agency administrative support to all OGE operating programs in the area of personnel, payroll, fiscal resource management, facilities and property management, travel management, procurement, publishing and distribution, printing, information resource management, telecommunications and office automation support, person-nel security and funding mandatory overhead expenses necessary for the operation of the agency.

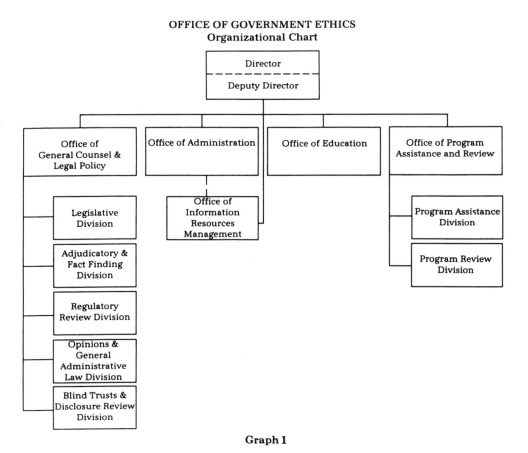

OFFICE OF GOVERNMENT ETHICS
Organizational Chart

Graph 1

2. Office of General Counsel and Legal Policy

2.1 Overview of Responsibilities

The Office of General Counsel and Legal Policy at OGE is responsible for establishing and maintaining a uniform legal framework of Government ethics for executive branch employees, and for assisting agencies in its implementation. To accomplish this broad purpose, the general counsel staff:

- assists the Director in coordinating with the White House and Congress all ethics policies and requirements for the executive branch, including liaison on pending legislation and regulations;

- reviews public financial disclosure reports of Presidential nominees, as part of the Senate confirmation process;

- develops and issues a regulatory system to carry out the ethics program requirements established by executive orders and statutes;

- provides interpretive guidance on the administrative ethical standards of conduct, the criminal conflict of interest statutes, the Ethics Reform Act of 1989 (Public Laws 101-194 and 101-280), and other ethics-related matters, to agency ethics officials, employees, and the public, by means of written and oral opinions;

- fulfills a consultative role of assisting agency ethics officials with the application of Government ethics to specific factual situations;

- coordinates with the Department of Justice in enforcing the criminal conflict statutes, and manages OGE's corrective action enforcement authority;

- augments the OGE Office of Education's role, by providing official speakers and panelists at forums for Government employees and the public, and at regional and Washington, DC training seminars for agency ethics officials;

- administers the qualified blind trust program for the entire executive branch, as well as the issuance of certificates of divestiture to permit deferral of tax on certain capital gains realized incident to Government service; and

- provides house counsel legal services for OGE in carrying out its own agency functions.

2.2 Staffing Organization and Utilization

Attorney staffing has remained fairly constant throughout this two-year period, averaging ten full-time equivalents (FTEs). While the attorneys are cross-trained to perform all general counsel functions, some specialization has developed, as a means of promoting consistency and expertise.

All ten attorneys shared the daily work of providing interpretive guidance, opinions, and consultations necessary for agency ethics officials to transform theoretical ethics principles into practical applications. Additionally, all were involved to some extent in providing house counsel advice at OGE; handling Privacy/Freedom of Information Act and other administrative law matters; and coordinating enforcement through informal liaison with the Department of Justice and use of OGE's corrective action authority. Time spent performing these functions equated to 3.5 attorney FTEs.

These same attorneys also specialized to perform one or more of the other major tasks of the Office of General Counsel and Legal Policy:

- drafting and coordinating with various agencies on new regulations and forms (2.75 FTEs);

- reviewing public financial disclosure reports (SF 278) for Presidential nominees requiring Senate advice and consent, and preparing the Director's certification to the Senate (1.25 FTEs);

- conducting White House liaison on ethics policy, reviewing legislation and coordinating the Director's written comments and testimony to Congressional committees, and serving as liaison to the news media (1.0 FTE);

- serving on a frequent basis as official lecturers, instructors, and panelists on Government ethics, both in Washington, DC and at regional sites around the country (.75 FTE); and

- certifying and monitoring all qualified blind trusts created in the executive branch, issuing all executive branch certificates of divestiture under authority of the Ethics Reform Act of 1989, and resolving legal issues arising out of ethics agreements entered by advice-and-consent nominees (.75 FTE).

These responsibilities are depicted by FTEs in Graph 2a, as the Attorney Utilization Plan for 1990-1991.

During this period of calendar years 1990 and 1991, the Office of General Counsel and Legal Policy maintained its support and paralegal personnel staffing at three. This included one full-time financial disclosure specialist, who coordinated all Presidential nominee reports with the White House, and two paralegal/clerical assistants, who processed correspondence, performed legal research, assisted with the review and tracking of requests for

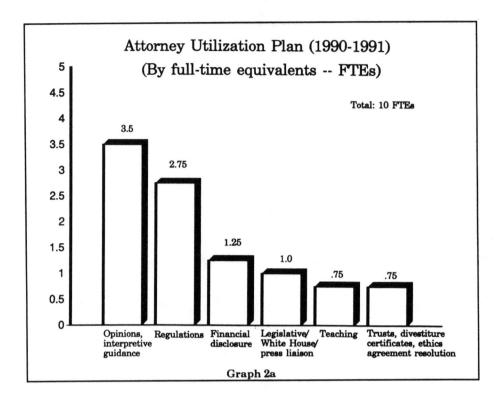

Graph 2a

certificates of divestiture, augmented attorney processing of Freedom of Information Act and Privacy Act requests, maintained statistics, and provided general support and assistance to the attorneys and to OGE's Office of the Director.

2.3 Accomplishments during 1990 and 1991

I. Opinions and Interpretive Guidance

A. Background

The general counsel staff executes OGE's responsibility of interpreting ethics laws and administrative standards of conduct, by means of both oral and written opinions. Assigned attorneys provide telephonic and personal consultation for agency ethics officials as guidance in resolving conflict of interest issues in individual cases, research and prepare written opinions on ethics issues which are unique or of widespread interest, coordinate with the Department of Justice to enforce criminal conflict statutes, offer general guidance to Government employees and the public on Government ethics issues, and advise the Director and other staff members on legal matters.

This area of responsibility encompasses the conflict of interest statutes at U.S.C. § § 202-209, which restrict employees in representing others to the Government, acting in matters where they have a conflicting financial interest, accepting a supplementation of their Government salaries for performance of duty, and certain representational activity to the Government after leaving employment. Also within the general counsel attorneys' interpretive responsibility are the statutes which were part of the Ethics Reform Act of 1989 – public financial disclosure revisions, gift restrictions, travel reimbursement authority, certificates of divestiture for deferral of tax on certain capital gains, and restrictions on outside income and honoraria. The attorneys are also called upon to provide ethics advice in relation to numerous other statutes, such as the Foreign Gifts Act, the Federal Advisory Committee Act, and procurement integrity legislation.

In addition to guidance concerning statutes, one of the major advisory roles of the general counsel attorneys concerns the administrative standards of ethical conduct, embodied in Executive Order 12674 of April 12, 1989, as amended by Executive Order 12731 of October 17, 1990, and the implementing regulations at 5 C.F.R. Part 735 (to be replaced in 1992 by Part 2635).

B. Specific Accomplishments

Time spent by all general counsel attorneys in providing written opinions and oral interpretive guidance accounted for an average of 33 percent of their workload during calendar years 1990 and 1991. Graph 2b depicts that time usage and shows a further breakdown by subject matter.

The majority of both oral and written advice was given to agency ethics officials, who are responsible for counselling individual employees and for maintaining agency Government ethics programs.

General counsel attorneys did provide some telephonic advice directly to employees and former employees, based on referral from their agency ethics office or in cases where agency advice is not readily available. The general public, the news media, and Congressional staffs also frequently sought OGE attorneys' interpretation on executive branch ethics issues. Additionally, general counsel attorneys coordinated interpretive telephonic advice provided by non-attorney desk officers in the Office of Program Assistance and Review at OGE, who serve as an alternate point of contact within OGE for agency ethics enquiries.

Advice on the conflict of interest statutes accounted for 13 percent of the attorney workload. The two conflict statutes about which advice was most often sought were 18 U.S.C. § 208 (financial conflicts) and 18 U.S.C. § 207 (post-employment restrictions). Financial conflict issues under § 208 focused on when an employee should be considered as having an interest

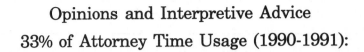

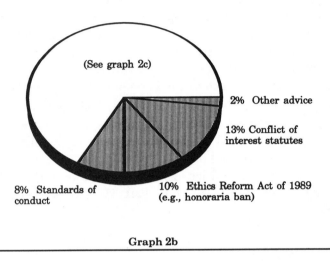

Opinions and Interpretive Advice

33% of Attorney Time Usage (1990-1991):

(See graph 2c)

2% Other advice

13% Conflict of interest statutes

8% Standards of conduct

10% Ethics Reform Act of 1989 (e.g., honoraria ban)

Graph 2b

which could be directly and predictably affected by the outcome of a Government matter in which he may participate, and how to best resolve such conflicts. The Office of General Counsel and Legal Policy coordinated all consultations required by Executive Order 12674 on when an agency might appropriately grant conflict waivers under § 208(b).

Post-employment advice under 18 U.S.C. § 207 most often involved issues of whether a matter being undertaken by the former employee should be viewed under the statute as the same matter in which he was involved while with the Government, whether the matter involved specific parties, whether his actions equate to representation, and application of the statute to former senior employees.

In calendar years 1990 and 1991, the general counsel staff was virtually besieged with requests for guidance on the honoraria ban, 5 U.S.C. App., which was part of the Ethics Reform Act of 1989. That ban became effective on January 1, 1991, and it engendered unprecedented inquiries, complaints, and requests for interpretive assistance. Private associations and employee interest groups, individual employees, the press, and agency ethics officials all sought help in understanding the ban, as did Congressional offices, where the level of constituent concern was high.

Considerable interpretive assistance was also offered on other specific provisions of the Ethics Reform Act of 1989 which authorized agencies to accept certain travel reimbursements for official attendance at meetings (31 U.S.C. § 1353); revised public financial disclosure requirements (5 U.S.C. App.); and provided new authority for granting certificates of divestiture (26 U.S.C. § 1043). The latter two topics are discussed in more detail below, in section II. Ethics Reform Act interpretation, including the honoraria ban, accounted for 10 percent of the attorney workload.

Ethics restrictions under procurement integrity legislation (41 U.S.C. § 423) also brought a steady flow of requests for guidance, as did the unique status of special Government employees appointed under 18 U.S.C. § 202, especially those who serve on committees created under the Federal Advisory Committee Act (5 U.S.C. App.).

Next to statutory interpretation, general counsel attorneys advised most frequently on the administrative standards of ethical conduct, especially since the implementing regulations have been under major revision as a result of Executive Order 12674 issued in 1989. This advice on standards of conduct constituted 8 percent of the attorney workload. As in the past, questions about gifts from outside sources predominated. Agency ethics officials frequently sought OGE's advice on the propriety of accepting food, entertainment, and tangible gifts, and the appearance concerns associated with acceptance. The gift restriction also brought questions from the private sector on when such items as food and refreshments could be given to executive branch employees.

Other standards of ethical conduct on which advice was most commonly provided were the prohibition on using public office for private gain or giving preferential treatment, restrictions on outside activities (such as fundraising) and employment, guidelines for using Government assets and information, exceptions to the general prohibition on gifts to superiors, and avoiding appearances of impropriety.

Advisory responsibilities which the general counsel staff performed also included assisting the Director with coordination of ethics enforcement efforts in the executive branch. This entailed discussion and liaison with the Department of Justice and agency ethics officials, in accordance with 5 C.F.R. § 2638.603, which requires that potential criminal violations of title 18 of the United States Code be referred to the Attorney General, as directed by law, and that agencies maintain a dialogue with OGE to insure that followup agency disciplinary or corrective action is taken, where appropriate. Additionally, this advisory role which general counsel attorneys performed in assisting the Director with executive branch enforcement involved exercise of authority under Subparts D and E of 5 C.F.R. Part 2638 to recommend investigation of possible employee ethics violations; to review agency reports of investigation, make findings, and recommend disciplinary action; and to order and monitor corrective action for employees and for agency ethics programs.

II. *Documents and Miscellaneous Services*

The time devoted by general counsel attorneys to all tasks other than advice and interpretation accounted for an average of 67 percent of their workload during calendar years 1990 and 1991. Graph 2c depicts that time usage, and shows a further breakdown by subject matter. Regulation drafting and coordination accounted for fully 33 percent of the workload. Other document-oriented and miscellaneous services performed by OGE's attorneys included reviewing and certifying public financial disclosure reports for advice-and-consent Presidential nominees (11 percent of the workload); providing liaison with the White House and Congress on ethics policy, legislation, and regulations, and with the new media (8 percent of the workload); certifying and monitoring qualified blind or diversified trusts and issuing certificates of divestiture for the entire executive branch, and resolving legal issues in ethics agreements of advice-and-consent Presidential nominees (7 percent of the workload); serving as official speakers, lecturers, panelists, and trainers on Government ethics topics (5 percent of the workload); and all other miscellaneous tasks, such as reviewing requests under the Freedom of Information Act and Privacy Act, responding to OGE's *Government Ethics Newsgram*, conducting legal research, maintaining professional and technical skills, and personnel administration (3 percent of the workload).

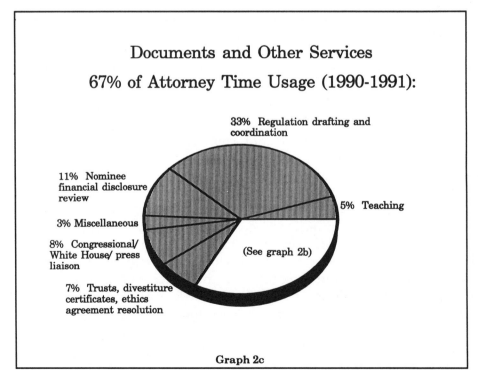

Documents and Other Services

67% of Attorney Time Usage (1990-1991):

33% Regulation drafting and coordination

11% Nominee financial disclosure review

3% Miscellaneous

8% Congressional/ White House/ press liaison

7% Trusts, divestiture certificates, ethics agreement resolution

5% Teaching

(See graph 2b)

Graph 2c

Discussion and amplification of these services follows in subsections A through E.

A. Development of Regulations

Calendar years 1990 and 1991 brought a dramatic increase in the amount of time spent by general counsel attorneys on developing, coordinating, and issuing new ethics regulations and related standard forms. This increase, which is unparalleled since the two-year period immediately following OGE's creation in 1978, was a direct result of OGE's 1988 reauthorization (P.L. 100-598), the Ethics Reform Act of 1989, and Executive Order 12674. As shown in Graph 2a, 2.75 attorney FTEs were dedicated to regulation work, with five attorneys devoting considerable amounts of time.

Preparation of a regulation entails painstaking draftsmanship, skilled negotiation with the Department of Justice and the Office of Personnel Management (with whom OGE's regulations must generally be coordinated, according to statutory and executive order direction), coordination of policy considerations with the White House and the Office of Management and Budget, compliance with intricate requirements for publication in the *Federal Register*, and analysis and detailed written discussion of public and agency comments after initial publication.

General counsel attorneys have worked particularly long hours on the following major regulations which were published in 1990 and 1991 in proposed, interim or final form:

Regulation	Basis	Citation
Corrective action and agency reports	1988 OGE Reauthorization	5 C.F.R. Part 2638 (Subparts D-F)
Certificates of divestiture	Ethics Reform Act of 1989	5 C.F.R. Part 2634 (Subpart J)
Honoraria ban	Ethics Reform Act of 1989	5 C.F.R. Part 2636
Standards of ethical conduct	Executive Order 12674	5 C.F.R. Part 2635

The attorneys have also labored to insure that other less voluminous regulations and notices were published during this period, such as an OGE

179

Privacy Act system notice, technical adjustments to 5 C.F.R. Parts 2637 and 2638, a regulation on OGE organization and functions incident to OGE's status as a separate agency by reason of its 1988 reauthorization (5 C.F.R. Part 2600), and partial implementation of the new post-employment provisions of the Ethics Reform Act of 1989 (5 C.F.R. Part 2641). In addition, general counsel attorneys have worked closely with the Federal Acquisition Regulation Council to produce regulations implementing the procurement integrity legislation (48 C.F.R. Part 3); with the General Services Administration to produce regulations implementing provisions of the Ethics Reform Act of 1989 which authorized agency acceptance of certain travel reimbursements (41 C.F.R. Part 301-1); and with OGE's Office of Education to produce an ethics training regulation for the executive branch (Subpart G of 5 C.F.R. Part 2638), to fulfill the purposes of Executive Order 12674. Beyond these regulatory achievements, OGE attorneys prepared and published in 1991 a completely revised executive branch public financial disclosure form (SF 278), to comply with new requirements in the Ethics Reform Act of 1989. At the close of this two-year period, they had also nearly completed and coordinated financial disclosure for the executive branch, along with a new standard form for confidential disclosure, in furtherance of requirements in both the Ethics Reform Act of 1989 and Executive Order 12674.

Work has also commenced on regulations to implement 18 U.S.C. § 208 (financial conflicts), § 209 (salary supplementation ban), and the complete Ethics Reform Act revisions to § 207 (post-employment restrictions), as required by Executive Order 12674 and the Ethics Reform Act. Additionally, general counsel attorneys have begun work on OGE agency regulations to implement statutes such as the Freedom of Information and Privacy Acts and the Equal Access to Justice Act, incident to OGE's establishment as a separate agency under its 1988 reauthorization.

B. Nominee Financial Disclosure Review

One of the OGE Office of General Counsel and Legal Policy's most time-sensitive responsibilities is the process of reviewing and certifying to the Senate all public financial disclosure reports (SF 278) for advice-and-consent Presidential nominees, as required under the Ethics in Government Act of 1978 and revised by Title II of the Ethics Reform Act of 1969 (see 5 U.S.C. App.). Besides the five attorneys who spent some of their time with review of SF 278s (for an equivalent of 1.25 attorney FTEs), one paralegal staff member devoted full time during this period to the coordination of Presidential nominee financial disclosure reports with the White House and the Senate confirmation committees. Also, staff members of OGE's Office of Program Assistance and Review augmented the pool of nominee SF 278 reviewers by conducting some initial coordination and review and then submitting their work-product to the general counsel staff for final approval.

These non-attorney resources should be considered as additional to the attorney assignments and workloads reflected in graphs 2a and 2c for nominee financial disclosure reviews.

An average of 75 to 100 SF 278 forms were pending at OGE for general counsel at any given time throughout this two-year period. Because OGE's responsibility begins during the prenomination phase while the White House is conducting various background checks on potential nominees, many of those SF 278s were in draft form but were being actively reviewed at OGE.

The review process entails working closely with agency ethics officials, and on occasion the nominee personally, to insure that all disclosures required by law are complete, and that any potential conflicts under the statutes or standards of conduct which those disclosures reveal are identified and resolved. Once a disclosure statement has been determined by the Office of General Counsel and Legal Policy to be complete, all potential conflicts have been resolved, and the President has announced nomination, the disclosure form is certified by the Director and the OGE reviewer prepares an opinion letter by which the SF 278 is forwarded to the appropriate Senate committee.

In 1990 and 1991, 677 nominee reports were coordinated and reviewed, of which 634 were certified to the Senate. The remaining 43 were reviewed but not certified, either because the President decided not to go forward with the nomination or because the individual withdrew from consideration. Of those nominees for whom reports were certified to the Senate, 215 entered into one or more ethics agreements, whereby they promised to complete action to resolve potential conflicts within 90 days of confirmation. Such action typically includes executing a recusal statement describing official Government matters in which they will not participate, divestiture of financial interests, resignation from outside positions, the seeking of a waiver under 18 U.S.C. § 208(b) for insubstantial conflicting financial interests, or the establishment of a qualified blind or diversified trust. These agreements are entered pursuant to authority in the financial disclosure provisions of Title II of the Ethics Reform Act of 1989 and regulatory guidance in Subpart H of 5 C.F.R. Part 2634. Graph 2d displays pictorially the most significant of these statistics on nominee financial disclosure reports, by calendar year.

C. Blind Trusts, Certificates of Divestiture, and Ethics Agreement Resolution

Title II of the Ethics Reform Act of 1989 restated and revised existing authority for the establishment of qualified blind and diversified trusts in the executive branch. Regulatory guidance from OGE is maintained at Subpart D of 5 C.F.R. Part 2634. The general counsel staff is responsible for overseeing the process by which employees may establish such trusts as a mechanism

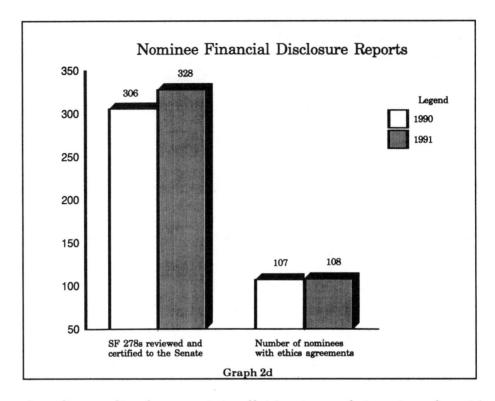

Nominee Financial Disclosure Reports

Graph 2d

of avoiding conflicts between their official actions and the private financial interests of themselves, their spouses, and their dependent children. This entails guidance to employees and their family members who are considering the use of a blind or diversifed trust under this authority, as well as to their representatives, fiduciaries, and trustees; reviewing and approving for the Director's certification all such trusts which are created; and conducting regular monitoring, which includes review of required periodic reports and determining when adjustments to or terminations of trusts may be required.

Because of the close scrutiny which must accompany this blind and diversified trust program, there were several hundred calls and conferences between the general counsel staff and the parties involved during this two-year period. At the end of 1991, approximately 30 active blind or diversified trusts existed, which was typically the count throughout this entire period.

Title V of the Ethics Reform Act of 1989 (26 U.S.C. § 1043) authorized OGE to issue certificates of divestiture for those executive branch employees (including their spouses, dependent or minor children, and certain trustees) who are required to divest assets because of a determination that such divestiture is reasonably necessary for them to perform their Government responsibilities free of conflicts. When such certificates are issued, the recognition of capital gains from the sale of those assets can be deferred for tax purposes, under the Internal Revenue Service Code, provided that all procedural steps are followed, such as reinvestment in permitted property within a specified period of time. Detailed rules are set out in Subpart J of 5 C.F.R. Part 2634. During 1990, which was the first year in which any certificates of divestiture were issued, the OGE general counsel staff processed and approved 107 certificates of divestiture; for 1991, the figure was 87 certificates. See Graph 2e.

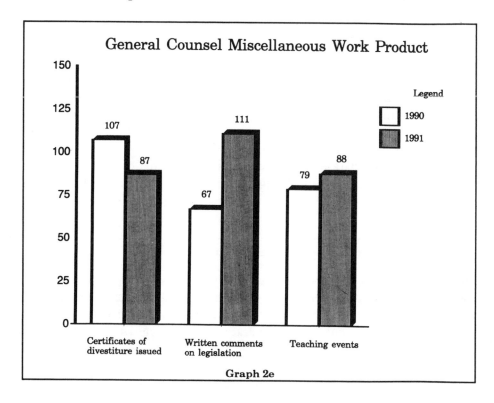

General Counsel Miscellaneous Work Product

Graph 2e

As discussed above in subsection II. B., 215 advice-and-consent Presidential nominees entered into ethics agreements in 1990 and 1991, whereby they promised to complete certain actions to resolve potential conflicts within 90 days of confirmation. This included steps such as execution of a recusal statement, divestiture, resignation, seeking a conflict waiver under 18 U.S.C. § 208(b)(1), or establishing a qualified blind or diversified trust. Despite attempts to make these agreements as precise as possible, legal issues frequently arise during the 90-day period in which they are being implemented. General counsel attorneys provided assistance to agency ethics officials and individual appointees in resolving these issues, such as specifying language for recusal reports or waiver grants to meet statutory requirements; determining what constitutes full divestiture; clarifying the strict requirements of qualified trust establishment; and coordinating substitute agreements if promised actions become infeasible.

In addition to the .75 attorney FTE which is devoted to qualified trusts, certificates of divestiture, and ethics agreement resolution, one paralegal provided considerable support in the processing, review, and maintenance of records which are required. This work should be considered along with that reflected for attorneys by Graphs 2a and 2c.

D. Congressional, White House, and Press Liaison

One of OGE's responsibilities is to insure that legislative initiatives related to Government ethics are properly coordinated with existing statutes and administrative standards on ethics, and that they are fully evaluated to determine their usefulness and feasibility. In carrying out this mission, the general counsel staff reviews and comments on proposed legislation, and it offers suggestions for statutory changes to improve the existing system, including the initiation of legislation. This includes liaison with Congressional staffs, the Office of Management and Budget, the White House, and all interested agencies. It also involves drafting and coordinating the Director's written comments on legislative proposals and on the comments of other agencies on such proposals, as well as coordinating testimony by the Director and OGE staff members before Congressional committees.

In 1990, general counsel attorneys prepared formal comments on 35 separate pieces of legislation, with a total of 67 written responses. In 1991, the number of legislative proposals which they reviewed nearly doubled: they prepared formal comments on 68 separate pieces of legislation, with a total of 111 written responses. Graph 2e reflects this significant rise in legislative liaison work. Additionally in 1991, there were 6 hearings on legislation involving ethics matters for which the general counsel staff either prepared testimony or personally presented it.

The Office of General Counsel and Legal Policy also maintained active liaison with the White House Executive Office of the President on general ethics policy and requirements for the executive branch, including proposed regulations and other guidance. General counsel attorneys also served as the primary liaison between OGE and the news media, to answer their inquiries and keep the public abreast of Government ethics developments in the executive branch.

Three OGE attorneys were involved with these legislative, White House, and press activities, equaling one attorney FTE, as depicted in Graph 2a. Additionally, one paralegal provided extensive administrative support to the attorneys on legislative liaison matters.

E. Official Speaking and Lecturing

The Office of General Counsel and Legal Policy lends legal expertise to OGE's Office of Education, to assist in fulfilling its training mission. In 1990 and 1991, this included attorney participation in seminars at the White House in Washington, DC and at various locations around the country for agency ethics officials. It also included service as speakers, lecturers, and panelists at meetings and seminars. These meetings were sometimes public forums composed of professional or trade associations interested in Government ethics, but many also involved groups of Government attorneys and other employees.

As depicted in Graph 2a, the equivalent of a .75 attorney FTE was devoted to training. However, that is somewhat misleading, since four attorneys served in this capacity on a frequent and regular basis, involving time to prepare and make the presentation, as well as some associated travel. Additionally, six other attorneys were assigned on an occasional basis in these educational efforts. During this two-year period, general counsel attorneys taught seminars, panels, and other training sessions on 167 occasions. As graph 2e indicates, the number of times when general counsel attorneys were assigned to perform these teaching functions rose slightly in 1991, as compared to the previous year.

3. Office of Program Assistance and Review

As provided in Title IV of the Ethics in Government Act of 1978, as amended, OGE's responsibilities include 'monitoring and investigating compliance with the public financial disclosure requirements of ... the Act' and 'monitoring and investigating individual and internal review requirements established by law for the executive branch'. The Act also provides that the Director of OGE may order corrective action on the part of agencies and employees, and establishes the processes for undertaking such corrective action. Moreover, under the implementing regulations at 5 C.F.R. Part 2638, OGE is to monitor agency compliance with the public and confidential reporting requirements and evaluate the effectiveness of programs designed to prevent conflicts of interest. Part 2638 also prescribes detailed procedures for implementing OGE's corrective action authority.

To carry out these responsibilities, the Office of Program Assistance and Review serves as the overseer for executive branch agency ethics programs. It consists of two separate divisions: the Program Review Division (PRD) and the Program Assistance Division (PAD). Management analysts in PRD monitor agency and employee compliance with executive branch ethics laws and regulations through periodic agency ethics program reviews. Ethics specialists in PAD assist agencies in the development, maintenance and improvement of their ethics programs. Consequently, the two divisions often work in tandem, with PAD assisting agencies in implementing ethics program recommendations stemming from reviews conducted by PRD. Although the divisions are interrelated, each one will be described separately.

PROGRAM REVIEW DIVISION (PRD)

3.1 Overview of Responsibilities

PRD conducts on-site headquarters and regional ethics program reviews to determine whether an agency has an effective ethics program tailored to its mission. The reviews are acomplished in accordance with detailed review guidelines, and are scheduled in advance in an annual program plan. The guidelines provide a step-by-step approach to examining each of the ethics program elements at an agency, while the program plan specifies the reviews to be conducted during the year, both at headquarters offices in Washington, DC and at various offices and military facilities in the regions. Approximately four weeks are spent at the headquarters of an agency during a review, while reviews at regional offices or military facilities have durations of from one day to a week.

Reviews entail a thorough review of all elements of the ethics program, including specific ethics issues tailored to the mission of the agency. Individual ethics program elements which PRD examines include:

- Ethics program structure and staffing
- Public financial disclosure reporting systems
- Confidential financial disclosure reporting systems
- Ethics education and training
- Ethics counselling and advisory opinions
- Outside employment and activities
- Post-employment training and counselling

Within the parameters of executive branch laws and regulations, the review determines the type of program, procedures and internal controls that will give that agency the strongest ethics program. Following the review, a report is sent to the agency head and the designated agency ethics official (DAEO) containing recommendations to improve the ethics program. Agencies are to respond to OGE within 60 days concerning the actions they are taking or plan to take on OGE's recommendations. To confirm that the agency has acted on OGE's recommendations, PRD then conducts a follow-up review six months from the date of the report. [1]

3.2 Staffing Organization and Utilization

PRD is staffed by management analysts under the supervision of a division chief and and audit manager (the first of at least three audit managers to be hired). Reviews are conducted in teams of two to three management analysts, one of whom is a senior analyst serving as the 'team leader'. These analysts constitute a cadre of seasoned professionals with a variety of Government backgrounds, as well as individuals new to the Government who bring a fresh perspective to the workplace.

With the recognition by Congress that OGE should increase the frequency of agency ethics program reviews, PRD has been one of the fastest growing divisions at OGE. Consequently, the staffing level of PRD increased from 4 management analysts at the end of calendar year 1989 to 15 at the end of calendar year 1991. This increase took place primarily in the last six months of 1991 but its impact has already been felt in the number of reviews completed and in progress. By the end of fiscal year 1993, PRD hopes to have approximately 35 management analysts in place which will enable more frequent and in-depth reviews to be conducted.

In addition to conducting program reviews, management analysts in PRD participate in OGE-sponsored training sessions for ethics practitioners, answer random phone calls from the ethics community, outside organizations, and the general public, and conduct special projects as assigned by the Director of OGE.

3.3 PRD Accomplishments

During 1990 and 1991 PRD staff issued reports on 5 cabinet-level departments, 2 agencies within departments, and 10 independent agencies; reviewed 51 regional offices/military facilities in 10 regions; and conducted 17 six-month follow-up reviews. At the end of 1991 field work was completed for six headquarters reviews and three additional headquarters reviews were in progress. Graph 3 indicates the number and types of reports issued and follow-up reviews conducted during 1990 and 1991. For a detailed listing of individual agencies see Appendix A.

For the past two years PRD's reviews have concentrated on the ethics program structure and staffing. This was done to ensure that agencies were providing the necessary commitment and resources to the program for it to be administered effectively. In the past OGE found that the root cause of many

---

1 To verify that agencies are implementing OGE report recommendations within a reasonable time, PRD developed and maintains a computerized audit tracking system.

187

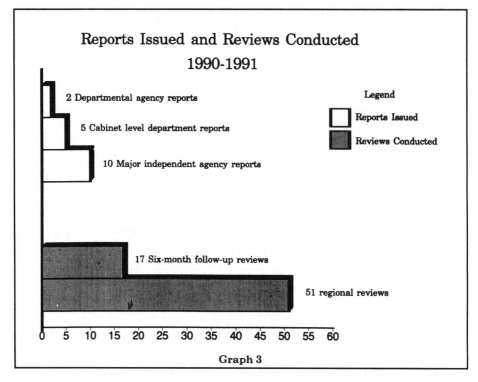

deficiencies in ethics programs could be traced to the lack of commitment and resources from the agency leadership. OGE also knew that a sound structure had to be in place for agencies to adapt to the new standards of conduct, training requirements, confidential financial disclosure rules, and other regulations to be issued by OGE in 1992.

As a result, OGE recommended to many departments that they establish either an Office of Ethics or a full-time ethics position with adequate staff resources to manage the program in all agency components. Departments such as Agriculture, Veterans Affairs, and Labor, and the U.S. Postal Service responded to these reviews by restructuring their ethics programs and/or adding more full-time staff.

Another major area in which OGE concentrated its reviews was agencies' efforts to educate and train employees on ethics, and their plans for implementing OGE's new training regulations once issued in final form. While agencies had made some improvements in their training programs, OGE emphasized that agencies had to start planning now as to how they will train employees under the new regulations.

3.4 Future Review Plans

With increased OGE resources in 1992 and 1993, PRD plans to review agency ethics programs more frequently and in greater depth. This will include evaluating how effectively agencies are implementing OGE's new regulations. PRD reviews will not only help agencies build their new programs, but will give OGE feedback as to where it must fine-tune the regulations for practical issues that may arise.

In addition to reviews of specific agencies, PRD plans to perform single-issue audits where it may, for example, determine how a cross-section of Federal agencies has implemented the ethics training regulations, or measure the impact of the new standards of conduct regulations in the area of teaching, lecturing and writing.

PROGRAM ASSISTANCE DIVISION (PAD)

3.5 Overview of Responsibilities

The Program Assistance Division (PAD) works with executive branch agencies to develop and maintain strong ethics programs that meet every requirement of executive branch ethics laws and regulations. In addition, PAD has primary responsibility for tracking, collecting, and reviewing the annual and termination public financial disclosure reports (public reports) of approximately 1,000 Presidential appointees confirmed by the Senate and approximately 125 DAEOs. To carry out its responsibilities, PAD:

- operates a desk officer system which assigns an OGE management analyst to each agency to act as a liaison between the agency and OGE;

- lends assistance to OGE's Office of General Counsel and Legal Policy in its review of public reports submitted during the nomination process for Presidential appointees requiring advice and consent of the Senate;

- works closely with agency ethics officials to ensure that all public reports are accurate and complete, in accordance with the Ethics in Government Act and implementing regulations, and that the filers are free of any ethics problems;

- processes waivers to be granted by agencies under § 208 of title 18, U.S.C., when such waivers are submitted to OGE's Office of General Counsel and Legal Policy for consultation in accordance with the provisions of Executive Order 12674, as modified by Executive Order 12731;

- provides advice to agency ethics officials on various substantive ethics issues as they arise or on technical matters, by telephone and/or through personal contact;

- plays an active role in implementing recommendations made by OGE following a PRD review of the ethics program;

- tracks, collects and reviews annual and termination public reports of all Senate-confirmed Presidential appointees;

- tracks and ensures compliance with agreements made by Presidential appointees during the confirmation process;

- processes requests, pursuant to the Ethics in Government Act, for filing exemptions and extensions on public reports, as well as requests for waivers of the $200 late filing fee;

- collects and makes available to the public semiannual reports required of agencies under 31 U.S.C. § 1353 which detail payments of more than $250 which the agency has accepted from non-Federal sources for travel, subsistence, and related expenses;

- processes agency requests for confidential financial disclosure coverage of additional positions; and

- releases publicly available financial disclosure reports to members of the press and of the general public who request them.

3.6 Staffing Organization and Utilization

PAD is staffed by seven management analysts and an ethics assistant who serve under the supervision of a division chief and a senior ethics officer. Six management analysts work as desk officers.

Initially, four desk officers worked individually to meet the needs of over 100 departments and agencies. In 1990 and 1991, three new employees were added to the desk officer staff. At the close of 1991, six members of the PAD staff were assigned in three teams, with each team member designated as the primary contact for a specific number of agencies.

3.7 The Public Financial Disclosure Tracking System

PAD developed and maintained an effective computerized tracking system for all public reports filed with OGE. This system has greatly improved the speed and accuracy of the review process.

PAD reviewed a total of 775 public reports in 1990 and 949 reports in 1991. Over the two-year period, 75 percent of the reports reviewed were annual filings and 22 percent were termination filings.

In addition to tracking and reviewing public reports, PAD staff releases publicly financial disclosure reports to members of the public who request them. In 1990 members of the press and of the general public requested 419 reports of 263 different executive branch officials whose reports were maintained by OGE. In 1991, 754 reports were requested, covering 592 officials.

Another task associated with the nomination process is the tracking of ethics agreements made by Presidential appointees during the confirmation process. These agreements concerning the financial interests of appointees, their spouses, and their dependent children are made to bring the filers into compliance with applicable ethics laws and regulations and to avoid conflicts of interest with their Government positions. Nominees are to certify, with documentation to OGE, that such agreements have been satisfied within 90 days of their confirmation.

In 1990, of the 306 nominees whose financial disclosure reports were approved and sent to the Senate by OGE, nominees made 203 agreements affecting their financial interests. In 1991, 108 of the 328 such nominees made 175 ethics agreements. Over this two-year period, the following types of agreements were made:

- Recusal: 139 nominees agreed to recuse themselves from acting on matters involving financial interests held by them or their spouse or dependent children;

- Resignation: 107 nominees agreed to resign from outside positions;

- Divestiture: 59 nominees agreed to divest of financial interests such as stocks, bonds or other securities;

- Waiver: 37 nominees agreed to seek waivers under 18 U.S.C. § 208(b), where their financial interest was not viewed as so substantial as to effect the integrity of their services to the Government;

- Severance payments: 32 nominees made agreements concerning severance payments from prior employers; and

- Blind trusts: 4 nominees agreed to set up blind trusts pursuant to the Ethics in Government Act.

3.8 Desk Officer System

PAD's desk officer system began in January 1990, with the goal of providing to agency ethics officials a strong link with OGE. In order to familiarize agencies with the relatively new desk officer system, PAD desk officers held 79 meetings with DAEOs and their staffs in 1990 and 1991. Through these visits to the agencies, desk officers acquired a better understanding of the agency as a whole, as well as the needs and ethics issues of concern to that particular ethics program.

In their role as liaisons, desk officers handle not only technical matters for their agencies but also various substantive ethics issues as they arise. This role requires extensive time on the telephone as well as personal contact with agency ethics officials. For example, desk officers handled over 20,000 telephone calls, both incoming and outgoing in 1991 alone.

Some of the technical duties that the desk officers handle include processing correspondence and requests from agencies to OGE regarding the technical requirements of ethics laws and regulations. Typical correspondence from agencies includes requests, pursuant to the Ethics in Government Act, for public report filing exemptions and extensions, requests for waivers of the $200 late filing fee on public reports, and requests, pursuant to 5 C.F.R. § 735.403(d), for confidential financial disclosure coverage of additional positions. PAD desk officers also collect the semiannual reports required of agencies under 31 U.S.C. § 1353, which detail payments of more than $250 which the agency has accepted from non-Federal sources for travel, subsistence, and related expenses as authorized by that statute. These reports are made available by agencies under § 208 of title 18, U.S.C., when such waivers are submitted to OGE's Office of General Counsel and Legal Policy for consultation in accordance with the provisions of Executive Order 12674.

In addition to the technical duties described above, desk officers provide advice and assistance to agency ethics officials, both in establishing effective programs and in resolving specific ethics issues that arise. For example, desk officers participated in agency training courses and conferences and consulted with agency ethics officials on the development of a financial disclosure tracking system.

In providing advice and assistance, personal contact with the ethics staff of agencies and their various components is of primary importance. In addition to frequent contact with the agencies, this liaison role necessitates frequent contact between OGE's desk officers and other offices and divisions within OGE, such as its Office of General Counsel and Legal Policy, its Office of Education, and its Program Review Division. For example, desk officers play a consultant role in offering ideas and suggestions on implementing recommendations made by OGE following a PRD review of an ethics program.

In summary, desk officer involvement with agencies during 1990 and 1991 ranged from technical advice on the proper review of financial disclosure reports to participation in agency training courses and conferences. As agencies become increasingly familiar with the resource available to them in their desk officer, PAD anticipates that this involvement with the agencies will continue to increase.

4. Office of Education

Section 402(b)(14) of the Ethics in Government Act of 1978, as amended, makes the Director of OGE responsible for 'providing information on and promoting understanding of ethical standards in executive agencies'. [1] Under implementing regulations at 5 C.F.R. § 2638.203(b)(6), each Designated Agency Ethics Official (DAEO) must ensure that an education program for agency employees concerning all ethics and standards of conduct matters, including post-employment matters, is developed and conducted in coopera-tion with the education program of the Office of Government Ethics.

4.1 Overview of Responsibilities

The Office of Education insures that quality ethics education programs are provided to almost 5 million executive branch employees and materials are made available to facilitate these programs. In order to accomplish this goal the Office of Education:

- provides classes for trainers and practitioners in both Washington DC and the field;

- provides specialized training classes for the White House as well as executive branch agencies;

- produces the *Government Ethics Newsgram*;

- creates other ethics materials and media;

- provides guidance for agencies in the design of their ethics training programs;

- reviews annual agency ethics plans;

- designs and implements conferences and meetings;

- encourages joint agency cooperation in the creation of materials and implementation of classes;

- coordinates and analyzes the annual ethics survey reports to OGE and edits the biennial report to Congress; and

- acts as liaison for OGE with public/private groups including Federal courts, state and local governments, corporations, professional associations, and institutions of higher learning.

4.2 Administrative Structure and General Training

The Office of Education is staffed by five people, the associate director, the

---

1 The Senate Report on the Ethics in Government Act stated that this was perhaps the most important function performed by OGE.

deputy associate director, two management analysts, and one management assistant.

The office provides ethics classes for ethics practitioners and trainers in the Washington DC area and regions across the nation. Since the last biennial report, the number of training sessions as well as the size of the classes significantly increased. In 1990 OGE conducted 25 ethics training sessions in Washington DC and the regions for 688 ethics practitioners. In 1991 OGE conducted 30 sessions for 1,062 ethics practitioners. The number of individuals trained increased 84 percent from 1989 to 1991. A numerical representation of training sessions and individuals trained is shown in Graph 4a.

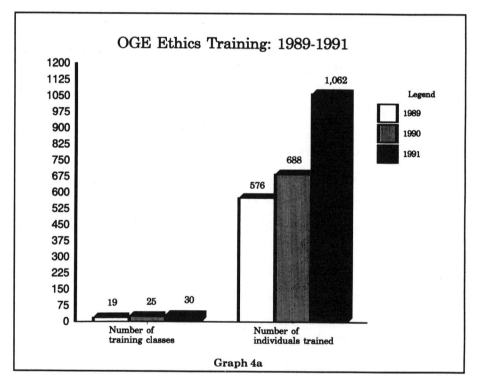

Graph 4a

The average class size grew from 27 practitioners in 1989 to 43 in 1991, which is an increase of 59 percent. Yet given OGE's responsibilities for training agency ethics personnel and trainers, this expansion hardly kept up with demand. As noted in Chapter 5,[2] the total number of ethics practitioners increased from 6,293 in 1989 to 8,803 in 1991, which is an increase of 40 percent.

---

2 Chapter 5 entitled 'Summary of Executive Branch Ethics Programs' is omitted from these extracts reproduced here in Volume 1: *Government Ethics*.

OGE continues to use the same general model for the training sessions. Each ethics class is three and one half hours long, and generally taught by a management analyst and an attorney from OGE. The design of the training session has basically remained the same: a mixture of lecture, videotape, slides, and case studies. Of course, the content of the classes has changed to reflect new laws and regulations.

The makeup of these classes included not only ethics practitioners, but also staff from agency Inspector General offices and U.S. Attorneys. Reflecting the part-time nature of the ethics community, the students spend approximately 22 percent of their time on ethics issues.

Individuals who attended the training reported an overall positive response to the course. Every attendee was asked to fill out an evaluation form on the instructor and the course materials. Using the thermometer scale with one being 'poor', four being 'good' and seven being 'excellent', OGE has consistently received scores that were better than 'good'. The average score for 1989 was 5.3, the average for 1990 was 5.5, and the average score for 1991 was 5.0. Graph 4b depicts these scores. Although the rating went down slightly in 1991, the office was not surprised by the results. The slightly lower scores can be attributed to a variety of factors, but most notably may be attributed to a significant increase in class size.

In addition to the training sessions for ethics practitioners, the Office of

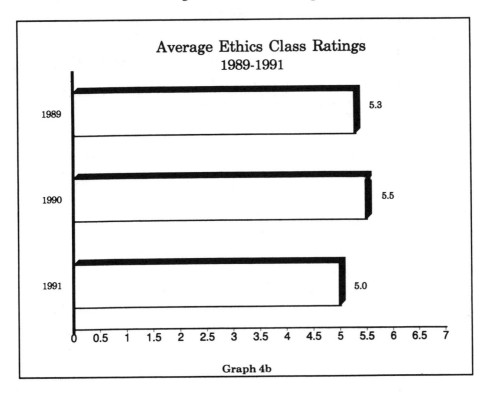

Graph 4b

195

Education either provided or utilized staff from other OGE offices and divisions to deliver speeches, participate on panels, and make other appearances on ethics. Such presentations varied from courses at the Justice Department Legal Education Institute, to speeches before Federal Executive Boards, to presentations for Voice of America. In 1990 OGE staff made presentations to 7,449 participants at 96 different events. In 1991 OGE personnel addressed 9,652 participants in 136 sessions. A graphic representation of the number of presentations provided by offices within OGE during 1991 is shown in Graph 4c.

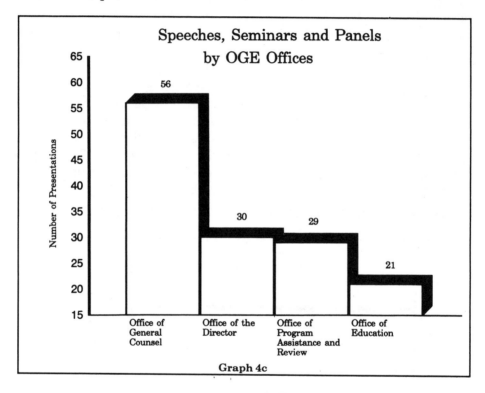

Graph 4c

4.3 Achievements

The Office of Education produces a quarterly publication, the *Government Ethics Newsgram*. It is an informal publication where individuals can get current information on new ethics regulations and details on major issues and events in the ethics community. It is specifically written to be readable and accessible to both the technical and the lay community. The *Government Ethics Newsgram* is available to anyone in the ethics community; it is also available to people outside the Government upon request and without cost. Currently, the distribution for the *Government Ethics Newsgram* is about 3,000, with several hundred more distributed after publication because of individual requests.

The office organized the first national conference for executive branch ethics officials in eight years. This conference focused on the new standards of ethical conduct, program issues, enforcement, and ethics resources. The conference covered two and one-half days, with over 194 senior ethics practitioners from 77 agencies in attendance.

The overall response to the conference was positive. Again using a thermometer scale with a top score of 7, the average response to the conference was 6.1. The responses were so encouraging that the office has begun planning the second annual conference scheduled for September 14-17, 1992.

The office also produced a pamphlet outlining the mission of OGE. This pamphlet contains a brief description of the roles of each office within OGE and the overall goals of the organization, and is available to the public.

The Office of Education published a proposed regulation on ethics training requirements in late 1990 and will be finalizing the regulation in the spring of 1992. This regulation establishes the executive branch requirements for an initial ethics orientation for all Federal employees and an annual ethics training session for specific categories of employees identified under Executive Order 12674, as modified. The regulation also requires agencies to submit annual training plans to OGE.

The Office of Education developed its own 'in-house' training series for new OGE employees. Each series was presented over four days for one and one-half hours a day. The topics included: an overview of ethics, the statutes, the standards of conduct, financial disclosure and the auditing process.

The office completed work on a form for notification to OGE of criminal referrals to the Department of Justice on conflict of interest statutes. This form was the result of concern by the Inspectors General about Privacy Act considerations in notifying OGE of any referral of a conflicts case pursuant to 28 U.S.C. § 535 and 5 C.F.R. § 2638.603.

The office distributes, collects, and analyzes the annual agency ethics program questionnaire. The office designed this questionnaire to assist agencies in complying with statutory requirements in the Ethics in Government Act of 1978, as amended (5 U.S.C. App. § 402(e)(1)). The questionnaire is sent to all executive branch agencies and departments with a DAEO. The analysis of the 1990 and 1991 results can be found in Chapter 5. [2]

4.4 Future Projects

The office has been actively planning the production of additional video tapes to be used in ethics training. These video tapes will be produced not only to train the trainers, but also for the trainers to use as a supplement in classes for all executive branch employees. The Office of Education is also developing an ethics library that will encompass the available ethics material in the Federal Government.

In addition to the annual conference, the office has also begun plans for a mini-conference and an international conference. These conferences will focus on the new standards of conduct and obtaining a better understanding on how ethics programs are implemented in other countries. [3]

---

3 These Chapters 1-4 of the Second Biennial Report to Congress: United States Office of Government Ethics (March 1992) are reproduced in full. Chapter 5 of the Report and Appendices A and B are omitted.

NOTE   1

Summary of Graphs and Abbreviations

GRAPHS   *Page*

Graph 1   - Office of Government Ethics Organizational Chart...................... 171

Graph 2a - Attorney Utilization Plan (1990-1991)... 174

Graph 2b - Opinions and Interpretive Advice 176

Graph 2c - Documents and Other Services... 178

Graph 2d - Nominee Financial Disclosure Reports.. 182

Graph 2e - General Counsel Miscellaneous Work Product 183

Graph 3   - Reports Issued and Reviews Conducted 188

Graph 4a - OGE Ethics Training: 1989-1991 194

Graph 4b - Average Ethics Class Ratings 195

Graph 4c - Speeches, Seminars and Panels by OGE Offices 196

ABBREVIATIONS

C.F.R.	-	Code of Federal Regulations
CSS	-	Career Senior Service
DAEO	-	Designated Agency Ethics Official
DOJ	-	Department of Justice
FTE	-	Full-time Equivalent
IG	-	Inspector General
OGE	-	U.S. Office of Government Ethics
PAD	-	Program Assistance Division
P.L.	-	Public Law
PRD	-	Program Review Division
U.S.C.	-	United States Code

VOLUME I   GOVERNMENT ETHICS

PART III

Government Ethics:

Secrecy, Access to Information and Privacy

10

Public Sector Ethics, with Specific Reference to Secrecy in Government from the Perspective of the Experience of India [1]

by Professor R. B. Jain, Head of the Department of Political Science, University of Delhi, India

The term 'ethics' is referred to, generally, as the art of determining what is right or good. Raziel Abelson in his essay in the *Encyclopaedia of Philosophy* has stated three different interpretations of this term, signifying (a) a general pattern or 'way of life', (b) a set of rules of conduct or 'moral' code, and (c) inquiry about ways of life and rules of conduct. [2] Although all these interpretations of the word 'ethics' are inter-related in this paper, I shall use the term more in the nature of a set of rules of conduct or moral code governing public actions of public and business officials.

From the background of Indian experience, I shall attempt to show that, despite fundamental differences in the approaches to public sector and business ethics, it becomes very difficult for public officials to hold on to their moral values in the face of diverse pressures from political, business and public interest groups and the compulsions of a democratic society. In the ensuing conflicts, it is the public sector ethics that seem to receive the most battering against the manipulations by no-hold-barred business practices, often in the garb of the so-called business 'ethics'.

This paper concerns a discussion on public sector ethics with specific reference to secrecy in Government from an Indian perspective. In *Teaching Ethics:* Volume III *Environmental Ethics* (forthcoming 1993) I contribute another paper devoted to the study of the Bhopal Gas disaster in India from the ethical standpoints of both India and the United States. In that paper I inter-relate and bridge the two topics of Secrecy in Government and Business/Environmental Ethics.

---

1 A paper delivered at the International Conference on Business and Public Sector Ethics, held under the auspices of the Centre for Business and Public Sector Ethics, Cambridge, England, 12-15 July 1989.

2 See Raziel Abelson, 'History of Ethics" *Encyclopaedia of Philosophy* (New York, Macmillan and Free Press, 1967), Vol. 3.

1. Public Sector Ethics

In the bureaucratic parlance, it was Max Weber who classified ethics into 'ethics of ultimate ends' and 'ethics of responsibility'. According to Weber, 'ethics of ultimate ends' comprehends life in totality, and is rigid, eternal and universal; its source is usually divine and for actions under its dictates, responsibility always rests with God. 'Ethics of Responsibility', on the other hand, is human, more predictable, and demands personal accountability of the actor. Weber sees an abysmal contrast between the conduct that follows the maxim of an ethic of ultimate ends – that is, in religious terms 'The Christian does rightly and leaves the results with the Lord' – and conduct that follows the maxim of an ethic of responsibility, in which case one has to give an account of the foreseeable results of one's action. [3] Although many scholars have labelled Weber's approach to public ethics as Machiavellian inasmuch as he does not rule out the possibility that morality would have to be sacrificed at the altar of expediency, it is not an exaggeration to say that all practical affairs of men require some moral principles to fill the gap left by legal inadequacies. In other words, 'all human actions, irrespective of place, objectives and commitments have moral connotations.' [4]

'The problem of ethical conduct for public officials', as Professor Stahl has put it, 'arises by virtue of the power and influence that he commands and the commitment he undertakes of loyal and disinterested service to the public'. [5] The power of public officials in modern times has greatly increased the proliferation of State activities and consequent increase in the power of the State to regulate the growing business of the welfare of its citizens. Subsequently, the scope of the use of administrative discretion not only has widened, but the increased chances of its possible unscrupulous use has the inherent tendency to corrupt and to be a major source of moral irregularities. Thus, for many scholars, the fundamental ethical problem of public officials is not to define conflict of interest, or to decide when to resign in protest, rather it is to determine how officials can use their discretionary power in a manner consistent with the values of a democratic régime. [6]

Public officials have an obligation to serve the public in a manner that strengthens the integrity and processes of a democratic society. Such a

---

3 See H. H. Gerth and C. Wright Mills *From Max Weber: Essays in Sociology* (New York, Oxford University Press, 1958) pp. 119-20.

4 Ibid. See also Robert Golembiewsky *Men, Management and Morality: Towards a New Organisational Ethics* (New York, McGraw Hill Book Co. 1965).

5 See O. Glenn Stahl *Public Personnel Administration* (New York: Harper & Row, 1976) p. 271.

6 See for example John A. Rohr *Ethics for Bureaucrats: An Essay on Law and Values* (New York, Marcel Dekker Inc., 1978), Chapter 1.

principle has at least three different implications for administrative performance. It means that (a) all the people must be served, equally and impartially, (b) this must be achieved with full respect for and reliance on
representative institutions, and (c) internal administration in public agencies
must lie consistent with these modes of behaviour. [7] Accordingly, being non-
elected officials, administrators are exempt from the discipline of the ballot
box but, as men and women who share in governing a democratic republic,
they are obliged morally to respond to the values of the people in whose
names they govern.

In his multi-dimensional activities, an administrator is not any more 'desk-
tied' or 'tongue-tied'. He is not only an implementor of public policy but in
almost all cases its formulator as well. His involvement in the entire political
processes is deep and of far-reaching consequences. In his role as 'Policy-
maker, policy adviser, programme-manager, programme implementor,
interest aggregator, interest articulator, agent of political communication,
adjudicator, agent of political socialization', he is constantly under pressure
from organised public and private interests, political leaders, members of the
citizenry and the communications media. There are many constraining factors
which may restrict his behaviour in terms of the prevailing norms of a
democratic system.

It goes without saying that ethics in government can be no better than
they are in the society. Although administrative behaviour is influenced considerably by the values cherished by that society, it is also true that public
officials can set the tone for the rest of the community. Certainly,
Governments, and even private organisations, can exercise care to employ
persons of integrity and encourage their employees to maintain high ethical
and other standards of performance. There are far too many examples in
every administrative system of dishonesty, unethical conduct, arbitrariness,
and a 'public-be-damned' attitude on the part of career and political officials
at all levels of government, which justify the need of an awareness that
organisations – be they public or private – are *moral* as well as *technical*
orders, and that the ethical quality of the ways administrative ends are pursued is just as important as the goals themselves. [8] In recent years there has
been an increasing realisation among scholars and practitioners of administration and organisation theory, therefore, that public services also stand in
need of a code of ethical conduct, just as other professions like the law,
medicine and journalism have codes of ethics for their practitioners.

---

7 Stahl, n.5. *op. cit.*, p. 271.

8 See Abraham Kaplan *American Ethics and Public Policy* (New York, Oxford University Press,
1963) for a discussion on how a public personnel system can contribute to the development of
public service ethics and ideals; see Felix A. Nigro and Lloyd G. Nigro *The New Public Personnel
Administration* (Ithaca, Ill. F. E. Peacock Publishers, Inc., 1976) pp. 323-26. Also see Stahl, *op.
cit.*, Chapter 16.

2. Components of Ethics in Public Life

Having thus identified the need for ethics in public administration, it is appropriate now to discuss the nature of the elements that constitute the core of ethical conduct on the part of administrators. Many of the complaints of declining morals and erosion of values will disappear if administration has the comprehension and realisation of two basic essentials of administrative behaviour, namely:- (a) there is no abuse of administrative discretion or willingness on the part of the administrators to further the objectives of special interest groups as opposed to the public interest and (b) there is expression of intellectual integrity in administration in long range thinking. The value orientation of administration is, however, an evolving concept and the total value system must be conditioned by a sense of social responsibility, so that a moral positive profile of administration may become manifest. [9]

2.1 Ethical Conduct: A Matter of Individual Responsibility

To a great extent, ethics in public life depend very much upon certain mental attitudes which an individual develops which, in turn, produce moral excellences that determine his ethical behaviour in administration. The responsibility for developing the right attitudes and values of ethical behaviour rests primarily on the individual public servant which I call the development of an internal 'character ethics'. In general, certain characteristics of highest moral character can be identified as courage, clarity of vision and understanding; fairness of judgement; generosity of mind; conversely, it can be asserted also that an excessive impersonality; arrogance, and inaccessibility on the part of the public official may lead to some unethical traits of bureaucratic behaviour.

Bailey has suggested three moral qualities that he calls 'the operative virtues', which support ethical mental attitudes. These are: (a) the quality of optimism which enables a public servant to deal with the vast complexity of choices without becoming paralysed to action, (b) courage which can be identified as abiding by principles in an unpopular cause; ability to rise above special favours requested by friends; willingness to make decisions contrary to expert opinion; the courage to decide and (c) fairness tempered with charity; that is, the ability to play fair and place principle above personal needs for recognition, status and power. Charity is the virtue which compensates for the inadequate information in decision-making and for the subtle importunities of self in the making of judgements designed to be fair. [10]

---

9 For a detailed exposition of these views see T. N. Chaturvedi 'Value-orientation in Human Problem Solving' *Management in Government* Vol. 15 (July-September 1981) pp. 107-16.

10 For a detailed discussion on the subject see Stephen K. Bailey 'Ethics and the Public Services' in Roscoe C. Martin (ed.) *Public Administration and Democracy* (Syracuse: Syracuse University Press, 1965) pp. 283-88.

Thus, one could argue that an ethical public conduct requires public officials with proven qualities of heart and character arising from their internalised value systems and also from the externalised socio-cultural system. Such a value system incorporates a clear concept of public trust and an appreciation of the unique obligations of the public services.

2.2 Unethical Behaviour

Public ethic is a related concept. It reflects a society's perspective on human conduct and pronounces actions good or bad by reference to some standard or criterion as imposed by, or specially relevant to, that society. Thus, unethical conduct on the part of public officials 'can be determined only in relation to an act, attitude or behaviour judged contrary to the practices commonly advocated by a certain State at a given time in the field of political and administrative morality.'[11]

Thus, it is difficult to define in any absolute terms what constitutes unethical conduct on the part of a public official. But there seems to be considerable agreement on the view that such behaviour on the part of the administrators may constitute (a) those activities which are contrary to the legal norms of a country and therefore punishable under the law (strictly speaking, however, this may not be constituted as unethical conduct, but as an illegal act as it is punishable by law), (b) those activities which are contrary to the basic principles of ethics/morality held (though not necessarily practised) by the society and (c) those activities which are undertaken because of the latent perceived pressure felt by a person under the obligations of loyalty, devotion, ties of kinship, affection, caste, religion or race. Unethical practice, then, may include such activities as favouritism, nepotism, conflict of interest, influence peddling, seeking pressure by using official position, favours to relatives and friends, leaking or misusing government information, engaging in political activities or misusing government property for personal gains.[12]

2.3 The Societal Constraints

Unethical behaviour on the part of the administrators is mostly the resultant product of the constitutional, political, the psychical, the socio-economic and the administrative environment prevailing in a society. Professor Stahl has put it most appropriately in the following words: 'As often as the facts have

---

11 See for details Yves Chapel, *The Comparative Study of Administrative Measures for the Eradication of Corruption* – Research Prospectus (International Institute of Administrative Sciences, Brussels, June 1972), Unpublished Report, p. 12; and also O. P. Dwivedi *Public Service Ethics* (International Intitute of Administrative Sciences, Brussels, June 1978).

12 See Dwivedi, n. 21, p. 9.

been pointed out, there is still a failure on the part of the general public to appreciate that a public service can hardly be expected to rise much above the level of its environment, that it derives most of its temptations for wrong doing from that environment, and that on top of all this, a double standard is applied to public officials as contrasted with men in private life. Informed and fair-minded persons will certainly concede that we expect higher standards of conduct from our public servants than we do from businessmen.' [13] Each of the environmental factors enumerated earlier delineates the ethical from unethical conduct on the part of public administrators.

An off-shoot of unethical conduct is the phenomena of administrative corruption which prevails to a lesser or greater extent in all societies. It is not necessary here to spell out the ways in which each of these factors acts in building a corrupt political and administrative environment. Ultimately, it is the society as a whole which bears responsibility for unethical conduct in public affairs. They, who complain of corruption but busy themselves with seeking special benefits not available to the general public, are the more serious corruptors. As one discerning statesman has put it, 'Until the citizen's own moral code prevents him from debasing himself by procuring corruption of public servants, the problem of corruption and morality in public life will remain very real and earnest.' [14] This correlation has been illustrated emphatically by the Sanatham Committee Report on Corruption in India.

In some administrative systems, unethical practices are listed in the codes of bureaucratic behaviour as prohibitions for administrators. Certain administrative systems lay more emphasis than others on ethical and positive aspects of employees' codes of conduct. For example, the Federal Government of the United States has, through an Executive Order, urged its public employees to avoid any action that might result in, or create the appearance of, (a) using public office for private gains, (b) giving preferential treatment to any organisation or person, (c) impeding government efficiency or economy, (d) losing independence or impartiality of action, (e) making government decisions outside office channels, and (f) affecting adversely the confidence of the public in the integrity of the government. [15] The other practices listed as prohibitive for public officials are provided under various statutes. These include: prohibition regarding outside employment; restriction on financial interests; prohibition against soliciting or accepting gifts; prohibition in respect of employer's indebtedness, prohibition against an employee using official information that has not been made public in order

---

13 Stahl, *op. cit.*, p. 279.
14 Ibid, p. 281.
15 *United States Code Standards for Ethical Conduct.* Executive Order No. 11222, 8 May 1965.

to further a private interest and certain other political restrictions. Some countries provide a number of positive value orientations in their employees' code of conduct, which are supposed to exhort them to upgrade the quality of service from time to time, perpetuate and sustain the interest that is given in performing assigned duty, instil a sense of common responsibility in the public service, establish a healthy and efficient environment/atmosphere in the service and strengthen the relationship between all categories of government servants. [16]

3. Governmental Secrecy: The Ethical Dimension

One of the ethical predicaments confronting public officials is the problem of secrecy is government. Most officials face what is known as the dilemma of discretionary secrecy in the dissemination of information on government and administrative decisions. Despite the existence of various public laws relating to secrecy in Government or a Freedom of Information Act, the decision to withhold administrative information or to refuse access to documents is at the discretion of the Executive Government. The latter is free to withhold information not only for legitimate reasons, such as protection of national security or personal privacy, but also to protect itself from wrong doing, or even to avoid a minor embarrassment or inconvenience. Instead of the general principle that all administrative information is open to the public except for those matters which are specifically required by law to be kept secret, the traditional principle is that all administrative information is considered to be secret unless the Government decides to release it, and the Government also has control over the timing and form of its release.

There is a widespread belief prevalent in many Western countries that democracy would progress if the 'administration's filing cabinets were open under some sort of judicial control' and the administrative documents were made available for inspection by the ordinary members of the public. This arrangement, it is argued, would lead to a more open, democratic process of administrative decision-making and, at the same time, serve as a control mechanism on the bureaucracy's corrupt and arbitrary behaviour. Thus, citizens in many countries have claimed a 'right to information' as against the Government's need for administrative secrecy in certain areas. Many scholars have felt that the present balance between the two conflicting claims favours too much secrecy, and that a public right to access of administrative documents ought to be established by a specific law. To delineate the boundary between warranted and unwarranted secrecy and to enquire into the lines on which a satisfactory balance could be struck between the legitimate

---

16 See for example, *'Guide to Excellence in Service'* brought out by the Government of Malaysia in a document dated 1 January 1979, emanating from the Prime Minister's Office.

requirements of the citizens, science, and industry for freedom of information and the need of the Government (for quite specific and justifiable reasons) to keep certain information confidential or even strictly secret, is the key problem in public administration today, which has defied a universally acceptable solution. [17]

The provision in certain countries that computer records holding highly personal information about citizens are to be classified as documents for purposes of public access, has raised new problems converging on the issues of 'privacy' versus 'secrecy'. While, on the one hand, the easy availability of computer information may be regarded as a danger to personal privacy, on the other, its centralisation and difficulty of access by the average citizen makes it easier to withhold. Thus, the argument about secrecy and publicity has continued, and is a live subject of discussion in respect of Parliamentary procedure and governmental operations.

In modern thinking, secrecy belongs to the group of phenomena which, while ubiquitous in politics, is considered morally objectionable, or at least, an instrument of potential misuse, such as corruption and betrayal (treason). Secrecy has been condemned traditionally by the more radical liberal and democratic thinkers, and publicity has been claimed as being essential to desirable public lire. Immanuel Kant was inclined to make publicity the touchstone of one's acting morality; secrecy carried the implication of something questionable; and presumably morally obnoxious. Bentham thought that Parliamentary debates required publicity and was prepared to make it an absolute standard. It is evident from available literature that secrecy is found throughout public life, and that some types of secrecy, that is, secrecy under some circumstances, in some situations, is functional, whereas in others it is dysfunctional. [18]

In the debates over these issues often it is overlooked that secrecy is a main behavioural aspect of an effective bureaucracy, whether governmental or private. A good many arguments on behalf of privacy in fact are meant to protect the secrecy of industrial and commercial operations. Rules and regulations looking towards secrecy have played a considerable role in the development of bureaucracy. The determined effort of organisations to keep secret their important evidence in controversial and competitive situations shows that such secrecy (privacy) is functional. [19]

---

17 The extent of administrative secrecy prevailing in many developed societies has been presented admirably by Professor Rowat in his edited work *Administrative Secrecy in Developed Countries* (London, Macmillan 1977). See also Rosamund M. Thomas *Espionage and Secrecy: The British Official Secrets Acts 1911-1989 of the United Kingdom* (Routledge, 1991 and Routledge, Chapman and Hall Inc. 1992).

18 Carl J. Friedrich 'Secrecy Versus Privacy: Democratic Dilemma' in Ronald Pennock and John W. Chapman (eds.) *Privacy* (New York, Atherton Press, 1971), pp. 105-6.

19 Ibid, n. 18, p. 111.

Friedrich considers privacy as a special form of secrecy. Since secrecy is endemic in all social relations, it is also there in politics. But the functionality of privacy and secrecy are dependent upon the system of which they form a part, and hence their evaluation must vary. At the same time, secrecy acts as a factor of systems influencing each other, and the destruction of privacy and enlargement of official secrecy, and indeed the entire apparatus of the secret police State, has forced democratic States to adapt to the world of totalitarian competition, to increase official secrecy, and to reduce privacy by the institution of police and investigatory methods resembling those of the autocratic order. Friedrich argues that 'Thereby they have endangered their systematic order and hence their internal security.' [20] In his opinion, making the innermost self secure is more vital to the security and survival of a constitutional order than any boundary or any secret. It is the very core of the constitutional reason of State. Insight into this need for maintaining privacy against all clamour for official secrecy is still missing in many quarters and the trend has been in the opposing direction. The functionality of officials and of private secrecy is in a delicate balance. It is difficult at the present time to assess the eventual outcome of the conflict between these two claims for secrecy. [21]

4. Secrecy in Government: The Indian Experience

Secrecy in the Indian Government is a continued legacy of the British Government since the Nineteenth century onwards. As early as 1843, the then Central Government in India run by the East India Company issued a notification asking its personnel not to communicate to the outside world any paper or information in their possession. Some years later, the Government of India felt compelled to reissue the earlier notification, as the practice of circulating governmental information to the press had become more widespread. In July 1875, the Central Government laid down detailed instructions in a bid to regulate the contemporary administrative behaviour in relation to the emerging press in India. Under these rules, the government officials were not permitted to become proprietor of any newspaper or periodical. Although officials were not prohibited absolutely from contributing to the press, the Government wanted them to confine themselves within the limits of temperate and reasonable discussion. Officials were prohibited, however, from making public, without previous sanction of the Government, any documents, paper or information which might have come into their possession in their official capacity. And it was the Government which ultimately decided, in cases of doubt, whether any engagement by the civil servant with the press, was consistent with the discharge of his duties to his

---

20 Ibid
21 Ibid, pp. 119-20.

employer. In a circular Number 214, issued to officials on 16 August 1884, the House Department charged officials to be discreet and intelligent in disclosing official information, and in cases of doubt, to apply to higher authority.

4.1 Application in India of the British Official Secrets Act

The first Official Secrets Act was passed in Britain in 1889, the unique feature of this statute was that it was applicable to any part of Her Majesty's dominions including India.

The British statute was re-enacted for India in 1889 under the title of the Indian Official Secrets Act, with such adaptations of language and penalties as the nomenclature of the Indian statute book permitted. The Indian Act of 1889 covered a much wider area than the Resolution of 1885 and was directed against espionage as well as against any person to whom official information ought not, in the interest of the State, to be communicated at that time. The over-riding objective of the 1889 Indian Act was to prevent the disclosure of official documents and information. An act of espionage was punishable with transportation for life or for any term not less than five years or for imprisonment for a term up to two years. The offences covered by the Act were: (i) the wrongful obtaining of information in regard to any matter of State importance, and (ii) the wrongful communication of such information. The Act was made far more severe through its amendment in 1904, which made all offences under the Act cognisable and non-bailable. Around this time, upholding of secrecy by officials was incorporated in the Government servants' conduct rules as well.

4.2 The Indian Official Secrets Act of 1923

The British replaced their Officials Secrets Act of 1889 by the Official Secrets Act of 1911, which together with the exigencies of World War One prompted the enactment of a new Act for India. The Indian Official Secrets Act was passed in 1923. [22] First, it was directed against espionage, the provisions relating to which were made more favourable to the State, and an individual could be punished on evidence. Secondly, the Act also related to communication of official information to outsiders. The Act made it a penal offence for any person holding office under the Government wilfully to communicate any official information to any person, other than a person to whom he is authorised to communicate it. Futhermore, it is an offence for any person to *receive* such information In other words, the statute sets out to punish both the 'thief' and the receiver of the stolen goods. This provision is contained

---

22 For accurate details of the espionage provisions of the British Official Secrets Act of 1911, and the British Official Secrets Act of 1920 (an Amending Act), on which the Indian Act of 1923 is based, see Rosamund M. Thomas *Espionage and Secrecy* op. cit.

in section 5 of the Act of 1923, which has some of the most Draconian provisions still in operation in the country even forty years after independence. It has been said that over two thousand different worded charges can be brought under it.

Section 5 of the 1923 Indian Act covers all that happens within the Government; all information which a civil servant happens to learn in the course of his duty is official, and is thus covered under it. This section leaves nothing, and nothing escapes it. [23] The Act makes mere receipt of official information an offence. The fact that the information might have been communicated to a person contrary to his desire, is irrelevant and does not immunise him in the least. Further, section 5 relates not only to civil servants, but also to other persons. This section categorises four situations in which other persons may also be caught:

1. Government contractors and their employees. The information that they learn in their capacity is 'official' for purposes of this section of the Act.

2. Any person in possession of official information which has been made or obtained in contravention of the Official Secrets Act.

3. Any person to whom official information is entrusted in confidence by a civil servant.

4. Any person coming into possession, by whatever means, of a secret official code word or pass word, or of information about a defence establishment or other political place. [24]

After independence, the Indian Official Secrets Act, 1923 was amended only once in 1967 primarily to make most of the offences punishable with greater sentences of imprisonment and to make most of the offences cognisable offences.

5. Secrecy and Espionage

The term Official Secret has not been defined in the Act. The Bombay High Court in a case observed that the expression 'official secret' is ordinarily understood in the sense in which it is used in the Official Secrets Act and has reference to secrets of one or the other Department of the Government or the State. [25] Budget papers are official secrets, until the budget is actually

---

23 Section 5 of the Indian Official Secrets Act, 1923 is akin to the old 'catch all' section 2 of the British Official Secrets Act, 1911. The latter was repealed and replaced by the new British Official Secrets Act of 1989, which reverses the 'catch all' principle, replacing it by more *specific* – yet complicated – provisions.

24 S. R. Maheshwari 'Secrecy in Government in India' *Indian Journal of Public Administration*, Vol. 25 (October-December 1979), p. 1108.

25 *R. K. Karanjia Vs. Emperor*, AIR 1946, Bom., 322, at 324, Cr. L. J. 744.

presented in the legislature. Contravention of maintenance of the budget's secrecy would amount to an offence. The fact that, on a subsequent date, the budget proposals have to be made public would not detract from the secrecy of these proposals until such time as they are announced in the Parliament.[26] The Kerala High Court in another case held that budget papers are official secrets which cannot be published until the budget is actually presented in the legislature and the contravention of the same would amount to an offence under the Act.[27] The disclosure of the government departmental examination papers also constitutes an offence under the Official Secrets Act.

A number of public officials have been punished under the Official Secrets Act on charges of espionage. Recently, three High ranking Pakistani intelligence officials masquerading as diplomatic corps personnel posted at the Pakistan chancery in Delhi carried out dangerous espionage operations, securing through blackmail, secret codified documents revealing Indian Air Force squadrons striking power. The codified documents secured by intercepting 'classified mail' revealed strategic locations of Indian Air Force squadrons, their striking power, allotment of MI-S helicopters and AN-12 aircrafts, flight timings and senior officers 'positions' at airforce stations and in the Defence Ministry. The IAP man maintained till the end that he never knew that the three Pakistanis were Pakistani intelligence officers. He was sentenced to ten years rigorous imprisonment in November 1979 by the Additional Sessions Judge of Delhi, Shri P. L. Singla, under sections 3 and 5 of the Official Secrets Act 1923 read with section 120B of the Indian Penal Code.[28]

In another case in August 1978, an Indian Army Officer, holding the rank of Lieutenant Colonel had been arrested on charges of having traded military secrets with a Pakistan agency across the actual line of control, according to official sources. The Officer, who headed the Indian military intelligence wing in Kashmir, was accused of having prepared a twenty-page document which was seized at a place in Western Kashmir in July 1979. Described as highly classified, the document contained complete information about strategic and operational strength of the Indian Army in the Northern command.[29]

In a third case, one former Lieutenant Colonel of the Indian Army, Mr Nirmal Puri who retired from the services, was arrested in January 1989 under the Official Secrets Act on charges of passing defence secrets and

---

26 *Nandlal More Vs. State*, 1965(1), Cr. L. J. 393 *at 408*.

27 *The Hindustan Times*, 29 August 1979. For details, see O. P. Motiwal 'Secrecy in Government in India' in *The Indian Journal of Public Administration*, Vol. 25, (October-December 1979).

28 *The Hindustan Times*, 30 September 1979.

29 *The Hindustan Times*, 30 September 1979.

classified information while in the services and faced trial along with one arms dealer, Mr Vinod Kumar Khanna. [30]

Section 5 (1) of the Indian Official Secrets Act thus is very comprehensive in its nature. It applies not only to government servants but also to all persons who have obtained secrets in contravention of the Act. Regarding section 5 (4) of the Act and section 4 (1) of the Press (Emergency Powers) Act, an invitation to the public contained in an article or advertisement in newspapers to send official secrets to the editor of a newspaper for payment, comes within section 4 (1) of the Press Act as well as section 5 (1) of the Official Secrets Act. Together, these two provisions act as a prohibition against an invitation inviting any person to commit an offence of passing secrets to the press.

The above cases demonstrate that the application of the Official Secrets Act had been quite severe in cases of alleged espionage or passing of documents to an outsider who is taken to be an enemy agent. In many cases like the Larkin Brothers' espionage conviction, doubts have been expressed that the documents alleged to have been passed to the agent were not really classified, as most of the information contained therein was freely available elsewhere in printed papers.

6. Secrecy and the Press

The Indian press has not claimed any right to publish information likely to be useful to the enemy in times of war or any confidential information likely to endanger public safety in times of emergency. However, the Indian Press, equally, is not ready to accept the claim that any circular or note or instruction becomes a prohibited secret because it is marked 'secret' or confidential. The press has claimed the right to publish confidential government information when its publication is in the public interest and the two basic limitations do not apply. It is a matter of professional honour and distinction for a newspaper to expose secret moves when the public interest justifies such exposure. The press on numerous occasions has protested against the lack of any clear and precise definition of 'official secrets' as far as it concerns publication. [31]

In a Seminar organised by the Delhi Journalist Association in New Delhi on 22nd April 1989, a number of journalists condemned the Official Secrets Act, especially section 5, as an obnoxious instrument cutting at the free flow of information and called for its immediate repeal in the interests of the unfettered functioning of democracy and the people's right to know. [32]

---

30 *The Hindustan Times*, 29 August 1979.

31 M. Chalopathi Rau, 'Official Secrets and Freedom of Information in India' *Indian Journal of Public Administration*, Vol. 25 (October-December 1979), pp. 1095-96.

32 'Demand to Repeal Secrets Act' *The Hindustan Times*, New Delhi, 23 April 1989, p. 7.

In a resolution passed unanimously at the end of the Seminar, the Government was reprimanded for not only maintaining a Draconian law introduced by the British in 1923, but also for suddenly threatening to enforce it. Any new law, the resolution said, should sharply define, 'national security' and 'public interest', so that they do not become shields of the Government.

The editor of the *Indian Express*, Arun Shourie, known for his investigative journalist coups, has been responsible for building up 'public opinion' on the subject. Shourie favours publication in defiance of the Official Secrets Act, and the destruction of the notion that the Government is the sole guardian of patriotism. He has made scathing attacks on several sections of the Official Secrets Act, and argued that it was nurtured by the Government, not for national security but for convenience. The Thakker Commission Report, for instance, he maintained, was being used to keep the former President, Mr Zail Singh, silent. To prove his point, Shourie maintained that on every single occasion the Government has lied going back as far as the Bhagalpur Blindings in the 1980s and the Antulay scandal.

Nikhil Chakravarty, another veteran journalist at the Seminar, observed that 'we do not have freedom of the press as a fundamental right' but it is covered under freedom of expression. He called for mobilising opinion against laws inhibiting freedom of expression and information and advised journalists not to be scared of the Official Secrets Act, but challenge it. Dina Nath Mishra of the *Nav Bharat Times* charged the Government with sitting on vital information and passing out trivial and superficial materials for public consumption.

A prominent lawyer Rajiv Dhawan observed that the Official Secrets Act had not been challenged since its introduction in 1923. That was because no Government had ever dared to threaten and use it. The Act is so sweeping that it contradicts itself. In the forty-two years of post-British India, not one journalist has been prosecuted successfully for violating section 5, its all embrasive core. In 1952, two *Indian Express* columnists were arrested for publishing a Government report on the evasion of excise duties by a private textile firm. The charge, which could not subsequently be proved, was the violation of the Official Secrets Act. According to the practising lawyer, Kapil Sibal, if one is arrested under such a law one could not defend oneself. In one of the cases, he was defending a client accused under the Official Secrets Act and demanded to know what the rule was for classifying a document as secret, if one existed. The Government counsel took the rule book out of his brief case but refused to open it. It was marked 'secret' too. The judge said nothing could be done to force him to reveal it. Sibal feels that the entire Act, not just section 5, is unconstitutional. [33]

---

33 *The Times of India*, 23 April 1989.

6.1 Disclosure of Thakkar Commission Report

The current controversy about the Official Secrets Act arose on account of the fact that the *Indian Express* editor, Arun Shourie in February 1989, had published in his paper part of the secret Thakkar Report, which investigated the assassination of Mrs Indira Gandhi in which some aspersions were cast on the role of her close aide, Mr R. K. Dhawan. Earlier in 1987, the Government had amended the Inquiry Commission Act, so as to permit the Government not to have to table any Report of an Inquiry Commission in the House of the Parliament, in cases where it considered that it would not be in the interest or the security of the State to do so. The Government, on that basis, withheld the Thakkar Commission Report from being made public on the floor of Parliament. But the Report somehow was leaked to the press by an interested party; and some excerpts from it were published in the *Indian Express*. With the re-appointment of R. K. Dhawan, as an Officer on Special Duty in the Prime Minister's Office, in March 1989, the issue was raised by the opposition in the House forcing the Government to table the report in the Lok Sabha, the lower House of the Parliament. Although the Report ultimately cleared R. K. Dhawan on his alleged complicity in the assassination of Mrs Gandhi, the whole episode left both the ruling party and also the opposition parties in a battered condition. The ruling party lost its credibility for not being able to stick to its position, and unnecessarily making an important document a 'classified one', away from public gaze, and the opposition parties were criticised for making a mountain of the mole hill.

6.2 Privacy Versus Freedom of Information

Although in India, the issue of 'privacy versus freedom of information' has not yet assumed a major debatable proportion, developments in the Indian political system over the last five years or so point to the fact that, in the coming decade, in all likelihood, this issue will be the pre-runner of other information-related issues on which a coherent and a rational public policy will be needed. The events leading to the declaration of emergency in 1975, the developments that took place during 1975-79, the efforts of the Shah and other enquiry commissions to unearth the correct information for public consumption and the personal, legal and political conflicts in which the public officials (both political and administrative) find themselves while discharging their lawful obligations have certainly highlighted the need for some legislative instrument to strike a proper balance between these two basic and seemingly conflicting propositions. Such balance is needed, especially in the context of an administrative system, which has traditionally been notorious for its conservatism and secrecy.

Thus, the protection of privacy requires not only a degree of consensus in the total population about the rights of the individual, who may be poor, uneducated, and of minority groups, and about adequate laws to recognise these rights, but also considerable efforts are required by those who exercise influence and wield power, governmental or otherwise, to enforce the laws and to encourage compliance with the moral, general, and social norms of respect for the individual. However, the emphasis on the right to privacy should not obscure the fact that Governments and other collectivities have legitimate concern over private aspects of their members' lives. Laws establish only guidelines for the competition between the autonomy of the individual and his government; the understanding of that competition requires further study of the functions of privacy for individuals, for collectivities, and for the relationships between the two. [34]

In the final analysis, as Snyder contends, we must assure freedom and integrity of the flow of information in our society; for in a community which has grown so large and complex we cannot personally experience its reality; we will have to depend upon the reality inferred from the data flow to inform our decision-making. To the extent that data is complete, correct and timely, our decision will be as correct as our collective decision-making process will permit. To the extent that the information is incorrect, incomplete or substantially delayed, our decisions will be enforced inadequately, and subject to greater error. And, during the coming decades, we will have precious little margin for error. [35] There is thus an immediate and strong case in India, put forward by some exponents, to amend the Official Secrets Act, as also the enactment of a positive Freedom of Information Act, so as to be in tune with the changing public ethics and legal norms.

---

34 Arnold Simmel 'Privacy' in *International Encyclopaedia of the Social Sciences* Vol. 12, pp. 480-86.

35 David P. Snyder 'Privacy: the Right to What?' *The Bureaucrat* Vol. 5, July 1976, p. 225.

NOTE 1

THE OFFICIAL SECRETS ACT, 1923

(19 OF 1923)

(As modified up to the 1st December 1983)

[PART I]

[PART II.—SUBORDINATE LEGISLATION BEING PUBLISHED SEPARATELY]

GOVERNMENT OF INDIA

Ministry of Law, Justice and Company Affairs

LIST OF AMENDING ACTS AND ADAPTATION ORDERS

1. The Repealing Act, 1927 (12 of 1927).

2. The Government of India (Adaptation of Indian Laws) Order, 1937.

3. The Indian Independence (Adaptation of Central Acts and Ordinances) Order, 1948.

4. The Adaptation of Laws Order, 1950.

5. The Part B States (Laws) Act, 1951 (3 of 1951).

6. The Indian Official Secrets (Amendment) Act, 1967 (24 of 1967).

LIST OF ABBREVIATIONS USED

A.O. 1937	..	.. *for*	Government of India (Adaptation of Indian Laws) Order, 1937.
A.O. 1948	..	.. ,,	Indian Independence (Adaptation of Central Acts and Ordinances) Order, 1948.
A.O. 1950	..	.. ,,	Adaptation of Laws Order, 1950.
Cl.	..	.. ,,	Clause.
Ins.	..	.. ,,	Inserted.
P.	..	.. ,,	Page.
Pt.	..	.. ,,	Part.
Reg.	..	.. ,,	Regulation.
Rep.	..	.. ,,	Repealed.
S.	..	.. ,,	Section.
Sch.	..	.. ,,	Schedule.
Subs.	..	.. ,,	Substituted.
w.e.f.	..	.. ,,	with effect from.

THE OFFICIAL SECRETS ACT, 1923

19 OF 1923[1]

[*2nd April*, 1923.]

An Act to consolidate and amend the law [2]* * * relating to official secrets.

[1]*   *   *   *   *   *

WHEREAS it is expedient that the law relating to official secrets [1]* * * should be consolidated and amended;

It is hereby enacted as follows:—

[4][**1.** (*1*) This Act may be called the Official Secrets Act, 1923.

(2) It extends to the whole of India and applies also to servants of the Government and to citizens of India outside India.]   Short title, ext at and application

2. In this Act, unless there is anything repugnant in the subject or context,—   Definitions.

(*1*) any reference to a place belonging to Government includes a place occupied by any department of the Government, whether the place is or is not actually vested in Government;

[5]*   *   *   *   *   *

(2) expressions referring to communicating or receiving include any communicating or receiving, whether in whole or in part, and whether the sketch, plan, model, article, note, document, or information itself or the substance, effect or description thereof only be communicated or received; expressions referring to obtaining or retaining any sketch, plan, model, article, note or document, include the copying or causing to be copied of the whole or any part of any sketch, plan, model, article, note, or document; and expressions referring to the communication of any sketch, plan, model, article, note or document include the transfer or transmission of the sketch, plan, model, article, note or document;

(3) "document" includes part of a document;

(4) "model" includes design, pattern and specimen;

(5) "munitions of war" includes the whole or any part of any ship, submarine, aircraft, tank or similar engine, arms and ammunition, torpedo, or mine intended or adapted for use in war, and any other article, material, or device, whether actual or proposed, intended for such use;

---

[1]For Statement of Objects and Reasons, *see* Gazette of India, 1922, Pt. V, p. 210; and for report of Select Committee, *see ibid.*, 1923, Pt. V, p. 61.

Extended to Berar by Act 4 of 1941; to Goa, Daman and Diu by Reg. 12 of 1962, s. 3 and Sch., to Dadra and Nagar Haveli by Reg. 6 of 1963, s. 2 and Sch. I; to Pondicherry by Reg. 7 of 1963, s. 3 and Sch. I and to Lakshadweep by Reg. 8 of 1965, s. 3 and Sch.

[2]The words "in the Provinces" omitted by the A.O. 1950.

[3]Paragraphs 1 and 2 of the Preamble omitted, *ibid.*

[4]Subs by Act 24 of 1967, s. 2, for s. 1.

[5]Cl. (*1A*) ins. by the A.O. 1937, omitted by the A.O. 1948.

(6) "office under Government" includes any office or employment in or under any department of the Government ¹* * *;

(7) "photograph" includes an undeveloped film or plate;

(8) "prohibited place" means—

(a) any work of defence, arsenal, naval, military or air force establishment or station, mine, minefield, camp, ship or aircraft belonging to, or occupied by or on behalf of, Government, any military telegraph or telephone so belonging or occupied, any wireless or signal station or office so belonging or occupied and any factory, dockyard or other place so belonging or occupied and used for the purpose of building, repairing, making or storing any munitions of war, or any sketches, plans, models or documents relating thereto, or for the purpose of getting any metals, oil or minerals of use in time of war;

(b) any place not belonging to Government where any munitions of war or any sketches, models, plans or documents relating thereto, are being made, repaired, gotten or stored under contract with, or with any person on behalf of, Government, or otherwise on behalf of Government;

(c) any place belonging to or used for the purpose of Government which is for the time being declared by the Central Government, by notification in the Official Gazette, to be a prohibited place for the purposes of this Act on the ground that information with respect thereto, or damage thereto, would be useful to an enemy, and to which a copy of the notification in respect thereof has been affixed in English and in the vernacular of the locality;

(d) any railway, road, way or channel, or other means of communication by land or water (including any works or structures being part thereof or connected therewith) or any place used for gas, water or electricity works or other works for purposes of a public character, or any place where any munitions of war or any sketches, models, plans, or documents relating thereto, are being made, repaired, or stored otherwise than on behalf of Government, which is for the time being declared by the Central Government, by notification in the Official Gazette, to be a prohibited place for the purposes of this Act on the ground that information with respect thereto, or the destruction or obstruction thereof, or interference therewith, would be useful to an enemy, and to which a copy of the notification in respect thereof has been affixed in English and in the vernacular of the locality;

(9) "sketch" includes any photograph or other mode of representing any place or thing; and

²*   *   *   *   * ,

(10) "Superintendent of Police" includes any police officer of a like or superior rank, and any person upon whom the powers of a Superintendent of Police are for the purposes of this Act conferred by the Central Government ³* * *.

---

¹Certain words omitted by Act 24 of 1967, s. 3.
²Cl (9A) ins. by the A.O. 1950, omitted by Act 3 of 1951, s. 3 and Sch.
³The words "or by any Local Government" omitted by the A.O. 1937.

3. (*1*) If any person for any purpose prejudicial to the safety or interests of the State—

(*a*) approaches, inspects, passes over or is in the vicinity of, or enters, any prohibited place; or

(*b*) makes any sketch, plan, model, or note which is calculated to be or might be or is intended to be, directly or indirectly, useful to an enemy; or

(*c*) obtains, collects, records or publishes or communicates to any other person any secret official code or pass word, or any sketch, plan, model, article or note or other document or information which is calculated to be or might be or is intended to be, directly or indirectly, useful to an enemy [or which relates to a matter the disclosure of which is likely to affect the sovereignty and integrity of India, the security of the State or friendly relations with foreign States];

he shall be punishable with imprisonment for a term which may extend, where the offence is committed in relation to any work of defence, arsenal, naval, military or air force establishment or station, mine, minefield, factory, dockyard, camp, ship or aircraft or otherwise in relation to the naval, military or air force affairs of Government or in relation to any secret official code, to fourteen years and in other cases to three years.

(*2*) On a prosecution for an offence punishable under this section [2]* * *, it shall not be necessary to show that the accused person was guilty of any particular act tending to show a purpose prejudicial to the safety or interests of the State, and, notwithstanding that no such act is proved against him, he may be convicted if from the circumstances of the case or his conduct or his known character as proved, it appears that his purpose was a purpose prejudicial to the safety or interests of the State; and if any sketch, plan, model, article, note, document, or information relating to or used in any prohibited place, or relating to anything in such a place, or any secret official code or pass word is made, obtained, collected, recorded, published or communicated by any person other than a person acting under lawful authority, and from the circumstances of the case or his conduct or his known character as proved it appears that his purpose was a purpose prejudicial to the safety or interests of the State, such sketch, plan, model, article, note, document, [3][information, code or pass word shall be presumed to have been made], obtained, collected, recorded, published or communicated for a purpose prejudicial to the safety or interests of the State.

4. (*1*) In any proceedings against a person for an offence under section 3, the fact that he has been in communication with, or attempted to communicate with a foreign agent, whether within or without [India], shall be relevant for the purpose of proving that he has, for a purpose prejudicial to the safety or interests of the State, obtained or attempted to obtain information which is calculated to be or might be, or is intended to be, directly or indirectly, useful to any enemy.

---

[1]Ins. by Act 24 of 1967, s. 4.
[2]Certain words omitted by s. 4, *ibid.*
[3]Subs. by s. 4, *ibid.*, for "or information shall be presumed to have been made".
[4]Subs. by Act 3 of 1951, s. 3 and Sch., for "the States".

(2) For the purpose of this section, but without prejudice to the generality of the foregoing provision,—

(*a*) a person may be presumed to have been in communication with a foreign agent if—

(*i*) he has, either within or without [India], visited the address of a foreign agent or consorted or associated with a foreign agent, or

(*ii*) either within or without [India], the name or address of, or any other information regarding, a foreign agent has been found in his possession, or has been obtained by him from any other person;

(*b*) the expression "foreign agent" includes any person who is or has been or in respect of whom it appears that there are reasonable grounds for suspecting him of being or having been employed by a foreign power, either directly or indirectly, for the purpose of committing an act, either within or without [India], prejudicial to the safety or interests of the State, or who has or is reasonably suspected of having, either within or without [India], committed, or attempted to commit, such an act in the interests of a foreign power;

(*c*) any address, whether within or without [India], in respect of which it appears that there are reasonable grounds for suspecting it of being an address used for the receipt of communications intended for a foreign agent, or any address at which a foreign agent resides, or to which he resorts for the purpose of giving or receiving communications, or at which he carries on any business, may be presumed to be the address of a foreign agent, and communications addressed to such an address to be communications with a foreign agent.

Wrongful communication, etc., of information.

5. (*1*) If any person having in his possession or control any secret official code or pass word or any sketch, plan, model, article, note, document or information which relates to or is used in a prohibited place or relates to anything in such a place, [or which is likely to assist, directly or indirectly, an enemy or which relates to a matter the disclosure of which is likely to affect the sovereignty and integrity of India, the security of the State or friendly relations with foreign States or which has been made or obtained in contravention of this Act,] or which has been entrusted in confidence to him by any person holding office under Government, or which he has obtained or to which he has had access owing to his position as a person who holds or has held office under Government, or as a person who holds or has held a contract made on behalf of Government, or as a person who is or has been employed under a person who holds or has held such an office or contract—

(*a*) wilfully communicates the code or pass word, sketch, plan, model, article, note, document or information to any person other than a person

---

¹Subs. by Act 3 of 1951, s. 3 and Sch., for "the States".

²Subs. by Act 24 of 1967, s. 5, for "or which has been made or obtained in contravention of this Act.".

to whom he is authorised to communicate it or a Court of Justice or a person to whom it is, in the interests of the State, his duty to communicate it; or

(*b*) uses the information in his possession for the benefit of any foreign power or in any other manner prejudicial to the safety of the State; or

(*c*) retains the sketch, plan, model, article, note or document in his possession or control when he has no right to retain it, or when it is contrary to his duty to retain it, or wilfully fails to comply with all directions issued by lawful authority with regard to the return or disposal thereof; or

(*d*) fails to take reasonable care of, or so conducts himself as to endanger the safety of, the sketch, plan, model, article, note, document, secret official code or pass word or information;

he shall be guilty of an offence under this section.

(*2*) If any person voluntarily receives any secret official code or pass word or any sketch, plan, model, article, note, document or information knowing or having reasonable ground to believe, at the time when he receives it, that the code, pass word, sketch, plan, model, article, note, document or information is communicated in contravention of this Act, he shall be guilty of an offence under this section.

(*3*) If any person having in his possession or control any sketch, plan, model, article, note, document or information, which relates to munitions of war, communicates it, directly or indirectly, to any foreign power or in any other manner prejudicial to the safety or interests of the State, he shall be guilty of an offence under this section.

¹[(*4*) A person guilty of an offence under this section shall be punishable with imprisonment for a term which may extend to three years, or with fine, or with both.]

6. (*1*) If any person for the purpose of gaining admission or of assisting any other person to gain admission to a prohibited place or for any other purpose prejudicial to the safety of the State— *Unauthorised use of uniforms; falsification of reports, forgery, personation, and false documents.*

(*a*) uses or wears, without lawful authority, any naval, military, air force, police or other official uniform, or any uniform so nearly resembling the same as to be calculated to deceive, or falsely represents himself to be a person who is or has been entitled to use or wear any such uniform; or

(*b*) orally, or in writing in any declaration or application, or in any document signed by him or on his behalf, knowingly makes or connives at the making of any false statement or any omission; or

(*c*) forges, alters, or tampers with any passport or any naval, military, air force, police, or official pass, permit, certificate, licence, or other document of a similar character (hereinafter in this section referred to as an official document) or knowingly uses or has in his possession any such forged, altered, or irregular official document; or

---

¹Subs. by Act 24 of 1967, s. 5, for sub-section "(*4*)"(w.e.f. 10-7-1968).

(*d*) personates, or falsely represents himself to be, a person holding, or in the employment of a person holding, office under Government, or to be or not to be a person to whom an official document or secret official code or pass word has been duly issued or communicated, or with intent to obtain an official document, secret official code or pass word, whether for himself or any other person, knowingly makes any false statement; or

(*e*) uses, or has in his possession or under his control, without the authority of the department of the Government or the authority concerned, any die, seal or stamp of or belonging to, or used, made or provided by, any department of the Government, or by any diplomatic, naval, military, or air force authority appointed by or acting under the authority of Government, or any die, seal or stamp so nearly resembling any such die, seal or stamp as to be calculated to deceive, or counterfeits any such die, seal or stamp, or knowingly uses, or has in his prossession or under his control, any such counterfeited die, seal or stamp;

he shall be guilty of an offence under this section.

(2) If any person for any purpose prejudicial to the safety of the State—

(*a*) retains any official document, whether or not completed or issued for use, when he has no right to retain it, or when it is contrary to his duty to retain it, or wilfully fails to comply with any directions issued by any department of the Government or any person authorised by such department with regard to the return or disposal thereof; or

(*b*) allows any other person to have possession of any official document issued for his use alone, or communicates any secret official code or pass word so issued, or, without lawful authority or excuse, has in his possesion any official document or secret official code or pass word issued for the use of some person other than himself, or, on obtaining possession of any official document by finding or otherwise, wilfully fails to restore it to the person or authority by whom or for whose use it was issued, or to a police officer; or

(*c*) without lawful authority or excuse, manufactures or sells, or has in his possession for sale, any such die, seal or stamp as aforesaid,

he shall be guilty of an offence under this section.

(3) A person guilty of an offence under this section shall be punishable with imprisonment for a term which may extend to [1][three years], or with fine, or with both.

(4) The provisions of sub-section (2) of section 3 shall apply, for the purpose of proving a purpose prejudicial to the safety of the State, to any prosecution for an offence under this section relating to the naval, military or air force affairs of Government, or to any secret official code in like manner as they apply, for the purpose of proving a purpose prejudicial to the safety or interests of the State, to prosecutions for offences punishable under that section [2]* * *

---

[1]Subs. by Act 24 of 1967, s. 6, for "two years".
[2]Certain words omitted by s. 6, *ibid.*

7. (*1*) No person in the vicinity of any prohibited place shall obstruct, knowingly mislead or otherwise interfere with or impede, any police officer, or any member of ¹[the Armed Forces of the Union] engaged on guard, sentry, patrol, or other similar duty in relation to the prohibited place.

Interfering with officers of the police or members of the Armed Forces of Union.

(*2*) If any person acts in contravention of the provisions of this section, he shall be punishable with imprisonment which may extend to ²[three years], or with fine, or with both.

8. (*1*) It shall be the duty of every person to give on demand to a Superintendent of Police, or other police officer not below the rank of Inspector, empowered by an Inspector-General or Commissioner of Police in this behalf, or to any member of ¹[the Armed Forces of the Union] engaged on guard, sentry, patrol or other similar duty, any information in his power relating to an offence or suspected offence under section 3 or under section 3 read with section 9 and, if so required, and upon tender of his reasonable expenses, to attend at such reasonable time and place as may be specified for the purpose of furnishing such information.

Duty of giving information as to commission of offences.

(*2*) If any person fails to give any such information or to attend as aforesaid, he shall be punishable with imprisonment which may extend to ³[three years], or with fine, or with both.

9. Any person who attempts to commit or abets the commission of an offence under this Act shall be punishable with the same punishment, and be liable to be proceeded against in the same manner as if he had committed such offence.

Attempts, incitements, etc.

10. (*1*) If any person knowingly harbours any person whom he knows or has reasonable grounds for supposing to be a person who is about to commit or who has committed an offence under section 3 or under section 3 read with section 9 or knowingly permits to meet or assemble in any premises in his occupation or under his control any such persons, he shall be guilty of an offence under this section.

Penalty for harbouring spies.

(*2*) It shall be the duty of every person having harboured any such person as aforesaid, or permitted to meet or assemble in any premises in his occupation or under his control any such persons as aforesaid, to give on demand to a Superintendent of Police or other police officer not below the rank of Inspector empowered by an Inspector-General or Commissioner of Police in this behalf, any information in his power relating to any such person or persons, and if any person fails to give any such information, he shall be guilty of an offence under this section.

(*3*) A person guilty of an offence under this section shall be punishable with imprisonment for a term which may extend to ⁴[three years], or with fine, or with both.

11. (*1*) If a Presidency Magistrate, Magistrate of the first class or Sub-divisional Magistrate is satisfied by information on oath that there is reasonable

Search-warrants.

---

¹Subs. by the A.O. 1950, for "His Majesty's Forces".
²Subs. by Act 24 of 1967, s. 7, for "two years".
³Subs. by s. 8, *ibid.*, for "two years".
⁴Subs. by s. 9, *ibid.*, for "one year".

ground for suspecting that an offence under this Act has been or is about to be committed, he may grant a search-warrant authorising any police officer named therein, not being below the rank of an officer in charge of a police station, to enter at any time any premises or place named in the warrant, if necessary, by force, and to search the premises or place and every person found therein, and to seize any sketch, plan, model, article, note or document, or anything of a like nature, or anything which is evidence of an offence under this Act having been or being about to be committed which he may find on the premises or place or any such person, and with regard to or in connection with which he has reasonable ground for suspecting that an offence under this Act has been or is about to be committed.

(2) Where it appears to a police officer, not being below the rank of Superintendent, that the case is one of great emergency, and that in the interests of the State immediate action is necessary, he may by a written order under his hand give to any police officer the like authority as may be given by the warrant of a Magistrate under this section.

(3) Where action has been taken by a police officer under sub-section (2) he shall, as soon as may be, report such action, in a presidency-town to the Chief Presidency Magistrate, and outside such town to the District or Sub-divisional Magistrate.

Provisions of section 337 of Act 5 of 1898 to apply to offences under sections 3, 5 and 7.   [1]12. The provisions of section 337 of the Code of Criminal Procedure, 1898[2] shall apply in relation to an offence punishable under section 3 or under section 5 or under section 7 or under any of the said sections 3, 5 and 7 read with section 9, as they apply in relation to an offence punishable with imprisonment for a term which may extend to seven years.]

Restriction on trial of offences.   13. (1) No Court (other than that of a Magistrate of the first class specially empowered in this behalf by the [3][appropriate Government] which is inferior to that of a District or Presidency Magistrate shall try any offence under this Act.

(2) If any person under trial before a Magistrate for an offence under this Act at any time before a charge is framed claims to be tried by the Court of Session, the Magistrate shall, if he does not discharge the accused, commit the case for trial by that Court, notwithstanding that it is not a case exclusively triable by that Court.

(3) No Court shall take cognizance of any offence under this Act unless upon complaint made by order of, or under authority from, the [4][appropriate Government] [5]* * * or some officer empowered by the [2][appropriate Government] in this behalf.

[6]*   *   *   *   *   *

(4) For the purposes of the trial of a person for an offence under this Act, the offence may be deemed to have been committed either at the place in which the same actually was committed or at any place in [7][India] in which the offender may be found.

---

[1]Subs. by Act 24 of 1967, s. 10, for s. 12.
[2]*See* now the Code of Criminal Procedure, 1973 (2 of 1974). s. 306.
[3]Subs. by the A.O. 1937, for "Local Government".
[4]Subs., *ibid.*, for "Governor-General in Council".
[5]The words "the Local Government" omitted. *ibid.*
[6]Proviso omitted by Act 24 of 1967, s. 11.
[7]Subs. by Act 3 of 1951, s. 3 and Sch., for "the States".

¹[(5) In this section, the appropriate Government means—

(*a*) in relation to any offences under section 5 not connected with a prohibited place or with a foreign power, the State Government; and

(*b*) in relation to any other offence, the Central Government.].

14. In addition and without prejudice to any powers which a Court may possess to order the exclusion of the public from any proceedings if, in the course of proceedings before a Court against any person for an offence under this Act or the proceedings on appeal, or in the course of the trial of a person under this Act, application is made by the prosecution, on the ground that the publication of any evidence to be given or of any statement to be made in the course of the proceedings would be prejudicial to the safety of the State, that all or any portion of the public shall be excluded during any part of the hearing, the Court may make an order to that effect, but the passing of sentence shall in any case take place in public. *[Exclusion of public from proceedings.]*

²[15. (*1*) If the person committing an offence under this Act is a company, every person who, at the time the offence was committed, was in charge of, and was responsible to, the company for the conduct of business of the company, as well as the company, shall be deemed to be guilty of the offence and shall be liable to be proceeded against and punished accordingly: *[Offences by companies.]*

Provided that nothing contained in this sub-section shall render any such person liable to such punishment provided in this Act if he proves that the offence was committed without his knowledge or that he exercised all due diligence to prevent the commission of such offence.

(2) Notwithstanding anything contained in sub-section (*1*), where an offence under this Act has been committed by a company and it is proved that the offence has been committed with the consent or connivance of, or is attributable to any negligence on the part of, any director, manager, secretary or other officer of the company, such director, manager, secretary or other officer shall also be deemed to be guilty of that offence and shall be liable to be proceeded against and punished accordingly.

Explanation.—For the purposes of this section,—

(*a*) "company" means a body corporate and includes a firm or other association of individual; and

(*b*) "director", in relation to a firm, means a partner in the firm.]

16. [*Repeals.*] *Rep. by the Repealing Act*, 1927 (12 *of* 1927), *s.* 2 *and Sch.*

---

¹Ins. by the A.O. 1937.
²Subs. by Act 24 of 1967, s. 12, for s. 15.

11

Information Law, Policy and Ethics: The Canadian Federal Government Experience

by Robert Peter Gillis, Director, Information Management Practices, Treasury Board of Canada

Canada has not escaped the ferment of the last two decades concerning information law and policy. As in other Western democracies, Canadians have been treated to a spate of discussion papers, royal commissions, task force reports, recommendations from standing committees, Government responses, draft Bills and final legislation.[1] The issues themselves are very familiar – the perceived need for greater access to government information, the related question of government accountability and transparency in transactions, the concurrent need for the protection of personal information, and the question of the adequacy and fairness of controls on sensitive government activities, particularly law enforcement and the security services.

The reasons behind this ferment are myriad. To some considerable extent, it results from the fears, concerns, and opportunities which spring from the final advent of that condition which has been dubbed the 'information society'. Government institutions have been fast to embrace the new information technology but politicians and bureaucrats have been much less sure about the legal and policy frameworks that are appropriate for melding traditional democratic concepts with modern social, political, and technological circumstances.

The fact remains, however, that information is the grist of modern governments. Without it, they cannot develop their policies or run their programmes. Some of this information is generated within government, but a much more significant amount is provided from outside. In some cases, information is submitted to obtain a benefit of some kind. In other cases, its provision is required by law. In still others, it is provided to advance common interests. At the same time, government in all modern industrialised

---

1 A good overview of this discussion is provided in Canada, House of Commons, Report of the Standing Committee on Justice and Solicitor General on the Review of the Access to Information Act and the Privacy Act, *Open and Shut: Enhancing the Right to Know and the Right to Privacy*. Chapter 1, (Ottawa, 1987).

countries, has become more complex. Its responsibilities have become more extensive and its powers and influence more pervasive, affecting more directly the lives of its citizens. The diversity and complexity of the issues involved, perhaps, is best illustrated by a quick journey through the most influential Canadian public documents of the last twenty years which have served to pace and direct debate and policy formation in this important field to look at how Canada has reacted to these at the Federal level, and finally to discuss some ethical matters which have arisen from this reaction.

1. The Events leading up to the Major Reform in Canadian Information Law and Policy at the Federal Level

The limits and consequences of this debate were stated clearly in the fine report of the Task Force on Government Information entitled *To Know and Be Known*, published in 1958. This group was established by Prime Minister Pierre Elliot Trudeau to look into the operation and the activities of Departmental information services and their advertising programmes at home and abroad. This would not appear to be fertile ground for sounding the first shot in the debate over information law and government accountability. The task force members – D'Iberville Fortier, Bernard Ostry, and Tom Ford – were, however, individuals not accustomed to taking a narrow approach to issues. The report took as its theme the discontent of the late 1960s and the 'developing tragedy' surrounding 'the lack of imaginative information for people who wish to participate in democratic action'. In brave terms, the report declared that: 'the information that the government gives to the people must be relevant to what the people require to be ... critical and constructive in the affairs of State; the information that the people give to the Government must be relevant to what the Government requires in order to do what the people want done.'

The task force went on to set clearly the themes that take us up to the present day:

> 'No one who gives any thought to the way democracies work can seriously question such hoary ideas. The arguments arise over how much information the people should have; over who should funnel it to them; over the dignity of Parliament and its duty to inform the people; over Cabinet solidarity; the status of the M.P.; official secrecy; and the proper roles for the press, television, Radio ...' [2]

Having raised these important issues there was little hope they could be resolved in one fell swoop. The task force is best remembered as the genesis of Information Canada, an innovative centralised approach to the provision

---

2 Canada, *To Know and Be Known: the Report of the Task Force on Government Information* (Ottawa, 1969), Vol. 1, p. 43.

of government information and service to the public, which was never able to rise above the perception that it was a Government propaganda machine. Its lasting contributions have been its prescient definition of the issues and the fastening on Canadian public policy of the 'duty to inform'. As the task force put it, Canadians should have the right 'to full, objective and timely information and the obligation of the State to provide such information about its programmes and policies (should) be publicly declared'. [3] Adoption of this principle of the 'duty to inform' moved information policy to a new level.

In 1972, protection of personal information emerged as an issue with the publication of the seminal study by the Federal Departments of Communications and Justice entitled *Computers and Privacy*. [4] The study grew out of concerns about the dangers posed by new information technology to personal privacy, and the problem of surveillance and Orwell's controlled society. While the report concluded that computerisation had not progressed to a state currently where it posed an actual threat to the privacy of Canadians, the potential existed for a technological revolution which could bring about this condition. The report raised awareness of the need for new legal and policy safeguards for the individual citizen confronting a faceless bureaucracy armed with computers to improve efficiency and, in the process, invade the citizen's informational privacy. The Trudeau Government reacted to the concerns raised by *Computers and Privacy* and the continuing visceral reaction to the ever spreading use of the social insurance number, the identifying device introduced in the 1960s for purposes of administering tax, pension, and unemployment benefits, with rudimentary privacy protection legislation.

Known as Part IV of the Canadian Human Rights Act, this legislation provided citizens with a right of access to personal information about themselves, which had been used by a government institution for an administrative purpose, and to correct or notate such information when they disagreed with it. [5] Exemptions were provided to the right of access where it might prove injurious to international relations, national defence or security, or Federal-Provincial relations; would disclose a Confidence of the Queen's Privy Council for Canada; would likely disclose information obtained by an investigative body; protection for penal information, solicitor/client privilege, and a few other special interests.

Basically, Part IV was not very adventurous legislation. The provisions stressed the right of access at the expense of fair information practices to

3 Ibid, p. 54.
4 Canada, Departments of Communications and Justice *Computers and Privacy* (Ottawa, 1972).
5 See Canada, Treasury Board, *Index of Federal Information Banks, 1979* (Ottawa, 1979).

control collection, use and disclosure of personal information by Government Departments. Nevertheless, it too broke new ground. The legislation did base a right of access in law; for the first time it began to codify those types of information which the Government would refuse to release and to describe these by injury and class tests; it identified Cabinet Confidences as a problem area; the legislation established the first requirements for a general accounting of personal information holdings by Departments; but, most important of all, it tackled the difficult problem of Ministerial responsibility by giving powers to the head of each Ministry to make decisions regarding access. Review of such decisions was by a Privacy Commissioner, who had strong investigatory powers, reported to Parliament but could not order disclosures. The Act stopped short of outright court review of decisions. All these features would appear later in more thorough-going access and privacy legislation.

While privacy legislation was unfolding, freedom of information initiatives were having a much more difficult time gaining any acceptance in Canadian public policy. The declarations of the Task force on Government Information were alright as statements of problems and intent, but the question remained how to seek solutions within established norms and political traditions. The 1970s, however, witnessed a growing mistrust of governments and bureaucracies which appeared to be distant from the public and lack any accountability for actions taken. These perceptions and problems are, to a great extent, still with us, but in the 1970s in Canada, with our proximity to the United States with its Watergate scandal and dirty tricks campaigns, political pressure became intense for freedom of information reform. Indeed, freedom of information became a rallying cry in the media for basic political reform that a simple access Act could not hope to fulfill. This development would cause considerable difficulties when access legislation was introduced finally in the early 1980s.

Faced with these rapidly changing circumstances, the Trudeau Government opted for administrative policies. In 1973, it tabled in Parliament a set of guidelines entitled *Notices of Motion for the Production of Papers*. [6] Its specific purpose was to assist government officials in responding to requests for information from Members of Parliament and the public. The guidelines established that information 'should' be produced unless it fell into one of sixteen exceptions. These exceptions involved the normal fields of defence, international relations, security, and Federal-Provincial relations but also went on to identify Cabinet documents and 'internal departmental memoranda'. The guidelines explained that such memoranda should be drafted in a way which separated recommendations from factual and analytical material,

---

6 Canada, Department of the Secretary of State, *Legislation on Public Access to Government Documents* (Ottawa, 1977) p. 31.

in order that the latter material could be released. Still very sound advice to public servants.

Later in the same year, another directive was issued dealing with access to public records. [7] These guidelines affirmed Ministerial control over the transfer of historical records to the then Public Archives of Canada (now the National Archives of Canada) and over public access to such records. These two sets of guidelines were referred eventually, along with a Private Member's Bill on freedom to information, to the Standing Joint Committee on Regulations and other Statutory Instruments. This Committee met throughout 1974 and 1975 and was influenced very much in its deliberations by a Tory Member of Parliament, Ged Baldwin, who was to win the title of the father of freedom of information legislation in Canada. The Committee endorsed the concept in late 1975 and the House of Commons approved its report in February 1976.

These events put pressure on the Government to act. It tabled a so-called Green Paper in mid-1977 which explored various options for freedom of information legislation. [8] It is fair to say that this discussion paper was not a good representation of events as they had now developed. Its recurring theme was worry over how to preserve Ministerial control over release and refusal of information. Obviously, the Government remained strongly opposed to independent review of Ministerial decisions to withhold information and would only later decide to experiment with the limited review mechanism set out in Part IV. The Green Paper was given to the Joint Committee for study. In mid-1975, it came out resoundingly in favour of legislation containing a broad right of access and only a very few narrow and specific exemptions. This position was supported by the Canadian Bar Association (CBA), which produced a model draft Bill. Public debate on the issue intensified, led by a number of national interest groups, as the Liberal Government declared that its own Bill would be ready soon in preparation for a Federal election campaign in the Spring of 1979.

Before turning to the events of the early 1980s which were to result in major changes to Canadian information law, it is necessary to review briefly one other report. This is the work of the *Commission of Inquiry Concerning Certain Activities of the Royal Canadian Mounted Police*. [9] Established in 1977 and known as the McDonald Commission after its Chairman, Mr Justice D. C. McDonald, the Commission investigated several instances of alleged criminal activities by the Security Services of the Royal Canadian Mounted Police

---

7 Ibid, p. 35.

8 Canada, Department of the Secretary of State, *Green paper on Legislation on Public Access to Government Documents* (Ottawa, 1977).

9 Canada, Commission of Inquiry Concerning Certain Activities of the Royal Canadian Mounted Police, Second Report, *Freedom and Security Under the Law* (Ottawa, 1981).

(R.C.M.P.), particularly in dealing with separatist activities in the Province of Quebec. The title of the Commission's second report, *Freedom and Security Under the Law*, published in 1961, gives a good flavour to the extensive hearings. They ranged over how the security services should be mandated and controlled in a democratic State; how the R.C.M.P. should go about obtaining personal information, particularly from other Government Departments and the Provinces; use of intrusive technologies to collect evidence, security screening techniques, and amendments to the Official Secrets Act. There is not space in this paper to deal in detail with security issues but it is important to bear in mind that the efforts at reform of information laws during this period were played out against a back-drop of critical study of accountability in an area that every Government finds most sensitive.

2. The Major Changes in Canadian Information Law and Policy at the Federal Level

It is time to turn now from those events which led up to the major reform in Canadian information law and policy at the Federal level in Canada and deal briefly with those changes. As we have seen, there was considerable study of information issues during the 1970s. Study, however, can be a mask for delay where no political consensus exists for action. Essentially, there was a need to break a log-jam. This was done during the short duration of the Conservative Clark Government in 1979. The Tories had espoused the Joint Committee's position on freedom of information and now set about quickly drafting legislation as a priority of the new Administration.

The Bill is commonly known as C-15 and was entitled the Freedom of Information Act. [10] This draft Bill, modelled in part, on the Canadian Bar Association's work, rapidly moved the debate from one of philosophy to hard political realities. It created an enforceable right of access subject to specific and limited exemptions; met the objection of Ministerial responsibility by making each Minister the head of his or her institution for purposes of the Act; provided a strict, class exemption for Confidences of the Queen's Privy Council for Canada; carried forward the idea of an information Ombudsman as the first level of appeal and provided recourse to the Federal Court for final review of access issues. The Clark Government also contemplated, but never introduced, a new Privacy Act, which would have provided strong guarantees for the protection of personal information as a counterbalance to the right of freer access. It was planning also to deliver on a Tory pledge to better control collection and use of the social insurance number.

Bill C-15 is important because it presented the first comprehensive attempt to balance a strong right of access with exceptions which provided

---

10 Canada, Bill C-15, 31 at Parliament, 28 Elizabeth II, 1979.

effective protection for those public and private interests which it was vital to protect in defence of good government. It dramatically shifted the debate from if it could be done to how it could be done. For many this would be admitted only grudgingly but in reality a major milestone had been passed.

The Clark Government was defeated in the House before it could pass C-15 into law. It mattered very little, however, for the reform of information law was underway. A reconstructed Trudeau Government indicated in the Throne Speech that it would be proceeding with an Access to Information Act, a revamped Privacy Act and amendments to the Federal Court Act and Canada Evidence Act to remove broad provisions which permitted a Minister to escape giving evidence on certain subjects by simple certification. Amendments were contemplated also to the Official Secrets Act but these were never proceeded with.

With this agenda, the period 1980 to 1981 became truly a water-shed in Canadian law and policy. When is added to this the decision to move forward with legislation to create a new Canadian Security and Intelligence Service, establish its mandate in law and to create a Security Intelligence Review Committee to look at the Service's activities each year, including its collection and use of information, for purposes of reporting to Parliament, then these few years take on even greater importance. This is not to say that this was a period of calm deliberation. The conflicts in Parliament were substantial. If there was a basic consensus to proceed with reform of information law and policy, the charting of the route and the speed of progress left ample room for political dispute.

Bill C-43, the Liberal Government' s access and privacy legislation, enjoyed the fetching title *An Act to enact the Access to Information Act and the Privacy Act, to amend the Federal Court Act and the Canada Evidence Act, and to amend certain other Acts in conseqence thereof.* [11] They spent two years in Parliamentary Committee, where over a hundred briefs were presented by interested individuals, associations and other interest groups. Many amendents were presented and, at the eleventh hour, the Prime Minister intervened to indicate that the Bill would die on the order paper unless the Opposition consented to the exclusion of Cabinet Confidences from the legislation. There remained too much worry that the Acts would serve to erode the Cabinet solidarity so vital to Westminster-style government. This amendment was dubbed the 'Mack truck' clause by the Opposition members for driving a hole in the legislation. [12] Nevertheless, shortly afterwards all party agreement was secured to move the Acts through Parliament before the end of the session.

---

11 Canada, An Act to enact the Access to Information Act and the Privacy Act, to amend the Federal Court Act and the Canada Evidence Act etc. 29-30-31 Elizabeth II, Chapter III, 1982.

12 *Ottawa Citizen*, 9 June 1982 *'Gutted' FOI Bill Angers Opposition.*

The passage of this legislation was truly the equivalent of crossing the Rubicon. The Acts mark a movement, however tentative, from the tradition of absolute secrecy in the practice of government, where the touchstones have been the Official Secrets Act and the public servant's oath of secrecy, to an ethic marked by attention to balancing a number of competing interests. To attempt to find the appropriate balance between the need to keep secret those activities vital to the proper functioning of a Westminster-style government while recognising and meeting an equally legitimate public right to know, about particular government activities. To protect personal, business, and other private interest information shared with the Government but to balance against this need a public interest in disclosure, particularly when such information relates to public health, public safety, or protection of the environment. To meet the pressing need to investigate and carry on surveillance of individuals and groups which pose a threat to the peace and security of the nation but to do so within the rule of law and by means which do not violate ultimate right to informational privacy of other citizens. These are but a few of the difficult issues involved in coming to a new ethical position on information issues in a public policy milieu which no longer can rely on absolute secrecy as its prime basis of operation. It has been said that access and privacy legislation are having and will continue to have an impact on the practice of politics in Canada equivalent to that of Auditor General's Act and the Charter of Human Rights and Freedoms. [13] Some may still look back longingly to a simpler, golden age before access and privacy but there is little room for back-tracking; rather there is a constant need to take stock of the new environment and to search out new verities to govern these most difficult and complex challenges to the practice of modern government.

Having identified these two Acts, as major catalysts for change, it is necessary to briefly describe their structure and intent before turning to their administrative impact.

2.1 The Access to Information Act

There is no doubt that the Access to Information Act has replaced the Official Secrets Act as number one in the information law firmament. There are public commentators who would contend that this is little more than a name change. As discussed above, this is not a fair assessment. A more fair critique is that any régime based on legal rights to promote public access to information is by its very nature confrontational and, thus, frustrates good communication between a Government and its citizens. There is a good deal of truth in this contention but it can also be argued that there is very little bite behind any access régime that does not have an ultimate guarantee in law.

---

13 Toronto *Star*, 5 July 1988, *National Affairs* by Carol Goar.

The public policy challenge is to balance both sides of the equation – easy access to non-exempt information and effective, inexpensive ways to make decisions on whether or not to refuse release of information of a type which Government Departments may wish to keep closer to their vest. It is somewhat of an axiom that the success a Government has in doing the former will ease its job in establishing credibility when it feels it must withhold information from the public.

The Access to Information Act captures both thoughts in its purpose statement. It demonstrates its close descent from Bill C-15 in setting out an enforceable right of access, in accordance with the principles that government information should be available to the public, that necessary exceptions to that right should be limited and specific, and that decisions on the disclosure of information should be reviewable independently of government. [14] The preamble goes on, however, to state that this Act is intended to complement and not replace existing procedures for access to government information and is not intended to limit in any way access to the type of government information that is normally available to the general public. [15]

This dual purpose statement gives the Act a much more pervasive effect than might otherwise be the case. There is a presumption that information normally will be available to the public on request, either informally or through formal application under the legislation, unless an exemption applies to it. The Act then goes on to establish the formal processes for making access requests. It sets time limits; an application fee and charges for searching, preparing and photocopying records; and procedures for notifying applicants. The Act also defines what is a government record in a very inclusive manner so that it covers every media including computer data, draft documents, and so-called personal records, such as desk calendars, when they are used in the conduct of public business. It does not cover, however, published materials which are dealt with under government communications and information management policies, which require that publications be indexed adequately and made available for public reference.

The heart of the Act is its exclusion and exemption provisions. As hinted at above, these exemptions serve not only to determine what will be released and refused to public access under the legislation but also set a 'bottom line' to what Parliament considers to be that information which a Government has a right to withhold in any circumstances. If there are no grounds for excluding or exempting a record under the Act, there is no other legal reason by which to refuse disclosure. This fact has a profound impact on broader information policy.

---

14 29-30-31 Elizabeth II, Chapter III, schedules 1, s. 2.

15 Ibid. See also the paper by Rosamund Thomas 'Access to Information: the Experience of Other Countries' in this Volume, Appendix III, pp. 599-633.

Without going into the technicalities of these exceptions to the right of access, protection is provided in the following areas. Absolute protection is given to Cabinet Confidences by excluding them from the Act and by surrounding protection in the Canada Evidence Act which ensures non-disclosure through a certification process. A major effort has been made in Canada to ensure the confidentiality of Cabinet proceedings, which has long been embodied in constitutional conventions. The only broadening of access rights in this area has been to give the Auditor General some access to financial analyses outside portions of Cabinet documents which make recommendations to Ministers. [16]

Mandatory protection is given to information obtained 'in confidence' from the government of an international organisation of States, a foreign government, or Provincial, Regional, or Municipal government; personal information obtained or compiled by the Government; confidential business information; and information which is prohibited from disclosure under another Act of Parliament. With the exception of the latter point, these can generally be referred to as provisions dealing with interests outside the Canadian Government. Normally, information can be released where the affected party consents. In the case of business information absolute protection is given only to trade secret documentation, while confidential financial, commercial, scientific, or technical information must be shown to be treated consistently in a confidential manner in order to qualify for exemption. This exemption is also modified by specific overrides for product or environmental testing and authorisation to disclose information which is not a trade secret where the public interest in health, safety, or protection of the environment outweighs in importance damage to the business interest involved. The whole business information exemption turns around a complicated notification procedure worked out with the interests involved and is easily the most difficult exemption for Government Departments to deal with. [17] For those areas traditionally thought of as the heart of government activities, protection is a little more varied. For law enforcement, information obtained or compiled by an institution qualifying as a Federal investigatory body, which is less than twenty years old, is given pretty rigorous protection with discretion lying with the head of the investigatory body. For other enforcement and regulatory bodies the discretion to refuse is given but must be exercised in the context of an injury test to the enforcement or investigatory activity. For international affairs, defence, and detection, prevention, or suppression of subversive or hostile activities, again an injury test is used, combined with exercise of discretion. Similar tests are involved with

---

16 Canada, Order in Council, P.C. 1985-3783 27 December, 1985.

17 Canada, Treasury Board, *Interim Policy Guide The Access to Information Act and the Privacy Act* (Ottawa, 1983), Part II, pp. 65-81.

Federal-Provincial affairs and economic interests of the Government of Canada. In these situations, the injury must be demonstrated to be specific, current and probable.

Finally, an exemption is provided for advice, recommendations and accounts of consultations and deliberations, as well as a few other types of documentation prepared internally to government. This has also proven to be a controversial exemption because it is based on a class description of 'advice' documents and the discretion of the head of the institution. Public criticism has been that it covers too much, while those in Government are not sure that it is effective in protecting the frankness of exchanges between Ministerial and senior Departmental staff which is essential to good, effective government in a Westminster-style government. It should be noted that advice provided by consultants hired out of public funds is not covered by this exemption. This is by no means a full and comprehensive look at the exemption criteria set out in the Act but it does give a flavour of how they operate and indicate that a vast amount of information is not subject to any restriction.

2.2 The Privacy Act

Turning to the Privacy Act, a different but equally important purpose statement guides its application. Its purpose is to protect the privacy of individuals with respect to personal information about themselves held by a government institution and to provide individuals with a right of access to such information. [18] It is wondered sometimes why Canada chose to relate access and privacy legislation so closely. The reason is fairly simple. The Access to Information Act contains a prohibition against the disclosure of personal information except in very limited circumstances usually involving consent. There is no 'unwarranted invasion of privacy' such as in American legislation. Privacy in information is viewed as an equal, if not more important, right than the public's right to know. Thus, there is no right to personal information in the access legislation and all releases are made under the Privacy Act.

The exemption criteria governing access by individuals to information about themselves are almost identical to those in the Access to Information Act. Of course, there is no exception for business information and, more importantly, no outright exemption for advice. This difference is based on the principle that as a basic right individuals should know what is being said and who is saying it when the Government is making a decision about them. It is also for this reason that the definition of personal information in the Act extends to 'the views or opinions of another individual about the individual' involved. There is one exception to the general rule and that

---

18 29-30-31 Elizabeth II, Chapter III, Schedule 2, s. 1.

relates to the 'peer review' process for grants and awards, where the academic community declared that it was not ready for this type of openness. This does not mean, of course, that criminals or espionage agents can find out what advice is being given about them. Such information can be exempted under an appropriate subject related provision, rather it means that advice cannot be refused in a blanket manner.

The guts of the Privacy Act, however, is its 'code of fair information practices'. This code, set out in sections 4 to 8 of the legislation, has been developed in recognition of the principle that the right of the individual to privacy includes the right to control the collection, use and disclosure of information about him or herself and, when exceptions to this principle exist, to know what information has been collected, what uses can be made of it and to whom and for what purposes the information may be disclosed. [19]

The code operates basically on three simple yet far-reaching axioms. First, no personal information can be collected by a government institution unless it relates directly to an operating programme. Second, in most cases (law enforcement being one obvious exception) information is to be collected directly from the individual to whom it relates and a declaration made as to the purposes for which it is to be put. Personal information is to be used for the purposes for which it has been obtained or compiled or for use consistent with those purposes, unless the individual consents to other uses. Disclosure to other third parties is permitted under a few restricted circumstances specified in the Act such as to assist in lawful investigations, to assist in legal proceedings, to meet agreements with other governments, and to Federal Members of Parliament to aid the individual to whom the information relates. It must be emphasised, however, that no right of access is established for third parties. Instead, discretion lies with an institution as to whether or not it will disclose the information. An equally important principle is the accounting and publication for public inspection of all purposes, uses, consistent uses and disclosures of personal data, including exempt data such as that from security and law enforcement agencies.

The code of fair information practices brings Canadian Federal activities into line with the OECD Privacy Guidelines. This is fine but the question of compliance is a reasonable one. Under both Acts, the head of each government institution, in most circumstances the Minister, bears ultimate responsibility for administering their provisions. Appeal lies under both Acts to the Federal Court of Canada but this only generally applies to questions of access to specific information. The vast majority of independent review lies at the first level with the two information Ombudsmen, the Information Commissioner and the Privacy Commissioner. The Ombudsman concept has

---

19 *Interim Policy Guide*, Part III, Section 7.

been adopted to try to solve complaints under the Acts without the high costs of going to court. The experiment has been reasonably successful.

Both Commissioners are servants of Parliament and report to it annually. They are classic Ombudsmen in that they have investigative and subpoena powers similar to a Judge or the Superior Court but in the end they only make a recommendation to the Minister heading the institution involved. The Information Commissioner generally investigates specific complaints from applicants about refusals of access, fees and other relevant matters. On the other hand, the Privacy Commissioner does handle specific complaints but also is given extensive powers to audit Departments in how they are applying the code of fair information practices. Thus, as the Access to Information Act impinges on how the Government protects information and releases it, the Privacy Act introduces through the audit function a 'privacy conscience' into the heart of those government operations dealing with personal information.

2.3 Other Statutory Activity

These formal structures and legal dicta would have been enough on their own to stimulate considerable attention to information policy issues. They have been combined with other factors, however, to make the need for that attention absolutely essential. The Official Secrets Act still sits as an 'eminence grise' behind all information law. Not substantially amended since 1911, it remains useful in cases of espionage and misuse, retention, or possession of information crucial to the national interest but usually has proved too heavy a hand to use in modern 'leaking' cases. The latter have tended to be dealt with under the breach of trust and theft provisions of the Criminal Code. [20] It should be noted, however, that a public servant, operating with authority under the access and privacy legislation and in good faith, is not subject to prosecution under the Official Secrets Act.

The Criminal Code is coming into play also as a deterrent against the misappropriation of personal information, with amendments in 1985 creating offences to preserve the integrity of computer systems and services, though it does not seem likely that there will be amendments to make the unauthorised appropriation of information an offence. [21] Reference should be made also to the revised Copyright Act, which retains a strong Crown Copyright provision thus enabling the Government to carry out publishing arrangements, including the publishing of computer databases in cooperation with the private sector, and to the new National Archives of Canada Act, which establishes strong legal requirements for the transfer of

---

20 *Revised Statutes of Canada 1985*, Chapter 0-5, an Act respecting official secrets.

21 Canada, *Access and Privacy: The Steps Ahead* (Ottawa, 1987) pp. 3-4.

all government records of historical significance to the National Archives. [22]

This statutory activity has heralded a trend in Government Departments to give a much higher priority to information issues. Not only have Departments had to deal with access and privacy matters but they have had to cope with the challenges posed by end-user computing to traditional file keeping and the desire of civil servants and the public alike to have access to a host of data systems both within Departments and outside. This activity has necessitated also a more coordinated public policy approach within the Federal Government. This new approach started with very specific problems. Policies had to be written and implemented to administer the access and privacy legislation, Justice lawyers had to make legal interpretations of particular provisions, the Privy Council Office had to make judgements about what was and was not a Cabinet Confidence. This development has grown into a central policy and coordination system; where the Privy Council Office is responsible for maintaining the integrity of the approach to Confidences; the Department of Justice has a role in maintaining a broad overview of the application of the two Acts; and Treasury Board Secretariat has the job of developing access and privacy policies to facilitate administration of the legislation within the broader context of information management plans and strategies. This arrangement is represented in Figure 1. It is a somewhat complicated structure but one which provides for a broader policy consideration which both places access and privacy requirements in perspective and allows many issues surrounding modern information practices to be addressed in a more integrated fashion. The final part of this paper discusses some of the major ethical dilemmas posed by the attempt to reform public policies in regard to information practices.

3. Ethical Dilemmas posed by the Attempt to Reform Public Policies at the Federal level in regard to Information Practices

Figure 2 provides an overview of how the various information spheres are being drawn together and related to one another in a policy sense at the Federal level in Canada. Those policies are bound primarily to each other, however, by an ethical steel cord which stresses balance, in the sense equipoise between the contrasting needs of open government and effective government, equity, fairness, and transparency. This paper has described, in

---

22 Canada, An Act respecting the National Archives of Canada and records of government institutions of Canada and to amend other Acts in relation thereto, 35-36 Elizabeth II, Chapter 1, 25 March 1987, and Consumer and Corporate Affairs Canada and Department of Communications, from *Gutenberg to Telidon: A Guide to Canada's Copyright Revision Proposals* (Ottawa, 1984) p. 8.

general terms, how these basic ethical principles have been pushed to the forefront in Canadian Federal information practices through passage of the Access to Information Act and the Privacy Act. They are kept there, in large part, by an on-going Parliamentary review which has been built into both pieces of legislation and the creation of information Ombudsmen, in the offices of the Information and Privacy Commissioners, who serve and report to Parliament. This very public attention has raised and continues to raise information practices issues which demand public policy solutions and the search for those solutions slowly strengthens and tightens that cord. A sampler of issues from the last five years follows.

3.1 Fair Information Practices

Considerable space was devoted under heading Two in this paper to describing the 'code of fair information practices' set out in the Privacy Act. Simply put, it embodies the ethical principles that an individual should have a general right, mitigated only by limited law enforcement and security exceptions, to have personal information collected directly from him/herself, to know what it will be used for, to be able to ensure its accuracy, and to know to whom it will be disclosed. Even in the law enforcement and security areas additional protection has been added through the 1985 Statute Law (Canadian Charter of Rights and Freedoms) Amendment which ended powers to enter premises, including private dwellings, without a warrant to authorise such entry. [23] The key principle here is informing individuals what is being done with their personal information and, where this is not possible, to have a due process to ensure an invasion of privacy is legitimate.

Fairness in information practices was resented initially by Departments as cumbersome and inefficient. Anything short of strong legal requirements would have been difficult to implement initially. These practices are accepted now as a normal way of carrying on government activities and are being implemented in fields beyond personal information where greater transparency is being demanded. Perhaps, the most difficult area to control in the use of personal information is the technological advances which make relatively easy the matching or linkage of such data for administrative purposes. In Canada, an additional complication is the national social insurance number, which is viewed by many as a prime device for linking together personal information banks and thus creating a national identifier. In this field, as in the others, informing the public about how information is being used and what is planned in matching or linkage is the key to fairness and, usually, avoiding complaints. The Federal Government has just introduced a new data matching policy which features notification of the Privacy Commissioner in advance and public accounting for all matching activities. The same policy

---

23 *The Steps Ahead*, p. 4.

also limits the use of the social insurance number in Federal programmes and requires Departments to tell an individual under what authority they are collecting it. Departments cannot refuse a right, privilege or benefit due an individual because he or she has refused to provide the number, unless its provision is required by law. In this way, the Canadian Government is trying to ensure that the Privacy Act remains on the 'cutting-edge' in selling standards for effective controls on the collection, use and disclosure of personal information. [24]

3.2 The Openness/Secrecy Conundrum

There is an axiom in freedom of information that there are always too many exemptions for those seeking access and never enough for the government institution which controls the records being requested. Under heading Two in this paper there was considerable discussion about how the exclusions and exemption criteria in the Access to Information Act prescribe the 'bottom line' on the types of information which the Federal Government normally will hold closer to its vest. This is not, however, a static concept but rather an uneasy truce where the competing and compelling public interests in openness and of effective government are debated.

During the period 1986-87, Federal access and privacy legislation underwent a detailed review by a Parliamentary Committee. That committee came to the conclusion that the balance between openness and secrecy in the Access to Information Act was not aligned properly. It recommended that all current mandatory exemptions be altered to an injury basis; that Ministerial discretion to refuse information be tightly circumscribed; that most exemptions include an override geared to arguments based on release in the public interest, and that Cabinet Confidences be included under the scope of the Act as a new mandatory exemption. [25] These recommendations, which were endorsed by all committee members, including those from the Governing party, were designed to alter significantly the balance of competing interests agreed to by Parliament in 1982.

In responding to these recommendations the Government did not retreat from its commitment to effective freedom of information legislation. It declared firmly that 'there is a compelling public interest in openness, to ensure that the Government is fully accountable for its goals and that its performance can be measured against these goals ... It ensures fairness in government decision-making and permits the airing and reconciliation of divergent views across the country.' But the Government went on to say that it believed the Access to Information Act already achieved the greatest

---

24 Ibid and Canada, Treasury Board, *Policy on Data-matching and Control of the Social Insurance Number*, (Ottawa, TBS Circular 1989-12, 1989).

25 *Open and Shut*, Chapters II and IV.

amount of openness presently possible. It concluded with the declaration that it is important to remember that there is also a compelling public interest in effective government and that the rights of third parties and individuals must be recognised. There is a need to protect vital State and private interests. There is also the need to find the appropriate relationship between open government and the Parliamentary system of government, which is dependent on the collective and individual responsibility of Ministers and their confidential relationship with officials. [26]

Balance of competing interests and the slow adaptation of Parliamentary democracy to the information age will mark the pace of this important debate in Canada and elsewhere.

3.3 Government Security Policy

In Canada, as in other countries with similar legislation, access and privacy Acts impact directly on security policies. Put at its simplest, if an institution cannot refuse public access to a document there is no reason to classify it, employ expensive measures to protect it from access, and subject its creators or custodians to intrusive security screening procedures.

In 1986, a major effort was made to revamp Canadian Departmental security policy with these principles in mind. [27] The security system itself was breaking under its own weight. There was no authoritative standard as to what types of information deserved classification for security protection, the military/international affairs classifications were used across government and this resulted in the security screening of thousands of individuals who would never come in contact with any information vital to the national interest. The system lacked sense, was expensive and was becoming more so as the demand for security clearances mounted annually, and was ineffective in providing security protection.

The first reform was to establish clearly that the security classification system would apply only to national interest information, that is information which concerns the defence and maintenance of the social, political and economic stability of the country. This category of information is circumscribed by the exemption criteria of the Access to Information Act dealing generally with Federal-Provincial affairs, international affairs, defence, security, and national economic matters. This reform has reduced substantially the number of security clearances required annually by public servants while enabling the government to concentrate on the information and assets requiring strict security measures. Almost coincidental with this policy reform, the legislation creating the Canadian Security and Intelligence

---

26 *The Steps Ahead*, pp. 30-31.

27 Canada, Treasury Board, *Government Security Policy* (Ottawa, Circular 1986-40, 1986).

Service made major changes to the security screening process itself which were intended to bring into it principles of equity, fairness and balance.

The first change was to define tightly a threat to the security of Canada as including activities such as espionage, sabotage, detrimental foreign-influenced threats, internal threats of violence against Canada or another State, and violent overthrow of the State but excluding lawful advocacy, protest or dissent, unless carried on in connection with the other activities. This change served to limit the reasonable grounds for refusing a clearance somewhat. The more substantial change was to add due process to the whole procedure by permitting an individual who has been refused a security clearance to seek redress of his or her case before the independent body set up to review security matters, the Security Intelligence Review Committee.

The second reform of security policies was to create a new category of sensitive information based on the remaining exemptions of the access and privacy legislation. The majority of information falling into this category involves law enforcement, confidential business documentation, and personal data. It has been created largely because of the heightened awareness of the value of such information and real instances where sensitive documents have been stolen by employees. The most serious incident in this regard was the theft of 16 million tax files stored on microfiche. [28] Employees handling this type of information do not receive security clearances but rather undergo a less intrusive reliability check done by Departmental officers. This check still, however, involves finger-printing and may also require a credit check, depending on the nature of the job. Due process for refusals is given through the normal employee grievance process. Once again, balance is the operative word in finding appropriate ways to protect classified and sensitive information from a variety of threats to its unauthorised use and providing personnel screening which is effective but has an effective appeal process to protect the employee.

3.4 Disclosure in the Public Interest

Access and privacy legislation recognises the public interest in disclosure in two separate areas; one dealing with confidential business information and the other with personal information. Both provisions are extremely difficult to apply because they bestow on the head of an institution the discretion to release to the public documentation which would otherwise be exempt on a mandatory basis. For reasons of space, this paper will cover only the issue of confidential business information.

The provision relates to the important issues of public health, public

---

28 Toronto *Star*, 23 November, 1986, *Diminishing privacy is a part of life in information age.*

safety, or protection of the environment. The test is a rigorous one for these interests must 'clearly outweigh in importance' the prejudice or injury to the business interest involved. It may be fairly asked why if this information is so vital to public health, safety, or protection of the environment, it is being released under access legislation. However, as is the case for other matters, the formal access tests pervade informal activities. The provision is so difficult because it asks an institution potentially to breach the trust of a business with which it carries on some type of activity and may regard, to some extent as a client, in favour of another client – the public. This dilemma may cause some particular catharsis for civil servants, especially those employed in regulatory agencies, who have to clarify carefully in their own minds the mission and role of the institution for which they work. In some instances, the conduct of the business will mitigate the difficulty of the decision. If there is evidence of illegality, breach of statutory authority or wilful misconduct, then the decision is easier. When the problems tend to be more minor, but continue despite continued warnings from the regulator, then it is much more difficult to make a decision.

It is not surprising that government institutions try to avoid decision-making of this nature. In cases which have tended in the direction (for example, meat inspection reports and aircraft maintenance reports), there is a precedent, so far up-held in court, of releasing information collected by inspectors through observation, while protecting confidential information provided by the business. Test results, including those on tainted tuna, which forced the resignation of a Minister and the closure of a fish plant, were released in compliance with the Access Act. Again balance and equity come into play in making extremely difficult judgements about which public interest should prevail. [29]

3.5 Duty to Inform/User Pay

This issue delves into slightly different ethical questions. Questions that are only beginning to be explored in Canada. This paper began with reference to the 'duty to inform'. [30] As a principle, this continues to form a crucial part of Federal information policy in Canada. It underwrites the important principle that the Access to Information Act complements and does not replace existing informal procedures for obtaining information. These informal requests come in millions each year through telephone enquiries, letters to Ministers and many other channels. It is essential that government institutions respond

---

29 *Interim Policy Guide*, Part II and Canada, Federal court, Trial Division, Order in the matter of Piller Sausages and Delicatessens Ltd. and the Minister of Agriculture and the Information Commissioner of Canada and Jim Romahn, 8 September 1987; and Order in the Matter of Air Atonabee Ltd. and the Minister of Transport, 19 October 1988.

30 *To Know and be Known.*

in a way which ensures that such requests or even a small proportion of them do not surface as formal access requests. Such a result would lead to a litigious system detrimental to good communication and lead to scarce resources being directed to processing access requests.

Government policy also clearly states, however, that provision of information is costly and should be undertaken only where there is a clear duty to inform or where the user is willing to pay for it. It further stipulates that the full cost of providing information to serve the proprietary interests of individuals should not be borne by taxpayers at large. [31] The policy reflects the fact that information is an expensive good to collect, compile, prepare, produce, and disseminate and that in a time of scarce resources user charges are an increasingly important way to defray costs.

The concept is that such charges will be reduced or waived where information

— is needed to make use of a service or programme;

— is required to understand a major new priority, law, policy, programme, or service;

— explains rights, entitlements, and obligations;

— informs the public about dangers to health, safety, or protection of the environment;

— is personal information or the fees have been waived under the Access Act.

This concept seems fair but it raises for some fears that government information will become so expensive that it will be available only to those who can afford it. This could be a major question of equity and fairness in the future, especially as more and more information is made available through specialised technologies. Does the rich or specially equipped citizen have more information rights than others?

The question of user charges also presents itself under the Access to Information Act. Figure 3 shows who makes actual access requests. The greatest majority are made by businesses, which candidly admit they are spying on their competitors or selling the information. This spying by businesses is not unique to Canada. In the United States, it is estimated that over seventy percent of their approximately 400,000 freedom of information requests are made by businesses. This raises the larger issue of whether or not such use falls within the original spirit of the legislation. It is contended here that it does not. These requests are being made so that information can

---

31 Canada, Treasury Board, *Communications Policy of the Government of Canada*, Chapter 480, *Administrative Policy Manual* (Ottawa, 1988).

be repackaged and sold; to aid the competitive position or other proprietary interests of businesses; or to meet the requirements of social interest groups. All these reasons for acquiring information are quite legitimate but there is considerable room to question whether such applicants deserve to obtain it under the generous fee system now operating under the Act, which was designed to not penalise individuals in obtaining information by which to better exercise their democratic rights. In the United States, they have gone to a multi-tiered fee system to meet this problem. This fee system is a complicated way to restore more appropriate uses of freedom of information legislation but discrimination between types of applicants also may be the only way to stop giving away expensive information to commercial users.

3.6 Public Service Values

By way of conclusion, it is appropriate to turn to the subject of public service values. There is in the Canadian public service a morale problem. In this, it does not seem to differ from other countries. Studies have found that the lower levels of the management cadre have a considerably diminished job satisfaction the further they are from the Deputy Minister and have less enthusiasm for the challenges and rewards of their jobs though they tend to have loyalty to the Canadian public and are oriented to quality of service and service to the public. [32] Earlier in this paper, there was discussion about the change brought about in 1983 with the proclamation of the Access to Information Act and the Privacy Act. Traditional values centred on the Official Secrets Act and the oath of office were replaced by much more complex and much less clear rules. There were some public servants who genuinely believed more openness was necessary but many more found a sense of security and self-worth in the traditional approach and were loath to admit that it was not coping well with the needs of a modern democracy.

Thus it is fair to say that, while the retreat from secrecy was not a major factor to the decline in public service morale, it has contributed to a sense of general malaise. Part IV of the Canadian Human Rights Act caused a minor tremor when it required that public servants be accountable to individuals for decisions they made about them. This accountability still rankles with some public servants but usually only when they are dealing with a chronic complainer or a troublesome employee. Most can see the value of fair information practices because they appreciate the complexity of modern government, its potential to unwittingly trench on individual rights, and probably, also, can see the day when they personally may need the protection of the Privacy Act.

---

32 Notes for Remarks by Paul M. Tellier, Clerk of the Privy Council and Secretary to the 1988 APEX Symposium, Ottawa, Canada, January 21, 1988, 'The Obligations of Public Service'.

The Access to Information Act is another matter. It cuts to the quick of traditional public service culture. Requests arrive in what is, at best, an unstructured manner and, at worst, a capricious one. They land on a bureaucracy already stretched by budgetary restraint, carry the power of law to compel a reply, and often come from a well-known critic of the Department or a professional requestor. But this is really only a superficial condition. Access requests can also cause considerable unease, along with resentment. They peel back the layers of bureaucracy to reveal who made the decision, who was involved in giving the advice, and whether all the options were properly considered. This probing is not a welcome condition for anyone and it can, at times, be most difficult for a public service bred to official secrecy and anonymity. Indeed, given the circumstances, it can be said that the Canadian public service has borne up reasonably well during its six years' experience under the new rules.

Perhaps it is the perception that protection for the deliberative privilege (the ability to give advice and carry on consultation and deliberation) has been eroded, which has been most troubling. Protection of this 'deliberative space' at Ministerial and senior bureaucratic levels is essential in a Westminster-style government. The Canadian access legislation does provide wide protection in this area but any request probing into this sensitive realm brings concerns about the chilling effect on the deliberative process and warnings about advice becoming grey, less frank or being given orally as opposed to written.

All too often elaborate and wasteful shell games are indulged in to hide the sources of advice and recommendation. There are also threats to destroy documents after use and, at the extreme, as with one American law enforcement officer, to take sensitive documentation home and store it under his bed to remove it from the ambit of freedom of information. The trick is to guarantee and preserve the 'deliberative space' while conceding considerable transparency and opportunity to debate divergent views. This balancing process is best done outside the formal scope of access to information. It really requires close attention to the wider responsibility to ensure a flow of information so that citizens can fully understand, respond to and influence policy development and implementation. Only when this flow of information is occurring on a regular basis will absolute protection for the 'deliberative space' gain credibility with the public. This is nothing more than a restatement of the 'duty to inform'. It is, perhaps, appropriate that this paper should at long last return to the principles of 'To Know and Be Known' because the 'duty to inform', at its broadest, captures the essential ethics of fairness, equity, transparency and balance between the compelling public interests of open and effective government necessary for information practices in a modern democracy. The challenge is considerable but failure to meet it will leave public policy, like Matthew Arnold, in the *Grande*

Chartreuse, 'wandering between two worlds, one dead the other powerless to be born'...[33]

Postscript [34]

The general trends discussed in this paper have not changed since it was written in 1989; nor has the challenge set forth in the conclusion. Canada will be entering its first decade of access to information and privacy legislation in 1991. The need for balance in applying such legislation remains, as does the need for fulsome communication of government information outside legislative frameworks, and the absolute requirement for responsive consultative government to underpin effective democracy.

The growth of access and privacy legislation as a visible expression of these needs has continued unabated in Canada over the last few years, with Provincial jurisdictions in British Columbia, Alberta and Saskatchawan moving to join the other Provinces and the Federal Government in this legislative field. At the Federal level, the twin forces of public service reform and budgetary restraint have led to an emphasis on enhancing service to the public through re-engineered programme delivery and application of information technology. Part of this strategic direction is the improved provision of information about government policies, programmes and services and the wider dissemination of government databases. In the meantime, the Access to Information Act and the Privacy Act are entrenched as legislation giving important rights to Canadians and their administration is now integrated as part of the operation of government.

---

33 See Matthew Arnold, 'Stanzas from the Grande Chartreuse' (1955) in William Frost ed. *Romantic and Victorian Poetry* (N. J. Englewood Cliffs), pp. 336-342.

34 Mr Gillis delivered this paper at the Inaugural Conference of the Centre for Business and Public Sector Ethics, Cambridge, England 13 July 1989. His 'Postscript' was written in 1992 during the course of publication of this Volume I: *Government Ethics.*

NOTE 1

Key Players in the Co-Ordinated Public Policy Approach to Information Law in the Federal Government of Canada

---

1. PCO[1] – Cabinet confidences

2. Minister of Justice – Legal Aspects of the legislation

3. President of TB[2] – Government-wide administration

4. Government Institutions

---

1   Privy Council Office
2   Treasury Board of Canada

NOTE   2

Users Access to
Canadian Federal Information Act

Users Access to Information Act		
	1986-87	1987-88
Business	30%	42%
Media	20%	11%
Academic	20%	4%
Other	30%	43%

NOTE   3

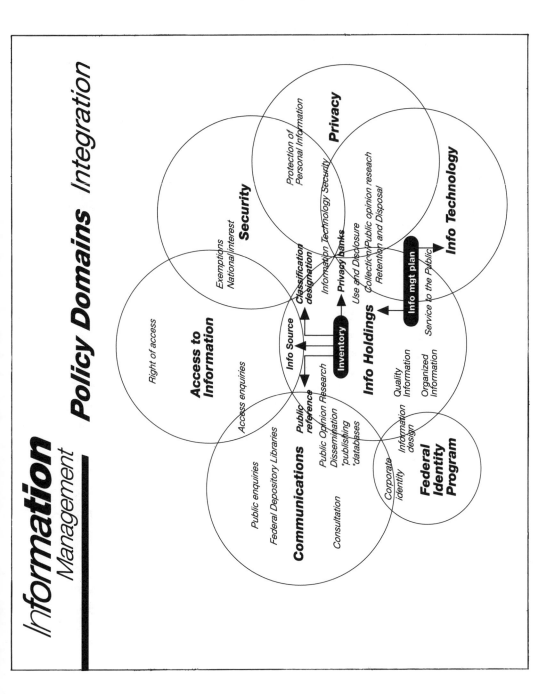

12

The Official Secrets Acts of the United Kingdom 1911-1989

by His Honour Judge David H. D. Selwood
(Director Army Legal Services (UK) 1990-1992)

Introduction

These remarks on the Official Secrets Acts of the United Kingdom 1911-1989 are intended to be no more than supplementary to the excellent and comprehensive book by Dr Rosamund Thomas on this subject.[1] In making these points I speak as a criminal law specialist with a particular interest in military law aspects.

1. The application of the Official Secrets Acts of the United Kindgdom 1911-1989

Many servicemen serve their country outside the United Kingdom. It is worth noticing that section 10 of the 1911 Official Secrets Act applied that Act to offences committed in any part of His Majesty's dominions or when committed by British officers or subjects elsewhere and gave jurisdiction to any competent British court in the place where the offence was committed or in England. The Official Secrets Acts of 1911 and 1920 were extended to Northern Ireland by the 1939 Act. Section 16 of the 1989 Act applied most of the provisions of that Act to acts done by a British citizen or Crown servant overseas and the Act extends to Northern Ireland.

For the soldier, however, all offences under these Acts can be tried by court-martial, wherever committed, under section 70 of the Army Act 1955.

2. Jurisdiction

The effect of these provisions is to confer concurrent jurisdiction on military courts-martial and all competent British courts at home and overseas. The question of which court, whether military or civil, has the primary right to exercise jurisdiction is the subject of well established principles.

---

1 Rosamund M. Thomas *Espionage and Secrecy: the Official Secrets Acts 1911-1989 of the United Kingdom* (London, Routledge 1991 and New York, Routledge Chapman & Hall Inc. 1992).

It is under those principles that decisions have been taken regarding the trial of the comparatively few officers and soldiers who have been tried by courts-martial both at home and overseas, and to try others (Dr Thomas has referred extensively in her book *Espionage and Secrecy: the Official Secrets Acts 1911-1989 of the United Kingdom* to the so-called Cyprus spy trial) [2] before civil courts.

In practice many offences against the Official Secrets Acts, which might otherwise fall to be dealt with under military jurisdiction are dealt with under other provisions, most commonly under section 69 of the Army Act 1955 and their equivalent sections in the other Service Discipline Acts. These sections deal with the offence of conduct to the prejudice of good order and military discipline and in this context the word 'conduct' includes 'neglect'. The loss of sensitive documents or other dealings with such documents incompatible with duty can often be disposed of in that way.

In addition, there are other offences created by other sections of the Service Discipline Acts which can be charged, for example:-

i) Section 25 of the Army Act 1955 – knowingly and without lawful excuse to communicate with or give intelligence to the enemy or knowingly and without lawful excuse to fail to make known to the proper authorities any information received from the enemy;

ii) Section 60 of the Army Act 1955 – without lawful authority disclosing or purporting to disclose information useful to an enemy.

It may be of interest to note that under section 25 (2) of the Army Act 1955 and its equivalent provisions in the other Service Discipline Acts, offences under section 25 of communicating with the enemy or failing to make known communications from the enemy, if committed with intent to assist the enemy, attract the death penalty. 'Enemy' includes all persons engaged in armed operations against any of Her Majesty's forces co-operating therewith and also includes armed mutineers, armed rebels, armed rioters and pirates. It follows that offences created under section 25 are not in law limited to time of war or international armed conflict.

It is also interesting to note that, although a prosecution under any of the Official Secrets Acts requires the consent of the Attorney General or the Director of Public Prosecutions, section 204A of the Army Act 1955 and its equivalent in the other Service Discipline Acts, provides that no enactment requiring the fiat or consent of the Attorney General or the Director of Public Prosecutions in connection with any proceedings shall have effect in

---

2 See also the paper on 'Military Ethics' in Part I of this Volume, pp. 67-100, by Mr James Stuart-Smith, CB, Q.C., recently the Judge Advocate General of the Forces (Army and Royal Air Force).

relation to proceedings under (The Army Act 1955). Despite this provision, however, there is close consultation between the military authorities and the Office of the Attorney General in connection with offences which could lead to prosecutions under the Official Secrets Acts on the issue of jurisdiction.

3. Evidence

Section 99 of the Army Act 1955 and its equivalent provisions in the other Service Discipline Acts apply the rules observed in civil courts in England to proceedings before courts-martial, subject to certain modifications. This means that the military lawyer is likely to have a practical insight into some of the problems of evidence discussed by Dr Thomas in her book *Espionage and Secrecy*. On this basis I would like to take up some of those problems.

Dr Thomas has discussed in Chapter Five of her above-mentioned book evidence of admissions made by those suspected of offences, pointing out that sometimes these admissions are subsequently withdrawn, sometimes they lack corroboration, sometimes they appear unreliable because of the way in which those admissions are obtained. She has discussed also the question of the evidence of spouses and the question of the evidence of defectors or informers.

From the practical criminal lawyer's point of view I believe that none of these problems, save possibly one with which I will deal in a moment, are by any means unique to prosecutions under the Official Secrets Acts.

Problems relating to admissions made by accused persons are too well known and too topical for there to be any need for me to rehearse them. The cases of the Guildford Four and the Birmingham Six are two of the star cases which have been subject recently to a great deal of debate. To a lesser degree, however, such cases occur before Crown Courts and courts-martial with great regularity. They do not attract so much attention.

The situation with regard to the difficulties arising from admissions and confessions has been greatly improved since the advent of the Police and Criminal Evidence Act 1984 and the Codes of Practice issued under that Act, not least the Code dealing with the tape recording of interviews. Both in the Crown Court and before courts-martial there has been a significant decrease in the number of challenges to the admissibility of admissions. Problems no doubt will persist, but I would submit that they arise from the nature of the kind of evidence we are considering rather than the nature of the offences which are charged.

The one area where I suspect difficulties arise as a result of the nature of the alleged offence is where problems over admissibility of admissions stem from the type of investigation into the incidents which have given rise to the charges.

There is a problem over the conduct of investigations in national security cases. A judgement has to be made where there has been a breach of security as to what is the primary aim of the investigation:

i) The need to maintain security

or

ii) The rights of the individual suspect

(I prefer the word 'rights' to the word 'interests' used by Dr Thomas).

Authority has to consider how serious the breach of security is. What is the potential damage or the actual damage? What is the extent of the compromise of the material? From this analysis, answers can be found to the question whether it is more important to discover the extent and scope of the breach and what can be done to limit the damage or whether it is more important to bring the alleged offender(s) to trial with the best possible chance of achieving a settled conviction. It will depend upon the answers to these questions as to which course the investigation will take. Should the suspect, for example, be interrogated without regard to the provisions of the Police and Criminal Evidence Act 1984 and the Codes of Practice, in order to obtain as much useful information from him as possible, or should he be questioned in accordance with that Act and the Codes and accorded all his rights?

If the decision is that security issues are predominant, then the criminal investigators and prosecutors will have to do their best with what they finally get after whatever damage limitation exercise is possible in the circumstances has been completed by the security authorities. Such an exercise may, and often will, weaken the prosecution case.

Of course it is perfectly possible for the criminal investigator to start again after those concerned with security have finished with the suspect. Not all breaches of the Police and Criminal Evidence Act provision or the Codes will taint further interviews.

The problem is not a new one – it has certainly been one of long-standing in the Armed Forces where advice constantly has been given to military police and provost services on how to cope with such a predicament over many, many years. The essential requirement is for close harmony between those charged with investigating security aspects of breaches and those charged with investigating the criminal aspects. Although the Army believes in separation between the police and security functions, it also believes in the closest possible co-operation between those who carry out those functions and realises how essential it is for each group to understand the needs of the other. In the Royal Air Force the police and security functions are discharged by the same group of people (the Provost and Security Services) and in those circumstances they can hardly help being aware of the needs of both aspects of investigation. So far as the Home Office police forces are concerned, the existence of a Special Branch drawn from serving police officers also ensures an awareness of the difficulties which can arise.

It is when the criminal investigatory function and the security function are muddled and investigators are unable to make up their minds what aim they are pursuing that serious problems arise. My sole point here, however, is that the experts in the Armed Forces and in the Civil Police are fully aware of these problems and that the judgements which they have to make are sometimes very difficult. It is easy to criticize the consequences, but better to understand and sympathise. [3]

---

3 These remarks were first made at the discussion group on laws of armed conflict at the Institute of International and Comparative Law on 22 April 1991 on the occasion that Dr Rosamund Thomas gave a paper based on her book *Espionage and Secrecy*, ibid.

13

Confidentiality of Information

Discussion by A. J. MacDonald, Deputy Under Secretary,
Ministry of Defence, the British Civil Service

From the perspective of a Government Department – namely the Ministry of Defence, I wish to discuss in turn the following three matters: *information; Government contracts;* and *physical assets.*

1. Information

I shall put four propositions to you:

i. *Information is the most precious commodity in which we deal.*

Government needs information to do its job properly. However, Government usually is unable to share that information with interested by-standers. Civil servants have to learn this principle from experience, not from formal training.

This principle applies not just to policy matters. Business confidences are crucial to British Government. 'Commercial-in-Confidence' is a much respected classification with Departments to protect business information passed to them.

The damage which occurs when matters go wrong is as follows:-

— If Ministers feel that confidences are not being respected, a reduced sharing of views and thoughts between Ministers and civil servants follows:

— If a company suspects that its confidences are not being respected that company will not seek Government help – and Government services (for example, export assistance) are thereby rendered impotent.

ii. *Preserving confidentiality should not present difficulties to Government servants.*

A mechanism for an appeal to a higher authority is available to those civil servants concerned on grounds of conscience. Resignation by a civil servant is also available, but this option is rarely used, being mainly a path for the disaffected to take;

iii. *There is tension between natural conservatism of Government servants towards retaining information and the demands for more information from public bodies.*

It can be incongruous to find that information which is strictly held secret one day is, officially, front page news the next.

iv. *A dilemma arises if a civil servant learns, from confidential information, that a company is behaving less than honourably.*

It is fortunate that, in the United Kingdom, high standards of ethics exist in business life.

Nevertheless, when receiving information, an individual civil servant cannot take the view that he was given the information as an individual, not as a representative of Government.

I would expect those same principles to apply to companies in their dealings with Government or with each other:

— Information is precious;

— Trust is precious;

— The dividing line between secrecy and publication may appear strong but can, in special circumstances, become blurred.

2. Government Contracts

There are special requirements put on those holding Government contracts. The needs of Government Departments are clear, and I doubt whether companies are disadvantaged by them:

i. *Honesty in carrying out contracts, and honesty of information given to Government Departments.*

Because of excess profit scandals of the 1960s, the Ministry of Defence has a team for investigating accounts. I hope that recent moves to competition will reduce that need.

ii. *Respect for confidentiality of Government information.*

The Ministry of Defence is not alone in this requirement – any company employing sub-contractors seeks the same! I am pleased to say that companies do respect our wishes – my colleagues could not recall an occasion when that respect has been broken.

If a company decides, in our democratic State, to deal with Government, it has to accept that this brings responsibilities. The Ministry of

Defence does ask company executives to sign the Official Secrets Act if they are to have accesss to classified information. I am not aware of this requirement causing problems – the option of not bidding for Ministry of Defence contracts is always there for those who object! If a company does not want its products used by the Ministry of Defence, it need not sell to us.

iii. *Compliance with export controls.*

Companies do exporting, not the Ministry of Defence. We cannot make companies export. We do look to ensure that legal actions are taken by companies.

3. Physical Assets

i. *The analogue of the private sector is relevant.*

Companies are fairly suspicious of outsiders trying to gain access to material which they regard as sensitive. Company sites are not National Parks (private sector long led the way in the use of electronic identification (ID) cards);

ii. *There are a few instances where special measures are needed.*

Terrorist threats are very real. The onus is on the Government to keep to a minimum the instances when, say, the Ministry of Defence Police are used on private contractors' premises – whilst at the same time ensuring that materials of value to terrorists and violent criminals are adequately protected.

14

Export Controls: The 'Super Gun' Affair

by John Meadway, Under Secretary, Department of Trade and Industry, British Civil Service [1]

The field of export control is a grey area, in that the application of one rule, that is, the respect by Government of the commercial confidentiality of information received in its regulatory function, would produce one result, which might be called black; whereas the freedom of the press might produce another, which would be called white. When the going gets difficult the result tends to be a compromise and so grey may be a reasonable description.

The obvious examples to use to discuss the subject currently arise from exports to Iraq. Some of the recent case work of the Department of Trade and Industry (DTI) in this field has attracted much public interest and this is likely to continue for some time. In discussing the subject at all, I have to take some liberties with certain obligations of confidentiality. Firstly, the 'Super Gun affair' is under examination at the moment by the House of Commons Select Committee on Trade and Industry; and evidence the Department of Trade and Industry has submitted to this Committee is not yet published. [2] To refer to the affair, therefore, would be a breach of Parliamentary privilege and also rather unwise since Ministers and ex-Ministers and civil servants, such as myself, do not yet know whether, before long, we shall be giving oral evidence to the Committee. Secondly, certain matters to do with the export of machine tools to Iraq are formally *sub judice* at the moment in that certain persons and companies have been charged with various offences by Her Majesty's Customs and Excise and the cases have not yet come to trial. [3]

---

1 As delivered, the paper concluded with a summary of developments up to then in the Matrix Churchill case. Since this case is now the subject of an Inquiry under Lord Justice Scott, set up in November 1992, which may involve the author, this paper has been edited, and that summary deleted from this published version in Volume 1: *Government Ethics*.

2 This Committee had now reported, see Trade and Industry Committee Second Report: *Exports to Iraq: Project Babylon and Long Range Guns* HC 86 (1991-92). DTI evidence: *Memoranda of Evidence* HC 607 (1990-91): *Minutes of Evidence* 26 November 1991, HC 86-i, 27 February 1992, HC 86-xv.

3 These controversial cases have now come to trial. For example, the Matrix Churchill trial collapsed in court in December 1992, after it appeared that the three accused (former executives of the Midlands-based machine tool company) had not attempted 'to sidestep' the Export of Goods (Control) Order 1991. See *The Times* 18 December 1992.

I should explain that the basic rule of the Department of Trade and Industry about individual export licence applications is that we do not comment on them, either in response to press questions or in response to Parliamentary Questions. The usual form of words is 'it has not been the practice of successive Governments to disclose such information'. The underlying justification is commercial confidentiality.

You might conclude that the above rule, combined with the *sub judice* rule, the desirability of not making comments that might prejudice law enforcement investigations which have not yet reached the stage of charges and becoming formally *sub judice,* and Official Secrets obligations as they bite on relations with other Governments and security and intelligence matters, might prevent us saying very much about these subjects. But, the level of political and public interest in these two affairs made this impossible and for discussion I have identified all the Parliamentary statements that Ministers have made orally in the House and in response to written Parliamentary Questions, to try and see if I can discern any principles which have guided us in deciding how much white has to go into the black to produce the appropriate shade. As further context, the United Kingdom export control system is outlined in Note 1 to this paper, on page 268.

To set the Department of Trade and Industry policy in context, it is necessary to set out the 'Super Gun' story in brief outline. 'Brief' is the word: both 'The Gun' and 'machine tools' have been the subject of very full treatment on British Television by the *Panorama* [4] and *Insight* [5] techniques.

1. The 'Super Gun' Affair

From the export licensing point of view the saga of the gun started in June 1988 when the Member of Parliament, Sir Hal Miller, telephoned the office of the then Minister of Trade, Mr Alan Clark, about some very large tubes to be made in Sheffield. He wanted to know whether they required export licences and he conveyed some disquiet about possible military applications. The Department of Trade and Industry's export licensing staff referred him to the technical side of the Ministry of Defence (MOD) and there was considerable contact between the Ministry of Defence and a senior metallurgist in the firm. They discussed a range of possible military uses especially in connection with rockets, but none made sense for the size, weight and technical specification of the metal; and since no one could pin-point a specific military application, the answer had to be given that licences were not required.

---

4 *Panorama:* BBC television, 3 September 1990 and 18 February 1991.
5 *Insight: Sunday Times* 22 April 1990 and 16 December 1990.

A couple of months later the two firms involved asked the Department of Trade and Industry Export Licensing Unit in writing whether or not licences were required for some tubes, of which they sent in drawings, saying that the purpose was the polymerisation of polyethylene, that is a process undertaken in the petrochemical industry. There was nothing in the papers to link this enquiry with the discussions a couple of months before, and the papers came in approximately four levels further down the organisation than the Hal Miller enquiry – which had been dealt with on the telephone as far as the Department of Trade and Industry was concerned. This later enquiry rang no alarm bells as to a potential military application; it was established that the item was not a controlled industrial item and clearance was given to the effect that an export licence was not needed.

In 1989 Government as a whole became increasingly aware of the scale and sophistication of the Iraqi procurement operation in the West and in particular an effort by an Iraqi controlled company to acquire some advanced technologies by taking over an aircraft component factory[6] in Northern Ireland was thwarted by refusal of government financial assistance. But, it was not until March turned into April 1990 that the picture began to fall together, some of the tubes were impounded by Customs at the point of export and Ministry of Defence experts confirmed that they were parts of a cannon of unprecedented size. This was when, in political terms, the balloon went up and the line of answers and statements starts.

If one analyses Mr Ridley's statement to the House of Commons of 18 April 1990 it departed from the usual practice in three ways. Firstly, it went into considerable detail about enquiries from named firms about licensability of particular goods; secondly, he commented on the stage at which we understood our firms had been paid; and, thirdly, he commented on the nature of business of the consignee, that is the Space Research Corporation. Mr Ridley resisted intense pressure to elaborate, stating that it was not possible to go further into details and it would be wrong to answer some of the questions that were being put to him, as this could prejudice the possibility of criminal proceedings at a later stage.

Masses of written Parliamentary Questions were put down and a substantial inter-Departmental exercise on answering them was started. The only ones that were answered in this period were those asking when Ministers, including the Prime Minister, knew that there was a problem about the order and that was answered with a reference to the current month – April 1990. On 25 April, Customs laid charges against certain people and the subject became formally *sub judice* and subsequently thirty-eight Parliamentary

---

6 For the proposed acquisition of the Learfan factory, see Trade and Industry Committee Report op. cit. para 93 *et seq.*

Questions were answered by saying that it would be inappropriate to give any further information in the light of the criminal charges laid against individuals and in the light of the continuing investigations by Customs and Excise.

In November 1990 Customs dropped the charges and Mr Sainsbury [7] made a brief statement in the course of Debate on the Import and Export (Control) Bill, which was coincidentally before Parliament at that time for the purpose of making the 1939 Act permanent. The statement added hardly anything towards what had been said previously but referred to two areas where procedures were being improved. Thereafter, Mr Lilley said that he would answer questions on the 'Super Gun' appropriate to the Department of Trade and Industry when this would not help the Government of Iraq or other would-be evaders of export controls.

Subsequent to that, specific answers were given on details of dealings with the firms concerned, including the dates of letters, and on what advice was given about an order which appeared just before the balloon went up, for what appeared to be aiming equipment. Ministers stated which Departments were involved in dealing with particular applications and what information we had, or rather did not have, on the activities of the Space Research Corporation. But other questions attracted the traditional line to the effect that answering them was not the practice; dealings with the Export Control Guarantee Department were not dealt with substantively in replies and we refused to go into a full history of our dealings with the companies concerned, or list what companies were mentioned in documents they have put in, or to go into the technical specification and composition of the steel.

What policy can be discerned here in this 'Super Gun' case? The 18 April 1990 statement was made under very severe political pressure and we did not feel the Department of Trade and Industry could refuse to discuss the dealings the firms and Sir Hal Miller had had with us, when they were shouting the odds about them from the housetops practically hourly. The statement that the business of Space Research Corporation was not exclusively military partly explained why our suspicions had not developed earlier.

What was the common theme when we departed from the usual practice not to answer particular questions, in the recent period after the *sub judice* block was lifted? I suggest it was to protect commercial confidences which were not in the public domain, such as business other than the gun, and other potentially commercially sensitive details that were not in the public domain.

2. Conclusion

As an overall conclusion, therefore, in these very unusual circumstances we

7 Minister for Trade, *HC Hansard* 29 November 1990, cols. 1059-1063.

abandoned the general rule not to comment on particular licence applications or answer the questions about them and dealt in substance with what others had placed in the public domain and in the period while the possibility of prosecution was being protected, that is in the period to April 1990 before charges were laid, we asserted the conclusion that the tubing was a gun but avoided going into the argument that led us to that conclusion. This was logical in terms of minimising exposure of detail that would be germane to a prosecution.

NOTE   1

United Kingdom Export Control Régime: Extract from the Second Report of the Trade and Industry Committee Report, House of Commons HC 86 (1991-92) entitled 'Exports to Iraq: Project Babylon and Long Range Guns'

UK export controls are administered by the Export Control Organisation in the DTI. Goods whose export requires a licence are listed in the Export of Goods (Control) Order made under the Import, Export and Customs Powers (Defence) Act 1939. The UK imposes export controls for a variety of reasons: [1]

EXPORT CONTROLS

Maintenance of collective security of UK & NATO allies

Maintenance of national security

Foreign policy requirements

International treaty obligations and commitments

UK non-profileration policy

Concerns about terrorism or internal repression

National heritage

These policy reasons mean that a number of Government Departments, apart from the DTI, are involved in the process of granting and enforcing export licences. Advice is sought from the Ministry of Defence, the Foreign and Commonwealth Office and the Department of Energy on licence applications which involve, for instance, military equipment, nuclear items or chemical weapon precursors[2]. Custome & Excise are responsible for the enforcement of export restrictions. [3]

'The law places the onus for applying for an export licence on the company contemplating the export. [4] A company may approach the DTI for advice *whether a licence is required* (known as a rating inquiry). It may also *make a licence application.*

The Export Control Organisation was set up under a unified management structure in the latter part of 1988 as a result of an internal review completed in 1987. It brought together three units: (i) the Export Licensing Unit which considers export licence applications; (ii) the Sensitive Technologies Unit which provides technical advice on whether equipment or technology is subject to UK export control regulation; [5] and (iii) a Policy Unit. In addition to specialists employed in the Sensitive Technologies Unit, the Export Control organisation may call upon the expertise available in the Department, particularly staff in the Industrial Research Establishments and Line Divisions (one of which was the Industrial Minerals and Metals Division). Advice is also available from other Departments. [6] Simple rating inquiries are filtered by an Enquiry Unit. [7] More complex cases are referred to the Sensitive Technologies Unit and details circulated to other Government Departments. [8]

As regards interdepartmental cooperation, the main forum for discussions is provided by the Restricted Enforcement Unit. Sensitive cases (including rating inquiries and licence applications) are considered in fortnightly meetings of the Restricted Enforcement Unit (REU) on which DTI, MoD, Customs & Excise and FCO are represented. [9]

---

1 Evidence p. 5 HC 607 1990-91.

2 Evidence p. 6 HC 607 1990-91 (DTI).

3 Evidence HC 86-ix p. 302.

4 Evidence p. 5 HC 607 1990-91 (DTI).

5 Export Control organisation Annual Report 1990 (October 1991).

6 QQ 8.46 (Mr Meadway).

7 Evidence p. 18 HC 607 1990-91 (DTI).

8 Evidence p. 6 HC 607 1990-91 (DTI).

9 These extracts are taken from pages vi-vii of the Trade and Industry Committee's above-mentioned Report, and in that Report these paragraphs are numbered 12-16.

15

Confidentiality and Security in the British Nuclear Fuels Industry: Some Special Problems

by Dr W. L. Wilkinson, recently Deputy Chief Executive, British Nuclear Fuels plc [1]

1. Background to British Nuclear Fuels [2]

British Nuclear Fuels manufactures nuclear fuel for nuclear reactors and intermediates and also reprocesses spent fuel. It carries out this business on an international scale and sales now exceed £1,000 million per annum from a total workforce of fifteen thousand.

2. Disclosure of Information

Clearly, we have some special problems in the nuclear industry concerning confidentiality. Nevertheless, in British Nuclear Fuels our approach is that all information should be available to the public *unless* there are sound reasons for withholding it on a case-by-case basis. This practice is the reverse of the traditional approach adopted by many organisations in the past, including my own.

For many years British Nuclear Fuels was accused of being secretive – not surprising in view of our origins, but since 1986 our policy has been centred on openness. We have accepted a commitment to disclose any Company information on request *except* that which would jeopardise:-

a. security

b. necessary commercial or legal confidentiality

c. personal privacy

This policy is subject to an overriding qualification that the resources

---

1 This paper was delivered on 24 May 1991 at the Third Conference held by the Centre for Business and Public Sector Ethics, Cambridge. Dr Wilkinson is currently a Non-Executive Director of BNFL, but has retired from the post of Deputy Chief Executive which he held in May 1991[*Editor*].

2 British Nuclear Fuels Plc is known as BNFL. British Nuclear Fuels is still a *public* sector company, unlike the gas and electricity industries of the United Kindom, which now are *privatised.*

necessary to produce the information cannot be allowed to rise to a level disproportionate to the importance of the information and the purpose for which it is requested. We have had to invoke that qualification only four times in five years, a fact which reflects well on the common sense of the public, the Press and, for that matter, the environmental activists.

Without being too smug, we at British Nuclear Fuels believe that this practice is especially noteworthy in an industry which, in the past, has been criticised for obsessive secrecy. The recognition of our policy of openness and honesty has had a beneficial effect on our public reputation.

3. Physical Security of Nuclear Materials

The basis of security concerning nuclear materials is the nuclear Non-Proliferation Treaty and this Treaty is enforced by the signatories. There are, of course, some notable exceptions, that is countries who are not signatories.

The basis of safeguarding nuclear materials is that all plants which are capable of producing materials which could be of use in nuclear weapons, such as plutonium, enrichment uranium and tritium, are subjected to inspection by independent inspectors of Euratom and the International Atomic Energy Agency (IAEA), during both the design and operational phases.

This is a very comprehensive process requiring special instrumentation and surveillance by on-site inspectors after the plant has gone into operation. The need to safeguard nuclear materials results in a number of constraints, such as:-

a. British Nuclear Fuels cannot do business with countries who are not signatories to the Non-Proliferation Treaty.

b. The United States of America plays a dominant role and puts end-use restrictions in nuclear fuel which originates from the United States.

c. The sale of technology has to be restricted to ensure that countries do not build up a capability for producing nuclear materials.

4. Commercial Security

Commercial security is not really a problem. Clearly there is a lot of commercially sensitive information in a Company like British Nuclear Fuels and we protect this accordingly. We believe that we do not over-classify material and we do not use commercial sensitivity as a device for not being open with information.

5. The Law of Discovery

Whilst discovery is not a breach of confidentiality or leakage in the terms contemplated for this Conference, the results for a Company can be very similar. We are compelled at British Nuclear Fuels to produce to our opponents through the English courts, material which may be very damaging to our Company. A manager may, in the privacy of his office, write a report today 'for authorised distribution only', dealing very frankly with the Company's problems. That report has to be produced in the future if legal proceedings are started and the document may relate, in some way, to an issue in the action. If the Board of British Nuclear Fuels has considered the document, then any written record of the Board's proceedings also have to be produced.

There is a legal obligation in the English courts placed on the Plaintiffs and their lawyers only to use the documents for the purposes of the particular litigation, but one is dependent upon their personal ethics!

6. Medical Information concerning British Nuclear Fuels' Employees

Another problem facing British Nuclear Fuels concerns the basis for co-operating in the provision of confidential medical information which may be required for epidemiological studies of employees. The Company's response should provide for the safeguard of the right of privacy of the individual but also comply with the procedures for access to such information as recommended by, for example, the Royal College of Physicians of London.

The following safeguards are found necessary at British Nuclear Fuels:-

a. there must be ethical committee [3] approval for the study

b. the Chief Medical Officer within British Nuclear Fuels [4] or nominated deputy shall retain control over the process of accessing BNFL information, and such accessing should be done by the Occupational Health Department staff at British Nuclear Fuels

c. there should be support from the relevant trade unions and staff associations at British Nuclear Fuels for co-operation in the study

d. the study must be carried out by a defined group of investigators [5] who must identify what classes or items of information are required and the rationale

---

3 Such ethical committees exist nationally and regionally in relation to all United Kingdom medically-related studies.

4 The current Chief Medical Officer at British Nuclear Fuels Plc is Dr Andy Slovak.

5 The group of investigators may be internal within British Nuclear Fuels, or external, or a combination of both.

e. the medical notes must not be removed from the appropriate department at British Nuclear Fuels

f. the Chief Medical Officer within British Nuclear Fuels or nominated deputy shall have the responsibility and right to verify data abstracted from medical records for which consent has been given

g. an individual worker has the right to see what information has been requested about him/herself and the right to opt out of any study at his/her request.

h. the workforce at British Nuclear Fuels should be informed of these safeguards and of any analysis of the study affecting them prior to any release of details. [6]

---

6 Dr Wilkinson delivered this Conference paper in May 1991. At the time this Volume went to press in Autumn 1992, an English High Court is hearing allegations against British Nuclear Fuels. The allegations, *inter alia*, are that radiation levels endured by the workforce at the BNFL Sellafield reprocessing plant, (which is forty-two years old and was called Windscale originally), were grossly underestimated by the Company. The above-stated allegation was made on the first day of a test case which began in late October 1992, in which two families are seeking £10 million damages, claiming that their children's cancers were caused by the effects of radiation on their fathers' sperm before the children were conceived'. The allegation made in court is that the children's fathers had been exposed to radiation by working at the BNFL plant in Cumbria, England. Up to 40 other cases depend on the test case, which is expected to last at least six months. See *The Times* 27 October 1992.

This High Court case presents for BNFL the further problem, identified by Dr Wilkinson in this paper under heading 5, of the Company being compelled to produce, through the English courts, material to their opponents which may be very damaging to the Company. Such material may deal frankly with the Company's problems and would have been written for Company purposes, and not for an action in a court of law. *[Editor]*

16

Confidentiality of Information

Discussion by John Mayne, [1]
recently Principal Finance and Personnel Officer,
Department of Health, British Civil Service

1. Categories of absolute confidentiality of information

It is very interesting that we are discussing the contrast with business. I suppose business is just as secretive as, perhaps even more so sometimes than, the Government. But I should like to speak about health matters, although I am not a health expert. If you look at the Department of Health, there are various aspects of confidentiality about which one would have relatively few qualms. First, about the absolute nature of medical confidentiality; about people's medical records, where there is a clear category, and under the Official Secrets Act, no problems at all. Most people would agree with that, I would have thought. There are other areas where the Department of Health is regulating, monitoring and so on; for example, the management of the National Health Service. Within reason I think one can be very open about this. On drugs licensing, once you have actually licensed the drug, the whole process by which the drug is tested ought, I think, to be open. While you are licensing, I think you can probably get into all sorts of discussions which you would not want to put wholly into the public presses. I shall come back to that in a minute in a different context. If you think of the Social Services Inspectorate, which inspects the Social Service Departments of Local Government, looking at child abuse cases and so forth, again there are clearly areas where everyone would say: 'Let us keep certain things confidential'.

There are other areas where the timing of publication is terribly important: this is particularly the case with my other example of public health matters, which are highly political, far more political, I think, than almost any other area of government that I have every had anything to do with. When one goes home and looks at the 'Nine O'clock News' and five items on the news are all to do with your Department, you begin to wonder whether you can actually control matters. We have had a spate recently of public health issues: salmonella; the threat that listeria poses to the 'cook/chill' business which is not insignificant if you happen to be Marks and Spencer and have

---

1 This discussion took place at the Second Conference of the Centre for Business and Public Sector Ethics held in Cambridge, 14 May 1991.

ninety percent of the cook/chill business but none of your products actually has any or significant amounts of listeria in them; the difficult position of the Chief Medical Officer, only within a week of today, in explaining that at a particular time the link between listeria, pregnant women and their unborn children, had not been proven and therefore the Government could not give advice on the link; Bovine Spongiform Encephalopathy, where there is a possibility that an organism present in sheep has been transmitted to cows, and therefore possibly could be transmitted to the human chain; water purity, which had the whole of the Oxford area boiling its water in a panic – actually you have to boil water for, I believe, about five minutes before you can actually get rid of the bugs they were worrying about in the reservoirs around Oxford and who, with an electric kettle, can boil water for five minutes? – difficult problems like that. Even more recently, we have had hazlenut yoghurt and botulism.

2. The timing of the release of information

Now I think that the only point I would bring out is that we have got to have confidentiality about these issues for a time, for crucial moments, where Ministers are in the position of saying 'what am I going to do about this thing and this morning? How can I deal with it without actually making everybody panic? Without creating a political harrouche that can't be controlled? I do not think you ought to spill out information on politically sensitive issues, but you should give people enough information about the issues when you judge that it is the right time to do so. Of course, you would say I am being a bureaucrat, aren't I, because I would want to have that amount of control. But I think control is terribly important in those particularly sensitive areas, because we have had enough unproductive hassle, about such issues with many people being unnecessarily worried as to whether they are at risk. I shall tell you a little story about journalists: you can put out any piece of paper you like about these particular issues, listeria or whatever, and you can say: 'The following people are at risk: pregnant mothers, young children and those whose immune systems are suppressed', and the press always add: and old people!

3. Parliament: Select Committees of the House of Commons.

Regarding the question of whether a British civil servant should appear, and be questioned by a Select Committee of Parliament, or whether he should take refuge in confidentiality, there are clearly times when a Select Committee will ask very difficult questions and you will have to say, as I said when I was first confronted with that question, 'I am not prepared to answer that question'. What I meant was that I was not briefed to answer that question.

But since officials are ready to answer questions of fact, I would like personally to see the process greatly developed. I look sometimes with admiration at the American system, though it clearly puts a considerable strain on the Administration and I should not want the British system to go that far. But I have always found that when I have appeared before a Select Committee, [2] I, as a professional, regard myself as having to be the greatest living expert in that particular area of government. There can be no questions that I cannot answer. So, a tremendous amount of briefing goes on. And I have always regretted, when I have come out from such an appearance, that I have not used up many of the hosts in my locker. You can usually find out roughly what is going to be asked and you can deal with the first question; then the first supplementary comes and you can answer that. But what I have always wanted to do at that particular point is to say 'Look, I have actually briefed myself fully; I want to tell you all about it'. But, of course, I am not allowed to do that, and the information is never extracted from me. I would like to see Parliament much better informed and enable Members of Parliament, if they were prepared to put the time into briefing themselves, to engage in a useful discussion and exchange of information with officials. I think there could be much more information made available in this way. [3]

---

2 For the current Memorandum of Guidance for British officials appearing before Select Committees, see this Volume, pp. 282-86.

3 The latest public health issue in 1993 to be publicised by the media in the United Kingdom concerns apple juice. In February 1993, the press expressed fears about the safety and quality of apple juice, believing quantities of this juice, still on sale in British shops, to be capable of causing cancer. The British Government was challenged by the media on the ground of 'cover up', with allegations made that the adverse effects of certain apple juices were known to the Government, yet the Government had not insisted upon the withdrawal of this juice from shop shelves.

Three comments are required here. First, as John Mayne has made clear in this discussion, *timing* is critical in regard to when the media, and the public, are informed about health issues. Second, the current Minister, William Waldegrave, who is responsible in British Central Government for the Citizen's Charter, is reported to be planning now 'to open up' Central Government Departments to keep people informed. He is planning to order British civil servants to publish regular reports on any harmful products. Third, these types of health issues draw attention to the different systems and procedures prevailing in individual countries to deal with both the public policy, and the scientific evidence, associated with potentially and/or actually dangerous products. For example, the United States and Britain have adopted different methods of making such assessments and consequently different timing and actions in connection with banning products. Whether these products be goods, drinks, pharmaceutical drugs or others.

The balancing of, on the one hand, the interests of business companies and, on the other hand, the public interest, is one of today's key ethical dilemmas facing Governments. [Editor]

17

What are the Proper Limits to which People in Official Positions should be able to go to Communicate with each other, Parliament, and the Media?

by David E. R. Faulkner CB,
recently Deputy Secretary, Home Office, British Civil Service [1]

1. Communications between those in official positions, Parliament and the Media

This paper is concerned with issues of secrecy, confidentiality and openness as they affect the day to day work of public officials in Government Departments. It does not address the content or jurisprudence of official secrets legislation but it does consider the professional standards of public officials and the dynamics of ordinary working situations where the exchange of information is involved.

The United Kingdom has the reputation of having one of the most secretive systems of public administration in the developed world. And yet Ministers and officials spend a great deal of time and energy in explaining what they do to Parliament, the media and the public more generally. My own Department – the Home Office – by reputation one of the most secretive in Whitehall – has in the last few years made special efforts to explain itself and its policies to the wider world, through the publication of White and Green Papers and discussion documents, through its evidence to Select Committees and its replies to their reports, through open days, and through conferences and meetings of various kinds. This effort has been recognised and appreciated by many of those who have been involved, but there is still a sense that more is needed.

A Government Department, or any public sector institution, needs to be open and accessible for two main reasons. One reason is to achieve its policy or operational objectives, which will depend on understanding, commitment and a sense of common purpose, certainly among its own staff and very often

---

1 Mr Faulkner gave this paper at the Fourth Conference of the Centre for Business and Public Sector Ethics, Cambridge, on 'Confidentiality of Information and Leakages' held on 27 November 1991. Since then, he has retired from the Home Civil Service.

among other organisations or individuals on whom it depends. The other reason is public confidence, where the institution will rapidly loose respect and credibility if its integrity, and its efficiency and effectiveness, cannot be adequately demonstrated.

For the most part, the procedures for these purposes are well established and operate without raising serious questions of propriety – through management and trade union channels to the staff; through correspondence and consultation with operational services and representative organisation; through Ministers to Parliament and its Select Committees; and through public relations branches to the media. Some information is required to be disclosed by statute, and some has become the subject of custom and practice, but to a very large extent it is for Departments to decide what information to provide. The United Kingdom does not have a Freedom of Information Act, and other organisations are not usually in a position to insist on what information they are entitled to receive – although Select Committees are better placed than most.

2. Pressures not to disclose Official Information

The arrangements can come under strain from two main directions. Within Government Departments there will be concern to prevent disclosure of material which by its nature is unsuitable, or the material is in itself unsuitable to prevent its premature disclosure, or disclosure by an inappropriate individual or on an inappropriate occasion (for example in anticipation of a formal announcement or statement in Parliament). Circumstances in which disclosure may nevertheless take place include inadvertence or a well intentioned wish to be helpful, to (conceivably but very rarely) a deliberate attempt to subvert the policy concerned or to embarrass the Minister or official involved. Very occasionally the disclosure may be to expose an actual or supposed scandal or deception ('whistle-blowing'), or for personal gain.

Outside Government, there may be dissatisfaction over a Department's reluctance to share information to which an organisation considers itself to be entitled, believes should be put on public record, or thinks would advance the campaign or programme on which it is engaged or which it supports (and to which the Department itself may be equally committed). The reasons here may be more complicated. There may be a considered judgement that the information is too sensitive or confidential to be disclosed; the main examples are probably material protected by the Official Secrets Act, details of confidential discussions among colleagues or with Ministers, commercial matters, and personal information about individuals. Or there may be a handling judgement that the information should be withheld until there is a carefully planned formal announcement, or until it can be given simultaneously to all interested parties. Or the judgement may be that the person or organisation is simply not to be trusted. Or that disclosure will start a debate which would be troublesome and difficult to control. Or the official concerned may be just too busy or too harassed to spare the time, or may feel awkward about making the necessary contacts or lack confidence in handling the situation which might follow. There is a range of possible circumstances, explanations and justifications, extending from properly considered judgements to more questionable judgements and to possible weaknesses in the system or in the individuals involved. Experience of these situations is part of the daily life of many middle ranking and senior civil servants, and of those with whom they are in regular contact.

3. Sanctions against Improper Disclosure

A Department's sanctions against improper disclosure include the criminal law (for example if theft or fraud is involved or the Official Secrets Acts apply): internal disciplinary procedures; various forms of formal or less formal guidance; and the professional culture of the organisation. In practice the criminal law will apply only in the rarest of cases; and Civil Service disciplinary procedures may not be suitable unless, for example, the disclosure has taken place in deliberate defiance of an explicit instruction (which however could include the instructions relating to the handling of classified papers). The strongest influence in most situations will be the professional culture of the Department or of the branch or division concerned.

The most significant feature of the new Official Secrets Act 1989 is that it substitutes for the blanket provisions of the old section 2 a set of specific provisions related to particular types of information. There are often specific prohibitions on disclosure – for instance to protect personal information gained for census and similar purposes. But, as a general rule, so far as the criminal law is concerned, information is now 'open' unless it is explicitly protected by the Act, as distinct from being 'closed' unless its disclosure has been properly authorised. However little it may have been used, the old section 2 created a presumption of secrecy; its repeal should remove one obstacle to the development of a professional attitude of mind in which the presumption is for disclosure in the absence of good reasons to the contrary.

4. Management for Quality requires successful Commmunication and Openness

Such an attitude is an essential ingredient of the modern approach to 'managing for quality' or to 'total quality management' in the public and private sectors. This approach has influenced to some extent the 'Next Steps' initiative and the development of the Citizens Charter, [2] and it is likely to

---

2 For details, see paper in this Volume by Mr Hayden Phillips, CB, recently HM Treasury.

become an increasingly significant part of Civil Service management over the next few years. Other ingredients of this approach are the organisation's accessibility to those who use or come into contact with it, their 'empowerment' to influence the quality and level of service they receive, and the application of those principles not only to the organisation's 'customers' but also to its own staff and the staff's 'ownership' of the policies and practices which result. It will be necessary always to protect confidences, especially in the Civil Service context, confidences between colleagues and between officials and Ministers, but an organisation cannot commit itself to managing for quality if its managers retain an attitude of mind which contains a general presumption of secrecy or confidentiality.

The openness involved in managing for quality, and increasingly required for effective performance, whether or not it is part of a formal 'quality' programme, can be very demanding. Senior and middle ranking civil servants have to handle a wide range of contacts and a wide range of pressures resulting from them. These contacts include Ministers, senior colleagues, their own staff, other Government Departments, Parliament, operational services, representative bodies, interest groups, and the media. Few civil servants have the time, the energy, or often the skill to operate successfully with all these contacts all the time. Some aspects have to be sacrificed. For the official concerned, the internal contacts – especially Ministers – usually will take priority, but the Department's credit and creditability will eventually suffer if the external contacts are for too long neglected.

Successful communication between officials and external contacts requires mutual confidence and respect. This statement is especially true in relation to the media. A few, but only a few, Civil Service jobs (apart from information service posts) necessarily involve regular contact with the media, and a civil servant who actively sought media attention would be viewed usually with suspicion both by his colleagues and by Ministers. Most civil servants, however, are keen, and rightly keen, that matters for which they have responsibility should be reported accurately and sensitively, and they are, or should be, ready to brief the media for that purpose whenever the occasion requires. Very often the task will fall to Ministers or information officers, but direct contact between the media and an official with relevant responsibilities and experience may sometimes be helpful. The media themselves certainly find it so. Nonetheless, the official will feel badly let down if what then appears is a catchy news story claiming the discovery of a disagreement between officials and Ministers or between Government Departments, or the failure of some aspect of the programme which is being reported. Nothing undermines an official's . professional relationship with Ministers or his colleagues so much as a story of that kind, and no official can afford to be open with the media if he thinks that may be the result.

5. Conclusions

To sum up, the proper limits of the information which can be communicated between public officials, Parliament and the media are at present to a considerable extent matters of professional and political judgement and confidence. That judgement should be exercised on the basis of a presumption of openness in the absence of good reasons to the contrary, and it needs to be exercised within the context of a clear understanding of what can or cannot reasonably be expected. The main elements of that understanding are that disclosure of certain types of information should never be expected or permitted – broadly those indicated on pages 278-79; and that disclosure should not be expected in circumstances where it would be premature, or give a particular advantage to one interested party. It is for consideration, and perhaps debate, how far this understanding should be codified in legislation (for example in a Freedom of Information Act),[3] in an administrative code of practice, or for purposes of Civil Service discipline; and how far it should be left to professional and political judgement, reinforced by the development of professional standards and practices in the context of the wider developments which are now taking place in Civil Service management.

---

3 See the paper in this Volume by Mr Robert Peter Gillis in respect of the Canadian Federal Government experience of an Access to Information Act. Unsuccessful attempts have been made in Britain by Private Members of the House of Commons to introduce a Freedom of Information Bill in Britain. The most recent attempt, still in progress, is 'The Right to Know' Bill which was introduced by Mark Fisher, MP, and passed its Second Reading in the House of Commons on 19 February 1993. This Bill is now in Committee stage, but may be defeated by the Government on its Third Reading.

Memorandum of Guidance for Officials Appearing before Select Committees (March 1988) [1]

1. Introduction

A Memorandum of twenty-five pages, [2] (together with earlier supplementary guidelines of April 1987 and further annexed material), was issued in March 1988 by the Cabinet Office, to assist British civil servants who may be called upon to give evidence before, or to prepare memoranda for submission to, Parliamentary Select Committees. While this Memorandum of Guidance is primarily intended to cover the Select Committees of the House of Commons, it is also generally applicable to Select Committees of the House of Lords. It may not always be literally applicable to the Public Accounts Committee, in view of the special position of Accounting Officers and the access of the Comptroller and Auditor General to departmental records. Supplementary guidance on the procedure to be followed in respect of the Commons Select Committee on European Legislation (and the corresponding House of Lords Select Committee on the European Communities) and on the handling of European Community documents is issued separately by the Cabinet Office. Guidance in dealing with the Joint and Select Committees on Statutory Instruments is provided in 'Statutory Instrument Practice'.

2. Select Committee System

2.1 General Description

The scope of the Select Committee system of the House of Commons has varied from time to time. The significance of the title is that the Committee's membership is 'selected' for a particular task, generally of enquiry. The main practical House distinction lies between such Committees, with their role of investigation and scrutiny, and 'Standing Committees', concerned with the examination of particular legislation and with their procedure based

---

1 This Memorandum of Guidance (known as the Osmotherly Rules) supersedes GEN 80/38.

2 Only brief extracts are reprinted here in Volume 1: *Government Ethics* of this twenty-five page Memorandum. The annexed material, not reprinted here, includes Annex E which is further guidance dated 19 August 1975 from the then Head of the British Civil Service, Sir Douglas Allen, (later Lord Croham), to civil servants concerning 'Disclosure of Classified Information to Select Committees'.

on debate rather than the taking of evidence. Most Select Commitees (hereafter referred to as 'Committees' are embodied in the Standing Orders of the House. Others are on a sessional basis, and can be established and their work completed within a matter of weeks or months. Some are Committees with a purely House function (for example, the Committee of Selection), with which Departments will not normally come into contact. The principal Commons Select Committees with which this Memorandum is concerned are those related to Government Departments (see below); the Public Accounts Committee; the Committee on the Parliamentary Commissioner for Administration; the Committee on European Legislation; and the Services Committee (concerned with House administration). Certain coordinating functions on behalf of the various Commons Committees are carried out by the Liaison Committee; the normal Government contact with this is through the Leader of the House and the Government Chief Whip.

The House of Lords has two major Select Committees – the European Communities Committee and the Science and Technology Committee – which are re-appointed at the beginning of every session. Both Committees have sub-committees and there is power to co-opt additional members to these sub-committees. In addition, there is generally one ad-hoc Select Committee in the Lords, also appointed on a sessional basis, which undertakes enquiries into matters of policy, or into Private Members Bills (Overseas Trade and the Infant Life Preservation Bill are recent examples). Ad-hoc Select Committees do not have sub-committees, they cease to exist once they have reported, and now rarely last more than one session. All these Committees take oral and written evidence from Departments. The terms of reference of the Lords Select Committees are set out in the sessional order of the House which appoints them. Additionally, the terms of reference for specific inquiries by Sub-committees of the Science and Technology Committee are determined by the Select Committee itself. Lords Committees have an inherent power to send for witnesses. Documents are produced voluntarily. An Order of the House would be required to compel witnesses to attend or produce papers and none has in recent times been necessary.

2.2 Committees Related to Government Departments

The House of Commons Committees related to Government Departments and the principal Departments concerned are:

Agriculture	Ministry of Agriculture, Fisheries and Food
Defence	Ministry of Defence
Education, Science and Arts	Department of Education and Science
Employment	Department of Employment

Energy [3]	Department of Energy
Environment	Department of the Environment
Foreign Affairs	Foreign and Commonwealth Office
Home Affairs	Home Office
Scottish Affairs	Scottish Office
Social Services	Departments of Health and Social Security
Trade and Industry	Department of Trade and Industry
Transport	Department of Transport
Treasury and Civil Service	Treasury, Office of the Minister for the Civil Service, Board of Inland Revenue, HM Customs and Excise
Welsh Affairs	Welsh Office

The Committees on Foreign Affairs, Home Affairs and the Treasury and Civil Service each have power to appoint one investigative sub-committee. A joint sub-committee may be set up from time to time to consider any matter affecting two or more nationalised industries, with members drawn from the departmental Committees concerned. Matters within the responsibilities of the Secretary of State for Northern Ireland will be considered by the existing Committees as necessary.

The general terms of reference of these Committees are as set out in Standing Order No. 130. The Committees are responsible for the interpretation of their own terms of reference. The Committees are entitled to examine the expenditure, administration and policy of the principal Government Departments, and also of their 'associated public bodies'. The terms of the Standing Orders do not define 'associated public bodies' but the then Chancellor of the Duchy of Lancaster said in his speech on 25 June 1979 that:

'The Government also accept the Procedure Committee's view that the Committees must be able to look at the activities of some public bodies that exercise authority of their own and over which Ministers do not have the same direct authority as they have over their own Departments. The test in every case will be whether there is a significant degree of ministerial responsibility for the body concerned.'

Associated public bodies therefore include all nationalised industries, fringe bodies and other Governmental organisations within the responsibilities of the Department or Departments concerned for which Ministers are

---

3 The House of Commons' Select Committee on Energy no longer exists in the 1990s. Other small changes have occurred since April 1987, when this Memorandum of Guidance was issued. For example, the Department of Health is separate now from the Department of Social Security. [Editor].

ultimately answerable. They do not, however, include bodies for which Ministers are not answerable to Parliament, even though these bodies may be in receipt of Government funds. There will no doubt be borderline cases, but in general the existing principles of Parliamentary accountability can be applied.

The work of Parliamentary Committees, whether Commons or Lords, is the concern of the House that appointed them and on whose behalf they conduct their enquiries. Therefore, questions about the work of a Committee, for example, how or when the Government will respond to a Committee's report, will normally only be raised in the relevant House. It is, however, acceptable for reference to be made in either House, in debates or during questions, to the substance of Committee reports and to their recommendations.

Annex A

Guidelines for Officials giving Evidence to Departmental Select Committees [4]

Officials who give evidence to departmental Select Committees do so on behalf of their Ministers in accordance with the principles that civil servants are accountable to Ministers, and that it is Ministers who are accountable to Parliament. In giving evidence, civil servants are therefore subject to the instructions of Ministers and remain bound to observe their duty of confidentiality to Ministers.

2. In the course of Select Committee inquiries into the expenditure, administration and policies of Departments and their associated bodies, the evidence given by officials will normally be concerned with explaining the policies and actions undertaken by Ministers, and by Departments on their behalf, and the reasons for those policies and actions. Sometimes, however, a Select Committee's inquiries may involve questions relating to what has been done by individual civil servants. On such occasions, the principles of Ministerial accountability are still applicable, even if officials have acted outside or contrary to the authority given to them by Ministers.

3. Subject to the general principles set out above, official witnesses should in all Select Committee inquiries be as helpful as possible in answering questions concened with the establishment of the facts of what has occurred in the making of decisions, or the carrying out of actions in the implementation of Government policies.

---

4 These guidelines supplement, and should be read in conjunction with, the Memorandum of Guidance for officials appearing before Select Committees, and will be incorporated in future editions of that guidance.

4. There may however be occasions when questions put by members of a Select Committee in the course of an inquiry appear to be directed to the 'conduct' of individual civil servants. 'Questions directed to the conduct' in this context means more than the establishing of facts about what has occurred; it carries the implication of allocating individual criticism or blame. In such circumstances, in accordance with the principles of Ministerial responsibility, it is for the Minister to look into the matter and if necessary institute a formal inquiry. Such an inquiry into the conduct and behaviour of individual civil servants and consideration of disciplinary action is properly carried out within a Department according to established procedures designed and agreed for the purpose, and with appropriate safeguards for the individual. It is then for the Minister to be responsible for informing the Committee of what has happened, and of what has been done to put the matter right and to prevent a recurrence. Evidence to a Select Committee on this should be given not by the individual civil servant or servants concerned, but by the Minister or by a senior official specifically designated by the Minister to give such evidence on his behalf. This would include the result of any disciplinary or other departmental proceedings against individual civil servants.

5. It is agreed that Select Committees should not act as disciplinary tribunals. Accordingly, if in the course of an inquiry a Select Committee were to discover evidence that called in question the 'conduct' of an individual named civil servant, the Committee should be asked not to pursue their own investigation into the 'conduct' of the person concerned, but to take up the matter with the Minister, for whom it would then be to deal with it on the lines described above.

6. If, when officials are asked to give evidence to a Select Committee, it is foreseen that the inquiry may involve questions about the 'conduct' of the individual officials in question or about other individual named officials, it should be suggested to the Committee that it would be appropriate for a Minister or a senior official designated by the Minister to give evidence, rather than the named officials in question. Any question which appears to relate to the 'conduct' of individual civil servants, such as the allocation of blame for what has occurred, can then be answered by the Minister or designated senior official. If an official giving evidence to a Committee is unexpectedly asked questions which he or she believes are directed at his or her individual 'conduct', or at the 'conduct' of another named individual civil servant, or if the official is uncertain whether or not questions fall into this category, the official should indicate that he or she wishes to seek instructions from his or her Minister, and the Committee should be asked to allow time for the Minister's instructions to be sought.

28 April 1987

NOTE 2

Code of Practice currently enforced by the Press Complaints Commission of the United Kingdom [1]

All members of the Press have a duty to maintain the highest professional and ethical standards. In doing so, they should have regard to the provisions of this code of practice and to safeguarding the public's right to know.

Editors are responsible for the actions of journalists employed by their publications. They should also satisfy themselves as far as possible that material accepted from non-staff members was obtained in accordance with this code.

Whilst recognising that this involves a substantial element of self-restraint by editors and journalists, it is designed to be acceptable in the context of a system of self-regulation. The code applies in the spirit as well as in the letter.

1. Accuracy

i. Newspapers and periodicals should take care not to publish inaccurate, misleading or distorted material.

ii. Whenever it is recognised that a significant inaccuracy, misleading statement or distorted report has been published, it should be corrected promptly and with due prominence.

---

1 Currently, the Press Complaints Commission is charged with enforcing this non-statutory Code of Practice which was framed by the newspaper and periodical industry of the United Kingdom. The Code is published in full in *Report No. 1* January–June 1991 of the Press Complaints Commission. [However, in January 1993 the latest report by Sir David Calcutt QC was published into Press and Privacy. The Calcutt report (1993) recommends *inter alia* a tough new *statutory* Code of conduct for newspapers, and a law of privacy obliging journalists to abide by a *statutory* Code. The Calcutt report is seen by some as an indirect attack on the Press Complaints Commission, which is considered to have failed in its attempt to discipline newspapers by the above *non-statutory* Code. The press, by contrast, fears that if the Government decides to turn the Calcutt conclusions into legislation, it will curb substantially the powers of the British press. A criticism of the Calcutt findings (1993) by the press is that the report does not recognise that newspapers consider they have a duty 'in the public interest' to investigate individuals, or public or private bodies, involved in possible corruption or scandals. Conversely, others complain about invasions into privacy by the press. *Editor]*

iii. An apology should be published whenever appropriate.

iv. A newspaper or periodical should always report fairly and accurately the outcome of an action for defamation to which it has been a party.

2. Opportunity to reply

A fair opportunity for reply to inaccuracies should be given to individuals or organisations when reasonably called for.

3. Comment, conjecture and fact

Newspapers, while free to be partisan, should distinguish clearly between comment, conjecture and fact.

4. Privacy

Intrusions and enquiries into an individual's private life without his or her consent are not generally acceptable and publication can only be justified when in the public interest. This would include:

i. Detecting or exposing crime or serious misdemeanour.

ii. Detecting or exposing seriously anti-social conduct.

iii. Protecting public health and safety.

iv. Preventing the public from being misled by some statement or action of that individual.

5. Hospitals

i. Journalists or photographers making enquiries at hospitals or similar institutions should identify themselves to a responsible official and obtain permission before entering non-public areas.

ii. The restrictions on intruding into privacy are particularly relevant to enquiries about individuals in hospital or similar institutions.

6. Misrepresentation

i. Journalists should not generally obtain or seek to obtain information or pictures through misrepresentation or subterfuge.

ii. Unless in the public interest, documents or photographs should be removed only with the express consent of the owner.

iii. Subterfuge can be justified only in the public interest and only when material cannot be obtained by any other means.

In all these clauses the public interest includes:

a. Detecting or exposing crime or serious misdemeanour.

b. Detecting or exposing anti-social conduct.

c. Protecting public health or safety.

d. Preventing the public being misled by some statement or action of an individual or organisation.

7. Harassment

i. Journalists should neither obtain information nor pictures through intimidation or harassment.

ii. Unless their enquiries are in the public interest, journalists should not photograph individuals on private property without their consent; should not persist in telephoning or questioning individuals after having been asked to desist; should not remain on their property after having been asked to leave and should not follow them.

The public interest would include:

a. Detecting or exposing crime or serious misdemeanour.

b. Detecting or exposing anti-social conduct.

c. Protecting public health and safety.

d. Preventing the public from being misled by some statement or action of that individual or organisation.

8. Payment for Articles

i. Payments or offers of payment for stories, pictures or information should not be made to witnesses or potential witnesses in current criminal proceedings or to people engaged in crime or to their associates except where the material concerned ought to be published in the public interest and the payment is necessary for this to be done.

The public interest will include:

a. Detecting or exposing crime or serious misdemeanour.

b. Detecting or exposing anti-social conduct.

c. Protecting public health and safety.

d. Preventing the public from being misled by some statement or action of that individual or organisation.

ii. 'Associates' includes family, friends, neighbours and colleagues.

iii. Payments should not be made either directly or indirectly through agents.

9. Intrusion into grief or shock

In cases involving personal grief or shock, enquiries should be carried out and approaches made with sympathy and discretion.

10. Innocent relatives and friends

The Press should generally avoid identifying relatives or friends of persons convicted or accused of crime unless the reference to them is necessary for the full, fair and accurate reporting of the crime or legal proceedings.

11. Interviewing or photographing children

i. Journalists should not normally interview or photograph children under the age of 16 on subjects involving the personal welfare of the child, in the absence of or without the consent of a parent or other adult who is responsible for the children.

ii. Children should not be approached or photographed while at school without the permission of the school authorities.

12. Children in sex cases

The Press should not, even where the law does not prohibit it, identify children under the age of 16 who are involved in cases concerning sexual offences, whether as victims, or as witnesses or defendants.

13. Victims of crime

The Press should not identify victims of sexual assault or publish material likely to contribute to such identification unless, by law, they are free to do so.

14. Discrimination

i. The Press should avoid prejudicial or pejorative reference to a person's race, colour, religion, sex or sexual orientation or to any physical or mental illness or handicap.

ii. It should avoid publishing details of a person's race, colour, religion, sex or sexual orientation, unless these are directly relevant to the story.

15. Financial journalism

Even where the law does not prohibit it, journalists should not use for their own profit financial information they receive in advance of its general publication, nor should they pass such information to others.

ii.   They should not write about shares or securities in whose performance they know that they or their close families have a significant financial interest, without disclosing the interest to the editor or financial editor.

iii. They should not buy or sell, either directly or through nominees or agents, shares or securities about which they have written recently or about which they intend to write in the near future.

16.   Confidential sources

Journalists have a moral obligation to protect confidential sources of information.

18

Privilege, Proceedings and Information given to Parliament

by Robert Rogers, a Deputy Principal Clerk,
House of Commons, Westminster [1]

Introduction

I think I must approach this subject in a responsive way rather than in a prescriptive way, because there is nobody who is entitled to give the view of the House of Commons on anything, far less on the sensitive subject of access to information. But I hope that I shall manage to be slightly more helpful than the Clerk of the House a little over a hundred years ago who, on a hot and frustrating Summer's evening after the House had spent four days on a second reading (these days second readings normally only occupy one sitting) of an Irish Bill, just as agitation for Irish Home Rule was reaching its pitch in the early 1880s. The Speaker suddenly realised late in the evening that he could see a procedural disaster about to open up in front of him. He leaned forward to the Clerk of the House, and said 'Sir Denis, Sir Denis, what do I do?' And the Clerk of the House gathered his gown around him, picked up his books, adjusted his wig and went and stood beside the Speaker's Chair. The Speaker began to relax on the assumption that some panacea was about to be presented to him, and Sir Denis Le Marchant said, 'I advise you, Sir, to be extremely careful' and disappeared behind the Chair. We now do try to be a little more helpful!

I shall concentrate my remarks on two subject areas, first, to give you a very brief survey of privilege, and, second, I should like to deal also with the handling of information, that category of information which is requested on behalf of the House by Select Committees.

1. Privilege

I shall look at privilege mainly from the point of view of the House of Commons, although it is common to both Houses of Parliament and it is very largely cognate with, and has the same origins as, the privilege which attaches to a court. This is not surprising, since Parliament is itself the High Court of Parliament and it is in order to protect its affairs, its doings, and to protect

---

1 This talk was given by Robert Rogers at the Fourth Conference of the Centre for Business and Public Sector Ethics held in Cambridge on 27 November 1991.

Members when they are actually in the service of the House doing their duty as Members, that privilege has developed.

Now I think I must caution you immediately against a feeling that privilege is some cloak which can be spread over everything which is even remotely Parliamentary. It is not, it is very precise, as precise as anything with edges as fuzzy as those of privilege can be. Privilege is for the purpose of facilitating and protecting the work of the House and of Members when they are involved in that work, when they are performing their duties. And so privilege relates to things like the freedom of speech in proceedings in Parliament (and I shall come to that definition in a moment), the freedom from molestation, and the freedom of the House as a whole from interference in its work. Perhaps a topical example of that would be the question of leaking of draft Reports of Select Committees. But again I shall come back to that in a little more detail later.

Now do not run away with the idea that we have in this country some broad immunity which is applied to all Members of Parliament, as soon as they are elected, or as soon as they have taken the oath or affirmed. That is the case in some countries. Interestingly, it is the case in the European Parliament, but it has been tested and indeed has survived recent tests in a way which I think is leading the European Parliament to compare other systems in Community countries. And, as it happens, a colleague of mine is giving evidence at this moment, before the European Parliament's Committee on Rules of Procedure on exactly this point, comparing the European Parliament system and our own at Westminster.

A Member who commits an offence for which he does not have the protection of privilege in the United Kingdom is entirely answerable before the law, even if the Member has committed the offence in circumstances which he may reasonably think are so closely connected with his parliamentary duties as to deserve some sort of protection of privilege. There was a case not long ago where a Member was hurrying for a Division and driving his car at huge speed across the carriageway going through Hyde Park, and he was stopped by a policeman. He said to the policeman 'You have no power to stop me. I am a Member of Parliament, I am going to a Division in the House, please let me pass.' And the constable, to his great credit, stood firm and said 'I don't know anything about that, Sir, please turn your engine off and get out of your vehicle.' And the Member, in turn, was greatly disabused about the application of the privilege and the extent of the protection it could afford him, because he was fined and his licence was endorsed.

And there he had put himself in a position where he was indeed going to something, a Division in the House, which would be a proceeding in Parliament, but he was acting in pursuance, as it were, of his private arrangements in how he got from A to B in order to take part in a proceeding. He was not taking part, at that time, in a proceeding.

Now the touchstone is certainly the question of what is proceedings in Parliament. But that itself is a moving target. And, indeed, privilege is not defined anywhere in statute, nor is it defined in any judgment, any *ex-cathedra* pronouncement of the House of Commons. And, of course, from time to time, the view of the courts as to what constitutes privilege and the view of the House as to what constitutes privilege may differ, but that is something we have to live with. There is no mechanism for approximating the two, some conferential system whereby we are going to arrive at a definition of what it is. I have to say that I am always attracted by grey areas in rules, because they turn out to be very much more profitable and advantageous than defining exactly where the rule starts and stops.

There was a surprising judgment by Mr Justice Popplewell not long ago, to the effect that an entry in the Register of Members' Interests was not a proceeding. Now the Register itself is published by order of the House, [2] so, at the very least, I would have thought that the application of the principle in *Stockdale and Hansard*, and indeed probably the Parliamentary Papers Act 1840, would have led him to a contrary view. But, as it happened, that is still on the record but as an event, rather than something which remains in conflict with the House's own view of its privileges.

There has been undoubtedly a narrowing of the application of privilege and of the effect of privilege. When I first went to the House the *locus classicus* was the Garry Allighan case, now forty years in the past, where a Member was eventually expelled from the House for his misconduct; but the relevance of this particular case to what I am saying is that 'the proceedings in Parliament' which formed part of that case were actually a private party meeting. I do not believe that the House today, in the context of having narrowed and refined Parliamentary privilege – in a certain degree I think in response to what is thought outside the House to be acceptable – would sustain that very broad definition of proceedings in Parliament. A party meeting just happens to be taking place in the precincts. It is not a committee of the House, it is not something which the House has ordered to be done, it is not a debate, which are the sort of criteria that have to be applied now.

There has always been an interplay of statute law and privilege case law. I suppose the most obvious example is the Bill of Rights, Article 9: no proceedings being questioned or impeached in any court or place outside Parliament. But there are many other examples. I quoted earlier the Parliamentary Papers Act, there is the Parliamentary Oaths Act 1866; and so on. But, those are merely a meshing of the two perceptions of what privilege is.

In regard to punishment, I think that the limitations that the House has to face in terms of punishing a contempt, a breach of privilege, have led to a

---

2 For details of the Register of Members' Interest, see this Volume, Appendix Part 111, pp. 570-96.

much more cautious application of privilege rules. The House has the power to imprison, but the last time anyone was imprisoned was a hundred years ago. I think if the House attempted to imprison somebody today there would be a severe credibility problem about the way in which the House had reached that decision. Indeed, about some civil and human rights issues, which might be involved in terms of being tried.

The House of Commons does not have the power to fine, although the House of Lords has the power to fine, although they have not done it for a long time. Most of the other recourses of the House of Commons, where there has been a breach of privilege, really tend towards the comic. It is now forty years since somebody was rebuked at the Bar of the House, but I think that in contemporary practice, a newspaper editor might well relish the opportunity of being rebuked at the Bar of the House. And so that has rather lost its sting! And it is twenty-five years since a Member stood in his place in order to be rebuked by the Speaker, and I think that probably that is open to the same sort of criticism.

So, the really severe sanction that the House of Commons still possesses, is of course over its own Members, for an abuse of their position, or for breaches of privilege which they themselves commit. The relevant twin weapons here are of suspension for such period of time as the House sees fit, or, in an extreme case, expulsion. And undoubtedly those are serious weapons. But they are weapons which it would be difficult to criticise the House for using, because the House is, in expelling or suspending a Member, merely regulating its internal proceedings.

The recent trend has been towards a greater caution with which the House has been operating. The definition of proceedings has been narrowing. In this connection, it might be relevant to mention the question of unsolicited documents, whistle-blower documents, received by Select Committees. Now I have been in the position of opening my post and seeing on my desk documents which made it quite clear to me, on the face of those documents, that the person who had sent them to me in my official capacity had committed certainly an offence under the Theft Act and, in all probablility, an offence under the old section 2 of the Official Secrets Act 1911 (now repealed by the Official Secrets Act 1989).

Please note that I cannot be prescriptive about privilege, I can only describe the pattern of what the House has in the past seen as a breach of privilege, and that is always the test. There is no book in which one can look up and say, yes, *that* is definitely a breach of privilege, *that* is not.

But in that aforementioned particular case of the documents I received, I would not advise, and did not advise, the Committee that those documents, and the receipt of those documents, attracted any privilege whatever, any protection of privilege. It would be a different matter, and I am glad to say that this still remains theoretical because we did not test it, to write to the person concerned and say please send us some more, because then you have engaged in a proceeding since the person concerned becomes *de facto* a witness and witnesses are protected by sessional order, as well as by ancient usage, against any criminal prosecution or civil proceeding in respect of the evidence which they give to a Select Committee. But let me leave that there.

The second area in which I have seen the House definitely drawing in its horns is on the question of leaks. The Committee of Privileges has investigated a number of leaks of primarily, Select Committee documents or Select Committee Reports over the years. Indeed, we now have a new system, perhaps as a result of the proliferation of such leaks a few years ago, whereby in the first instance the inquiry is one for the leaked-against committee itself to undertake. Such an inquiry happened most recently in the case of the Health Committee and the draft Report which we are led to understand was transmitted to the Department of Health. Once the Committee has reported that there has been an interference with its work, then, automatically, the matter is referred to the Committee of Privileges.

In the past, the Committee of Privileges has been very ready to recommend to the House sanctions against the people to whom the information was leaked. And the House has taken a broader view, and has said, no, these journalists are only doing their job. Sanctions would be unenforceable, because it would bring the whole process of punishing for this sort of offence into disrepute. Also, it is contrary to natural justice in a sense, if somebody is doing the job that they are paid for. What you have to do is to finger the leaker rather than the 'leakee'.

2. Information given to Parliament

And after that crime against the English language, perhaps I ought to move on to the question of information given to Parliament. I shall take, as my starting point, that some of the time-hallowed ways that Parliament seeks information from the Executive are now deeply flawed. This great jewel in the crown of Parliamentary procedure – Parliamentary Questions – 'I Shall Ask a Question in the House' is, I am afraid, tinged with the rosy mists of nostalgia. I do not believe that it is, any more, a very effective proceeding, because it has changed its character. It is an exchange of views. It is a process of assertion and counter assertion, rather than a truly inquisitorial function.

I think that one of the reasons for this change may well be that the House is extremely large and, as such, that underlines its theatrical qualities, which can be of great use when a Minister is under pressure at the despatch box. I do not say that the system of Parliamentary Questions should be written off.

But the complexity of Government and the need to look in detail at what Government is doing over a long period of time, not perhaps headline-grabbing stuff, means that the present system makes the task difficult. The lens is the House of Commons, as a whole. In the Chamber, through which it examines Government policy, through which it scrutinises the Executive, and this is not sufficient to carry out the job that the House of Commons ought to be doing.

In this respect I think that Select Committees, and particularly the post-1979 Select Committees, are an advantage. [3] Remember that Select Committees have a very long history. Indeed, most of the Parliamentary side of the Civil War was run by a Select Committee – and Parliament still won. But since 1979, the key thing about it has been not that the powers of Select Committee changed, because they did not one jot, but it was a rationalisation of the system, an extension of the system into fourteen Departmental Select Committees. I think a burgeoning of confidence grew amongst Members that this new system gave them a tool to do something which many of them had yearned for before, but did not have the means to tackle.

3. The role of Select Committees

I have been talking about the inquisitorial function, and certainly the Standing Order which sets the committees up talks about investigating the expenditure, administration and policy of Government Departments. Do not, however, under-estimate the role of Select Committees (a) in providing a forum for debate and discussion in a remarkably open way on Government policy, and on the views of those who are affected by Government policy and (b) as providers of information. A remarkable amount of information is produced in the evidence which the Select Committees publish and I think that that is a role which certainly should not be under-estimated.

David Faulkner, of the Home Office, referred earlier to culture. I have to say immediately that, when I proceed to talk about the provision of information by Government it is with my recent six years' experience on the Defence Committee in mind, and perhaps it may be said by some that the approach of the Ministry of Defence towards the giving of information to Parliament is not of the most user-friendly character. So forgive me, because I am talking about the Ministry of Defence and do not extend my remarks to other Government Departments and, certainly, not to the Home Office!

We are discussing what are the proper limits to which people in official positions should go in communicating information. Obviously, one criterion of this issue is: what does Parliament need? As an Officer of the House, I

---

3 For a list of the post-1979 Select Committees, see this Volume, pp. 283-84.

have to take the view that it is what Parliament says it needs, what a Select Committee says it needs in order to discharge the Order of Reference which the House has given it. Clearly, I recognise also the powerful constraints on Government, which David Faulkner has explained. Immediately I would make a distinction between those things which are secret, and those things which are sensitive.

But taking secrets first, rather surprisingly the Defence Committee found very little difficulty. We had regular access to secret information and the great mass of it was in terms of the progress of particular defence projects. I have to say that the Committee did not really approach this in an attitude of prurience, shall we say, seeking to find information. They did apply a need to know principle but, of course, I equally recognise that it was the Committee's view of what they needed to know and nobody else's.

But, basically, there was not very much of a problem. Problems did arise, of course, in the arguments that we used to have with the Ministry of Defence over the declassification of evidence. Clearly, the Commons' Defence Committee was not seeking to have some highly classified matter which bore on national security broadcast to the winds. But the Committee was also seeking information in areas where no reason for classification at all could be seen, and, particularly, where the information was freely publicly available. There was a recent case in the Committee, after I left it, where officials refused to answer in public session on the number of Tornadoes which were serviceable, although under the confidence building measures they had had to give that information to the Soviet High Command! That was a quirk. I am not criticising officials, because they had to follow the rules in this case and they found themselves, I am quite sure, in a very embarrassing situation of which they were fully aware, but they played the game by the rules.

The area which I think is particularly difficult is that of embarrassment, sensitivity, where nothing but loss, rather than profit, is foreseen by the Government. Please be assured that I am talking about Governments of any party. Let us take, as the first area, advice to Ministers, which David Faulkner touched on. [4] I have no difficulty with what is clearly advice to Ministers and, indeed, the classic arguments against revealing it seem to me to be very powerful. You should not prejudice the process of government reaching a decision on something. You should not associate individual officials with particular courses of advice, particularly since those may be politically highly sensitive. It is embarrassing for the official, and may make the official's job

---

4 For the paper delivered in Cambridge on 27 November 1991 at the Fourth Conference of the Centre for Business and Public Sector Ethics by David Faulkner, then Deputy Secretary at the Home Office, see this Volume, pp. 277-81.

much harder to do, and may mean that the advice which the Minister is getting is interpreted as being party political advice. I think that is embarrassing and not very helpful.

And so I do not think that there is any difficulty with matters which clearly fall into that category of advice to Ministers. But, there is an area, of course, which is up to the subjective judgement of a Department as to whether it makes information in that area available to Select Committees. And I shall give you a couple of examples which my former Committee found extremely trying.

One example was during our enquiry into the future of the brigade of Gurkhas. [5] We went so far in that case as to append the exchanges to the Report. The Committee thought that if the Gurkhas cannot be in Hong Kong after 1997, could they be sent elsewhere, say as in the case of Brunei where the Sultan meets all the costs of the Brunei battalion. Perhaps this might happen somewhere else, perhaps this might be a relatively elegant solution to the difficulty of what to do about the Gurkhas after 1997? I was asked to ask the Ministry of Defence: 'Has the Ministry investigated the possibility of deploying Gurkhas to any country where they have not so far been stationed? Are such deployments still under consideration?' *Answer* – the Gurkhas have exercised in a wide range of locations. In principle, and given sufficient training, there is no reason why Gurkha infantry should not be able to fulfil any of the United Kingdom's current war roles. Clearly, the deployment options available is one of the factors that will determine the future of the Gurkhas, with particular consideration being given to the need to meet the operational requirements of the Army and defence as a whole.

The Defence Committee tried again: 'It may be that the above answer is intended to be the answer to some different question and appears in the memorandum by mistake. The Committee will be grateful to know 1) whether the possibility of deploying Gurkhas, other than on exercise, to any country where they have not so far been stationed, has been considered by the Ministry? 2) if so, which countries? 3) What is the present status of any such possibility? The Committee will be content with a classified answer to these questions should one be necessary.'

Reply by the Ministry of Defence: 'As you acknowledge, question 3 of your letter reiterates an earlier request for information. We have tried to be as helpful as possible in our answer, while staying within the conventions regarding the advice on policy options given to Ministers and on which Ministers have not taken a view.'

---

5 See Defence Committee, First Report, (Session 1988-89), *The Future of The Brigade of Gurkhas* HC 68 (London, HMSO 8 February 1989).

The Defence Committee tried a third time: 'I have to say that I do not understand the paragraph of your letter relating to question 3 in my letter of 12th January. This question does not relate to advice on "policy options given to Ministers". It does not ask what deployments have been recommended to Ministers. The three points of question 3 are purely factual, and I would be grateful if you could explain why the Ministry is unable to provide answers.'

Reply by the Ministry of Defence: 'Existing Government policy,' said the Ministry of Defence, 'is reflected in the current deployment pattern of Gurkhas given in an earlier memorandum and we have made it clear that deployment options will be one of the factors to be taken into account in determining the future of the Gurkhas. As we have also made clear, no option for the future deployment of the Gurkhas in principle has been excluded from consideration. Therefore, it would be inappropriate for us to go beyond what was said in the memorandum forwarded with my letter of 18th January. I hope this clarifies the matter.'

Now, of course, I am being exceptionally unfair, and I do not wish to pillory, but really I am quoting that example to you as, I hope, a vivid example of where perceptions on "advice" change reality. The interpretation of advice, on one side, is perfectly straightforward, no doubt. On the other side, it is equally straightforward. Unfortunately, they are not identical interpretations!

Now another example was that of the long-term costings, a key document for financial planning in the Ministry of Defence, and one which, when changes occur, can have enormous effect, both on industrial activity in terms of slowing down the pace of performance of a contract and on service dates. Accordingly, it is highly sensitive. But the character of the information and its classification is no higher than anything that the Committee routinely received. But, once again, that was seen by the Ministry of Defence as advice to Ministers, although it occupied a role in the Ministry of Defence which was clearly different. I shall not attempt to define its role any more closely for the moment, but it was different from the business of recommending a course of action to a Minister, or providing an analysis of a problem upon which a Minister then would have to decide.

I do not wish to treat this lightheartedly and I equally recognise that there are two perfectly valid views, but I hope that just going through some of these examples gives a flavour of the interpretative difficulties which can arise.

The other point, which again David Faulkner mentioned, was the question of discussions between Departments. Here again, the Memorandum of Guidance for officials giving evidence before Select Committees [6] is very

---

6 For extracts from the Memorandum of Guidance for officials appearing before Select Committees of Parliament, see this Volume, pp. 282-86.

precise on not revealing conversations between Ministerial colleagues or between Departments. But let me give you an example of where perhaps this is not an entirely appropriate attitude to take. We were doing an inquiry into the future of deployments in the South Atlantic and what sort of level of deployment would be required, what the threat was and things of that sort. Clearly, there were two separate interests. One was the Ministry of Defence, which took a view about the military threat and wished to save some money because a) it was expensive and b) in personnel terms there was a great deal of turbulence in long deployments to the South Atlantic. And the other was the Foreign Office, which wished to have a presence there for other reasons, including negotiating fishing licences, and things of that sort.

Now, the Defence Committee asked questions which were designed to bring out the two themes; not unusual, all sorts of Government decisions have to involve the complex weighing of competing priorities. But the Government absolutely refused to answer on what the Foreign Office might have said. It was through the Ministry of Defence, and through them alone, that the Committee received their evidence.

Clearly, there are two sides here again. Understandably, Government sees a Committee saying what did *you* say, and then what did *you* say, as possibly an attempt to insert a very damaging wedge and to threaten the principle of collective responsibility. But of course Departments within themselves make similar judgements. 'We would have liked to have done that, but we could not afford it.' It seems an artificial distinction when the two priorities within Government as a whole, which we are frequently told is a seamless concept, nevertheless cannot be compared as perhaps they should, because of that rule.

And I do not want to criticise the Memorandum of Guidance unduly, but I hope that those two features of advice to Ministers and discussions between Departments will illustrate, again, some of the problems that exist.

I shall conclude with two final points. One is the very difficult area of the extent to which civil servants appearing before Select Committees appear only, as it were, as manifestations of the Ministers to whom they are responsible. Now clearly here, the Westland case is the *locus classicus* and I should have a close interest in this case because I drafted the Committee's report. And, in that context, I recommend Rosamund Thomas's survey. [7] I think probably that those difficulties cannot be considered separately from the question of accountability.

Ministerial accountability has moved on since the Crichel Down case, [8]

---

7 Survey by Dr Thomas is reproduced in this Volume, Appendix Part I, pp. 383-408.
8 See R. Douglas Brown *The Battle of Crichel Down* (London, The Bodley Head 1955).

and a new way of approaching it has got to be developed, and is developing. But, as the Defence Committee said in its report, accountability on the part of Ministers does not mean just accepting a general responsibility for what took place and then, if pressured into it, resigning. Accountability involves accounting to Parliament in detail for actions taken as a Minister. I think here there are questions which relate to the roles and answerability of those who serve in the 'Next Steps' agencies.

I should not like you to think that I am advocating a complete transparency between Select Committees and Government, so that Select Committees can look at anything and interfere with anything. I am not advocating micro-management by Select Committees, who are not skilled in it, and, indeed, are not there to do it; they are there to carry out a form of policy audit and financial review. I would not advocate micro-management at all and I think it is sometimes seen in Whitehall as something of a spectre. I think Select Committees are there to create, if one can give it this name, a *climate of accountability* where the possibility of Parliamentary review and investigation is never far from the minds of those who are making policy decisions.

Finally, I ought to say that Select Committees have come a long way since the story which I hope is apocryphal, but I fear not, of the Committee which was given a Departmental briefing and after chart after chart, and graph after graph, had been unfolded and the briefing was at an end, there was one of those embarrassing silences when nobody has quite understood what has happened and nobody really wants to ask a question. The Chairman thought he had better do something and he said to the Permanent Secretary 'Sir John, it's an extremely interesting briefing, it's given us a lot of food for thought, perhaps you could begin by explaining to us this steady trend which is shown in column 8 of that chart?' And there was an even more uncomfortable silence and the Permanent Secretary said, 'that Chairman, is the date'.

19

Free Speech – Prince of Rights?

by the Honourable Sir John Laws, [1] *Justice of the High Court, Queen's Bench Division, formerly Treasury Devil*

1. The Relationship between Law and Morals

Controversies in and out of the courts about confidentiality and free expression demonstrate that this is an area where questions of law and questions of morals are apt to run into each other. The Government might say (as it did in the *Spycatcher* [2] case) that a newspaper intending to publish the unauthorised memoirs of a former member of the Security Service would breach its legal right to protect confidential information, and there is a public interest in maintaining the confidence; the newspaper might say (as they did) that the public interest requires publication. This is a legal dispute, of which, of course, the court is the judge. Yet there are moral overtones: different people will have very pointed perceptions about the right answer in such circumstances – irrespective of what the law says about it.

Now take the case of the doctor: he may receive confidences from his patient which, ordinarily, he would regard it as his duty to keep. But there might be powerful reasons for breaking it; the welfare of other patients of his might be affected; there might be in the rare case an over-riding public interest. If the doctor's decision to break the confidence ever fell to be litigated, I incline to think that the court might not have too much to say about it: if the doctor had made a careful and considered decision, the judge would be unlikely to second-guess his conscience or professionalism. So here the ties between law and morals, or at any rate professional ethics, are much looser. Contrast, again, the case of a commercial confidence: its owner is in general entitled to protect it by recourse to law; sometimes public interest questions can arise, but more usually the case turns on whether the information was truly confidential or whether for some reason the defendant was entitled to use or publish the material. To all such questions, the law will

---

1 Sir John delivered this discourse before his appointment to the Bench, as an after-dinner speech on 14 May 1991 at the Second Conference of the Centre for Business and Public Sector Ethics held in Cambridge that day on the topic of 'Confidentiality of Information (and Leakages)'.

2 For full details of this case, see Michael Fysh, Q.C. (Editor) *The Spycatcher Cases* [1989] 2 F.S.R. 3, 27, 81 and 181. See also Rosamund M. Thomas *Espionage and Secrecy: the Official Secrets Acts 1911-1989 of the United Kingdom* (Routledge 1991 and Routledge, Chapman and Hall 1992), Chapters 3 and 4.

provide the answer. While moralists will have views about commercial confidences, they are unlikely to be so stark as in the newspaper case; and, unlike the medical case, the ethical perceptions of the defendant will have little or no part to play in the adjudication of the court.

What is to be learned from these instances? First, that the relationship between law and morals in this area is not unitary, but diverse; secondly, that interests of a very different kind are engaged in the different types of case. These facts make the search for principle a sophisticated task, in which in some quarters there is a temptation to be captious and partisan. Professor Hare [3] has said that thinking about moral questions has this in common with other intellectual activity, that it can be done well or badly, and this is true; it means that knee-jerk reactions are nearly always unhelpful.

2. The Search for, and Importance of, Moral Principles

In the search for principle, the first step, I think, is this: that breach of confidence is always on the face of it - *prima facie*, to use the legalism - unconscientious: that it stands in need of justification. There is often a confusion in conversations about ethics between the notion of an absolute rule and the notion of a principle. Diehards in many fields will assert the existence of absolute rules, for fear that without them morals are trivialised and become matters of mere opinion. Others will say - especially in areas of private conduct - that morality is a subjective concept in which one person's opinions have no more value than anyone else's. Both views are crude and jejune. If a developed society is not to fall victim either to the Scylla of dogmatism or the Charybdis of a louche philosophy in which decency is a joke word, it will recognise that moral questions cannot be resolved by adherence to either side of so barbarous an antithesis. Rather, it will vouchsafe and underwrite the importance of principles: not doing violence; not telling lies; not treating another unkindly; not, indeed, breaking confidences. But these are not absolute rules, because it is in the nature of a principle that there may be circumstances in which the principle should not apply: self-defence is an answer to violence; courtesy and kindness may require a lie; necessary criticism may be unkind; the public interest may dictate a breach of confidence. Thus, though such a breach may always require to be justified, justification will sometimes be at hand. It is in the tension of this debate that issues concerning the breach of confidence must be confronted.

3. The Media: Partners in the Rule at Law?

Then we have the question, who is to decide whether a confidence can rightly be breached? I have been discussing moral perceptions, but here we

---

3 R. M. Hare *Moral Thinking* (Oxford University Press 1981).

have an issue about how our society should be ordered as a matter of compulsory rule. There are newspaper editors who believe that the courts have no business, generally, making orders which have the effect of a prior restraint against an intended publication. Now, such a man is obviously entitled to think that the American system, in which such orders are rarely available, is greatly to be preferred to the British. That is one thing. But suppose he takes this position: that because he feels it his right – even his duty – to publish first and have questions asked afterwards, he will resort to a trick or device to prevent the case being aired before a judge until after publication. Here, he makes himself the judge: he says he knows better than the judge, or, at least, that he is *morally* entitled to baulk the possibility that the judge, not he, will decide whether the publication should go ahead. This I think is a very questionable position. The newspaper is taking a view based on its perception of the public interest. Society cannot live with decisions about the public interest, which may affect many citizens, unless the decision is made by a body with the constitutional authority to make it. The media are not, in this, merely private parties to litigation with their own axe to grind. They would not like it, but they, to an extent at least, should be partners in the rule of law.

The importance of the foregoing observations is related not merely to the possibility that the media might behave dishonourably; rather, it is that the last guardian of the public interest in confidence cases has to be the court. It is true of doctors, businessmen, newspapers. It is true of the Executive, though not of the Legislature, because of our doctrine of Parliamentary Sovereignty. It is a first principle which should not be forgotten in discussions about the ethics or the law of confidence.

There is another distinction to be made. I have referred to businessmen, doctors, and the press. There is a distinction, looking at these examples, between confidence cases which engage issues of freedom of expression, as the Strasbourg Convention would call it, and other confidence cases which do not. A doctor's dilemma about revealing a patient's confidence is not a question about freedom of expression. Nor is an ex-employee's decision whether or not to use information he has gained from his employer. But when the media are concerned whether or not to publish something they have obtained, freedom of expression is the badge under which their case is written. And it is true as well of issues of censorship.

4. Censorship

Censorship should be a problem about confidences, pure and simple, and is worth looking at. Remember the debates we had in the 1960s. We have to some extent moved past them: about the rights and wrongs of prohibiting allegedly indecent material. Now that was a debate, whatever side of it one felt loyal to, which was not about what the law should be. It was about rules we ought to have. It was not about whether there was a moral right to disobey the law. Compare the position of the journalist who declines to reveal his sources; there has been some interesting and important litigation about that. He declines to reveal them even under order of the court. Paradoxically, that case is one in which the court may be requiring a breach of confidence. The journalist does not necessarily say that the law should be any different from what it is. He says something other than that. He says, rather, that he is morally entitled to ignore it, to disobey it. He will, as is sometimes put, go to the stake for it. Now where is the principle in that? He will refuse to obey an injunction and he will expect the approbation of his peers in doing so. It is because he disagrees with the court. Why should he have a better claim to anyone's approval than the publisher who publishes some, let us say, erotic work in defiance of an injunction, in the belief that it is a work of art which the judge has no business to suppress.

These are questions that can throw light on the individual moral judgment to be made, to say nothing of the legal judgment, in the various cases that can arise. Of course, this is not merely about what confidence should be kept. This is about, as Humpty Dumpty would have said, who should be master. I fear that my song is that in the end you have to let the court be the master. If you do not, the citizen's rights, not the judge's, are what are infringed. It is easy to entertain the pronouncement of rights such as life itself, and to echo them and mark flags on their backs, but these rights are, funnily enough, like the bloodless shades on the banks of the Styx, voiceless, ineffective, unless there are lying behind them other rights and in particular the right to live in a social régime that is ordered by the law. The law very wisely gives place to the professional decision of doctors and others in other circumstances that you would perhaps be better able to imagine than I. The law, I think, must conform its principles to the age in which it operates. It must speak a language which is not private, obscure and remote, but which is part of the lingua franca of the people. It must see that its authority is not resented or repudiated but, in the end, welcome.

The law, as a whole, has achieved these aims. Too many stories abound about judges who have not heard of the Beatles, Gaza or other instances. There was one judge, a very distinguished commercial judge, a brilliant lawyer, who however knew nothing of machinery, in particular he knew nothing of motor cars. He had to his chagrin to try an accident case and the man came to give evidence and told the judge 'I was driving along the road and I changed down in order to accelerate and gather speed'. A little later he said 'I came to a hill and I was to go down the hill so I changed down in order to lower my speed'! The judge cast away his pencil and said to Counsel 'This is an obviously incredible witness who contradicts himself in front of the court in such a manifest way'.

Now this is a trivial example of what may be a lack of judicial understanding. There are other stories, of course. But this is only to say that we have judicial imperfections, of which there are many, and the judges must cure them. So they must! What it is not to say is that in the end, where we have problems, ethical problems that travel into the law about confidence, there is another master than the law. For there is none and the answer, an alternative answer, is not only a denial of the simple form of legal rights, it is a denial of democratic rights. It is a denial of a citizen's right to live under an established system with a balanced division of power. And so in the end if the law is sometimes an ass, as clearly it sometimes is, anyone thinking he is above it, is a bigger one.

20

Free Speech – Prince of Rights?

*Reply to the Honourable Mr Justice Laws by Sir John Bourn, KCB,
Comptroller and Auditor General, the National Audit Office* [1]

I am delighted to be asked to respond to a very interesting talk that we have had from John Laws. If I have understood him correctly, he has with his own great skill, sketched out the way, when we face ethical dilemmas, we can proceed. On the one hand, we see a possible solution lying in the application of dogma and, on the other hand, a possible solution lying in relativism. But, instead, we should look for a middle way, a principle, and we should reflect that principles sometimes conflict and therefore we should turn to the court to make the choice between them. By the courts, I think, he must ultimately mean a wise man, a judge. Now I am all in favour of turning to wise men, because as the Comptroller and Auditor General, surely I must place myself in this category! A claim which I boldly assert and you will be kind enough on this occasion not to deny me.

But I am conscious, as I say this, that I ought to explain who I am, because I know colleagues from overseas, and some of those from the United Kingdom, do not have any very clear idea of what the Comptroller and Auditor General does. [2] I shall use my own experience to elaborate on what John Laws has said.

1. The role of the Comptroller and Auditor General as a wise man'

Like everything in Britain, the Comptroller and Auditor General goes back a long way and, indeed, I go back to 1314 and I started as an official in the court of the King. It was the task of my predecessors to, as it were, sit on the treasure chest of the King and if you wanted to do something interesting, you would have applied to my predecessor for the money to do it. And if he thought that your request accorded with the policy of the King, he

---

1 Sir John Bourn delivered this reply as an after-dinner speech on 14 May 1991 at the Second Conference of the Centre for Business and Public Sector Ethics held in Cambridge that day on the topic of 'Confidentiality of Information (and Leakages)'. The Honourable Mr Justice Laws gave his talk, to which Sir John Bourn here responds, before he was appointed to the Bench. [*Editor*].

2 For the detailed paper delivered in July 1989 at the Inaugural Conference of the Centre for Business and Public Sector Ethics by Sir John Bourn entitled 'Government Accounting, Standards and Ethics: The British Experience', see this Volume pp. 20-47.

would give you the money and if he didn't he would not. You can see from this description that this was a job in Medieval times of great attraction, so that if you got it right you would end up as a Duke and a millionaire. Of course if you got it wrong, it was the Tower of London and your head off! And although I have to say life is not quite so exciting at the headquarters of the National Audit Office today, there is still a residual function which derives from that activity.

And it is that, as the Comptroller General of the Receipt and Issue of Her Majesty's Exchequer, every day I receive a request from the Treasury for the funds to keep the Government going for the day. And when I approve this request, if I do, as lying within what Parliament intends (because democracy has moved on and I now work for Parliament rather than the monarch), I send an instruction to the Governor of the Bank of England to, as it were, put it in the Government's current account for the day.

So that will give you some idea of my duties. But it is true to say, as well, that the title which I bear as Comptroller and Auditor General, does have a certain ring to it and does, I have noticed on being introduced to people, induce a certain reaction of panic and alarm! This was underlined for me particularly when some months ago I visited a hospital, because I thought that the Comptroller and Auditor General ought not to sit among his books of account; he ought to go out and see the world where the truth might be supposed to lie – not on pieces of paper in his accounts. And I went to visit a hospital. I said to the Department of Health that I should like to go and see a hospital and they said what a good idea. And when some weeks later they said we have carefully selected a hospital and I was invited not to go to the hospital down the road, Westminster, or across the river at St Thomas's. Instead, I was invited to go to the Pilgrim Hospital in Lincolnshire, which I was very pleased to do.

I went there and we had an excellent day, in which I had all the details of the finances of the region and the district explained to me, and then, in a way the most exciting part of the day, I was handed over to the nursing staff to walk the wards. And, rather like a parcel, I passed from one sister to another and we were going down one of these enormously long wards that you have in hospitals and the sister stopped at the bedside of an elderly gentleman who was looking pretty pale and wan as he lay on the bed. And the sister bent over him and she said 'This is the Comptroller and Auditor General, he's come to visit you.' And the look of horror and alarm! At the very best I had come with a bill, but more likely he was dead already and some acolyte of St Peter had come to make the final reckoning!

But I say that to give you some flavour of what sort of wise man I am supposed to be. I am, of course, in the role of Comptroller and Auditor General, a kind of accountant, a kind of auditor. I have reflected about my own position, in the context of this Conference on 'Confidentiality of

Information (and Leakages)' and it seemed to me that the auditor is, in a way, a kind of licensed leaker.

2. The Comptroller and Auditor General as a 'licensed leaker'

The auditor is a person who examines the activities of an organisation from a privileged position of access to confidential matters, and he reports upon them in public. That is true of the auditor of a public limited company and it is certainly true of the Comptroller and Auditor General, who reports on the accounts and the activities of the Departments of Central Government and a wide range of other bodies.

Now is this licence, as it were, to break confidences and to put into the public arena privileged information, something that should worry us, or is it something that we should be pleased about? Is the licensed leaker a contributor to the liberty of the people, or is he in fact someone who over-turns the orderly conduct of business, someone who releases into the public domain matters which are handled more expeditiously on a confidential basis? And of course there has been, in the development and the history, I think, of the accountancy profession, certainly in the development and the history of the Comptroller and Auditor General, a degree of such over-turning. Note the answer to this question; because the auditor is a licensed leaker, he is indeed given privileged access, he is indeed expected to report publicly. And perhaps this is what makes him bearable; he is required to do so hedged about by a number of conventions, practices and laws.

If I take my own case, for example, yes I do report on the accounts of Government Departments, but I am required to report on their performance in relation to specific purposes. I am required to report on them in terms of auditing their accounts and saying whether they have produced value for money. I am not supposed to report on them for other purposes, saying whether I approve or disapprove of what they are about, or whether their activities will lead to human happiness. Value for money is what I am supposed to do. And whether the accounts are a true and fair record of the disbursement of funds. So, I am limited in what I may say, in terms of the purposes to which I am directed.

Then, I am limited also in terms of the access to the materials of the Departments at which I look. I can ask for all the information I want, but it must be in terms of my purposes, it must be in terms of auditing the accounts. To audit the accounts, it is my unfettered right to ask for what I think I need. Interestingly enough, so far as my duties to look for value for money are concerned, I may ask for what I reasonably require. There are not yet any decided cases, and I hope that there never will be, which attempt to define what is reasonable. But nonetheless, one sees that the access I have is hedged around this way.

There are other limits, which fall into a third category, that hedge me about. One limit is that I am not to question Government policy in what I do. I am to fashion my comments on the accounts and to comment on value for money without criticising the Government's policy objectives. I may find from my examination of implementation and management that the policy is such a nonsense and it could not possibly ever be put into effect in such a way that it is economic, effective and efficient. But I may not write that down in words that appear to cast a stone at the Government's policy objectives.

Another area in which I am limited relates to my staff, and I am limited there in that my staff, as I am, are required to be bound by the Official Secrets Acts; not surprising in this country, because they do have access to the papers and records of Government Departments. My staff are also professional accountants. I have to say that I am not. The eccentricities of the British constitution allow someone to be the Comptroller and Auditor General who is not in fact an accountant! But my staff are professional accountants and therefore they have a duty to obey the ethical precepts of the accountancy profession.

Finally, there is also a spirit or convention which affects the way in which I report, so that, for example, when I comment on the activities of a Government Department, I may say that, for example, a particular Defence project has not achieved the delivery, time and cost that was intended, but by convention I do not say this is the fault of Mr Snookes, the Director General of Missile Systems, and I do not lay blame at the door of individuals in that way. But this is just a convention of the office.

Now I have mentioned all these in reasonable detail, because I think they are important in understanding the work of somebody like the auditor, and there are other people in this position in society who, as it were, are licensed leakers. They have the right, apparently, to say what they wish. But, in fact when you look at the way in which they set about it, you see built into the system within which they operate, a whole series of limitations and conventions. And I suppose what we have to ask, and what we have to decide, is whether these conventions are in fact devices to emasculate the auditor, so that what he says is done in words which are so opaque, that they carry no real meaning? Are these devices to emasculate the auditor, or are they devices to make his presence feasible, and possible, and consistent with the conduct of good business? I suppose the answer must be that this is a matter for continuing debate and perhaps this is a matter which the Centre for Business and Public Sector Ethics, Cambridge, and this Conference, must attend to. Because I think that what we do have to do, in such positions as my own, is consider what is my remit and the conventions which support it, or undermine it. And to look over a period of years as to how appropriate they are, and to enquire whether they need modification as times change.

And so the thought, that I would like to put before you, building I hope with some reasonable consistency on developing the argument put forward by John Laws, of asking how should wise men behave, that is to say that usually when such people are appointed in our society they appear to be given a licence to speak out, but this licence is abridged and we have to ask whether the abridgement is productive to the public benefit, or is the constraint a reduction in the public benefit? And that, I think, is what a Centre, such as your own, might attend to, and attend to it by looking not only at the broad and exciting questions of confidentiality and some of the cases, which of course, must engage us, but also to look at the detail of the position of people who have access to information and some duty to report it. I have spoken about the position of the Comptroller and Auditor General, but I might have given a rather similar discussion of the position of the tax inspector, or the position of the policeman in handling the information that he receives from informers, and a great range of other people in society.

PART IV

Government Ethics:

Concepts, Education and Training

21

Ethics in Governance:
The United Kingdom 1979-1990

by Andrew Dunsire,
Emeritus Professor of Politics, University of York, England

Introduction

What is ethical governance? If governments can ever be said to be acting immorally (as distinct from the persons involved), how are such actions to be recognised? How, once recognised, can correction be applied? These would seem to be the questions to be addressed. However, they may not have universal answers; it would be a safer bet for a political scientist to assume that the answers to such questions are culture-specific. Let me therefore say that ethical dilemmas or controversies in governance are exemplified by government policies or strategies that run counter to the expectations of enough people in a culture concerning what it is 'right' for a government to do. In this paper I shall try to elicit a specific set of answers by describing what worried a lot of people in the United Kingdom about some of the actions of the Thatcher Government and of its civil servants, but setting that discussion within a framework that may well have wider applicability.

1. Ethics in governance: a hierarchical model

I propose the following model.[1] It seems to me that people employ a hierarchy of expectations of right conduct in their government, a hierarchy in the same sense as Maslow's 'hierarchy of needs'[2] – that is, we would expect the lower to be met before we went on to consider whether the higher were or should be met. Thus, on the lowest level of expectation we look for government to be awake, alert, vigilant and diligent in seeing what needs seeing to, whether it be protection from external enemies or filling in holes in public roads; and from all public servants, a day's work for a day's pay. We might hope also for effectiveness: effort accurately directed, services that work. Laziness, inattentiveness, carelessness and desultoriness are faults wherever they are found, as are bumbling, lack of coordination, poor

---

1 I have used a similar scheme in discussing the narrower subject of 'Bureaucratic Morality in the United Kingdom' – see A. Dunsire *International Political Science Review* Vol. 9 (3) 1988 pp. 179-91.

2 A. Maslow 'Motivation and Personality' (New York, Harper and Row 1954).

control. I call this most basic level of governmental ethics the level of *competence*. The least the people ought to be able to expect is government that can get things done (irrespective of whether they agree with what is being done).

It is quite a step up to the next level of expectation, which concerns the idea that the government acts on the nation's or the people's behalf, governance as a trust. Public officials, more so than others, should have clean hands, and do nothing that cannot stand up to investigation afterwards. It is at this level that questions of honesty, probity and rectitude arise; including, of course, the classic area of 'corruption', encompassing extortion, bribery, malversation, nepotism and the other standard 'Weberian' crimes. Where the notion of 'property' obtains at all, stealing is usually a crime, though in many cultures stealing public property is often considered less of a sin than taking your neighbour's possessions, at least at petty levels. The same may be true of nepotism: while formally prohibited, it may be actually enjoined by traditional values. But corruption at higher levels, using public office to line one's own pockets, while it may be no surprise, is usually seen as wicked, a betrayal of trust, unethical governance.

But there is a positive as well as a negative aspect of care for the public purse. A Government ought to make the best use of public resources; therefore it ought on the one hand to search for economies, 'value-for-money', efficiency; and on the other, to maximise the return on the employment of national resources so as to increase national welfare. But national resources extend beyond money: a good Government ought to care for the environment, and consider its powers held in trust not only for the present generation, but for those who come after. This is why I call this second level of governmental ethics *stewardship*.

Accountability of this kind can be distinguished, then, from a higher order of moral expectation, associated with governmental authority or power over the lives of citizens: that government should act justly as between individuals and groups. Official rhetoric in all régimes usually asserts that the government is the government of 'all the people', and that it is the welfare of the whole country that is behind every exercise of official discretion. For some institutions of the State, for example judges and magistrates, the obligation to investigate both sides of any case, to use due process, and arrive at impartial judgment, is almost paramount; but the ethic of equity is present to some degree for all manifestations of government. This is the level of *fairness*.

The highest level of ethical expectation concerns what I shall call *honour*. The expectation can be expressed simply enough: governments should not tell lies, they should keep their bargains, they should be loyal to the constitution and to the civilised understandings of public life. In so far as we are talking about politicians, we have to make room for the 'professional lie' or necessary renege (*cf* the 'professional foul' in association football). Yet there are limits; honour consists in keeping well within these limits.

Civil servants, for their part, have a duty to obey and not to obstruct their political masters. But more significantly, we impose an obligation on them to be resourceful and imaginative in the deployment of their knowledge and experience, in not only obeying instructions, but taking the merest hints of these instructions and developing them, making them workable, suggesting superior methods, even superior objectives. They should 'learn the mind of the Minister' to such a degree that they can carry out the wishes of the Minister even when none have been expressed (the 'doctrine of anticipated reactions'). [3] In the United Kingdom an even more stringent obligation has applied: the civil servant has been expected to give this 'professional' loyalty equally sincerely to whatever government is in political power. [4]

As I see it, all four levels of obligation apply at all levels of the government hierarchy. Those at the base of the pyramid of rank have no more of a dispensation from the obligations of governmental honour than do Cabinet Members from the requirements of competence. But forms and incidences differ. Similarly, the ethics of stewardship and fairness apply throughout government, but special structures may be needed at grades where most actual cash is handled, where individual cases are determined, and so on. By the same token it is at the top where the greatest virtue in governmental honour is needed.

2. Coping with transgressions: a hierarchical model

If this four-level hierarchy of expectations seems to provide reasonable categories for the ordering of a discussion of ethics in governance in the United Kingdom, perhaps the discussion of how we try to cope with transgressions should also be based on a model. A fairly simple ascending-systems model will cope reasonably well: for *competence*, control within the bureaucracy or the Cabinet – ordinary supervision or management; for *stewardship*, control via cross-cutting agencies or inspectorates, that is, functional or procedural control; for *fairness*, control through courts of law or social institutions such as mass media; and for *honour*, ultimate control through the supreme democratic machinery of elections, aided more proximately by élite socialisation processes.

With that introduction, we proceed to an assessment of governmental ethics in the United Kingdom in the last decade, under these four heads.

---

3 C. J. Friedrich *Constitutional Government and Politics* (New York, Harper and Brothers 1937) p. 16.

4 It should be noted, however, that since 1979 a Conservative Government has been in power without interruption, which is unusual for the United Kingdom which, normally, operates as a two Party system of government.

3. Governmental Competence

The British State apparatus is not, by and large, an incompetent or undisciplined one. From time to time charges of incompetence were levelled at the Thatcher Government by political opponents, mainly for not thinking through the implementation consequences of an ideology-driven policy change, such as in the ever-shifting exemptions and interim palliatives of the replacement of the local property tax with a community charge or poll tax; or the embarrassing escalation in the cost of decommissioning the Magnox nuclear reactors; or blunders in selling off ordnance plants without proper valuation, leading to inordinate profits for asset-stripping buyers; or chaos in the Passport Office as a result of staff cuts and bungled computerisation; or the obstinate reliance only on interest rates in the management of the economy. It is easy, also, to find instances of lack of co-ordination to castigate, as with any modern government. But the effectiveness of governance in the United Kingdom in the last decade – the ability to carry through what has been decided, in the large scale privatisation programme, for instance – is not seriously in question.

At the individual case level, too, 'maladministration' in the form of inordinate delay, insufficient consideration, perverse rule-following and the like, seems containable. Cases investigated by the Parliamentary Commissioner for Administration and fellow-Ombudsmen are in the hundreds rather than the thousands annually, the bulk of them concerning two Ministries, Inland Revenue and Social Security, which have the longest interface with citizens. These Ombudsmen cannot make awards to successful complainants; they can only draw the attention of managements to their shortcomings.

The most disturbing cases of poor management and discipline in recent years have not been in the tax or benefits fields, however, but in policing. Allegations of 'police brutality' after any disturbance or demonstration have become almost routine; but discounting the political animus, there have been several well-authenticated and admitted cases of excessive police violence causing severe injuries and even deaths, as well as a long catalogue of unproven allegations about deaths-in-custody, unprovoked assaults, carrying of irregular weapons, and so on. The creation of an independent Police Complaints Authority in 1985 has not stilled criticism; complaints against policemen are still investigated by other policemen, and awards are only recommendations to management. Both the indiscipline and the allegations perhaps can be put down to reaction, within society and within the service, to a fairly massive shift in the police role, from crime to public order, within the present generation. [5]

---

5 R. Reiner *The Politics of the Police* (Brighton, Wheatsheaf 1985) and 'Dixon's Decline: Why Policing has become so Controversial' *Contemporary Record* Vol. 3 (1) pp. 2-6. See also J. Benyon *The Police: Powers, Procedures and Proprieties* (Oxford, Pergamon 1986) and *The Roots of Urban Unrest* (Oxford, Pergamon 1987).

4. Governmental Stewardship

One of the unmistakeable marks of Mrs Thatcher's style of government was her air of unimpeachable rightness, which whatever its origins [6] has invested many of her policies and programmes with ethical overtones, and aroused vehement opposition that often seems to go beyond the merely party-political. Her fervent rejection of 'consensus politics' and seeming predilection for confrontation rather than negotiation similarly goes against – and is so intended – the grain of post-war British politics. Neo-corporatism is not dead (the National Economic Development Council still exists), but it is consigned to a backwater; and the trade unions are regarded as the enemy within. What this means is that the Government accepts full responsibility, and not shared responsibility, for major economic and other policies; stewardship is undivided. But many are growing more and more uneasy about this style of governance, Conservatives among them; not on economic or pragmatic grounds, but on what can only be called moral or quasi-moral grounds.

There are two main focuses of this feeling; one, the perception that for Mrs (now Baroness) Thatcher, 'private' is good and 'public' is bad, that collective provision is always and inevitably inferior to individual provision; two, certain aspects of the privatisation programme. The first leads to the widespread distrust of the Government's treatment of the National Health Service and Social Security schemes; Mrs Thatcher's assurance that 'the Health Service is safe in our hands' was simply not believed. A poll in September 1989 (*Guardian/ICM* poll on political attitudes) [7] showed seventy percent of respondents disagreeing with a proposition to that effect, including 56% of Conservative voters who disagreed or expressed no preference (as against only 40% of Conservatives who agreed, and four percent who did not know). The ethic of a *caring* State is strongly entrenched, and the encounter with a Government which does not accept it raises ethical questions.

The perception that the Government's preference for 'market solutions' made it indifferent to environmental degeneration was similarly not wiped out by Mrs Thatcher's partial espousal of the 'Green' cause in 1989. The September poll indicated that seventy percent of all voters, and seventy-five percent of Conservative voters, agreed with the view that 'The Government should give a higher priority to environmental policy even if this means higher prices

---

6 H. Young *One of Us: A Biography of Margaret Thatcher* (London, Croom Helm 1989). See also L. Abse *Margaret, daughter of Beatrice: A Politician's Psychobiography of Margaret Thatcher* (London, Jonathan Cape 1989).

7 *Guardian* 18 September 1989.

for some goods'. Here again, concern for the environment has strong ethical elements, and a Government not doing enough in that field is seen as betraying a trust. [8]

Opinion on privatisation is heavily influenced of course by party allegiance. But any observer of the British scene in the last five years or so would have to report a sense of baffled outrage in many comments by ordinary voters, in such media as letters to the editor and television 'vox pop' interviews, at what is perceived as dissipation of public assets; a tone precisely caught by Lord Stockton's (former Conservative Prime Minister Harold Macmillan) remark about 'selling off the family silver'. The selling of publicly-owned manufacturing companies like Amersham International and even of transport firms like British Airways and the National Freight Corporation passed without arousing such feelings. With the floating of telephone and gas shares the arguments centred on other aspects, to which we shall return. But the current moves to privatise water services (water supply, river and flood management, and sewage treatment) [9] have set up waves which again have a strong ethical element – it is perceived as *wrong* to sell, so that private entrepreneurs can make money out of, such a fundamental public service. Opinion Polls show opposition to the whole idea of water privatisation running at over eighty percent.

This may not prevent a great many of the same people applying for water shares when they go on sale, so advantageous are the terms likely to be – which raises another ethical issue: is it right for the Government to use tax proceeds to advertise and float such give-away offers, and does this not amount to 'bribery of the nation'? Estimates are that the Government's advertising campaign preceding the gas flotation cost £25 million, and that advertising by the Water Authorities Association and by the Government together will amount to £60 million – at a time, Labour critics say, when money cannot be found to enable Britain to meet European standards of water quality. (The Government expects to raise £7 billion from the sale). Whatever one's views about such assertions, there is no doubt that they constitute a debate about the ethics of government.

Turning to less elevated political concerns – what one might designate as administrative rather than political wrongdoing: probably most British people (and possibly most people in other countries too) see the United Kingdom public service as among the least *corrupt* in the world. Maybe they are right, but a perusal of Alan Doig's book *Corruption and Misconduct in Contemporary British Politics* (1984) may at least given them pause. Its four

---

8 See Volume III: *Environmental Ethics* in this series of *Teaching Ethics* (forthcoming 1993, Centre for Business and Public Sector Ethics, Cambridge).

9 Many of these services have now been privatised. *[Editor]*

hundred pages are full of reports of trials of public officials and elected representatives within the previous twenty years for corrupt practices of one kind and another. Some were celebrated cases such as the Poulson Affair (a system-building city-centre developer of the 1960s who embroiled a network of city councillors in petty bribery) [10] and the Metropolitan Police scandals in the 1970s (several convictions of London Drugs Squad and Obscene Publications Squad officers, some of high rank); [11] many were obscure cases concerning market-stall letting, driving-test examiners, and the like. It is clear that British public life is by no means free from corruption, whatever the position may be relative to other countries.

Similar cases, mainly in local government, continue to appear, as in the conviction in September 1989 of the Liverpool City Architect for illegally accepting gifts of work on his own house in return for favouring a particular firm for public contracts. But it is again police cases which give most cause for disquiet. In August 1989 the West Midlands Chief Constable disbanded his entire Serious Crimes Squad after trials collapsed amid allegations that officers had regularly fabricated evidence. A Detective-Sergeant and five other officers belonging to the Kent police force were punished in September 1989 and a further twenty-eight officers admonished after a four-year inquiry into falsification of crime clear-up figures. In October 1989 four Irish people, imprisoned fifteen years ago after being convicted of pub-bombing in Guildford, were released by the Appeal Court when it was revealed that Surrey police officers fabricated confessions and withheld alibi evidence; Law Officers of the Crown were alleged to be implicated in a cover-up. Pressure grew for the re-opening yet again of the case of the 'Birmingham Six', whose conviction for another pub-bombing in 1974 was widely thought to be equally insecure, and in which West Midlands crime squad officers were involved.

No comparable series of breaches of trust exists for other arms of the public service, in particular the Civil Service itself. Individual cases, especially in the field of property management, surface every now and again, but at a rough estimate the total number of non-trivial cases in all Central public bodies taken together would hardly get into three figures. It is debatable whether it is the fairly stringent system of rules and audit checks, or the relative lack of opportunity and temptation in most agencies of government, or the general climate of social opinion, or the high personal and corporate moral standards obtaining in most of the public service, which is most responsible for this state of affairs.

---

10 R. Fitzwater and D. Taylor *Web of Corruption* (London, Granada 1981).

11 B. Cox, J. Shirley and M. Short *The Fall of Scotland Yard* (Harmondsworth, Penguin Books 1977).

The *positive* understanding of governmental stewardship takes it beyond the mere avoidance of malversation of office or misappropriation of public funds into the avoidance of *waste* of public money and, further, the search for the maximisation of public benefits in any expenditure or organisational change. Here the ethical problem with Mrs Thatcher's Government was an interesting one, that of 'overfulfilment'.

Formally, the detection and correction of extravagance in public spending, in Central Government and public bodies, has since 1861 been the province of the Public Accounts Committee of the House of Commons, assisted from 1866 by the Exchequer and Audit Department (now the National Audit Office), [12] and, in local government, the District Audit (now the Audit Commission). The annual reports of both bodies are a salutary record of overspending and mismanagement, and in recent years not in terms of *correctness* only, but of value-for-money.

Attempts to eliminate 'organisational slack' are equally venerable, dating from Pitt's Economical Reform of the 1780s. The more recent story of the rise and fall of Planning, Programming, Budgeting, Systems (PBBS's) British counterparts PAR and PES (Programme Analysis and Review, Public Expenditure Survey) has been well told. [13] It was under a Labour government that 'VFM auditing' became a catchword, and it was Edward Heath, Mrs Thatcher's predecessor as Conservative leader, who invited a team of businessmen to become temporarily part of the government machine. But the most notable step was Mrs Thatcher's creation in the Prime Minister's Office of what is now the Efficiency Unit, originally under Sir Derek Rayner (later Lord Rayner), the former head of one of Britain's most successful retail firms, Marks and Spencer. The 'Rayner Scrutinies' laid less emphasis on programme objectives and coordination, more on the simple uncovering of extravagance and waste, using the energies of keen young high-fliers, who could thus bring themselves to favourable notice. [14]

Mrs Thatcher came to office pledged to go much further than this, however, and to 'roll back the State'. The first manifestation of this commitment was

---

12 See paper in this Volume by Sir John Bourn KCB, Comptroller and Auditor General of the National Audit Office, pp. 20-47.

13 G. K. Fry *The Changing Civil Service* (London, George Allen and Unwin 1985); A. G. Gray and W. I. Jenkins (eds.) *Policy Analysis and Evaluation in British Government* (London, Royal Institute of Public Administration 1983); and A. G. Gray *Administrative Politics in British Government* (Brighton, Wheatsheaf Books 1985).

14 L. Chapman *Your Disobedient Servant: the continuing story of Whitehall's overspending* (London, Chatto and Windus 1978). Also (Harmondsworth, Penguin Books 1979); Rosamund M. Thomas 'The Politics of Efficiency and Effectiveness in the British Civil Service' *International Review of Administrative Sciences* Vol. L No. 3 (Autumn); and C. Ponting *The Right to Know: the inside story of the Belgrano Affair* (London, Sphere Books 1985).

the drive to reduce the size of the Civil Service, which in five years went down from 732,000 to 599,000, a drop of eighteen percent. It is true that most of the saving came from blue-collar rather than white-collar groups in the Civil Service [15] but it is still quite a notable achievement. At the same time a number of internal changes stepped up the 'managerialisation' of the senior Civil Service, with increasing emphasis on output measurement and performance rewards. [16] The latest manifestation of this commitment is what has been called the 'privatisation of Whitehall itself', the creation of a potentially large number of 'independent executive agencies' somewhat on the Swedish pattern. [17]

The upshot of all this relentless pressure for trimming, pruning and paring of government apparatus is a perception and fear of deterioration of the quality of public services, expressed in lack of maintenance of school and hospital buildings, roads, sewers and other infrastructure; and in increasing water and atmospheric pollution because of the relaxation of controls. This is a classic case of 'conflict of goals', where the otherwise-laudable pursuit of efficiency is seen as being 'taken too far', at the expense of safety, security, and public health – another betrayal of stewardship. In the same public opinion poll quoted earlier, 58% of all voters, agreed that 'It is better to pay higher taxes and have better public services than lower taxes but worse services'.

5. Governmental Fairness

British people have a standing reminder of what British people are capable of, in respect of governmental unfairness: Northern Ireland. Leave aside the present violence and political intractability, and there is left a reprehensible history of fifty years (1922-1972) of inequitable distribution of whatever the self-governing provincial State had to offer; gerrymandering in electoral districts, gross bias in public appointments, highly selective allocation of public housing, and so on – in favour of the majority group, the Protestants or Unionists, and to the detriment of the minority, the Catholics or Republicans. From the outside this looked like official corruption of government, thinly legitimated by 'majority rule' so that United Kingdom control mechanisms were rendered inoperative. [18] Since 1972 the governance of Northern Ireland has been in the hands of the British Government directly,

15 A. Dunsire and C. C. Hood *Cutback Management in Public Bureaucracies* (Cambridge and New York, Cambridge University Press 1989).
16 L. Metcalfe and S. Richards *Improving Public Management* (London SAGE 1987).
17 K. Jenkins, K. Caines and A. Jackson *Improving Management in Government: The Next Steps* Efficiency Report to the Prime Minister (London, HMSO 1988).
18 P. Arthur *The Government and Politics of Northern Ireland* (London, Longman second edn. 1984). See also R. Rose *Governing without Consensus: an Irish Perspective* (London, Faber and Faber 1971).

and discrimination against Catholics has undoubtedly decreased; but the province remains a source of troubles on the human rights as well as the terrorism front.

Distributional questions – who gets what, when, how, in Lasswell's immortal phrase – are the very stuff of politics. It is to be expected that, in a two-party system, the winning party will use the tax and other systems of governance to reward its followers at the expense of its opponents. As in so many other contexts, the matter only enters the ethical sphere when a majority or substantial minority perceives the balance to have been tilted rather too much. And whereas it is generally seen as virtuous in a Government to transfer resources from the rich to the poor, it is otherwise when the net effect is a transfer in the other direction. The combined effect of Mrs Thatcher's Government's large tax cuts and smaller benefits (for example, freezing of child benefits for many years) is widely seen as robbing the poor to give to the rich. By the same critics, privatisation of publicly-owned industries is seen as a transfer of the benefits of ownership of property from the community to the wealthy. The two perceptions can be put together, as in this letter to the editor of *The Guardian:*

'When you look at the privatisation of British Gas or British Telecom, they were really nothing more than Government-organised larceny: the transfer of ownership from the entire population to the wealthiest, and predominantly Conservative, sector. Nearly all of the recently privatised organisations were profit making enterprises – geese that regularly and reliably laid golden eggs which went into the public purse to benefit the entire population. The government then undervalued them and sold them. Who to? Why, richest twenty percent of the population. Now the geese are still laying golden eggs, but for the benefit of only twenty percent of the population, if that.

This might seem a satisfactory state of affairs in that the well-off twenty percent did at least pay money for their shares. However, when we examine what the government then did with the money, we can see the whole sordid business in a different light. The proceeds of the sale of shares went directly into the much publicised tax cuts. And who benefits there? Not the unemployed or the low-paid – they don't earn enough to pay income tax. The middle income sector? Yes, a penny or two in the pound. And the well-off twenty percent of the population? They received the benefit of a massive cut – the 60 percent rate reduced to 40 percent. In effect everything they paid for their shares in the gas and telecom business was immediately handed back to them ... When they talk of 'privatisation', what they really mean is stealing a national asset and making a present of it to the wealthiest sector of society.' [19]

---

19 *The Guardian* 23 September 1989.

Other perceived Ministerial breaches of time-honoured expectation concerned the Secretary of State for Education's unilateral abrogation of the negotiating machinery for teachers' salaries (the Burnham Committee) and its replacement by a nominated advisory board; and the Secretary of State for Health's imposition, after negotiations broke down, of a new contract on the nation's doctors in general practice.

Great emphasis is laid in the United Kingdom on the fairness and procedural correctness of transactions between civil servants and individual citizens. The main formal organs of control, the Common Law courts, supplemented by an array of administrative tribunals and other channels of remedy, are efficacious enough in ensuring it once a citizen has surmounted the financial and other hurdles of bringing a case before them. It is a matter of opinion whether these remedies already amount to at least the foundations of a proper system of Administrative Law, as some judges think: [20] social welfare appeals, in particular, are precariously grounded. Legislatively, the ancient doctrine of 'Redress of Grievance Before Supply' still survives in Question Time in the House of Commons, and in other opportunities for Members of Parliament to raise their constituents' complaints about their treatment by bureaucracy.

Not only self-seeking conduct but *any* form of bias or lack of even-handedness in a discretionary situation in principle would be *legal* grounds for the reversal of the decision at the least. The extent to which these moral/legal expectations are disappointed can be gauged by perusal of the Law Reports and the annual reports of the Parliamentary Commissioner for Administration and his counterparts in local government and the health service – multiplied by whatever factor one thinks appropriate to represent the 'rest of the iceberg'. It is not, perhaps, a worrying total. Yet in the public opinion survey already quoted several times, when respondents were asked to express agreement or disagreement with the proposition that 'There is one law for the rich and one for the poor', 71 percent agreed, 51 percent agreeing 'strongly' (as against 66 percent and 42 percent in 1988). Among Conservative voters, 52 percent agreed with the proposition. The editorial comment was 'The sense of living in an unfair society has strengthened over the past year'.

Race and sex discrimination are combatted by the Commission for Racial Equality and the Equal Opportunities Commission respectively. Again, the sharpest anxiety in the racism field has been caused by the police. Policemen even at the lowest ranks have a great deal of discretion – whether to 'notice' a violation, whom to stop and search, whether to arrest or caution, and so on. At higher ranks, policing strategies, and tactics in relation to riot control

---

20 H. W. R. Wade *Administrative Law* (Oxford, Clarendon Press fifth edn. 1982) p. 589.

or strike picketing, are clearly discretionary. Official reports and independent research studies have been heavily critical on all these points in recent years; and the existence of a degree of racism among police officers, especially in the big cities, is generally recognised. [21]

One of the best antidotes to unfairness in governance is publicity and *openness*. The United Kingdom government and bureaucracy is one of the most secretive in the world, starting always from the assumption that official information is privileged and not to be released unless a clear advantage to Government can be demonstrated in so doing, rather than the opposite spirit. The Official Secrets Act of 1911, whose section 2 made the unauthorised disclosure of *any* official information a criminal offence, is now completely discredited, politically, judicially, and as a safeguard of security; but its replacement by the Official Secrets Act 1989 makes things worse, from the point of view of openness, by restricting the criminal offences to a reasonable list but taking away any 'public interest' defence, and placing a 'duty of confidence' on civil servants.

The movement for a Freedom of Information Act continues to gain adherents, including many former top civil servants, and party leaders while in Opposition; but the dam is still unbreached. The currently most acute public anxieties about secrecy concern food safety and nuclear power – costs of decommissioning, accidents, incidence of leukaemia, and so on, but the list of fields where it has been formally announced that disclosure would be against the public interest is long and often amusing. [22] So long as the official passion for secrecy in Britain is unquenched, the claim of governmental fairness cannot be fully demonstrated, because the control mechanisms (civil and administrative law, political and representative bodies, pressure groups, the media), like all control mechanisms, need information about what is going on, as well as what ought to be going on, before their correcting devices can operate. This topic of secrecy and freedom of information is covered in detail in Part III of this Volume I: *Government Ethics*. Some views differ from mine expressed above in this paper.

6. Governmental Honour

To expect that governments should tell the truth, keep their bargains and not subvert the constitution is probably too starry-eyed. May be the

---

21 See the paper on Police Ethics in this Volume I *Government Ethics* by Neil Richards 'A Plea for Applied Ethics' pp. 657-79.

22 D. Wilson ed. *The Secrets File: the case for freedom of information in Britain today* (London, Heinemann 1984). See also David G. T. Williams *Not in the Public Interest* (London, Hutchinson 1965) and Rosamund M. Thomas *Espionage and Secrecy: the Official Secrets Acts 1911-1989 of the United Kingdom* (London and Routledge 1991 and Routledge, Chapman and Hall 1992), [*Editor*].

important thing is that they should not be so insouciant as to be caught out. All's fair in love, war, and political survival. But the argument is certainly one of ethics in governance, and the threshold is again not an absolute one, but one where enough people say that 'They've gone too far this time'. A number of recent cases in Britain have raised anxieties: some concerning civil servants, some the police and armed forces, some the judges, some Cabinet Members. Collectively they mark what it may not be too extreme to regard as the politicising of constitutional guarantees.

First, the constitutional position of civil servants. The question 'To whom (or what) does a civil servant owe loyalty?' is not to be answered simply, in the United Kingdom today. About one hundred years ago it became generally accepted (without formal document) that in return for permanency and pension, civil servants would serve the Government-of-the-Day with equal zeal, whatever its platform and policies. [23] This is usually called 'political neutrality'; but it by no means implies that the civil servant is *neutral* between one political party and another, occupying some no-man's-land or middle ground; it requires the civil servant to give unstinting loyal service to only one party, that which is in power. There were many among early Socialists to doubt that this could be given to a Socialist Government by 'mandarins' of the class and educational background that dominated the Civil Service then; and there are several Labour ex-Ministers today, who claim that top civil servants concealed information from them while in office, and obstructed their clear wishes. [24] Others have alleged that Civil Service Departments have effectively managed their Ministers so as to substitute their own preferences, and even that they have in practice dictated the policies of all governments since the War. [25]

Top civil servants may have their views, and are expected to offer a searching critique of any policy proposals put forward by their Minister or anyone else – but always in the Minister's interest, never in their own or that of the Department, let alone that of any outside rival interest; and always in confidence. We may all 'know' that reality fails to live up to these high expectations, at least sometimes; but few will deny that these are the ethical prescriptions which apply. To avoid public misapprehension, no senior civil servant, and no civil servant who deals directly with members of the public (and this applies also to the police), may run for Parliament or local council

---

23 H. Parris *Constitutional Bureaucracy* (London, Allen and Unwin 1969).

24 A. Benn 'Manifestos and Mandarins' in W. Rodgers et al *Policy and Practice: The Experience of Government* (London, Royal Institute of Public Administration 1980) and A. Benn *Arguments for Democracy* (Harmondsworth Penguin Books 1982).

25 Eleventh Report of the House of Commons Expenditure Committee 1976-77 *The Civil Service* (London, HMSO HC. 535-1 1976). See also H. Young and A. Sloman *No, Minister: an Inquiry into the Civil Service* (London, British Broadcasting Corporation 1982).

elected office, or be a member of (let alone hold office in) a political party. Local government officers may not be members of their own councils; but the extent to which some people who are officers or servants of one authority are notoriously politically-active members of a neighbouring local authority has given cause for anxiety. [26]

Two developments have put this position under strain. The first concerns a civil servant's options when what his Minister is doing is in the civil servant's view unconstitutional. The most celebrated recent case was that of Clive Ponting, a senior civil servant in the Ministry of Defence, who felt that his Minister was seriously misleading the House of Commons, and sent a copy of a secret document to a Member of Parliament. He was found out, and tried under the Official Secrets Act. The judge ruled that 'the interests of the State', the crucial phrase in the Act, would only mean the policies of the Government-of-the-day, as laid down by the Minister, and that it was no part of Ponting's duties to go beyond these. Despite this the jury acquitted Ponting, an outcome that was seen as public approval for the view that civil servants *do* have a higher duty than loyalty to their Minister – namely, loyalty to Parliament, perhaps, or the Crown, or 'the people'. The official position was stated by the Head of the Civil Service, Sir (later Lord) Robert Armstrong during the trial: if a civil servant were asked to do something against his conscience, he should take the matter to his Departmental superior, and then if necessary to his Permanent Secretary. If the problem were still unresolved, the civil servant should resign, but maintain silence. This doctrine of omertá can do little to resolve the dilemma of the public-spirited official, and might be thought to lend itself too easily to the official cover-up. [27]

The question arose again in 1986, in connection with another 'leak', during the 'Westland Affair'. This was an attempt by an American company, Sikorsky, to take over the British firm Westland Helicopters, with the support of the firm's directors and employees, but against the personal opposition of the Defence Secretary Mr Michael Heseltine. Although the Government's position was officially a neutral one, in fact Mrs Thatcher and the Industry Secretary Mr Brittan were in favour of the Sikorsky bid; and at a crucial point Mr Brittan's Head of Information section, with the knowledge of the Prime Minister's Private Office, was instructed to leak to the Press a critical but confidential letter from the Government's lawyers to

---

26 *The Conduct of Local Authority Business:* the Widdicombe Report (London, HMSO Cmnd. 9797 1986). See also the current code of conduct for British civil servants covering political activities, pp. 458-62 of this Volume, Appendix Part I. *[Editor]*

27 See C. Ponting *The Right to Know* op. cit. and Rosamund M. Thomas 'The British Official Secrets Acts 1911-1939 and the Ponting Case' *Crim. L. R.* [1986] pp. 491-510. The Armstrong Memorandum is reprinted in this Volume 1: *Government Ethics*, pp. 58-62.

Mr Heseltine. The civil servant protested, but did what she was told. Both Mr Brittan and Mr Heseltine resigned over the affair. [28]

A case of another sort concerned the Government's extravagant attempts in 1987 to stop the publication in Australia of a book on British Intelligence by Mr Peter Wright, a former member of MI5, although much of what it contained was already public knowledge. The legal basis of the Government's submission was not the Official Secrets Act, but the alleged breach of confidence involved. [29]

The second development which has brought the official doctrine under strain is a different one. It was alleged that under Prime Minister Thatcher 'professional loyalty' among top civil servants was ceasing to be enough, and that what was rewarded instead was *commitment* to the outlook and policies of her Government. Instances are quoted of named civil servants, promoted from Under Secretary to Permanent Secretary over the heads of 'less reliable' senior people who were not convinced monetarists, it was said at the time. However, much of this is unfavourable construction rather than unchallengeable fact. A recent report concluded that rumours about politicisation are groundless. [30] The Prime Minister made no secret of her wish to divert Civil Service attention away from concentration upon policy advice to Ministers, and towards better management of their Departments. The current 'blue-eyed boys' may well be those who genuinely espouse managerialism; but this need not be reprehensible, even if distasteful to the doubters.

It will be different, however, if the commitment an officer is expected to share is a rooted antipathy to public sector trading, or to trade unions, or even to rail travel; such attitudes in a senior civil servant, if made manifest, might well render him or her unacceptable to a successor Government of a different colour. Where to draw the line is not easy. But a number of recently-retired civil servants of very high standing were saying a few years ago that the threshold of the tolerable has been decisively crossed, and that a cadre of party-political mandarins, coming in and going out with their Ministers as in most other countries, is the only solution to the impossible position that many senior civil servants now feel themselves to be in. [31]

---

28 M. Linklater and D. Leigh *Not Without Honour* (London, Sphere Books 1986). See also Rosamund M. Thomas 'The Duties and Responsibilities of Civil Servants and Ministers: A Challenge within British Cabinet Government' *International Review of Administrative Sciences* Vol. 52 No. 4 December 1986 pp. 511-38 and reproduced in this Volume, pp. 383-408.

29 For details of the Peter Wright case see, for example, Rosamund M. Thomas *Espionage and Secrecy* op. cit.

30 Royal Institute of Public Administration *Top Jobs in Whitehall: Appointments and Promotions in the Senior Civil Service* (London, RIPA 1987). Readers should note that in 1992 the RIPA ceased to function, having become insolvent. *[Editor]*

31 See J. Hoskyns 'Conservatism is not Enough' *Political Quarterly* Vol. 55 1984 pp. 3-16 and D. Wass *Government and the Governed* (London, George Allen and Unwin 1984).

Professor Trevor Smith has highlighted another 'slippage in the standards of conduct within the higher social strata', in the increasing frequency with which high-ranking civil servants are moving, on early retirement, into lucrative boardroom posts in private-sector companies with which they previously had official dealings. The rule is that such appointments cannot be accepted within two years of retirement except by permission; but permission is seldom refused. As Professor Smith says, 'The objection is not just the danger of partiality in negotiating government contracts and similar malpractice but it is also a question of propriety, seemliness, becoming conduct or call it what you will'. [32] There is no outright *corruption* alleged; the question is one of *honourable behaviour*.

Among other *causes célèbres* outside the ambit of Civil Service propriety was the 'Stalker Affair'. This concerned a Manchester Deputy Chief Constable appointed to investigate charges of an illegal and unethical 'shoot-to-kill' policy against the Royal Ulster Constabulary in Belfast in their unending struggle with Republican terrorists. The story involved the intelligence services, secret tapes, stake-outs and all the other ingredients of a fictional thriller. But as Stalker was approaching the crucial phase of his investigations he was suddenly withdrawn from the investigation and suspended, on the basis of charges of personal misconduct (which were subsequently shown to be trivial). Stalker later resigned and wrote his own account. [33] The inquiry was eventually completed, and several Ulster officers were reprimanded; but the reports were not published.

An alleged 'shoot-to-kill' policy was also the ground of another such 1987 scandal, involving Irish Republican Army (IRA) terrorists again, but this time the SAS commando of the British Army and British Government Ministers. An 'active service unit' of three IRA persons was ambushed in Gibraltar on information that they had planted a car bomb designed to explode during a military ceremony, and shot dead on assumptions that they were about to draw weapons. There was no car bomb, and they were unarmed. Various discrepancies in the accounts of witnesses and between the official versions of the British and Spanish authorities were uncovered by investigative journalists (notably in a television documentary *Death on the Rock*, which the Government attempted to suppress). Allegations were made that instructions came direct from Downing Street.

Many will ask what all the fuss is about, that since the Irish Republican Army shoots and bombs to kill, why should not the security forces? But the question is not whether we should have a shoot-to-kill policy: it is officially

---

32 T. Smith *British Politics in the Post-Keynesian Era* (London, Action Society Trust 1986) p. 20.

33 J. Stalker *Stalker* (London, Harrap 1987).

denied that any such policy exists; and the ethical doubts arise where official action appears to be inconsistent with official proclamation, and the gap is unconvincingly filled.

At the time of writing it is the case of the 'Guildford Four' which creates worry over the role of senior judges as protectors of the law and of the rights of citizens. The words of the late Lord Denning, a former senior judge, in an earlier case ('The Birmingham Six'), are being recalled:

> 'Just consider the course of events if this action is allowed to proceed to trial ...
> If the six men win, it will mean that the police were guilty of perjury, that
> they were guilty of violence and threats, that the confessions were involuntary
> and were improperly admitted in evidence and that the convictions were
> erroneous ... This is such an appalling vista that every sensible person in the
> land would say: it cannot be right these actions should go any further'.

In other words (as it was widely interpreted), it is better that the Six stay in prison than that the integrity of the judicial system and the police be shown to be impugned. Yet point by point the freeing of the Guildford Four does just that, after similar statements by another judge (Lord Roskill) in rejecting their previous appeals. A string of cases, in which not only did the conviction rest on disputed police evidence but where rejection of appeals also rested in effect on the need to maintain public confidence in the judicial system, are now being raised again. Hugo Young, a respected journalist and biographer of Mrs Thatcher, mused in his *Guardian* column about whether judges ever felt they should apologise when they got it so badly wrong:

> 'If it occurred to him (improbably) that he might have made a mistake, he
> could certainly not conceive of the system being strengthened by his admitting
> as much. In senior judges, private arrogance has a habit of being converted into
> a pillar of the constitution. Until some serving judges speak with passion for
> the opposite position, it will be hard to believe that they have honestly addressed
> the frailty of the system over which they preside.' [34]

Finally, the *honour* of the then Prime Minister herself (as distinct from her personality and style) was openly impugned by the other Prime Ministers of the Commonwealth present at the recent meeting in Malaysia, after her curious behaviour in signing a joint declaration on the South African issue and hours later giving out a press statement signifying her total dissent from its principles. The word 'betrayal' was used of her treatment of the former Chancellor of the Exchequer Mr Lawson. A former Lord Chancellor in her Government, Lord Hailsham, was reported as saying: 'It is not legitimate to use your press office, if you are Prime Minister, in the way in which some-

---

34 *The Guardian* 24 October 1989.

times I fear it has been used, in order to undermine the authority of Ministers.' The Downing Street office may not have been corrupted, but it has been used unscrupulously: 'this is dishonourable conduct towards colleagues'. The honour of other Cabinet Members, in respect of deceitfulness, breaking promises, and abandonment of conventions, is also brought into question. Politics is a rough game.

It is clear that the customary mechanisms of *homoeostasis* in this field, whatever they are, are not working well. New institutions have been proposed: for civil servants, an 'Inspector-General' to whom troubled bureaucrats could take a Ponting-type problem, and a Royal Commission to look into the matter of Civil Service loyalty, ministerial involvement in appointments and the public accountability of officials including the heads of the new non-ministerial agencies; for police, a stronger lay component in the working of the Police Complaints Authority, and a new Royal Commission; for judges, a special tribunal to investigate alleged miscarriages of justice free from what the Court of Appeal evidently regards as its responsibility to maintain public confidence in the system.

But what would such new institutions replace? What were the customary mechanisms that are apparently not now working? The answer is certainly not 'elections', in these areas, for we do not elect our civil servants or judges, and we do not choose our Cabinet Members except at second or third hand. Elections are too remote and infrequent a sanction altogether to serve as a monitor. Some have pointed to the declining influence of 'public school ethics' – that blend of parental deprivation at an early age, ritual beating, and the cult of open-air sport which, it is often supposed, was the common inheritance of English 'gentlemen' between the accessions of Victoria and Elizabeth II. The country is now run, it is complained, by people who went to State schools – what can you expect? This is manifestly too narrow a view of what has 'gone wrong' and yet it may be a paradigm.

For a century, the cohesiveness of British public life – that is, in sectors other than manufacturing – was indeed assisted by the integration of formal relationships with a second reticulation, generically called the 'old boy network' because it stemmed from public-school (that is, élite private-school) ties. This, like other freemasonries, had its beneficial properties; the more channels there are, the more likely are important messages to get through; and gossip is a powerful medium not only of peer-group maintenance but of peer-group control. But the old-boy network, again like other freemasonries, can also be seen as a conspiracy against the public interest, and has been under relentless attack not only from the Left but also from the New right, as a species of restraint of trade.

But élite socialisation processes in Whitehall and Westminster did not depend only on pre-entry formation. They took whatever human material they were presented with and got to work on it from scratch if necessary.

Few Members of Parliament from however proletarian a background proved immune to its embrace. Nonconforming behaviour became 'boorish', almost unthinkable. The Civil Service took its recruits to the 'mandarinate' straight from university and saw to it that thereafter, with very few exceptions, they had no experience whatsoever of life outside Whitehall, while subjecting them to early exposure to the heady delights of high places close to Ministers. Young civil servants by these processes soon learned what was expected of them by their seniors. Moreover, they were few enough to know each other, to form their own networks; Whitehall is a 'village'. [35]

In the last decade, it is these very socialisation processes themselves which have been blamed (by Mrs Thatcher and her followers) for many of the ills of late twentieth century Britain. She herself does not derive from either landowning-family or banking-family connections, and is said to have little time for the traditional 'Tory grandees' who dominated Conservative politics for so long. 'Conviction politics' will have no truck with the 'post-war consensus', of time-honoured consultation processes such as Royal Commissions (Mrs Thatcher appointed not one), and urges instead a quite different ethos on Whitehall, the ethos of managerialism and success. Ministers now refuse to behave according to the old lights of *noblesse oblige,* and welcome confrontation. Young civil servants now decline to adopt the traditional protective coloration. The *cynicisms* of some top civil servants, in regard to the relationship between Whitehall and company boardrooms, is unedifying.

Replacing the old 'public service ethic' (which could easily and unselfconsciously be identified with the preservation of existing class and group privilege) by a public sector adaptation of the market-oriented managerial ethic is a legitimate aspiration: it may well be 'what the country needs' at this time. But the control mechanisms of the market have not been installed, perhaps cannot be installed, in place of the earlier conventions of the constitution we are discussing under 'governmental honour' – unless, indeed, the general election is a form of political market mechanism.

The role of general elections in democracy is a vexed question, not least in the United Kingdom. But there may be some merit in the market metaphor if what is being bought and sold is not policies and programmes or even ideologies, and not favours promised to a series of interest groups, but rather the people's trust in the persons proposed to them to undertake governance, in an ethical rather than an economic coin, and on the world stage as much as the national one. From this point of view, a party presiding over governance seen by enough voters as simultaneously incompetent, profligate, unfair and dishonourable can surely not survive, whatever their policies and promises.

---

35 H. Heclo and A. Wildavsky *The Private Government of Public Money* (London, Macmillan 1974).

If this should look at all likely in present circumstances, we may yet see the reappearance of a traditional Tory control mechanism: the deputation of 'grandees' waiting on the Leader to indicate gently but firmly that the time has come for change.

Conclusion

In any world-wide comparison, it would probably remain true that standards of ethics in governance in the United Kingdom are relatively high on an absolute scale, and that the conduct of elected representatives and public servants on the whole does not normally fall very much below them. I am obliged to conclude, nevertheless, that present trends in governmental ethics in the United Kingdom give cause for some anxiety. The mechanisms of control are still in place and coping with disruptive forces at the lower levels reasonably well; but at the higher levels the mechanisms are old-fashioned and inappropriate for the job they now have to do, while what should replace them has not yet become clear. The question is whether measuring performance and rewarding success can in the United Kingdom reliably replace, whether at bureaucratic or ministerial level, the old-fashioned processes of socialisation into 'the ideal of public service'.

[*Editor*: This paper, delivered at the Second Conference of the Centre for Business and Public Sector Ethics, held in Cambridge on 14 May 1991, relates to Mrs (now Baroness) Thatcher's period in office as Prime Minister from 1979-1990. The paper does not seek to cover any new developments under the new Conservative Prime Minister, Mr John Major. The views expressed in this paper are those of Andrew Dunsire, Emeritus Professor, and may differ, at least to some extent, from the views of British civil servants and others set out, for example, in Part III of this Volume 1: *Government Ethics.*]

22

The Concept of Trust

Discussion by Andrew Dunsire,
Emeritus Professor of Politics, University of York, England

The world runs on trust. As Niklas Luhmann[1] puts it, if a man really believed in not trusting anyone, he would not even get up in the morning. We go through life perforce trusting other people to know what they are doing, from the milkman to the brain surgeon, because our own experience does not provide us with a critique.

It is perhaps more important than that. Karl Deutsch,[2] Hart[3] and Luhmann,[4] and several others, have made the point that governance is a bit like banking or car driving: banks can lend out a lot more than they get in from depositors, drivers can drive through a busy crossing at some speed if the traffic light is at green, and governments can require compliance with many more laws than they have the strength to enforce, because people habitually trust others. People have confidence in their expectations that their money will be safe with the bank, that other drivers, wanting to avoid accidents, usually stop on the red, and that the government will not pass laws without good reason behind them. Authority is to power as credit is to cash. A habit of obeying pays off, and the role of fines and arrests is marginal.[5]

The corollaries are that if the people suddenly come to believe that their money is not safe in the bank, the bank collapses; if the habit of driving through red lights spreads, accidents increase and telltale cameras and so on

---

1 Niklas Luhmann *Vertrauen. Ein Mechanismus der Reduktion sozialer Komplexität* (Revised edn. 1973 Stuttgart: Ferdinand Enke. English translation, introd. Guianfranco Poggi, in *Trust and Power* (Chichester, John Wiley 1979) p. 4. This discussion by Andrew Dunsire on 'The Concept of Trust' took place at the Second Conference of the Centre for Business and Public Sector Ethics, held in Cambridge on 14 May 1991.

2 Karl Deutsch *The Nerves of Government: Models of Political Communication and Control* (New York and London, the Free Press of Glencoe 1963) p. 121.

3 H. L. A. Hart *The Concept of Law* (Oxford, Clarendon Press 1961) p. 52.

4 Niklas Luhmann *op. cit.* p. 24.

5 Karl Deutsch *op. cit.* p. 123.

have to be installed; if government loses authority, it may still have the right to pass laws but it will have to use more power to enforce them; the role of fines and arrests will become more important.

'Trust' relates to our expectations about the world and the behaviour of people in it. We may have no particular expectations about a person, but if we find him or her to have been consistently honest and reliable in the past, we are likely to take the risk of placing trust in that person in the present and near future. But that trust is contingent: it needs constant reinforcement, or confirmation that our expectations are being borne out; and one bad disappointment with that person can destroy the relationship.

About other people we may have expectations even before we know them. We are usually disposed to trust members of our own family, *because* they are family; they are as it were entitled to have our trust until we learn otherwise. This presumptive trust extends to whole classes of people, such as professionals and tradesmen, whom we believe to have been certified by an authority to practice their profession or trade, and so to be entitled to our trust in matters connected with that profession or trade. This presumption about the class of people will persist even if we find cause to be disappointed in the behaviour of one or two members of it. But although the presumption ought perhaps to concern only their 'official' or job-related behaviour, their trustworthiness in our eyes is liable to be affected by purely personal behaviour which we find unacceptable – that is, presumptive trust is also, at the margin, contingent.

In my preceding paper entitled 'Ethics in Governance: the United Kingdom 1979-1990' I employ the concept of *trust* as a concomitant of the notion of *office*, in the ancient sense of 'appointed task', more or less as Bentham used it in the *Panopticon*, [6] in contrasting 'contract-management' and 'trust-management', the former meaning the same as we now do in the idea of 'contracting out', the latter being equivalent to 'management by one holding an office or duty to do so'. (In that understanding, by the way, the present usage in the designating of Hospital 'Trusts' is almost a contradiction in terms, since it marks a change *from* trust *to* contract as the basis of health management). [7]

The idea of holding an *office*, in this sense, confers trust upon the officeholder, presumptively, from clients and outsiders just as does professional certification; but it also embodies expectations by the principal, or body conferring the office, of certain standards of behaviour on the part of the agent,

---

6 Jeremy Bentham (1791) *Panopticon, or the Inspection House,* in John Bowring (ed.) *The Works of Jeremy Bertham* 10 vols. (Edinburgh, William Tait 1843).

7 See British National Health Service Reforms, information available from the Department of Health and London, HMSO).

or office-holder, which are contingent. The office *is* a trust, in the legal sense of trusteeship: trust implies responsibility. There is, for example, a civil law of confidentiality which gives an employer the right to expect that an employee will not without permission release information about the business acquired in the course of duty – the doctrine used by the British Government in the Australian courts in connection with their charges against Mr Peter Wright. [8]

My treatment of confidentiality of information in the preceding paper's suggested hierarchy of governmental and bureaucratic ethics does not, however, fall under 'trust' or 'stewardship' but under 'professional honour'. Let me in these remarks concentrate on this one narrow issue, because it is the subject of the conference, although the discussion of the meaning of 'trust' would cover many other issues and situations of presumptive trust.

The world runs on trust, but some worlds run on that particular variety of trustworthiness I am calling professional honour more than others. Perhaps obviously, if information is a business's stock-in-trade rather than physical artefacts or manual dexterities, confidentiality of business information is liable to be seen as a crucially important element in the behaviour expected of an office-holder. Hence the counter-businesses of military, political and industrial espionage, and the prestige of investigative journalism, which all thrive on breaches of that trust. Banking, too, prides itself on confidentiality of information, and breaches are considered heinous – perhaps precisely because they threaten the basis of that other more general confidence on which credit hangs.

The trust relationship between the principal and the agent, in such milieux as banking, the professions and government, thus has several aspects. The agent owes a duty to the principal (or in some cases the professional peer-group), but also enjoys the trust of (and therefore has responsibility towards) clients and in a wider sense the general public. The principal has legitimate expectations of the trustworthiness of the agent's behaviour, but is also dependent upon retaining the confidence of clients or citizens upon which ultimate authority or credit is based.

The likelihood of conflicts arising is evident. We are used to the expression 'conflict of loyalties', and this is a parallel. In the classic case, conflict arises between the agent's consciousness of duty to the principal and of responsibility to clients or citizens, arising out of the presumptive trust which people repose in the office or profession. Conflict is acute especially where the duty of confidentiality which the principal exacts is precisely aimed at

---

8 See, for example, Rosamund Thomas *Espionage and Secrecy: the Official Secrets Acts 1911-1989 of the United Kingdom (Routledge 1991 and New York, Routledge and Chapman Hall 1992).*

preventing the escape of information which if known might imperil authority or confidence or credit in general – and the agent nevertheless feels it is time the whistle were blown, because that general confidence is in fact misplaced. The model just constructed does not say whether or when such a 'breach of confidentiality' or trust is justified; it merely labels the elements perhaps a bit more consistently and comprehensively.

And yet it seems intuitively true that some 'leaks' are honourable and some are dishonourable, and some may become dishonourable which were not always so. I am told that 'insider dealing' was more or less the done thing at one time, whereas it is now a crime. Whistle-blowing, where the agent at the cost of a breach of trust reveals criminal or unethical conduct in his agency, is generally considered honourable by the press and people outside the agency, although experience shows that the whistle-blower is usually ostracised by colleagues, and life made so intolerable that he or she eventually resigns. Yet a whistle-blowing leak, paradoxically, may *increase* general confidence in the system; it may confirm the rightness of presumptive trust in the system even as it exposes individual wrongdoing within it – providing the system then recognises the wrongdoing and takes steps to correct it. If this does not happen, general confidence is further eroded: indeed, the rightness of *distrust* is confirmed.

It may be that 'political' leaks in government, to gain party advantage, are seen as 'part of the game', and not particularly dishonourable, especially when compared with betraying industrial or military secrets – and selling secrets is surely marginally more dishonourable than spying for ideological reasons. Breach of confidentiality may be considered more honourable where the agent patently makes no material gain from it and willingly risks material loss than when it is all done to make money. And so on: such blame-chopping is easy to do. My own prescription would be something like this: breach of a duty of confidentiality is justified when and only when the secrecy clearly is aimed at concealing conduct which itself is a breach of the wider trust enjoyed by the business or profession or government. I believe in encouraging whistle-blowing.

23

Ethics for Public Sector Administrators: Education and Training

by Professor O. P. Dwivedi, Chair, Department of Political Studies, University of Guelph, Canada

Introduction

Teaching ethics in public policy and administration courses, and training public sector administrators in ethics may be relatively a new idea, but it certainly is not a passing fad. It is a response to the emergence of an all-encompassing and over-powering administrative State which has given rise to many ethical dilemmas where none existed before. It is also a response to the public loss of faith, trust and honesty in government. Further, it relates to public demand for open government, social equity and justice, and reflects a changed expectation about the sincerity and integrity of public officials. In this paper, an attempt has been made to assess these emerging concerns in the context of moral dimensions of public sector management, unethical conduct and conflict of interest, and administrative theology. The need for education and training for public sector ethics is then examined; and finally, some challenges are discussed which may affect the future of ethics in government.

1. Moral Dimension of Public Sector Management

The contemporary interest in the moral dimension of government is attributable to several factors: (1) the continued growth, until recently, in size, scope and complexity of government and its resultant negative attributes (generally referred to as an overpowering leviathan in the form of the administrative State); (2) insistence of the public on open and accountable government; (3) demands for enhancing and protecting individual rights and freedoms; (4) a general feeling of disappointment with the conduct of elected public officials, and frustration with the erosion of the concept of service and the doctrine of vocation among public servants; (5) growing cynicism about the capacity of government leaders to protect the quality of the environment, and in their ability to enhance human dignity; and (6) a deep feeling that people in politics and administration are not to be trusted. These and related factors have increased the demand for a more moral and accountable government and administration. However, the contemporary moral outrage expressed world-wide by the public in the 1970s and 1980s is of a different variety compared to the demands of Civil Service reforms in the West during the late nineteenth century and early 1900s when the emphasis was to transform the Civil Service from a corruption-riddled nest of patronage to a professional service. Those earlier reforms, coupled with the growth of the administrative State, gave immense discretionary power to public officials. [1] The use and abuse of that power in recent times has created demoralising and dehumanising tendencies in public bureaucracies. The growing public outrage is a reflection of such tendencies in government and administration.

Deriving from this situation and at the heart of the morality issue is the fear that people have regarding the power of government and its possible abuse. In a sense, people are afraid that an unknown quantity of risk is confronting them, and they would like not only to reduce the 'moral risk' in government but also to assess and manage such a risk. The use of power and authority by public officials is the key to the public concern. Any instance of unethical activity by a public official adds to the growing loss of ·public faith in the fairness and objectivity of both elected and appointed public servants. To the public, examples of patronage appointments, organisational brutality and use of power to either obstruct or delay the desired action, conflict of interest and unethical conduct are the symptoms of that widespread malady. These observations are especially relevant to situations where opportunities may arise for administrative excesses and the arbitrary use of power. Safeguards, checks and balances, must be instituted, whereby the actions of public servants are scrutinised regularly and openly, and where any infraction is immediately and appropriately dealt with. If the administrative apparatus is to serve the people, the public officials must be accountable, not only for the services rendered, but also for the manner in which they are delivered.

Some important questions, however, arise from this assertion. Are public servants aware of the ethical implications of the power they exercise? What values should they choose in the exercise of their responsibilities? [2] Clearly their choices will vary, depending in large part on their conscience, family and religious background, their country, their government, and the particular Department in which they are employed. But, in the absence of

---

1 For the impact of the administrative State, see Emmette S. Redford *Democracy in the Administrative State* (New York: Oxford, 1969); O. P. Dwivedi, ed. *The Administrative State in Canada* (Toronto: University of Toronto Press, 1982); and the two classics by Dwight Waldo *The Administrative State* (New York: Ronald Press, 1948), and F. M. Marx *The Administrative State: An Introduction to Bureaucracy* (Chicago: Chicago University Press, 1957).

2 See Gerald E. Caiden 'Ethics in the Public Service: Codification Misses the Real Target', *Public Personnel Management*, 10 (April 1981), pp. 146-52.

any agreed values, public servants are left in a void which increases the ethical predicaments they face in the exercise of discretionary power and the management of public programmes.

Obviously, there is an urgent need to develop the public's awareness of the abuse of power and authority by public officials in some countries, as there is a need for constant vigilance in those nations that have achieved responsible and accountable public services. Consequently, the prime goal of any administration ought to be to ensure that both elected representatives and appointed public servants are held responsible for the proper exercise of power. The abuse of power in the public sector undermines public confidence and trust in government, reduces the capacity of government to fulfil its functions effectively, subverts ethical responsiveness to the citizenry, and imposes an unnecessary financial burden on the public. The capacity of a political system to prevent, detect, punish and control such abuses has a direct bearing on its legitimacy and the moral basis of its authority. [3]

2. Unethical Conduct and Conflict of Interest

Modern government functions as a protector of its citizens against uncertainties (domestic and external) of human existence, a provider of essential welfare and an arbiter of competing sectional or other special interests. In carrying out its task, government necessarily depends upon the sense of justice and fair play of its employees and officials. We tend to judge a government (and while doing so we essentially judge those who run the government) by the extent to which it furthers the public interest; by the extent to which it allows participation by its citizens in the processes by which they are governed; and by the extent to which it encourages the pursuit of ideals of the good life. This means all persons, not some privileged people, be they Ministers or public servants.

Any deviation or appearance of deviation from the above gives people a cause to believe that the system is favouring some persons to the detriment of others in a way that is not equitable and moral, even though it may be legal. Thus, a conflict may emerge between an unethical act (that may not necessarily be illegal) which advances a personal interest and a just act which is in the best interests of society. Both an individual citizen and/or a public official may be involved in such a conflict. For example, an individual citizen may seek some special favour not available to others by enticing a government employee to make deviations from the established norm. On the other hand, a public official may try to further his/her

---

3 O. P. Dwivedi 'Ethics and Administrative Accountability', *Indian Journal of Public Administration*, 29 (July-September 1983), p. 516.

private interest by exploiting the official position and the influence. In both cases, much depends upon the willingness of a public official to succumb to such temptations. In summary, then, unethical conduct or a conflict of interest can exist only if someone is willing to exploit the public office or is capable of being influenced to let his/her name and office be exploited for the purpose.

Exploitation of a public office, and the resultant unethical behaviour may include the following activities:

a. those activities which are contrary to the legal norms of a country and therefore punishable under the law;

b. those which are contrary to the basic principles of ethics/morality held (though not necessarily practised) by that society; and

c. those which are undertaken because of the latent, manifest or perceived pressures felt by a person, under the obligations of loyalty, devotion, ties of kinship, affection, caste, politics, religion, or race.

Thus, unethical conduct includes not only those practices which are unquestionably criminal acts – such as bribery and misappropriation of funds – but also other activities such as patronage, nepotism, conflict of interest, influence peddling, seeking pleasure by using the official position, favours to relatives and friends, leaking or misusing government information, and engaging in any unsanctioned political activity.

It is desirable to define the meaning of an unethical conduct. [The following definition has been adapted from the author's *Public Service Ethics* Brussels: International Institute of Administrative Sciences, 1978, p. 8]:

> '*An unethical conduct denotes a situation whenever a public official (a Minister or a public servant), individually or collectively, exploits the official position (or give the appearance of doing so) in a way which compromises public confidence and trust in the integrity of that office in particular and the government in general, or lets others (such as relatives or friends) use the name of such positions towards some form of private gain at the expense of common good.*' [4]

The above definition does cover those situations where a public official may not receive any direct financial gain for himself but may be able to help a relative, friend, and others, including the demands of a superior officer, in administration or in politics.

---

4 O. P. Dwivedi, *Public Service Ethics*, Brussels: International Institute of Administrative Sciences, 1978, p. 8.

In 1986, in Canada, a Cabinet Minister, Sinclair Stevens, was found in such a situation. A Commission of Inquiry was appointed, chaired by Mr Justice William Parker. Justice Parker, in his report, decided first to differentiate between the 'real' and 'apparent' conflict of interest. According to Justice Parker:

> 'A real *conflict of interest denotes "a situation in which a Minister of the Crown has knowledge of a private economic interest that is sufficient to influence the exercise of his or her public duties and responsibilities" '.* [5]

And

> 'An apparent conflict of interest exists where there is a reasonable apprehension, which reasonable, well-informed persons could properly have, that a conflict of interest exists.' [6]

The Judge concluded that 'Mr Stevens' conduct during his tenure as a Minister of the Crown demonstrated a complete disregard for the requirements of the guidelines and code [*Conflict of Interest Guidelines* released by Trudeau in April 1980, and *Conflict of Interest Code*, applied by Mulroney effective from January 1986] and the standard of conduct that is expected of public office holders'. [7]

Regarding the effectiveness of guidelines and code of conduct, the Judge said:

> '. . . no conflict of interest system can, by itself, guarantee ethics in government or prevent dishonourable conduct on the part of Cabinet Ministers or other public office holders. Ultimately, public trust and confidence in the integrity of government depends on the integrity of individual public office holders and their individual sense of honour.' [8]

Of course, the scope of such guidelines raises some basic questions: Should the immediate members of a public servant's family be prohibited from working in the same agency/Department or from seeking contracts or licenses from that Department? Should such prohibition on family members be extended to cover the entire government operations? And what should a public official do after he leaves the government service: should he avoid seeking employment in all those business firms which are in any contractual relationship with his former Department only or with the

---

5 Canada, *Commission of Inquiry into the Facts and Allegations of Conflict of Interest Concerning the Honourable Sinclair M. Stevens* (Commissioner: Justice W. D. Parker), Ottawa: Supply and Services Canada, 1987, p. 29. See also pp. 451-88 in this Volume I: *Government Ethics*.

6 *Ibid*, p. 35.

7 *Ibid*, p. 342.

8 *Ibid*, p. 361.

entire government? Should there be a waiting period, and how long should it be?

And to what extent is it appropriate for a public official to sell his expertise out of office hours by becoming a consultant or partner in a private business? Under what circumstances would such an activity impair his usefulness as a public servant? When does service in a trade union or staff association become incompatible with public interest? Further related questions can be raised; for example, why it is possible for a businessman to escape the public wrath when he bends or evades laws and regulations; whereas a public office holder must always be beyond any shadow of suspicion of moral turpitude? This double standard is perhaps justified on the grounds that a businessman's unethical activities are not all far-reaching and comprehensive as compared to those in the public sector. That is why citizens cannot rely on a blind faith in their public officials' integrity but instead must have a healthy measure of cynicism and vigilance. But, once that faith disappears; it may begin the slow death of the democratic government because our system *is* based on the maintenance of public confidence and trust in the integrity of public officials. Such a trust is crucial for the proper functioning of a democratic government. At the same time, it should be noted that the achievement of high standards of morality among public officials is central to maintaining that public trust and confidence. Thus, it is the public officials who by accepting the responsibility of holding a public office open themselves to severe public scrutiny of their behaviour. It is they who are liable to misuse the power and authority entrusted to them. And it is they who, by their own doing (although involuntarily sometimes), may cross the limits of legal norms, ethical guidelines, and expected moral standards. Consequently, it is they who are to be held answerable for acts (both by commission and omission) committed. No State should be a shield for unethical, illegal, improper, and immoral activities of any public official.

3. Administrative Theology

As mentioned earlier, there is much public cynicism and general distrust about the conduct of government and public officials. The prevailing view is that the concept of service has weakened if not altogether disappeared from their ranks. What can be done to recapture that sense of mission, dedication, and service which used to be the hallmarks of our public officials? In this section, the concept of 'theology of administration' (or administrative theology) is discussed as a possible source of enhancing that mission and dedication towards a moral government and its statecraft. [9]

---

9 This section draws from O. P. Dwivedi 'Moral Dimensions of Statecraft: A Plea for an Administrative Theology' *Canadian Journal of Political Science* 20:4 (December 1987) pp. 699-709.

The 'theology of administration' may be seen as a study of concepts and practices relating to matters of ultimate concern in statecraft. Administrative theology, on the one hand, subsumes administrative ethics which 'involves the application of moral principles to the conduct of officials in organisations'. [10] Administrative ethics, in turn, is related to (and is generally influenced by) political ethics. 'Administrative theology, on the other hand, drawing on the doctrine of vocation (or callings) and the concept of service, relates to the sense of mission which a public official is supposed to undertake, to serve the public, perform duties and fulfil obligations'. [11] The objective of this concept is based on three specific elements.

First, the term 'theology' is used here in a most ecumenical way. As most of the modern States exhibit multi-cultural diversity, the administrative theology can strengthen the moral dimension of government by drawing at least one special feature from all high religions of the world. That feature is the concept of service. In all religions, people have been exhorted to serve others; in each religion as well as in all cultures, this doctrine is considered to be the ultimate concern of all human beings. Thus when such a concern is expressed through a vocation such as public administration whose ultimate aim is to serve humanity and to protect the public good, it acquires the desired prerequisite of a moral government.

Secondly, the term draws on the doctrine of vocation and callings which is evident in all major religions of the world. For example, a similar doctrine of vocation was prescribed several thousands of years ago by Lord Krishna in *Bhagavad Gita*: 'One must perform his prescribed duties as a vocation, keeping in sight the public good'. [12] The doctrine, as it relates to statecraft, and specifically to duties and obligations of public officials, is still greatly relevant and requires urgent revival.

Third, the use of the term 'administrative theology' could relate to different interpretations to established norms of modern secular bureaucracy. For example, the concepts of 'neutrality' and 'objectivity' in this context would not mean total disinterest and noninvolvement as well as avoidance of morality; rather they would require sympathetic involvement of public officials in protecting, enhancing and serving the public good. It also means displacing or minimising such traits of the administrative State as impersonality, authoritarianism, red tape, and bureaucratic oppression by believing in the vocation of public service as a true calling to be a servant of mankind. For all religions agree that the true measure of a religious man and woman is whether he or she is able to serve others.

---

10 Dennis F. Thompson 'The Possibility of Administrative Ethics' *Public Administrative Review* 45 (September-October 1985), p. 555.

11 O. P. Dwivedi 'Moral Dimensions of Statecraft . . .' *op. cit.* p. 703.

12 *Bhagavad Gita* Chapter 3, Verse 20.

These three major elements suggest that administrative theology can be an important dimension of moral government and administration. Religious precepts can be a formidable force to support any democratic form of government so long as we are not compelled to accept either theocracy or orthodoxy that suppresses the acknowledgment of other viewpoints, leads to a unidirectional handling of public policy and administration and suppresses existing democratic values.

Is 'administrative theology' possible? The two most serious obstacles to administrative theology come from the foundations of the modern State and administration – the separation of the State from religion, and the presumption of the neutrality of administrative action. Neither of these needs to be displaced in order to include administrative theology as one of the basic elements of education and training as well as standards and requisites of performance of administrators; also, by introducing such an element, we might find ourselves in a self-consciously moral society which would have to put duties and obligations first, and relegate individualism and selfishness to a subordinate place in the democracy.

The moral foundation of any public service organisation in a democracy requires that administrators and public officials show a genuine care for their fellow citizens. Devoid of such a moral foundation, a situation could emerge akin to the Nazi bureaucracy when State administration was enlisted in the cause of evil led by self-righteous people in government who sacrificed the moral obligation of the profession of serving the public. [13] What happened then is simply not acceptable. Because democratic values such as equality, law, justice, right and freedom have moral connotations, and demand an unwavering commitment to serve from those who govern. Public officials are obligated to uphold these values (which may be enshrined in a nation's constitution or considered as self-evident truths), particularly because in the final analysis the appropriate implementation and enforcement of government policies and programmes rests upon their shoulders. *Thus, they have a primary moral obligation to serve.* This is *the* basic premise upon which depends the normal functioning and survival of a democratic system of government. Public administrators have an obligation to serve the public in a manner which strengthens the integrity and processes of a democratic society. This is a resolve which draws on the doctrine of vocation as it relates to administrative theology.

The essence of this concept is in the identification of the strongest asset in any individual, that is, serving others. The basic thrust of the concept

---

13 Hannah Arendt has very aptly demonstrated the absence of any moral qualm among those public servants of the Third Reich who knew about the transportation and murder of Jews. See, *On Violence* (New York: Harcourt, Brace and World, 1969).

discussed above is to motivate people in government so that they can make a full contribution of their capabilities in better serving their country and the public:

> *'The plea is addressed mainly to those who are the backbone of the statecraft – public servants – and the objective is to create an environment, an administrative culture, in government so that public servants as well as Ministers are able to respond to the challenge of moral government. But such an environment will not result by itself unless there is a change in the management philosophy, attitudes of public service unions, and conduct of elected and appointed public servants – all to be oriented towards the broader aims of this plea: achieving excellence by serving others.'* [14]

4. Education and Training for Public Sector Ethics

The premise for education and training for public sector ethics is based on the view that the conferral of administrative or discretionary power on public servants is the source of ethical problems in the public management and behaviour of public servants. [15] Are public servants aware of the implications of the exercise of power and the ethical dimension that it entails? And what values should public servants choose in the exercise of their functions? Surely the possibility exists that two public servants may give interpretations to societal values that are mutually exclusive. And finally, will the public servant not respond to those values and beliefs to which he/she subscribes and chooses to respond? Would it not also depend upon how he perceives his obligations, to self, family, his conscience, his religion, country, organisation, and the like? Thus, public servants, facing these dilemmas, are left with a void if there is no common denominator or general appreciation of what appropriate values are to be adhered to, and what is the landscape of those values. That void can be easily filled in by providing a training for public service ethics where a common appreciation of such values can be exemplified to remove ambiguity and conflict in values. That training would have to be in two parts: (a) a seminar organised by a central agency with a common theme, and providing a generalised approach to the public service ethics; and (b) a workshop organised by the Department or agency with emphasis on specific aspects of ethical concerns which an employee may face while working in that environment. Such a training programme should be able to alert public servants to the sensitivity and seriousness of the issue. Of course, the following questions will emerge while planning for such a training programme.

---

14 O. P. Dwivedi, 'Moral Dimensions of Statecraft . . .' *op. cit.* p. 707.

15 This section draws from O. P. Dwivedi 'Teaching Ethics in Public Administration Courses' *International Review of Administrative Sciences*, 54 (March 1988) pp. 119-27.

Can a teaching and training programme which provides a perspective on the use of power, public service values and responsibility help public servants to better appreciate the ethical dimensions of public sector management? Can one 'teach' ethics and values? How, and at what level (pre-entry or post-entry public service training or both) should ethical maturity be developed? And if the ethical dimension of public sector management is based on a convergence of societal and individual values, how can this be approached? Further, there are instances to indicate that public servants tend to get offended by the suggestion that they should attend seminars/courses on ethics and values. This attitude seems to be based on the view that unless a person is already facing an ethical problem, or is going to be involved in an unethical dealing, then why would one volunteer for such a course or a training programme? The reluctance appears to arise from the fact that during their educational preparation for entry into the public service, not many public servants as students received sufficient exposure to the importance of ethics and values of public sector management. And once they joined the government employment, their initial training period supported the prevailing myth that value-laden decisions were actually in the domain of politicians while public servants purportedly work in a fact-filled environment; thus there was little need or purpose in teaching students and training public servants about a matter which would have little relevance to their work. This constricted view of the public servants' universe - separation of value-saturated environment of politicians and fact-filled universe of public servants – has continued to persist in nearly all countries. However this myth is no longer applicable as discussed in the previous section of this paper. Thus there is an urgent need to develop a suitable programme of education and training on ethics and values of public service responsibility.

4.1 Public Sector Ethics Course Curriculum

It has been recognised that a course curriculum on public sector ethics will be difficult to prepare, particularly if the comparative and international dimensions are to be included. However, if basic agreement can be reached about major aspects that ought to be included, then preparation for such a course will not be too difficult. For example, the education and training objectives may include the following:

a. enhancement of standards of objectivity, effectiveness, impartiality, integrity, and probity in the conduct of public business within the context of maintaining a professional public service dedicated to achieving a high degree of competence and efficiency;

b. fostering the responsiveness and accountability of public servants;

c. encouragement of conduct which prohibits the use of public office for self-interest or private gain or for improperly giving preferential treatment or disclosing confidential information to any person or group; and

d. standards of conduct which embody respect, fairness, social equity, and justice by public officials and employees in their decision-making process, and in their contact with members of the public. [16]

Once an agreement is reached about the general principles and objectives, a course curriculum can be prepared. [The author has prepared a broad outline of such a course curriculum which was published by the *International Review of Administrative Sciences* in 1988]. This Volume 1: *Government Ethics*, edited by Rosamund Thomas, provides an alternative model. It should be realised that any training programme should not be mounted as a one-shot event but as a continuous training activity. Further, the format should vary according to the level of responsibility and accountability although there ought to be a commonality of some basic topics. Moreover, teaching material should emphasise the relationship between theory and actual cases; this should be done by simulation of events, role playing, case studies, and other pedagogical methods. Finally, a team consisting of academics and practitioners should be involved in course preparation, instruction, seminar/ workshop organisation, and course evaluation.

Based on the above, a curriculum should aim to (a) raise the right questions and not to presume to provide the 'right' answers; (b) provide a setting in which the experience and sentiments of practitioners in specific time and space situations can be interrelated with logic and sentiments of theoreticians of ethics and morals; (c) provide a comparative perspective by drawing out and incorporating the different views and results under different economic, political and cultural settings; (d) help public servants to consciously confront the values that are cherished in their politico-administrative and societal environment; (e) help internalise a perspective on power, values and accountability that supports the ethical dimension of public management; [17] and (f) assist in understanding the relationship between obligations, responsibility and accountability of holding public office.

The basic objective of the suggested education and training programme, to summarise, is to strengthen the resolve of public servants to make their actions more responsive to the needs of the public. This way they would be

16 O. P. Dwivedi and E. A. Engelbert 'Education and Training for Values and Ethics in the Public Service: An International Perspective' *Public Personnel Management*, 10 (April 1981), pp. 140-141.

17 J. A. Worthley 'Ethics and Public Management: Education and Training', *Public Personnel Management*, 10 (April 1981), pp. 45-46.

able easily to exhibit moral maturity which involves a sensitivity to questions of personal and social responsibility, and an ability to distinguish moral judgements from expressions of personal or conventional preferences. [18]

5. Emerging Challenges

Three major challenges influencing the domain of public sector ethics are discernible: (1) spiritual guidance for secular affairs, (2) growing scepticism about government credibility, and (3) towards a moral administration. These are briefly discussed below.

5.1 Spiritual Guidance for Secular Affairs

The separation of Church from State had meant that the affairs of State were to lie outside the proper sphere of religion. It has also meant that no spiritual guidance was sought on any public policy and administrative issue. Further, somehow it was assumed that while religion dealt with the world hereafter, politics and administration were to concern mostly life before death. This separation between Church and State (which was not universally shared by all world religions and cultures) finally influenced the twin domain of politics and administration when dichotomy between the two became an accepted fact in teaching, training, research and practice of the two professions. Of course, the rise of scienticism with emphasis on rational objectivity and quantification equally affected the schism. Slowly, amoralism started influencing the domain of politics and administration, and its decision-making system. The process which began by hailing the separation of State and Church went perhaps too far in the other direction whereby the neglect of ethics and values in education, research and practice of statecraft was either condoned or at the best never questioned. It was not realised that the absence of spiritual guidance would strengthen the process of amoralism, selfishness, individualism, and materialism. That process, when applied to the secular domain, gives birth to ethical relativism, and removes or weakens such desirable attributes of public morality as individual self-discipline, sacrifice, compassion, justice, equity, and striving for the highest good. These attributes draw on the spiritual guidance which world religions and cultures provide. Thus, such a guidance is a necessary and desirable condition for a moral government:

'If justice, equality, equity and freedom are to be maintained, proximate political and administrative acts must have moral standards by which they can be judged. All government acts, if they are to serve the present and

---

18 O. P. Dwivedi, 'Ethics and Values of Public Responsibility and Accountability' *International Review of Administrative Sciences*, 51 (1985), pp. 65-66.

future generations well, must be measured against some higher law. That law cannot be a secular law because it is framed by imperfect people in their limited capacities and therefore limited in vision. That law has to be, perforce, based on the principles of higher spiritual and philosophical foundations.' [19]

For too long, those foundations have been weakening and are in the state of desuetude. The time has come for the spiritual guidance to be respected in the matter of public policy and State affairs.

5.2 Growing Public Scepticism About Government Credibility

Political activity was made illegal for the Federal public servants of Canada in 1917. But in 1967, the law was changed thereby permitting many aspects of political activity. On the other hand, a few decades ago, there was no law, a code of conduct, or even guidelines on conflict of interest. But nowadays, it has become a matter of great public concern and illegal. Thus, the level of acceptance of political activity has grown in perhaps the same proportion as the level of intolerance of conflict of interest has increased. Another example is the extent of corruption in government and its exposure. In the past, there was more corruption in politics and administration compared with today. But the corruption of bygone days did not receive the same kind of public scrutiny. Nowadays, even a slight deviation from the perceived official norm becomes a matter of great public concern and heated debate. There is clearly today a deeper cynicism in the public about the credibility of government. Consequently, any remote possibility of a conflict of interest is seen by the public as yet another example of deception and unethical activity in government. Not surprisingly, there is a great deal of scepticism concerning the morality of governmental action and the ethics of its officials. This is eroding public trust and confidence. And unless these are restored, moral government will remain a distant dream. Restoration of that public trust and confidence will depend upon how public officials are able to demonstrate the highest standards of ethics and responsibility in the use of power entrusted to them. Towards this, they (the elected as well as appointed public servants) will need to reinforce the sense of mission to serve the public, by acknowledging the place of administrative theology, and by acquiring the necessary education and training in public service ethics and responsibility. Such is the task ahead for those who wish to be involved in the complex and overly-sensitive world of statecraft.

---

19 O. P. Dwivedi 'Moral Dimensions of Statecraft . . .' *op. cit.*, p. 705.

5.3 Towards A Moral Administration

Moral administration does not mean that its officials exhibit only the negative obligations such as to do no harm, to avoid injury or to keep out of trouble. On the contrary, the notion of public sector ethics suggests that administrators actively undertake actions which are socially just and moral. Only by proactively pursuing the goals of social justice, equity and human dignity, can the officials and the State be moral and just. In the past, there was emphasis on negative obligations and admonitions that warned public officials to avoid waste, injustice and abuse of authority. Today, in addition to the above, the administrators need to subscribe to ethical ideals and personally exercise moral judgement in their duties. [20] By demonstrating the highest standards of personal integrity, honesty, fairness and justice, public officials can inspire public confidence and trust, which are the key ingredients of a moral government.

These ingredients can be strengthened by at least three means. Education and training in virtue and morality of holding a public office is the prerequisite. The second means to strengthen the moral resolve of a public servant is the existence of a code of conduct and ethical guidelines to assist a public servant in resolving a possible situation of ethical dilemma. Public servants should be aware of the conduct expected of them not only by the State which employs them but also by the public. A set of principles and guidelines which have force of law should be developed, and an office be established for enforcement and resolution of conflicts. Finally, there is a need to resurrect the concept of service and vocation so that a public administrator can rise above individualistic leanings and become a true 'public servant'. [21] Exemplary action against improprieties and malfeasance committed by either the elected or appointed officials would not only reduce such behaviour but would also have a salutary effect on the morale of all concerned, including the public.

It should be noted that the morality which determines political and administrative action is multidimensional. It is rooted in our civilisation, and derives from its spiritual foundations. It draws from the community of nations and various cultures, and influences the universe that we know of:

> *'The confidence and trust in the democracy can be safeguarded only when the governing processes exhibit a higher moral tone, deriving from the breadth of*

---

20 For a discussion on ethical ideals of public service, see Rosamund M. Thomas *The British Philosophy of Administration*, (Cambridge: Centre for Business and Public Sector Ethics, 1989); and Andrew Dunsire, 'Bureaucratic Morality in the United Kingdom', *International Political Science Review*, 9 (July 1988), pp. 179-191.

21 O. P. Dwivedi 'Moral Dimensions of Statecraft . . .' *op. cit.*, p. 705.

morality. This calls for a commitment on the part of elected and appointed officials to moral government and administration.' [22]

Actually, we get a moral government by creating those conditions within which a moral government can operate by making it possible for officials to acquire the necessary traits, and by the practice of the same. An exemplary public servant, to be specific, is not simply one who obeys the laws and behaves within the confines of legality of that action, but is also one who strives for a moral government. Such is the duty for those who are members of the difficult and complex world of government. This is the essence and basis of a moral State, and its activities. Only by demonstrating the highest standards of personal integrity and morality, can public officials inspire public confidence and trust, the true hallmarks of moral government. [23]

---

22 O. P. Dwivedi 'Conclusion: A Comparative Analysis of Ethics, Public Policy, and the Public Service', in *Ethics, Government and Public Policy: A Reference Guide*, eds. James S. Bowman and Frederick A. Elliston (New York: Greenwood Press, 1988) p. 318.

23 This paper was presented at the Inaugural Conference of the Centre for Business and Public Sector Ethics held in Cambridge, England, 12-15 July 1989.

The Teaching of Ethics in American Government Classes

by Professor Leicester R. Moise, Department of Political Science, University of Louisville, United States

Introduction

The title of the paper, 'The Teaching of Ethics in American Government Classes,' has an almost innocent simplicity. From one point of view instruction of ethics seems the right or ethical thing to do when teaching undergraduates in American government. But as is the case in many issues, the simple problem is more complex.

Intellectual interest in ethics and politics began during the Grecian period. During the age of the Greek philosophers politics and ethics were interrelated, almost inseparable. One concept of this earlier age was that the procedures of thoughts of politics and ethics were useful, for by this process groups of individuals who thought and accomplished good, transformed themselves toward goodness whether their activities accomplished personal or political objectives. Centuries later the Machiavellian age brought a series of new questions which complicated the ethics issues as outlined by the classical philosophers. Politics and ethics were separate and there was not any requirement for the individual who was ethical in his or her personal life to transmit this ethical behaviour into decisions of the State or government. [1]

During the last part of the nineteeth century and accelerating rapidly in the first six decades of this century the academic community gradually became dominated by the development of empirical or positive science. Donald Warwick in *The Teaching of Ethics in the Social Sciences*, and Douglas Sloan in a *Hastings Report* article, outline the decline of ethics and rise to domination of positive/empirical concepts in the academic community. In tracing the role of ethics courses, Warwick concludes that there was a triumph within the academic community of positivism by the year 1930. Warwick states:

---

1 Rosemarie Tong *Ethics in Policy Analysis* (Englewood Cliffs: Prentice Hall, 1986) pp. 35-44.

'The essential tenet of logical positivism is that truth of statement of fact must be established by observation ... To have any meaning, ethical statements must fall within the compass of observation or otherwise be derived from science, as from empirically based theory ... The moral equation was simple: science = objectivity: objectivity = value neutrality; ergo science = value neutrality ... Courses in ethics in the social sciences were non-existent.' [2]

Sloan contrasts objective free social science with the personal ideals of academics of the 1930s. He writes:

'Most social scientists not only held that social science is totally objective, value-free enterprise, but ethical values themselves are an expression of subjective preferences. Ethical values were seen as noncognitive, nonrational ... many (faculty) were committed as individuals to humane and democratic ideals derived from religious and cultural sources they were no longer willing to recognize ...' [3]

A brief resurgence of ethical/moral behaviour expected for public officials occurred in the United States in the period after the First World War. In America some educators wished to train generations of political officials entrusted with a sense of civic responsibility. The extension of these ideas were sometimes reminiscent of Plato's guardians, for the American period was one which stressed that 'the paramount need of American society ... was for guided social change under the direction of trained experts.' [4]

The academic interest in ethical concerns was shortlived. Facts were not values, and the value-free influence of positive/ empirical approach retained a dominant position in the social science community. A return of interest for political ethics began over a decade ago. Sloan indicated that interest in ethical matters tends to be cyclical. He writes:

'Even as concern with the teaching of ethics has time and again flagged and even at one point disappeared in higher education, it has without fail ... reappeared at another, for the issues with which it deals have been integral to the entire enterprise.' [5]

While scholarly work written in the last decade on the relationship of ethics and politics indicates a resurgence of the issue in the academic community, Warwick suggests that political ethics has moved only from oblivion to ambivalence. [6]

---

2 Donald P. Warwick *The Teaching of Ethics in the Social Sciences*, (Hasting on Hudson: The Hastings Center, 1980) pp. x, 27, 29.

3 Douglas Sloan, 'The Teaching of Ethics in the American Under-graduate Curriculum,' *Hastings Center Report*, Vol. 12, Number 1, December, 1979, p. 20.

4 Sloan, p. 24.

5 Sloan, p. 21.

6 Warwick, p. 36.

1. Ethics

James Rachel asks a fundamental question in his essay titled 'Can Ethics provide answers?' Rachel indicates that philosophers who have disagreed on this fundamental question are divided into two positions. One position is affirmative while the other side indicates that there are only ethical questions. Rachel's major conclusion is that ethics must be limited to matters about things we care about when reason is a vital factor and when we are concerned about what we ought to do. [7]

Alasdair MacIntyre's article in *The Hastings Report* describes the search for the foundations of ethics as frustrating because of the failures of modern analytical moral philosophy, and the relatively short lived moral indignation over social or political issues. [8]

References to the work of Rachel and MacIntyre indicate the difficulty about reaching agreements on basic ideas. Basic ideas and definitions often create legitimate differences among scholars since basic premises should shape the examination of the questions and the issues involved. So it is with ethics and politics.

Despite difficulties many scholars do develop basic definitions for ethics and politics. A combination of ideas from three sources provides the definition of ethics for this study. Ethics concerns moral values that relate to human conduct and questions about judgements of right and wrong. [9]

Politics is also the subject of controversy but one widely used definition is that politics is about power, who gets it, how, and the manner in which authoritative decisions are made about public issues and policies. This type of definition is close to a Hobbesian approach since the emphasis is on the human drive for power.

While the two definitions offer contrasting values, they are still related. This relationship is described by Claes Ryn as follows:

'When a government is conceived as based on nothing but a prudential,

---

7 James Rachel, 'Can Ethics Provide Answers,' *Applied Ethics and Ethical Theory*, David Rosenthal and Fadloe Shehadt, (eds.) (Salt Lake City: University of Utah Press) 1988, p. 24.

8 Gerald C. MacIntyre, Jr., 'Why is the Search for the Foundations of Ethics So Frustrating,' *Hastings Center Report*, Vol. 19, Number 4, August, 1979, pp. 16-17. MacIntyre also indicates that contemporary practitioners are pale shadows of earlier philosophers. This paper can but mention the main element of the questions that MacIntyre raises.

9 General definition is a composite from: Mortimer Adler and Seymour Cain, *Ethics: The Study of Moral Values*, (Chicago: Encyclopedia Britannica, 1962) preface; Robert C. Beck, (ed.) *Perspectives in Philosophy*, (New York: Holt, 1975) p. 563; John Dewey, *Critical Theory of Ethics*, (New York: Hillary, 1951) p. 1.

pragmatic effort to settle disputes peacefully, when the ethical perspective is pushed aside ... the result is a distortion of political reality.' [10]

This work is not primarily about theories of ethics or politics though the basic concepts of both form a foundation for the study. A major question of this study is:

'What ethical theories can provide a framework for use in the applied area of politics and government, specifically in the instruction of American government classes?'

There has been an increasing number of books and articles in the past two decades about political ethics. While this study uses a variety of sources, a key theoretical work on the relationship of ethics and politics is Dennis Thompson's, *Political Ethics and Public Officials*. This study is not limited to the Thompson ideas; however, the Thompson book and other sources are used by this study to develop a focus and basis for a political ethics framework appropriate for undergraduate students in American government classes.

Thompson's work indicates that the issue of ethics and politics is best considered from the point of view of what demands ethics makes on politics. The justification is that ethical principles require a person to act on universally accepted principles which apply to almost any context including politics. Thompson indicates that politics is a co-operative effort by individuals directed toward a common good. Democracy has a mutual dependency with ethics and democratic politics receives reinforcement support from political ethics. The reverse is also true, democratic politics is a support system for political ethics. In democracies, Thompson indicates ethical conflicts arise out of the representational and organisational characteristics of public office. Decisions by public officials should be responsible and promote the general welfare of citizens despite defective governmental structures. Despite structural defects, Thompson concludes that political ethics can provide a link between the structure of government and the political officials. [11]

2. Methodology

Basic questions arise from the renewed academic interest in politics and

---

10 Claes G. Ryn, *Democracy and Ethical Life*, (Baton Rouge: Louisiana State University Press, 1978) p. 21.

11 Concepts from: Dennis Thompson, *Political Ethics and Public Office*, (Cambridge: Harvard University Press, 1987); Dennis Thompson, 'Moral Responsibilities of Public Officials: The Problem of Many Hands,' *American Political Science Review*, Vol. 74, Number 4, December, 1980.

ethics. This paper deals with one: The teaching of ethics. Examinination of this issue is restricted to instruction of American government classes at institutions of higher education in the United States.

To examine the current level of concern and information about ethics and politics, the author used a questionnaire to examine student attitudes, did a content analysis of thirty American government textbook glossaries and indexes, and examined other political science materials. The content for the past decade of a number of journals, and books was examined to provide a research base for the development of ethics theory and concepts and their relationship to political systems and public officials. A benchmark text in American government was selected for topical content analysis. As a result of the research of ethics/politics books and articles, a suggested framework is developed for ethics instruction in American government classes.

2.1 The Student Questionnaire

Public opinion polls often report on the low public esteem for public officials. A Harris poll in 1980 indicated that only 11 percent of citizens had confidence in the Congress, and 78 percent of citizens thought Members of the Congress used unethical methods. [12]

A questionnaire developed by the author was designed to examine the perceived attitudes about political ethics. The tested group were undergraduate students in American democracy classes. The test was taken by the students during April, 1988. Thirteen questions sought student responses in ethical behaviour patterns of what should be and what are the behaviour patterns of political systems and political actors. The specific questions are listed in Note 1 together with the data on the student responses. Of the 700 students enrolled in American government classes 426 students answered the questionnaire. Because the questionnaire was taken only by University of Louisville students, the results are of limited value until administered by some appropriate random sample.

The questionnaire also asked a series of demographic questions. The analysis of two demographic variables is included in the survey results. Details of the results are in Table One on page 360 in Note One.

Questions 1, 2, 3 and 11 examined student attitudes about what *should* be the ethical behaviour of the American political system (1), all elected political officials (2), major national political officials in the Executive branch and the Congress (3), and ethical goals established by the constitution (11). Questions 4 through 7 examined the student's perceptions of what *are* the ethical behaviour patterns of executives (4), congressmen (5), judges (6), government workers (7). Questions 8, 9, and 10 examined student attitudes

---

12 *Congressional Ethics*, Washington: Congressional Quarterly, Inc., 1980, p. 1.

about ethical concerns in public policies of defence and security (8), economic prosperity (9) and domestic programmes (10). Questions 13 examined eight variables in the political decision-making process to determine how ethical concerns ranked with students. Question 12 asked if students thought the higher education curriculum should have an increased emphasis of the teaching of ethics.

A summary of the major questionnaire results is as follows:

Questions one and two reveal that students perceive a slight difference between the political system and political officials in regard to ethical behaviour in the American democratic setting. While the medians were an identical 8.0 the mean was 8.014 for public officials compared to 7.706 for the political system.

A comparison of question three (should be ethical) with questions 4 to 7 (do behave in an ethical manner) indicates that students perceive a modest difference in the expectation of ethical political behaviour with the reality of political behaviour by political officials. The mean for question 3 was 7.703 while all four categories, executives, congressmen, judges and public servants had lower means. Civil servants ranked the lowest in student estimates of ethical behaviour with a 5.572 mean. Congressmen were slightly better with a 5.583 mean, with executives like the President at 6.656. Judges were classified by students as the best in ethical behaviour of the four groups with a 7.049 mean, a score which was the closest to the mean for expected ethical behaviour of public officials.

Questions 8, 9, and 10 related to perceptions of policy issues and ethical behaviour. In general the means for these three questions were lower than expected ethical behaviour of the political system and lower than the ethics behaviour of public officials since none of the three questions had a mean which reached 6.0. Domestic policy mean was 5.958, the highest, followed by 5.706 for economic prosperity. The students perception of ethical behaviour for defence and security policy had the lowest mean for any question on the survey at 5.594.

Question 11 tied the Constitution to ethical behaviour and was developed to test both common good concepts, and to determine perceptions about the ethical standard set by the Constitution's Preamble. The analysis of the student answers indicated that this question had the second highest mean (7.733) on the questionnaire. The mean was close to those for expected ethical behaviour for the political system and public officials (Questions 1 and 2).

Question 12 asked about student perceptions for teaching of ethics. The result indicated a perceived need for additional instruction in this area, though the mean at 7.287 was lower than the three questions on expected ethical behaviour and the role of the Constitution (Question 11).

Combining the defence/security policy area with the question on ethical behaviour of public officials indicates that students perceived that administrative civil servants involved in defence and security matters have the lowest political ethical pattern of behaviour for public officials.

Table One
Student Political Ethics Questionnaire Data

Question Number (topic)	Mean	Median	SD
#1 (Ethics-Political System)	7.706	8.000	1.974
#2 (Ethics-Political Officials)	8.014	8.000	1.960
#3 (Ethical Decisions)	7.703	8.000	1.986
#4 (Exec. Ethical Behaviour)	6.656	7.000	2.016
#5 (Rep. Ethical Behaviour)	5.583	6.000	1.987
#6 (Judge Ethical Behaviour)	7.049	7.000	2.052
#7 (Civ. Serv. Eth. Behaviour)	5.572	5.000	2.011
#8 (Sec/defence Ethics)	5.594	6.000	2.179
#9 (Economic Ethics)	5.706	6.000	2.025
#10 (Domestics Ethics)	5.958	6.000	2.098
#11 (Constitution Ethics)	7.733	8.000	2.004
#12 (Teaching Ethics)	7.287	8.000	2.108

Question 13 sought to rank student perceptions about ethical behaviour with a number of political decision-making policies. The results indicate that students think that national political leaders should make decisions by the following ranking:

1. Ethical factors: 23.8%
2. Legal and Constitutional Issues: 22.4%
3. Economic Costs: 18.0%
4. Trustee for people: 12.7%
5. Ideology: 11.8%
6. Party; 7.5%
7. Election/personal ego: 5.6%

2.2 Demographic Analysis

The questionnaire asked students a number of demographic questions. Two categories are:

1. Gender
2. Underclassmen (freshmen/sophomores) and upperclassmen

Data on the first eleven questions was used to examine variance of these two demographic categories. The results were checked for significance by the

Kruskal-Wallis One way Anova test. A standard of .025 was used as a level of significant variation. The results of this statistical test indicated:

a. There are not significant differences in student opinion of political ethics based on gender on ten of eleven of the test questions. The only question where there was a gender difference in student perceptions was Number 6 (Judicial) where the mean ranking was higher for men at 223.52 compared to 184.06 for women.

b. The means for women on the ethical expectation questions, 1, 2, and 3 were higher than those for men. But on the ethical behaviour questions about political officials the means were higher for men. This suggests that women may have higher expectations for ethical behaviour than men and that women may evaluate ethical performance by political officials more harshly than do men.

c. There are not significant differences in under or upperclassmen opinions of political ethics for nine of the eleven test questions. Questions seven (Civil servants) and eleven (Constitution) were the only questions where there was a difference. The mean rankings were higher at 211.67 (7) and 213.10 (11) for underclassmen than the means of 179.14 (7) and 176.80 (11) for upperclassmen.

d. The means for upperclassmen on expectations for ethical performance (questions 1, 2, 3) were higher than the means for underclassmen. The means for ethical performance by public officials were perceived as lower by upperclassmen when compared to underclassmen. This suggests that upperclassmen have higher ethical expectations for ethical behaviour than underclassmen and evaluate ethical performance more harshly than underclassmen.

e. Combining the two issues suggests that upperclassmen women have the highest expectations, but are the most disappointed in the ethical performance of public officials.

3. Glossary/Index References in American Government Texts

The glossaries and indexes of thirty American government texts were examined for references to ethics or political ethics. A list of the texts, by author's name, and the data of this survey, is in Note Two.

Of the twenty-six volumes which have a glossary, none has a glossary reference or definition for ethics or political ethics.

In the indexes of the thirty texts listed by author in Note Two, none has an index for political ethics. Just fifty percent (15 of 30) have an ethical reference, all of which relate to applied political ethical questions. The references lack any substantial discussion of political ethics as an issue in its own right. The most common reference (nine) is to the 1978 Ethics Act. Seven ethics references refer to Congressional ethics. There are only four precise references to Presidential ethics and the other two refer in a general way to bureaucratic ethics or the common good concepts. There were no direct index references to judicial or legal ethics. This content analysis indicates that the renewed interest in political ethics has not made an impact on texts used for instruction in American government classes and that the more value-free positivism approach still dominates American government textbooks. The survey of University of Louisville American government students' results indicate that students want more instruction in political ethics. The American government texts are not providing this perceived need.

The relative lack of references to ethics or political ethics in American government texts is generally similar to what occurs in some other American political material. Two examples are:

1. Two recent articles in the publication, *News For Teachers of Political Science*, have little reference to political ethics in their discussions of the purpose of political science undergraduate education.

2. Neither the 1985 Membership Directory nor the 1988 Biographical Directory of the members of the American Political Science Association have a category which allows a faculty member to list ethics or political ethics as an area of teaching or research.

The American Political Dictionary does have references to ethics in three categories which reflect, in a general way, the major ethics references from the textbook index analysis of Appendix Two. The three areas noted in the political dictionary relate to the following:

1. Ethics Codes which concern the codes of financial behaviour of Congressmen.

2. Ethics Committees which deal with Congressional Committees.

3. The Ethics in Government Act of 1978 which defines the issues of financial disclosure for all senior government officials and the restrictions for a one/two years on conflict on interest relating to employment after government service. [13]

The limited information in the textbooks and other material reviewed contrasts with the student perception of a need for more political ethics instruction. What study framework can be suggested to implement the study

---

13 Jack C. Plano and Milton Greenberg *The American Political Science Dictionary*, (New York: Holt, 1985) pp. 206, 292. The publication, *Congressional Quarterly*, periodically has articles relating to Congressional and public officials violations of the 1978 Ethics law.

of politics and ethics in American higher education and in American government classes?

4. Ethics Instruction in Political Science

Until the last decade or so, the study of ethics in American Universities has been left to the Philosophy Department. This decision did not result in additional instruction, since one reseacher discovered in 1964 that only 27 of 100 American universities required even one course in philosophy or ethics as a graduation requirement. [14]

There are a variety of questions involved if a determination is made to enhance the teaching of ethics in politics and government. The most elementary question is: Can it be taught: The *Hastings Center Report* published a number of articles on this topic. An article by a psychologist indicates that ethical moral learning is a cognitive process that occurs in the stages of human growth and development. The final two stages of moral development are the points where the individual recognises institutions and groups. One assessment tool for research in this area is the Defining Issues Test (DIT). Not too surprisingly, philosophers and political scientists record the highest DIT scores. The research indicates that moral judgement DIT scores increase with education but individuals level out after leaving school. [15]

This research would tend to indicate that education at the University level is a maximum point for the development of ethical and moral skills and analysis based on such factors as reasoning and decision-making.

Another Hastings Center report warns of the pragmatic problem of testing for ethics performance/knowledge. This report states that:

> 'Testing may cancel out one reason students have liked ethics courses: in these courses they have a chance to think on their own . . . Testing might orient teaching more toward force feeding of knowledge' [16]

These articles indicate the value of ethics instruction in higher education and warn of the possibility of a negative influence of traditional testing methods.

One way to proceed is to develop specific courses such as legal ethics, medical ethics, media ethics, bureaucratic ethics. These courses provide a pattern for the development of political ethics.

Two examples of administrative ethics are the separate suggestions by O. P. Dwivedi and Charles R. Embry. Dwivedi's work outlines the need for

---

14 Sloan, p. 32.

15 James R. Rest 'A Psychologist Looks at the Teaching of Ethics' *Hastings Center Report*, Vol. 9, Number 1, February, 1982, pp. 31-32.

16 Carol Levine 'Do Ethics Testing Get a Passing Grade' *Hastings Center Report*, Vol 13, Number 3, June, 1983, p. 33.

teaching in ethical and moral values. He establishes a specific set of goals for the course curriculum which can be applied in a comparative and international basis. Dwivedi's plan includes a philosophical outline, the clarifications of norms and values, the role of power and authority, the rights and obligations of public servants and their accountability. [17] Embry's outline centres on the American administrative culture and his ethics course includes a variety of humanistic/literary works as well as political research documents. His ethics course proposals include concepts of the ancient philosophical tradition, American régime and public administrative ethics, specific cross-cultural influences, including references to such groups as southern white, black Americans, native Americans and hispanic Americans. His outline concludes with a framework for ethical decision-making. [18]

The other tact is one suggested by Donald Warwick in his article in *The Hastings Center Report*. Warwick states that specialised political ethics courses should be part of Graduate School curriculum. At the undergraduate level 'the teaching of ethics should be integrated into all form of teaching rather than confined to a separate course.' [19]

The study of political ethics could emphasise more abstract ethical theory matters as indicated by the courses in the field of philosophy and/or in the American journal, *Ethics*. Two recent books by Daniel Callahan and Bruce Jenning's, *Ethics, The Social Sciences, and Policy Analysis*, and Norman Bowie's, *Ethical Issues in Government* suggest a different solution. They combine ethics theory with applied issues. Because of a renewal of interest in political and governmental ethics, Bowie indicates that there are a number of applied questions:

1. Should Legislators serve constituents or conscience?

2. What are the proper bounds of government regulation?

3. Is cost-benefit analysis an ethically proper tool for public policy decisions

4. What is the government's obligation to inform the public? [20]

The edited book by Callahan and Jennings indicates that the social sciences obtained a prominent role in the public policy process. Positivist views

---

17 O. P. Dwivedi 'Teaching Ethics in Public Policy and Administrative Courses' *Public Policy and Administrative Studies*, Guelph, University of Guelph, 1986, pp. 198-207.

18 Charles R. Embry 'Ethics and Public Administration' *News for Teachers of Political Science*, American Political Science Association, Number 42, Summer, 1984, p. 10.

19 Warwick, p. 49.

20 Norman E. Bowie 'Preface' *Ethical Issues in Government*. Norman E. Bowie, (ed.) (Philadelphia: Temple University Press, 1981) p. ix.

related well to the assumption that policy was a technical problem. Ethics issues arose only within the context of intellectual honesty, collecting and reporting data accurately. This approach disguises hidden individual group value judgements. [21] Another article in the Callahan and Jennings book was written by Robert Bellah. Bellah suggests that issues be examined, not so much from the perspective of a value-free technology, but should have as a basic component rationality, reason and ethical/moral considerations. [22]

4.1 Political Ethics/American Government

Four concepts of ethics instruction make a simple matrix system of choices:

Table Two
Political Ethics Teaching Matrix

Political Course Ethics Theory	Existing Courses Applied/Cases-Ethics
Political Course Applied/Cases-Ethics	Existing Courses Ethics Theory

All four of these approaches have valid reasons for adoption. This study applies ethics theory and applied ethics to an existing course. This approach is justified by research of the publications about ethics and politics, the analysis of the American government textbooks and the other materials, and, to a limited extent, the results of the student survey administered to University of Louisville students. The specific study example is applied to American government classes, though the principles may be applicable to other political sciences classes in the United States and other democratic nations.

The following list of ethics frameworks does not encompass all possible ethics approaches which can be derived from ethical theories. The five suggested ethics theories/concepts are ones which logically can be defended as appropriate for American government classes. The five ethics frameworks are:

1. Classical Political Democratic Ethics

2. Ethics and the Individual: Ethical Egoism

21 Daniel Callahan and Bruce Jennings, 'Introduction' *Ethics, the Social Sciences and Policy Analysis* Daniel Callahan and Bruce Jennings, (eds.) (New York: Plenum, 1983) pp. xiii-xix.

22 Robert W. Bellah 'Social Sciences as Practical Reason' *Ethics, the Social Sciences, and Policy Analysis,* Daniel Callahan and Bruce Jennings, (eds.) (New York: Plenum, 1983) pp. 37-64.

3. Utilitarian Ethics and the Theory of Justice

4. The Consequences of Dirty Hands/Moral Responsibility of Many Hands

5. Applied Ethics in Public Policy

The author recognises that the five framework set has problems. For example, the dirty-hands, many hands set overlaps with the other four sets. The consequential concepts inherent in the dirty-hands/many hands framework overlap into both deontological, egoistic factors and the utilitarian framework. The purpose of relating an ethical framework to political issues/concepts is not the justification of any one ethical conception or the comparative merits to other theories or concepts. The purpose of the alignment of political matters with ethics concepts is to provide the student with one method of *how* to examine politics and ethical issues.

These five ethics frameworks were applied to a one American government 'benchmark' text. The text selected is authored by James MacGregor Burns, J. W. Peltason and James Cronin, a text published in thirteen editions.

The benchmark text contains parts/chapters which can be used to relate ethical frameworks to political context. The political areas of the text and the related ethical approach are listed in Table Three.

Table Three
Ethics and American Government

Benchmark Text Area	Ethics Framework
(1) Chapters and documents such as the Constitution Declaration of Independence and *The Federalist,* and the democratic system.	Classical/Political democratic ethics
(2) Chapters and amendments to Constitution dealing with individual citizen rights, citizens beliefs, interests groups, voting, elections and political parties.	Ethical egoism
(3) Chapters on the Executive, administrative, regulatory institutions of government.	Consequences of dirty hands/many hands
(4) Chapters on the Congress and Judiciary.	Utilitarianism and the theory of justice

| (5) Chapters on public foreign policy, defence security, economic issues and domestic policy. | Applied ethics/policy analysis and case studies |

*The table is one plan to relate the pairings of political topics to an ethical framework. The author does not mean to suggest that the alignment is the only possible matrix. The absence of other ethics theories and frameworks is not intended to indicate they lack validity or justification in a political ethics general framework.

A brief defence of the pairings in Table One requires an overview of the ethical concepts which can be used to justify the pairings of the political issues with the ethical analysis framework.

5. Pairing Number One: Constitution and Classical Political Democratic Ethics:

Much of the ethical and philosophical reasons for the adoption of the American Constitution rested with political philosophers and their ethical judgements. W. J. Mackenzie traces early democratic political ideas to a variety of authors including Aristotle, Plato, Augustine, Aquinas, Hobbes, Spinoza, Hegel, Machiavelli, Locke and Rousseau. [23] One of many possible illustrations of the relationship of the classics to the Constitution is from John Locke. Locke wrote:

> 'Man being ... by nature, all free, equal, and independent, no one can be ... subjected to the political power of another, without his consent ... And, thus every man, by consenting with others to make one body politic under one government, puts himself under obligation, to everyone of that society, to submit to the determination of the majority ... The first and fundamental positive law' ... is the preservation of society, and (as far as will consist with the public good) of every person in it.' [24]

Two American ethics' scholars have summarised ethical concerns about democracy as follows:

> '... democracy ... with all its faults and all its dangers, is the only form of government under which nations ... can ... go ... on to a higher level of civilisation, levels at which a life of reasonable dignity and happiness shall be within the reach of the great majority of mankind.' [25]

---

23 W. J. M. MacKenzie *Politics and Social Sciences* (Baltimore: Penguin, 1967) pp. 40-53.

24 John Locke 'A Priori-Liberalism' *Political Ideologies*, James A. Gould and William H. Truitt, (eds.) (New York: Macmillan, 1973) pp. 38, 39.

25 William McDougal *Ethics and Some Modern World Problems* (New York: Plenum, 1924) p. 10.

'Representative democracy is committed to respecting the boundaries of the individual ... yet establishing a mutual moral permeability between the public and nonpublic.' [26]

The conception of humanity developed in both positive and negative examples by democratic political philosophers can be used in classes to enhance the ethical justification for the Constitution, including the governmental structure, and the individual rights and duties which it established. A contemporary example of a breakdown in ethical behaviour is the May, 1989 resignation of James Wright as speaker of the House of Representatives. In his resignation address to the Congress, the central theme was the responsibility and obligation of an elected official to be a trustee for the better good of the people of a democratic society.

6. Pairing Number Two: Individuals and Ethical Egoism

Philosopher William Frankena in his book, *Ethics*, indicates about ethical egoism that:

> ... *'ethical egoism is an ethical theory ... the tenants of the ethical egoism ... (are) that an individual's one and only basic obligation is to promote for himself the greatest balance of good over evil ... an individual should go by what is to his own private advantage ... ethical egoists ... have often been hedonists ... identifying good or welfare with happiness and happiness with pleasure.'* [27]

Egoistic and deontological theories are often divided into two major subdivisions: acts and rules. From the act viewpoint each circumstance varies and the uniqueness of the circumstances means that no general guideline can cover all conditions. Rule deontology indicates that general standards for truths establish rules which cover circumstances. This contrast can be developed into a variety of possible ideas about the role of the individual and factional groups in America.

One American classroom example would be to question the ethical conditions for individuals/factions as outlined in Numbers 10 and 51 of *The Federalist*. Major emphasis of these Madisonian works is the idea that individual and/or factional ambition is checked by the ambition of another individual or faction. The ambition checking ambition concept can be related to self-interest egoism. One possible contemporary social science work which could use an ethical egoism approach is the individual choice and group decisions, which are a part of James Buchanan and Gordon Tullock's, *Calculus*

---

26 George Kateb 'The Moral Distinctiveness of Representative Democracy' *Ethics*, Vol. 91, Number 3, April, 1981, p. 91.

27 William Frankena, *Ethics* (Englewood Cliffs: Prentice-Hall, 1963) pp. 16-17.

of Consent. This book is usually associated with economics and politics. Their work begins with basic questions from political philosophy and centres on what the State ought to be. The model which they develop is about the theory of collective choice, a theory founded on an individualistic methodology. [28]

7. Pairing Number Three: Executives and the Consequences of Dirty Hands, Many Hands

The recurring dilemma for political leaders of democracies is the issue of what political philosopher Dennis Thompson describes as the dirty hands and many hands issue.

The dirty hands issue is the problem that officials in democracies may be required to act in public life in a manner contrasting with their private ethical standards. Thompson writes that ... 'public life may require officials to act in ways that would be wrong in private life, raising the classic problems of dirty hands.' [29] A 1988 example occurred during the Presidential campaign when Vice-President Bush authorised the use of the Horton political campaign advertisement. The Horton advertisement was about a black American released from prison on parole who committed a murder after release. Did Mr Bush find the advertisement offensive and in violation of his personal standard of behaviour?

A President may have to lie about economic policy regarding Government tax or spending policy. Is President Bush ethically obligated to resist tax changes to help resolve the American Government's budgetary deficit, or is he ethically obligated to complete his campaign pledge of 'read my lips, no new taxes!'

In theory, democracies require the consent of the governed, and the failure to communicate truthfully by the executives can create problems on the justification of decisions, and is related to both consequential and deontological issues. Thompson concludes that 'if the deal is worth making, it is because on balance it promotes the public good ...' [30]

The many hands concept attempts to deal with the problem that almost all political matters are not limited to the decision of one individual. Most

---

28 James M. Buchanan and Gordon Tullock, *The Calculus of Consent* (Ann Arbor: The University of Michigan Press, 1965) p. 1. The concepts in *Calculus of Consent* are advanced and this type of material is normally used in Graduate School courses. While it probably cannot be used in typical American government classes, it might be appropriate for honours classes. Including this level of material does illustrate the practical problem the teacher faces with some of the ethical/political references, i.e. How does the teacher maintain the academic integrity of the information and yet make it understandable to typical students?

29 Thompson 'Moral Responsibilities ...' p. 905.

30 Thompson *Political Ethics* ... pp. 15, 41.

decisions involve a number of persons or groups. When many people, or groups, are involved, the decisions which often are ascribed to hierarchical or some collective model do not consider the range of moral, ethical considerations. [31]

One of Thompson's examples of ethical issues is the resignation of American Secretary of State Cyrus Vance in 1980 after the aborted attempt by the American military to rescue the hostages held by Iran. Thompson writes that 'he (Vance) resigned not only because he disagreed with Carter's plan, but also – let us assume – because he had deceived our allies'. [32]

Thompson suggests that Vance's resignation is an example of a public official declining to 'dirty his own hands.' [33] This analogy is probably quite appropriate in the Vance case and can be illustrated by other resignations and behaviour of public officials in many democratic nations. However, I suspect that some students when presented with the ethical behaviour of Mr Vance, would argue that the democratic political systems create higher ethical performance levels than many elected and appointed officials have as individuals. The behaviour of Mr Vance and other positive illustrations would be offset to extensive numbers of less than ethical behaviour by other public officials. The right model, is not clean individual (ethical) hands versus dirty political hands, but relatively dirty individual hands of elected or appointed public officials in a democratic political system of cleaner hands. In other words, democratic political systems enhance ethical standards to an expectation beyond the capability of many elected or appointed public officials. Recent examples suggesting this concept are the questions over the ethics of: (1) many Congressmen including former speaker James Wright, and (2) many of the public officials involved in the Iran-Contra affair, whose behaviour was brought out during the Congressional Committee hearings and the trial of Colonel Oliver North.

These unethical individuals are shielded by what Thompson calls the collective responsibility of the many hands involved in making public policy decisions. Thompson writes that:

> 'Many political outcomes are the product of the actions of many different people, whose individual contributions may not be identifiable at all ... The second step is the claim that no one individual can be morally blamed for these outcomes. At the final step, proponents of the argument diverge, offering two different conclusions ... every individual associated should be charged with moral responsibility and the other holds that only the collectivity can so be charged.' [34]

---

31 Thompson 'Moral Responsibilities ...' p. 905.
32 Thompson *Political Ethics* ... p. 18.
33 Thompson *Political Ethics* ... p. 18.
34 Thompson *Political Ethics* ... p. 44.

8. Pairing Number Four: Utilitarianism and the Theory of Justice

Some faculty members teach ethics indirectly. Others may be more direct, using the classical utility and justice concepts, and perhaps quote or use the ideas of John Stuart Mill and Jeremy Bentham. Utilitarian ideas are generally associated with common or public good as an ethical criteria for political action. This study uses philosopher Frankena's definition which states that utilitarianism is a:

> '... standard of right, wrong, and obligation ... (which has) the principle of utility or beneficence, which says quite strictly that the moral end to be sought in all we do is the greatest balance of good over evil.' [35]

Two subsets of utilitarianism are, as in the case of egoism, act and rule dimensions. A major aspect of act utility is the emphasis on the effect of the act, beneficial or detrimental. This very brief overview of utilitarianism and the act/rule division cannot provide the true dimension of the meaning of utilitarianism but a logical extension of the main aspect of the idea is that in democratic societies, the political system and political officials should make decisions which are of utility or benefit for the greatest good. [36]

The theory of justice is related to the common good idea but at the same time challenges utilitarianism. Allen Buchanan's discussion of John Rawl's theory of justice provides such a counterpoint. Buchanan indicates that the justice theory of Rawls suggests that utilitarianism is divided into classical and average theories. Classical utilitarianism states that increasing total utility relates to individual preferences for happiness or satisfaction. In contrast, average utilitarianism is centred on the need to develop a per person average utility. [37]

Rawlsian justice is based on two principles:

1. Each person is to have an equal right to the most extensive total system of equal liberties ...

---

35 Frankena, p. 33.

36 A common theme is that acts and institutional behaviour must be judged by the effect of decisions on human welfare, David Lyons, *Ethics and the Rule of Law*, (Cambridge: Cambridge University Press, 1978) p. 111; A rule utilitarian is one who states that correct action is that allowed by the moral code which society holds and increases or maximises the total benefit for society. Richard B. Brandt 'The Real and Alleged Problems of Utilitarianism' *Hastings Center Report*, Vol. 13, Number 2, April, 1983, p. 39.

37 Allen Buchanan 'A Critical Introduction to Rawl's Theory of Justice' *John Rawls' Theory of Justice*, H. Gene Blocker and Elizabeth H. Smith, (eds.) (Athens: Ohio University Press, 1980) p. 6.

2. Social and economic inequalities are to be arranged so that they are to the greatest benefit of the least advantaged. [38]

This theory of justice is controversial, one point being the 'difference' principle of unequal social and economic opportunities. The contrast of ethical values posed by this dichotomy lends itself to the issues of the American Congressional and judicial systems. The two organisations of American government must make decisions which contrast utilitarian and judicial values. One practical American example of recent time is the challenge to Affirmative Action programmes, which began with the Alan Bakke case. Bakke charged reverse discrimination when his admission to a California medical school was denied because of quota system for minorities. While the Supreme Court did not make a landmark, or major precedent decision which upset the congressionally approved Affirmative Action programmes, the consideration of any such cases poses issues of justice for the disadvantaged.

Utility and justice ethical theories can be used to examine both the judicial and Congressional actions for the possible precedence of which has priority, the utility of all members of society, or the Rawlsian theory of justice that the system must ethically be based on the greatest advantage for the least advantaged.

9. Fifth Pairing: Applied Ethics and Public Policy

Scholars interested in ethical theory often relate their ideas to questions of an abstract nature. These types of issues are a major part the American journal, *Ethics*. Many philosophers question the application of ethics since there is no single theory of ethical behaviour but a group of defensible concepts. [39] Despite theoretical difficulties, the field of applied or normative ethics attempts to deal with specific cases. Applied ethics has been defined as:

> '... the attempt to analyse and understand several aspects of an actual situation, such as the roles of the relevant agents, how those roles have changed, what grievances are felt by whom, and the rights, powers and responsibilities attached to those roles.' [40]

The transfer of applied personal ethics to public policy ethics is not as simple as it may seem. For most individuals, ethics is about personal behaviour. Albert Jonsen and Lewis Butler suggest that 'policy makers may not readily conceive of public morality in other terms than private morality

---

38 A. Buchanan, p. 9.

39 David Rosenthal and Fadlou Shehadi *Applied Ethics and Ethical Theory* (Salt Lake City: University of Utah Press, 1988) pp. ix-xxii.

40 Rosenthal and Shehadi, p. xiii.

of individuals in public life.' [41] These scholars suggest that there are two major tasks for public ethics as it relates to public policies:

1. Articulation and elucidation of the relevant moral principles associated with the policy problem

2. Ranking the moral options for policy choices [42]

Some of applied ethical issues are quite obvious. Two study examples are about public policy and the individual, and in a second example, the future of collective society. The individual ethical policy example is the debate in some State Legislatures over Bills which contain the statement on the right to die. These Bills are usually of three types, legalising euthanasia, rights of competent patients, and clarifications of incompetent patients. [43] The collective ethical decision example is in security and defence. Political officials are faced with ethical issues in nuclear, bio-chemical and conventional weapons systems which may affect the world population. For example, philosopher Richard Barbour states about the ethics of nuclear war and the limited war policy that 'its very real risks outweight its intended benefits, and (I) urge it be reconsidered, revised, or replaced.' [44]

Other public policy debates may not make the role of ethical considerations as obvious, but in the final analysis, no public policy is without an ethical concern. Warwick suggest five ethical principles for public officials:

1. Public orientation should relate to the public interest.

2. Reflective choice which brings decisions out of routine individual and organisational limitations.

3. Veracity and trust which should guide public officials.

4. Procedural respect for laws, regulations and precedents which form a basis for the administrative bureaucracy.

5. Restraint of means which may seem to the public officials to accomplish the goal but has the effect of reductions in citizen trust of government. [45]

---

41 Albert Jonson and Lewis H. Butler 'Public Ethics and Public Policy' *Hastings Center Report*, Vol. 5, Number 4, August, 1975, p. 20.

42 Johnson and Butler, p. 22.

43 Jonas B. Rubitscher 'The Right to Die' *The Hastings Center Report*, Vol. 2, Number 4, September, 1972, pp. 11-14.

44 Richard Barber 'Ethics and Nuclear War' *Organisational Policy and Development*, Leicester R. Moise (ed.) (Lousville: University of Louisville Center for Continuing Education, 1984) p. 231.

45 Warwick, pp. 115-124.

The failure to follow ethical guidelines by public officials is part of the reason for the establishment in 1986 of a new journal, *Corruption and Reform*. This journal contains articles dealing with the problem in nations around the world. The editorial of the first edition asks the question, why study corruption? The answer given by the editors is that 'people make mistakes ... and they choose, at times, to deliberately break cultural and legal rules.' [46] Major public policy areas, security, domestic issues, and economic prosperity offer an extensive number of cases, sometimes with corruption issues, for the application of normative ethics. For example in the economic area, a major text in economics by Paul Samuelson has no index reference to ethics. But the application of economic concepts has ethical questions. Charles Wolf, Jr. writes that:

'I ... suggest that it makes far better sense to talk about the economics of morality than about the immorality of economics ... I ... argue that there is a fundamental sense in which the notions, concepts, framework embodied in price theory are likely to be central if we are to deal with ethical and moral issues in a usable and practical way in policy analysis.' [47]

10. Conclusion

This study is limited to the application of politics and ethics to the student attitudes, text materials and a possible ethics curriculum for American government classes.

The study reveals that:

1. Index and glossary references in American government texts about ethics occur in less than half the texts.

2. Where text references do occur, they are brief and usually related to the 1978 Ethics Act.

3. Text information reflects not the recent development of concern about political ethics, but the value-free emphasis of the positivist era.

4. University of Louisville student perceptions are that ethics should be a vital factor is making political decisions, which is in contrast to the lack of emphasis in American government textbooks.

5. A sample of student attitudes in University of Louisville American government classes indicates a variance in their perceived attitudes about political ethical expectations and performance of public officials

---

46 'Corruption and Reform: An Editorial Essay' *Corruption and Reform* Vol. 1, Number 1, 1986, p. 5.

47 Charles Wolf, 'Ethics and Policy Analysis' *Public Duties: The Moral Obligations of Government Officials,* Joel L. Fleishman, Lance Liebman and Mark H. Moore, (eds.) (Cambridge: Harvard University Press, 1981) p. 139.

6. Ethical performance by public officials on policy issues is perceived by University of Louisville students as lower than other areas. Performance by civil servants in defence and security issues ranked the lowest in student perceptions.

7. There are not significant variations in political ethical student perceptions by gender or whether students are under or upperclassmen for the eleven relevant questions when taken as an entity. Analysis of question-means does indicate that upperclassmen have higher ethical expectations for the political system and public officials but expect lower levels of ethical behaviour when compared to underclassmen.

The study developed a suggested curriculum for American government classes using five ethical concepts. This plan is but one of a number of possible applications of ethics theory to political matters. While the pairings are subject to legitimate discussion and critique, the plan does offer one method on *how* students can study the relationship of ethics and politics.

These study conclusions are more precise but do not significantly vary from the more general suggestions made by Donald Warwick for ethics teaching in the social sciences. Warwick's suggestions included enhanced ethics instruction in undergraduate courses by social scientists teamed with or co-operating with ethics scholars, and serious attempts should be made to upgrade the quality of literature for instruction in ethics in the social sciences. [48]

11. Comments

The comments are divided into two areas: the first concerns politics and public officials; the second relates to teaching political ethics.

What are possible applications of this study to politics and public officials? First, the perceived attitudes suggest that practising public officials should enhance ethical concerns when deciding public policy issues. Which ethics theory or approach they adopt is a legitimate issue, but ethical and moral factors deserve higher ranking than presently considered. For the relatively low level of concern for political ethics on public policy decisions, the academic community must share responsibility with public officials. The emphasis on empiricism, positivism and value-free judgements permitted an emphasis on technology and cost analysis at the expense of ethical concerns. The renewed interest in political ethics among some academics should help in achieving a better balance in factors influencing public policy. [49]

---

48 Warwick, pp. 49-52.

49 Rosamund Thomas 'British Administration, History, Culture and Values' *Public Policy and Administrative Studies*, O. P. Dwivedi (ed.) (Guelph: University of Guelph, 1988) p. 121. Another suggestion by Thomas is that neglecting ethical values is a step backward for civilised societies.

The academic works suggest a revitalisation of ethics and politics in the American academic community. Students perceive a need for more ethics instruction. Unfortunately, as students progress with their education, their political ethical expectation and judgement about the behaviour of public officials declines. In the final analysis the decision about ethics teaching in higher education political science classes is itself an ethical question. Philosophers and other ethics scholars tend to conclude that basic moral and ethical principles cannot be proved as valid or true. Nevertheless, the author concludes, along with Ethics' scholar, Dan W. Brock, that some coherent form of ethics is justified and is related to public policy issues. [50] Earlier in this article this paper used the concept of one scholar who suggested that political ethics had moved from oblivion to ambivalence. For the 1990s and the next century it is time to move political ethics from ambivalence to reality. [51]

---

50 Daniel Brock 'Truth or Consequences: The Role of Philosophers in Policy-Making' *Ethics*, Vol. 97, Number 4, July, 1987, p. 790.

51 This paper was presented at the Inaugural Conference of the Centre for Business and Public Sector Ethics held in Cambridge, England, 12-15 July 1989. The aim of the Inaugural Conference, and later Conferences held by this Centre, which follow the research method developed under the Centre's auspices, is to produce literature for *Teaching Ethics*. *[Editor]*

NOTE 1

Student Survey

This is a survey about college student attitudes toward political ethics. In general the questions are meant to ask you about the ethical behaviour of political leaders and the political systems.

Answer on a scale of 1 to 10. Ten (10) means that you agree to the highest degree with the statement with declining importance down to 1 which would indicate your highest level of disagreement with the statement.

1. American democracy requires the ethical behaviour of government political system.   1,2,3,4,5,6,7,8,9,10

2. American democracy requires the ethical behaviour of elected political officials.   1,2,3,4,5,6,7,8,9,10

3. National elected leaders such as the President and Members of Congress should make decisions based on ethical considerations.   1,2,3,4,5,6,7,8,9,10

4. Political executives like the President behave in an ethical manner.   1,2,3,4,5,6,7,8,9,10

5. Elected representatives such as Senators or Congressmen behave in an ethical manner.   1,2,3,4,5,6,7,8,9,10

6. Judges in the Federal courts behave in an ethical manner.   1,2,3,4,5,6,7,8,9,10

7. Civil servants and government workers behave in an ethical manner.   1,2,3,4,5,6,7,8,9,10

8. National government public policy on security and defence reflects ethical factors.   1,2,3,4,5,6,7,8,9,10

9. National government public policy of economic prosperity reflects ethical factors.   1,2,3,4,5,6,7,8,9,10

10. National government public policy on domestic programmes reflects ethical factors.   1,2,3,4,5,6,7,8,9,10

11. 'We the People of the United States in order to form a more perfect union, establish justice, insure domestic tranquility . . . and provide for the general Welfare, and secure the Blessings of Liberty, do ordain and establish this Constitution for the United States.'

    The preceding statement from the Preamble to the Constitution establishes the ethical goals for

political policies and decisions made for the public   1,2,3,4,5,6,7,8,9,10
or common good for all American citizens.

12. The college curriculum should increase the oppor-   1,2,3,4,5,6,7,8,9,10
tunities for the teaching of ethics.

For question 13 use a percentage figure for one or more of each
category.

13. How much emphasis in making public policy decision should national political leaders give to:
(A to H should total 100%)

A. ethical factor percentage ....
B. ideological factor percentage ....
C. partisan party politics percentage ....
D. personal ego/election needs percentage ....
E. legal/constitutional issues percentage ....
F. economic/budget costs percentage ....
G. trustee for common good percentage ....
H. Other (please list)

Demographic Data:

This survey must be a representative sample of student opinion on political
ethics. Would you please provide the following information

14. What is your undergraduate major area of study. Please list ....

15. Regarding your age, were you on January 1, 1989:

(1) 16 to 19 (2) 20 to 25 (3) 25 to 30 (4) 30 to 40 (5) Over
40

16. Which of the following are you:

(1) Male (2) Female

17. Which of the following are you:

(1) American Indian (2) Asian (3) Black/African American (4) Hispanic
(5) White

18. Which of the following are you:

(1) Freshman (2) Sophomore (3) Junior (4) Senior (5) Graduate
student

19. Which group best describes the income of all members of your
household last year before taxes? This figure should include salaries,
interest, pensions and all other income.

(1) Less than $7,000 (2) $7-11,999 (3) $12-19,999 (4) $20-29,999 (5) 30-
39,999 (6) 40-49,999 (7) 50-75,000 (8) Over 75,000 (8) don't know or
no report

20. Do you think of your self as:

    (1) An atheist or non believer (2) Baptist (3) Jewish (4) Moslem (5) Protestant (6) Roman Catholic (7) None of the previous

21. Would you describe your political attitudes as:

    (1) Liberal (2) Moderate (3) Conservative (4) None of the previous

22. Regarding a political party would you generally identify

    (1) Democratic (2) Republican (3) Independent (4) Other political party (5) No interest in political party.

NOTE 2

Content Search: Ethics or Political Ethics

Book Author Number	Glossary	Index	1	2	3	4	5	6	7
#1 Aldrich	n	n							
#2 Burnham	n	y				4			
#3 Burns	n	y		2					
#4 Cummings	n	y		2	3				
#5 Curry	n	y		2	3				
#6 Ebenstein	x	y				4			
#7 Edwards	n	y	1						
#8 Gitelson	n	n							
#9 Janda	n	y		2	3				
#10 Katznelson	x	n							
#11 Ladd	n	n							
#12 LeLoup	n	y				4			
#13 Lineberry	n	y	1						
#14 Lipsetz	n	y		2		4			
#15 Mackenzie	x	n							
#16 Morlan	n	n							
#17 Parenti	n	n							
#18 Patterson	n	n							
#19 Pious	n	n							
#20 Prewitt	n	n							
#21 Pynn	n	n							
#22 Ross	n	n							
#23 Schmidt	n	y		2		4			
#24 Shea	n	n							
#25 Skidmore	x	y		2	3				
#26 Stephenson	n	y				4			
#27 Stone	n	y		2				6	
#28 Weissberg	n	n							
#29 Welch	n	y		2		4		6	
#30 Woll	n	n							
Totals	0	15	2	9	4	7	0	2	0

1= Public Good, 2= 1978 Ethics in Gov Act, 3=Executive or
Presidential political ethics, 4=legislative or
congressional political ethics, 5=judicial or legal
political ethics, 6 Bureaucratic ethics 7= public policy
ethics

American Government Text Books [1]

---

1 The full authors' details, titles and publishing details of the 30 American Government Text
Books, listed above, are marked with an asterisk in the Bibliography of this Volume 1: *Government Ethics.*

VOLUME I   GOVERNMENT ETHICS

APPENDICES

Appendices
Contents

Appendix Part I: 381
    GOVERNMENT ETHICS:
    GENERAL

Chapter

1   The Duties and Responsibilities of Civil   383
    Servants and Ministers: a Challenge within
    British Cabinet government
    Dr Rosamund M. Thomas, Director, Centre for
    Business and Public Sector Ethics,
    Cambridge

2   The Ethic of the Profession   409
    Peter Hennessy, Professor of Contemporary
    History, Queen Mary and Westfield College,
    University of London

3   *R v. Lord Chancellor's Department ex parte*   416
    Nangle:
    Stuart-Smith L.J.

4   Judicial Review and Civil Servants: Contracts   435
    of Employment Declared to Exist
    Sandra Fredman and Gillian Morris

5   United Kingdom Civil Service Management   441
    Code – Personnel Management Volume
    4. Conduct and Discipline (February 1993)

Appendix Part II: 469
     GOVERNMENT ETHICS:
     CONFLICT OF INTEREST

Chapter
6   Conflict of Interest: A Modern Antidote   471
           Jean-Pierre Kingsley, then Deputy Secretary,
           Personnel Policy Branch, Treasury Board
           of Canada

7   Commission of Inquiry into the Facts of   479
           Allegations of Conflict of Interest Concern-
           ing the Honourable Sinclair M. Stevens
           Commissioner: The Honourable W. D. Parker

8   Conflict of Interest Issues in Canada: the   517
           1991 Review
           Georges Tsaï, Assistant Deputy Registrar
           General of Canada

9   Conflict of Interest in Canada, 1992: A   528
           Federal,   Provincial   and   Territorial
           Perspective
           Georges Tsaï, Assistant Deputy Registrar
           General of Canada

10   Disclosure of Financial Interests by Members 559
           of Parliament (Westminster): The John
           Browne Affair
           Michael Ryle, former Clerk of Committees,
           House of Commons (Westminster)

11   House of Commons (Westminster) Select   569
           Committee on Members' Interests (Extracts
           from the First Report, Session 1991-1992,
           London HMSO HC 326 4 March 1992)

Appendix Part III: 597
      GOVERNMENT ETHICS:
      SECRECY, ACCESS TO INFORMATION
      AND PRIVACY

Chapter

12   Access to Information: the Experience of   599
      Other Countries
      Dr Rosamund M. Thomas, Director, Centre for
      Business and Public Sector Ethics,
      Cambridge

13   Independent Review of Administrative   634
      Decisions on the Merits – Successes and
      Strains in the Australian Experience
      Robert K. Todd, recently President of the
      Australian Capital Territory Administrative
      Appeals Tribunal

14   Independent Review of Administrative   645
      Decisions on the Merits – Successes and
      Strains in the Australian Experience
      Commentary by Robert K. Todd, recently
      President of the Australian Capital Territory
      Administrative Appeals Tribunal

Appendix Part IV: 651
      GOVERNMENT ETHICS:
      CONCEPTS, EDUCATION AND
      TRAINING

Chapter

15   The Public Interest   653
      Walter Lippman

16   A Plea for Applied Ethics   657
      Neil Richards, Tutor, Chief Police Officers'
      Course, Police Staff College, Bramshill,
      England

VOLUME I   GOVERNMENT ETHICS

APPENDIX PART I

Government Ethics:

General

APPENDIX I

1

The Duties and Responsibilities of Civil Servants and Ministers: a Challenge within British Cabinet government [1]

by Dr Rosamund M. Thomas, Director, Centre for Business and Public Sector Ethics, Cambridge [2]

Disclosures of official information, [3] particularly in the cases of Clive Ponting and Westland, were the subject of four publications in the mid 1980s. [4]

---

1 This revised article is based on one published originally in *International Review of Administrative Sciences* Vol. 52 (1986) pp. 511-538.

2 Dr Rosamund Thomas is Director of the Centre for Business and Public Sector Ethics, Cambridge, under whose auspices Volume I *Government Ethics* is published.

3 Section 2 of the British Official Secrets Act 1911 (recently reformed by the Official Secrets Act 1989) made it a criminal offence *inter alia* for a civil servant to communicate official information without authority (i.e. an *unauthorised* communication or in colloquial terms a 'leak'). However, Ministers and senior civil servants are *authorised* in some circumstances to communicate information in connection with their job.

4 *The Ponting case*: Clive Ponting, a senior civil servant in the Ministry of Defence, passed without authority two official documents about the sinking of the *Belgrano* in the Falklands war to Mr Tam Dalyell, Labour MP. Ponting had developed differences with Departmental colleagues about how/what information should be provided to Mr Dalyell who had written to Mr Michael Heseltine, then Secretary of State for Defence, requesting detailed information about the sinking. Moreover, Mr Ponting had differences with colleagues about what information should be given to the Commons Select Committee on Foreign Affairs, which was investigating the sinking of the *Belgrano*. Therefore, in July 1985, Ponting took it upon himself to pass without authority the two documents to the Member of Parliament. One document was marked 'CONFIDENTIAL' but the civil servant removed all markings to hide the source. Mr Dalyell gave the two leaked documents to the Commons Select Committee on Foreign Affairs (whose chairman returned them to the Secretary of State for Defence) and also disclosed them to the press and they were published. In early 1984 Clive Ponting was tried and acquitted at the Central Criminal Court, London, on a charge under the old section 2 (1) of the Official Secrets Act 1911.

The Westland Affair: The Westland affair did not involve a criminal offence because the disclosure was authorised. In January 1986 selected extracts from a 'CONFIDENTIAL' letter written by the Solicitor-General to the then Secretary of State for Defence, Mr Michael Heseltine, were disclosed by officials from another Department (Trade and Industry) to the Press Association shortly before the start of the Westland press conference. This was done without the knowledge of the Minister involved (i.e. Mr Heseltine) but on the authorisation of the then Secretary of State for Trade and Industry (Mr Leon Brittan). The method of disclosure was on an 'unattributable basis' and the extracts discredited Mr Heseltine's view.

(Footnote 4 ➜)

The first report was from the Commons Treasury and Civil Service Committee of May 1986 whose subcommittee enquired into the Ponting situation. During the subcommittee's enquiry the Westland affair broke and provided another topic for its study. The second publication was the Government's Response of July 1986 to the Treasury and Civil Service Committee's report. The third report was from the Commons Defence Committee, also of July 1986, relating to the Government's decision-making over the Westland Public Limited Company, and the fourth was the Government's Response to the Commons' Defence Committee's report on Westland, published in

→ Disagreements had arisen among Cabinet Ministers about the policy to be adopted in respect of the future of Westland Helicopters. Two alternative financial reconstruction solutions existed; one favoured the American-backed Sikorsky-Fiat group and the other preferred a consortium of European manufacturers. The Prime Minister and Mr Brittan promoted the Government's policy which was to permit the decision about Westland's future to be made by the Westland Board and the Westland shareholders. Mr Heseltine wanted a European solution and refused to uphold the collective decision of the Cabinet as to the way the decision should be dealt with. On 6 January tendacious parts of the Solicitor-General's letter were disclosed by the DTI officials to the Press Association (after consultation with officials in the Prime Minister's Office). Both the Prime Minister and Mr Brittan agreed later that the method of disclosure was wrong (e.g. without Mr Heseltine's permission) but Mr Brittan accepted full responsibility for his officials' actions and confirmed that he had authorised the disclosure. At the Cabinet meeting on 10 January, Mr Heseltine resigned because of differences with Cabinet colleagues and some time later Mr Brittan resigned following his involvement in two controversial incidents, one being the disclosure of the Solicitor-General's letter.

The four publications referred to in this article are:

i. House of Commons, Treasury and Civil Service Committee Report, *Civil Servants and Ministers: Duties and Responsibilities*, Seventh Report, Session 1985-6 (London: HMSO. Ordered to be printed 12 May 1986. HC 92-1 *Report* and HC 92-11 *Minutes of Evidence*).

ii. *Civil Servants and Ministers: Duties and Responsibilities. Government's Response to the Seventh Report from the Treasury and Civil Service Committee* above (London: HMSO Cmnd 9841, July 1986).

iii. House of Commons, Defence Committee, *Westland plc: The Government's Decision-Making*, Fourth Report, Session 1985-6 (London: HMSO 23 July 1986 HC 519 *Report*).

iv. *'Westland plc: The Defence Implications of the Future of Westland plc (and) The Government's decision-making'. Government's Response to the Third and Fourth Reports from the Defence Committee* above (London: HMSO Cmnd. 9916, October 1986).

A fifth publication appeared later on 'Ministers and civil servants'. It is the First Report, Session 1986-87, from the Treasury and Civil Service Committee (London, HMSO 1 December 1986, HC 62). It challenged the Government's Response to the Commons Defence Committee's report on Westland plc on the subject of accountability, in which the Government maintained that a Parliamentary Select Committee is not a suitable instrument for investigating and passing judgement on the conduct of an individual civil servant (see this paper p. 387).

For further details of the Ponting and Westland cases, see Rosamund M. Thomas, 'The British Official Secrets Acts 1911-1939 and the Ponting Case', in *Criminal Law Review*, August 1986; and Geoffrey Marshall, 'Cabinet Government and the Westland Affair', *Public Law*, Summer 1986.

October 1986. All four publications raise wider issues of the duties and responsibilities of civil servants and Ministers, as well as the workings of the British system of Cabinet government and the constitutional conventions' underlying it.

1. Loyalty and Accountability

1.1 Loyalties and Responsibilities

On the matter of loyalty, the report from the Treasury and Civil Service Committee refers to the 'Armstrong Memorandum', a Note of guidance to officials by Sir Robert (later Lord) Armstrong, then Cabinet Secretary and Head of the Home Civil Service, following the Ponting case. The Armstrong Memorandum restates a number of long-standing principles intended to guide civil servants on such issues as to whom they owe their allegiance and loyalty. They are reminded that they are servants of the Crown and owe their allegiance 'first and foremost to the Minister'. The Treasury and Civil Service Committee points out (quoting from Ponting's oral evidence to its subcommittee) that loyalty is not a one-way system of civil servants being loyal to Ministers. It must be a 'two-way street' of Ministers having responsibilities towards officials. Accordingly, the committee recommended that guidelines should be formulated, setting out the duties and responsibilities of Ministers to Parliament, to whom the former must be fully accountable, *and* to the Civil Service. The committee proposed that the Prime Minister, after consultation with leaders of other political parties, should draw up and publish such guidelines. This recommendation seems sensible but it was rejected by the Government in its response to the Treasury and Civil Service Committee's report. The Government's reply was that Ministers are aware of the principles that govern their relations with Parliament and civil servants, and: 'It goes without saying that these include the obligations of integrity.' [5] If the Government's statement is correct, one wonders what happened to integrity in the Westland affair during November and December 1985 and January 1986. The Defence Committee's report criticised severely the method of disclosure, authorised by the then Secretary of State for Trade and Industry (Mr Leon Brittan), of selectively leaking a letter addressed to another Minister (Mr Michael Heseltine, then Secretary of State for Defence) and written to the latter by the Solicitor-General and classified 'CONFIDENTIAL'. The Defence Committee concluded that the selected extracts released on an unattributable basis from the Department of Trade and Industry by officials were aimed at causing maximum damage to Mr Heseltine's case and to his personal credibility.

An additional point made by the Treasury and Civil Service subcommittee

---

5 See House of Commons, Treasury and Civil Service Committee, *Minutes of Evidence Vol. II*, p. 109; and *Government's Response* to the above committee's report, paragraph 11.

(not carried by the full committee) refers to the position of the Prime Minister in the chain of loyalties which in some circumstances could be crucial but is not defined by the Armstrong Memorandum. The role of the Prime Minister brought the subcommittee briefly to the subject of distinctions between traditional Cabinet Government, in which collective decisions are binding on Cabinet members, and 'Prime Ministerial government', in which a premier may take an *over-riding* position, or *dissent* by an individual Cabinet Minister may undermine the convention of collective decision-making (as with Michael Heseltine in the Westland affair). The subcommittee saw the Westland case not as one of Prime Ministerial government but rather as an extreme example within Cabinet Government where the Civil Service is answerable to the Prime Minister as well as to Departmental Ministers. However, the subcommittee pointed out that such a situation is not covered by the Armstrong Memorandum. The Defence Committee also mentioned the breach of collective Cabinet decision-making in the Westland affair and reports adversely on Mr Heseltine's personal crusade supported by the resources of his Department, for one particular solution 'which was diametrically opposed to the Government's stated policy.' [6]

1.2 Accountability

Concerning accountability, the Treasury and Civil Service Committee was uncertain about what recommendation(s) to make. It noted that the constitutional convention whereby a Minister accepts responsibility for a mistake made by his Department and offers his resignation is waning, yet no clear alternative exists. Hence the committee invites and recommends that the Government, and other parties, [7] reconsider the crucial concept of accountability and produce specific proposals. The Government's response refuted this view, maintaining that Ministers were never expected to resign over every mistake made by their Department – although they are responsible to Parliament and action is taken to remedy the fault and prevent its recurrence.

The Defence Committee also discusses accountability. It defines a Minister's accountability to Parliament not as a *general* responsibility leading in certain circumstances to his resignation but involving *accounting in detail* for actions as a Minister, which may include naming individual civil servants who have acted improperly. The above definition of accountability is open to debate and raises the further issue of the *anonymity* of civil servants. Since 1979, when the new Commons Select Committees were created, named officials have been appearing increasingly before them to give evidence –

---

6 House of Commons Defence Committee, *Report*, paragraphs 105 and 126. The Armstrong Memorandum is reprinted in this Volume 1: *Government Ethics*, pp. 58-62.

7 Other parties, such as the Constitutional Reform Centre and the Institute of Directors considered the Treasury and Civil Service Committee's Report.

even though they do so on behalf of their Ministers. This development is a move away from the traditional convention of anonymity whereby the Minister speaks for the actions of his Department and shields officials from the glare of publicity and personal identification. In both the Westland affair and the debate on the tin industry in 1986 officials were identified in the press and in the Commons, and the Defence Committee regards the 'fiction of anonymity' as inappropriate in instances such as these where the conduct of individual civil servants has become a matter of wider controversy. [8]

The Government's Response to the Defence Committee justifiably expressed concern about discarding the convention of anonymity and naming individual civil servants 'if they have done amiss'. The Government pointed out that there are a variety of procedures for disciplining the individual civil servant if he has acted improperly, together with the safeguards and rights of appeal. The Government did not consider a Select Committee of Parliament to be a suitable instrument for investigating and passing judgement on the conduct of an individual official and believed that the role of Select Committees should not be extended to cover such enquiries. Moreover, such investigations contradict the basic principle whereby the civil servant is accountable to Parliament. In its reply a few months earlier to the report from the Treasury and Civil Service Committee, the Government dismissed any attempt to make civil servants (rather than the Departmental Minister) directly accountable to Parliament (other than in the exceptional case of the Accounting Officer) on the ground that it 'would be difficult to reconcile with the Ministers' responsibility for their Departments and the civil servants' duty to their Ministers. [9] Moreover, the Government distinguishes between internal accountability within Departments and the external accountability of the Minister to Parliament. Obviously the two Select Committees differ from the Government about the meaning and extent of Executive accountability to Parliament. The very least that can be done now is to propose that the separate Note of guidance issued earlier to officials on how to answer questions before Select Committees of Parliament be integrated with, or set alongside, the Armstrong Memorandum, since appearances before such committees can create dilemmas for civil servants and affect the relation between them and their Departmental Ministers.

1.3 A Code of Ethics for Civil Servants?

The Armstrong Memorandum sets out the procedures a civil servant should follow when faced with a dilemma of conscience, such as that facing Clive

---

8 See Defence Committee's *Report*, paragraphs 236 and 238. Although neither Sir (later Lord) Robert Armstrong nor Ministers named any of the five officials involved in the Westland case, the latter's names appeared in the press.

9 See *Government's Response* to the Defence Committee's Report, paragraphs 39-44. See also *Government's Response* to the Treasury and Civil Service Committee's report, paragraph 13.

Ponting or Sarah Tisdall, a former clerk in the Foreign Secretary's office who was sentenced to six months' imprisonment in March 1984 for leaking documents to *The Guardian*. The stated procedure is to consult a superior officer, or 'in the last resort the Permanent Head of the Department, who can and should if necessary consult the Head of the Home Civil Service'. [10] Mr Ponting thought that the Permanent Secretary in the Ministry of Defence was aware of his views but chose not to take up his case. In the Westland affair, the Permanent Secretary in the Department of Trade and Industry was not in London at the time that the official, who was instructed to make known to the press the content of the Solicitor-General's letter, felt disquiet and because of the urgency involved could not be consulted. Nor was the Departmental Principal Establishment Officer available for consultation. The committee concluded therefore that the 'Armstrong procedures' are insufficient and reported that the First Division Association (the Civil Service trade union representing higher civil servants) has drafted a Code of Ethics to help aggrieved civil servants. The code covers 'much the same ground' as the Armstrong Memorandum but is an alternative perspective. The committee did not favour an abstract code of principles and recognised the value in a code only if it relates to ' a wider and more specific range of circumstances than is provided for either in the FDA draft or in the Armstrong Memorandum. The FDA draft would have been no more use to the officials caught up in the Westland affair than was Sir Robert's Note of guidance'. [11] Thus the committee recommended that the Head of the Home Civil Service should enter into discussions with the Civil Service trade unions to produce an agreed text for a new Note of guidance for civil servants. The Government's Response endorsed the Armstrong Memorandum but nevertheless stated that Sir (later Lord) Robert had agreed to enter into discussions with Civil Service trade unions on this matter.

2. An Appeals Mechanism

2.1 Internal Appeals

The Treasury and Civil Service Committee proposed that *internal* review procedures should be improved to remove what it termed a gap in the Armstrong Memorandum – namely, that created if the Permanent Secretary should reject the civil servant's approach or is absent. The committee recommended that this gap should be filled by the Head of the Home Civil Service who should make it wholly clear that 'he is prepared personally to consider appeals from officials who have followed his procedures but whose dilemmas

---

10 Treasury and Civil Service Committee, *Report* Vol. I, paragraph 4.1.

11 Ibid, paragraphs 4.8 and 4.9.

remained unresolved'.[12] The committee noted that if this proposed improvement does not work in practice, the arguments advanced by its sub-committee (but held in abeyance) for a new system of *external* review should be considered. The Goverment's reply accepted in principle that the Head of the Home Civil Service should be willing personally to consider appeals from officials who have followed his procedures but find their crises of conscience unresolved. Again, this internal appeals mechanism was made one of the subjects for discussion by Sir Robert Armstrong and representatives of the Civil Service unions. The Government commented that Mr Ponting did not follow procedures and failed to take his problem either to his Permanent Secretary or to the Head of the Home Civil Service.

2.2 External Appeals

A new system of *external* review urged by the subcommittee, but not adopted by the full committee and rejected in the Government's Response,[13] features a Parliamentary Commissioner for the Civil Service to be appointed 'to consider individual cases where civil servants have been unable to resolve ethical or constitutional dilemmas through the normal Civil Service channels', that is, an Ombudsman.[14] The system proposed by the subcommittee would take the following form. An aggrieved civil servant, such as Clive Ponting, would appeal in writing to the commissioner who would investigate his case and, if necessary, refer to the relevant Select Committee. The commissioner would have access to all appropriate persons, papers and records. Both the Government and the civil servant would be expected to comply with any judgement reached and the House of Commons would ensure that such judgements were enforced. However, if one or more of the parties found the commissioner's recommendations unacceptable, the commissioner would be empowered to make a special report to Parliament explaining the circumstances. The subcommittee's arguments for external review contained in the proceedings at the end of the report are more radical than those for improved internal review accepted by the full committee and published in the main body of the text. The arguments for external review are more radical because (1) complaints about the security services are *not* excluded from this proposal, which could lead to sensitive security matters being

---

12 Ibid, paragraph 4.16. The *Government's Response* to the Treasury and Civil Service Committee's report (paragraph 19) draws attention to the need for some safeguard to prevent 'merely frivolous or vexatious appeals to the Head of the Home Civil Service'.

13 The *Government's Response* (paragraph 19) also rejected other proposals for an external appeals mechanism put forward in evidence to the Treasury and Civil Service subcommittee by the First Division Association and by Sir Douglas Wass (for example, for an Inspector General for the Civil Service).

14 Treasury and Civil Service Committee, *Report* Vol. I (Proceedings of the Committee) p. xxxviii.

presented to the relevant Select Committees and to Parliament which, in turn, could lead to leaks of national-security-type information under external review. Even the presentation *in camera* of sensitive information to a Select Committee could have its dangers, as these committees are no more 'leak-proof' than the Civil Service; and (2) the strengthening of Parliament over the Executive in the proposed external review system may complicate further the relationship between civil servants and Ministers. This opinion was stated in evidence by Sir Robert Armstrong and is a valid argument. [15] Certainly, some alternative forms of external review could be considered (besides that of a Parliamentary Commissioner), if an improved internal review system proves unsatisfactory. However, an outside person or persons, independent of both the Executive and Parliament, may be the answer – for example, a notable High Court judge.

3. The Politicisation of the Civil Service

3.1 Senior Appointments

The Treasury and Civil Service Committee in its report expressed ambivalence on this subject. It acknowledged the expanding use within the British Civil Service of political and other appointees and yet did not equate this development with 'politicisation' to which it gives the precise definition of *'partisanship'*. [16] Again the committee noted the increasing interest being taken by Ministers and the Prime Minister (all of whom are *party political*) in senior appointments within Government Departments but still found no convincing evidence of 'politicisation'. The present system of appointments is that the top two positions of Permanent and Deputy Secretary are 'made by the Prime Minister on the advice of the Head of the Home Civil Service and after consultation with the appropriate Minister. Senior appointments below that level are decided by the Permanent Secretary in consultation with the Minister. [17] The Treasury and Civil Service Committee proposes that Ministers should be able to take an active part in selecting the key officials who are going to work with them in planning and carrying out their policies, and maintains that this Ministerial involvement happens already, and should be recognised openly. The practice may exist to an extent now, but is it wise to endorse and encourage it?

A brief analysis of the Civil Service is required here to determine whether the practice of Ministerial involvement in appointments occurs and, if so, whether it should be encouraged. Five points should be noted about Civil Service appointments. First, direct Ministerial patronage in senior appoint-

---

15 Ibid, paragraph 4.14

16 Ibid, paragraph 5.7.

17 Ibid, paragraph 5.11.

ments is not new. A more radical proposal was considered in 1978 by Mr James Callaghan, then Prime Minister, to introduce a new class of senior civil servant (albeit 'outsiders') into Whitehall by this method rather than by open competition based on merit. [18] And Ministers in the past have taken a keen interest in the highest Civil Service appointments, as revealed in the diaries of Richard Crossman and Barbara Castle. Second, structural changes in the organisation of Civil Service Departments in 1981, which will be discussed again later, have meant that Sir (later Lord) Robert Armstrong, then Cabinet Secretary *and* Head of the Home Civil Service, *and* adviser on top appointments, was closer to the Prime Minister than was Sir Ian Bancroft, [19] when Head of the Service and Permanent Secretary of the Civil Service Department (now disbanded). Third, the then Prime Minister, now Baroness Thatcher, made it her personal responsibility to visit Government Departments, talk to officials, and get to know the sort of top official she preferred, which in 1982 and 1983 led her critics to refer to 'political interference'. [20] Others replied that the Prime Minister was only exercising her responsibility for approving top appointments and was choosing on the basis of 'temperament' not 'conviction' from among the best candidates. [21] However, the extent to which the process of approval permits a Prime Minister to reject names with the call to 'think again', as was rumoured, is open to question. [22] Fourth, Baroness Thatcher took a prominent interest in management generally in the Civil Service (not simply top appointments). This direct involvement by the then Prime Minister, and Ministers, in Civil Service *management (as distinct from policy)* breaks with tradition. Fifth, during Margaret Thatcher's two Administrations an unusually large number of Permanent Secretary vacancies arose – because of the retirement of top officials who joined the Service immediately after the Second World War. By chance, this historical event gave Mrs (now Baroness) Thatcher the occasion to approve their successors. [23]

Should the practice of Ministerial involvement in senior appointments be encouraged? In recent years fewer able applicants have entered the administration trainee scheme (leading to senior Civil Service posts), with a high

---

18 See *The Times*, 31 May 1978. In 1977 a study group established by the Labour Party's National Executive committee, chaired by Mr Eric Heffer, MP, urged future Labour governments 'to abandon the principle of a politically neutral Civil Service'. See *The Times*, 23 May 1977.

19 Sir Ian was Head of the Civil Service Department, 1978-82. He became Lord Bancroft after his retirement from the Service in 1982.

20 See, for example, *The Times*, 4 November 1982.

21 See *The Times*, 2 November 1982, and letter to the editor of *The Listener* (26 May 1983) from Sir Patrick Nairne (former Permanent Secretary and later The Master, St Catherine's College, Oxford).

22 See article by Michael Cockerell in *The Listener*, 19 May 1983.

23 Ibid.

'wastage' rate of these trainees leaving after, say, five years. [24] If the apex of the hierarchy in future should be reserved for 'politically-selected' staff, it may reduce further the incentives, opportunities, and *career* expectations of those civil servants who do not wish to be 'politically active or labelled'. Therefore, wider personnel management issues are at stake. Although the Treasury and Civil Service Committee appeared not to wish to move towards *partisanship*, its suggestions on senior appointments would lead in time to the rotation of staff at the top two levels of the Civil Service, with officials changing as Ministers come into and go out of office. If rotation at the top does not occur, then the civil servants involved may have acquired a 'party political' complexion which could make it difficult for them to work with Ministers of an alternative party. One reason for devising the Northcote-Trevelyan principles last century, on which today's Civil Service is still largely based, was to conquer problems of Parliamentary patronage, partisanship and corruption – which has been almost wholly accomplished. [25] Furthermore, the Civil Service Commission was established then as a independent body to deal with recruitment generally and to safeguard the merit principle. However, recently the Civil Service Commission has been replaced, by virtue of two Orders-in-Council of 1991 which created: (1) an Office of the Civil Service Commissioners (OCSC) and (2) Recruitment and Assessment Services (RAS).[26] These changes in recruitment methods to the Service already represent significant alterations. It would be sad if, in order to follow a current vogue for 'politicisation', this country turns its bureaucracy back towards the problems of the nineteenth century by undermining its career Civil Service. The merits of continuity and the lack of both corruption and vested interests which, on the whole, characterise the British Civil Service would be put at risk. Unfortunately, the 'Yes, Minister' programmes have

---

24 See *The Times*, 14 May 1984, referring to the results of an unpublished Rayner scrutiny on the Civil Service Commission which cited 'high wastage' of administration trainees.

25 Patronage in respect of Civil Service appointments was not eradicated until the early twentieth century.

26 Unlike some countries, the Civil Service Commission in the United Kingdom has had responsibility only for *recruitment* to the Service, and not for wider matters of standards of conduct. The first Civil Service Commissioners were appointed in 1855 to run the open competitive examination to test merit and to give approval for the appointment of those duly qualified. The Commissioners set up an office – the Civil Service Commission – and recruited the necessary staff. The Civil Service Commission retained its independent existence as a Government Department until 1968, when, on the recommendation of the Fulton Report, it merged with the personnel management divisions of the Treasury to form the Civil Service Department (which subsequently was incorporated into the Cabinet Office, and now forms the Office of Public Service and Science). In 1982 the Civil Service Order-in-Council was changed and, again, in 1991 two new Orders-in-Council were made (for the Home Civil Service and the Diplomatic Service respectively) further extending the role of Departments and the new Executive Agencies in recruitment to the Service. (See Note 2 to the paper by Mr Hayden Phillips, this Volume, pp. 63-66).

exaggerated the view that the Minister is in the hands of his officials. More likely, it is that continuity and experience of the governmental machine give senior civil servants greater knowledge in some areas than an incoming Minister possesses, but officials are there *to advise* and implement. Indeed, the implementation of controversial policies like 'privatisation' demonstrates that civil servants do assist and advise Ministers to carry through their goals – even though personally some officials may dislike the policies. [27]

The Government warned in its Response that the wording about senior appointments in the committee's report 'carries a significant risk of increasing politicisation, which (like the Committee) the Government wishes to avoid'. Therefore, it put forward its commitment to a career Service, stating that it desired to go no further than the present arrangements for appointments. However, the Government acknowledged the rare exception where a Minister finds he cannot work with a particular official in which instance he/she is advised to talk to the Permanent Secretary, to the Head of the Home Civil Service, or to the Prime Minister. [28]

3.2 Outside Appointments and Press/information Officers

Two further recommendations by the Treasury and Civil Service Committee were, first, that there should be regular intakes of permanent and temporary people of ability from outside into the higher Civil Service. The other proposal was that the positions of press and information officers should be made political appointments, if Ministers require the incumbent to act in a political way. Clearly the committee had the Westland affair in mind when making the latter proposal, but it is idealistic of its members to believe that an effective career Service can be preserved alongside these numerous developments. Such an achievement would be difficult. Also the committee associated appointments from outside the Service with the French system of government, but this practice is more akin to the American system. In the United States the 'in-out' tradition prevails but there are differences between that country and Britain: the United States' Federal public service is dominated by 'specialists', who sometimes have a too narrow vision, rather than by 'generalists' and it is easier to interchange them with staff brought in from

---

27 Many countries have a high regard for the British Civil Service. Mr Christopher Tugendhat, giving evidence before the Treasury and Civil Service subcommittee and drawing on his European Community experience, said that the British and French Civil Services were regarded as 'the two best' and the British Civil Service is 'very much admired' for its objectivity, fairness and 'non-politicisation'. See Treasury and Civil Service Committee, *Minutes of Evidence*, pp. 199-201.

28 William Beveridge, writing earlier this century, likened the one-to-one relationship between the Permanent Secretary and the Minister to a 'marriage', but declared that a 'divorce' was difficult to obtain. See Rosamund M. Thomas *The British Philosophy of Administration* (Cambridge, Centre for Business and Public Sector Ethics 1989) pp. 43-45.

outside spheres such a law firms and businesses. Also American Federal bureaucrats hold more higher degrees and professional qualifications, and take more 'mid-career' degrees and other courses than their British counterparts, which facilitate relations with 'outsiders' on common professional grounds. Nevertheless, the United States experiences problems of finding sufficient able staff to fill the political appointments in the Federal Service (once the initial pool has been used up) and there is a high rate of turnover among appointees who stay on average just over two years. Also conflicts of interests occur with these 'in-out' practices (known as 'revolving door' problems). Furthermore, an increasing number of jobs have been brought within the career Civil Service with appointment by merit (that is, the selection of the best candidates according to qualifications and ability), while the number of political appointments has been reduced substantially. At the time of the New Deal, for example, the merit principle applied to little over half the Federal employees but by 1977 ninety-two percent of Federal employees were under merit systems. One reason for this and other Civil Service reforms in the United States has been revived anxiety about partisan spoils practices (that is, the distribution of public offices by a successful political party on its accession to power as rewards to its supporters rather than by merit). During the Nixon Administration, in particular, abuses in senior appointments through political and personal favouritism took place, leading experts in government to conclude that Watergate might not have happened if more care had been taken about the qualifications and quality of certain politically appointed officers. Later, criticisms arose again about favouritism and partisanship under the Reagan Administration with inexperienced people being appointed to senior posts in the Federal service. [29] In Britain conflicts of interest and problems of vetting staff and of national security are likely to arise if 'temporary' intakes enter the Service and then return to, say, business companies. Inside knowledge of governmental processes and possible access to classified information would contribute to these problems. Other difficulties would include the need to increase salaries to compete with those in business and other professions, as well as a lack of continuity in policy advice and the risk of partisanship. [30]

Although the Government's reply to the Treasury and Civil Service Committee did not elaborate as above on foreign systems, it declared a preference for the British system and maintained that the Civil Service should be

---

29 See James W. Fesler *Public Administration: Theory and Practice* (Englewood Cliffs, NJ: Prentice-Hall, 1980), pp. 90-91. See also Luc Rouban, 'La Politique de la Haute Fonction Publique aux Etats-Unis: Grandeur et Decadence du Senior Executive Service' *Revue Française d'Administration Publique*, April-June 1986 No. 28, p. 299.

30 Both short tenure and a high rate of turnover among political appointees characterise the United States Higher Public Service. For example, see *International Herald Tribune*, 3 September 1986, regarding problems in American foreign policy advice due to these reasons.

capable of providing staff with the necessary qualifications and expertise for the public service. However, the Government did favour increasing secondments between the Civil Service and industry, commerce and other organisations as well as continuing limited joint training arrangements. Also it recognised that in a few cases 'a particular requirement at a particular time' may be met more appropriately by an outside appointment (as at present) but argued that these are *not political* appointments – rather they must be based on qualifications and expertise in accordance with the requirements of the Civil Service Commissioners. [31] An additional proposal not mentioned in any of the reports would be to give greater importance to personnel management in the Service, together with more flexibility of age limits for recruitment to permanent posts and, as mentioned earlier, to have strengthened the Civil Service Commission which until recently dealt with recruitment generally.

Concerning press and information officers, the Government's Response was that they should be regarded in the same way as other career civil servants and not in party political terms. Indeed, Departmental press officers who are asked to behave in a manner which oversteps the line are advised to consult their Permanent Secretary, or, presumably, in his/her absence, the Head of the Home Civil Service.

3.3 A Minister's Policy Unit

Another proposal put forward by the Treasury and Civil Service Committee was for a Minister's policy unit. This recommendation follows the Continental style of government (for example, France, Italy and Belgium) and would involve a smaller degree of change in this country than one based on the American system. In France a Minister is assisted by his *cabinet*, which is a body composed of some ten to fifteen persons, mainly civil servants and other advisers. [32] According to the committee the concept would be adapted in Britain so that a Minister's policy unit would focus less on *political* activities as in France and more on helping a Minister to increase his control over the Department and to implement his policies with *greater efficiency and effectiveness*. Also the unit would assist his collective role within the Cabinet and enable wider thinking on policy issues. The unit would be appointed by

---

31 *Government's Response* to the Treasury and Civil Service Committee's Report, paragraph 31. For more recent 1991 changes to the Civil Service Commission, see Note 2 to the paper by Mr Hayden Phillips, this Volume pp. 63-66.

32 The size of ministerial *cabinets* had been increasing so, during the Fifth Republic, President Giscard d'Estaing imposed 'limits on the membership of all staffs except his own and that of his Prime Minister'. Thus, the French Prime Minister's *cabinet* may have thirty or more staff (i.e. more than double the size of a Minister's *cabinet*). See H. Machin, 'France', in F. F. Ridley (ed.), *Government and Administration in Western Europe* (Oxford: M. Robertson, 1979), p. 83.

an incoming Minister and include his Parliamentary Private Secretary to maintain contact for the Minister with backbenchers; a number of civil servants to keep the Minister in contact with his Department; and a group of Special Advisers to provide a link with the party organisation and to give policy advice. In effect it would be an expansion of the Minister's Private Office. The committee recommended that experiments with the policy unit should be undertaken in several Departments and considered such a unit is needed particularly since the Central Policy Review Staff was abolished. Again this type of proposal has been circulating in various forms since the 1970s when, for example, a Labour Party national executive committee report argued for more special advisers on the model of the French *cabinet* system and, later, Sir John Hoskyns's call for teams of civil servants and 'outsiders' working together in Government Departments on strategic thinking. [33] These proposals contain a number of points which require careful attention. Much would depend on the use made of the policy unit or similar body. It might cause friction with civil servants in the Department, as has been known in France, [34] and become 'party political' over time, creating difficulties when officials return to their main Departmental work, and the role of the Permanent Secretary and other civil servants might diminish. No doubt the unit would add complexity to Minister – civil servant relations.

The Government's reply to the Treasury and Civil Service Committee envisaged no constitutional difficulty in introducing an experiment to formalise and extend the present arrangements whereby a Minister in charge of a Department 'may have a Parliamentary Private Secretary, a Private Office, and one or two Special Advisers'. [35] But the Government suggested that by looking abroad the committee underestimated the role that Ministers of State and Parliamentary Private Secretaries play in the British system of government. Most Departments have between two and seven Ministers in addition to the Minister in charge, who share the load of Parliamentary and Departmental work and provide political advice for the Minister heading the Department. The French author A. Dutheillet de Lamothe made a similar point in 1965, enquiring whether the need for ministerial *cabinets* was not a result of 'the absence of, or . . . the very negligible part played on the Continent by Junior Ministers (Parliamentary Secretaries) or Parliamentary Private Secretaries and Permanent Secretaries'. The French Civil Service does not

---

33 For example, see *The Times*, 29 September 1983; 18 October 1983; 27 March 1984; and, later, a seminar chaired by Sir John Hoskyns at the Institute of Directors on 'Reskilling Government' held on 8 September 1986.

34 See Professor F. F. Ridley's evidence to the Treasury and Civil Service subcommittee, *Minutes of Evidence*, 29 January 1986, paragraph 570.

35 *Government's Response* to the Treasury and Civil Service Committee's Report, paragraph 31.

have Permanent Secretaries. The nearest equivalent in France to the British Permanent Secretary, the permanent career civil servant who heads a Department of State, is the General Secretary. Most State Departments in France do not possess a general secretary. Thus, a main function of a ministerial *cabinet* is *to co-ordinate* the work of the various *departmental* divisions (particularly total money, manpower and materials) as well as *interdepartmental* activities. In French Ministries which have a general secretary, relations between the latter and the ministerial *cabinet* can be difficult, involving problems of 'concurrent authority'. [36]

The Government's Response to the Treasury and Civil Service Committee's proposal of a Minister's policy unit was cautious, making four key points:

i.   More thought requires to be given to the functions of the unit and its relationship to the rest of the system. The Government stated that it did not propose to take the initiative towards such an experiment but it did not dismiss the possibility of 'further evolution of existing arrangements'. It remained unconvinced of the need for formalisation and claimed that some Ministers in charge of a Department prefer to have no Special Adviser [37] but 'rely on the other Ministers and on their Parliamentary Private Secretaries'.

ii. The Government agreed with the committee that numbers working in the proposed unit should be limited on the grounds of cost and efficiency. In the case of Special Advisers the Government's view was that there should not be more than one per Department.

iii. The unit should not insulate Ministers from the advice of their permanent civil servants or interfere with the Permanent Secretary's 'overall accountability to the Minister for the effective implementation of the Minister's policies and management of the Department'.

iv. The Prime Minister's approval should continue to be sought for the employment of Special Advisers in order to ensure consistency in practice. Invariably the latter are from outside the Civil Service and should be appointed, as now, 'for terms which expire with the end of the Administration ... (and) ... should continue to be subject in general to Civil Service conditions of service'. [38]

---

36 A. Dutheillet de Lamothe, 'Ministerial Cabinets in France', *Public Administration*, Vol. 43, Winter 1965, pp. 366-72.

37 The Treasury and Civil Service Committee *Report* (paragraph 5.23) refered to this as a 'patchy and unsystematic use of Special Advisers'.

38 *Government's Response* to the Treasury and Civil Service Committee's Report, paragraphs 30-35.

Despite the Government's reference to no constitutional convention being altered by this experiment, it is likely that those officials within the Minister's policy unit would become 'politicised' to a greater extent than under our present arrangements, as happens in the French *cabinet* system. No precise political allegiance is required by staff in a *cabinet* in France but they have to display total commitment to the Minister's policy. The loaning of senior civil servants (usually of a young age) is possible in France because officials have more freedom to take 'open political stances'. Most civil servants are permitted 'to join political parties and participate in their activities; they obtain leave to fight elections and, if selected, to serve in Parliament'. Therefore, some French civil servants move temporarily into politics to become Mayors, Deputies or Ministers. Another characteristic is that senior civil servants in France transfer into business, without necessarily breaking their connection with the Civil Service. They pervade the managements and boards of directors of private firms and public enterprises – with firms competing for their managerial skills. However, there is no such pervasion in the reverse direction of business managers and industrialists into the Civil Service: [39] thus, the French system is the opposite of the American. The main reason why senior civil servants are in demand in France lies in the prestigious technical and administrative *corps* within the Service and the competitive selection, higher education and professional training for them. Examples of the administrative *grand corps* are the Council of State (which is the expert adviser to the government on the legality of regulations and decrees and final court for administrative matters), the Court of Accounts and the Finance Inspectorate (both dealing with audit and control of public spending). Apart from their primary functions, members of the technical and administrative *grand corps* are deployed in high posts throughout the Civil Service (monopolising key posts in Government Departments), in ministerial *cabinets*, and in the private and semi-private sectors. Thus, after a period in a *cabinet*, senior civil servants in France (especially members of the *grands corps*) have a wider range of job opportunities both inside and outside the Service than would be the case in Britain. Whether one sides with the Treasury and Civil Service Committee or with the Government on these matters, another constitutional convention is under challenge – the political neutrality of British civil servants. A study group of the former Royal Institute of Public Administration examined the 'politicisation' of the Civil Service and its report remains of considerable interest: see *Top Jobs in Whitehall: Appointments and Promotions in the Senior Civil Service* (RIPA, 1987).

---

39 Machin, op. cit. Note 30, pp. 83-106.

4. Management/organisation in the Civil Service

4.1 The dual role of the Cabinet Secretary and Head of the Home Civil Service

Overall Ministerial responsibility for the Civil Service resides with the Prime Minister as Minister for the Civil Service, whereas the day-to-day running of the Service is split between the Minister of State, Treasury (pay and manpower); and the Minister of State, Privy Council Office (personnel management, efficiency and organisation). This arrangement came about under Margaret Thatcher's Administration when, in 1981, the Civil Service Department was disbanded and its functions and responsibilities divided up. A new but weaker Management and Personnel Office (without a Minister of its own) was established and attached to the Cabinet Office, so making the Cabinet Secretary also Head of the Home Civil Service and giving him *executive* functions far beyond those of heading a *recording and informing* secretariat. The Treasury and Civil Service Committee favoured a single Minister for the Civil Service, who will provide specific leadership for the Service. Additionally it recommended that the post of Head of the Home Civil Service should be filled by a full-time Permanent Secretary working to the proposed Minister for the Civil Service and separate from the post of Secretary of the Cabinet, presumably a Department for the Civil Service as in the past. The task of this new Permanent Secretary would include the improvement of morale in the bureaucracy. The proposal is intended also to avoid alleged conflicts of interests between the two roles and the heavy burden of responsibilities contained in the combined executive posts.

The Government responded that it preferred its own post-1981 reorganisation with the Prime Minister as Minister for the Civil Service. Furthermore, it argued that frequent institutional change causes disruption. On the proposal to separate the posts of Cabinet Secretary and Head of the Home Civil Service the Government disagreed, seeing benefits in the existing arrangement. At present the Permanent Secretary for the Cabinet Office (including Management and Personnel Office), of all the Permanent Secretaries, is closest to the Prime Minister and is responsible to him/her (and to the Minister of State, Privy Council) for aspects for which he/she, as Minister to the Civil Service, has particular responsibility (although he is *not* the latter's Permanent secretary). The Government maintained that he is well placed to advise the Prime Minister on top appointments in the Service and other matters. The Government rejected the committee's idea that morale is a matter for one person, stating that it concerns the government as a whole and senior management generally. No reply was given on conflicts of interests between the two roles, although the Government referred to one which would arise if the Head of the Home Civil Service, or other Permanent Secretaries, 'take up a public position in advocating the interests of the Civil Service, if to do so would appear to put them in conflict with the

Government-of-the-day. [40] On the workload the Government replied that it is 'manageable provided that the incumbent delegates sensibly'. [41]

The Defence Committee raised again the issue of the dual role of the Secretary of the Cabinet and the official Head of the Home Civil Service, pointing to at least a *potential* conflict of interest in the Westland case. The committee noted that the Chief Press Secretary at No. 10 Downing Street reports to the Prime Minister, but if he has the kind of problem which it is appropriate to refer to the Prime Minister he would go to the Cabinet Secretary. Hence, the Head of the Home Civil Service finds himself having to enquire into the conduct of someone whose direct Civil Service superior he is. The Government's Response to the Defence Committee pointed out that the Head of the Home Civil Service 'has never supervised the day-to-day work of members of the Prime Minister's Office: he is their superior only as a result of the Prime Minister's Office being treated for "pay and rations" purposes as part of the Cabinet Office (Management and Personnel Office)'. Thus, the Government maintained that the dual role of the Secretary of the Cabinet and Head of the Home Civil Service creates no problem which would not have been faced by his predecessors as Head of the Service. [42] [For the latest 1991 allocation of responsibilities, as set out in the Civil Service Order-in-Council 1991, see Note 2 to the paper by Hayden Phillips, this Volume, pp. 63-66 *Editor*].

4.2 A Prime Minister's Department in Britain?

The subject of a Prime Minister's Department was not raised in the reports but it has bearing on Minister-civil servant relations. While Britain may not have Prime Ministerial government, the reorganisation of 1981 which placed the Management and Personnel Office within the Cabinet Office and united the roles of Head of the Home Civil Service and Cabinet Secretary, strengthened the centre, a development which may be thought by some to be akin to a Prime Minister's Department. But what would be a Prime Minister's Department in Britain? In 1970 Edward Heath, then Prime Minister (Conservative), set up the Central Policy Review Staff (CPRS) with a view to it assisting the Cabinet collectively to improve its decision-making. In 1974 Harold Wilson, as Prime Minister (Labour), took a major step in increasing the assistance to the Prime Minister by creating a new policy unit located at No. 10 Downing Street. This was the first time in British peacetime history that a Prime Minister had established 'a systematically organised

---

40 *Government's Response* to the Treasury and Civil Service Committee's Report, paragraph 40.

41 Ibid, paragraph 41.

42 Defence Committee's *Report*, paragraphs 214-15; and *Government's Response* to the Defence Committee's Report, paragraph 32.

personal bureau'. It comprised seven members, brought in from outside as temporary civil servants who, although *specialists*, gave services which were 'political, party-oriented and personal', a group committed to the Prime Minister personally and to the Government-of-the-day. Some commentators argued in the early 1970s that the Prime Minister needed a fully-fledged Department and a suggestion was put forward for a merger between the Cabinet Office (together with the CPRS) and the then Civil Service Department. In 1973 Harold Wilson said that he favoured a Prime Minister's Department, but also feared that the growth of a No. 10 machine would make it harder for the Prime Minister 'to keep his eye on the main problems'. [43] Certainly, in the United States the Executive Office of the President, of which the White House Office is a unit, has expanded greatly. In 1937 the original proposal was for a maximum of six presidential assistants as against 350 staff in the White House Office in 1980, and 1,570 in the Executive Office of the President. [44]

Between 1977 and 1978, James Callaghan (Labour Prime Minister) considered creating a Prime Minister's Department but decided against it. [45] During Margaret Thatcher's Administration the first head of the Downing Street Policy Unit was Sir John Hoskyns and by 1982 there was talk again of creating a Prime Minister's Department by, for example, merging the Downing Street Policy Unit with the CPRS. [46]

Debate has continued on this subject. Arguments against a formal, structured Department include (1) such a bureaucratic organisation, especially if large, might develop 'a view and momentum of its own' and to control it the Prime Minister may require another set of personal assistants, [47] and (2) it would be a major constitutional change which 'would mark a final transition from Cabinet to Prime Ministerial government. And that in certain conceivable Parliamentary situations could be a step towards tyranny'. [48] Another argument is whether a Prime Minister's Department would be 'part of the existing Whitehall machine, and thus part of the Cabinet Office, or whether it should be a separate, parallel body'. [49]

Thatcher rejected the idea of a Prime Minister's Department [50] and, in

---

43 George W. Jones, 'Harold Wilson's Policy-makers', *The Spectator*, 6 July 1974.

44 Fesler, op. cit. Note 27, pp. 57-60.

45 See *The Times*, 2 March 1983, for report of a seminar at the then Royal Institute of Public Administration on this subject.

46 See *The Observer*, 7 November 1982; and *The Times*, 8 March, 1984.

47 Jones, op. cit. Note 41.

48 See letter to the editor of *The Times* by Sir Paul Osmond, 12 December 1980.

49 *The Observer*, 7 November 1982.

50 Margaret Thatcher replied during Commons Questions that she did not intend to set up a Prime Minister's Department. See *The Times*, 12 November 1982.

1983, abolished the CPRS – although a few of its people were transferred to her personal Policy Unit. [51] Thus, there is no formal structured Prime Minister's Department separate from the Cabinet Office in Britain, though the Prime Minister's modestly-sized Policy Unit still exists together with other staff (for example the Prime Minister's Private Office and small group of press officers). However, the reorganisation of 1981 which expanded the Cabinet Office and created a dual role for the Cabinet Secretary, needs to be exercised with care to avoid giving substance to the charge of a Prime Minister's Department or Prime Ministerial government. It is necessary for the Prime Minister not to use his/her influence for political ends in Civil Service appointments, or in other matters, beyond the normal practices of British Cabinet government. The Government's Response to the Treasury and Civil Service Committee stated (perhaps belatedly) its support for the career Civil Service and British Cabinet government.

4.3 Other Management/organisational issues

Three other management issues are evident from the Westland and Ponting cases. First, the delegation of authority. The Government's Response to the Treasury and Civil Service Committee relied on sensible delegation of authority as the answer to attaining a manageable workload for the Cabinet Secretary and Head of the Home Civil Service. Yet, the Westland affair highlighted a weakness in the delegation of authority within the Department of Trade and Industry. The Defence Committee reported that of the three individuals who could have been consulted by Miss Bowe – the press information official faced with the dilemma of releasing extracts from the Solicitor-General's letter – the first, the Permanent Secretary, then Sir Brian Hayes, was out of London. The second, the departmental Principal Establishment Officer, 'was not available to consult' so she discussed the matter with the third most senior official involved in the disclosure. The committee stated that 'Sir Robert Armstrong suggested that if the official concerned had had the opportunity to consult Sir Brian Hayes matters might have been different'. [52] Surely this case shows the need for clear delegation of executive authority within a Government Department by senior staff to cover possible events likely to arise during their absence or unavailability.

Another management, or organisational, issue concerns conflict between Central Government Departments. Professor Peter Self wrote on this topic in his book *Administrative Theories and Politics* (1972), well ahead of these recent example. [53] The Westland affair demonstrates not only a breakdown

---

51 See *The Times*, 10 July 1984.

52 Defence Committee *Report*, paragraph 174.

53 Peter Self, *Administrative Theories and Politics* (London: George Allen & Unwin, 1972), Chapter 3, 'Administrative Competition and Co-ordination'.

in collective Cabinet decision-making but also conflict between two major Departments: the Department of Trade and Industry and the Ministry of Defence. Similarly, during the Falklands crisis, and the sinking of the *Belgrano* (the subject underlying the leak by Mr Ponting), conflict and poor communications between the Ministry of Defence and the Foreign Office is apparent. Such conflicts and competition need to be recognised and tackled by the Government and the Civil Service if future problems are to be avoided. [54]

Third, morale in the Service requires more attention. Both the report by the Treasury and Civil Service Committee, and the Government's Response to it, comment on morale, but offered different solutions for its improvement. It is not sufficient to pay lip-service to the need to restore morale; it is necessary to understand the factors which have caused its decline in the Service and seek to remedy them as well as to appreciate the texts of management theorists which advocate leadership, example from the top, and good personnel management to inspire employees – whether in government or private organisations. Too much emphasis has been placed in recent years on 'value for money' in the Civil Service and too little on personnel management and morale, despite warnings since 1979 of a decline in the latter. [55] Finally, the direct involvement of the then Prime Minister, and other Ministers, in the *management* of Government Departments rather than concentration on policy matters, as mentioned earlier, represents a change from the traditional relation between civil servants and Ministers.

5. Open government

5.1 Freedom of Information

On the basis of limited enquiries into open government, the Treasury and Civil Service Committee concluded that the Government had *not* put forward a convincing case against some form of Freedom of Information (FOI)

---

54 For details of strained relations between the Ministry of Defence and the Department of Trade and Industry, see Third *report* from the House of Commons Defence Committee, Session 1985-6, 'The Defence Implications of the Future of Westland plc' (London, HC 518, 23 July 1986), paragraphs 174 and 175. See also the *Government's Response* to the Third and Fourth Reports from the Defence Committee, Session 1985-6, on Westland which underestimated the problems of Departmental conflicts.

55 Chester 1. Barnard is an example of a management theorist who wrote on leadership, see his book *The Functions of the Executive* (Cambridge, Mass.: Harvard University Press, first published 1938; thirtieth edn 1968). For warnings of flagging morale in the British Civil Service, see *Daily Telegraph*, 10 October 1979; *The Times*, 5 June 1980; *The Times*, 31 May 1983; and *The Times*, 2 December 1983. The United States has suffered a similar problem of low morale among public servants. The major problem is identified as the fact that American Presidents in recent years have devalued the profession of public service. See *International Tribune*, 3 September 1986.

Act for this country. Certainly the Government would have benefited from restating its case, both by demonstrating what information had been released already and by drawing on evidence from other countries about problems connected in practice with FOI-type legislation. Furthermore, the committee assumed that there is a link between having an FOI Act and fewer leaks of official information.

The Government's reply stated that its policy was to make as much information available as possible, commensurate with the requirements to protect national security and other sensitive information. The Government also pointed out that the new Select Committee system of post-1979 makes considerably more information available than previously. On freedom of information legislation, the Government neither was convinced about its need nor believed that such legislation would lead to more effective government. It agreed with the committee that the advice of civil servants to Ministers should remain confidential and, since this category of information would be exempt from any FOI or Access Act, the Government doubted if FOI legislation would have any bearing on relations between Ministers and their officials. The Government was correct that the confidentiality of advice tendered by Ministers of the Crown and officials is specifically protected under an exemption clause in, for example, the New Zealand Official Information Act of 1982. On the committee's assumption that a FOI Act would reduce leaks, the Government did not comment but it appears to be a false correlation. Research by this author reveals that the experience of the United States negates the view that a FOI Act prevents leaks. [56]

5.2 Official Secrets

On the issue of leaks the Treasury and Civil Service Committee stressed that it did not condone those by civil servants aimed at frustrating the policies or actions of Ministers. However, to deal with unauthorised disclosures it supported the principle of a new, narrower criminal law to protect only 'matters which injure the State' [57] and suggested leaving less serious matters to internal discipline rather than court action (as proposed by the Franks Committee in 1972). Although maintaining that section 2 of the Official Secrets Act 1911 was unenforceable, the full committee held back from recommending its repeal, recognising the need before annulling that legislation to devise the precise form of any future legislation. [Section 2 of the Official Secrets Act 1911 has been repealed since this Treasury and Civil Service Committee's Report of 1986 by the new Offical Secrets Act 1989: see Rosamund Thomas *Espionage and Secrect: the Official Secrets Acts 1991-1989 of the United Kingdom* (Routledge, 1991). *Editor*].

---

56 See Rosamund M. Thomas, 'Access of Information: the Experience of Other Countries' this Volume Appendix Part III, pp. 599-633.

57 Treasury and Civil Service Committee, *Report*, paragraph 6.11.

Conclusions

Numerous constitutional conventions underlying Cabinet government – indeed the very system itself – have been challenged by recent episodes in political and administrative behaviour and in proposals by the Treasury and Civil Service Committee and others to reform Minister-civil servant relations. Conventions are principles of *political* practice, in contrast to *laws*, which provide the rules for institutional relationships in British government. Although these conventions have been called 'fictions' because they some-times cloak the real events, like dissension among Cabinet Ministers, they are nonetheless the seams of the constitution without which it would fall apart. Thus, it is important to identify each of the conventions under attack.

The *collective responsibility of the Cabinet* suffered a blow in the Westland case. The convention of the *anonymity of British civil servants* has been chang-ing since 1979, when the new Select Committees were established, but would alter further if civil servants were named to a greater extent or more radical recommendations to increase the accountability of civil servants were acted upon. The *political neutrality of officials* is at risk from proposals put forward by the Treasury and Civil Service Committee, and by Sir John Hoskyns, [58] Norman Strauss, [59] and others, which would 'politicise' the upper ranks of the Civil Service. If the idea of a fully-fledged Prime Minister's Department were to be put forward again, it would move Britain from Cabinet govern-ment to Prime Ministerial government by strengthening considerably the assistance to the premier beyond that of the Cabinet collectively. Freedom of information legislation, if introduced in the future, would require the con-vention of the *confidentiality of advice tendered by civil servants to Ministers* to be reconsidered, to see how it could be incorporated as an exemption into such a statute so that this type of official information would not be released to the public as of right. In July 1986 the unattributable briefings to the press by a number of the staff at Buckingham Palace (alleged to refer to the Queen's personal opinions about the Government's policies and which, moroeover, were at variance with those of her Prime Minister) [60] represent an abuse, albeit indirect, of the convention that *the right of the sovereign to coun-sel, encourage and warn her Government should be exercised in confidence*. Other traditions of British government are undergoing change: the loyalty of civil servants to Ministers (and vice-versa?) has been breached in unauthorised disclosures by, for example, Clive Ponting and Sarah Tisdall; the direct involvement of Departmental Ministers in management as well as policy-

---

58 For example, Sir John Hoskyns's 'Let's end this Whitehall farce!', *Daily Mail*, 20 October 1982.

59 See N. Strauss, 'Why Whitehall Fails the Inner Cities', *The Times*, 6 November 1985; and *The Times*, 6 April 1984.

60 *The Sunday Times* of 20 July 1986 carried this report and Mr Michael Shea, then the Queen's Press Secretary, was believed to have spoken to the press.

making is a change; even the Prime Minister's small Policy Unit carries the danger referred to by Sir Francis Pym (in *The Politics of Consent*) of creating a system 'which deliberately pits Downing Street against departments'. [61]

Nevil Johnson, an expert on government, pointed out in a letter to *The Times* that constitutional constraints should not be viewed as 'an old suit of clothes' to be discarded and changed, and he labels those who appear to hold this view, like Sir John Hoskyns, as 'oddly naive'. [62] Professor Griffith, writing to *The Listener* from the London School of Economics, took another academic lawyer to task, calling him 'one of a dangerous breed', because the latter asserted that the 'real secret' of the constitution 'is that the flexibility provided by the pivotal role of the vague and slippery conventions *allows each generation* to develop *its own* constitution. Constitutional moments of crisis or imagined crisis are *the golden opportunity* for developing the principles *which we want* to guide *our* political life'. John Griffith explains that 'this picture of you and me seizing on the Westland affair or the Queen's alleged distaste for her Prime Minister's policies to reshape our destiny is pure fantasy, invented to support the myth that political power resides in the people'. [63] It is clear that three types of change exist within these constitutional developments. First, *evolutionary intentional change*: that is, limited modifications to the constitution – for example, the creation of fourteen new Select Committees of the House of Commons to parallel and monitor the main Executive Departments which, to a degree, has eroded the anonymity of civil servants. Second, *radical intentional change*: that is, fundamental constitutional alterations – for example, proposals put forward by Sir John Hoskyns and others which reject a permanent career Civil Service based on political neutrality in favour of transferring aspects of the French *cabinet* system to British government and other recommendations which would 'politicise' the Service. Third, *abuses of normal constitutional conventions*: for example, Mr Heseltine's personal crusade in the Westland case 'which was diametrically opposed to the Government's stated policy' and breached the convention of collective Cabinet responsibility. It is important to note these different types of change so as to be alert to whether the threat to the constitution is a matter of abuse or intended change. Writers earlier this century regarded the permanent career Civil Service as a 'constitutional check' on any extreme measures which a political party may seek to push through, especially since the House of Lords as a constitutional check was limited! [64]

---

61 Sir Francis Pym, *The Politics of Consent* (London: Hamish Hamilton, 1984); see *The Times*, 18 June 1984.

62 Letter to the editor of *The Times* from Mr Nevil Johnson, 17 October 1983.

63 Letter to the editor of *The Listener* (21 August 1986) from Professor John Griffith. The stress on the words in italics was made by John Griffith.

64 See, for example, Graham Wallas, *Human Nature in Politics* (first published 1908. Reprinted London: Constable, 1962), pp. 262-81.

Constitutional change may not be appropriate, yet retaining the *status quo ante* with regard to the British Civil Service may not be the answer either. Would-be reformers think that to modernise and lead this country the Service must play a more skilful role in advising and supporting politicians. However, changes could be made which would not abandon our long-standing constitutional conventions. For example, in 1918 the Machinery of Government Committee (chaired by Viscount Haldane) put forward a recommendation, based on the 'staff' principle which operates in the British Army and Navy, for a research unit to be set up in each Department whose duty would be to study the future and provide strategic thinking and planning 'as preliminary to the settlement of policy and subsequent administration'. [65] It is worth re-reading the committee's report and reconsidering this idea. Such research units would meet Sir John Hoskyn's call for more strategic thought, being composed of permanent officials with the purpose of providing 'the *continuous* acquisition of knowledge . . . in order to furnish a proper basis for policy' [66]. But these units would not create the problem experienced in the United States and France of *short-term* policy being offered, which often happens when politicians are responsible for appointing policy advisers, who then leave office with them. Moreover, these proposals would not threaten the convention of political neutrality. The 1918 Haldane Committee stressed the need to pay particular attention to the methods of recruiting staff to the research units and urged that more specific research studies be conducted by these units and by other bodies linked to the Executive Departments, either directly or by means of grants to outside specialist institutions. [67] Other changes could be made which would retain a career Service on merit. Greater priority could be given to personnel management in the Service, without restructuring the Executive Departments: for example, improving leadership and morale and removing rigidities like the strict age barrier for recruitment to permanent posts. In the United States a number of ethical problems arose in the 1970s because of a failure to enforce the merit principle: for example, Civil Service Commissioners sometimes engaged in favouritism and preferential treatment, and a revival of the partisan spoils system occurred. The Reform Act of 1978 divided the Civil Service Commission into two, with one new body established to enforce, that is, protect, the merit principle. [68] In other words, if recruitment according to merit diminishes, ethical problems can grow. Another change which could be introduced into the British Civil Service (taken from the French system) is

---

65 *Report of the Machinery of Government Committee* (London: HMSO, Cd. 9230, 1918), p. 6.

66 Ibid, p. 16.

67 Ibid, pp. 25-7.

68 See David T. Stanley, 'Civil Service Reform in the United States Government', *International Review of Administrative Sciences*, No. 3-4, 1982, pp. 305-06.

increased professionalisation of training. Training in France includes periods of field administration which acquaint the official with local people (and their problems) for whom he will administer policies. More secondments in the field for Whitehall officials during initial training, and in normal work careers, would be advantageous. The Treasury and Civil Service Committee's report of 1986 on Minister-civil servant relations raised wider issues which affect the Service as a whole. In the past a Royal Commission or similar *independent* body would have been set up to examine the Civil Service and to make recommendations. It is one matter for the new Parliamentary committees to enquire into certain *routine* operations of the Executive Departments which they monitor, but another matter for them to advance proposals which, if implemented, would *reshape the entire Service.* [In fact recent changes during the late 1980s and early 1990s, like the new Executive Agencies set up by the 'Next Steps Initiative'; the Citizens Charter 1991-2; the Civil Service Orders-in-Council 1991; and the Civil Service (Management Functions) Act 1992, all have altered radically the British Civil Service – *Editor*].

APPENDIX I

2

The Ethic of the Profession

by Professor Peter Hennessy [1]

The best and wisest discourse on Civil Service ethics I have ever encountered (and the best speech ever made at a trade union conference, incidentally) was delivered in this very hall at the First Division Association (FDA) Annual Conference of 1969 by Derek Morrell, a senior Home Office official. How we could have done with him and his insights in the 1970s and 1980s. It might be an idea in this twentieth anniversary year of that speech, which was delivered a few months before Morrell's death, if the FDA reprinted his words in *FDA News.* [1]

1. The Ethical Context

As overtures go that was pretty grim stuff. Ethics is not comic opera material (though I'm sure Gilbert and Sullivan could have done something with it, after all they got a laugh out of the Northcote Trevelyan Report in *Iolanthe* when the Queen of the Fairies suggested that 'a Duke's exalted station be attainable by competitive examination.') There is, however, a nice mix of gravity and levity in the vignette a friend of mine in the Service repeated for me when I told him I was to deliver this lecture. My friend, in what context I don't know, fell into conversation about an official's motivation with a retired Under Secretary from one of the social Departments. 'When it comes to advising Ministers', the renewable sage declared, 'you must seek to be detached and objective. You must think about what would be in the public interest. Usually by this stage the course of action to recommend is obvious. If it isn't you must ask the $64,000 question – "what's in it for me?"'

I'm no ethical philosopher but that, I suspect, just about sums up the dilemma of any professional throughout the ages who's tried to live and work by some kind of code whether it be a chivalric one or a monastic one or Bertie's famous 'Code of the Worsters'.

It's intriguing to think what the development of an ethical culture tells

---

1 These extracts are taken from a Lecture under this title, given by Peter Hennessy on 31 May 1989, at the Royal Commonwealth Society in London and published in *The Bulletin of the Council of Civil Service Unions* Vol. 9 No. 7 pp. 102-5. It formed the 1989 First Division Association GCHQ Memorial Lecture. The FDA is the staff association which represents higher civil servants in Britain. Recently, Peter Hennessy has been appointed Professor of Contemporary History, Queen Mary and Westfield College, University of London.

you about a society or a nation. Some would argue that truly vibrant, red-in-tooth-and-claw societies don't bother with that kind of thing and that they get big by not bothering. That only when they go soft or lose their sense of their direction do they start asking 'what are we here for?' and 'what is the meaning of life?'

I don't subscribe to that view for a minute. It doesn't fit nations or empires on the make. Even in an understated nation like ours the years of our imperial zenith were laden with scholars and proconsuls, businessmen and missionaries banging on with a variety of justifications – peace, progress, good order, free trade, the scriptures – for what the Englishman was doing abroad with his 'White Man's Burden' at any particular time in the nineteenth century. And I never noticed the superpowers of the twentieth century, whether they be Stalin's Russia, Hitler's Germany or Roosevelt's America, going quiet and coy about their mission in the world. Perhaps the Japanese in this, as in other things, are the exception in preferring, these days, to quietly trade us into extinction with never a word said.

I'm wandering. Back to tonight's business. The ethic of the British Civil Service. There is an ethic. But, as is the British way, it's not written down anywhere. *The Civil Service Pay and Conditions of Service Code*, vast though it is, [2] doesn't attempt to capture in words anything as important as this. The only person to have put it on a page successfully is the remarkable Derek Morrell on this platform twenty years ago. 'We stand committed to neutrality of process', he said:

> 'We profess that public power is not to be used to further the private purposes of those to whom it is entrusted. It is to be used solely for the furtherance of public purposes as defined by constitutional process...
>
> We have evolved rules for the appointment and promotion of staff, for the control of public money, and for other formal accountabilities, such that even the temptation to use public power for private ends has, in these areas, been very largely eliminated.' [3]

Morrell believed officials paid a high price for this ethic in suppressing a part of their inner selves and I'll come back to that in a minute.

Even if the Cabinet Office did put something on paper in addition to the Armstrong Memorandum on the duties and responsibilities of civil servants (which, characteristically, says what you can't do as opposed to what you are

---

2 A new series of briefer Codes has replaced *The Civil Service Pay and Conditions of Service Code*. See the new Civil Service Management Code (Section 4 on 'Conduct and Discipline, dated February 1993) reprinted in this Volume pp. 441-67.

3 I am grateful to Sue Corby for supplying me with a text of Derek Morrell's speech from FDA files when I was preparing my *Whitehall* volume.

there to do) [4] – even if a Butler Memorandum came round on the meaning of official life, the key element would not be that scrap of paper. It would be the genetic code of professional expectations transmitted from one generation to another in a way that often happens when a relatively small group of people, such as the senior ranks for the Civil Service, spend many years in very close contact one to another. It's now and always will be more of a personal than a paper phenomenon.

I'm keen that it should continue to exist and be transferred, as if it were a piece of ethical technology, from one generation to the next for two reasons:

i.   I believe it to be crucial to keeping our entire system of Central Government clean and decent.

ii. As an outside observer, I by and large like what I see of that ethical technology.

2. A Genetic Code

It's now incumbent on me to tell you what I conceive that genetic code to be. Let me rattle off a list in which every item matters and contributes to a sum much greater than its parts.

- *Probity.* We have, by any test, a remarkably incorruptible Civil Service. Of the 155 countries of the world recognised as such by the United Nations I suspect you could only say that with certainty about 15 to 20 of them. An honest Civil Service, in which Departmental tills are hand-free zones, is a pearl of great price. Here it's taken for granted. If it could no longer be taken for granted the country would be impoverished in a moral as well as a financial sense.

- *Care for evidence.* The Civil Service is an evidence – driven profession. This can be very inconvenient because politics isn't. Constant care has to be taken to prevent anyone – including the Minister through the private office door – from tampering with official statistics. The trouble arises, as always, where evidence tends to give way to hunch and, equally dangerous, to wishful thinking because not everything is susceptible to measurement by the Central Statistical Office.

- *A respect for reason.* A civil servant cannot believe political will is all, because politics is the art of mobilising prejudice. Reason is the enemy of prejudice. Mind you, this can be taken too far. In June 1940 after France had fallen every 'reasonable' policy analyst would have advised the British Empire to raise the white flag while it still had a chance of preserving

---

4 Sir Robert Armstrong, *The Duties and Responsibilities of Civil Servants in Relation to Ministers, Note by the Head of the Home Civil Service*, Cabinet Office, 25 February 1985. See also the paper in this Volume by Mr Hayden Phillips, Note 1, pp. 58-62 *[Editor]*

some of itself intact – and every policy analyst would have been wrong.

- *A willingness to speak truth unto power.* If a civil servant can't tell the powerful Minister he or she is plumb wrong and why, nobody can. That's part of what you're paid for; that's why you have what amounts to tenure; even though in the end you have to do what the Minister says. This brings me to

- *A capacity not just to live with the consequences of what you believe to be a mistaken course, but to pursue it energetically.* The former Head of the Diplomatic Service, Lord Vansittart, captured this requirement when he said: 'The soul of our Service is the loyalty with which we execute ordained error.' [5] This, however, is the bit of the job Derek Morrell found most difficult. 'So far as concerns our private aspirations in the field of public policy', he said, 'we cling to the myth which science has now abandoned. We still do not accept the reality of our individual humanity; we have not therefore evolved rules of procedure such that we can contribute all that we are to a process having public and not private outcomes. And the price which we and the public pay for pursuing a myth is heavy. Speaking personally', Morrell went on, 'I find it yearly more difficult to reconcile personal integrity with a view of my role which requires the deliberate suppression of part of what I am. It is this tension, and not overwork, which brings me, regularly, to the point where I am ready to contemplate leaving a service which I care about very deeply.' I know exactly what Morrell meant by that. It captures to perfection the reason why I could never be a civil servant. It is, however, a dilemma which can never be resolved so long as we keep a career Civil Service in being which is constitutionally subordinate to Ministers and ministerial policy. In the end Ministers must prevail.

- Side by side with this, however awkward it may be to fit in, has to go at the very least *an appreciation of the wider public interest.* This is very difficult. It lay at the heart of the Ponting dilemma. It will always be a dilemma for two reasons: one's definition of the public interest tends to coincide with one's personal views of what is right and proper; and what do you do if the Minister acts in a contrary fashion? He or she is elected, after all, and you are only appointed. Perhaps a better way of describing this bit is to call it

- *An awareness, necessary at all times, of other people's life chances.* Government, uniquely, is involved in policies and programmes which affect directly and sometimes ultimately all 56 million of us. Inefficiency in delivery of benefits which are an individual citizen's entitlement can, at best, be a matter of personal distress to the person deprived and, at

5 Lord Vansittart, *The Mist Procession*, (Hutchinson, 1958) p. 313.

worst, a matter of life and death. This interlocks with another piece of the ethical jigsaw, that of

- *Equity and fairness.* This has been of great advantage to Britain. It's best looked at, in terms of the 'pensioner in Orkney' or the unemployed and angry teenager in Skelmersdale' tests – the requirement being that however remote or 'difficult' the recipient of services might be they have the same entitlement to careful, reliable individual treatment as the conveniently located and the personally charming.

This brings me to the three flying buttresses, essential to the stability of the entire system, which also shore-up the requirement that you shall always be a *constitutional* Civil Service under the control of a higher authority of elected Ministers accountable to Parliament.

- A constant and careful concern for the law.

- A constant concern for Parliament – its needs and procedures. No lying and no misleading.

- A concern for democracy. You may not like the kind of people it places above you but coups or any kind of destabilisation are out.

All these may strike you either as self-evident or thoroughly Pollyanna-ish. I don't mind if they do. Clichés, conventional wisdoms, democratic pieties sometimes pass the tests of truth and necessity where clear or novel formulations do not.

But there's another reason for putting them in separate little packets. Wrap them into a bundle and you get what is a pretty good professional ethic by anyone's standards. You get something else – a public service motivation which means, however meagre the pay in relative terms, however dark the corridors, however tatty the offices, that State service continues to attract a share of the best, the brightest and the decently-motivated year in year out. And, despite those worrying indications of a talent haemhorrage in early to mid-career, a high proportion still stay for a working lifetime.

3. Motivation

One of the silliest clichés of the business community in the 1980s has been that 'if you pay peanuts, you get monkeys'. If that was true now, or had ever been true, nobody with a dozen grey cells and the energy to rub them together would have been attracted to the higher Civil Service in the past one hundred and twenty years. And, as we all know, in City and industrial terms, you can pay people in sacks of gold-plated peanuts and still get monkeys. Motivation by other means than pay – the public service impulse, in other words – is an area in which the private sector can learn from the Civil Service. But few on either side realise it and even fewer say it.

413

Taken together, these public sector impulses – like probity and incorruptibility – are very easily taken for granted. Hence they are ignored. Hence the possibility of their dissipation, if not disappearance, is enhanced.

Are all these good things in jeopardy as we approach the 1990s? I'm not about to chain myself to the Cabinet Office front door to irritate Sir Robin Butler[6] and alert a nonchalant world about imminent danger. But there are some causes for concern if not alarm.

Much of my concern arises from the polarisation of British politics in the last twenty years. This may well be easing now thanks to Labour's policy reviews. I'm sure it will ease tangibly the day the present Prime Minister is replaced with whoever it is who goes to the Palace to kiss hands and whatever their party. Nonetheless, we are living *now* with the accummulated stresses of the Seventies and Eighties.

When the gap between the parties competing for power widens beyond a certain point, the nineteenth century model of a permanent, politically-neutral career Civil Service begins to creak and groan as it stretches to bridge it. In recent years there was never a possibility of Britain quitting NATO but there was a real possibility of our leaving the European Community and of our ceasing to be a nuclear weapons State. Either of those outcomes could have seen resignations as could the restoration of capital punishment within the ranks, at least, of the Home Office and the Prison Service. Then the ethical technology, or part of it, would have ceased to be transferrable. People would have reached a personal breaking-point.

4. Politicisation

There was another price to be paid for polarisation. After an election at which the Government changed hands, incoming Ministers tended to think their officials were in the pockets of their outgoing rivals. Two ways were found for remedying this: the importation of a number of special advisers sharing to a high degree the political philosophy of the Minister who had recruited them; and the taking of a greater interest in top appointments from within the career Civil Service.

I do not believe that this so-called 'one of us approach' has amounted to a political test. It's more a matter of temperament – of a 'can do' spirit, of energy and commitment which is all about personal drive but not in the sense of ideological drive. I reached my conclusions some time before the Royal Institute of Public Administration's equivalent of a Royal Commission reached theirs but out findings were identical.[7] Yet the problem remains real

---

6 Sir Robin Butler is the current Head of the Civil Service and Secretary to the Cabinet. He has written the Foreword to this Volume 1: *Government Ethics [Editor]*.

7 My conclusions can be found in Hennessy, *Whitehall*, pp. 623-34, and the RIPA's in *Top Jobs in Whitehall; Appointments and Promotions in the Senior Civil Service,* Report of an RIPA Working Group, (RIPA, 1987).

and live because Margaret Thatcher has created the impression of politicising the Permanent Secretaries and, in the irrational, non-evidence-driven world of politics, it's impressions that count.

There is now a possibility of some future Labour Secretaries of State despatching their inherited Permanent Secretaries on gardening leave. Dr John Cunningham, Labour's environment spokesman, for example, is on record as saying of Sir Terry Heiser, Permanent Secretary at the Department of the Environment, 'there would either have to be a remarkable change of attitude towards local government and the exercise of power by Mr Heiser or he'd have to go. Frankly, from what I know of his view and attitudes over the last five years, I couldn't see he and I working together if I was to be Secretary of State for the Environment.' [8]

If I was the Head of the Home Civil Service I would be deeply alarmed by statements of that kind from Members of the Shadow Cabinet. If a purge took place in the first weeks of a new Government, the basis of the nineteenth century settlement of the Civil Service question would have crumbled probably beyond repair. In their defence, new Labour Ministers would cite the Thatcher experience. They would be wrong but it would seem a plausible enough alibi to many Members of the political nation. I'm very keen for there to be 'new blood' in the Civil Service up to and including the top (and I hope this new 'Next-Steps' agencies will facilitate this). But I don't want it to be injected by those methods and for those reasons. The key to the 'new blood' case should be merit – a richer mixture of skills – not party political acceptability. That way lies the patronage State and all the enormities of pre-Gladstone Whitehall. Losses would outweigh any likely gains.

It's as well to consider these matters way ahead of an election in relatively quiet times. Ethical issues tend to come to the fore at moments of crises – Suez, Ponting, GCHQ, Westland – when the body politic exudes more heat than light. That's why I've never believed the ethics question is a soft option for Civil Service staff associations when there's little joy to be had on the pay-and-conditions front. Because it goes to the heart of the matter, what the profession of a civil servant is all about.

---

8 Peter Hennessy, 'Whitehall Watch: Why new members could mean wholesale change', *The Independent*, 9 January 1989.

21 R v. Lord Chancellor's Department ex parte Nangle [1]

100 *Contracts of employment*
102 *Formation of contract*
10000 *Judicial review*

22 The facts:

Mr Nangle was employed as an executive officer. In November 1989, it was alleged that he had assaulted and sexually harassed a young woman in his department. An oral hearing was held and Mr Nangle was notified that the charge had been upheld and that it had been decided that he should be transferred to another department with a withdrawal of increment. An internal appeal against this decision was rejected, although the loss of increment was reduced from 12 months to three.

Mr Nangle was granted leave to move for judicial review on grounds that both decisions were reached in breach of the rules of natural justice and there was a procedural impropriety. The respondents sought an Order that the application be dismissed on grounds that the application of disciplinary procedures to a Crown servant is not a matter of public law appropriate for determination by way of judicial review.

It was accepted on behalf of the applicant that he had no remedy on public law if he was employed by the Crown under a contract of service. However, the applicant relied upon paragraph 14 of the Civil Service Pay and Conditions of Service Code,
23 which states: "For the most part, the relationship between the civil servant and the Crown remains one regulated under the prerogative and based on personal appointment. As such, a civil servant does not have a contract of employment enforceable in the courts but rather a letter of appointment, and technically the Crown still retains the right to dismiss a civil servant at
24 pleasure."

The High Court, Queen's Bench Division [Divisional Court] (Lord Justice Stuart-Smith, Mr Justice Turner) on 27 March 1991 dismissed the application for judicial review.

---

1 Reprinted from [1991] IRLR 343.

The Divisional Court Held:

25

171

200

4300

102

10000

The applicant was employed by the Crown under a contract of service since his employment had the necessary intention to enter into legal relations. *R v Civil Service Appeal Board ex parte Bruce,* in which the Divisional Court held that a civil servant's appointment was not pursuant to an enforceable contract of employment since there was no intention to create legal relations, would not be followed.

The relationship of employer and employee must of its very nature be one that involves an intention to create legal relations, unless such intention is clearly excluded either expressly or by necessary implication. An intention to create legal relations in such a context means an intention to enter into a contract legally enforceable in the courts, and the converse is that the relationship is purely voluntary or is binding in honour only.

Where the documents show that the parties entered into a relationship involving obligations, rights and entitlements which go both ways then prima facie the court will hold that they intend these obligations to be enforceable and not merely voluntary. In such a business situation there is a heavy onus upon the party asserting a lack of intention to create legal relations.

The mere fact that someone has no private law remedy does not mean that they have a public law one. The crucial element is whether the dispute has a sufficient public law element.

In the present case, the internal disciplinary proceedings of the Lord Chancellor's Department are quite different from those of a tribunal, such as the Civil Service Appeal Board, set up under prerogative or statutory power. They are of a domestic nature, similar to that which might occur in the case of any large employer.

In the present case, with the exception of paragraph 14 of the Civil Service Pay and Conditions of Service Code, it was plain beyond argument that the parties intended to create legal relations. Paragraph 14, which states that "a civil servant does not have a contract of employment enforceable in the courts", had to be read in context. Its purpose is to describe a state of affairs as it was believed to be, not to limit or exclude rights or obligations or to restrict or exclude the enforceability of such rights or obligations. The documentation lay down rights, obligations and entitlements dealing with matters which are the stock in trade of a contract of employment such as pay, pensions, hours, holidays, sick leave and discipline. Paragraph 14 of the Code could not be construed as meaning that all those matters were to be voluntary only and not legally enforceable or even that such was the intention of the Crown.

Moreover, there was fundamental inconsistency in the applicant's argument in that it was difficult to see how the parties could have intended that their relationship should not be governed by private law, but did intend that they should be governed by public law. They either intended their relationship to have legal consequences or they did not.

As the applicant was employed by the Crown under a contract of service, he had no remedy in public law. However, he was entitled to sue for damages for breach of contract if he could establish failure to comply with provisions of the disciplinary code.

10000 In any event, the disciplinary decisions impugned did not have a sufficient element of public law to justify the exercise of the Court's jurisdiction in judicial review.

Cases referred to:

R v East Berkshire Health Authority ex parte Walsh [1984]
IRLR 278 CA
Kodeeswaran v Attorney General of Ceylon [1970] AC 1111 PC
R v Civil Service Appeal Board ex parte Bruce [1988] ICR 649
DC
Inland Revenue Commissioners v Hambrook [1956] 2 QB 641
HC
Reilly v The King [1934] AC 176 PC
McLaren v The Home Office [1990] IRLR 338 CA
Lam Yuk-ming v Attorney General [1980] Hong Kong LR 815
Hong Kong Court of Appeal
Street v Mountford [1985] AC 809 HL
Rose and Frank Co v J R Crompton and Bros Ltd [1923] 2 KB
261 CA
Rogers v Booth [1937] 2 AER 751
President of the Methodist Conference v Parfitt [1984] IRLR 141
CA
Davies v Presbyterian Church of Wales [1986] IRLR 194 HL
Edwards v Skyways Ltd [1964] 1 WLR 349 HC
R v Panel on Take-overs and Mergers ex parte Datafin plc [1987]
1 QB 815 CA
R v Derbyshire County Council ex parte Noble [1990] IRLR 332
CA
*R v Secretary of State for the Home Department ex parte
Benwell* [1985] IRLR 6 HC
*R v Secretary of State for Foreign and Commonwealth Affairs ex
parte Council of Civil Service Unions* [1985] IRLR 28 HL
R v Secretary of State for the Home Department ex parte Attard
[1990] WLR 641 CA

Apearances:
For the Applicant:
E TABACHNIK QC and N GRIFFEN, instructed by Pattinson & Brewer
For the Respondent:
J LAWS, instructed by The Treasury Solicitor

1   LORD JUSTICE STUART-SMITH: In 1974 the applicant
joined the Lord Chancellor's Department. In 1989 he was
an executive officer in the Protection Division of the Public
Trust Office. In November of that year it was alleged that
he had assaulted and sexually harassed a young woman in
his department. The matter was investigated, purportedly
in accordance with the laid-down procedures. On 19 December 1989 there was an oral hearing. By letter dated 11
January 1990 the applicant was notified that the Head of

Personnel Management Division had upheld the charges and decided that the applicant should be transferred to another department with a withdrawal of increment for 12 months.

2   The applicant appealed to the Permanent Secretary. The appeal was heard on 9 February 1990 by an officer delegated by the Permanent Secretary. By letter dated 19 February 1990 the applicant was told that his appeal had been dismissed by the Principal Establishment and Finance Officer acting by delegated authority. The loss of increment was however reduced from 12 months to three.

3   The applicant sought leave to move for judicial review of the decisions of 11 January and 19 February 1990. He alleges that both decisions were reached in breach of the rules of natural justice and that there was procedural impropriety. Kennedy J granted leave to move on 8 June 1990. By notice of motion dated 7 August 1990 and subsequently amended the respondents seek an Order that:
'This application for judicial review be dismissed on a preliminary point of law: that the application of disciplinary procedures to the appellant as a Crown servant is not a matter of public law appropriate for determination by way of judicial review.'

4   Two main questions arise on this motion: (i) Is the applicant employed by the Crown under a contract of service? If he is, it is accepted by Mr Tabachnik QC on his behalf that he has no remedy in public law, the case being indistinguishable from *R v East Berkshire Health Authority ex parte Walsh* [1984] IRLR 278; (ii) If the applicant is not employed under a contract of employment is there a sufficient public law element in the case to justify the exercise of the Court's jurisdiction in judicial review?

5   **Question 1**
It is common ground between the parties that the plaintiff's employment in the department involved two of the necessary ingredients of contract, namely offer and acceptance and consideration. The point at issue is whether there was in addition an intention to enter into legal relations. It is also common ground that the Crown can enter into a contract of employment with its servants. See *Kodeeswaran v Attorney General of Ceylon* [1970] AC 1111 and *R v Civil Service Appeal Board ex parte Bruce* [1988]

ICR 649, a case much relied upon by Mr Tabachnik. At p.660B May LJ said:

'Nevertheless there is in my view nothing unconstitutional about civil servants being employed by the Crown pursuant to contracts of service, and if the Cabinet Office's reappraisal continues on the present lines I anticipate that this is what will happen. Such a situation would in my view be wholly consistent with a modern and realistic view of the position of civil servants vis-à-vis the Crown.'

And see also per Roch J at p.665C.

6   It is necessary to set out in a little more detail the documentation relating to the applicant's employment. His letter of appointment is dated 31 December 1973 and includes the following extracts:

'I am now pleased to offer you appointment as an unestablished clerical officer in the Statistics Section of the Lord Chancellor's Department with effect from Monday 4 February 1974. This appointment is subject to the receipt of satisfactory references and the completion of a three-month trial period.'

7   There is then set out his salary and other conditions of pay:

'I attach a leaflet containing a short summary of the main conditions governing your appointment. Please let me have in writing your acceptance of the offer of appointment on these conditions.'

8   In a document Appendix A enclosed with the letter entitled 'Conditions of service' it is stated:

'The following is a short summary of the main conditions governing your appointment but these are contained more fully in the staff handbook with which you will be supplied in due course. Any significant changes will be notified by means of LCD News which is circulated weekly.

Every appointment to the department is held at the pleasure of the Crown and conditions of service can therefore be altered from time to time and appointments can be terminated without notice. Unless, however, you are dismissed on disciplinary grounds, and provided you have served continuously for 13 weeks or more, you will receive at least five weeks' notice of termination of appointment. If you decided to leave, you would be required to give not less than one month's notice. The appointment is also subject to the receipt of satisfactory references and such other enquiries as it is necessary to make.'

9   At Appendix B there is a statement of 'Superannuation benefits'. It is unnecessary to refer to the provisions in detail, they are couched in the language of entitlement.

10   The Lord Chancellor's Department staff handbook runs to some 162 paragraphs. After a brief introduction there are three main heads: 'Conduct and discipline', 'Career' and 'Conditions of service'. Many of these terms and conditions are of a similar nature to those that might be found in any contract of employment; many are in terms of obligation and it is plain that it is intended that non-compliance by the employee may be regarded as a matter of discipline and dismissal or action short of dismissal.

11   The appointment was also subject to the Civil Service Pay and Conditions of Service Code. In the introduction is to be found:

'(i) Under Article 5 of the Civil Service Order in Council 1969, the Minister for the Civil Service is empowered to make regulations for controlling the conduct of Her Majesty's Home Civil Service. Instructions given in the exercise of this power are communicated to departments by the Civil Service Department as part of a consolidated Code. Such instructions stem mainly from two sources, legislation which binds the Crown or which, although not binding the Crown, Ministers have undertaken to supply as though it were so binding; and agreements reached in negotiation with the National Staff Side or with staff associations in accordance with custom and practice extending back over more than 50 years. Rules and guidance so issued are mandatory on employing departments. In some instances, the method of application of the rules is precisely defined, in others, the principles to be observed are defined and the method of application is left to departments.

(ii) Within the Civil Service, the employer/employee relationship exists between the individual civil servant and his employing department. For convenience of departments, this Code collects together the results of negotiations with employees' representatives, and the rules for their application, on all matters of pay and conditions of service which are handled by the Civil Service Department on behalf of all employing departments. It also contains a statement of accepted principles of conduct which have statutory backing or are based on expressed government policy.'

12 Under the heading 'Legislation affecting the conditions of service of civil servants':

'11. The Civil Service has evolved under the Royal prerogative and, except as regards superannuation, does not rest on a codified statutory basis. In legal theory, all civil servants form part of the personal staff of the Sovereign and it is still true to say that on appointment civil servants, as servants of the Crown, hold office during the pleasure of the Crown.

14. For the most part, the relationship between the civil servant and the Crown remains one regulated under the prerogative and based on personal appointment. As such, a civil servant does not have a contract of employment enforceable in the courts but rather a letter of appointment, and technically the Crown still retains the right to dismiss a civil servant at pleasure. Recently, however, the legal position of civil servants has been radically changed by the growing trend for legislation to apply to the Civil Service either directly, by the provisions of the Acts themselves, or by governmental assurances that the conditions applying to civil servants will not be less favourable than those applying to other employees.'

13 After considering the cases of *Inland Revenue Commissioners v Hambrook* [1956] 2 QB 641, the well-known dictum of Lord Atkin in *Reilly v The King* [1943] AC 176, 180 where he said that the Crown's power to dismiss its servants without notice at will 'is not inconsistent with the existence of a contract until so determined and the decision of the Privy Council in *Kodeeswaren v Attorney General of Ceylon* [1970] AC 1111, May LJ in *ex parte Bruce* concluded that the authorities were in a confused and uncertain state. It is to be noted, however, that there does not appear to have been any suggestion in any of the authorities prior to *ex parte Bruce* that the reason why there was no contract between the Crown and its civil servants was due to an absence of intention to enter into legal relations; rather it was due to doubts as to the constitutional position of the Crown and its ability to bind itself in contract with its servants who were historically regarded as members of the Sovereign's household, and the belief that the ability to dismiss its servants at will was inconsistent with contract.

14 The first of these propositions was laid to rest in the *Kodeeswaren* case; although that case might have been

decided on principles of restitution and quasi contract, it is plain that in fact it was not; it was decided that the civil servant in *Ceylon* had a claim in contract (see per Lord Diplock at p.1123G). The second proposition is rebutted by the dictum of Lord Atkin to which we have referred in *Reilly's* case.

15   Mr Tabachnik founds his argument in the case on paragraph 14 of the Civil Service Code and the decision in *ex parte Bruce*. He also submits that the letter of appointment points in terms to an appointment rather than a contract. In our judgment the use of the word 'appointment' is neutral and certainly does not negative an intention to create legal relations. Many contractual relationships of employer and employee are described as appointments.

16   Mr Tabachnik also relies on the attitude of the Crown in previous cases, where it is probably true to say that in the majority it has either been assumed that there was no contract or it was argued that there was none. An example of the latter is *McLaren v The Home Office* [1990] IRLR 338. In that case Mr Tabachnik took the contrary position to that which he takes in this case. He argued that a prison officer was employed under a contract of employment and could bring a private law claim. The Crown argued that any claim the plaintiff might have should be pursued by judicial review and sought to strike out the claim. The Court of Appeal held that it was arguable that there was a contractual relationship and refused to strike out the pleading. It should be noted that paragraphs 11 and 14 of the Civil Service Code applied equally in *McLaren's* case. But we cannot see how the Crown's attitude in other cases – which may or may not have been mistaken – can be relevant to the question whether the parties intended to create legal relations in this case.

17   Mr Tabachnik has also referred to a number of statutes which affect employees of the Crown, in particular: the Equal Pay Act 1970; the Industrial Relations Act 1971; the Trade Union and Labour Relations Act 1974; the Employment Protection Act 1975; the Sex Discrimination Act 1975; the Race Relations Act 1976 and the Employment Protection (Consolidation) Act 1978.

18   It is true that these Acts are not applied to civil servants simply by providing that the Acts shall bind the Crown. It is done in a somewhat more circumspect way. For example,

in the Employment Protection (Consolidation) Act 1978 it is provided by s.138:

'(1) Subject to the following provisions of this section, Parts I (so far as it relates to itemised pay statements), II, III ... V ... VIII and this Part and s.53 shall have effect in relation to Crown employment and to persons in Crown employment as they have effect in relation to other employment and to other employees.

(2) In this section, subject to subsections (3) to (5) "Crown employment" means employment under or for the purposes of a government department or any officer or body exercising on behalf of the Crown functions conferred by any enactment.

(3) This section does not apply to service as a member of the naval, military or air forces of the Crown ... but does apply to employment by any association established for the purposes of [Part VI of the Reserve Forces Act 1980] ...

(7) For the purposes of the application of the provisions of this Act in relation to Crown employment in accordance with subsection (1):

(a) any reference to an employee shall be construed as a reference to the terms of employment of a person in Crown employment;

(b) any reference to a contract of employment shall be construed as a reference to the terms of employment of a person in Crown employment;

(c) any reference to dismissal shall be construed as a reference to the termination of Crown employment.'

19   For our part we do not derive any assistance from this legislation which is equally consistent with the presence or absence of a contractual relationship, though scarcely consistent with an absence of intention to create legal relations.

20   Mr Tabachnik drew our attention to the decision of the Hong Kong Court of Appeal in *Lam Yuk-ming v Attorney General* [1980] Hong Kong LR 815 in which it was held that a civil servant did have a contract of employment. In that case there was a somewhat similar provision to paragraph 14 of the Civil Service Code; but the Court held that it did not apply to the plaintiff's contract. At p.828 Roberts CJ said:

'In versions A, D and E (but not versions B and C) it is stated that "these regulations" do not constitute a contract between the Crown and its servants. The Crown submitted that the phrase "these regulations", in its context, referred only to Colonial Regulations, and not to the other regulations listed earlier in the relevant sub-paragraph. We think that this is correct. The phrase is not appropriate to include Orders, Department Instructions or Ordinances, all of which appear earlier in the paragraph. Conversely, the limited terms of this disclaimer can be taken as inferring an intention that such other instruments as are referred to in that paragraph are intended to form part of such a contract. That case is therefore distinguishable on its facts.'

21   Mr Laws submits correctly, in our judgment, that the question whether there is an intention to create legal relations is to be ascertained objectively, and where the terms of the relationship are, as here, to be derived solely from the documents, depends upon the construction of those documents. It is possible for a party to believe mistakenly that he is contractually bound to another when in fact he is not; and conversely to believe that he is not when he is. His belief is immaterial. While this remains a subjective belief uncommunicated to the other party, this is plainly correct. But where such a belief is expressed in the documents it must be a question of construction of the documents as a whole what effect should be given to such a statement.

22   Mr Laws also relied on the principle that the label which the parties give to their relationship is not conclusive of its legal nature; see for example *Street v Mountford* [1985] AC 809. But in that case there was no dispute but that the parties were legally bound in contract; the question was as to the true legal nature of the agreement and not whether there was an intention to be legally bound at all.

23   We accept that the concept of an intention to create legal
102   relations in this context means an intention to enter into a contract legally enforceable in the courts. But the converse of the situation is that the relationship is purely voluntary or is binding in honour only. See for example *Rose and Frank Co v JR Crompton and Bros Ltd* [1923] 2 KB 261 and the religious cases such as *Rogers v Booth* [1937] 2 AER 751, *President of the Methodist Conference v Parfitt* [1984] IRLR 141 and *Davies v Presbyterian Church of Wales* [1986] IRLR 194.

24
102

Where the documents show that the parties enter into a relationship involving obligations, rights and entitlements which go both ways then prima facie the court will hold that they intend these obligations to be enforceable and not merely voluntary.

25
102

In such a business situation the onus is upon the party asserting a lack of intention to create legal relations and the onus is a heavy one (*Edwards v Skyways Ltd* [1964] 1 WLR 349 per Megaw J at p.355 and see Chitty on Contracts, 26th Edition, Volume 1, paragraph 129).

26
102
10000

With the exception of paragraph 14 of the Code it seems to us plain beyond argument that the parties intended to create legal relations; this is consistent with the *Kodeeswaran* and *Lam Yuk-ming* cases. Moreover, the earlier authorities, supported by the Opinion of Lord Goddard CJ in *IRC v Hambrook*, do not turn on an absence of intention to create legal relations. In our judgment paragraph 14 has to be read in context. It is to be found in a section of the Code which is dealing with legislation affecting conditions of service of civil servants; it is merely part of the introduction to the legislation referred to. The purpose of the section is to describe a state of affairs as it is believed to be; not to limit or exclude rights or obligations or to restrict or exclude the enforceability of such rights or obligations. Paragraphs 11-13 merely describe the historical evolution of the Civil Service; paragraphs 14 and 15 introduce the legislation that is thereafter referred to. The very legislation, to much of which we have earlier referred, shows that there are legal consequences of the relationship. The documentation lays down with great clarity rights, obligations and entitlements, dealing with such matters as pay, pensions, hours of attendance, holidays, sick leave, discipline and many other similar matters which are the stock in trade of a contract of employment. We cannot construe paragraph 14 of the Code as meaning that all these matters are to be voluntary only and not legally enforceable or even that such was the intention of the Crown. In our judgment it is merely descriptive of what was believed to be the position. It makes no difference that the terms are described as conditions of service as opposed to terms and conditions of contract. The relationship of employer and employee, master and servant, which plainly exists here must of its very nature be one that involves an intention to create legal relations, unless such intention is

clearly excluded either expressly or by necessary implication, and is in the religious appointments cases. In our
judgment read in its proper context paragraph 14 does not
have this effect. Moreover, it seems to us that there is a
fundamental inconsistency in Mr Tabachnik's argument.
We find it difficult to see how the parties can have intended
that their relationship should not be governed by private
law, but did intend that they should be governed by public
law. They either intended their relationship to have legal
consequences or they did not.

27　　For these reasons we have come to the conclusion that we
should not follow the reasoning of the Divisional Court in
ex parte Bruce and that the first question should be answered in favour of the respondent. This is not a matter of
public law; if the applicant can establish breach of contract
by failure to comply with the express or implied provision
of the disciplinary code which has resulted in loss, he can
sue for damages for breach of contract.

28　**Question 2**
But what is the position if we are wrong on Question 1?

29　　In deference to the extensive argument that has been
addressed to us, it is incumbent upon us to deal with this
question. In the absence of a legally enforceable contract
the applicant is clearly in a stronger position.

30　　The statement of the law to found in the judgment of
Lord Donaldson MR in *R v Panel on Take-overs and Mergers ex parte Datafin plc* [1987] 1 QB 815 provides the logical
starting point for the discussion. At p.838E he said:
　　'In all the reports it is possible to find enumerations of
　　factors giving rise to the jurisdiction, but it is a fatal
　　error to regard the presence of all those factors as
　　essential or as being exclusive of other factors. Possibly
　　the only essential elements are what can be described as
　　a public element, which can take many different forms,
　　and the exclusion from the jurisdiction of bodies whose
　　sole source of power is a consensual submission to its
　　jurisdiction.'

31　　Mr Tabachnik submitted that the relationship of employer and employee may fall into one of four categories:
1. A purely casual and informal association where A volun-
teers to work for B. No private contractual law rights exist

and public law right has no application.

2. Where there is a contract of employment or a contract for services, whether the employer is in the private or public sector, all rights arise out of the contract, they are consensual and exist only in private law. There are no public law remedies. See *ex parte Walsh* and *R v Derbyshire County Council ex parte Noble* [1990] IRLR 332.

3. There may be a relationship where the terms are governed entirely by statute in which case the employer's powers are regulated entirely by public law and there are no private law rights. Mr Tabachnik suggested that an example of this was the position of the judges, perhaps more especially the circuit judges.

4. Where the relationship is not a purely voluntary one that falls into category 1 and the parties have chosen not to regulate their relationship by contract according to private law, nevertheless he submits a framework of law regulates their relationship. Into this category come civil servants and prison officers. In its dealings with civil servants the Crown acts under the prerogative power pursuant to the Civil Service Orders in Council of 1969, 1978, 1982. The latter provides by paragraph 4:

'As regards her Majesty's Home Civil Service –

(a) The Minister for the Civil Service may from time to time make regulations or give instructions . . .

(ii) for controlling the conduct of the Service.'

32   It is pursuant to this power that the Civil Service Code is promulgated. In these circumstances submits Mr Tabachnik a complaint in relation to disciplinary proceedings, albeit conducted by the employer and not before some independent body such as the Civil Service Appeal Board (CSAB), is justiciable in public law.

33   In support of this fourth proposition Mr Tabachnik relied on the dictum of May LJ in *ex parte Bruce* at p.660C where he said:

'In the instant case, however, in the absence of a contract of service between the applicant and the Crown I think that one is bound to hold that there was a sufficient public law element behind the applicant's dismissal from his appointment with the Inland Revenue and the hearing of this appeal by the CSAB to entitle him to apply for judicial review of the latter and he has obtained leave to do so.'

34   But it is to be noted that this case relates to a decision in which the CSAB was involved and not to purely internal departmental disciplinary proceedings.

35   Mr Tabachnik submits that there is no difference in principle between the two because they both flow from the Civil Service Code. We do not agree. The CSAB is an independent body set up under the prerogative. It has four functions:
'i. to decide whether a department's decision to retire an individual early or to dismiss is fair;
ii. to act as the Appeal Board for civil servants who have been refused permission by their departments to undertake political activities;
iii. to consider appeals against a proposal to withhold superannuation benefits under rule 8.2 of the PCSPS;
iv. to consider appeals against a departmental decision not to pay compensation in cases of dismissal on grounds of inefficiency.

36   Under paragraph (i) it entertains appeals from the employer's decision in relation to certain matters. Its decision is not that of the employer. The applicant has no direct relationship with the CSAB; he has to invoke its jurisdiction by way of appeal. That is typically a body that is amenable to judicial review. The disciplinary proceedings within the department result directly from the employer/employee relationship and result in a decision of the employer.

37   Mr Tabachnik also relies on the judgment of Woolf LJ (with whose judgment McCowan LJ agreed) in *ex parte McLaren*. If I may respectfully say so, there is in this judgment a most helpful and penetrating analysis to be found. Mr Tabachnik submits that this case falls squarely within Woolf LJ's second category.

38   At p.86 at E he said:
'There can, however, be situations where an employee of a public body can seek judicial review and obtain a remedy which would not be available to an employee in the private sector. This will arise where there exists some disciplinary or other body established under the prerogative or by statute to which the employer or the employee is entitled or required to refer disputes affect-

ing their relationship. The procedure of judicial review can then be appropriate because it has always been part of the role of the court in public law proceedings to supervise the inferior tribunals and the court in reviewing disciplinary proceedings is performing a similar role. As long as the "tribunal" or other body has a sufficient public law element, which it almost invariably will have if the employer is the Crown, and it is not domestic or wholly informal, its proceedings and determination can be an appropriate subject for judicial review.

An example is provided here by the decision of the Divisional Court in *R v Civil Service Appeal Board ex parte Bruce* [1988] ICR 649. If there had not been available the more effective alternative remedy before an Industrial Tribunal, the Divisional Court would have regarded the decision of the Civil Service Appeal Board in that case as reviewable upon judicial review. The decision of this Court which has just been given in *R v Secretary of State for the Home Department ex parte Attard*, The Times, 14 March 1990 is another example of the same situation.

There, what was being considered by this Court were the powers of a prison governor in connection with disciplinary proceedings in respect of prison officers. The prison governor's disciplinary powers in relation to prisoners are reviewable only on judicial review (see *Leech v Deputy Governor of Parkhurst Prison* [1988] AC 533) and they can also be reviewed on judicial review where they affect a prison officer on the application of that officer.'

39   In the last lines of this passage is a reference to the case of *R v Secretary of State for the Home Department ex parte Benwell* [1985] IRLR 6, a decision of Hodgson J. It is clear that Woolf LJ regards this as an example of his category 2. *Ex parte Benwell* is an important decision, because if the reasoning is correct it is indistinguishable from the present case. That was a case where a prison officer had been dismissed on the decision of the Home Secretary for breach of the Code of Discipline. The Code was drawn up by the Home Secretary under the provisions of s.47(1) of the Prison Act 1953 and the Prison Rules made under it. But it is immaterial that the source of the power is statutory as opposed to the prerogative: *R v Secretary of State for Foreign and Commonwealth Affairs ex parte Council of*

Civil Service Unions [1985] IRLR 28. It is therefore a case of internal disciplinary proceedings, albeit the matter went at one stage on appeal to the CSAB. The complaint was against the Home Secretary; but it makes no difference whether the political head of the department is involved or his officials. *Benwell's case* raised no general question of policy or interpretation of the law applicable to prison officers generally; it related solely to the propriety of the proceedings and decision in his case. Mr Laws submits that it was wrongly decided, although the decision may be supportable on the grounds stated by Hodgson J at p.13, 49 where he said:

> 'In this case, however, it is my opinion that in making a disciplinary award of dismissal, the Home Office (to use a comprehensive term to include the department and the Secretary of State so distinguished by the respondent itself in this case) was performing the duties imposed upon it as part of the statutory terms under which it exercises its power.'

40 It should be noted that it was contended by the applicant in *ex parte Benwell* that the relationship was not a contractual one. It is not apparent that for the Crown it was contended otherwise. Mr Tabachnik further relies on the decision of the Court of Appeal in *R v Secretary of State for the Home Department ex parte Attard* [1990] WLR 641. That again was a prison officer's case. There was no argument that judicial review was not the appropriate remedy. But the question in that case turned on the interrelationship between the Home Office staff handbook which was intended to be applicable to all non-industrial Home Office staff, and the Code of Discipline for Prison Officers. Mr Laws accepts that whether or not there was a contract of service between the applicant and the Crown (a point which was not argued) this was an issue of public law justiciable by judicial review just as the question whether the employees at GCHQ should have the right to be a member of a trade union or the legitimate expectation of consultation before such right was withdrawn was an appropriate issue for public law in the *CCSU* case.

41 Mr Tabachnik's argument is undoubtedly a formidable one, especially since *Benwell's* case appears to have been endorsed by the majority of the Court of Appeal in *McLaren's* case.

42 Nevertheless, Mr Laws confronts it. He submits, cor-
10000 rectly in our judgment, that the mere fact that someone has
no private law remedy does not mean that they have a
public law one. The crucial element is whether the dispute
has a sufficient public law element. He submits that this
was merely an exercise of internal discipline, such as might
occur in the case of any large employer and it has no wider
implication in public law (which distinguishes the case
from *Attard's* case and the *CSSU* case). Even in cases
where there is a contract of employment involving a public
body or the Crown, the nature of the issue may be such that
it affects many others or the wider public, such as for
example questions of policy or interpretation of legal powers which will be justiciable in judicial review, subject only
to the discretion to refuse it where an equally effective
remedy lies in private law. This is the third category
referred to in Woolf LJ's judgment in *McLaren*. Moreover,
he submits that even if there is no contract, the submission
to the disciplinary proceedings is in truth a consensual one,
since it arises out of the relationship of a master and
servant, employer and employee and is part of the terms
and conditions accepted by the applicant when he entered
the Crown's service.

43 It is no answer to this submission to say that even where
an applicant makes application to a tribunal (whether set
up under the prerogative as in the case of the Criminal
Injuries Compensation Board or the CSAB or more usually
under statutory power) for redress of some kind, the applicant is consenting to the jurisdiction of the tribunal. There
is an essential difference between the acceptance as part of
the terms of appointment of the internal disciplinary code
of the employer on the one hand and an ad hoc submission
to the tribunal such as the CICB whose jurisdiction arises
only by virtue of the application made to it.

44 Here the submission by the applicant to the disciplinary
powers of the Permanent Secretary or his officials arises
out of the terms of appointment, albeit on this hypothesis
the terms are not intended to have legally enforceable
consequences. There are no cases, submits Mr Laws, except
perhaps *Benwell*, where the sole source of power is the very
agreement that the parties have made though the existence of an agreement may be a necessary condition without
which public law issues do not arise. For example, an

agreement between parties as to how noxious waste is to be disposed, which is a private law contract, may call into play the Minister's power to control the disposal of waste; the exercise of these powers may be subject to judicial review.

45

10000

In my judgment, Mr Law's[2] submissions are compelling. The internal disciplinary proceedings of the Lord Chancel-lor's Department are quite different from those of a tribunal, such as the CSAB, set up under prerogative or statutory power. They are of a domestic nature and on the hypothesis that there is no intention to create legal relations, which we do not accept, they are informal. The decision in *ex parte Bruce* that the CSAB was subject to judicial review, save only that in the exercise of the Court's discretion it was not appropriate to grant it because there was an alternative and more effective remedy from the Industrial Tribunal, was, if I may respectfully say so, clearly correct. And that as May LJ said at p.660 at C to D was so, even if there was a contract of employment.

46

For this reason also we would hold that the decisions impugned do not have a sufficient element of public law for them to be subject of judicial review. [3]

---

2 For the contribution to this Volume I: *Government Ethics* by John Laws (now the Honourable Mr Justice Laws), see pp. 303-07.

3 The above case and its headnote have been reproduced with kind permission of the Industrial Relations Services, Eclipse Group, London, N5, tp reprint from *Industrial Relations Law Reports* [1991] p. 343.

4

Judicial Review and Civil Servants: Contracts of Employment Declared to Exist

by Sandra Fredman and Gillian Morris

Analysis

Recent developments in judicial review have given renewed inpetus to the debate as to whether civil servants have contracts of employment. The leading case of *R. v. East Berkshire Area Health Authority, ex parte Walsh* [1] held that a claim which arises from a contract of employment will not usually have sufficient public law content to warrant judicial review. This means that the availability of judicial review to civil servants largely depends upon whether or not they have contracts. The Crown has taken differing stances on this issue according to the nature of the plaintiff's action. [2] In *Bruce*, [3] the Divisional Court held that civil servants did not have contracts because there was no intention to create legal relations, an essential ingredient of contract. By contrast, in the latest case on this issue, *R. v. Lord Chancellor's Department, ex parte Nangle*, [4] the Divisional Court held that the requisite intention does exist, despite a statement in the Civil Service Pay and Conditions Code which indicates the contrary. [5] In other words, civil servants do, after all, have contracts of employment. If *Nangle* is correct, the door will be shut on judicial review of decisions relating to most aspects of civil servants' employment. [6]

The applicant in *Nangle*, an executive officer in the Lord Chancellor's Department, was subjected to disciplinary procedures in connection with allegations that he had assaulted and sexually harassed a young woman in his

---

1 [1985] Q. B. 152.

2 Contrast *McLaren v. Home Office* [1990] I. C. R. 824 and *R. v. Civil Service Appeal Board, ex parte Bruce, infra,* n. 3: for other examples, see S. Fredman and G. Morris 'Civil Servants: A Contract of Employment?' [1988] P. L. 58.

3 *R. v. Civil Service Appeal Board, ex parte Bruce* [1988] I. C. R. 649 (upheld on different grounds: [1989] I. C. R. 171).

4 [1991] I. R. L. R. 343.

5 Para. 14. See also *Editor's* Note in this Volume, p. 440.

6 Some aspects remain subject to review: see *e.g. C. C. S. U. v. Minister for the Civil Service* [1985] A. C. 374; *ex parte Bruce* (*supra*, n. 3); *R. v. Civil Service Appeal Board, ex parte Cunningham* [1991] I. R. L. R. 297 (C. A.).

Department. After exhausting the internal procedures, which included an oral hearing and an appeal to the Permanent Secretary, the applicant applied for judicial review of the relevant decisions, on the ground of breach of natural justice. The Crown argued that the application of disciplinary procedures to a Crown servant was not a matter of public law appropriate for determination by way of judicial review.

It was accepted by the applicant, on the basis of *ex parte Walsh*, [7] that if he was employed under a contract of employment, he had no remedy in public law. The main question, therefore, was whether he was so employed. Stuart-Smith L.J. giving the judgment for the court, noted that two of the necessary ingredients of contract, namely offer and acceptance, and consideration, were clearly present. Accepting that there was no constitutional bar to civil servants having contracts of employment, [8] and that a contract was not inconsistent with the doctrine of dismissal at will, [9] he held that the central question was whether there was an intention to enter legal relations. The major obstacle to such an intention was the statement in paragraph 14 of the Civil Service Pay and Conditions Code that 'a civil servant does not have a contract of employment enforceable in the courts'. In *Bruce*, [10] this factor was relied upon as evidence of an absence of intention. Stuart-Smith L.J., however, considered that the question whether there was an intention to create legal relations was to be ascertained objectively; it was quite possible for a party to believe mistakenly that he or she was not contractually bound. Where the documents showed that the parties had entered into a relationship involving mutual rights and obligations, then there would be a strong presumption that the parties intended to create legal relations, especially in a business context. [11] In the present case, Stuart-Smith L.J., believed that it was 'plain beyond argument' that the parties did so intend, and the purpose of paragraph 14 of the Code was merely to describe a state of affairs as it was (wrongly) believed to be. Thus, he refused to follow *Bruce* and held that there was a contract of employment. The result was there was no public law issue. If the applicant could establish breach of contract by failure to comply with the disciplinary code, he could sue for damages.

The emphasis on intention to create legal relations as a criterion for determining civil servants' status is relatively new, having surfaced for the first time in *Bruce*. The enunciation of this principle in *Nangle* exemplifies the argument that it is nothing more than a judicial construct, enabling the courts to demarcate relationships which they consider to be legally enforce-

---

7 *Supra*, n. 1.

8 *Kodeeswaran v. Att.-Gen. of Ceylon* [1970] A. C. 1111; *ex parte Bruce, supra*. n. 3.

9 *Reilly v. R.* [1934] A. C. 176. 180.

10 [1988] I. C. R. 649 (D. C.)

11 *Edwards v. Skyways Ltd.* [1964] 1 W. L. R. 349.

able from those which they prefer to exclude from the realms of judicial activity. Family relationships, [12] spiritual appointments [13] and collective agreements [14] have for various policy reasons been considered to be inappropriate for judicial enforcement. The converse is true for ordinary commercial relationships, where the presumption in favour of enforceability is strong enough to overcome all but the most explicit statements. [15] In *Nangle*, far from there being an agreed intention to be bound, the parties were genuinely unsure of the status of their agreement, and were awaiting a definitive statement from the courts. Indeed, before *Bruce*, the Cabinet Office, acting on legal advice, were engaged in drafting new pages for the Code stating that civil servants were employed under contracts. However, the draft was shelved following the decision in *Bruce*, the hope being that the Court of Appeal would finally clarify the matter. That court unfortunately declined to do so, deciding the case on a different point. [16]

Stuart-Smith L.J. was therefore correct in stating that the relevant paragraph in the Code was merely an expression of what the government believed to be the case. However, it is difficult to see how he could go on to conclude that, despite the mistaken belief that there was no contract, it was 'plain beyond argument that the parties intended to create legal relations'. That notion that intention can somehow be objective sheds little further light on this conclusion. It would have been more accurate to acknowledge that the court is responsible for characterising a relationship as legally binding or not, as the case may be. Such an acknowledgement would have enabled the court to discuss why a relationship should give rise to legal consequences, rather than obscuring the issue behind a notional intention.

It is striking too that, as in previous cases, [17] the parties' stance on the contractual issue was entirely pragmatic and expedient: the applicant arguing against the existence of a contract, and the Crown maintaining the opposite in order to bar judicial review. This reverses the stances taken in the recent case of *McLaren v. Home Office*, [18] an application under the ordinary writ procedure, where the Crown based its case of the absence of contract whereas the applicant claimed the converse. [19] This shows that the material used for

---

12 *Balfour v. Balfour* [1919] 2 K. B. 571.

13 *Davies v. Presbyterian Church of Wales* [1986] 1 All E. R. 705 (H. L.).

14 *Ford Motor Co. Ltd. v. A. U. E. W.* [1969] 2 Q. B. 303.

15 *Edwards v. Skyways Ltd. (supra.* n. 11): *Rose and Frank Co. v. Crompton Brothers* [1925] A. C. 445.

16 *R. v. C. S. A. B., ex parte Bruce* [1989] I. C. R. 171 (C. A.).

17 *Supra.* n. 2.

18 *Supra.* n. 1.

19 For other examples, see Fredman and Morris, *supra.* n. 2 It is difficult to see how such conflicting claims by the Crown could be defended by the Attorney-General in the House of Commons.

practical purposes is not the contractual status of civil servants, but the implications of this for the disinction between private and public law. In certain circumstances, judicial review is a preferable route for an aggrieved employee; in others, contract holds out greater advantages. [20] For example, terms and conditions which have contractual effect can only be varied with the consent of the employee. In public law, by contrast, the stability of conditions of employment is only protected by the doctrine of legitimate expectation, which may be defeated by national security or public policy arguments. [21] Thus in *McLaren v. Home Office*, [22] a claim for breach of contract was more useful to the applicant prison officer than one in public law, both because of the longer time limit for claims by writ, and because his claim concerned his substantive terms and conditions of employment. On the other hand, procedural justice plays a more clear-cut role in public law than under contract. The courts have been reluctant to imply natural justice into a contract of employment, [23] and will certainly not do so to improve on a procedure specified in a contract. At public law, natural justice is more readily implied, giving rise in some cases to more extensive rights than those available in private law. [24] In *Nangle*, it appears that the formal procedures had been properly followed, so that a claim for breach of contract (if one existed) would not have been sustainable. At public law, however, it may have been arguable that these procedures were in breach of natural justice. The different remedies available in public and private law may also influence an applicant's choice of procedure. Although the increased readiness of the courts to grant injunctions in respect of private law contracts has brought contract closer into line with public law remedies such as certiorari, there remain significant limitations on injunctive relief. [25]

In this light, the debate about the existence or absence of a contract for

---

20 See also Fredman and Morris 'Public or Private? State Employees and Judicial Review' (1991) 107 L. Q. R. 298, 299-302; and B. A. Walsh 'Judicial Review of Dismissal from Employment: Coherence or Confusion?' [1989] P. L. 131.

21 The *C. C. S. U.* case (*supra.* n. 6); *Hughes v. Department of Health and Social Security* [1985] A. C. 776.

22 *Supra.* n. 2.

23 *Ridge v. Baldwin* [1964] A. C. 40. This attitude is relaxing somewhat: see *Malloch v. Aberdeen Corporation* [1971] 1 W. L. R. 1578; *Stevenson* v. *United Road Transport Union* [1977] I. C. R. 893; and it has been suggested that the boundaries should be further extended: see Woolf L.J. in *McLaren v. Home Office* and *R. v. Derbyshire County Council, ex parte Noble* [1990] I. C. R. 808 (C. A.).

24 For example, the right to consultation in the *C. C. S. U.* case (*supra.* n. 6.).

25 For example, *Jones v. Lee* [1980] I. C. R. 310; *Irani v. Southampton Health Authority* [1985] I. C. R. 590; *Powell v. Brent Council* [1988] I. C. R. 176; *Hughes v. London Borough of Southwark* [1988] I. R. L. R. 5. On limitations, see *Dietman* v. *Brent Council* [1988] I. C. R. 842; Fredman and Morris *The State as Employer* (1989), pp. 58-60.

civil servants, as with other public service groups, [26] seem tangential to the real issue: whether the action properly belongs in public or in private law. Cases subsequent to *Walsh* have attempted to draw the line in a more subtle and complex way. In particular, Woolf L.J. in *McLaren v. Home Office* [27] and *R. v. Derbyshire County Council, ex parte Noble* [28] has stated that the distinction between public and private law depends upon the subject-matter rather than on contract. In *Nangle*, a similar line of reasoning was followed in the alternative argument. In case he was wrong on the contractual question, Stuart-Smith L.J. went on to consider the situation if there was no contract. In such circumstances, he argued, there was still an insufficient public law element to justify judicial review: the absence of a private law remedy does not guarantee that the gap will be filled by public law. He stressed that in the present case, the disciplinary proceedings were internal, arose directly out of the employment relationship, and could arise in the same form in the private sector. By contrast, the Civil Service Appeal Board was an independent body, set up under the prerogative, whose decision was not that of the employer, and with whom the applicant had no direct relationship. The latter was amenable to judicial review, as decided in *Bruce*,[29] but not the former. The distinction, therefore, seems to depend on whether or not the particular issue, here disciplinary proceedings, flows directly from the employment relationship, and could occur in the same form in the private sector.

While such a formulation is a welcome departure from the contractual test, it too has its problems. In relation to civil servants, the Civil Service Appeal Board is susceptible to review. In practical terms, it is difficult to see why a civil servant who appeals to the Board (which has jurisdiction only in cases of dismissal or compulsory premature retirement) should have superior remedies to one who is disciplined solely according to internal procedures, [30] especially in the context of dismissal at will. On a more principled level, Stuart-Smith L.J.'s distinction depends on the assumption that elements of the employment relationship which occur in the same form in the private sector should be litigated in private law only. However, as we have argued elsewhere, [31] the fundamental problem is the rigid delineation in *O'Reilly v.*

---

26 Fredman and Morris, *supra.* n. 25. Chap. 3.

27 *Supra.* n. 2.

28 *Supra.* n. 23.

29 *Supra.* n. 3. *R. v. C. S. A. B., ex parte Cunningham* (*supra.* n. 6.)

30 Since Nangle was given a disciplinary penalty short of dismissal, he had no right of appeal to the C.S.A.B. A similar point could be made in respect of prison officers: judicial review is available for discipline under the Prison Rules but not otherwise (contrast *R. v. Secretary of State for the Home Department, ex parte Attard. The Times,* March 14, 1990; and *McLaren v. Home Office, supra.* n. 2.).

31 Fredman and Morris, *supra.* n. 20.

Mackman [32] and *Walsh* [33] between private and public law, with their conse-quences for the parties' procedural choices. The relationship between the State as employer and its employees gives rise to issues in both public and private law, which are too closely connected to permit demarcation in any logical manner.

As far as the principle of a contract of employment for civil servants is concerned, there seems to be no intrinsic objection to this. [34] However, if the decision in *Nangle* is to become established law, the doctrine of dismissal at will should be abolished. [35] This doctrine, which has been found not to be inconsistent with a contract [36] undermines even the limited remedies avail-able under contract for ordinary employees, giving the Crown the right, for example, to alter terms and conditions unilaterally. The doctrine has long become anachronistic. In practice, civil servants enjoy *de facto* security of tenure, they are protected in most cases under the laws against unfair dis-missal, and frequently as regards a decision affecting a group of civil servants, there will be a legitimate expectation of consultation, mitigating the full force of dismissal at will. The arguments for the removal of the principle of dismissal at will are strengthened by the fact that possession of a contract brings disadvantages for civil servants: it exposes them to the possibility of suits for breach of confidence, strengthening the hand of the Crown in cases such as *Spycatcher*, and, under the present law, removes the protection of judi-cial review. Confirmation of a contract for civil servants without the aboli-tion of dismissal at will would subject them to additional obligations without endowing them with extra rights. [37]

[*Editor:* Sandra Fredman is a Fellow in Law at Exeter College, Oxford and Gillian Morris is Reader in Law at Brunel University. This article is reprin-ted, with kind permission of the authors, from *Public Law* [1991] 485-490. Please note that the *Civil Service Pay and Conditions of Service Code,* referred to in this article on page 436, has been superseded by the *Civil Service Manage-ment Code.* For details of the new *Code,* see this Volume of *Government Ethics,* pp. 441-67.]

---

32 [1983] 2 A. C. 237.

33 *Supra.* n. 1.

34 For policy arguments to the contrary, see Fredman and Morris, *supra.* n. 2 at p. 61.

35 And see Fredman and Morris, *supra.* n. 25. pp. 68-71.

36 *Reilly* v. *R., supra.* n. 9 at p. 180; *Kodeeswaran, supra.* n. 8 at p. 1123.

37 This analysis by Fredman and Morris was published first in [1991] *Public Law* pp. 485-490.

5

United Kingdom Civil Service Management Code [1] – Personnel Management Volume:

4. Conduct and Discipline

Conduct

4.1 General Principles and Rules

4.1.1 Civil servants are servants of the Crown and owe a duty of loyal service to the Crown as their employer. Since constitutionally the Crown acts on the advice of Ministers who are answerable for their departments and agencies in Parliament, that duty is for all practical purposes owed to the Government of the day. A fuller account of the constitutional position is given in the Armstrong Memorandum. [2]

Authority

4.1.2 The Minister for the Civil Service is responsible for the central framework, outlined in Sections 4.2 to 4.4, which governs the conduct of civil servants. Departments and agencies are responsible for defining the standards of conduct they require of their staff and for ensuring that these fully reflect the central framework.

Principles

4.1.3 The central framework derives from the need for civil servants to be, and to be seen to be, honest and impartial in the exercise of their duties. They must not allow their judgement or integrity to be compromised in fact or by reasonable implication. In particular:

    a.   civil servants must not misuse information which they acquire in the course of their official duties or disclose information which is held in confidence within government;

---

1 As issued by the United Kingdom Civil Service, February 1993 (Issue 1). Copyright HMSO. In addition to Section 4 on 'Conduct and Discipline' reprinted here, the other Sections 1-3 of the Civil Service Management Code: Personnel Management Volume cover matters: 1. Recruitment; 2. Appointments and Secondments; 3. Career Management; 5. Health and Safety; 6. Equal Opportunities; 7. Leaving the Service; and 8. Early Retirement

2 The Armstrong Memorandum is reprinted as Note 1 to the Chapter by Mr Hayden Phillips in this Volume, pp. 58-62. The Memorandum normally forms Annex A to the *Civil Service Management Code – Personnel Management Volume: 4, Conduct and Discipline.*

441

b. civil servants must not take part in any political or public activity which compromises, or might be seen to compromise, their impartial service to the Government of the day or any future Government; and

c. civil servants must not make use of their official position to further their private interests, or receive gifts, hospitality or benefits of any kind from a third party which might be seen to compromise their personal judgement or integrity.

4.1.4 The central framework does not seek to prescribe a comprehensive code of conduct. It does not deal, for example, with such issues as isolated neglect of duty, failure to obey a reasonable instruction or other forms of misconduct which may properly be dealt with under disciplinary arrangements (see paragraph 4.5.5).

Rules

4.1.5 Departments and agencies must define the standards of conduct they require of their staff. They must:

a. make clear to staff their duties and obligations and the penalties they may incur if they fall short of them;

b. comply with the rules in Sections 4.2 to 4.4;

c. ensure that the rules they lay down for their staff fully reflect the standards of conduct described in Sections 4.2 to 4.4 and incorporate any additional rules necessary to reflect local needs and circumstances.

4.1.6 In drawing up, and in interpreting, their own standards of conduct, departments and agencies must pay full regard to the need for staff to conform, and to be seen to conform, to the principles in paragraph 4.1.3.

4.2 Confidentiality and Official Information
Rules

4.2.1 Departments and agencies must remind staff on appointment, retirement or resignation that they are bound by the provisions of the criminal law, including the Official Secrets Acts, which protect certain categories of official information, and by their duty of confidentiality owed to the Crown as their former employer.

Standards of conduct to be reflected in local staff regulations

4.2.2 Civil servants are expected to be prepared to make available official information which is not held in confidence within Government, in accordance with Government policy and departmental or agency instructions. They must not, without relevant authorisation, disclose official information which has been communicated in confidence within Government or received in confidence from others.

4.2.3 Civil servants must continue to observe this duty of confidentiality after they have left Crown employment.

4.2.4 Civil servants must not take part in any activities or make any public statement which might involve the disclosure of official information or draw upon experience gained in their official capacity without the prior approval of their department or agency. They must clear in advance material for publication, broadcasts or other public discussion which draws on official information or experience.

4.2.5 Civil servants must not publish or broadcast personal memoirs reflecting their experience in Government, or enter into commitments to do so, whilst in Crown employment. The permission of the Head of their Department and the Head of the Home Civil Service must be sought before entering into commitments to publish such memoirs after leaving the service.

4.2.6 Civil servants must not seek to frustrate the policies or decisions of Ministers by the use or disclosure outside the Government of any information to which they have had access as civil servants.

4.2.7 Civil servants must not take part in their official capacities in surveys or research projects, even unattributably, if they deal with attitudes or opinions on political matters or matters of policy.

4.2.8 Civil servants who are elected national, departmental or branch representatives or officers of a recognised trade union need not seek permission before publicising union views on an official matter which, because it directly affects the conditions of service of members of the union as employees, is of legitimate concern to their members, unless their official duties are directly concerned with the matter in question. In all other circumstances they must conform to the standards set out above.

Crown copyright

4.2.9 Under the Copyright, Designs and Patents Act 1988 copyright in any works made by civil servants in the course of their employment is Crown copyright. Civil servants must obtain prior permission from their Head of

Department or Agency Chief Executive before entering into any arrangements regarding the publication of any articles or materials which they have produced as part of their official duties. The Head of Department or Agency Chief Executive will, except in those cases specified in paragraph 4.2.10, need to refer the matter to HMSO to consider the copyright implications.

4.2.10 In the case of papers submitted for publication in learned journals or in the proceedings of conferences or seminars, or where departments or agencies have been granted specific delegated authority by HMSO, they may deal direct with the matter without recourse to HMSO provided that:

a. they ensure that the source is adequately acknowledged; and

b. the copyright is not assigned to the publisher.

4.2.11 If a work is created by a civil servant entirely in his or her own time and is clearly unconnected with his/her official duties, then Crown copyright is not an issue. If the civil servant independently writes a book relating to his/her official duties, the situation is more complex. In this context, the department or agency would need to ascertain:

a. whether the author produced all or part of the work during official time;

b. whether the work is based on Crown copyright sources; and

c. if there are any security implications.

4.2.12 If the civil servant writes a book in his or her own time, unrelated to his/her official duties, but wishes to incorporate extracts of Crown copyright material within the work, permission to reproduce that material must be sought, either from HMSO or from the sponsoring department if the appropriate delegation of authority exists.

Payment to the author

4.2.13 If the work is to be published:

a. by HMSO. The department or agency may agree a payment with the author, with the consent of the Cabinet Office (OPSS);

b. by an outside publisher. All such cases should be dealt with by HMSO, who will take into account the department's or agency's views, unless exceptional delegation of authority has been granted to the department or agency to cover the authorisation of full publishing agreements.

4.2.14 If the work is Crown copyright in its entirety (i.e. has been prepared by a civil servant in the course of his or her duties, or has been commissioned by an outside contractor and copyright has been formally assigned to the Crown), the author will not be entitled to any additional remuneration from sales of the publication. This applies equally whether the work is published officially or by an outside publisher under licence from the Controller of HMSO.

4.2.15 Departments and agencies should be aware that HMSO produce guidance material on Crown copyright which can be obtained from HMSO's Copyright Section.

4.3 Standards of Propriety

Rules

4.3.1 Departments and agencies must not, unless the civil servant has fully disclosed the measure of his/her interest in the contract and senior management has given permission, let contracts to:

a. any civil servant in the department or agency;

b. to any partnership of which a civil servant in the department or agency is a member; or

c. to any company where a civil servant in the department or agency is a director (except as a nominee of the department or agency).

To enforce this rule, departments and agencies must require their staff to report relevant business interests.

4.3.2 Departments and agencies must ensure that civil servants who are bankrupt or insolvent are not employed on duties which might permit the misappropriation of public funds.

4.3.3 Departments and agencies must not sell surplus Government property to civil servants who have been able to get special knowledge about the condition of the goods because of their official duties; or have been officially associated with the disposal arrangements; or at a discount that would not be available to a member of the public.

4.3.4 Departments and agencies must require staff to seek permission before accepting any outside employment which might affect their work either directly or indirectly and must make appropriate arrangements, which reflect the Business Appointments Rules (Annex A) and any local needs, for the handling of such requests.

4.3.5 Departments and agencies must inform staff, taking into account the principle in paragraph 4.1.3(c), of the circumstances in which they need to report offers of gifts, hospitality, awards, decorations and other benefits and of the circumstances in which they need to seek permission before accepting them. In drawing up such rules departments and agencies must draw the attention of staff to the provisions of the Prevention of Corruption Acts 1906 and 1916.

4.3.6 Departments and agencies must consult the Foreign and Commonwealth Office if a civil servant is offered a decoration or medal by a foreign government.

Standards of conduct to be reflected in local staff regulations

4.3.7 Civil servants must familiarise themselves with, and as appropriate abide by, the rules on the acceptance of outside appointments by Crown servants (Annex A).

4.3.8 Civil servants may freely invest in shareholdings unless the nature of their work is such as to require constraints on this. They must not be involved in taking any decision which could affect the value of their private investments, or the value of those on which they give advice to others; or use information acquired in the course of their work to advance their private financial interests or those of others.

4.3.9 Civil servants must therefore declare to their department or agency any business interests or shareholdings (including directorships) which they or members of their immediate family (spouse, including partner where relevant, and children) hold, to the extent which they are aware of them, which they would be able to further as a result of their official position. They must comply with any subsequent instructions from their department or agency regarding the retention, disposal or management of such interests.

4.3.10 Civil servants who become bankrupt or insolvent must report the fact to their department or agency. Civil servants must let their department or agency know if they are arrested and refused bail, or if they are convicted of any criminal offence. This does not apply to a traffic offence unless an official car was involved, or the penalty included imprisonment or disqualification from driving.

4.3 Annex A: Rules on the Acceptance of Outside Appointments by Crown Servants

Introduction

1. The Business Appointments Rules have been drawn up to provide for the independent scrutiny of business appointments which individuals propose to take up in the first two years after they leave the service. The aim of this scrutiny is to protect individuals, and government more generally, from claims that, in accepting particular appointments, they are breaching the trust that has been placed in them in the course of their official duties.

2. While it is in the public interest that people with experience of public administration should be able to move into business or other bodies and that such movement should not be frustrated by unjustified public concern over a particular appointment, it is also important that when a Crown servant accepts a particular outside appointment that there should be no cause for any suspicion of impropriety. Most applications submitted under the rules are approved without condition. In some cases, however, approval may be made conditional upon a waiting period or other conditions. Each case, and each appointment, is considered on its merits.

3. Against this background, the aim of the rules is:

   a. to avoid any suspicion, no matter how unjustified, that the advice and decisions of a serving officer might be influenced by the hope or expectation of future employment with a particular firm or organisation; or

   b. to avoid the risk that a particular firm might gain an improper advantage over its competitors by employing someone who, in the course of their official duties, has had access to technical or other information which those competitors might legitimately regard as their own trade secrets or to information relating to proposed developments in Government policy which may affect that firm or its competitors.

4. For the most senior grades, the Prime Minister decides whether conditions should be applied to business appointments and, if so, wht they should be. In view of their access to policy issues at the highest levels, Grades 1 and 1A and their equivalents are required to wait a minimum of three months after leaving the Service before they take up business appointments. The Prime Minister is advised by the Advisory Committee on Business Appointments, an independent committee appointed by the Prime Minister comprising people with experience of the relationships between the Civil Service and the private sector.

5. Applications at Grade 3 level or its equivalent are considered by the Head

of the Home Civil Service. Other applications are considered either by departments alone or by departments in consultation with the Cabinet Office (OPSS). A sample of applications from officers at Grade 3 level and below are reviewed by the Advisory Committee to provide an assurance that the rules are being applied consistently and effectively.

6. It is important to recognise that the imposition of conditions does not imply anything improper in your relationship with the prospective employer. Rather, it is an indication that an immediate move from Crown service to the employer, or one without conditions, might be open to criticism or misinterpretation. Experience has shown that employers generally are content to accept such constraints as being reasonable in an open society which places a high premium on the integrity and impartiality of its civil and military services. The aim of the application of the rules is to maintain public trust in those services and in the people who work within them.

Who must apply?

7. Civil servants must obtain Government approval before taking any form of full, part-time or fee-paid employment:

   a. in the United Kingdom, or overseas in a public or private company or in the service of a foreign government or its agencies;

   b. within two years of leaving Crown employment; and in the following circumstances:

   - if they are Grade 3 or above; or

   - if they have had any official dealings with their prospective employer during the last two years of Crown employment; or

   - if they have had official dealings of a continued or repeated nature with their prospective employer at any time during their period of Crown employment; or

   - if they have had access to commercially sensitive information of competitors of their prospective employer in the course of their official duties; or

   - if, during the last two years of Crown employment their official duties have involved advice or decisions benefitting that prospective employer, for which the offer of employment could be interpreted as reward, or have involved developing policy, knowledge of which might be of benefit to the prospective employer; or

> – if they are to be employed on a consultancy basis – either for a firm of consultants or as an independent or self-employed consultant – and they have had any dealings of a commercial nature with outside bodies or organisations in their last two years of Crown employment.

8. The rules do not apply to:

a. unpaid appointments in non-commercial organisations; or

b. appointments in the gift of Ministers.

9. Approval is required for:

a. the initial appointment; and

b. any further appointment within two years of leaving Crown employment.

10. Staff on secondment from the Civil Service to the private sector are subject to the rules in the same way as other members of the Civil Service.

11. Staff on secondment to the Civil Service from the private sector are also subject to the rules in the same way as civil servants unless they return to their seconding company at the end of their secondment and remain with that company for two years.

12. Equivalent rules apply to members of the Armed Services and the Diplomatic Service.

13. The rules do not apply to Special Advisers.

Reporting offers of employment

14. Staff considering any approach from an outside employer offering employment for which apporval would be required under these rules – or which seems likely to lead to such an offer – must report the approach as follows:

> – Grade 1 (or equivalent): report to the Minister in charge of the Departments;
>
> Grade 3 (or equivalent) and above: report to the Head of the Department;
>
> staff below Grade 3 (or equivalent): report to a senior member of staff at least two grades higher.

15. Staff in sections concerned with procurement or contract work should report any such approach, particularly where it emanates from an outside employer with whom they or their staff have had official dealings, *whether or not* they are considering taking it up.

Applications

16. Staff who need to get approval before taking up an outside appointment must apply to their department (or former department) using the standard form available from the department.

Approval of applications

17. Applications under these rules will be granted either:

    a. unconditional approval; or

    b. approval subject to conditions. These may apply for up to two years, the duration depending on the circumstances of the case. They may include:

        – a waiting period, effective from the final date in Crown employment before taking up the appointment;

        – an absolute or qualified ban on involvement of the applicant in dealings between the prospective employer and the Government;

        – a ban on involvement by the applicant in dealings between the prospective employer and a named competitor (or competitors) of that employer;

        – in the case of consultancies, a requirement to seek official approval before accepting commissions of a particular nature or from named employers

18. All applications from grades 1 and 1A (or equivalents) which are referred to the Advisory Committee are subject to an automatic minimum waiting period of three months between leaving Crown employment and taking up an outside appointment, unless the applicants are in posts to which they have been appointed from outside the Civil Service on a limited period contract. Applicants in the latter category will not be required to serve the *automatic* waiting period, although approval of applications may be subject to waiting periods or other conditions in the same way as any other application.

19. In cases where it is proposed to impose a waiting period or other conditions, applicants should be given the opportunity of having an interview with an appropriate Departmental officer if they so choose.

Procedures for departments

Making staff aware of the rules

20. Departments must:

   a. draw the attention of staff to the existence of the rules on appointment. There is a paragraph about the rules in the schedule to the model letter of appointment which may be used for this purpose. Departments are advised to take special care to ensure that staff recruited from outside the Crown service either on secondment or on a limited period appointment are made aware of their position under the rules on appointment;

   b. include a copy of the rules in Departmental Staff Handbooks;

   c. issue regular reminders to staff about the rules and the circumstances in which they apply at all levels targeted on particular staffing areas as necessary;

   d. ask staff at Grade 3 level (or equivalent) and above to acknowledge in writing that they have seen and are conversant with the rules – and to provide a further, similar acknowledgement on retirement or resignation from the Crown Service or at the end of a period appointment;

   e. remind all staff of the rules:

   – on retirement

   – on resignation

   – at the end of a limited period appointment

(In the case of staff who resign or come to the end of a limited period appointment this should normally take the form of providing them with a copy of the rules and an application form. The OPSS model application form incorporates the relevant extracts from the rules for this purpose.)

21. Departments are advised:

   a. to take all opportunities provided by letters of resignation, exit interviews and requests for references to check whether an application under the rules is necessary; and

   b. to ensure that personnel and line managers of staff working in areas which involve contact of a commercial nature with outside organisations, particularly on procurement or contract work, are issued with regular reminders to monitor resignations by staff employed in those areas to ensure that applications are made where necessary.

Applications

22. Departments must ensure that application forms are completed for all requests for approval for outside appointments under the rules. For this purpose:

　　a.　the applicant must be asked to supply:

　　　　　－　full details of the proposed employment;

　　　　　－　details of any official dealings with a prospective employer or with any other company, including any competitors of the prospective employer; and

　　b.　departments must ensure that they seek the comments of a countersigning officer who can verify, as far as possible, the information supplied by the applicant.

23. Departments are strongly recommended to adopt the revised Cabinet Office (OPSS) model form for applicants.

Procedure for dealing with applications

24. The procedure for dealing with applications varies according to the grade of the applicant.

　　Grades 1, 1A and 2. All cases must be referred to the Head of the Home Civil Service.

The application may be approved without reference to the Advisory Committee if the Head of the Home Civil Service and the Departmental Minister agree that such reference would be inappropriate, for example where the appointment is to a non-commercial body, such as a university.

The Head of the Home Civil Service, on behalf of the Prime Minister, will refer all other cases to the Advisory Committee.

　　Heads of Departments below Grade 2 (or equivalent). All cases must be referred to the Head of the Home Civil Service.

　　Grade 3 (or equivalent). All applications must be referred to the Cabinet Office (OPSS), who will then consult the Head of the Home Civil Service.

　　Grades 4 to 7 (or equivalent). The Cabinet Office (OPSS) must be consulted unless:

　　　　－ the applicant has had no official dealings with the prospective employer and there appears to be no risk of criticism; or

　　　　－ the employment is with a non-commercial organisation.

SEO (or equivalent) and below. The procedure must follow that set out for Grades 4-7, except that Departments do not need to consult the Cabinet Office where:

– the applicant has had no official dealings with the prospective employer in the previous two years, or at most dealings of a casual nature; and

– there appears to be no risk of the disclosure of commercially sensitive information; or

– the appointment is with a non-commercial organisation.

25. Any application may be referred to the Advisory Committee if the Head of the Home Civil Service and the Departmental Minister so agree.

26. When referring cases to the Head of the Home Civil Service or to the Cabinet Office (OPSS) departments must submit:

a. a copy of a completed and countersigned application form;

b. a covering letter, giving their own assessment of the application, including the outcome of any consultations with competitors of the prospective employer, and their proposed or recommended course of action.

Approval of applications

27. Decisions on all applications, other than those referred to the Prime Minister through the Advisory Committee, rest with the Minister in charge of the Department. The Minister may, however, approve arrangements under which defined categories of cases may be dealt with at a specified level without reference to the Minister.

28. There may be occasions when a Minister decides that the national interest is the overriding consideration, regardless of the circumstances of the case. In all such cases, the normal procedures for dealing with applications must first be followed, including reference to the Advisory Committee where that is appropriate. A decision that the national interest should override other considerations may only be taken by the Minister in charge of the Department or, in the case of applications referred to the Advisory Committee, by the Prime Minister.

29. Departments must:

a. inform prospective employers of any conditions which have been attached to the approval of an appointment;

b. make a careful record of all decisions to approve appointments under the rules, noting in particular the grade of the applicant and any conditions that were applied;

c. submit quarterly statistical returns of applications dealt with under the rules to the Cabinet Office (OPSS) in the form requested.

Guidance for departments

30. The rules are designed primarily to counter any suspicion that an appointment might be a 'reward for past favours' granted by the applicant to the firm, or that a particular firm might gain an unfair advantage over its competitors by employing someone who, had access to what they might legitimately regard as their own 'trade secrets'.

31. An appointment might also be sensitive because of the employer's relationship with the department and the nature of any information which the applicant possesses about Government policy.

The employer and the applicant

32. In most cases problems will only occur if the applicant has had some degree of contact with the prospective employer, giving rise to criticism that the post is a 'reward for past favours'. Departments are asked to take the following into account:

a. how much of this was in the course of official duties;

b. how significant a degree of contact was involved;

c. the nature of the proposed employment;

d. the connections between the new job and the applicant's previous official duties.

33. In order to establish whether the applicant was able to exert any degree of influence over the outcome of contractual or other dealings with the prospective employers, departments are advised to establish:

a. whether the individual was acting as a member of a team taking sole or joint responsibility;

b. whether the employer benefited substantially from such dealings;

c. whether contact was direct;

d. whether it was indirect as indirect (i.e. through those for whom the applicant was responsible, whether or not they normally worked for him or her).

34. Departments are advised to take into account contacts in the course of official duty which have taken place:

    a. at any time in the two years before resignation or retirement;

    b. earlier, where the association was of a continued or repeated nature.

35. Departments are advised to consider in particular, whether the applicant has been:

    a. dealing with the receipt of tenders from the employer;

    b. dealing with the award of contracts to the employer;

    c. dealing with the administration or monitoring of contracts with the employer;

    d. giving professional or technical advice about such contracts whether before or after they were awarded;

    e. involved in dealings of an official but non-contractual nature with the employer (important in a field where the Government as a whole or the applicant's department has a financial, policy or other special interest).

The employer and the Government

36. The relationship of the prospective employer to the government may be a relevant factor in considering applications. Departments are advised to pay special attention to appointments where the employer:

    a. has a contractual relationship with the department;

    b. receives subsidies or their equivalent from the department;

    c. receives loans, guarantees or other forms of financial assistance from the department;

    d. is one in which the Government is a shareholder; or

    e. is one with which Services or departments or branches of Government are, as a matter of course, in a special relationship.

Overseas employers

37. The same considerations apply to foreign publicly-owned institutions or companies as to their UK counterparts. If the prospective employer is a foreign government, departments are advised to consider whether the applicant has information that would benefit that government to the detriment of HM Government or to allies. This can arise where the person:

a. has been giving advice to HM Government on policies affecting the foreign government; or

b. would have been in a position to gain special knowledge of HM Government's policies and intentions concerning the foreign Government.

Government policy or business

38. Many civil servants, members of the Armed Services and members of the Diplomatic Service deal with private interests on behalf of the Government. They have special knowledge of how the Government would be likely to react in particular circumstances. Departments are advised to consider whether the applicant could be, or could be thought to be, significantly helpful to the employer in dealing with matters where policy is developing or legislation is being prepared in a way which might disadvantage competitors of that employer.

39. This applies, less generally, to specific areas where:

a. there has been a negotiating relationship between the Department and the employer;

b. the applicant has been involved in policy discussions within the department leading to a decision of considerable benefit to the employer;

c. the applicant has been involved in policy discussions within the department, knowledge of which might give the employer an improper advantage over its competitors; or

d. where there is a risk of public criticism that the applicant might have scope to exploit contacts in his or her former department for commercial purposes.

40. In such cases, departments are asked to consider the implications of the applicant's joining the employer, and be guided accordingly.

The employer and competitor's trade secrets

41. Appointments might be criticised on the grounds that the applicant had access to information about his or her prospective employer's competitors which they could legitimately regard as 'trade secrets'. Concern on this score can arise whether or not the applicant has had previous dealings with the prospective employer. Departments are strongly advised to consult competitors as a matter of course preferably using a standard letter based on the Cabinet Office (OPSS) model letter, to see whether they have any objections to the appointment.

Consultancies

42. Individuals who are to be employed on a consultancy basis – either for a firm of consultants or as independent, self employed consultants, competing for commissions in the open market ('brass plate' consultancies) should be treated in the same way as other applicants under the rules. Extra care is needed, however, in dealing with such applications.

43. In the case of applicants wishing to set up a 'brass plate' consultancy the question of 'rewards for past favours' does not arise in the usual way. But departments will wish to keep in mind the need:

  a. to counter any suspicion of impropriety that might arise if such individuals were to be given lucrative contracts by employers with which they or their former department had dealings.

  b. to protect 'trade secrets' to which such individuals may have had access. There may be circumstances in which it would be undesirable for an independent consultant to offer services to a particular employer where he or she has had access to the trade secrets of a competitor of the employer. The fact that the competitor might also be free to use the same consultant, but did not choose to do so would not make the information any less sensitive to negate the potential advantage which could be gained by the other employer.

44. In approving applications to set up 'brass plate' consultancies departments will, therefore, need to consider carefully the application of conditions in cases where such considerations apply.

45. In the case of applicants wishing to take up a salaried appointment with a firm of consultants, the 'rewards for past favours' question will relate almost exclusively to the question of any previous dealings between the applicant and the firm he or she is seeking to join. Departments will, however, need to consider the 'trade secrets' questions both from the point of view of any competitors of the consultancy firm and then, more generally from the point of view of the service which the applicant will be offering on behalf of the consultant. As in the case of self employed consultants it may be necessary to impose conditions on the appointment to protect the 'trade secrets' of firms with which the applicant or the department had dealings.

46. Departments will also need to consider whether to apply conditions limiting contacts between applicants proposing to work as consultants and their former departments. This may be particularly relevant in the case of staff at senior grades, where there is a risk of public criticism that they could be exploiting contacts in their former departments for commercial purposes.

4.4 Political Activities

Rules

4.4.1 Departments and agencies must make clear to staff any restrictions on their taking part in political activities. Political activities that may be subject to restriction are defined as follows:

    a. at national level: holding, in a party political organisation, office which impinges wholly or mainly on party politics in the field of Parliament or the European Parliament; speaking in public on matters of national political controversy; expressing views on such matters in letters to the Press, or in books, articles or leaflets; being announced publicly as a candidate for Parliament or the European Parliament; and canvassing on behalf of a candidate for Parliament or the European Parliament or on behalf of a political party; and

    b. at local level: candidature for, or co-option to, local authorities; holding in a party political organisation, office impinging wholly or mainly on party politics in the local field; speaking in public on matters or local political controversy; expressing views on such matters in letters to the Press, or in books, articles or leaflets; being announced publicly as a candidate for Parliament or the European Parliament; and canvassing on behalf of candidates for election or local authorities or a local political organisation.

4.4.2 Departments and agencies must allow civil servants in industrial and non-office grades the freedom to take part in all political activities. These staff are known as the 'politically free' category. The groups of staff to be included in this category are subject to the approval of the Minister for the Civil Service (Servants of the Crown (Parliamentary, European Assembly and Northern Ireland Assembly Candidature) Order 1987).

4.4.3 Departments and agencies have discretion to permit other staff to take part in local or national political activities in accordance with paragraphs 4.4.9 and 4.4.10 below. In exercising their discretion, departments and agencies must pay due regard to the guidelines and principles in Annex A.

4.4.4 In giving permission to participate in political activities to groups of staff or individuals, departments and agencies must make clear to them that the permission can be withdrawn at any time and without prior notice if there is a change in relevant circumstances.

4.4.5 Departments and agencies must give civil servants who are refused permission to take part in political activities, or who have permission to do so withdrawn, a full explanation of the reasons for the decision, and inform them of their right of appeal to the Civil Service Appeal Board (see Section 7.7, Appeals).

4.4.6 Departments and agencies must reinstate civil servants in the politically free group who resign to stand for election (see paragraph 4.4.20 below) provided they apply within a week of declaration day if they are not elected. If they are elected, they must still be subsequently reinstated if:

a. they cease to be a Member after an absence from the Civil Service of not more than 5 years; and

b. they have had at least 10 years service before their election; and

c. they apply for reinstatement within 3 months of ceasing to be a Member.

If the first two of these conditions are not met reinstatement is at the discretion of the department or agency, but departments and agencies are encouraged to treat applications sympathetically.

4.4.7 Departments and agencies have discretion to reinstate civil servants who are not in the politically free category following resignation to stand for election to Parliament or the European Assembly. Discretion to reinstate should normally be exercised only where it is possible to post staff, at least initially, to non-sensitive areas.

4.4.8 Where a civil servant is reinstated, the period of the break will not count for pay or superannuation purposes. Salary will not be payable during the break.

Standards of conduct to be reflected in local staff regulations

4.4.9 Civil servants at Grade 7 level and above, plus Administration Trainees and Higher Executive Officers (D) (the 'politically restricted' category), must not take part in national political activities (paragraph 4.4.1a). They must seek permission to take part in local political activities (paragraph 4.1.b) and must comply with any conditions laid down by their department or agency.

4.4.10 Civil servants outside the 'politically restricted' category (paragraph 4.4.9) and the 'politically free' category (paragraph 4.4.2) must seek permission to take part in national or local political activities (paragraph 4.4.1) unless they are in a grade or area that has already been given permission to do so by means of a specific mandate from the department or agency. Where they already have permission under such a mandate, they must notify the department or agency of intended political activities prior to taking them up. They must comply with any conditions laid down by their department or agency.

4.4.11 Civil servants must not take part in any political activity when on duty, or in uniform, or on official premises.

4.4.12 Civil servants must not attend in their official capacity outside conferences or functions convened by or under the aegis of a party political organisation.

4.4.13 Civil servants not in the politically free category must not allow the expression of their personal political views to constitute so strong and so comprehensive a commitment to one political party as to inhibit or appear to inhibit loyal and effective service to Ministers of another party. They must take particular care to express comment with moderation, particularly about matters for which their own Ministers are responsible; to avoid comment altogether about matters of controversy affecting the responsibility of their own Ministers; and to avoid personal attacks.

4.4.14 They must also take every care to avoid any embarrassment to Ministers or to their department or agency which could result, inadvertently or not, from bringing themselves prominently to public notice, as civil servants, in party political controversy.

4.4.15 Civil servants who are not in the politically free category and who have not been given permission to engage in political activities must retain at all times a proper reticence in matters of political controversy so that their impartiality is beyond question.

4.4.16 Civil servants do not need permission to take part in activities organised by their trade unions. Elected trade union representatives may comment on Government policy when representing the legitimate interests of their members, but in doing so they must make it clear that they are expressing views as representatives of the union and not as civil servants.

4.4.17 Civil servants given permission to take part in local political activities must tell their department or agency if they are elected to a local authority.

4.4.18 Civil servants given permission to take part in political activities must give up those activities if they are moved to a post where permission cannot be granted.

4.4.19 Civil servants are disqualified from election to Parliament (House of Commons Disqualification Act 1975) and from election to the European Parliament (European Assembly Elections Act 1978). They must therefore resign from the Civil Service before standing for election in accordance with paragraphs 4.4.20 and 4.4.21.

4.4.20 Civil servants in the politically free group are not required to resign on adoption as a prospective candidate. But to prevent their election being held to be void they must submit their resignation before they give their consent to nomination in accordance with the Parliamentary Election Rules.

4.4.21 All other civil servants, including civil servants on secondment to outside organisations, must comply with the provisions of the Servants of the Crown (Parliamentary, European Assembly and Northern Ireland Assembly Candidature) Order 1987. They must not issue an address to electors or in any other manner publicly announce themselves or allow themselves to be publicly announced as candidates or prospective candidates for election to Parliament or the European Assembly; and they must resign from the Civil Service on their formal adoption as a Parliamentary candidate or prospective candidate in accordance with the procedures of the political party concerned. Civil servants not in the politically free group who are candidates for election must complete their last day of service before their adoption papers are completed.

4.4 Annex A: Guidelines and Principles on Participation in Political Activities

1. In exercising discretion over participation by civil servants in the political activities described in paragraph 4.4.3, departments and agencies must pay regard to the following principles:

   a. permission should normally only be refused where civil servants are employed in sensitive areas in which the impartiality of the Civil Service is most at risk. Permission may be granted to individuals or groups to undertake either only national or only local political activities;

   b. permission should normally be granted in all other circumstances, provided departments and agencies are satisfied that the civil servants concerned are aware of the need to observe the principles set out in paragraphs 4.4.10 and 4.4.11 and the other rules governing the conduct of civil servants, including those relating to the use of official information.

2. In applying these principles, departments and agencies should regard posts as being 'sensitive' if:

a. they are closely engaged in policy assistance to Ministers (or to non-departmental Crown bodies) such as tendering advice or executing immediate Ministerial directives;

b. they are in the private offices of Ministers or senior officials or in areas which are politically sensitive or subject to national security;

c. they require the postholder regularly to speak for the Government or their department or agency in dealings with commercial undertakings, pressure groups, local government, public authorities or any other bodies;

d. the postholder represents the Government in dealing with overseas governments; or

e. the postholder is involved in a significant amount of face to face contact with members of the public who may be expected to know of the postholder's political activities and makes, or may appear to make, decisions directly affecting them personally.

3. Departments and agencies are advised to apply as helpful a postings policy as possible to staff who wish to become or remain politically active, provided the staff concerned understand that this may have the effect of limiting their range of experience; and to identify blocks of posts in which staff may be granted advance permission to take part in the political activities described in paragraph 4.4.3.

4. Where a civil servant is adopted as a parliamentary candidate and is therefore required to resign, departments and agencies may, at their discretion, make an ex-gratia payment equivalent to the period of notice to be given to the individual if the adoption process does not reasonably allow for the individual to give full notice.

Discipline

4.5 Rules and Code of Practice

4.5.1 The Minister for the Civil Service is responsible for the central framework outlined in paragraphs 4.5.2 to 4.5.15.

4.5.2 Departments and agencies are responsible for their own disciplinary arrangements within the central framework set out below. They must:

a. ensure that staff are aware of the disciplinary procedures that will apply to them and of the circumstances in which they may be invoked; and

b. reflect the rules at paragraphs 4.5.9 to 4.5.15 and Annex A in their own disciplinary procedures.

The attention of departments and agencies is drawn to the following as guides to the drawing up of their own disciplinary procedures:

a. the ACAS Code of Practice Disciplinary Practice and Procedures in Employment;

b. the Equal Opportunities Commission Code of Practice for the elimination of discrimination on grounds of sex and marriage and the promotion of equality of opportunity in employment; and

c. the Commission for Racial Equality Code of Practice: Race Relations.

These Codes of Practices are given significant weight in Industrial Tribunal cases.

4.5.3 Recognised trade unions have the right to make representations on procedural matters and on general principles underlying disciplinary action. Such representations may be made centrally and at departmental and agency level.

4.5.4. Disciplinary procedures may be invoked in certain circumstances in addition to, or instead of, criminal investigations or legal proceedings. Departments and agencies should consult their legal advisers before taking disciplinary action in parallel with criminal proceedings.

4.5.5. It is for departments and agencies to define the circumstances in which initiation of disciplinary procedures may be appropriate. It is not necessary to attempt to define every circumstance. However departments' and agencies' rules for staff must make clear the circumstances in which the application of the disciplinary procedures may be considered. These must include:

a. breaches of the organisation's standards of conduct or other forms of misconduct (see paragraph 4.1.4); and

b. any other circumstances in which the behaviour, action or inaction of individuals significantly disrupts or damages the performance or reputation of the organisation.

4.5.6 Rules and guidance on the limited efficiency and inefficiency procedures are given in Sections 7.1 and 8.2 respectively.

4.5.7 The sanctions applied as a result of disciplinary proceedings are a matter for the department or agency concerned, in the light of the circumstances of each case.

Rules
Disciplinary procedures

4.5.8 Subject to the following rules, the leval at which decisions are made whether or not to proceed with disciplinary action, the disciplinary procedures to be followed, and the arrangements for appeals, are matters for departments and agencies.

4.5.9 Disciplinary decisions must be taken by someone at least one level higher than the individual concerned and appeals must be heard by someone at least one level higher than the person making the disciplinary decision. Wherever possible, appeal decisions should be taken by someone independent of the original disciplinary decision.

4.5.10 Decisions concerning those at Grades 1 or 1A, equivalently ranked Chief Executives of agencies, and Heads of Departments must be taken by the Head of the Home Civil Service, after consultation with the Minister of the Department concerned and, as appropriate, the Prime Minister. Decisions concerning those at Grades 2 or 3, or the Chief Executives of agencies, must be taken by the Permanent Head of Department or Chief Executive. Individuals in these cases have a right of appeal to the Head of the Home Civil Service.

4.5.11 Decisions not to proceed with disciplinary action in cases of serious fraud, other than where the individual is being prosecuted, must be taken by the Head of Department or Chief Executive of the agency after consultation with the responsible Minister.

Trade union representation

4.5.12 Individuals must be granted the right to the assistance throughout the disciplinary proceedings of a trade union representative or colleague.

Appeals

4.5.13 Departments and agencies must make clear to individuals their rights of appeal against disciplinary decisions. They must allow staff who are dismissed to appeal to the Civil Service Appeal Board if they are eligible to do so (see paragraph 7.7.23, Appeals). They must allow a right of appeal under the personal grievance procedure (see paragraph 7.7.4, Appeals) to:

a. staff who are dismissed but ineligible to appeal to the Civil Service Appeal Board; and

b. staff who are not dismissed.

Suspension from duty

4.5.14 Individuals under criminal investigation or disciplinary procedures may be suspended from duty if necessary to protect the public interest. Pay may be withheld wholly or partly during suspension. During suspension, only basic pay (defined as that which would be paid during the first six months of sickness absence) may be paid, and departments and agencies have discretion to decide whether the individual on suspension should receive full basic pay or a proportion of it. Pay withheld during suspension may be forfeited wholly or partly as a result of a disciplinary decision. Any pay not forfeited must be paid retrospectively and reckoned under the Principal Civil Service Pension Scheme in the normal way.

4.5.15 Departments and agencies must apply, where appropriate, the rules that apply to the recovery of losses to public funds on dismissal and to the forfeiture of superannuation benefits in respect of dismissal for certain criminal offences. These rules are set out in Annex A.

4.5 Annex A: Recovery of Losses to Public Funds

1. On dismissal for an offence involving loss to public funds, any sums unpaid, for example in respect of salary or wages up to the last day of duty, or of income tax overpaid on salary may be withheld as a set-off against the loss. Similar set-offs should be made if someone who would have been dismissed for an offence resigns before the dismissal can be put into effect. The Inland Revenue should be notified of any sums so withheld in respect of income tax refund, and at the same time be requested themselves to withhold the refund of overpayment of tax. If the amount of tax from these sources is less than the loss to public funds, it may be possible to recover the balance from any superannuation benefits payable. Civil Service Pensions Division, HM Treasury should be consulted at an early stage and their authority obtained for the deduction to be made.

Forfeiture of Superannuation Benefits (see also Section 7.7)

1. Automatic loss of pension rights applies only where a civil servant is convicted of treason.

2. The Treasury exercises the power under rule 8.2 of the Principal Civil Service Pension Scheme to withhold superannuation benefits in whole or in part if a civil servant or former civil servant is convicted of:

   a. one or more offences under the Official Secrets Act 1989 for which the person concerned has been sentenced to a term of imprisonment of at least ten years or has been sentenced on the same occasion to two or more consecutive terms amounting in the aggregate to at least 10 years; or

   b. an offence in connection with any employment to which the PCSPS applies, being an offence which is certified by a Minister of the Crown either to have been gravely injurious to the State or to be liable to lead to serious loss of confidence in the public service.

3. The guaranteed minimum pension payable under the provisions of the Social Security Pensions Act 1975 must be paid in the case of 2b, but that element of a pension can be withheld if forfeiture is applied under 2a or as a result of a conviction for treason. Before the Treasury exercises this power to withhold superannuation benefits, the case will be discussed on a 'without prejudice' basis with the trade union side.

4. The Cabinet Office (Office of Public Service and Science) will normally advise Ministers on the certification of offences in accordance with paragraph 2. Cabinet Office Security Division should therefore be consulted at an early stage in any case in which criminal proceedings are pending and the charges are such that a withholding of superannuation benefits under either 2a or b will need to be considered. The decision on forfeiture is however a matter for the Treasury and Civil Service Pensions Division of the Treasury should be kept informed of discussions. Departments and agencies should subsequently notify both Divisions of the outcome of the trial and of the possibility of an appeal. If there is a conviction, the department or agency concerned may make recommendations about the forfeiture of superannuation benefits but these recommendations should not be made known to the individual(s) concerned. They should, however, be supplied with a copy of rule 8.2 of the PCSPS and advised that representations in writing about any matters relevant to the question of forfeiture may be submitted. Such representations may be made on their behalf by a colleague or trade union representative.

5. The department or agency concerned will be told whether or not it is proposed to withhold superannuation benefits and, if forfeiture is intended, what benefits will be withheld. The department or agency will be told also the period (normally 21 days) within which notice of intent to appeal must be made by the person concerned. It will be for the employing department or agency to pass that information to the person. Attention should be specifically drawn to the right of appeal and a further copy of rule 8.2 of the PCSPS should be provided. The individual should be advised that in the event of lodging an appeal full written representations may be made, prior to the hearing, to the Civil Service appeal Board, whose judgement on whether or not, or to what extent, superannuation benefits should be forfeited will be accepted by the Treasury. No action, therefore, should be taken either to pay superannuation benefits to a serving member of staff or to withhold them from somebody who is already retired until a final decision is promulgated by the Treasury.

VOLUME I   GOVERNMENT ETHICS

APPENDIX PART II

Government Ethics:

Conflict of Interest

Conflict of Interest: A Modern Antidote

by Jean-Pierre Kingsley, then Deputy Secretary,
Personnel Policy Branch, Treasury Board of Canada

1. The Public Interest in Perspective

Modern government serves a number of functions. It is, as Professor Dwivedi has observed, a protector of its citizens against uncertainties of human existence, a provider of essential welfare, and an arbiter of competing sectional or other special interests. [1]

Public servants play a key role in modern government, not only delivering the programmes implemented by Parliament, but also advising the Government of the feasibility of new measures and the successes or failures of current programmes. They enforce the laws that are passed and must do so without prejudice or favour to any one person. Public servants, regardless of levels or positions, are trustees for both elected representatives and the public at large.

It is essential that the advice public servants offer their superiors or Ministers be the most objective advice possible, offered without regard to personal or private considerations. Thus, individual public servants, their superiors and their Ministers must be confident that this advice has not been improperly motivated. Canadian citizens also must be confident that the public servants who provide them with services are objective in the execution of their duties. In order to carry out its roles, the Government must, of necessity, rely upon the sense of justice and fair play of its employer, the public.

Professionals are characterised traditionally as performing a service to the public, as being competent and having integrity in their work. While their expertise in areas of highly specialised knowledge or technical skills has been the basis for their duty to fulfil and discharge a public trust, the propriety of the use of that expertise is crucial to the maintenance of that public trust.

---

1 O. P. Dwivedi, *Public Service Ethics* (Brussels: International Institute of Administrative Sciences, 1978). Readers please note that Mr Kingsley recently was Assistant Deputy Registrar General of Canada, see this Volume pp. 105-20. He now holds the post of Chief Electoral Officer of Canada. This article was first published in *Canadian Public Administration* Vol. 29 No. 4 Winter 1986 pp. 585-92. *[Editor]*.

The term 'professional' has come to apply to more than just the traditional disciplines such as law and medicine, to the extent that it is not determined by the kind of work one does, but rather it embodies the attitude and behaviour with which one approaches and performs the work. In this context, all government personnel can and should conduct themselves as professionals. Implicit is the requirement to behave with integrity, demonstrate competence in work and dedicate oneself to the pursuit of excellence. Public service is different from anything else, because the ultimate employer is not a board of directors or even a privileged group of shareholders; it is the public; a neighbour; a friend; and even one's own family. Whatever the position, one is not working to make a profit for an owner, one works to serve everyone.

It would seem from this that a social contract exists between public servants and the public, just as surely as a social contract exists which permits the public to give its confidence to its elected representatives who take the actions they think are in the best interests of the public. This social contract is at the base of a representative democracy. For the public servant, this contract means the acceptance of a responsibility; it means one must carry out one's duties fairly and equally for all. A government official acts as a trustee for every Canadian, and as a trustee, it is important that this trust not be broken.

In the context of these roles and responsibilities, it is clearly unacceptable that a public servant allows a conflict of interest situation to arise. For a government officer, a conflict of interest situation is one wherein 'a public employee has a private or personal interest sufficient to influence or appear to influence the objective exercise of his official duties.'[2] How then, do governments and managers attempt to minimise the incidence of this destructive phenomenon?

2. Treatment at Various Levels of Government

In Canada, public servants at all levels, Municipal, Provincial, Territorial and Federal, are subject to a conflict of interest régime of one form or another. I would not suggest that each régime is a step in an evolutionary continuum, but I would like to mention some of the distinctions of each, starting with the Municipal level.

The Municipal Level

Michael Starr and Mitchell Sharp observed in their Task Force Report, *Ethical Conduct in the Public Sector*, in May 1984 that it is at the Municipal level in

---

2 Kenneth Kernaghan, *Ethical Conduct: Guidelines for Government Employees* (Toronto: Institute of Public Administration of Canada, 1975), p. 13.

472

Canada where by far the largest body of law and jurisprudence applies with respect to conflict of interest matters. For many years, provisions have been contained in the Municipal Acts or similar statutes in each Province and in the two Territories which are relevant to ethical conduct on the part of elected representatives. Recent practice has been to develop rules that are also applicable to Municipal employees.

In Newfoundland, Prince Edward Island, New Brunswick and the Yukon, conflict of interest at the Municipal level is covered by the Municipalities Act. Other Provinces have chosen to enact separate legislation governing conflict of interest matters at the Municipal level, such as an Act to Prevent Conflict of Interest in the Conduct of Municipal Government enacted in Nova Scotia in 1982, an Act Respecting Municipal Bribery and Corruption in the Province of Quebec, and the Municipal Conflict of Interest Act passed in 1983 in Manitoba. In general, provisions governing the conduct of members of Municipal councils require disclosure of conflicting interests on matters before council, and prohibit members from speaking to or voting on matters in which they have financial interest.

One can assume from the way most Provincial legislatures have enacted provisions to regulate this subject that concern for conflict of interest problems at the Municipal level is profound. That may well be because the risk of problems arising at the Municipal level is great, given the large number of highly specific matters local councils must deal with, for example, licensing, zoning, building permits and development approvals. They can give rise to a focusing of efforts by interested parties to influence members of council. In addition, councillors themselves may be involved in business activities while working as part-time councillors. These factors, among others, have presented Provincial legislatures with a recognition that a fairly specified legal framework is required, and they have tended to respond by providing one to guide the conduct of elected Municipal officials.

The Provincial and Territorial Levels

For the Provincial level, approaches to treatment of conflict of interest vary from one Province to another, and from the approach at the Federal and Municipal levels. While there is less legislation dealing with conflict of interest at the Provincial level than at the Municipal level, there are a fair number of Provinces that deal with conflict of interest through legislation.

The provisions of the Criminal Code dealing with conflict of interest, which apply in all Provinces and Territories as well as at the Federal level, provide a base for the treatment of conflict of interest at the Provincial level. As indicated, some Provinces, such as New Brunswick and Newfoundland, have enacted specific legislation dealing with conflict of interest. Others, such as British Columbia and Saskatchewan, have conflict of interest provisions built into their Public Service Acts. Various Provinces and the

Territories have developed relevant regulations or guidelines, which in some cases are in the process of evolution, while in others the employee's oath of office serves as the general framework.

The Federal Public Service Experience

I would like to turn now to the Federal public service. The Canadian experience has developed differently from the United States where, since 1965, ethical conduct of government employees has been regulated by a comprehensive list of activities under the heading 'Bribery, Graft and Conflict of Interest,' as contained in chapter II of the United States Code. In 1978 the United States formalised the codification exercise through passage and signing into effect the Ethics in Government Act.

In Canada, the first attempt to codify such conduct came as the 'Standard of Conduct for Public Service Employees' which was promulgated as a circular letter from the Secretary of the Treasury Board in 1973, and contained the conflict of interest guidelines which were proclaimed by order-in-council. In introducing the circular letter, the Secretary of the Treasury Board noted that:

> 'For many years, the Public Service of Canada has operated with very few formal published rules of conduct. There have, no doubt, always been generally accepted assumptions about what a public servant could do and what he should not do without prejudicing his usefulness as an employee of the Federal government. However, the increasing complexity of modern government has blurred the line between public and private matters to such an extent that a systematic and public set of standards is now required.'

Thus introduced, the conflict of interest guidelines were applied across the public service. The guidelines covered situations of actual or potential conflict of interest, but did not attempt to define them. Rather, the guidelines set forth certain principles, the violation of which would constitute conflict of interest situations. The onus was placed on individuals to conduct their activities in such a manner that the principles would be respected, the test being the scrutiny which could be brought to bear on the activities with the guidelines as the standards.

In early 1978 a set of post-employment activities guidelines were issued to complete the set of provisions. This policy applied to all new appointments to order-in-council positions, to senior executive and equivalent positions in the public service, to Ministers, their exempt staff, and Parliamentary secretaries, and to certain positions at more junior levels that the Minister responsible identified as being of a particularly sensitive nature.

In 1983 Prime Minister Pierre Trudeau struck a task force co-chaired by Michael Starr and Mitchell Sharp, with the mandate to:

> 'examine and report to the Prime Minister on the policies and practices that should govern the conduct of Ministers, Parliamentary Secretaries, exempt staff,

full-time Governor-in-Council appointees and public servants during and after their period of public service, having particular regard to the need to ensure both public confidence in and the integrity of the governmental process and the need to attract to government individuals of high calibre from all walks of life.'

The terms of reference of the task force were a strong reflection of the Canadian approach, recognising that,

1. the public interest required the recruitment to public office of highly qualified individuals from diverse backgrounds to participate in the public affairs and public administration of Canada;

2. such office holders should carry out their official duties and arrange their private affairs in a manner that conserves and enhances public confidence and trust in government;

3. after their period of public service such office holders should be able to return to fulfilling employment within the community-at-large; and

4. the actions of former office holders should not cast doubt on the probity and impartiality of the public policy process.

The report of the task force was presented in May 1984 to Prime Minister Trudeau. On September 9, 1985, Prime Minister Brian Mulroney introduced the conflict of interest and post-employment code for public office holders as part of his 'package of major initiatives on public sector ethics.' The Prime Minister took care to note that while some of the thinking, and even some words, of the authors of the task force report were enshrined in the new code, it was an evolutionary document, and bore the clear mark of the government-of-the-day.

In his opening statement, Prime Minister Mulroney indicated:

'It is a great principle of public administration – I could even say an 'imperative' – that to function effectively the government and the public service of a democracy must have the trust and confidence of the public they service. In order to reinforce that trust, the government must be able to provide competent management and, above all, to be guided by the highest standards of conduct.'

He further added, in his open letter to Members of Parliament and senators that:

'While ultimate accountability for ethical standards is that of the Government, the Code continues to place the onus of responsibility on the individual public office holder for his or her own conduct. What is expected of each individual is clearly stated in the Code, which also provides a clear basis for assessing those individual judgements, as well as prescribing penalties for those who fail to meet expected standards'.

Indeed, the new code marked a strengthening of the former conflict of interest and post-employment régime in that it:

- covered a broader population in a more definitive fashion than previously;

- included enforcement mechanisms that were lacking in the post-employment régime;

- placed an absolute prohibition on switching sides, just as a lawyer is barred from changing from one side of a case to the other;

- clearly allocated responsibility and provided for accountability;

- is fairer to individuals by taking into account both individual circumstances and the public interest; and

- is clearer and more precise, consolidating what was previously contained in five documents.

The conflict of interest and post-employment code for the public service, which took effect on January 1, 1986, is derived from the Prime Minister's code, and contains the same principles and represents an extraction of the provisions of the code which apply directly to persons for whom Treasury Board represents the Government as the employer.

While the principles of the new code are quite similar to those previously in effect, the new code emphasises the allocation of responsibility and the provision for accountability. A new feature, however, is that employees are required to sign a document certifying that they have read, understood and will observe the requirements of the code as a condition of employment. To aid employees in understanding the code, a videotape for instructional purposes was developed, and Departments have conducted training and information sessions for employees.

One of the prime difficulties under the conflict of interest code is the onerous responsibility it places on an individual of making a formal judgement concerning a real or potential conflict of interest situation – in other words, in arriving at the same conclusion as an 'impartial' public about such a situation.

The certification document which employees must sign provides a list of 'exempt' (i.e. not subject to confidential disclosure) and 'non-exempt' (i.e. possibly subject to confidential disclosure) assets and liabilities, and is designed to help employees examine their personal situation – holdings, liabilities and outside activities – in light of their official duties and functions. Employees can, in a systematic manner, determine whether they must file a confidential report or not. Where there is some doubt in an employee's mind as to whether particular circumstances can or might constitute a conflict of interest, the employee can consult with a designated departmental official and, based upon the information obtained, can arrive at a decision. In such circumstances, the employer rightly shares with the employee the judgement and the responsibility. Where circumstances so warrant, the designated official can direct the employee to divest assets or cease outside activities. In cases of dispute, redress mechanisms are available.

From a practitioner's point of view, one might ask, if the onus is on the individual to determine appropriate action, why it was necessary or desirable to heighten attention to this area for attention seems to get focused naturally when cases of public controversy arise. Personally, I feel that the ever-increasing complexity of modern government, the growing number of employees leaving the public service and taking up other careers, increased dual employment and part-time employment have blurred the lines in this area. Also, in North America over the past decade, there has been a marked trend toward emphasising the rights of the individual. This has resulted, with increasing frequency, in elected and non-elected public office holders being confronted with complex situations where their private interests may be confused with the public interest. It is imperative for all concerned to recognise quickly that for public servants, such conflicts must be resolved in the public interest.

I share the view that the success of any conflict of interest régime depends upon the goodwill and the sense of public service of public office holders. The correct balance between fairness to the individual and protection of the public interest is delicate and difficult to attain, but I do not feel that we need to legislate ethical behaviour. It is perhaps a bit like the signs one sees on the highways indicating there is a financial penalty for littering.

I would like to think that the vast majority of Canadians do not throw litter on the highway not because if they do, they face a fine, but rather, because a pristine travel route is a desirable feature of Canadian life.

3. Grey Areas: the Challenge for Management

How can one best deal with the grey areas? Conflicts of interest can occur in a variety of forms. Whether the elements are cases of actuality, potentiality or appearance, or some combination of these, they all can constitute 'conflict' situations. While terms such as real, potential and apparent can be defined and understood, it remains a difficult task to apply them to individual situations.

Prevailing circumstances can lead to very different results when applied to situations that on the surface appear similar. Such factors as the nature of the employee's duties, the degree of influence exercised on departmental decisions as they affect the public, the nature of client contacts, if any, and the like must all be weighed in themselves and in relation to the employee's personal interests.

Determination of conflict of interest is further complicated by the fact that such a conflict may exist notwithstanding the absence of wrongdoing on the part of the employee and notwithstanding that the employee's personal integrity, honesty or responsibility is above reproach. This presents a very delicate situation, which must be handled very carefully. However, when the private interests of an individual are at variance with his or her official duties and responsibilities to the Government, a conflict of interest exists and must be resolved in the public interest in all cases. The conflict situation can run the gamut from one in which the individual seeks to use a position in government or confidential information received in government in a fashion proscribed by law, to one in which all that is involved is the appearance of a conflict. Private and public interests need not be in competition or conflict for an ethical problem to exist. The public interest could be abused equally where the private interests of an office holder coincide with the public interest so as to mesh together, with the result that in serving the public purpose the individual benefits privately as well.

The question of conflict of interest has existed since the first form of government was established. Concern about the subject ebbs and flows in direct relation to the frequency and intensity of allegations about the way government business has been conducted or revelations about improper conduct. While the application of instruments such as the new Federal conflict of interest and post-employment code will reinforce the trust and confidence of the public, it would be naïve to suggest that conflict of interest will disappear. In fact, this instrument, which permits a heightened awareness and thus a decreased absolute incidence of inappropriate activities by public servants, may lead to an apparent increase of conflict of interest situations. However, I am confident that, on closer examination, the facts will show that the already high standard of conduct in the Federal public service will only increase as a result of the heightened awareness of what is expected.

Commission of Inquiry into the Facts of Allegations of Conflict of Interest Concerning the Honourable Sinclair M. Stevens [1]

by Commissioner : The Honourable W. D. Parker

Preface

The Honourable Sinclair M. Stevens resigned from the federal Cabinet on May 12, 1986, in the wake of conflict of interest allegations relating to his responsibilities as a Minister of the Crown. The conflict of interest allegations were made in the media and in the House of Commons and concerned Mr Stevens' activities as the Cabinet Minister responsible for regional economic development, foreign investment review, and privatization. The allegations referred to private financial dealings with the same individuals or firms that were doing business with Mr Stevens' Government Department and suggested numerous instances of conflict of interest on the part of Mr Stevens as a Minister of the Crown.

Following the initial news reports in late March and early April 1986, the allegations multiplied in number and became even more serious and wide ranging. In addition to the specific conflict of interest charges, there were more general allegations of influence peddling, breach of public trust, and corruption. As a result of the growing controversy, and shortly after Mr Stevens' resignation from the Cabinet, this Commission of Inquiry was established, and I was directed to inquire into the facts following these allegations and report on whether Mr Stevens was in real or apparent conflict of interest under the code of conduct governing public office holders.

This is my report. It is divided into twenty-seven chapters grouped under five parts. Part One consists of three introductory chapters, the first containing a discussion of the allegations and the terms of reference of the Inquiry. Well over one hundred allegations were made, but they can be grouped under five heads: one, that Mr Stevens was in a conflict of interest in his

---

1 The Preface, and Chapters 1, 26 and 27 from the above Report are reproduced here in full. The Report was published by the Ministry of Supply and Services Canada 1987, Canadian Government Publishing Centre, Ottawa, Canada.

dealings with Magna International Inc., a large manufacturing firm; two, that Mr Stevens was in a conflict of interest in his dealings with the Canada Development Investment Corporation and certain Bay Street investment firms; three, that Mr Stevens was in a conflict of interest with regard to the auto manufacturer Hyundai Corporation; four, that he was in a conflict of interest because he mingled private and public business; and five, that he failed to comply with the Conflict of Interest Guidelines for Ministers of the Crown and the régime that replaced these guidelines, the Conflict of Interest and Post-Employment Code for Public Office Holders.

Having summarized the allegations, I then describe in Chapter 2 the conflict of interest régimes to which Mr Stevens was subject as a Member of the Cabinet. This discussion of the two relevant conflict of interest régimes underscored the fact that in neither one was conflict of interest defined. I concluded that such a definition was essential if I was to discharge my mandate. In Chapter 3, I develop a set of definitions for real and apparent conflict of interest.

Part Two of the report deals with Mr Stevens' business interests and his involvement in these interests to September 1984, when he was appointed to the Cabinet. In the first chapter, Chapter 4, I briefly describe Mr Stevens' background and ministerial responsibilities. In Chapters 5, 6 and 7, I describe the York Centre group of companies, their overall financial condition, and Mr Stevens' role in the companies to September 1984. I conclude this part with a description of the steps taken by Mr Stevens in September 1984 to comply with the conflict of interest rules.

In Part Three I examine the extent to which Mr Stevens remained involved in private business matters after September 1984 and his appointment to the Cabinet. Eight specific incidents are examined. I also examine the roles that were played by Shirley Walker and Noreen Stevens and the nature and extent of their communication with Mr Stevens. With this background I am better able to draw conclusions about Mr Stevens' involvement in private business matters while a Minister of the Crown.

In Part Four I turn to the public side and the conflict of interest allegations. Chapters 20 to 24 are devoted to a detailed analysis of the allegations as set out under the five categories. I make certain findings under each category and draw certain conclusions.

Part Five completes the report. It contains my final comments and observations. Chapter 25 provides a detailed description of the inquiry process and the procedures that were employed. Chapter 26 contains a summary of my conclusions regarding the conflict of interest allegations. Chapter 27, the final chapter, is devoted to my recommendations for reform.

It is my hope that this final chapter will be of some assistance to those who are involved in the reform of the present sytem. This Inquiry has had a unique opportunity to explore the practical workings of the conflict of interest régime that is presently in place. My observations and recommendations emerge from the lessons of this Inquiry. Four issues with respect to conflict of interest kept arising during the course of the Inquiry: one, what assets and activities should Cabinet Ministers have to disclose and how should assets be divested; two, should Cabinet Ministers be obliged to declare their interests and withdraw when necessary from certain responsibilities; three, what should be required of spouses of Cabinet Ministers; and, four, what should the responsibilities be of the office of the Assistant Deputy Registrar General. These issues I discuss in some detail in the final chapter.

I must say in closing that the conduct of this long and complicated Inquiry and the preparation and writing of this final report would not have been possible without the cooperation of all those who participated in the process. I thank Commission Counsel and Commission staff for their effectiveness and their energy. I also thank Counsel for all the parties, and for the many witnesses who gave evidence in the Inquiry. Their sense of commitment and cooperation is recognized and much appreciated. Finally I wish to offer my personal thanks to those members of the public who gave evidence before me and thereby enabled me to make the findings of fact recorded in this report.

William D. Parker
Commissioner

1. The Inquiry, the Allegations, and the Terms of Reference

1.1 The Inquiry

On May 15, 1986, the Government of Canada by Order in Council P.C. 1986-1139 constituted a commission of inquiry appointing and directing me to inquire into and report on:

a. the facts following allegations of conflict of interest made in various newspapers, electronic media and the House of Commons, with respect to the conduct, dealings or actions of the Honourable Sinclair M. Stevens; and

b. whether the Honourable Sinclair M. Stevens was in real or apparent conflict of interest as defined by the Conflict of Interest and Post Employment Code for Public Office Holders and the letter from the Prime Minister to the Honourable Sinclair M. Stevens of September 9, 1985 . . .

Following my appointment I began the task of conducting this Inquiry. I engaged Commission Counsel and sufficient staff to assist with the investigation of the allegations. I issued an invitation to interested parties to come forward, and many did. Twelve parties were granted standing. All parties and almost all of the witnesses were represented by Counsel.

I then proceeded to hear all of the evidence. The public hearing process was lengthy and complex. It lasted from July 1986 to February 1987 and involved over 90 witnesses and thousands of pages of documents. After the public hearing phase concluded, I invited and received oral and written submissions from those wishing to make them and then began to work on this report. I am pleased to provide a more detailed description of the proceedings of the Inquiry in Chapter 25 of the report.

1.2 The Allegations

My first task is to set out the allegations. At the commencement of the Inquiry, Commission Counsel prepared and filed as exhibit 5 a book itemizing all of the various allegations made in the House of Commons and in the media. Exhibit 5 represents a list of all the allegations, in the words of the acting Prime Minister, 'both temperate and intemperate.' Counsel for Mr Stevens and the Government of Canada urged upon me that instead of adopting a checklist approach to these allegations, I should distil them into groups and I do so below. A comparison of the contents of exhibit 5 with the five categories of allegations listed below will demonstrate that there are intemperate allegations, for example, the allegation that Mr Stevens instituted 'a true system of payoff,' or that his Government Department was 'more open to corruption than most,' which are not encompassed in any one of the five categories. The reader will understand that such accusations were not supported by any evidence and have clearly not been made out. It is unnecessary for me to deal with them on an individual basis. What is left are the five categories of allegations about which evidence was tendered and with which I am required to deal.

The allegations may be summarized as follows:

1. It is alleged that, in his dealings as the Minister responsible for the Department of Regional Industrial Expansion (DRIE), Mr Stevens was in a position of conflict of interest with regard to:

   • loans, grants, and other assistance from that Department to Magna International Inc. (Magna); and

   • Magna's proposal to acquire an interest in Canadair Ltd. (Canadair);

   because his wife, Noreen Stevens, had obtained a $2.6 million loan for Cardiff Investments Ltd (Cardiff) from 622109 Ontario Inc., a numbered company controlled by Anton Czapka, a Magna-related individual.

2. It is alleged that, in his dealings as the Minister responsible for the Canada Development Investment Corporation (CDIC), Mr Stevens was in a position of conflict of interest with regard to:

- the appointment of the Canada Development Investment Corporation Directors and the decision to permit companies associated with certain directors to acquire CDIC assets;

- the award of, and approval of fees for, advisory contracts to Burns Fry Ltd. (Burns Fry) and Dominion Securities Ltd. (Dominion Securities);

- the award of, and approval of fees for, an advisory contract to Gordon Capital Corporation (Gordon Capital); and

- the sale of shares of the Canada Development Corporation (CDC);

because Noreen Stevens and Edward (Ted) Rowe, president of York Centre Corporation (York Centre), were approaching CDIC director J. Trevor Eyton, president of Brascan Ltd. (Brascan), and senior officials in Burns Fry, Dominion Securities, and Gordon Capital for financial advice or assistance on behalf of York Centre.

3. It is alleged that, in his dealings as the Minister responsible for Investment Canada, Mr Stevens was in a position of conflict of interest with regard to Hyundai Corporation (Hyundai):

- by waiving a commitment made to the Foreign Investment Review Agency to export certain quantities of goods from Canada; and

- by awarding substantial federal government assistance to Hyundai to establish an automotive assembly plant in Bromont, Quebec;

because of his companies' obligations to the Hanil Bank of Canada (Hanil Bank), a subsidiary of a bank in which Hyundai was a major shareholder, and his desire to ensure that a parts plant was built in his ·riding.

4. It is alleged that, in his dealings as a Minister responsible for DRIE and CDIC, Mr Stevens was in a position of conflict of interest because he mingled his private interest and the public interest.

5. It is alleged that Mr Stevens failed to comply with the Conflict of Interest Guidelines for Ministers of the Crown (guidelines) and the Conflict of Interest and Post-Employment Code for Public Office Holders (code) and an explanatory letter of the Prime Minister dated September 9, 1985 (letter), in that:

- the blind trust was not blind because he continued to have knowledge of his private business affairs and his spouse managed the assets in the blind trust; and

- the blind trust was an inappropriate method of divestiture for a closely knit 'family' business.

1.3 The Scope of the Terms of Reference

As noted earlier, this Commission of Inquiry was established to inquire and report on:

a. the facts following allegations of conflict of interest made in various newspapers, electronic media and the House of Commons, with respect to the conduct, dealings or actions of the Honourable Sinclair M. Stevens; and

b. whether the Honourable Sinclair M. Stevens was in real or apparent conflict of interest as defined by the Conflict of Interest and Post Employment Code for Public Office Holders and the letter from the Prime Minister to the Honourable Sinclair M. Stevens of September 9, 1985 ...

During the course of the Inquiry questions were raised by some counsel as to the scope of my terms of reference. The questions that were raised can be summarized under two heads:

- First, are some of the allegations that may involve conflict of interest too broad and general to be considered as allegations into which I am to inquire and report?

- Secondly, should I report on those allegations involving breaches of the blind trust or the code of conflict that are· not allegations of conflict of interest by themselves?

Inquiry into the General Allegations of Conflict of Interest

In construing the terms of reference, counsel for Mr Stevens urged that I ought to find that the words used in part (a) of the Order in Council, 'to inquire into and report on (a) the facts following allegations of conflict of interest', meant the facts relating to allegations of conflict of interest made in the media and the House of Commons. Further, it was argued that this 're-writing' of the Order in Council is necessitated if the terms of reference 'are to make sense'. Counsel for Mr Stevens argued that it follows from this interpretation that the terms of reference confine the scope of this Inquiry only to those specific allegations which are in fact allegations of conflict of interest made prior to Mr Steven's resignation on May 12, 1986. It is readily apparent that many allegations involving breaches of the code of conduct governing public office holders, including breaches of the blind trust, are not conflict of interest allegations per se.

In accordance with this interpretation, counsel for Mr Stevens submitted that there are basically only three allegations of conflict of interest that fall within the terms of reference. These are the allegations relating to Mr Steven's dealings with Magna, Hyundai, and certain Bay Street financiers. All counsel agree that the scope of the Inquiry extends to at least an examination of the facts relating to these allegations and the question of whether Mr Stevens was in these instances in a position of real or apparent conflict of interest.

Mr Stevens' counsel submitted that any consideration by me of the 'mingling of government and private business' as a fourth distinct allegation would be erroneous and outside the terms of reference. Counsel, in his written argument on behalf of Mr Stevens, stated that the mixing of government and private business:

> is not a separate allegation of conflict of interest but simply one way of defining conflict of interest. The phrase was used by John Turner during a radio interview. The statement was made to describe how he characterized Stevens' conduct relating to the Magna Allegation and the Bay Street Allegation. There are no facts forming part of this allegation as there are in the case of the other allegations, which further confirms that this is not an allegation the facts of which are to be investigated.

(Submission of Sinclair M. Stevens, p. 5)

On this basis, counsel for Mr Stevens submitted that incidents about which the Commission heard extensive evidence involving James (Jim) Stewart of the Chase Manhatten Bank, Angus Dunn of Morgan Grenfell & Co. Ltd. (Morgan Grenfell), Kenneth (Ken) Leung of Olympia & York Developments (Olympia & York), Thomas (Tom) Kierans of McLeod Young Weir Ltd, and Mr Stevens' Korean visit to the Hanil Bank are not within the terms of reference of the Commission and that I should therefore make no report regarding them.

Counsel for the Government of Canada did not join with counsel for Mr Stevens in seeking so restrictive an interpretation of the terms of reference. Counsel's written submission argued that the Order in Council 'is predicted on a *conflict* of interest, i.e. an improper mingling of a Minister's public duty and his private interest' and invited the Commission to decide whether the Minister was in real or apparent conflict of interest. As I understand this submission, the Government of Canada urged the Commission to investigate and report on all incidents of conduct that could give rise to a finding that Mr Stevens was in a position of real or apparent conflict. This of course would include incidents involving the mingling of public and private business as is said to have occurred with Jim Stewart, Angus Dunn, Ken Leung, Tom Kierans, and Mr Stevens' Korean visit to the Hanil Bank.

The interview referred to by counsel for Mr Stevens was the interview given to CFRB Radio in Toronto by John Turner, leader of the opposition, on May 12, 1986. It included the following statement: 'The tragedy of

Sinclair Stevens is that he mingled and his family mingled their own private family interest with the way they were handling their public interest, the way that Department was being managed' (Exhibit 224).

This very general allegation was made in the first few moments of the interview and well before any discussion of Mr Stevens' dealings with Magna or the Bay Street brokers. Although this was an allegation of conflict of interest, the question posed by counsel for Mr Stevens is whether either its generality or context preclude me from treating it as a separate and distinct allegation.

Although admittedly no facts form part of the allegation, its generality does not necessarily alter its character as an allegation. In this context it is noteworthy that the terms of reference themselves failed either to enumerate the instances of alleged conflict into which I was to inquire or to define the meaning to be attributed to the word allegation. In the absence of any definition or limitation, the word allegation ought to be given its natural and ordinary meaning without the artificial restriction suggested by counsel for Mr Stevens.

This broad interpretation of the word allegation is not only consonant with the ordinary and natural meaning of the word but also clearly reflects the intention of the government in drafting the terms of reference. A statement made by the acting Prime Minister, Erik Nielsen, to the House of Commons on May 14, 1986, in response to questions about the scope of the Inquiry is of some assistance:

> As I have assured the House on Monday, Tuesday, and again today, the terms of reference will take into account the allegations made in the House of Commons, both temperate and intemperate. They will take into account the allegations made in the newspapers, both temperate and intemperate. They will take into account the allegations made in the electronic media, both temperate and intemperate. It will be in the context of the conflict of interest Code of Conduct for public office holders, in addition to the Prime Minister's letter of September 9 to the former Minister and other members of his Ministry.

(Canada, House of Commons, *Debates*, May 14, 1986, p. 13,260)

Logic does not dictate that the absence of a specific factual underpinning to the allegation alters its character as an allegation. This is especially so in light of the terms of reference, which make it my obligation to find the facts in relation to these allegations.

I also reject the submission of counsel for Mr Stevens that it is clear from the context of Mr Turner's remarks that he was referring specifically to the loan made by Anton Czapka or to the approaches to Bay Street brokers. To the contrary, I find that the statement made by John Turner is sufficiently separated from the discussion of the Czapka loan or the Bay Street brokers to constitute an independent allegation that Mr Stevens mingled his private interest with his public duties as a Minister responsible for a Department of government. Therefore I decline to accept the submissions of counsel for Mr Stevens, and find that the mingling of private interests and public interest is indeed an allegation of conflict of interest that I must investigate and report on.

Allegations Relating to the Blind Trust or Code of Conduct

There remains the second issue involving the terms of reference of the Commission: whether I should inquire into matters of non-compliance with the guidelines and code or breaches of the blind trust which do not necessarily involve conflicts of interest, real or apparent. Counsel on behalf of the Government of Canada and Mr Stevens both submitted that these matters were outside the terms of reference of the Commission. In his written argument on behalf of the Government of Canada, counsel stated:

> *It is difficult to see how this allegation fits into the Commission's mandate except, indirectly, as part of the Commission counsel's attack on Mr Stevens' credibility. Undoubtedly the Guidelines and Code imposed on Mr Stevens a duty to establish and comply with the terms of the blind trust. But the mandate of this Commision is directed to the issue of whether specific allegations of conflict of interest – real or apparent – are well founded, not whether Mr Stevens observed the procedural steps contemplated by the Code as a precaution to prevent 'potential' conflicts from arising.*
>
> *... The Code itself draws a clear distinction between compliance 'in form' and compliance 'in substance'. Following the recommended procedures does not necessarily save a Minister from conflicts. Conversely, failure to follow recommended 'avoidance' procedures does not necessarily place a Minister in conflicts.*
>
> Section 5(2) of the Code says explicitly that:
>
> > *Conforming to this Code does not absolve public office holders of the responsibility to take such additional action as may be necessary to prevent real, potential or apparent conflicts of interest. (Exhibit 7, tab 7, p. 2)*
>
> Conversely, violations of a blind trust may put a public office holder in breach of the Code, and may expose him or her to potential conflicts, but a breach of the Code's procedural requirements does not itself amount to a conflict of interest.
>
> (Submission of the Government of Canada, pp. 19-20)

This submission is at first blush persuasive. However, it leaves unanswered those numerous allegations made in both the House of Commons and in the media which involved the Minister's compliance with the guidelines and those regarding his activities, or those of his spouse Noreen Stevens, which involved breaches of the blind trust. These allegations were summarized by Commission counsel in exhibit 5 and a sampling is sufficient to make the scope of these allegations apparent. They are as follows:

- Even though the Minister's interests had been placed into a blind trust, his family and former associates were still very much involved in their continuing operation.

- It's one thing if a Minister puts one hundred shares of a widely-held public company like Bell Canada into a blind trust; the trustee may sell them the next day and buy shares of Canadian Pacific and the Minister would never know. But it's another thing entirely when – as was the case with Stevens – a Minister's family firm is put into a blind trust; the trustee is obviously not going to sell it. So the Minister knows he still owns it and can conceivably take advantage of this knowledge. Or his wife can.

- The Minister's trustee must have been aware of the loan negotiations and approved them. If the trustee, National Trust, was not aware and did not approve, that would make even more ridiculous than now the use of the blind trust gimmick as a way of avoiding conflict of interest problems. It would mean that for all real purposes the trustee was the Minister's wife.

- Stevens and his wife short-circuited the system – when the spouse is an officer of their joint company, the barrier insulating the blind trust from the Minister is too easily broken. The private interests of the Minister and his spouse are indistinguishable and his blind trust is not nearly blind enough.

- The 'so-called' blind trust was a 'farce': 'it was not blind, it was not at arm's length, we had active participation by the Minister's spouse on his behalf ...'

- The Minister does not have a blind trust if his wife was part of the management.

- There cannot be a blind trust when the Minister's wife is running one of the subsidiaries, his law firm is attached to their own offices and his telephone number is the number of subsidiaries.

- Because of the contact between husband and wife, an arm's length relationship cannot be maintained between the Minister and his holdings. Handing his affairs over to his spouse was not sufficient.

- The Minister's blind trust looks like a 'transparent ruse' if his wife was still running the business – getting up in the morning and having toast and coffee with the Minister, and then setting off to seek million-dollar loans for one of his companies from people dealing with his Department. How blind was this trust!?

- The Assistant Deputy Registrar General did no investigation beyond speaking to the Minister.

(Exhibit 5, pp. 1-3)

My fact-finding mandate is described in paragraph (a) of the terms of reference. I am required to find the facts following allegations of conflict of interest made in the House of Commons and the media. I find that the words conflict of interest in the context of my fact-finding mandate extend to the facts of all allegations that relate to conflict of interest issues generically, such as breaches of the blind trust or procedural non-compliance with the code. This interpretation coincides with the interpretation given in the House of Commons by Erik Nielsen in answer to a question posed by another member of the House about the scope of this Inquiry. If the government had intended that I refrain from finding the facts relating to certain clear allegations such as that the blind trust was not blind, not blind enough, or a ruse, I have no doubt it would have made its intention known in unambiguous terms.

It is noteworthy that counsel for the government and counsel for Mr Stevens concede that evidence of Mr Stevens' knowledge of his financial interests is an essential finding of fact in any determination of whether he was in real or apparent conflict. However, the issue of Mr Stevens' knowledge and the manner in which it was obtained are also inextricably interwoven with issues regarding Mr Stevens' compliance with the guidelines and code. Therefore, on the view of my mandate urged by counsel for Mr Stevens and the Government of Canada, the facts of Mr Stevens' knowledge must be found by me in the discharge of my fact-finding mandate.

However, the effect of counsel's submission is that, although I should find the facts in relation to such matters as Mr Stevens' knowledge, I should stop there and not draw any conclusions about whether such facts disclose a violation of the guidelines or code. This is nothing short of inviting me to find facts in a vacuum, without identifying their ultimate meaning. Such a position is inconsistent with the effective discharge of my mandate, and I therefore hold that conclusions with respect to compliance are a necessary part of the fact-finding process with which I am charged.

Further, conclusions regarding Mr Stevens' compliance with the code have a significant bearing upon his credibility. Under oath at this Inquiry, Mr Stevens testified as follows:

Q. First of all, at page 2 of Exhibit 211, in your letter to the Prime Minister, which was dated May 11, 1986, in the second paragraph you wrote:

> *"I have repeatedly stated that I have complied fully with the provisions of the Conflict of Interest Code for public office holders, as well as with the provisions contained in your letter to Ministers, dated September 9, 1985".*

That was the text of your letter at the time, sir?

A. That is right.

Q. Would it be fair, and I want to be fair here, to confirm that your intent was to say that you complied fully with the Code that was in existence in 1984 when you were appointed to the Cabinet in addition to that which was in existence at the time that this letter was written?

A. I had fully complied with the Code in both instances, if that is the thrust of your question.

(Transcript, vol. 71, p. 12,141)

A few moments later, Mr Stevens was asked by Commission counsel about his present position:

Q. In respect of all of these statement that were made at the time, I gather from your evidence in chief, that, effectively, you reassert them at this stage in this Inquiry; is that right, sir?

A. Yes.

(Transcript, vol, 71, p. 12,147)

It is obvious that such assertions bear fundamentally on Mr Stevens' credibility. For this reason as well I find that the matter of whether Mr Stevens acted in violation of the guidelines or code of conduct or in breach of the provisions of the blind trust is one that I am duty bound to inquire into and report on.

In sum, I conclude that my terms of reference include general allegations of conflict of interest, such as the 'mingling of government and private business', and also the allegations relating to the blind trust.

26. Conclusions about Mr Stevens' Conflict of Interest

This chapter summarizes my principal conclusions under each of the five broad categories of allegations that were reviewed above. Before turning to these conclusions, however, I shall deal briefly with certain allegations of conflict of interest that were not pursued in this Inquiry.

26.1 Allegations Not Pursued in this Inquiry

The first allegation related to Mr Stevens' conduct between March 26 and May 12, 1986, that is, in the period between the first major news story and the date of his resignation from the Cabinet. It was alleged by certain members of Parliament that any dealings that Mr Stevens had as Minister involving Magna, Burns Fry, Dominion Securities, Gordon Capital, or Hyundai following the news reports of March 26, 1986 (about Hyundai) and of April 29 1986 (about the others), and his then clear knowledge of the $2.62 million loan and the York Centre search for financing, would be conflicts of interest and would remain so until the date of the Minister's resignation. This category of allegations can be disposed of quite briefly. Regarding Hyundai, I have found in this report that Mr Stevens was not in a conflict of interest in his dealings thereto. I also note that in any event Mr Stevens had no further dealings with Hyundai following the March 26 news story. Thus there could have been no subsequent occasions for conflict of interest. As for the Magna and Bay Street allegations, I have already found that Mr Stevens had knowledge of the $2.62 million loan and York Centre's involvement with Burns Fry, Dominion Securities, and Gordon Capital well before the publication of these allegations in the media on April 29. It thus goes without saying that any further ministerial dealings that Mr Stevens had with Magna, or with Burns Fry, Dominion Securities, or Gordon Capital, following these news reports could have amounted to further conflicts of interest. I find, however, that between April 29 and May 12, 1986, there were no such dealings.

There were two other conflict of interest allegations that were not pursued in this Inquiry. Both were made by members of Parliament and recorded in Hansard. The first related to de Havilland Aircraft. The allegation was that de Havilland was sold for a 'ridiculously low price.' The second related to the closing of a Quebec shipyard. The allegation was that there was a conflict of interest in Mr Stevens' decision to place the chairman of one shipyard in charge of planning the closure of another shipyard without first advising the latter. As things turned out, counsel for the members of Parliament in question advised Commission counsel in writing that neither of these allegations in fact had any relation to any alleged conflict of interest on the part of Mr Stevens. Hence, the allegations were not pursued further.

26.2 General Conclusions about Conflict of Interest

I am now in a position to summarize my general conclusions with regard to the five broad categories of allegations that were reviewed in this part of the report. For ease of understanding, I shall set out my conclusions under each of the five categories that were reviewed.

The Allegations of Conflict of Interest Relating to Magna

These allegations have been made out. I have found that from early April 1985, when Mr Stevens acquired knowledge of Mrs Stevens' negotiations with Mr Anton Czapka, until his resignation from public office, all of his dealings with Magna in his capacity as Minister of DRIE and Minister responsible for CDIC were occasions of real conflict of interest. In particular, I have found that Mr Stevens was in a position of real conflict of interest in:

- personally approving the applications for federal assistance to Multi-matic Inc., Master Precision, and Integram on April 17, 1985, at a meeting of the Economic Development Board (these applications totalled $5,033,000 in federal assistance);

- personally approving Magna's application for 10.2 million for the Class A Stamping plant on April 17, 1985, subject to approval by Treasury Board and contingent upon an equivalent provincial contribution;

- pressing for and authorizing the presentation to the Treasury Board of the application for federal assistance for the Class A Stamping plant in June 1985;

- entering into a cancellation agreement with Magna and recommending to Cabinet an amendment to the Enterprise Development Regulations enabling the cancellation of the Polyrim stock option in July and August 1985;

- becoming involved in January 1986 in a meeting to consider Magna's proposal concerning the privatization of Canadair; and

- decisions made, directions given, and agreements entered into, leading to the $64.2 million in federal assistance ultimately recommended for approval for the Cape Breton project in April 1986.

The Allegations Relating to CDIC and Bay Street

These allegations have been made out in part. I have found that Mr Stevens in his capacity as Minister responsible for CDIC was in a position of real conflict of interest with regard to:

- the appointment in October 1984 of Mr Trevor Eyton as a CDIC director;

- the approval in March 1985 of the financial advisory contracts awarded by CDIC to Burns Fry and Dominion Securities;

- the appointment in late April or early May 1985 of Gordon Capital as a financial adviser to the federal government on the CDC share sale.

I have found that with regard to the other allegations relating to 'Brascan,' and in particular to Mr Stevens' involvement in a 'reversal of policy' affecting Noranda and Eldorado, or to his involvement in the CDC share sale, Mr Stevens was not in a conflict of interest position.

The Allegations Relating to Hyundai

These allegations have not been made out. I have found that the allegations relating to Mr Stevens' dealings with Hyundai in his capacity as Minister responsible for Investment Canada were unfounded and that Mr Stevens was not in a position of conflict of interest.

The Allegations Relating to the Mingling of Private and Public Business

These allegations have been made out. I have found that Mr Stevens mingled his private interest with his public duties while he was a Minister of the Crown. Mr Stevens used his public office for private advantage and mixed government and private business on at least five occasions:

- in his dealings with the Chase Manhattan officials;

- in his meeting with Mr Angus Dunn of Morgan Grenfell;

- in his dealings with Mr Tom Kierans of McLeod Young Weir;

- in his telephone call to Mr Ken Leung of Olympia & York; and

- in his visit to the Hanil Bank in Seoul, South Korea.

On each of these occasions, I have found that he was in a position of real conflict of interest.

The Allegations Relating to Non-Compliance with the Guidelines, Code, and Letter

These allegations have been made out. I have found that the blind trust was not in fact blind. Mr Stevens remained knowledgeable about and involved with the York Centre companies and thus with the very assets that were in the blind trust. Both Mrs Stevens and Miss Walker conveyed information to Mr Stevens about the assets in the blind trust and, with Mr Stevens, remained involved in their management.

In sum, Mr Stevens' conduct during his tenure as a Minister of the Crown demonstrated a complete disregard for the requirements of the guidelines and code and the standard of conduct that is expected of public office holders.

493

27. Recommendations for Reform

This Inquiry has provided a unique opportunity to examine some of the practical workings of the conflict of interest régime that is in place at present for federal cabinet Ministers. Many of the provisions of the guidelines (Appendix E), and code (Appendix F), and letter (Appendix H) were subjected to examination, and their strengths and weaknesses were reviewed. It is in my view important that the lessons that were learned in the course of this Inquiry be recorded, and I therefore offer some final observations and suggestions for reform.

This was not the first inquiry to explore the topic of conflict of interest. The matter has been studied at both the federal and provincial levels. The leading federal study is *Ethical Conduct in the Public Sector: Report of the Task Force on Conflict of Interest* (1984). Known as the Starr-Sharp Report, it provided a comprehensive and sophisticated review of existing federal and provincial conflict of interest régimes, and set out proposals for reform.

There have also been a number of provincial studies arising out of inquiries into allegations of conflict of interest on the part of provincial cabinet Ministers. I note in particular in Manitoba, Mr Justice Freedman's *Report of the Commission of Inquiry in the Matter of Wilson D Parasiuk* (1986), and in Ontario, the *Report of the Standing Committee on Public Accounts on the Allegation of Conflict of Interest Concerning Elinor Caplan* (1986). A recent provincial study which I found particularly useful was the study conducted by the Honourable John B. Aird, former lieutenant-governor of Ontario, *Report on Ministerial Compliance with the Conflict of Interest. Guidelines* (1986). The Aird Report recommended a number of important reforms, some of which have been adopted by the Ontario government in the Members' Standards of Office Act, 1986, which received first reading on November 27, 1986.

The reform of conflict of interest codes has also been studied abroad. A number of recent studies describe experiences in the United Kingdom and in Australia. I have also reviewed with considerable interest the current approaches to conflict of interest at the federal level in the United States. These studies and reports have provided a useful context for my own conclusions about the directions for reform that the federal government might pursue.

It is important to emphasize that what follows is not a comprehensive study. Nor is it a detailed blueprint for legislative reform. What follows are my own views on the fundamental lessons learned over the course of this Inquiry and my suggestions for reform.

My suggestions will address the four basic conflict of interest issues affecting members of Cabinet that figured most prominently over the many months of public hearing.

- Disclosure and Divestment: the extent to which disclosure should be required; the appropriate vehicles for divestment; and the role, if any, of the blind trust.

- Recusal: the need to recognize a continuing obligation on the part of public office holders to declare their interests and withdraw from exercising certain duties or responsibilities (or recuse) whenever necessary.

- Spouses: the question of spousal compliance, and in particular whether spouses should be required to disclose their financial interests and activities.

- The Assistant Deputy Registrar General (ADRG); the reform of the office of the ADRG and the kinds of functions that a government ethics office should perform in principle.

I shall deal with each of these points in turn.

27.1 Disclosure, Divestment, and the Role of the Blind Trust

Requirements under the Present Code

As drafted, the Conflict of Interest and Post-Employment Code for Public Office Holders (Appendix F) sets out detailed but confusing requirements for disclosure and divestment. I have already analyzed these requirements in detail in Chapter 2. Nonetheless, a brief summary here may be useful. It will be recalled that the code requires adherence to certain 'compliance measures' (not defined) and sets out four 'methods of compliance'; avoidance, confidential report, public declaration, and divestment. The appropriate compliance method is determined in large part by the type and value of the assets involved. The code classified assets in three different ways: exempt, declarable, and controlled.

Exempt assets are assets and interests that are not of a commercial character but are for the private use of the public office holder and his or her family. Exempt assets are defined to include such things as private residences, automobiles, household goods, and other personal effects. Assets that are primarily of a private or personal nature are exempted from confidential report or public declaration.

Assets that are not exempt are of two types: declarable assets and controlled assets. The code requires the public office holder to make a 'confidential report' to the ADRG of all such non-exempt assets and all direct and contingent liabilities. The non-exempt assets are then classified as either declarable or controlled. Declarable assets are 'assets that are not controlled' and they include:

a) interests in family businesses and in companies that are of a local character, do not contract with the government and do not own or control shares of public companies, other than incidentally, and whose stocks and shares are not traded publicly;

  b) farms under commercial operation;

  c) real property that is not an exempt assets ...; and

  d) assets that are beneficially owned, and that are not exempt assets ...
     and that are administered at arm's length.

Declarable assets can be disclosed in a public declaration.

Controlled assets are defined as 'assets that could be directly or indirectly affected as to value by Government decisions or policy.' Controlled assets include:

  a) publicly traded securities of corporations and foreign governments;

  b) self-administered Registered Retirement Savings Plans, except when exclusively composed of exempt assets ...; and

  c) commodities, futures and foreign currencies held or traded for speculative purposes.

Controlled assets do not have to be disclosed, but they must be divested.

Controlled assets are usually divested either by selling them in an arm's length transaction, or by making them subject to a trust. Three kinds of trust arrangements are suggested; the blind trust, the frozen trust, and the retention trust. The frozen and retention trusts simply freeze the existing assets and transfer managerial responsibilities to the trustee. Only the blind trust provides for the possibility of complete divestment and true blindness.

Once these compliance measures have been completed, two documents must be filed in the Public Registry. The first is the public declaration, which sets out the declarable assets. The second is a summary statement, which sets out the methods of compliance used by the public office holder to comply with the code.

Problems with the Present Code

There are in my view four fundamental problems with the present code's disclosure and divestment provisions; first, they fail to provide for full disclosure; secondly, even as a system of partial disclosure and divestment, the provisions are flawed and inconsistent; thirdly, the provisions for blind trusts do not meet the objective of blindness; fourthly, although the provisions call for judgments on the likelihood of a conflict of interest arising, there is no definition of conflict of interest. Let me explain what I mean by each of these criticisms.

Failure to Provide for Full Disclosure

In my view the code does not provide an adequate public disclosure system, and in my suggestions for reform I shall develop my reasons for this view. Here I shall simply set out the present limits on disclosure. Although declarable assets must be divested or publicly disclosed, controlled assets need not be disclosed. Further, the ADRG is not able to assess all of a Minister's assets to assist him or her in classifying them. Those assets that are exempt in a Minister's opinion need not be disclosed confidentially to the ADRG. I note as a matter of interest that when the code came into force the ADRG himself advised Ministers that it would be prudent to continue to disclose exempt assets precisely for these classification purposes.

As far as disclosure of activities and positions is concerned, the code requires a Minister to disclose publicly only directorships and official positions. It is thus fair to say that the present code provides for a system of partial and uneven disclosure.

Flawed and Inconsistent Provisions

One of the principal problems with the current system of partial disclosure is the lack of workable criteria for deciding what has to be disclosed, how it has to be disclosed, or whether it has to be divested. Exempt assets are defined as '[a]ssets and interests for the private use of public office holders and their families and assets that are not of a commercial character.' Controlled assets are defined broadly as 'assets that could be directly or indirectly affected as to value by Government decisions or policy,' and declarable assets as effectively those that are neither exempt nor controlled. I believe that the broad and open-ended nature of the definitions of exempt and controlled assets, although designed to achieve laudable purposes, may leave doubt about how an asset should be classified and whether it need be disclosed confidentially, disclosed publicly, or divested. This ambiguity is, of course, undesirable.

Further, the language of the code leaves the occasions and proper methods for divestiture in some doubt as well. One section of the code states that *all* controlled assets are to be divested except those determined by the ADRG to be of such minimal value as not to constitute any risk of conflict of interest; another section of the code, however, requires divestment 'where continued ownership [of an asset] by the public office holder would constitute a real or potential conflict of interest.' These sections are at odds, and the ADRG is given no guidance or indeed mandate to exercise the suggested flexibility and discretion.

What is a proper method of divestment is also not clear. In one section the code states that arm's length sale and trusts, the most common of which are set out in a schedule, are 'usual'. Elsewhere, arm's length sale or trusts are given as the two methods of compliance by divestment. The result is muddle and confusion.

497

Provisions for Blind Trust Do Not Ensure Blindness

A major problem arises from the fact that the trusts suggested in the schedule to the code, and especially the blind trust, appear to be available indiscriminately for *any* controlled asset. Given the highly elastic definition of controlled asset, it seems that almost any asset could be placed into a blind trust, including a family business, even though, realistically, such an asset would never be sold by the trustee and the blind trust would never become blind.

Indeed, it is this imprecision in the definitions in the present code and the predecessor guidelines that allowed Mr Stevens to place what was effectively a family business into a blind trust, even though by any realistic measure the trust holding would never be divested and the blind trust would never be blind. I do not suggest for a moment that this imprecision in the definitions can excuse Mr Stevens' conduct with regard to the assets in his blind trust or excuse his breaches of the conflict of interest code. The guidelines and code are quite explicit in their prohibition of involvement in management. What Mr Stevens did was a clear violation of clearly worded provisions. Still, the fact that Gill and its holdings could satisfy the definition of a controlled asset and be placed into a so-called blind trust suggests that important questions relating to the role of the blind trust have neither been addressed nor resolved.

I shall set out later in this part my view on whether the blind trust should be retained at all.

No Definition of Conflict of Interest

I have noted earlier in the report the absence of a definition of conflict of interest. The omission is critical. Conflict of interest is discussed in more than a dozen provisions in the code but never once defined. Public office holders are required to arrange their private affairs and perform their official duties 'in a manner that will prevent real, potential or apparent conflicts of interest from arising.' But the key phrases are not defined.

I recognize that, for the vast majority of public office holders, conflict of interest has a common sense meaning that does not require extensive definition. The mingling of private and public business, for example, clearly involves a conflict of interest and is wrong by any measure. Some conflict of interest problems, however, are not as black and white. For the grey areas, which require subtle judgments, a clearly written and easily understood definition is needed. Both for reasons of information and education, and for ease of compliance, conflict of interest should be defined.

Public Disclosure as Cornerstone

In my view, public disclosure should be the cornerstone of a modern conflict of interest code. I recognize that the extent to which public office holders should make a public disclosure of private financial interests has been a matter of some debate both in Canada and abroad for a number of years. I am satisfied, however, that full public disclosure of public office holders' private financial interests and activities is the sensible direction for reform.

The point was made in the Aird Report: 'full public disclosure of all economic interests and relationships is the strongest weapon in the arsenal of any conflict of interest régime' (p. 38). I agree. If modern conflict of interest codes are to ensure that public confidence and trust in the integrity, objectivity, and impartiality of government are conserved and enhanced, they must be premised on a philosophy of public disclosure. In addition to the individual effort that is expected on the part of public office holders to avoid conflicts of interest, public confidence in the integrity of its public officials requires a healthy measure of public vigilance. Public vigilance, however, depends upon reasonable access to information, first, about the fact that a public duty or responsibility of public office is being exercised, and, secondly, about the existence of any related private interest on the part of the public office holder. The first is normally within the public domain; the latter needs disclosure.

In my view, public confidence in the integrity of government can best be assured by a system that requires disclosure of the public office holder's private financial interests. Indeed, public disclosure requirements are increasingly commonplace. Most of the provinces already have in place laws or guidelines that require some form of public disclosure.

The actual disclosure requirement – the nature and extent of public disclosure, the kind of assets, interests, and activities that should be disclosed, and so on – should be set out simply and clearly. If definitions are to be used, they should be clearly worded and easily understood. If distinctions are to be drawn among classes of assets or activities, then the distinctions should be principled, plainly drafted, and, again, easily understood.

The suggestion that public disclosure must be a cornerstone philosophy for any modern conflict of interest régime does not mean that public office holders would have to bare their souls. Canadians place a high value on privacy. We recognize that public office holders have and deserve to have a private life. Thus, it would not offend the principle of public disclosure to allow public office holders the right to keep private those assets that are truly personal, such as place of residence, household goods and personal effects, automobiles, cash and saving deposits, RRSPs, and so forth. The assets that are exempt under the present code are the kinds of assets that would continue to remain exempt under a public disclosure régime.

All other financial interests – all sources of income, assets, liabilities, holdings and transactions in real or personal property – would have to be disclosed in a financial disclosure statement that would be filed in the Public Registry and made available to the media and other interested citizens. The disclosure statement, to be effective, would have to be reasonably comprehensive, but it need not require the disclosure of net worth. What is important to disclose is not the public office holder's overall net worth or the dollar value of each and every asset, but the existence and general range of value of these assets. It is my view that it may be sufficient to disclose the source, type, and range of value for certain kinds of financial interests, rather than the exact dollar amount. By range of value I mean monetary categories, such as 'under $1000 to $5000,' or 'over $100,000.'

One could, for example, design a disclosure statement that required the public office holder to disclose on an annual and updated basis all sources of income, assets and liabilities, holdings and transactions in property, as well as activities and positions held. Important policy decisions, of course, would have to be made about which assets or liabilities would require disclosure by source, type, and exact dollar amount and which would need only source, type, and range of value.

I understand that this approach to financial disclosure requirements has been in place in the United States for nearly a decade. Under the Ethics in Government Act 2 U.S.C. 701 et seq. enacted in 1978, members of Congress and of the executive and judicial branches of the federal government are required to file financial disclosure statements listing assets and financial interests by source, type, and either exact dollar amount or range of value.

The U.S. Ethics in Government Act also requires public disclosure of all activities and positions held during the current calendar year, and in particular:

> The identity of all positions held on or before the date of filing during the current calendar year ... as an officer, director, trustee, partner, proprietor, representative, employee, or consultant of any corporation, company, firm, partnership, or other business corporation, company, firm, partnership, or other business enterprise, any non-profit organization, any labor organization or any educational or other institution other than the United States. This subparagraph shall not require the reporting of positions held in any religious, social, fraternal, or political entity and positions solely of an honorary nature. (pp. 21-22).

The public disclosure statement required under U.S. federal law must be filed on an annual basis and must be continuously updated as circumstances change.

By all accounts the U.S. disclosure requirements are working reasonably well. There have been criticisms relating to investigation and enforcement, but the requirements in principle have received wide-ranging approval. I was particularly interested to learn that the disclosure requirements have not discouraged 'good people' from entering politics or running for public office. For example, a study of members of the U.S. House of Representatives and Senate conducted by the Center for Responsive Politics in 1985 found no one who felt that financial disclosure affected his or her decision to seek public office. Further, the vast majority of senators and representatives interviewed said that they knew no one who declined to seek public office because of disclosure requirements. The disclosure obligation is seen as a reasonable requirement that quite properly attaches to the privilege of holding public office.

The actual design of a public disclosure requirement for Canadian Cabinet Ministers undoubtedly merits more study. My concern here is simply to emphasize the importance of having a principled and effective cornerstone for a modern conflict of interest code. That cornerstone in my view must be public disclosure.

The Role of the Blind Trust

Disclosure is only one part of an effective conflict of interest régime. Disclosure alone does not prevent conflicts of interest. Even with disclosure, there would still be occasions for conflicts of interest whenever the public office holder's private financial interests encroached upon the exercise of his or her public duties or responsibilities. To minimize the incidence and frequency of such occasions, most conflict of interest codes, even those premised on public disclosure, provide for divestment. The Starr-Sharp Report explained the rationale for divestment:

> In theory, divesting oneself of assets and business connections frees one for the execution of one's official responsibilities without any risk of a conflict of one's governmental responsibilities with one's personal economic interests...
>
> [Divestment] is a form of preventive medicine... [R]ather than an individual continually worrying about whether a particular decision will affect one of his or her specific vested interests, and rather than having the public perceive that a public office holder could be ensconced in a position to confer benefits upon himself or herself, it has been decided that the problem should be removed in advance by requiring divestment of certain types of assets and relinquishing of certain types of interests by those in authority (p. 63).

Disclosure, after all, does not affect the continuing obligation to recuse or withdraw from exercising a duty or responsibility of office when necessary. To avoid the debilitating effect of permanent or semi-permanent recusal from exercising the duties and responsibilities of office for which the public office holder was appointed, he or she must divest certain private interests. (Failing that, the public office holder should change portfolios or resign from public office altogether).

Thus, the present code requires that controlled assets be divested, usually

501

via arm's length sale or trust. If the divestiture is via arm's length sale, the problem is at an end. If a decision is made to use a blind trust, however, the problems continue. In my view, to make the trust effective, the Minister would still have to withdraw from the exercise of any duties or responsibilities of public office that might involve a conflict until advised that the problematic asset had been divested and, with regard to that asset, the blind trust was truly blind. But the likelihood of that happening in a timely fashion would depend on the likelihood that the blind trust asset would really be sold by the trustee.

The real difficulty with regard to divestment by way of blind trust stems from the definition of controlled assets – that is, the kinds of assets eligible for a blind trust. I noted earlier that this definition allowed Mr Stevens to place what was effectively a family business into a blind trust whose blindness understandably became the subject of immediate scepticism even apart from the evidence of Mr Stevens' knowledge of any involvement in the affairs of York Centre. It is simply wrong to provide such a vague and openended definition of the kinds of assets that can be placed in a blind trust.

However, a more important question is whether the blind trust should be retained at all. The Starr-Sharp Report (1984) cautioned that 'trusts are at best an imperfect instrument,' but concluded that it could 'see no feasible alternative to trusts as a means of temporary divestment of assets that could involve conflicts between public duties and private interests' (p. 114). Recently, however, a number of studies have begun to recognize the deficiencies of using blind trusts to avoid conflicts of interest. The Aird Report (1986) noted that 'the mechanism of the blind trust as currently utilized, has fallen into disrepute. In the public eye, the blind trust is too often a mere optical illusion' (pp. 5-6). Nonetheless, Mr Aird ultimately concluded that the blind trust was still viable and should be retained.

This aspect of his report was not adopted by the Ontario government. In the proposed Members' Standards of Office Act, 1986, described earlier, the blind trust is abolished. In his speech to the Ontario Legislative Assembly, the attorney general explained that the blind trust was being abolished because 'the blind trust mechanism requires a blind faith in its opaqueness that the citizens of this province are no longer able to share' (Ontario, Legislative Assembly, *Debates*, November 27, 1986). Instead, the act provides for a 'management trust' that Cabinet Ministers can establish to manage their business interests while they are holding public office. The management trust is designed to distance the Minister from his or her private business interests. There is no attempt to blind the Minister to the existence of these business interests – indeed, the Minister is informed of any material changes in the trust holding.

I have a number of serious concerns about the management trust. First, the management trust is a confusing and unnecessary device. The confusion will arise from the fact that the management trust has nothing to do with divestment and yet will be seen as an attempt to further true divestment. It must be remembered that even if a Minister places the management of certain assets into a management trust, the Minister still continues to bear the responsibility to prevent conflicts of interest with regard to the assets in the management trust. The assets have not been divested and yet the formality of a management trust will invite a misplaced confidence (both on the part of Ministers and the public) that something akin to divestment has been accomplished. This is undesirable.

Secondly, the management trust may be an unnecessarily formal mechanism for accomplishing what would occur in any event routinely and informally. A Minister seeking properly to comply with the requirement to devote full-time attention to the responsibilities of public office would necessarily have to turn over certain private interests, whether a farm, a business, or the management of a financial portfolio, to someone else while in public office. This can be accomplished now with oral or written agreements – formal management trust documentation is not needed and, if needed, it can be made available without the endorsement of a conflict of interest code.

In sum, I do not believe there is value in including in a conflict of interest code a trust mechanism that may easily be misunderstood and misapplied. To my mind, the hard decisions about which assets can be retained and which have to go must be made, and those that have to be divested should truly be divested.

Where such divestment is needed, the only real alternative to outright sale is divestment via a truly blind trust. But given the difficulties of design and definition, and the criticisms that have been levelled at the blind trust, can the blind trust still perform a meaningful role?

The only way that a blind trust can work as a legitimate vehicle for divestment is if its 'blindness' can be ensured. The only way that blindness can be ensured is by strictly limiting the kinds of assets or interests that can be placed into a blind trust. The Aird Report (1986) concluded that '[a]ny form of asset should be eligible for placement into a blind trust' (p. 53). With respect, I disagree. In my view, the only assets that should be placed into a blind trust are those that can truly and easily be sold by an arm's length trustee, such as publicly traded securities. The blind trust should never be used for any other kind of holding, and certainly not for anything like a family business or family firm.

Given this narrow category of eligible assets and given the reality that most public office holders could use the transition period to allow for a regularized divestment of a stock and bond portfolio, the question that remains is whether or not the blind trust option should be preserved for the public office holder who prefers, perhaps for market reasons, to retain a diversified portfolio of stocks and bonds, although blinded about its contents. On balance, I question the rationale for retaining an instrument as widely criticized as the blind trust for such a narrow compass of cases, and I urge its abolition.

If the blind trust is retained, however, it should be made clear, first, that only a very limited category of assets are eligible for inclusion, and, secondly, that even with a blind trust, the public office holder remains obliged to recuse any activities that could give rise to conflicts until notified that the original blind trust assets have been divested. Although perhaps obvious, it should also be made clear that the public office holder must neither obtain, nor seek to obtain directly or indirectly any information about the trust assets and must avoid any involvement with them.

In sum, it is essential that a modern conflict of interest policy deal with the concept of divestment from first principles: the theory behind divestment, how it can best be achieved, and when and under what circumstances a blind trust alternative should be permitted. The lingering policy question is whether the blind trust should be retained for a narrowly defined category of assets or abolished outright. In my view, as noted earlier, the blind trust should be abolished.

27.3 Declaration of Interest and Withdrawal (Recusal)

In addition to the twin mechanisms of disclosure and divestment, the code also requires Ministers to avoid certain situations giving rise to conflicts of interest and contains a number of statements of principle for their guidance. There is, however, no clear direction in the code as to what the proscription against conflict of interest means for the public office holder on a day-to-day basis. Granted, a number of general principles are set out that require public office holders to perform their official duties and arrange their private affairs 'in such a manner that public confidence and trust in the integrity, objectivity and impartiality of government are conserved and enhanced,' but these open-ended principles provide no real direction and fail to establish a workable system for achieving the desired objective.

It is a fundamental premise that Ministers should not deal with public duties and responsibilities of office in situations of conflict with their private interests. I suggest a twofold system for addressing this problem that tries to prevent occasions for conflict from arising and, should they occur, provides for an established procedure for their resolution.

My first suggestion is that a registry of interests (identical to a Minister's disclosure) be established by a Minister on entering office so that public activities involving or relating to these private interests could be handled by others without the Minister's involvement or knowledge. Such a registry would therefore contain the initial disclosure and updates. It would be open for inspection by the public but its primary use would be by officials designated to see that matters involving the disclosed interests never reached the Minister. In other words, where it is considered appropriate for a Minister to retain his private interests, or where such interests have not yet been fully divested by sale, there would be a formal system in place to prevent the Minister from dealing with or knowing of any public matter possibly affecting such interests.

The registry's primary purpose would be to formalize the areas in which a need for recusal is foreseeable and to minimize the incidents of interruption or inconvenience or the suggestions of impropriety, by providing for ongoing disclosure and formal withdrawal. The registry would act as a formal declaration of interests and provide a mechanism for withdrawal. I note that provisions for declaration and withdrawal are in place in some provinces in Canada. In one instance, there is even a system for recording these occasions as well. The federal government in the United States has also instituted a 'recusal agreement' system for the executive branch of government.

Nonetheless, occasions of conflict of interest could still arise in spite of the registry, and here I suggest that the further requirement of an ad hoc declaration and recusal be made clear and explicit, with guidance given as to who should be informed of the problem and how the Minister's public duty and responsibility is then to be handled. Such a system is designed to assist the Minister to resolve conflicts of interest in favour of the public interest by providing clear direction as to what he or she must do.

I am satisfied that the adoption of a formal system for recusal will enable Ministers to meet more easily the requirements to avoid or resolve conflicts of interest. Obviously the system will be useful only where recusal is not the norm for the particular Minister. Where a Minister's private interests are of such a nature or extent as to require routine withdrawal from public duties, divestment of the interests or declining or resigning the office will be necessary. Nonetheless, in the more usual case of a Minister with limited private interests, recusal will serve as a vital adjunct to the cornerstone of public disclosure.

27.4 Disclosure of Spouse's Financial Interests and Activities

The third area of concern is spouses. Elsewhere in this report I have had occasion to observe that the guidelines and code as drafted at present do not apply to spouses. Not only is the spouse not governed by the same conflicts régime as the Minister, but the guidelines and code place no restraint of any kind on a spouse's activities or dealings with property. The entire burden of ensuring that spousal activities and dealings with property do not create situations of conflict rests with the Minister.

In this regard, both Prime Minister Trudeau's letter of April 28, 1980 (Appendix G), and Prime Minister Mulroney's letter of September 9 1985

(Appendix H), impose a duty on a Minister to ensure, first, that a spouse's activities do not create a conflict for the Minister, and, secondly, that a spouse is not used as a vehicle to circumvent restrictions on the Minister's behaviour. To discharge this duty effectively, the Minister must remain sufficiently aware of a spouse's activities or dealings with property to take whatever action is necessary to avoid real or apparent conflicts. This duty, which is by its very nature ongoing, necessarily implies that, if issues of conflict do arise and no mutually satisfactory arrangement is reached between the spouses as to who will abstain from certain activities, it is the office holder who must withdraw from the performance of public duties.

Thus it can be seen that the régime at present in place for dealing with spousal interests and activities requires a clearly defined system of recusal for its effective implementation; this system it does not possess. A further difficulty with the present régime is the extremely high level of vigilance required of the public office holder. I am satisfied that in some cases, despite good faith and real effort, the office holder may have difficulty assessing the potential for conflict, real or apparent, arising from spousal activities or dealings with property. These inadequacies underscore the need to address the more fundamental issue of whether spouses of public office holders should themselves be governed by conflict of interest provisions, and, if so, of what kind.

The present federal conflict of interest régime is unique among conflict of interest régimes in Canada in expressly exempting spouses from its provisions. In nine provinces provision has already been made (and is also being retained in proposals for change) for disclosure of the financial interests of Ministers' spouses. It is also noteworthy that the approach taken to compliance by spouses by various federal governments has differed. In 1979 spouses were governed by compliance provisions which went so far as to require divestment of some types of assets. As the Starr-Sharp Report noted, serious objection was taken to such provisions by at least one spouse of a public office holder. In 1980 the régime was changed to its present form.

The objection to including spouses in a conflict of interest régime is that their inclusion is inconsistent with recognizing that independent spouses have separate professional, economic, social, and political interests. It is said that to require compliance is to treat a spouse as an appendage of an office holder and to treat his or her interests as secondary to those of the public office holder.

I find this argument misconceived in several respects. The present federal conflict of interest régime could just as well be interpreted as premised on notions of a nuclear family with only one spouse actively involved in economic pursuits. Such a premise would favour a régime that disregarded spousal activities and dealings with properties because the potential for such activities giving rise to a situation of conflict would be remote. Indeed, one does not have to go back too far in time to find a situation where women were systematically excluded from participation in economic activity by being denied access to professions, excluded from holding office, and severely limited in their right to deal with property. A conflict of interest régime premised on the assumption that the spouses in question would be women whose activities would be confined to the home could just as easily have led to the present requirements that spouses not be required to comply.

In any event, the reality of modern life is quite different. Women today are increasingly breaking down the barriers to full participation in economic activity. Women today do pursue independent careers. Indeed, marital relationships frequently involve spouses with separate professional, financial, social, and political interests. It is this very independence that gives rise to concerns about conflict of interest.

In acknowledging the modern reality of spousal independence, however, one must also acknowledge the existence and effect of the marital relationship. Spousal independence must be considered in the context of the modern institution of marriage. Major reform has occurred across Canada in the area of family law, which in varying degrees has sought to recognize marriage as a partnership of equals. These reforms endeavour to recognize the economic contribution of both spouses and the legitimacy of their interest in one another's financial activities. The effect of these changes has been to create régimes where each spouse has a clear pecuniary interest in the financial activities of the other. These legal changes have only enhanced the social reality that spouses usually have a profound impact upon one another.

Still, it is self-evident that no conflict of interest régime could or should require a spouse to divest property or to abandon a career or other social or political interests. Such a requirement would be an unjustifiable infringement of contemporary principles of equality. This, however, does not end the matter. Other jurisdictions that have grappled with these issues have identified a legitimate public interest in compelling spouses to disclose at least their financial activities while at the same time acknowledging their right to pursue and possess independent interests. By requiring such disclosure, the reality of marriage as an economic partnership is recognized and the public office holder's pecuniary interest in a spouse's financial activities is identified.

Even with a régime that is limited to dislosure, the question of whether the public interest in ensuring the integrity of decision making in government is sufficient to outweigh a spouse's interest in privacy remains. The public interest in ensuring integrity in government has increased along with the growth of government itself. The modern state is more directly involved in the affairs of its citizens than ever before, a fact that has led increasingly to demands for openness and accountability in governmental decision making.

With this growth in government has come a diminishing respect in recent years for its institutions. There exists in some segments of the community a perception, based in part upon extensive exposure to both national and international incidents, that public office holders lack integrity. One aspect of this perception is that public duties are sometimes discharged with an eye to private gain – either the office holder's or his or her family's. Whether such suggestions of impropriety in government are made in Canada or elsewhere, they have had an impact on the community's collective faith in the honesty of its elected officials. Therefore, provisions governing the conduct of public office holders, particularly at the Ministerial level, must acknowledge the need both to ensure that actual decision making is free from conflict as well as to enhance the community's perception that this is so. The importance of these concerns cannot be overestimated. They relate to the continued legitimacy of the state itself and the maintenance of the consensus necessary to govern.

It has also been argued that the effect of requiring disclosure of financial interests will be to hamper married women unduly from entering public life in circumstances where their husbands will have to make disclosure. This would be a very serious drawback if true. However, the validity of this assertion is difficult to assess. I have been unable to find any empirical data in Canada addressing this concern. It is of some significance that the Center for Responsive Politics study referred to earlier indicated that the fact that there are now more female members, and thus more male spouses, should not affect the disclosure laws that are in place at the federal level in the United States.

In light of these views, and despite any apparent unease men may have about being publicly scrutinized because of their wives' public profile, I am satisfied that a modern conflict of interest régime requires public disclosure of the financial interests of spouses, whether male or female. I am fortified in this conclusion by the fact that all Canadian provinces with rules for disclosure by office holders apply a disclosure requirement to spouses as well.

Disclosure of Spouse's Financial Interests

I do not propose that total disclosure of interests be required without regard to a spouse's right to privacy, but rather disclosure of only those kinds of interests that might reasonably be said to give rise to concerns regarding conflict of interest. Thus I would reject as unjustified a system of disclosure that made available information such as appears on an income tax return. In my opinion, no public interest is served by this type of disclosure. The disclosure of financial interests required of a spouse ought to be identical in scope to that required of the public office holder.

Although the financial interests of a spouse ought in general to be disclosed, at least one foreign jurisdiction has sought to recognize a narrow exemption from disclosure for a truly independent financial interest which is of no benefit to the office holder. Such provisions have been the subject of serious criticism because of the vagueness associated with any kind of 'benefits' test. It is readily apparent that income, although kept exclusively for the benefit of one spouse, may indirectly benefit the other in certain circumstances. Although the question of whether such an exemption is or can be made workable cannot be answered within the confines of this report, I am satisfied that, in principle, such an exemption is appropriate for ensuring spousal privacy in those rare cases of truly independent financial interests.

Disclosure of Spouse's Activities

One area of concern that has arisen in the context of this Inquiry is the question of public disclosure of certain spousal activities, such as positions held as an officer, director, employee, or consultant. Most régimes exempt disclosure of such activities on the part of the spouse, although they require such disclosure by the office holder. This exemption obviously rests upon considerations of the spouse's right to privacy. It has been suggested that disclosure of activities is unnecessary because reporting is required of significant sources of a spouse's earned income. In these circumstances, a spouse's connection to a company would become apparent in most cases.

However, I have doubts about exempting from disclosure any activities that have an avowedly commercial character *and* that it might reasonably be said could give rise to a conflict of interest on the part of the office holder. In my opinion, it would be preferable for these activities to be disclosed. To a large extent, such activities are already included in the public record by way of other mandatory government filings, for example, lists of officers and directors of incorporated businesses. In such circumstances, to require disclosure would not be an intrusion on a spouse's privacy. If such activities are not disclosed elsewhere but are of a commercial character, the public interest in monitoring and preventing conflicts through disclosure outweighs the spouse's interest in privacy in this narrow area. Such a requirement, however, should not require disclosure of activities of a purely religious, philanthropic, or political nature.

27.5 Office of the ADRG

The Inquiry heard a great deal of evidence about the structure and operation of the office of the Assistant Deputy Registrar General. The office of the ADRG was established in May 1974 and was made responsible for the administration of the federal government's rules on conflict of interest. It was located in the department of Consumer and Corporate Affairs.

In addition to its responsibilities for the administration of the conflict of interest code, the office of the ADRG was also given responsibility for various formal document procedures that are required of the Registrar General of Canada and for the use and safe keeping of various formal instruments such as the Great Seal of Canada.

As I have noted earlier in Chapter 2, the office of the ADRG was never intended to have an independent role or function in the conflict of interest area. Indeed, herein may lie the seed of some of the difficulties that have surrounded the operation of the office as brought to light during this Inquiry. Two points became clear as the Inquiry progressed: first, the administration of the federal conflict of interest régime would be better served if the office in charge could be given a separate and more visible status with a clearer and more appropriate focus, namely, conflict of interest alone; secondly, the demands of administering the federal conflict of interest régime in an effective and efficient manner require additional and more sophisticated resources.

In recent years, a number of federal and provincial studies have recommended the establishment of a conflict of interest office that would have a clearer mandate, broader powers, and a higher public profile than that of the existing ADRG. The Starr-Sharp Report recommended the establishment of an 'Office of Public Sector Ethics' headed by an 'Ethics Counsellor' (p. 201). The Aird Report recommended a 'Commissioner of Compliance' with wide-ranging investigative and enforcement powers (p. 6). In the United States, the 1978 Ethics in Government Act established an 'Office of Government Ethics' (p. 48).

It is not my purpose here to consider the various models or to make recommendations that may be seen as a detailed blueprint for the reform of the office of the ADRG. I leave these important policy decisions for Parliament. The questions that surround the reform of the office of the ADRG – where it should be located, how it should be structured, to whom it should be accountable, how it should be designed and staffed, what powers it should have, and so on – are questions that merit more detailed study.

My contribution here is to identify the kinds of functions that the Conflicts of Interest Office, whether it be an office of government ethics, a conflict of interest commissioner, or a redesigned ADRG, should perform in principle. Based on the lessons learned in this Inquiry, I suggest that in addition to providing information, education, and consultation, and giving advice, the office responsible for the administration of the federal conflict of interest law be empowered to perform two further functions:

- *Opinions and rulings.* The office should have the power to make rulings on questions that arise with regard to details of compliance; the office should have the ability to make judgement calls and the administrative

discretion to 'waive' the application of a technical compliance requirement when reasonable to do so; where appropriate the opinions and
rulings should be published and circulated.

- *Investigation and inquiry.* The office should have the mandate and sufficient resources to undertake follow-up investigations to ensure that
compliance is achieved, or initiate fresh investigations with regard to
allegations of non-compliance or conflict of interest; the office should
also have the capability to conduct independent inquiries when investigations disclose that further inquiry is warranted.

Related to the investigation and inquiry function, of course, is the question of enforcement and sanction. Should the office have the power to issue
a public report following an investigation, or to recommend or impose
sanctions or penalties? Or should these important policing aspects remain
within the traditional structures of Parliament? These are questions that in
my view are best left to parliamentarians and policy makers.

On the office of the ADRG, I am content to make two basic observations:
first, the office as structured at present needs to be redesigned; secondly,
whatever shape the new conflict of interest office takes, it must have a
clearer mandate, broader powers, and a higher profile so that it can have
greater impact in ensuring that the new conflict of interest system will be
understood, implemented, and enforced.

27.6 Final Observations and Proposals for Reform

I have referred throughout this part of my report to the need for new
federal conflict of interest rules. It is important that I make myself clear.
Conflict of interest is much too important to leave to the vagaries of
guidelines and codes. In my view, the time has come to move beyond codes
of conduct and establish conflict of interest rules that have the force of law.
I recommend that comprehensive legislation be enacted relating to conflict
of interest; that the legislation contain clearly worded definitions and directions; that conflict of interest be defined as suggested in Chapter 3 of this
report; that the compliance requirements be clearly drawn and easily
understood; and that the legislation be enforced when appropriate with
penal sanction.

Based on the lessons learned in this Inquiry, I suggest the following
specific recommendations for reform:

- The federal conflict of interest law should be based on the principle of
public disclosure.

- Public disclosure means disclosure by the public office holder upon
entering office, and continuously thereafter, of private financial
interests and activities, by source, type, and dollar amount, or range of

value, depending on the nature of the asset or interest being disclosed.

- The same financial interests and certain activities of a spouse should also be publicly disclosed in accordance with the guidelines suggested herein.

- The rules pertaining to disclosure and divestment should be set out in plain English and French so they can be easily understood.

- The blind trust should be abolished.

- The legislation should make clear that even with disclosure and divestment, the public office holder would have a continuing obligation to anticipate any remaining areas of potential conflict and to recuse when problems arise.

- A recusal registry system should be established in Departments of government; forseeable conflict areas would be identified in advance by the Minister so that problematic matters could be handled by others without his or her involvement or knowledge.

- The office of the ADRG should be given a clearer mandate, broader powers, and a higher public profile. Whatever shape the structure takes, the office should have clear responsibility for the administration of the federal conflict of interest law and should at a minimum be-empowered to perform the following functions: information, education, consultation, and advice; opinions and rulings; investigation and inquiry.

It is important to remember that no conflict of interest system can, by itself, guarantee ethics in government or prevent dishonourable conduct on the part of Cabinet Ministers or other public office holders. Ultimately, public trust and confidence in the integrity of government depends upon the integrity of individual public office holders and their individual sense of honour. Nonetheless, it is in my view important to provide clear conflict of interest rules that have the force of law and that provide useful direction for the vast majority of public office holders who do perform their duties and responsibilities in good faith and with integrity.

I recognize that the enactment of a federal conflict of interest law is a substantial undertaking and one that will necessarily involve much more than the four topics discussed herein. It is my hope, however, that my observations and suggestions for reform will be of assistance to federal parliamentarians as they consider the design and content of a much needed conflict of interest law.

NOTE 1

Abbreviations

ADRG	Assistant deputy registrar general
BB	Inquiry designation for Shirley Walker diaries, series 1
CBCA	Canada Business Corporations Act
CCERD	Cabinet Committee on Economic and Regional Development
CDC	Canada Development Corporation
CDIC	Canada Development Investment Corporation
CEIC	Canada Employment and Immigration Commission
CIBC	Canadian Imperial Bank of Commerce
DRIE	Department of Regional Industrial Expansion
EDB	Economic Development Board
ERDA	Economic Redevelopment Agreement
FIRA	Foreign Investment Review Agency
GPT	General preferential tariff
IRD program	Industrial and Regional Development Program
MOU	Memorandum of understanding
PIP	Petroleum Incentive Program
SMDC	Saskatchewan Mining Development Corporation
SW	Inquiry designation for Shirley Walker diaries, series 2
YCC	York Centre Corporation
YCPL	York Centre Properties Limited

NOTE 2

Commission of Inquiry
into the Facts of Allegations of
Conflict of Interest Concerning
the Honourable Sinclair M. Stevens

CANADA

Commission d'enquête
sur les faits reliés à des allégations
de conflit d'intérêts concernant
l'honorable Sinclair M. Stevens

Commissioner
The Honourable W.D. Parker

Counsel
David W. Scott, Q C

Administrator
T.R. Webb

Commissaire
L'honorable W.D. Parker

Conseiller juridique
David W. Scott, c.r.

Administrateur
T.R. Webb

**TO HER EXCELLENCY
THE GOVERNOR GENERAL IN COUNCIL**

MAY IT PLEASE YOUR EXCELLENCY

By Order in Council PC-1986-1139 dated May 15th, 1986,
I was appointed Commissioner to inquire into the matter of
alleged conflict of interest. I now beg to submit the attached
Report.

Respectfully submitted.

Commissioner

COMMISSION OF INQUIRY: STEVENS

P.C. 1986-1139

Certified to be a true copy of a Minute of a Meeting of the Committee of the

Privy Council, approved by Her Excellency the Governor General

on the   15th day of May, 1986.

       The Committee of the Privy Council, on the recommendation of the Prime Minister, advise that pursuant to section 37 of the Judges Act, the Honourable William Dickens Parker, be authorized to act as a Commissioner and that a Commission do issue under Part I of the Inquiries Act and under the Great Seal of Canada appointing the Honourable William Dickens Parker, to be a Commissioner to inquire into and report on

    (a)   the facts following allegations of conflict of interest made in various newspapers, electronic media and the House of Commons, with respect to the conduct, dealings or actions of the Honourable Sinclair M. Stevens; and

    (b)   whether the Honourable Sinclair M. Stevens was in real or apparent conflict of interest as defined by the Conflict of Interest and Post Employment Code for Public Office Holders and the letter from the Prime Minister to the Honourable Sinclair M. Stevens of September 9, 1985; and

       The Committee do further advise that the Commissioner be authorized,

    (a)   to adopt such procedures and methods as he may consider expedient for the proper conduct of the inquiry and to sit at such times and at such places as he may decide;

.../2

P.C. 1986-1139

- 2 -

(b) to engage the services of such staff and
     counsel as he may consider necessary or
     advisable, at such rates of remuneration and
     reimbursement as may be approved by the
     Treasury Board;

(c) to engage the services of such experts and
     other persons as are referred to in
     section 11 of the Inquiries Act who shall
     receive such remuneration and reimbursement
     as may be approved by the Treasury Board; and

(d) to rent office space and facilities for the
     Commission's purposes in accordance with
     Treasury Board policy; and

The Committee do further advise that the
Commissioner be directed to submit a report in both
official languages to the Governor in Council as soon
as possible, and to file his papers and records with
the Clerk of the Privy Council as soon as reasonably
may be after the conclusion of the inquiry.

CERTIFIED TO BE A TRUE COPY - COPIE CERTIFIÉE CONFORME

CLERK OF THE PRIVY COUNCIL - LE GREFFIER DU CONSEIL PRIVÉ

8

Conflict of Interest Issues in Canada: The 1991 Review [1]

by Georges Tsaï,
Assistant Deputy Registrar General of Canada

1. The Ethics Scene in Canada

Most North American managers and administrators recognise that organisational power tends to be much more diffused in recent years. Within Canada's Federal public service, a widespread programme of renewal (known as Public Service 2000) has accentuated this general trend. Like the private sector, where the pyramid of power is being flattened, the Government of Canada wants to simplify rules, to give line employees more responsibility, and so ultimately to improve service to the public. As a matter of policy, the Government has said that 'it is possible to be both service-oriented and to achieve fairness, prudence and probity by relying less on rules and regulations and more on the values and renewed personal responsibility and accountability of individual Public Servants working collegially'. [2]

The Government realises that this reliance on values – including ethical values – requires fundamental changes in attitudes. In a more volatile and dynamic environment, it is the values and ideas of an organisation that are controlling, not some manager with authority. Values provide a mutually shared structure of assumptions, a common language for aligning an organisation's leadership and its people.

Organisations, like individuals, have their own set of ethics. And just as personal ethics guide what an individual will do when faced with moral dilemmas, corporate ethics guide what an organisation will do when faced with issues of conflicting values. Corporate ethics help managers and employees answer the question: 'What should I do?'

---

1 This paper by Mr Georges Tsaï was presented on September 23, 1991 at the Thirteenth Annual Conference of the Council on Governmental Ethics Laws (COGEL) held at Hilton Head Island, South Carolina, United States of America.

2 *Public Service 2000: The Renewal of the Public Service of Canada (Synopsis)/Fonction publique 2000: le renouvellement de la fonction publique du Canada (synopsis)* (Ottawa: Government of Canada/ Gouvernement du Canada, 1990) pp. 4-5 (English); p. 5 (French).

And so our management training college, the Canadian Centre for Management Development, has integrated specific components on ethics into several courses over the past year, especially the orientation course for new public-service managers and various courses on leadership and ethics. As the Honourable Gregory Evans reminds us in his second annual report as Ontario's Conflict-of-Interest Commissioner, 'good government and good ethics are inseparably intertwined'.

More generally, I continue to see a growing sensitivity to ethical issues in Canadian business and professional life. This, of course, might simply be the optimism of Francis Bradley, the English philosopher for whom 'the world is the best of all possible worlds, and everything in it is a necessary evil'. [3]

Interest in applied ethics remains high. An additional Chair of Applied Ethics has been established at the University of British Columbia, privately endowed by a professional engineer. That university is also setting up the Canadian Business and Professional Ethics Network, a national computer-linked consortium of researchers and research users. Funding for that project came from the new applied ethics strategic-grant category created by the Federal Social Sciences and Humanities Research Council of Canada.

The University of Waterloo in Ontario has agreed to be the host institution for a new Centre for Accounting Ethics. It is funded in large part from fines levied by the professional accounting association in Alberta against members who have failed, as the phrase goes, to live up to the highest accounting standards. In the field of nuclear energy, the Federal Crown corporation, Atomic Energy of Canada Limited, together with the Ontario Crown corporation Ontario Hydro, have recently sponsored a major gathering of ethical specialists on the question of nuclear fuel waste-management and disposal.

Professional and business associations are increasingly turning to codes and guidelines as a way of regulating ethical behaviour. The Canadian Medical Association, for instance, has just adopted thirty-eight guidelines on relations between doctors and drug companies: a code described by CMA officials as the most far-reaching and specific in the world. The investment community continues to debate the merits of a one-year ban on incentive trips for mutual-fund salesmen, instituted by the Ontario Securities Commission. A new code of conduct that could be binding nationally has been drafted by the Investment Funds Institute of Canada for approval by the Canadian Securities Administrators.

And publications on applied ethics have proliferated, from the proceedings of a conference last year on ethics in government and business called *Do Unto*

---

3 'Preface' to *Appearance and Reality* (1893).

Others, to the first textbook on public-sector ethics, *The Responsible Public Servant*. COGEL members might also be interested in a special issue of the Canadian journal *Optimum*, devoted to ethics and the public spector. [4] Each of these publications in one way or another deals with the swings of the ethical pendulum that we observe in our daily work, between ethics as virtue and ethics as expediency – or as some have aptly put it, between Sir Thomas More and Machiavelli.

2. New legislation and regulations

To turn to new legislation and regulations, you may recall that last year my Office published *Conflict of Interest in Canada: A Federal, Provincial and Territorial Perspective*. Fortunately I had the foresight then to mention that the legislative and regulatory horizon is constantly shifting, and indeed it has, during the past year. The cover of that publication featured a maze, to which I am now going to add some further byways.

2.1 Federal

At the Federal level, the Government's proposed conflict-of-interest Bill C-46 died on the order paper when the House of Commons prorogued in May. [5] In our Parliamentary system this is a relatively common case of 'gone, but not necessarily forgotten'. That Bill would have established a three-person commission to extend new conflict-of-interest rules to all Parliamentarians; the commission would also have taken over the conflict-of-interest duties that my office now performs for Cabinet Ministers and Parliamentary Secretaries.

---

4 Kenneth Kernaghan, ed. *Do Unto Others: Proceedings of a Conference on Ethics in Government and Business* (Toronto: Institute of Public Administration of Canada, 1991), first published as a special issue of *Canadian Public Administration/Administration publique du Canada*, XXXIV. 1 (Spring/printemps 1991); Kenneth Kernaghan and John W. Langford *The Responsible Public Servant* (Halifax: Institute for Research on Public Policy and Institute of Public Administration of Canada, 1990); *Optimum: The Journal of Public Sector Management/La revue de gestion du secteur public*, XX. 1 (1991).

5 Since this paper was written by Mr Georges Tsaï, the most important development at Federal level has been the introduction on November 22, 1991 of Bill C-114 on conflict of interest rules for Parliamentarians. (This Bill is virtually identical to Bills C-114 (1988) and Bill C-46 (1989), both of which died on the Order Paper. A Joint Committee of the Senate and the House of Commons has undertaken recently a wide-ranging examination of the subject. The Special Joint Committee of the Senate and the House of Commons on Bill C-43 tabled its report in June 1992. Instead of a separate conflict of interest law for Parliamentarians, it proposed consolidating conflict of interest rules into a separate part of the *Parliament of Canada Act*. It also proposed a draft Bill to that effect. Therefore, if new clauses are enacted, they might be quite different from what is proposed in Bill C-43. See also the other papers in this volume of *Teaching Ethics*: Vol. I *Government Ethics* (Part II) on Conflict of Interests.

Amendments to existing Federal legislation have modified Canada's conflict-of-interest régime to some extent.

The *Parliament of Canada Act* has been changed, affecting Senators and Members of the House of Commons. As I reported last year, Parliamentarians were concerned about the powers of the police to investigate them. The Act now gives the Internal Economy committees of the Senate and the House of Commons the exclusive authority to determine the propriety of any use by Parliamentarians of funds, goods, services or premises made available to them for their Parliamentary functions.

In the course of any investigation concerning the use of Parliamentary funds, goods, services or premises, a peace officer may seek the written opinion of the appropriate committee; the committee may provide a peace officer with an opinion on its own initiative as well. If a peace officer applied to a judge for a formal process, including a search warrant, wire-tap authorisation, and a summons or arrest warrant, the judge 'shall be provided with the opinion and shall consider it in determining whether to issue the process'.

The Federal Minister of National Revenue has also taken a first step to amending the *Income Tax Act*. An Ontario case raised the problem of donations to Provincial politicians having been improperly channelled through a national non-profit association. As a result the Minister released a discussion paper proposing changes to the *Income Tax Act*, to tighten the rules on financial reporting and public disclosures for charities.

And finally, I have an item on ethics in the marketplace. The Federal Government recently made public some possible amendments to its business corporations law in the area of insider trading and tip-offs. A discussion paper is being distributed on the proposals, which are intended to send a clear signal to all market place participants that improper insider trading is not condoned by Canadian society. The proposals would also provide for greater harmonisation of Federal corporate law with current Provincial securities law.

2.2 Provincial and Territorial

Legislative and regulatory events at the Provincial and Territorial levels have been much more extensive this year. New acts from three Provinces have come into effect, a Territorial act has been introduced, and guidelines amplifying Ontario's conflict-of-interest act have been established.

In British Columbia, the *Members' Conflict of Interest Act* I discussed last year was promulgated in December 1990. Subsequently a report by the then Acting Ethics Commissioner (and now Commissioner), the Honourable E. N. Hughes, led directly to the resignation of the Premier of the Province, a governing-party leadership convention, and a new Premier's being installed, all in the space of three months.

Alberta's new *Conflict of Interest Act*, in effect since June [1991], flows directly from the recommendations of the Conflict of Interest Review Panel set up in 1989. It establishes the office of Ethics Commissioner, who is an independent officer of the Provincial Legislature. The law deals with Members, Ministers, their spouses and minor children, and certain corporate and partnership associations.

Alberta's Act requires both confidential and public disclosures, and lists of individual relationships. In addition, the Provincial Treasurer must report annually on any payments by the Crown to Ministers, Members and all those persons directly associated with them. The Ethics Commissioner has the full powers of Alberta's *Public Inquiries Act*, and penalties for a breach range from reprimand through fines to expulsion. The law provides for a six-month limitation on post-employment activities.

The third new Provincial statute is Nova Scotia's *Act to Regulate Conduct in Order to Avoid Conflict of Interest in Government by Members and Government Employees through Full and Open Disclosure*, given Royal Assent in July [1991]. This repeals and replaces the Province's 1989 *Conflict of Interest Act*. As the title suggests, it goes beyond the earlier legislation in requiring that all assets, debts and investments be reported annually and publicly, and extends to spouses and dependent children. All political contributions over $50 must be disclosed annually, and anonymous contributions are to be turned over to the Minister of Finance. A post-employment provision prohibits switching sides during a six-month limitation period. As with the earlier Act, the administrator is a judge designated by the Governor in Council.

The heavy emphasis on disclosure could derive in part from the situation of Nova Scotia's former Premier, who resigned on his elevation to the Senate of Canada. The new Premier acknowledged that his predecessor had been privately paid substantial sums of money to supplement his pay as Premier. In the first major case under the new statute, ironically, Judge A. M. McIntosh, the judge designated to administer the law, ruled that he could not hold an inquiry into payments to the former Premier because that individual was no longer a Member of the Legislature when the complaint was laid. The press had characterised this as a significant loophole.

In the Northwest Territories, *An Act to Amend the Legislative Assembly and Executive Council Act* was introduced in June [1991]. If passed, the amendments would deal directly with conflict of interest and provide wide-ranging guidelines for members, their spouses and their dependent children.

Ontario has seen new conflict-of-interest guidelines extending beyond the provisions of its 1988 *Members' Conflict of Interest Act*. Following a change of Government after an election in September 1990, the new Premier felt it advisable to introduce additional rules affecting Ministers, Parliamentary assistants, their spouses and dependents. The *'Premier's Guidelines with Respect to Conflict of Interest'* (18 February 1991) bring in more stringent provisions than the Act itself in the areas of contracts or agreements with the Government; disclosure; divestment; gifts, hospitality and benefits; communicating with the judiciary, tribunals and ministries; and land ownership.

3. Cases

Rather than attempt a transcontinental sweep of conflict-of-interest cases – out from under the national carpet, so to speak – I am going to start with what was suddenly the most publicised conflict-of-interest case in Canada this year. Then I shall review some of the other cases more briefly.

That dramatic case concerns Bill Vander Zalm of British Columbia. After he temporarily withdrew from Provincial politics, he purchased property and began developing Fantasy Garden World, a theme park. He then ran successfully for leadership of the governing Social Credit Party in 1986, simultaneously becoming Premier of the Province. Although he maintained that it was his wife's business, he in fact retained 83⅓% ownership.

In February 1991, court documents revealed that the Premier was directly involved in the sale of Fantasy Gardens, and that he may have arranged special privileges for the Head of the Taiwan conglomerate that had bought the Gardens. The Premier then asked the Acting Commissioner of Conflict of Interest to investigate the sale of Fantasy Gardens and this was carried out under the existing *Conflict of Interest Guidelines for Ministers and Parliamentary Secretaries*. Mr Hughes found that the Premier had mixed his private affairs with his public responsibilities in the following ways which amounted to conflict of interest on the part of the Premier.

i. Arranging a meeting with prospective buyers of the Gardens and senior government officials in which future investment possibilities in the Province were discussed.

ii. Arranging an official luncheon for the buyers at Government House with the Lieutenant Governor.

iii. Contacting the President of Petro-Canada, a Federal Crown Corporation, to discuss the purchaser's desire to acquire a lot adjacent to the Gardens but, at that time, owned by Petro-Canada.

iv. Impairment of the Premier's abilities to exercise his duties and responsibilities relevant to this matter in an objective way in the future in light of a $20,000.00 cash payment that passed from the purchasers to the Premier during the final negotiating session coupled with the lack of any reasonable explanation for the passing of this cash amount.

With respect to this activity, the Commissioner found that the Premier had played 'the primary and dominant role' in the sale of the Gardens and in the indicated ways, had breached the guidelines that the Premier had issued for Ministerial performance.

Commissioner Hughes' conclusion states that 'the Premier's problem stems not just from his inability to draw a line between his private and public life but in his apparently sincere belief that no conflict existed so long as the public was not aware of what was going on'. The Premier resigned forthwith.

Mr Vander Zalm then asked the British Columbia Supreme Court to set aside the Hughes report, on the grounds that the Commissioner was acting in a quasi-judicial capacity, and hence his conclusions could be reviewed by the courts. The Supreme Court found that Mr Hughes' investigation dealt with events that occurred before the new legislation was enacted; the investigation was actually carried out using the Guidelines in effect at the time. Because Mr Hughes was functioning as a respected adviser giving an informed opinion rather than as Conflict-of-Interest Commissioner, his report was not subject to judicial review. More recently, a charge of breach of trust has been laid against Mr Vander Zalm under the Criminal Code.

The other events I am going to mention received much less publicity than the Vander Zalm case. I begin at the Federal level.

- Two weeks ago, a criminal charge of influence peddling was laid against a Senator by the Royal Canadian Mounted Police. He has been accused of accepting illegal payments for helping an industrialist who was seeking Federal government grants.

- The Federally appointed part-time Chairman of a Harbour Commission resigned after allegations of conflict of interest were raised in the House of Commons. It was suggested that he received $400,000 in professional fees from a company for representing it in the sale of waterfront property to the Harbour Commission. An independent inquiry appointed by the Minister of Transport later found that he was in clear and continuing conflict of interest, and that he had violated the Harbour Commission's conflict-of-interest guidelines. The Royal Canadian Mounted Police subsequently charged him with one count of breach of trust, and the case is pending.

- A very senior Air Force officer was dismissed when he could not justify his use of government aircraft and travel expenses for personal purposes.

- The Department of External Affairs and the Royal Canadian Mounted Police are continuing an investigation into the improper conversion of full-fare airline tickets into discount tickets by public servants who pocketed the difference. As of mid-August, one hundred and twenty-seven employees had received reprimands, suspensions or fines, and $297,000 had been recovered.

- One case of post-employment activities concerned allegations about a former member of the Prime Minister's Office. The individual rejoined a private-sector consulting firm in which he had been a partner before his government employment. A large Crown corporation granted the company a $700,000 contract two months before he rejoined the firm. The former office-holder maintained that he had no role either in bidding for or awarding the contract, nor was he directly involved in its execution. The allegations were not pursued further.

- Under a little-used procedure of the Criminal Code, thirteen current and former Federal politicians and three high-level RCMP officials were charged with obstruction of justice and conspiracy to defraud the government. The charges were initiated by a private citizen acting as a self-appointed ethics watchdog. On September 16, 1991, all charges were dropped except those still being investigated against a former Minister.

- And finally, an update on the matter of confidentiality of information held by my Office: as I reported last year, a journalist requested access to records of all public office-holders for which the Assistant Deputy Registrar General is the designated official. On being denied access, including access under the *Access to Information Act*, the journalist asked the Federal Court of Canada to review the denial. The Court's trial division rules that the journalist's lawyer be given limited access to the files to argue why they should be disclosed. On appeal, however, the Court's appeal division has now overturned that ruling, and the action has been discontinued. This means that personal information provided to my Office remains confidential.

Provincially, a sample of specific events indicates the range of issues that attracted public attention over the past year.

- In British Columbia, a Cabinet Minister resigned in the aftermath of the Fantasy Gardens affair, when court documents revealed that he had supplied the former Premier with confidential information about the real-estate agent in the sale of the former Premier's theme park.

- Ontario's Conflict of Interest Commissioner, the Honourable Gregory Evans, was asked for an opinion following allegations that three Cabinet Ministers had not divested themselves of modest business interests in the form of rental properties. He held that such holdings did not constitute a business interest, on the grounds that they were 'simply a supplemental form of income'. Two Parliamentary Secretaries were treated similarly, and a third Parliamentary Secretary eventually resigned rather than sell his medical practice.

- Two Ontario Cabinet Ministers tendered their resignations – which were later refused – after it became known that they had written letters to the College of Physicians and Surgeons, expressing their opinions on a physician's possible suspension.

- The Patti Starr case in Ontario, to which I alluded during my review a year ago, has been resolved. Ms Starr faced thirty-three charges of violating the Province's election-finances law and eleven fraud-related charges, all stemming from her improperly channelling political donations through a national non-profit organisation. She pleaded guilty to one breach-of-trust and several criminal-fraud charges, and was convicted of eight charges under Ontario's *Election Finances Act*. She has been sentenced to six months in jail and fined $3,500.

- Also in Ontario, the Mayor of Ottawa assumed the Presidency of a new National Hockey League franchise, appropriately called the Ottawa Senators, and was widely criticised for holding two jobs. Although the Province's *Municipal Conflict of Interest Act* does not prevent a Mayor from holding a second job, he finally resigned his public office. In the meantime Ontario's previous Minister of Municipal Affairs appointed a panel to recommend tougher conflict-of-interest legislation for Municipalities.

- A New Brunswick Cabinet Minister resigned after allegations concerning his previous job. When he was Chairman of a large public-utility company, it awarded contracts to a company run by some of his political associates.

- A Cabinet Minister in Nova Scotia was acquitted of criminal charges laid after he revealed confidential medical information about a senior public servant. This public servant has raised wide-ranging allegations of political corruption. The resulting police investigation cleared a former Premier but led to charges against the public servant's predecessor and the director of a company which had renovated the legislature building.

- Finally, a Cabinet Minister in Newfoundland, who had also been involved in a controversy last year, resigned following allegations about an adviser. That individual allegedly helped a campaign worker get a government job by supplying a list of questions that were to be asked at an interview.

4. Conclusion

To summarise the events of the past year, I would say that in spite of the litany or alleged ethical lapses I have just recited, 1991 has been a good year. An awareness of ethical issues is undoubtedly permeating many areas of society. And there has been a good deal of legislative and regulatory activity, particularly on the Provincial scene: nine of Canada's ten Provinces now have specific conflict of interest statutes.

On the other hand – and in this business, there is always another hand – the cases that I have mentioned exemplify the usual roster of inexperience, blundering, lack of judgement, or simple ignorance. In the public mind, moreover, perceptions remain negative. A Gallup poll taken eleven months ago indicated that 65% of Canadians believe that corruption and favouritism in national politics were increasing, while only 6% felt they were decreasing and 22% said they were about the same.

Unfortunately – or may be fortunately – we cannot depend in our work on any generally accepted and immutable bottom-line of ethical behaviour. Conflict-of-interest rules will always reflect the fluctuating values and perceptions of society at large.

Quite obviously, we are – at least in North America – moving to more rigid rules. But we must, at the same time, move toward more sophisticated applications of these rules. If we do not, we risk discouraging experienced and competent persons from seeking public office.

I am not trying here to suggest that we have to become too easy on those who breach the rules. But I do think that a good measure of our success will depend on our ability to reconcile a sensible and reasonable approach with our overall objective which is to enhance public confidence in the integrity of the political system. In other words, to achieve the perfect balance between Machiavelli and Thomas More.

NOTE 1

Administration of the Conflict of Interest and Post-Employment Code for Public Office Holders

Office of the Assistant Deputy Registrar General of Canada

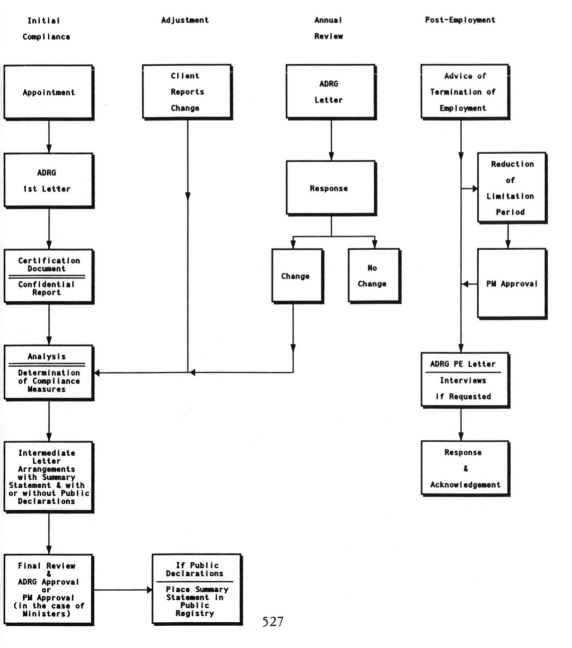

527

9

Conflict of Interest in Canada, 1992: A Federal, Provincial and Territorial Perspective [1]

by Georges Tsaï, Assistant Deputy Registrar General of Canada

Introduction

Conflict of interest issues are in all likelihood as old as the exercise of power itself. Plato recommended in *The Republic* that philosopher-kings and others holding public office relinquish their estates and content themselves with a salary just sufficient to support them. Nepotism has also attracted much attention, since this practice, apparently abused in the fifteenth century by Pope Innocent VIII, consists in favouring one's relatives and more particularly – etymologically speaking, at least – one's nephews.

Throughout the centuries and in different settings, kings have seized upon State monopolies, barons have held several offices simultaneously (frequently by inheritance) and certain heads of State have misused their positions of trust for personal advantage.

In Canada, conflict of interest questions have been part of our political drama since well before Confederation. Each generation of legislators has responded as it saw best to the complicated ethical issues raised by the demands of administering our intricate Parliamentary system.

In the past two decades, as a result of higher ethical expectations, pressures on all levels of government have intensified to adopt clear conflict of interest rules which would enhance public confidence in the integrity of public office holders and the public service.

---

1 The paper, printed here with small modifications, was first published by the Office of the Assistant Deputy Registrar General of Canada, 1992. (Minister of Supply and Services Canada 1992; Catalogue No. RG 15-7/1992 ISBN 0-662-59245-X.) Both the separate *Introduction* to the First Edition (1990) of this paper and the *Introduction to the 1992 Update*, have not been reproduced here in full, nor has the Appendix which lists the officers responsible for conflict of interest provisions, been reproduced. However, the other considerable updating by Mr Georges Tsaï of the conflict of interest provisions at the Federal, Provincial, and Territorial levels in Canada are reprinted in this 1992 update.

In 1974, the Federal government [of Canada] assigned the administration of its conflict of interest guidelines to the Office of the Assistant Deputy Registrar General. The Office continues to oversee the application of the Government's *Conflict of Interest and Post-Employment Code for Public Office Holders*. At the same time, many Provinces have passed formal conflict of interest laws, and all Provinces and Territories have a variegated array of codes, rules, directives, regulations, Orders in Council and guidelines in place.

This publication attempts to provide a single list of the major conflict of interest and post-employment requirements currently in effect in Canada, together with the various categories of public office holders to whom they apply.

1. The Federal Government [2]

The Federal government of Canada regulates potential conflicts of interest by a combination of Federal statutes, Parliamentary rules and administrative provisions. The nature of the governing authority in effect generally depends on the kind of public office held by an individual, although under Canada's Federal Parliamentary system it is possible for one office holder to be affected by a mixture of statutes, regulations and administrative provisions.

- **Cabinet Ministers** are normally members of the House of Commons (MPs) or of the Senate. As MPs, they are covered by the *Criminal Code,* the *Parliament of Canada Act* and the *Standing Orders of the House of Commons.* In addition, the *Conflict of Interest and Post-Employment Code for Public Office Holders* applies to all Ministers. Cabinet Ministers who are Senators are subject to essentially the same authorities, except that the *Rules of the Senate of Canada* apply, rather than the *Standing Orders of the House of Commons.*

- **Parliamentary Secretaries** are MPs, and as such are covered by the *Criminal Code,* the *Parliament of Canada Act* and the *Standing Orders of the House of Commons.* The *Conflict of Interest and Post-Employment Code for Public Office Holders* also applies to them.

- **Senators** are governed by the *Criminal Code,* the *Parliament of Canada Act* and the *Rules of the Senate of Canada.*

- **MPs** are subject to the *Criminal Code,* the *Parliament of Canada Act* and the *Standing Orders of the House of Commons.*

- A variety of full-time **Governor-in-Council appointees,** including **Deputy Ministers,** and Members of Cabinet Ministers' staffs known as

---

2 See also the other papers on this topic in this *Volume I: Government Ethics* by Mr Jean-Pierre Kingsley, pp. 105-20; Professor Andrew Stark, pp. 121-47 and Mr Georges Tsaï, pp. 517-527.

ministerial exempt staff, are subject to the *Criminal Code* and the *Conflict of Interest and Post-Employment Code for Public Office Holders*. Part-time Governor-in-Council appointees are subject to the *Criminal Code*, Part I of the *Conflict of Interest and Post-Employment Code for Public Office Holders*, and other compliance measures that may be established by their organizations.

- **Public servants** are governed by the *Criminal Code* and the *Conflict of Interest and Post-Employment Code for the Public Service*.

- Members of the **RCMP** are covered by the *Criminal Code*, certain provisions of the *Conflict of Interest and Post-Employment Code for Public Office Holders*, the conflict of interest provisions of the *Royal Canadian Mounted Police Act* and *Commissioner's Standing Orders*.

- Members of the **Canadian Armed Forces** are subject to the *Criminal Code*, certain provisions of the *Conflict of Interest and Post-Employment Code for Public Office Holders*, the *Code of Service Discipline* and orders concerning conflict of interest made pursuant to the *National Defence Act*.

1.1 Criminal Code of Canada

The *Criminal Code of Canada* is the Federal statute with the broadest application to conflicts of interest. All of the Federal public office holders considered in this survey, and indeed all Canadians, are subject to its general provisions on corruption, including bribery, fraud, breach of trust, and selling, purchasing or influencing appointments and offices.

Sections 119 and 120 of the *Criminal Code* forbid Members of Parliament, Members of Provincial legislatures, and public officers, among others, from accepting or giving 'any money, valuable consideration, office, place or employment for himself or another person in respect of anything done or omitted to be done or omitted by him in his official capacity'. The penalty is imprisonment for up to fourteen years. Section 121 forbids frauds upon the Government such as loans or benefits in exchange for co-operation, and forbids contractors from contributing to election funds in order to obtain contracts. Other offences include breach of trust by a public officer (s. 122), selling or purchasing offices (s. 124), and influencing or negotiating appointments or dealing in offices (s. 125). For each of these offences the penalty is imprisonment for up to five years.

1.2 Parliament of Canada Act

The *Parliament of Canada Act* contains several conflict of interest prohibitions specifically concerning Senators and MPs. Senators are forbidden by ss. 14-16 from being party to any contracts with the Government or from receiving or agreeing to receive direct or indirect compensation for services rendered to others in relation to any matter before Parliament, including trying to influence other Senators or MPs. The penalties are fines which range from $200 per day for contractual dealings to $2,000 for receiving prohibited compensation.

The conflict of interest provisions that apply specifically to MPs are set out in ss. 32-41. Sections 32 and 33 govern the eligibility of a Member to sit in the House of Commons, forbidding the acceptance of any other office, commission or employment in the service of the Government of Canada, with certain exceptions such as the offices of Cabinet Minister, Parliamentary Secretary or active service in the Armed Forces in wartime. Anyone who contracts with the Government or who works for such a contractor is not eligible to be a Member of the House of Commons, and shall not sit or vote in the House (ss. 34-40), although an MP may be a shareholder with a company having a Government contract that does not involve building any public work (s. 40). Section 41 is similar to the strictures on Senators in s. 16 and forbids MPs from receiving any compensation. The penalties include disqualification from sitting as a Member for five years after conviction and fines of $500 to $2,000.

In April 1991, the *Parliament of Canada Act* was amended to give additional powers to the Senate and House committees responsible for internal administration. These committees now have the exclusive authority to determine whether funds, goods, services or premises made available to Parliamentarians for carrying out their official functions were properly used. A peace officer investigating such matters may seek the opinion of the appropriate committee and a judge from whom a formal process is requested must consider the opinion of the committee, if one has been given.

1.3 Rules of the Senate of Canada

Under the *Rules of the Senate of Canada*, a Senator is not entitled to vote on any question in which the Senator has a pecuniary interest not available to the general public (s. 49). Nor shall a Senator who has any pecuniary interest in a matter referred to any Select Committee sit on that committee (s. 75).

1.4 Standing Orders of the House of Commons

Similarly, under the *Standing Orders of the House of Commons*, an MP may not vote on any question in which the Member has a direct pecuniary interest (s. 21); s. 22 requires public registration of any sponsored foreign travel; and s. 23 forbids bribery at elections and offering advantages to MPs for promoting a matter to be transacted in Parliament.

1.5 Conflict of Interest and Post-Employment Code for Public Office Holders

By far the most explicit provisions and requirements to prevent conflicts of interest at the Federal level are set out in the *Conflict of Interest and*

531

Post-Employment Code for Public Office Holders and a companion document for public servants, the *Conflict of Interest and Post-Employment Code for the Public Service.* Effectively applying to all Federal public office holders, the overriding objectives of both are the maintenance and enhancement of public confidence in the integrity of the people and institutions of government.

The Code, building on a series of earlier guidelines issued since 1964, was tabled by the Prime Minister in September 1985.

The Code provides for two sets of compliance measures: Category A public office holders, who are subject to the more stringent requirements, and Category B public office holders. Category A public office holders include Ministers of the Crown, Parliamentary Secretaries, full-time Governor-in-Council appointees and designated senior Members of ministerial exempt staff. Category B public office holders include Members of ministerial exempt staff who have not been designated as Category A, and all employees of a department for whom the Treasury Board is the employer.

The *Conflict of Interest and Post-Employment Code for Public Office Holders* requires every public office holder to conform to nine principles:

a. public office holders shall perform their official duties and arrange their private affairs in such a manner that public confidence and trust in the integrity, objectivity and impartiality of Government are conserved and enhanced

b. public office holders have an obligation to act in a manner that will bear the closest public scrutiny, an obligation that is not fully discharged by simply acting within the law

c. public office holders shall not have private interests, other than those permitted pursuant to this Code, that would be affected particularly or significantly by Government actions in which they participate

d. on appointment to office, and thereafter, public office holders shall arrange their private affairs in a manner that will prevent real, potential or apparent conflicts of interest from arising but if such a conflict does arise between the private interests of a public office holder and the official duties and responsibilities of that public office holder, the conflict shall be resolved in favour of the public interest

e. public office holders shall not solicit or accept transfers of economic benefit, other than incidental gifts, customary hospitality, or other benefits of nominal value, unless the transfer is pursuant to an enforceable contract or property right of the public office holder

f. public office holders shall not step out of their official roles to assist private entities or persons in their dealings with the Government where this would result in preferential treatment to any person

g. public office holders shall not knowingly take advantage of, or benefit from, information that is obtained in the course of their official duties and responsibilities and that is not generally available to the public

h. public office holders shall not directly or indirectly use, or allow the use of, government property of any kind, including property leased to the government, for anything other than officially approved activities, and

i. public office holders shall not act, after they leave public office, in such a manner as to take improper advantage of their previous office.

Compliance with the *Conflict of Interest and Post-Employment Code for Public Office Holders* is mandatory for Cabinet Ministers, Parliamentary Secretaries, full-time Governor-in-Council appointees and ministerial exempt staff. The Office of the Assistant Deputy Registrar General of Canada (ADRG), charged by the Prime Minister in 1974 with overseeing earlier conflict of interest guidelines, currently administers the Code as it applies to these public office holders.

A requirement of the Code is that every public office holder provide the Office of the ADRG with a written Confidential Report of all assets, liabilities and outside activities.

All assets must be reported, with the exception of certain exempt items such as a house which is for personal or recreational use, and fixed-income investments. Assets other than exempt items are considered to be of two kinds: declarable or controlled. Declarable assets are those that are not likely to give rise to a conflict of interest situation, and include, for example, ownership interests in family businesses and farms under commercial operation; a public declaration of them is made available in a Public Registry maintained by the ADRG. Controlled assets include publicly traded securities, futures, commodities and foreign currencies held for speculative purposes. All controlled assets must be divested, either by outright sale or by the establishment of a trust agreement.

Direct and contingent liabilities must be reported for review by the ADRG to ensure that no conflict of interest can arise.

Category A public office holders may only hold directorships or official positions in non-profit outside activities that do not give rise to an actual or perceived conflict of interest. All former activities held two years before appointment, including those in the private sector, must be reported for possible inclusion in the Public Registry. Category A public office holders may not practise a profession outside of their official duties; may not hold office in a union or professional association; may not actively manage or operate a business or commercial entity; and may not serve as a paid consultant.

Gifts, hospitality and other benefits must as a general rule be declined if they could influence the Category A public office holder's judgement or performance of official duties and responsibilities. Incidental items of nominal value received in the course of performing the duties and responsibilities of an office are acceptable, provided that they are within the bounds of propriety, a normal expression of courtesy or protocol, and do not bring suspicion on the office holder's impartiality. Other gifts, hospitality or benefits of nominal value received from Governments or in connection with an official or public event are permissible, as are those received from family members and close friends. Acceptable gifts worth more than $200, except for those received from family members and close friends, require a public declaration.

Category B public office holders are subject to specific compliance measures when assets, liabilities, outside activities, gifts, benefits and hospitality might give rise to a conflict of interest situation in respect of the office holder's official duties and responsibilities.

Public office holders subject to the post-employment obligations may not act for or on behalf of any entity, in respect of any specific on-going proceeding, transaction, negotiation or case to which the Government is a party and in which they participated. This prohibition is not limited in time, but by the resolution of the matter. For a period of one year after leaving office, or two years for Cabinet Ministers, they may not accept employment with an entity with which they had significant official dealings in their last year of public office. They may not make representations on behalf of a third party to any governmental entity with which they had significant official dealings during their last year of public office. And they may not provide advice for the commercial purposes of the recipient of the counsel on the programmes and policies of their former Department or agency unless that advice is based on information generally available to the public. Subject to certain conditions, a former public office holder may be granted a reduction of the limitation period on employment.

Four kinds of compliance measures are described in the Code: avoidance, the Confidential Report, public declaration, and divestment. The ADRG recommends to the public office holder the most appropriate compliance measures, taking into consideration the particulars of each situation and the office held by the individual. The Office has also developed precedents establishing comprehensive limits on participation in certain activities or the holding of certain assets. Under the Code, the Office has no investigative powers.

1.6 Conflict of Interest and Post-Employment Code for the Public Service

The *Conflict of Interest and Post-Employment Code for the Public Service* has been extracted from the *Conflict of Interest and Post-Employment Code for Public Office*

Holders, and is applicable to all public servants appointed under the *Public Service Employment Act.* It consists of principles, compliance measures equivalent to those described in the preceding section, applicable to Category B public office holders, and post-employment compliance measures for senior public servants only. Supplementary compliance measures may be required by Departments to meet their particular needs, subject to Treasury Board approval. It is administered by the Deputy Head of each Department.

1.7 Other initiatives

Bill C-43, *Members of the Senate and House of Commons Conflict of Interest Act,* received first reading in the House of Commons in November 1991. The proposed legislation was identical, except for certain minor changes, to that of previous bills C-46 (in 1989) and C-114 (in 1988). If passed, it would create a three-person independent Commission answerable to Parliament, and would introduce a new definition of conflict of interest:

> 'a Member has a conflict of interest when the Member, the Member's spouse or a dependant in relation to the Member has significant private interests, other than permitted private interests, that afford the opportunity for the Member to benefit, whether directly or indirectly, as a result of the execution of, or the failure to execute, any office of the Member'.

The Bill has specific provisions on Members' assets, income, activities, gifts and hospitality, as well as restrictions on post-employment activities of Ministers and Parliamentary Secretaries. The Bill sets out the requirement for Parliamentarians to file personal information statements concerning themselves, their spouses and dependants; the duty of the Commission to advise them on compliance measures and public declarations; and the Commissioner's power to investigate. After first reading, the subject matter of Bill C-43 was referred to a Special Joint Committee of the Senate and the House of Commons for review under a process known as 'pre-study'. The Special Joint Committee held hearings during the winter of 1991-1992, and issued its report on June 10, 1992.

The Committee's Report proposed less complex legislation that that of Bill C-43, and recommended that instead of a separate law, the new rules become a new part to the *Parliament of Canada Act.* The Report proposes that an independent office of Jurisconsult be created to advise Members concerning their obligations, ensure the public disclosure of Members' interests and investigate possible breaches.

The next steps in this legislative process are now to be determined by the Government.

2. Yukon

In the Yukon, conflict of interest provisions apply in the following manner:

- The **Commissioner of the Yukon**, who is appointed by the Federal Government, is subject to the Federal *Conflict of Interest and Post-Employment Code for Public Office Holders*.

- **Members of the Executive Council** are governed by the *Legislative Assembly Act,* and a specific Order in Council that deals with the terms and conditions under which they hold office.

- **Members of the Legislative Assembly** are covered by the *Legislative Assembly Act.*

- **Public servants** are guided by three policies: *Outside Employment Activities* (June 1972), *Conflict of Interest* (August 1978), and *Speaking in Public and Writing for Publication* (May 1982).

2.1 Legislative Assembly Act

The *Legislative Assembly Act* requires annual disclosure by all legislators, and their families, of income, assets, Yukon real estate, activities, and business interests.

2.2 Administrative provisions

The Federal *Conflict of Interest and Post-Employment Code for Public Office Holders* applies to the Commissioner of the Yukon, who is a Federal appointee.

Three policies apply to public servants: *Outside Employment Activities* (June 1972), *Conflict of Interest* (August 1978), and *Speaking in Public and Writing for Publication* (May 1982).

An Order in Council (March 1981) describes the terms and conditions under which a Member of the Executive Council holds office.

2.3 Other Initiatives

In June 1992, the Legislative Assembly gave final approval to Bill 82, *Public Government Act*. It is expected that the Act will be proclaimed in effect later in 1992.

Part II of the Act contains conflict of interest provisions governing Members of the Yukon Legislative Assembly, Cabinet Ministers, public servants, political staff of Ministers and caucuses, and board appointees. It is modelled on legislation put in place in other Provinces in the last few years and is consistent with other Canadian legislation designed to ensure that public officials avoid conflicts, and the appearance of conflicts, between their public duties and private interests.

The Act includes provisions, for the first time in the Yukon, for public servants, political staff, and board appointees; and strengthens the provisions for elected officials.

The Act defines conflict of interest and establishes those activities that are conflicts between public duties and private interests. It establishes a 6-month 'cooling off' period for former Ministers and public servants when they leave Cabinet or government service. It prohibits Cabinet Ministers and the Leader of the Official Opposition from carrying on business and other activities that could conflict with their responsibilities to the Yukon public; these provisions are now in law, rather than simply policy, as has been the case for Cabinet Ministers.

The Act requires, for the first time, that Cabinet Ministers and the Leader of the Official Opposition put their business interests in trust. It establishes the office of Conflicts Commissioner, who is responsible for providing advice to MLAs on avoiding conflicts of interest and investigating complaints. Finally, it maintains the system of public disclosure of MLAs' interests, a system now administered by the Conflicts Commissioner.

This legislation strengthens current provisions and covers all people in the service of the government, to ensure that public officials maintain the trust and confidence of the people they serve.

3. Northwest Territories

Conflicts of interest are regulated in the Northwest Territories as follows:

- The **Commissioner** as a Federal appointee is covered by the Federal *Conflict of Interest and Post-Employment Code for Public Office Holders*.

- **Members of the Executive Council (Ministers)** are subject to the *Legislative Assembly and Executive Council Act* and *Ministerial Administrative Guidelines and Procedures Respecting Conflict of Interest and Gifts*.

- **Members of the Legislative Assembly** are regulated by the *Legislative Assembly and Executive Council Act*.

- **Public servants** are covered by the *Public Service Act, Public Service Regulation No. 226* and the *Conflict of Interest Directive*.

3.1 Legislative Assembly and Executive Council Act

The *Legislative Assembly and Executive Council Act* applies to all Members of the Legislative Assembly, including Members of the Executive Council. In July 1991, Bill 47 was introduced, passed and promulgated, completely replacing Part III of the Act, which dealt with conflict of interest. The new Act is similar in many respects to other proposed or actual legislation at the Federal level (Bill C-43), the Yukon Territory, Ontario and British Columbia.

The new Part III requires Members of the Legislative Assembly to avoid any conflict of interest in the performance of their duties. It retains the provision that a Member must declare any conflict of interests and not participate in a meeting or perform any function of office that may affect the interests of the Member. It orders that Members may not hold contracts with the Government of the Northwest Territories. It provides for the public disclosure of gifts or benefits received by Members, as well as the public disclosure of their financial interests and those of their spouses and dependant children.

In terms of post-employment, the Act now requires that for one year after leaving office a former Speaker or a former Minister may not enter into a contract with a Department for which the former Speaker or Minister was previously responsible.

The amendment to the Act provides for the establishment of a Conflict of Interest Commission with powers to investigate any complaint of a conflict of interest. It also provides for a hearing into a complaint before a Commission of Inquiry, with final disposition of the matter by the Legislative Assembly.

3.2 Public Service Act

The *Public Service Act* restricts the political activity of public servants.

3.3 Public Service Regulation No. 226

Public Service Regulation No. 226 (November 1986), issued under the *Public Service Act*, puts constraints on public servants' outside business or employment activities.

3.4 Conflict of Interest and Post-Employment Code for Public Office Holders

The Federal *Conflict of Interest and Post-Employment Code for Public Office Holders* applies to the Commissioner.

3.5 Ministerial Administrative Guidelines and Procedures Respecting Conflict of Interest and Gifts

Ministerial Administrative Guidelines and Procedures Respecting Conflict of Interest and Gifts were issued in October 1988, and apply to all Members of the Executive Council.

There are four guidelines on gifts and items either received or presented by Ministers. Gifts must be worth less than $150 and be for the Minister as opposed to the office represented. Ministers should maintain an inventory of such personal gifts and other personal effects used in their office. The guidelines also direct how presentation items are to be acquired and paid for.

The seven ministerial guidelines concerning conflict of interest are similar to the principles of the Federal Code, although the guidelines are silent on post-employment requirements. To comply with the guidelines, Ministers must make a disclosure in writing to the Government Leader (equivalent to the Premier of a Province) within 90 days of taking office. The form of the disclosure is not rigid, but it should include all assets, interests or memberships that could give rise to a conflict of interest. The disclosure must confirm that necessary action has been taken to divest financial holdings or interests and positions (paid or unpaid) that would not be in compliance with the *Legislative Assembly and Executive Council Act* and the guidelines.

The guidelines and procedures are administered by the Deputy Minister of the Executive Council.

3.6 Conflict of Interest Directive

The *Conflict of Interest Directive* (June 1983) covers all public servants. It forbids undue exploitation of acquaintances employed by the public service for personal gain in outside business or employment, as well as unauthorized use of information, facilities or property. Senior public servants may not be directors or officers of companies holding contracts with the government. Payments or other benefits such as bribes are forbidden.

Deputy Heads of Departments are responsible for administering the directive.

4. British Columbia

British Columbia regulates conflict of interest through statutes and specific conflict of interest guidelines.

- **Members of the Legislative Assembly** (including **Cabinet Ministers** and **Parliamentary Secretaries**) are subject to the *Members' Conflict of Interest Act* and some sections of the *Constitution Act*, and they must comply with the *Financial Disclosure Act* at the time of seeking elected office.

- **Public servants** are subject to the *Standards of Conduct Guidelines for Public Servants*.

4.1 Constitution Act

The *Constitution Act* prohibits all Members of the Legislative Assembly from accepting any money from the Government except for the annual indemnity, expense allowance or salary for service as a Member of the Legislative Assembly. The Member may also accept reasonable out-of-pocket expenses incurred in the discharge of official duties. A Member of the Legislative Assembly may not be a director or senior officer, and in certain circumstances a shareholder, of any corporation or corporate affiliate contracting with the government.

4.2 Financial Disclosure Act

The *Financial Disclosure Act* requires all candidates for election to the Legislative Assembly, immediately prior to an election, to disclose assets (including land), creditors and interests to the Clerk of the Legislative Assembly, who must, upon request, produce the information for public inspection.

4.3 Conflict of Interest Guidelines for Cabinet Ministers

The *Members' Conflict of Interest Act* was brought into force on December 21, 1990 and applies to all Members of the Legislative Assembly, with specific rules for Cabinet Ministers. It underwent considerable amendment in June 1992.

The Act prohibits a Member from exercising an official power or performing an official duty or function if the Member has a conflict of interest or an apparent conflict of interest. It is stipulated that a Member has a conflict of interest when the Member exercises an official power or performs an official duty or function in the execution of his/her office and at the same time knows that in the performance of the duty or function or in the exercise of the power there is the opportunity to further his/her private interest. The Member has an apparent conflict of interest where there is a reasonable perception, which a reasonably well informed person could properly have, that the Member's ability to exercise an official power or perform an official duty or function must have been affected by his/her private interest.

The Act prohibits a Member from using insider information, or using the Member's office to seek to influence a decision, knowing it would further the Member's private interests.

The acceptance of gifts or personal benefits connected directly or indirectly with the performance of a Member's duties of office is prohibited except where the gift or personal benefit is received as an incident of protocol or social obligations that normally accompany the responsibilities of office. Gifts in excess of $250 in value must be immediately disclosed to the Conflicts Commissioner.

The Act establishes a 24 month prohibition for Cabinet Ministers, after they leave the office, from receiving from the government a contract or benefit for themselves, or for another person on whose behalf the former Cabinet Minister makes representations.

A Cabinet Minister or a Parliamentary Secretary is prohibited from engaging in employment or in the practice of a profession or carrying on a business, if any of these activities is likely to conflict with the Member's public duties. A Cabinet Minister or Parliamentary Secretary is also prohibited from holding an office or directorship, other than in a social club, religious organisation, political party, or Crown corporation.

A Conflicts Commissioner, who is appointed by a two-thirds vote of the Legislative Assembly, and who is an officer of the Legislature, is charged with administering the Act. This includes providing advice to Members on how to avoid conflicts of interest, overseeing a public disclosure system which requires that all Members, annually and within 30 days of material changes occurring, publicly disclose the nature of assets, liabilities and other financial interest of the Member, the Member's spouse and minor children, and any private corporations controlled by any of them. The Commissioner also undertakes investigations respecting allegations of breach of the Act by Members.

Allegations of breach of the Act can be brought to the Commissioner by a Member of the Legislature or by a member of the public. Where, after investigating such a complaint, the Commissioner finds that the Member has breached the Act, the Commissioner must report the results of the investigation to the Legislative Assembly with a recommendation as to the appropriate penalty. Penalties under the Act range from a reprimand to a declaration that the Member's seat is vacant. The Legislative Assembly can approve or reject the Commissioner's recommendation, but it cannot impose a punishment other than the one recommended by the Commissioner. The Legislative Assembly may request that the Commissioner give an opinion on any matter respecting the compliance of a Member of the Legislature with the provisions of the Act or of the portion of the *Constitution Act* referred to above. The Legislative Assembly or Cabinet can at any time request the Commissioner to undertake special assignments that he/she considers appropriate. What constitutes a special assignment has not been stipulated but it would seem to encompass matters that relate in some way to conflict of interest generally or that in some related way, impact on Members of the Legislature.

[*N.B. It should be noted that proclamation of the June 1992 amendments had not taken place when this publication went to print.*]

4.4 Standards of Conduct Guidelines for Public Servants

Standards of Conduct Guidelines for Public Servants were issued in February 1987 as a directive applying to all public servants employed under the *Public Service Act*. The directive enunciates principles very similar (in some cases, identical) to those of the Federal *Conflict of Interest and Post-Employment Code for Public Office Holders*.

Public servants must avoid conflict of interest situations, including those that could impair the employee's ability to act in the public interest, or where an employee's actions would compromise or undermine the trust which the public places in the public service. There are restrictions on gifts, and employees are not to divulge information not available to the general public unless prior authorization is given. Avenues are provided, however, for raising concerns related to contravention of a law, waste of public funds or assets, or dangers to public health and safety. The guidelines forbid public servants to sign affidavits related to information acquired from official duties, unless the affidavit is prepared or approved by a lawyer acting for the Government.

The public servant's Deputy Minister administers the guidelines.

5. Alberta

Conflict of interest is governed in Alberta by a statute and administrative provisions.

- **Members of the Legislative Assembly and the Executive Council** are governed by the *Conflicts of Interest Act*.

- **Deputy Ministers** are covered by the *Code of Conduct and Ethics for the Public Service of Alberta* and the *1975 Premier's Statement re: Senior Public Officials – Public Disclosure of Interest*.

- **Public servants** are covered by the *Code of Conduct and Ethics for the Public Service of Alberta*.

5.1 Conflicts of Interest Act

This Act, passed in June of 1991, regulates the conduct of Members of the Legislative Assembly, including Members of the Executive Council.

Members are in breach of the Act when they attempt to further their own interests by taking part in a decision, by using their office or powers to influence a decision of the Crown, or by using or communicating information not available to the public.

The Act established the Office of the Ethics Commissioner, who is an independent Officer of the Legislative Assembly.

Each Member must file with the Ethics Commissioner a statement setting out assets, liabilities, and financial interests. Information must be provided as it relates to the Member, the Member's spouse, minor children, and private corporations controlled by any of them. Members must also file information with the Commissioner on any fees, gifts, and benefits exceeding $200 from the same source in any calendar year.

A Member may seek the advice and recommendations of the Commissioner on any matter that might involve real, apparent, or potential conflict of interest. The Members may rely on the Commissioner's advice as protection from further action, provided that the full disclosure was made to the Commissioner.

Public disclosure statements are transferred to the Office of the Clerk of the Legislative Assembly, where these statements are available for examination by anyone.

Additional restrictions apply to Cabinet Ministers, who must divest any interests in publicly-traded securities by sale or by placing them in a blind trust. Alternatively, they may seek the approval of the Ethics Commissioner for their retention.

There is a six month 'cooling off' period during which a former Minister may not solicit or accept a government contract or benefit; accept employment or appointment to a board of directors or equivalent body; or act on a commercial basis in connection with any Department of the public service with which the former Minister had significant official dealings during the last year of service.

The Ethics Commissioner may receive a request for an investigation into an alleged breach of the Act by a Member from any person, any Member, or the Legislative Assembly, or from the Executive Council respecting an alleged breach by a Minister. The Ethics Commissioner may conduct an investigation or an inquiry. The Ethics Commissioner has the powers, privileges, and immunities of a commissioner under the *Public Inquiries Act*. The Commissioner may refuse or cease to investigate an allegation if the request is found to be frivolous, vexatious, or not made in good faith, or if there are insufficient grounds to investigate.

The Commissioner reports investigations to the Legislative Assembly through the Speaker, except where the request was received from Executive Council.

Where it is determined that there has been a breach of the Act, the Ethics Commissioner may recommend that the Member be reprimanded, that the Member be fined and the amount of the fine, that the Member's right to sit and vote in the Assembly be suspended, or that the Member be expelled from the Legislature. The Commissioner may also recommend no sanction if the breach was trivial, inadvertent, or committed in good faith. The Assembly may accept or reject the findings and recommended sanction of the Commissioner or substitute its own findings and impose its own sanction.

5.2 1975 Premier's Statement Re: Senior Public Officials – Public Disclosure of Interest

All Deputy Ministers and other comparable senior public officials must continue to make regular public-disclosure statements of land and business interests in Alberta in which they or their families own an interest. They may not own shares of public companies that might be materially affected by decisions of the Government of Alberta. They may, however, own shares through a trust arrangement where all decisions are made by the trustee. The Attorney General's office receives these disclosures. There are no post-employment restrictions on Deputy Ministers and comparable public officials.

5.3 Code of Conduct and Ethics for the Public Service of Alberta

The *Code of Conduct and Ethics for the Public Service of Alberta* was issued in 1983 and is administered by the Public Service Commissioner. The Code includes provisions on outside employment, investment and management of private assets including those of spouses and children, political activities, public statements, gifts, and dealings with relatives. The onus is on the public servants to reveal a real or potential conflict of interest situation to their superior.

6. Saskatchewan

Saskatchewan regulates conflict of interest by a specific Conflict of Interest Act, as well as other related statutes and guidelines.

- **Members of the Executive Council** are covered by the *Members of the Legislative Assembly Conflict of Interest Act* and by the *Legislative Assembly and Executive Council Act*.

- **Legislative Secretaries** are subject to the *Members of the Legislative Assembly Conflict of Interests Act*.

- **Members of the Legislative Assembly** are covered by the *Members of the Legislative Assembly Conflict of Interests Act* and by the *Legislative Assembly and Executive Council Act*.

- **Public servants** are governed by *The Public Service Act* and by the *Saskatchewan Public Employees Conflict of Interest Guidelines*.

6.1 Members of the Legislative Assembly Conflict of Interests Act

The *Members of the Legislative Assembly Conflict of Interests Act* applies to the conduct of all legislators. Section 3(1) prohibits legislators from holding other government offices. Certain exceptions as to 'other government offices' that legislators may hold are listed in s. 3(2), such as Members of the Executive Council; the Speaker; Chairpersons of Crown Corporations, and of the Public Accounts and other Legislative committees; and offices such as coroner, justice of the peace, notary public, official auditor or public trustee.

Sections 5 and 6 combine to prohibit Members of the Legislative Assembly from receiving benefits under government contracts.

Specific exceptions as to receiving benefits under a government contract are listed in s. 7, including legislators who are doctors, lawyers or dentists charging government plans for their services.

The Act also requires the annual filing of statements of disclosure as to certain assets and debts.

6.2 Legislative Assembly and Executive Council Act

The *Legislative Assembly and Executive Council Act* sets out instances where Members are not disqualified when they accept offices or remuneration from or under the Crown. The Act also provides that Senators and Members of the House of Commons are not eligible to stand for election to the Legislative Assembly.

6.3 The Public Service Act

The Public Service Act deals specifically with political activities of public servants, and its provisions are intended to ensure the political neutrality of the public service, and to maintain the right of a public servant to take part in political activities, such rights only being constrained by the requirement that the activities not impair the public servant's usefulness in the position in which the public servant is employed. The Act also addresses outside employment by public servants where the permission of a Public Service Commission is required.

6.4 Saskatchewan Public Employees Conflict of Interest Guidelines

The *Saskatchewan Public Employees Conflict of Interest Guidelines*, which have their foundation in s. 51 of *The Public Service Act,* apply to all employees appointed pursuant to that Act. The Guidelines contain a definition of conflict of interest, and deal specifically with outside employment; management of private affairs and investments; dealings with family, friends, business associates, former business associates and voluntary organizations; acceptance of gifts; use of information; and post-employment activities.

6.5 Other initiatives

In the Throne Speech of April 27, 1992, the Government stated its intention of having the Legislative Assembly adopt a Code of Ethical Conduct, and introducing a new *Members of the Legislative Assembly Conflict of Interests Act*.

7. Manitoba

Manitoba regulates conflict of interest by a specific Conflict of Interest Act and policy.

- **Members of the Executive Council, Members of the Legislative Assembly, Deputy Ministers** and **Assistant Deputy Ministers** are subject to the *Legislative Assembly and Executive Council Conflict of Interest Act*.

- **Public servants** are covered by the *Conflict of Interest Policy for Manitoba Government Employees*.

- **Employees of the Legislative Assembly** are subject to *Conflict of Interest Rules*.

7.1 Legislative Assembly and Executive Council Conflict of Interest Act

The *Legislative Assembly and Executive Council Conflict of Interest Act* applies to Members of the Legislative Assembly, Members of the Executive Council

(Ministers) and the following senior public servants: the Clerk of the Executive Council; Deputy Ministers or the equivalent; Assistant Deputy Ministers; chairpersons, presidents, vice-presidents, chief executive officers of Crown agencies; and persons designated by, or occupying positions designated by, the Lieutenant-Governor in Council by regulation. The Act extends to persons who occupy any of these positions on a temporary basis.

While a Member, Minister or senior public servant is in office, and for a period of one year after leaving office, the Act forbids the use of influence in awarding contracts or conferring benefits in which he or she, or a dependant, has a pecuniary interest. Upon leaving office, the Act prohibits entering into government contracts or receiving benefits for a period of one year except with Lieutenant Governor in Council approval; prohibits acting or advising on matters where advice was provided to the government for a period of one year; and, where the person accepts employment with a person or organization dealt with on an official basis in the year before he or she left office, imposes restrictions for a period of one year.

The Act forbids the use of insider information, which is defined as information not available to the general public, by present and former Members, Ministers and senior public servants. It also requires that a Member or Minister who has, or whose dependants have, a direct or indirect pecuniary interest in, or a direct or indirect pecuniary liability in relation to, a matter raised at a meeting, disclose the nature of the interest or liability, withdraw from the meeting without voting or participating, and refrain at all times from attempting to influence the matter.

Persons other than a Member or a Minister who breach the Act are guilty of an offence and, following conviction, may be fined from $1,000 to $10,000. The penalties which may be imposed on a Member or Minister for violating the Act, after a hearing by a Court of Queen's Bench Judge, include one or more of the following: disqualification from office; suspension from office for up to 90 sitting days; a fine not exceeding $5,000; or restitution to the government for any gain realized.

The Act requires that every Member and Minister file a statement of assets and interests (including assets and interests of dependants) with the Clerk of the Legislative Assembly within 15 days after the beginning of each session of the Legislature.

7.2 Conflict of Interest Policy for Manitoba Government Employees

The *Conflict of Interest Policy for Manitoba Government Employees,* introduced in March 1984, provides a set of general principles applicable to all Manitoba Government employees. The expressed intent of the Guidelines is 'to prevent employees from using, or appearing to use, public office for private gain'. They forbid a civil servant from having business or personal interests that could benefit from his or her official position or knowledge, or which could conflict with official duties. The civil servants are prohibited from acting in any matter where there is a personal interest incompatible with an unbiased exercise of official judgement and from placing themselves under obligation to others where preferential treatment might result.

Disclosure of all situations or matters where an employee has a conflict or a potential conflict of interest must be made to the employee's Deputy Minister or designate. An employee who disputes the application of the Guidelines by his or her Department may appeal to the Deputy Minister and then to the Civil Service Commission, whose decision is final.

7.3 Conflict of Interest Rules

The *Conflict of Interest Rules* apply to employees of the Legislative Assembly, who are not Members of the Provincial public service. The *Rules* have been adopted by the Legislative Assembly Management Commission, and are patterned on and almost identical to the *Conflict of Interest Policy for Manitoba Government Employees.*

8. Ontario

Ontario has a specific *Members' Conflict of Interest Act, 1988.*

- **Members of the Executive Council** and **Members of the Legislative Assembly** are subject to the *Members' Conflict of Interest Act, 1988.* **Cabinet Ministers** and **Parliamentary Assistants** are also subject to the *Premier's Guidelines* of 1990.

- **Public servants** are governed by the *Public Service Act* and a regulation made under the Act.

8.1 Members' Conflict of Interest Act, 1988

An Act Respecting Conflicts of Interest of Members of the Assembly and the Executive Council (Members' Conflict Of Interest Act, 1988) was proclaimed in September 1988, and applies to all Members of the Legislative Assembly and the Executive Council, and their spouses, minor children and private companies controlled by any of them. It is administered by a Commissioner, who is an officer of the Legislative Assembly.

A conflict of interest arises, under the definition of the Act, 'when a Member makes a decision or participates in making a decision in the execution of his or her office and at the same time knows that in the making of the decision there is the opportunity to further his or her private interest'.

The Act forbids use for personal gain of information gained in the execution of official duties and not available to the general public, or influencing others, and provides rules for acceptance of gifts and benefits, including their disclosure to the Commissioner if the value from any one source in twelve months exceeds $200. Executive Council Members in addition may not have outside employment, carry on a profession or business or hold offices or directorships other than in social clubs, religious organizations or a political party. A trust may be used for administering financial interests or a business of a Member of the Executive Council, and must be approved by the Commissioner.

Assets, liabilities and financial interests (including private business interests) as well as income and the sources of that income must be disclosed to the Commissioner within sixty days of election for the Member, spouse, dependant children and private companies, and thereafter annually. Certain information disclosed may be placed in a Public Disclosure Statement which provides exemptions for assets, liabilities, financial interests or income of a value of $1,000 or less.

A Member may seek the advice of the Commissioner about any obligations under the Act, and the Commissioner is empowered to make any inquiries he deems necessary to provide the Member with a written opinion or recommendations. The opinion and recommendations are confidential and may only be released by the Member or with the consent of the Member in writing.

On receiving a question from a Member of the Legislative Assembly concerning another Member's obligations, the Commissioner may investigate allegations of conflict of interest. The inquiry may be conducted under Parts I and II of the *Public Inquiries Act* and the Commissioner's report is filed with the Speaker of the Assembly, who presents the report to the Assembly. The Commissioner may recommend to the Assembly that a Member be reprimanded, or that a declaration be made that the Member's seat be vacated until an election is held.

Upon receipt of a question from the Executive Council with respect to a Member of the Executive Council, the Commissioner reports to the Clerk of the Executive Council, but is not empowered to hold an inquiry under the *Public Inquiries Act*, and cannot make recommendations.

Post-employment provisions specify that former Members of the Executive Council are forbidden for one year from accepting government contracts or benefits or lobbying for such contracts or benefits for themselves or others.

8.2 Premier's Guidelines

In December 1990, the Premier tabled a new set of Guidelines for Cabinet Ministers and Parliamentary Assistants, which extend beyond the present *Members' Conflict of Interest Act, 1988*. The Guidelines provide the following additional requirements.

- Parliamentary Assistants are subject to the same obligations as Cabinet Ministers under the legislation of 1988.

- Ministers cannot be involved in contracts with the government; however, immediate family members are eligible through open competitions with public disclosure of such contracts.

- Cabinet Ministers and Parliamentary Assistants must divest themselves of all financial interests, including business interests, unless divestment would cause undue hardship, in which case, the interests must be placed in a trust.

- All material changes in assets, liabilities and financial interest must be disclosed to the Premier, who will publicly disclose the information.

- There is a prohibition on acquiring land other than for personal, recreational or farm use.

- Upon declaration of a conflict of interest by a Minister at a Cabinet meeting, the Secretary of Cabinet shall publicly disclose the declaration after the Cabinet decision has been implemented.

- Gifts and benefits exceeding $100 must be reported.

- Guidelines were issued with respect to communication with judges, tribunals, prosecutors and police.

- Premier will make available to the Conflicts Commissioner confidential Cabinet documents as may be appropriate to the Commissioner's investigation of an alleged conflict of interest.

In February 1991, the Premier issued memoranda to Cabinet Ministers, Parliamentary Assistants and Caucus Members clarifying the Guidelines with respect to rental property, financial investments and registered retirement savings plans:

- Rental of rooms or apartments in owner-occupied property will not be considered a conflict of interest. However, ownership of rental property does pose the potential for conflict. Due to the economy, enforcing divestment would create hardships for many Members and as a result the ownership of a single-family dwelling, condominium or other such dwelling in addition to owner-occupied dwelling is permitted;

- Investments in specific companies, including debentures and stock, must be divested. Mutual funds administered by an arm's length financial institution are permitted;

- Self-administered registered retirement savings plans are prohibited, and must be converted to other forms of registered retirement savings plan investments;

- Genuine non-profit enterprises or shares in co-operatives that are bought as a condition of membership are not considered conflicts.

8.3 Public Service Act

The *Public Service Act* and *Regulation 881* (1989) made under the Act regulate the outside work and business undertakings of public servants.

8.4 Other initiatives

The Commission on Conflict of Interest is in the process of reviewing the present legislation and will recommend amendments to better define the obligations and responsibilities of Members.

By reference of the Legislature dated December 20, 1990, the Standing Committee on Administration of Justice was charged with the responsibility to 'review and make recommendations' with respect to the Premier's Guidelines. In September 1991, the Committee presented its Report containing comments and recommendations on the Guidelines and the *Members' Conflict of Interest Act, 1988*.

9. Quebec

Quebec regulates conflicts of interest by a combination of statutes and administrative provisions.

- **Members of the Executive Council** are subject to the *Act Respecting the National Assembly,* the *Executive Power Act,* the *Directives to Members of the Executive Council concerning Conflicts of Interest,* and the *Directives concerning Gifts and Donations*.

- **Members of the National Assembly** are governed by the *Act Respecting The National Assembly*.

- **Public servants** are covered in the *Public Service Act*.

9.1 Act Respecting the National Assembly

Chapter III ('Independence of the Assembly') of the *Act Respecting the National Assembly* applies to all Members of the National Assembly, including Members of the Executive Council. The Act forbids Members from receiving remuneration or benefits from other Governments in Canada or foreign States, except for service in the Armed Forces. If a Member has a personal, direct financial interest in a matter under consideration, the conflict must be declared before the Member may take part in debate and vote on the matter.

Members are forbidden from soliciting or accepting economic benefits in exchange for taking a position on a Bill, from using insider information, or from contracting with the government, except where circumstances clearly show no collusion or undue influence. Members may hold shares, bonds or debentures issued by the Government or by Crown corporations, if the conditions of ownership are the same as for any member of the public. Members may receive remuneration for professional, commercial or financial activities provided that the client is neither the government nor a public organization. If a conflict of interest exists, it must be resolved within six months.

9.2 Executive Power Act

The *Executive Power Act* forbids Members of the Executive Council (Cabinet Ministers) from being an officer or director of any commercial, industrial or financial corporation that does business with the Provincial Government. The sanctions include a fine and from two to five years' prohibition from sitting as a Member of the Executive Council or the National Assembly.

9.3 Public Service Act

The *Public Service Act* applies to all public servants, and establishes requirements for loyalty, ethics, impartiality, confidentiality and political neutrality. Chapter II, *Standards of Ethics and Discipline in the Public Service,* clarifies and expands on the relevant provisions of the Act. For example, professionals who are public servants normally are required to work exclusively for the public service, but the standards permit certain exceptions such as employment during leave without pay, part-time employment with the public service, or work as a teacher in the Quebec system of agricultural, immigrant orientation or tourism schools. The standards are administered by Deputy Heads of employees' Departments, and disciplinary measures include release from government service.

The Act forbids public servants from having direct or indirect interests in any undertaking that causes a conflict between personal interests and public duty. Public servants are forbidden from accepting gifts or other considerations for the performance of their official duties. They may not grant, solicit or accept undue favours or benefits and may not use State property. Information obtained by virtue of public office is to be used with discretion; confidential information must be kept confidential.

9.4 Directives to Members of the Executive Council concerning Conflicts of Interest

Cabinet Ministers are subject to the *Directives to Members of the Executive Council concerning Conflicts of Interest* enacted by the Prime Minister of Quebec in April 1986. These conflict of interest directives, which also apply to spouses and minor children, are similar to those of other Provinces. For example, outside professional, commercial or business activities are forbidden, as are contracts between a Cabinet Minister's company and the government (unless they hold a five percent interest or less). Speculation in real property in Quebec is forbidden, although property may be purchased for normal business purposes, such as farms and buildings. Ministers may not hold interests in public companies, except for in the case of a blind trust or in the form of investments in Registered Retirement Savings Plans that are not self-administered, the Quebec Stock Savings Plan, or mutual funds. They must make a disclosure of their interests to the Secretary General of the Executive Council within 120 days of appointment and annually thereafter. These disclosures are made available to the public on or about September 1st.

9.5 Directives concerning Gifts and Donations

Under the *Directives concerning Gifts and Donations,* issued by the Prime Minister of Quebec in December 1985, Ministers may accept gifts only if they are under $35.00 in value; otherwise they must be returned or given to the Government.

10. New Brunswick

New Brunswick regulates conflict of interest through a specific Act and regulation.

- **Members of the Executive Council, Members of the Legislative Assembly, Deputy Ministers,** certain **Executive staff members** and **Heads of Crown corporations** are governed by the *Conflict of Interest Act* and a *Conflict of Interest Regulation.*

- **Public Servants** are covered by guidelines.

10.1 Conflict of Interest Act and Regulation

The *Conflict of Interest Act* and the *Conflict of Interest Regulation 83-134* (September 1983) apply to all Members of the Legislative Assembly, Members of the Executive Council (Cabinet Ministers), Deputy Ministers and Heads of Crown corporations. Executive staff members who are ministerial appointees, but not including secretarial or other similar Members of a Minister's staff, are also subject to the Act and regulation.

Each of these public office holders must disclose to a judge designated by the Government 'all information pertaining to their involvement or the involvement of their spouses or dependant children with or ownership of real and personal property of any nature or kind, and all business and financial involvement of any nature whatsoever'. Exceptions are the primary residence, primary recreational property, automobiles, working farms, cash and domestic or personal-use items, and assets in a blind trust. The disclosure must be made before taking office, again when any change occurs to property or business interests, and annually.

The Act and regulation forbid Members of the Legislative Assembly, including Cabinet Ministers, from holding a second paid office in the Provincial government or full-time job in the Federal government; from being a director, officer or from holding more than 5% of the issued shares in any company doing business with the government; or from using privileged information for personal gain or for the gain of others.

Cabinet Ministers are forbidden to carry on any other business unless a designated judge determines that there is no conflict. In addition, Cabinet Ministers are not permitted to accept gifts or other benefits that could reasonably be deemed to influence their decisions or other duties. Preferential treatment and secondary employment also are forbidden. Similar rules exist for Executive staff members and for Deputy Ministers.

10.2 Public Service Guidelines

New Brunswick has conflict of interest guidelines for public servants which effectively substitute the Deputy Minister or Chief Executive Officer, as the case may be, for the designated Judge under the *Conflict of Interest Act* in receiving documents of discovery from selected employees.

11. Nova Scotia

Conflict of interest in Nova Scotia is governed by an explicit Act and other statutes.

- **Members of the Executive Council** and **Members of the House of Assembly** are subject to the *Members and Public Employees Disclosure Act* and the *House of Assembly Act*.

- **Public servants** are regulated by the *Members and Public Employees Disclosure Act* and the *Civil Service Act*.

11.1 Members and Public Employees Disclosure Act

The Act received royal assent on July 11, 1991 and covers all Members of the Legislative Assembly as well as all public employees. It repeals the former *Conflict of Interest Act*. Members must file regular disclosure statements for themselves, their spouses and their dependant children. The statement is to include assets, income and source, trusts, other interests, liabilities (with a few exceptions), liabilities due to the Member, spouse or dependant children, payments from any recognized political party or association, and gifts over $250. Use of insider information is forbidden and the Act requires recusal when a conflict arises.

The Act also covers political contributions to candidates as defined under the *Elections Act* and establishes general principles for public employees, including the recusal requirement.

Members and public employees are forbidden from switching sides on ongoing cases for six months after their departure from public office.

The Act provides for the designation of a Nova Scotia Supreme Court Judge (either active, retired or supernumerary) to administer the Act. This designated person may conduct inquiries and make recommendations respecting allegations of conflict of interest.

11.2 House of Assembly Act

The *House of Assembly Act* applies to all Members of the House of Assembly, including Members of the Executive Council.

The Act forbids other employment with the Federal or Provincial governments, or contracting directly or indirectly with the Province of Nova Scotia. Specified exceptions include temporary or part-time employment that requires special qualifications or professional skill, duties as a justice of the peace or notary public, active service in wartime in the Armed Forces, and activities as a shareholder of an incorporated company that has received a contract from the Province as the result of submitting the lowest bid. No Member may receive compensation for promoting a legislative Bill, or may either offer or accept a bribe. Penalties include imprisonment.

11.3 Civil Service Act

The *Civil Service Act* includes some conflict of interest matters such as improper influence and permission to run for Federal, Provincial and Municipal office on certain conditions. There is also a requirement that Deputy Heads and persons appointed to the Civil Service not undertake activities, assume responsibilities, or make public statements of a politically partisan nature or kind that could give rise to the perception that the Deputy Head or person appointed to the Civil Service may not be able to perform duties as a public servant in a politically impartial manner.

11.4 Other initiatives

On April 16, 1992, the Government tabled Bill number 205, which proposed some amendments to the *Members and Public Employees Disclosure Act*. The amendments, if passed, would permit the designated person to use the title of Conflict of Interest Commissioner, and would require disclosure of any trust which makes payments to the Member, spouse or dependant children. The Bill clarifies that post-employment restrictions would not apply to former public employees who have been laid off, and permits the Conflict of Interest Commissioner to deal with conflict of interest complaints against a former Member or employee if a complaint is made within two years of the individual's departure from public office.

12. Prince Edward Island

Prince Edward Island governs conflict of interest by an explicit Act.

- **Members of the Executive Council** and **Members of the House of Assembly** are subject to the *Conflict of Interest Act*.
- **Public servants** take and sign an Oath of Office.

12.1 Conflict of Interest Act

The *Conflict of Interest Act* applies to all Members of the Legislative Assembly, all Members of the Executive Council (Cabinet Ministers), their spouses, any individual with whom a Member may cohabit, and 'any other person whose primary source of financial support is the Member or Minister'.

The Act defines conflict of interest as seeking or receiving privileges or advantages for oneself or dependants by virtue of one's office; accepting any benefits that could reasonably be deemed to influence a decision related to official duties; making use for gain of oneself or others of privileged information; or holding an office or position incompatible with the disinterested performance of one's duties.

A disclosure statement must be filed with the Clerk of the Legislative Assembly within ten sitting days of the beginning of each session. The statement must include all assets or interests and debts over $2,000, and any contracts entered into with the Government and all gifts received worth $1,000 or more during the preceding two years.

Whenever a contract or other matter is discussed, in which a Member has a direct or indirect pecuniary interest, the Member must disclose the general nature of the interest and both withdraw from participation in the discussion and the vote, and refrain from attempting to influence. Use of insider information, bribery and influence peddling are expressly forbidden.

Allegations of conflict are investigated by a Standing Committee of the Legislative Assembly, and if a unanimous decision is not reached, the matter is referred to a judge of the Supreme Court. Penalties include restitution of pecuniary gain and declaring the Member's seat vacant.

12.2 Oath of Office

Public servants must take and sign an Oath of Office before a justice of the peace or commissioner of oaths, and attest to faithful and honest performance of duties and retention of confidential information.

Prince Edward Island has no conflict of interest guidelines for public servants.

13. Newfoundland

Newfoundland regulates conflict of interest through a specific Act and other statutory and regulatory provisions.

- **Members of the Executive Council** are subject to the *Conflict of Interest Act*, the *Legislative Disabilities Act* and the *Conflict of Interest (Ministers) Guidelines*.

- **Members of the House of Assembly** are governed by the *Conflict of Interest Act* and the *Legislative Disabilities Act*.

- **Designated public servants** and **members** and **employees of government agencies** are covered by the *Conflict of Interest Act* and all public servants and employees of designated agencies by the *Conflict of Interest (Public Employees) Regulations*.

13.1 Conflict of Interest

The *Conflict of Interest Act* applies to all Members of the House of Assembly, including Members of the Executive Council, designated public servants and Members and employees of designated government agencies.

When Members of the House of Assembly or an agency have conflicting interests with a matter under discussion, they may speak on the matter only if they begin by declaring the conflict with their interests or those of their spouses or minor children. Subsequently they may not vote on the matter unless the House of Assembly by resolution permits them to do so. Use of confidential information for personal gain or for the gain of others also is forbidden.

Every Member and public servant must file a disclosure statement upon appointment, afterwards within sixty days of any acquisition of an interest not previously reported, and annually on or before 15 January. The disclosure statement must include all land in the Province owned directly or indirectly in whole or in part by the Member or the public employee, by the spouse, and by any dependant children. Similarly all financial interests are to be reported, with the exceptions of shares of corporations (other than land development corporations) listed on a stock exchange where the value is less than $5,000.

The President of the Treasury Board is charged with administering the Act, but the Auditor General receives the disclosure statements. The Auditor General may relax the rules by listing a position as clerical, non-discretionary or non-decision making. Penalties on conviction include a fine of up to $1,000 and imprisonment for up to three months.

Samples of disclosure statements as well as positions designated as unlikely to have conflicts of interest are annexed to the Office Consolidation of the Act, as are relevant sections of the Federal *Criminal Code*.

The government has begun a preliminary review of the Act.

13.2 Legislative Disabilities Act

The *Legislative Disabilities Act* governs the activities of Members of the

House of Assembly respecting benefits from the government. In general, it prohibits a Member from benefitting directly or indirectly from any public service contract. Sanctions include forfeiture of a Member's seat and bearing financial responsibilities for the ensuing election. There are also exceptions to the application of the Act that must be examined in any individual case.

13.3 Regulations

Three regulations have been issued to carry out the provisions of the *Conflict of Interest Act:* the *Conflict of Interest (Ministers) Guidelines* (1982) and the *Conflict of Interest (Public Employees) Regulations* (1982 and 1984).

NOTE 1

Summary of Federal, Provincial and Territorial Perspective

1. The Federal Government ....

1. *Criminal Code of Canada* ....
2. *Parliament of Canada Act* ....
3. *Rules of the Senate of Canada* ....
4. *Standing Orders of the House of Commons* ....
5. *Conflict of Interest and Post-Employment Code for Public Office Holders* ....
6. *Conflict of Interest and Post-Employment Code for Public Service* ....
7. *Other initiatives* ....

2. Yukon ....

1. *Legislative Assembly Act* ....
2. *Administrative provisions* ....
3. *Other initiatives* ....

3. Northwest Territories ....

1. *Legislative Assembly and Executive Council Act* ....
2. *Public Service Act* ....
3. *Public Service Regulation No. 226* ....
4. *Conflict of Interest and Post Employment Code for Public Office Holders* ....
5. *Ministerial Administrative Guildelines and Procedures Respecting Conflict of Interest and Gifts* ....
6. *Conflict of Interest Directive* ....

4. British Columbia ....

1. *Constitution Act* ....
2. *Financial Disclosure Act* ....
3. *Members' Conflict of Interest Act* ....
4. *Standards of Conduct Guidfelines for Public Servants* ....

5. Alberta ....

1. *Conflicts of Interest Act* ....
2. *1975 Premier's Statement Re: Senior Public Officials – Public Disclosure of*
   – Interest
3. *Code of Conduct and Ethics for the Public Service of Alberta* ....

6. Saskatchewan ....

1. *Members of the Legislative Assembly Conflict of Interests Act* ....
2. *Legislative Assembly and Executive Council Act* ....
3. *Public Service Act* ....
4. *Saskatchewan Public Employees Conflict of Interest Guidelines* ....
5. *Other initiatives* ....

7. Manitoba ....

1. *Legislative Assembly and Executive Council Conflict of Interest Act* ....
2. *Conflict of Interest Policy for Manitoba Govement Employees* ....
3. *Conflict of Interest Rules* ....

8. Ontario ....

1. *Members' Conflict of Interest Act, 1988* .....
2. *Premier's Guidelines* ....
3. *Public Service Act* ....
4. *Other initiatives* ....

9. Quebec ....

1. *Act Respecting the National Assembly* ....
2. *Executive Power Act* ....
3. *Public Service Act* ....
4. *Directives to Members of the Executive Council concerning Conflicts of Interest* ....
5. *Directives concerning Gifts and Donations* ....

10. New Brunswick ....

1. *Conflict of Interest Act and Regulation* ......
2. *Public Service Guidelines* ....

11. Nova Scotia ....

1. *Members and Public Employees Disclosure Act* ....
2. *House of Assembly Act* ....

Disclosure of Financial Interests by Members of Parliament (Westminster): The John Browne Affair

by Michael Ryle, former Clerk of Committees, House of Commons

'Surely this place is about pressures' – The Speaker, November 12, 1984. [1]

1. Historical background

The House of Commons' concern to ensure that the personal or pecuniary interests of Members of Parliament do not get too closely mixed with their Parliamentary duties is of long standing. [2] In 1695 the Commons resolved that:

> *'the offer of money, or other advantage, to any Member of Parliament for the promoting of any matter whatsoever, depending or to be transacted in Parliament, is a high crime and misdemeanour and tends to the subversion of the English constitution'.* [3]

In 1858 the House resolved:

> *'That it is contrary to the usage and derogatory to the dignity of the House that any of its Members should bring forward, promote or advocate in this House any proceeding or measure in which he may have acted or been concerned for in consideration for any fee or reward'.* [4]

Despite the exhortations of the House, Members were for many years totally unrestricted in their Parliamentary actions by their personal or financial interests except when voting on private legislation or sitting on committees on Private Bills. [5] However, there was for many years a conventional

---

1 H. C. Deb., Vol. 67, col. 407.

2 For relevant studies, see G. Alderman *Pressure Groups and Government in Great Britain* (1984); A. Doig 'Influencing Westminster: Registering Lobbyists' (1986) 39 *Parliamentary Affairs* pp. 517-535; J. A. G. Griffith and M. Ryle *Parliament* (1989) pp. 55-68; and M. Rush 'Lobbying Parliament', (1990) 43 *Parliamentary Affairs* pp. 141-148.

3 C. J. (1693-97) 331.

4 C. J. (1857-58) 247.

5 See Erskine May's *Parliamentary Practice* (21st ed., 1989) (hereinafter referred to as 'May'), pp. 354-359 and 884.

obligation on Members to declare, when speaking in the House or in committee, any personal interest they might have in the subject under debate. [6]

By the 1960s, there was a growing feeling that not all Members were being as frank with their colleagues as they should be. [7] In 1969 a Select Committee on Members' Interests (Declaration) was appointed. It came down against a register, but it recommended that the conventions on declaring interests in debate should be made mandatory by a resolution of the House. [8] The report was not debated and the issues lapsed after the general election of 1970.

The problems did not go away, however, and on May 22, 1974, the House resolved:

'That, in any debate or proceeding of the House or its committees or transactions or communications which a Member may have with other Members or with Ministers or servants of the Crown, he shall disclose any relevant pecuniary interest or benefit of whatever nature, whether direct or indirect, that he may have had, may have or may be expecting to have.'

A second resolution authorised the establishment of a Register of Members' Interests and the appointment of a registrar and required all Members to furnish to the registrar such particulars of his registrable interests as might be required. A Select Committee, appointed to work out how this should be implemented, recommended that the register should:

'provide information of any pecuniary interest or other material benefit which a Member . . . may receive which might be thought to affect his conduct as a Member . . . or influence his actions, speeches or votes in Parliament'. [9]

It also recommended that Members should be required to register nine specific classes of pecuniary interest or other benefit. The register would be published periodically and be available for inspection by the public. A permanent Select Committee would control the compilation, maintenance and accessibility of the register. Neither the committee nor the registrar would look for cases where Members had failed to register or declare an interest;

---

6 See *Report of the Select Committee on Members' Interest (Declaration)* H. C. 57 of 1969-70, para. 34 and App. XXV.

7 See, *e.g.* F. Noel-Baker, 'The Grey Zone: The Problem of Business Affiliations of Members of Parliament' (1961-62) 15 *Parliamentary Affairs* pp. 87-93.

8 H. C. 57 of 1969-70, para. 114.

9 H. C. 102 or 1974-75, para 11.

they would act only on complaints submitted to them. The underlying principle was that Members were responsible for their entries in the register. As for enforcement, the committee concluded, 'There can be no doubt that the House might consider a refusal to register as required by its Resolutions or the wilful furnishing of misleading or false information to be a contempt.' [10]

The committee's conclusions and recommendations were broadly accepted by the House. [11] The Select Committee on Members' Interests was first appointed in February 1976 and is now a permanent committee under Standing Order No. 128. The Registrar of Members' Interests is also the clerk of the committee.

2. The present requirements

As far as debates in the House are concerned, and proceedings in all types of committee, Members are now required to declare all relevant interests, as set out in the resolution of the House of May 22, 1974. The requirement does not extend, however, to question time or to the tabling of questions, motions or amendments. In accordance with a resolution of June 12, 1975, any interest disclosed in the register is regarded as sufficient disclosure for the purposes of voting. [12] The limited restrictions on voting remain as stated above.

The requirements for entries in the register are more specific than those for declarations, although still significantly qualified. Members are not required to disclose the amount of any remuneration or benefit they may have, nor the interests of spouses or children, except in certain circumstances relating to shareholdings. [13] The nine classes of interest which Members must disclose, subject always to the general obligation to provide information of any relevant pecuniary benefit, may be summarised as follows:

i. remunerated directorships of companies;
ii. remunerated employments or offices;
iii. remunerated trades, professions or vocations;
iv. the names of clients when the interests include personal services by the Member related to his membership of the House;
v. financial sponsorships as a Parliamentary candidate or as a Member;
vi. certain overseas visits;

10 Ibid, para. 37.
11 H. C. Deb., Vol. 893, col. 735 (June 12, 1975).
12 For details of the declaration requirements, see May, pp. 385-386.
13 Introduction to the Register of Members' Interests.

vii. payments from or on behalf of foreign governments, etc;

viii. and or property of substantial value (excluding a Member's home);

ix. companies in which the Member or his spouse or infant children has a beneficial interest exceeding one-hundredth of the issued capital share. [14]

3. The John Browne Case

Between its appointment in 1976 and 1989, the committee received only three complaints. [15] The third, and much the most important, case was that of Mr John Browne. In May 1989, Mr David Leigh, a journalist, lodged a formal complaint that Mr Browne, the Conservative Member of Parliament for Winchester, had failed on a number of occasions to register, and where appropriate to declare, his pecuniary interests, as required by the resolutions of the House of May 22, 1974 and June 12, 1975. [16] The complaints considered fell under five heads:

i. That Mr Browne failed to declare a major shareholding in a company;

ii. That he failed to declare certain interests when speaking in a debate;

iii. That he failed to declare interests in respect of certain payments received from abroad, the most substantial being in excess of 88,000 United States dollars from the Saudi Arabian Monetary Agency;

iv. That he failed to register benefit received from a foreign organisation; and

v. That he failed to register his interest in a firm whilst lobbying Ministers and officials on their behalf. [17]

Despite the inherent complexities of the case, the basic task of the committee was essentially simple, namely to decide (a) whether Mr Browne had registered, if required, the various interests which were the subject of the

---

14 For full details, see Register of Members' Interests on January 8, 1990 (H. C. 115 of 1989-90) and May, pp. 386-388.

15 See H. C. 330 and 370 of 1983-84 and H. C. 428 of 1988-89. While this comment was in press, the committee reported on two further complaints, one concerning Mr Michael Grylls, Member of Parliament (H. C. 561 of 1989-90) and the other Mr Michael Mates, Member of Parliament (H. C. 506 of 1989-90).

16 H. C. 135 of 1989-90 (hereafter referred to as the 'Browne Report'), para. 1.

17 For full details, see Browne Report, para. 18.

complaints; and (b) whether he had declared all such interests when the resolutions of the House required such declaration. The committee was essentially concerned with discovering and assessing the facts; it would be for the House to pronounce judgement.

Select Committees are not courts of law. The rules of evidence do not apply; there is no restriction on its admissibility; evidence is not normally taken on oath [18]; those against whom charges have been made are not normally represented by counsel [19] and no witness has, of right, access to evidence given by other witnesses or knowledge of any charges made against him or her (although a Member of Parliament has a theoretical right to attend any meeting of a committee).

The committee took oral evidence from the complainant, Mr Leigh, on two occasions, and from Mr Browne on three occasions; a business associate of Mr Browne's gave evidence at one other meeting. Much of the written evidence considered by the committee was published with its report. The committee did its best to ensure that both parties were treated as fairly as possible. All material evidence given by the complainant, or upon his behalf, was sent to Mr Browne, and Mr Leigh saw all Mr Browne's replies and evidence given by him, with one exception. Both parties were given opportunity to make written comments on the other's evidence. [20] Mr Browne was not legally represented, but his solicitor came with him when he gave evidence.

The committee held nineteen meetings, all in private. The chairman's draft report was agreed to without amendment or division. The committee examined each of the five areas of the complaint and found that in several cases either the rules had not been breached or that the circumstances did not warrant further action. The committee did, however, uphold two of the more serious complaints, finding that Mr Browne, on receiving some 88,000 United States dollars from the Saudi Arabian Monetary Agency for a study he was writing for them, should have declared both the client relationship and the foreign payment. On the complaint that he failed to register his interest in a firm whilst lobbying Ministers and officials on their behalf and on behalf of their clients, while the committee found it difficult to get to the bottom of this matter because of the problems of getting evidence from abroad, it found beyond reasonable doubt that Mr Browne had in effect a 'client' relationship with one businessman which influenced his Parliamentary actions and conduct as a Member and which should have been declared in the register.

---

18 For exceptions, see May, p. 682.
19 For exceptions, see May, pp. 631-632.
20 Browne Report, para. 20.

The committee's report was debated on March 7, 1990. [21] In a personal statement, Mr Browne recognised that he had failed to register properly all his interest, and for this he apologised to the House. As far as the Saudi Arabian contract was concerned, he reaffirmed that he had not declared it because the work did not involve Parliament in any way whatsoever; having declared an interest in his company, he had not appreciated that the rule also applied to monies received from clients of that company. He accepted the committee's interpretation, but said that he was not alone in having misunderstood the rules. On the matter of the fifth complaint, he insisted that his agreement with the firm concerned did not involve any Parliamentary lobbying, but he now understood why the committee had found the relationship so close and he accepted its judgement.

The debate revealed a wide range of opinion on what punishment, if any, should be imposed on Mr Browne. [22] In the end the House rejected, by 237 votes to 67, an amendment to impose no penalty at all. It negatived without division an amendment requiring the Speaker to reprimand Mr Browne. It rejected, by 254 votes to 33, an amendment calling for his resignation. An amendment to suspend Mr Browne from the service of the House for three months was defeated by 189 votes to 111. Finally, the House agreed, without division, to endorse the findings of the committee and to suspend Mr Browne for twenty sitting days and also his Parliamentary salary for that period. It later became known that Mr Browne would not be seeking re-selection as the Conservative candidate for Winchester at the next general election.

4. Comments and conclusions

The debate on the John Browne case revealed widespread unease about the present rules on registration and declaration of interests. And since this case further concern has been expressed about a growing number of Members who have acquired financial interests since they entered the House which might well influence their Parliamentary activities. While many Members clearly feel that the present balance is properly struck, others believe that the time has come to tighten up the rules in some way to make it harder for private interests to prevail over public duty.

The debate also revealed anxiety about the way Select Committees work when examining the conduct of individual members. While the attempts of

---

21 H. C. Deb., Vol. 168, col. 889.

22 Comparison may be made with the debate held by the House on July 26, 1977 (H. C. Deb., Vol. 936, col. 332) on the report by a Select Committee inquiring into the conduct of Members of Parliament in relation to the Poulson group of companies at a time before the present rules of declaration of interest were introduced. And see G. J. Zellick (1978) P. L. 133.

the committee to give Mr Browne a fair hearing were not impugned, there was a feeling that proceedings more like those of a court of law should be adopted in these cases.

The House agreed to request the committee to report further on both these questions.

4.1 Procedure for consideration of complaints

Article 9 of the Bill of Rights protects the right of the House to regulate its own proceedings, including the conduct of its Members. It would substantially erode this position if adjudication of the registration or declaration of interests were to be transferred to the courts. [23] The judgement of Members who may have broken the rules of the House is best undertaken by their fellow Members, as with professional bodies, including those of the law.

If the consideration of complaints is to remain with the committee, it would be a mistake for it to attempt to copy the procedures of the courts; its Members are not necessarily lawyers and certainly not neutral judges. There is also an appeal from the decision of a court. If the committee were to seek to adjudicate like a court, there would be a demand for an appeal procedure that could not easily be met.

It is, however, important that the committee should ensure natural justice for the Member whose conduct is under review. It is clear that Mr Browne and other Members were not happy with the investigation procedures in his case. [24] Here are two suggestions. First, whenever the conduct of a Member is under examination, both the complainant and the Member should be represented by counsel if they so wish. Secondly, it might be desirable to separate more deliberately the prosecuting and adjudicating roles of the committee. One Member could be asked, with the assistance of the registrar, to lay the facts before the committee, and to lead its examination of witnesses as does the Attorney-General in the Committee of Privileges.

4.2 What interests should be registered or declared?

The concept of conflict of interests underlies the questions of registration and declaration. [25] It is of the nature of politicians that they should have interests of many kinds – the very fact that they represent constituencies,

---

23 The argument of Mr Tony Benn (H. C. Deb., Vol. 168, col. 913) that the principle was breached many years ago by the transfer of the trial of contested elections to the courts is misconceived. Election petitions relate to events outside Parliament and to the conduct of candidates, not elected Members; the registration and declaration of interests relate to the proceedings of the House and to the conduct of its Members.

24 H. C. Deb., Vol. 168, cols. 890, 905, 922, 935-937, 945-946, 956-958, 961-962.

25 The whole issue was clearly analysed by S. Williams in Conflict of Interest: the Ethical Dilemma in Politics (1985).

and that they wish to be re-elected, creates an interest – and they want to promote causes, to change the world, or to halt such changes; the totally disinterested Member of Parliament would be a poor creature indeed.

The challenge, therefore, is not so much to ensure, as Sir Geoffrey Howe has said, that there is never a conflict of interests, [26] but rather to seek to ensure that when such conflict of interests arises the Member makes the right choice and follows his Parliamentary obligations, not his personal interests.

There are three ways by which Members could be guided towards making the right choice. First, Members could be prohibited from having any interests which could conflict with their Parliamentary duties. This is essentially the rule that applies to Ministers and civil servants; it is also partially applied in the United States Congress, which attempts to limit the outside earnings of Congressmen. Secondly, Members could be barred from speaking or voting on any matter in which they have a personal or financial interest. Thirdly, there is the present Parliamentary solution of requiring that all relevant interests are made public in the hope that this will discourage Members from putting their personal interests first.

The first solution has its supporters in the House, [27] but the majority of Members appears – rightly in my view – to consider it acceptable, given the scale of Parliamentary salaries, that Members should be able to earn money outside so long as this does not conflict with their duties to the House and to their constituents. Some outside activities, for example in broadcasting or writing, are an integral part of political life. Experience in commerce or industry or teaching may also be valuable. Some payment for such activities seems fair. What appears to be less honourable is the practice of accepting directorships – and the fees – without doing any real work, so that the firm can have the assumed advantage of having a Member of Parliament's name on its notepaper. A prohibition on Members receiving any outside earnings would also be difficult to police or enforce and would lead to constant controversy.

The second possibility is also fraught with difficulties. Local councillors have executive responsibilities, in awarding contracts or deciding planning applications, for example, and it is essential that they take no part in such business when they are personally financially interested. The position is totally different in the House of Commons, where Members are debating matters of public policy and holding to account those who take executive decisions. In a sense all Members have an interest, on behalf of their constituents as well as themselves, in all questions of public policy and must be allowed to participate in their deliberation. Strictly enforced, the local government solution would bring the work of the House to a halt.

---

26 H. C. Deb., Vol. 168, col, 896.

27 See, *e.g.* H. C. Deb., Vol. 168. cols. 910-911, 932-933, 954-956, 973-976.

So we are left with the solution that the House has already adopted. Can it be improved? The main difficulty lies in deciding which outside interests are broadly acceptable and which are potentially harmful. This turns on three things: the size of the financial benefit received, the extent to which the Member's outside activities distract him from his Parliamentary duties, and his motives for assuming such interests.

The bigger the reward, the more likely is a Member to be influenced in the event of conflict. Publishing its size might serve to modify his vigour in furthering the interest of those outsiders with whom he is associated. All Members, when registering an interest in the form of a payment, should be required to declare the sum involved in their entry in the register; the same should apply to payments by clients of firms with which the member is connected.

The practice of putting outside activities before Parliamentary duties might also be discouraged if Members were required to include in the register an indication of the time they spend each week, while the House is sitting, on other forms of paid employment, although it is recognised that this information would be somewhat uncertain, and difficult for anyone to monitor.

The question of motive is the hardest of all, but it is central to any judgement of Member's conduct. The present register gives no indication of the reasons why a Member has acquired an interest. Mr White may register a directorship having sat on the board for many years, starting before he entered the House; he sometimes speaks in the House, declaring his interest, using his outside experience; but he does not try to help his company by his contacts or actions in the House. Mr Black entered Parliament with no experience in industry but, seeking ways of augmenting his salary, he let it be known that he was willing to help any business that wanted to establish contacts with Ministers and Members of Parliament and he accepted a directorship. He spends much of his time arranging social functions to which other Members are invited to meet people from his company, he takes representatives from the firm to meet Ministers, and he speaks from time to time on industrial questions in which his company is involved. When he considers it relevant, he declares his interest.

In the published register the two entries would be identical, merely revealing a directorship in the company concerned, but the cases are completely different. For Mr White, membership of the House is almost totally irrelevant to his directorship. For Mr Black, his membership is the sole reason for his directorship and one of his main purposes in the House is to further the interests of the company. Most people would see little wrong in Mr White's outside interest. Most people would consider Mr Black's position reprehensible: he is simply using his membership of the House to feather his own nest (worst of all, he may have entered Parliament for this very purpose). It is a question of motive, but the register and the rules of the House are blind to the distinction.

It is difficult to see what the House can do about this, as it is hardly realistic to require the registration of 'motives'. The House might, however, like to consider requiring registration of the date on which a directorship, consultancy or other outside appointment was accepted; this would at least identify those appointments taken up after a person entered the House.

Other changes which ought to be considered include the registration of the principal clients of companies (especially professional lobbyists) with which a Member is connected, and the provision of more information about companies and other bodies listed in the register; at present the significance of some entries is far from clear.

Whatever improvements may be made to the register, the primary responsibility for ensuring that the House, and the public, are properly informed about their interests rests with Members themselves, subject to the ultimate judgement of their fellow Members in the case of complaints. Members are required to register those interests or other benefits which *they* think might affect their conduct as Members; no one else can make this judgement (although the registrar is always ready to advise). Members must declare in the House and on the other occasions specified in the Resolution of May 22, 1974, any *relevant* pecuniary interests, etc.; and the Member himself is the judge of relevance.

In my view this must be accepted. It would not be tolerable, and it would challenge the whole ethos of a House of Honourable Members, to appoint a committee to investigate every entry in the register and every disclosure made by each Member – let alone those entries and disclosures that had not been made.

There is widespread concern that some Members are not as frank about their outside interests as they should be. More seriously, some Members may be using their membership for purposes which are alien to the service of Parliament or of their constituents. The House needs to heed these anxieties and tighten up its rules to ensure that it continues to be a place where Members can deal honourably with the pressures to which the Speaker referred. [28]

---

28 This analysis by Michael Ryle was first published in [1990] *Public Law* pp. 313-22.

House of Commons (Westminster) Select Committee on Members' Interests

Registration and Declaration of Members' Financial Interests

Session 1991-1992
(London HMSO HC 326
4 March 1992)

NOTE: The following are extracts (pages vii-xxxiii) from the First Report, House of Commons' Select Committee on Members' Interests, Session 1991-92, (London HMSO HC 326 4 March 1992). It should be noted that:

(a) Members of Parliament, Westminster, have no *statutory* duty to register and declare their financial interests. The methods set out in this First Report are *non-statutory* and

(b) In November 1992 Lord Wakeham, Leader of the House of Lords (Westminster), rejected calls to set up a Register of Members' interests in the Lords. See *The Times* 10 November 1992. *[Editor]*

FIRST REPORT

REGISTRATION AND DECLARATION OF MEMBERS' FINANCIAL INTERESTS

The Select Committee on Members' Interests has agreed to the following Report:

1. INTRODUCTION

Background to the Enquiry

1. The House has two distinct but related methods for the disclosure of Members' private financial interests: declaration of interest in debate, and registration of interest in a Register which is open for public inspection. The main purpose of declaration of interest is to ensure that fellow Members of the House and the public are made aware, at the time when a Member is making a speech in the House or in Standing Committee, or examining a witness before a Select Committee, of any past, present or potential future pecuniary interest which has a particular relevance to the Member's contribution. The main purpose of the Register is to give public notification on a continuous basis of those pecuniary interests held by Members which might be thought to influence their parliamentary conduct or actions. A copy of the Register, which is updated regularly, is open for public inspection, and is published annually as it stands on the day following the Christmas adjournment. The terms " declaration " and " registration ", although often confused in the House and outside, should not be used interchangeably but should distinguish clearly these two separate methods of disclosure; that is how we use the terms in this Report.

2. The procedure of the House for the disclosure of pecuniary interests is supported by a complaints procedure. In February 1990 the Committee laid before the House a Report relating to a complaint against a Member of the House,[1] which was debated by the House the following month.[2] This was the first occasion since the Register of Members' Interests was established in 1975 that the complaints procedure had been followed to this ultimate stage; and at the end of the debate the House, in addition to reaching a decision on the particular matter of the complaint, also agreed to the following Resolution:

" That this House requests the Select Committee on Members' Interests to study and report further on the questions raised by its Report (HC 135) relating to:
  (i) the definition of outside interests and the enforcement of obligations in relation to declarations of outside interests by honourable Members; and
  (ii) the procedures whereby complaints may be brought before the Select Committee and whereby the Select Committee investigates such complaints;

together with such other questions as might appear to it to arise therefrom."

3. The Committee's Report is made in response to that Resolution. Since the debate took place, the Committee has produced reports on the Interests of Members and Chairmen of Select Committees[3] and on Parliamentary Lobbying,[4] both of which remain to be debated by the House. We have been required also to report on three other complaints against Members.[5] During this Parliament the Committee has met on more than twice the number of occasions of any of our predecessors since 1975. In preparing this Report we have been able to draw on the experience gained and the evidence taken in those previous enquiries.

Evidence

4. We have also received written and oral evidence directed more specifically at the remit which the House gave us in March 1990. A list of the witnesses who gave oral evidence appears at page iv, and a list of the written evidence published as Appendices to the Minutes of Evidence appears at page vi. We are grateful to all those who contributed to our work in this way, and in particular to the Rt Hon Bernard Weatherill MP, Speaker of the House, who had an informal discussion with us and whose subsequent letter to the Chairman is published as Appendix 5. In addition to the published evidence, we also invited the views of Members of the House through a notice placed in the all-party whip. We wish to thank those who responded to our invitation.

---

[1] HC 135 (1989–90).
[2] HC Deb, Vol 168, Cols 889–976, (7 March 1990).
[3] HC 108 (1990–91).
[4] HC 586 (1990–91).
[5] HC 506 (1989–90); HC 561 (1989–90); HC 261 (1990–91).

Origins and purposes of the Register

5. On 22 May 1974 the House agreed to two resolutions relating to the disclosure of Members' personal pecuniary interests. The first resolution translated the established convention of declaration of interest in debate into a rule of the House: the second was a decision, in principle, to establish a compulsory Register of Members' Interests. The two resolutions are as follows:—

(i) That, in any debate or proceeding of the House or its committees or transactions or communications which a Member may have with other Members or with Ministers or servants of the Crown, he shall disclose any relevant pecuniary interest or benefit of whatever nature, whether direct or indirect, that he may have had, may have or may be expecting to have.

(ii) That every Member of the House of Commons shall furnish to a Registrar of Members' Interests such particulars of his registrable interests as shall be required, and shall notify to the Registrar any alterations which may occur therein, and the Registrar shall cause these particulars to be entered in a Register of Members' Interests which shall be available for inspection by the public.

6. At the same time, a Select Committee was appointed to determine the form and content of a Register and to propose arrangements for its administration. The Committee published its Report in December 1974,[1] and in June 1975 the House agreed to the main recommendations contained in the Report.[2] The first published edition of the Register appeared in December 1975.

7. The initiative to establish a Register was taken by the Government of the day. It formed part of a series of measures taken to restore confidence in standards of probity in public life following revelations made during the bankruptcy proceedings and subsequent trial of a prominent architect and others.[3] These measures mainly focused on local government. Legislation relating to councillors' conduct which had applied for many years had recently been revised and sections 94–97 and 105 and 107 of the Local Government Act 1972 and sections 38–42 and section 60 of the Local Government (Scotland) Act 1973 laid down rules, supported by criminal penalties, requiring members of local authorities to abstain from speaking or voting on any question in which they had a pecuniary interest, and providing for declaration of interest. In the same month that the Government placed its proposal for a Register of Members' Interests before the House, the report of the Prime Minister's Committee on Local Government Rules of Conduct was published. This discussed in some detail the merits of compulsory registers for members of local authorities, and concluded that such registers would have a value in requiring councillors to review their private interests periodically in the light of their public duties.[4] In December 1974, six days before the Select Committee on Members' Interests (Declaration) reported, a Warrant was issued appointing a Royal Commission on standards of conduct in public life in central and local government under the chairmanship of Lord Salmon.

8. Although, both in its criteria and in its specific recommendations, there is more than an echo in its Report of the proposals then being considered for local government, the Select Committee on Members' Interests (Declaration) of Session 1974–75 chaired by Mr Fred Willey[5] (the Willey Committee) sought to build upon the traditional practices of the House so far as it could. The Register it proposed was intended to establish a balance between a Members' public duty and the right of the Member and his or her family to a proper degree of personal privacy. On the basis of this principle the Committee rejected suggestions that Members should be required to publish their

---

[1] HC 102 (1974–75).

[2] The two relevant Resolutions (12 June 1975) are as follows:—

Resolved, That pursuant to the Resolutions of the House of 22nd May 1974, this House agrees with the recommendations made in the Report of the Select Committee on Members' Interests (Declaration) relative to the arrangements for the registration of Members' Interests, and with the recommendations contained in paragraphs 43 and 47 of that Report in relation to the declaring of such interests; and that a register of such interests be established as soon as possible in accordance with the proposals made in that Report.

Resolved, That, for the purposes of the Resolution of the House of 22nd May 1974 in relation to disclosure of interests in any proceeding of the House or its Committees—

(i) any interest disclosed in a copy of the register of Members' Interests shall be regarded as sufficient disclosure for the purpose of taking part in any Division in the House or in any of its Committees;

(ii) the term "proceeding" shall be deemed not to include the giving of any written notice, or the asking of a supplementary question.

[3] For a convenient summary of the trials of Mr John Poulson and others on corruption charges, see Keesing's Contemporary Archives, June 24–30, p 26583.

[4] Cmnd. 5636: esp paragraphs 55–64.

[5] Member of Parliament for Sunderland (North), 1945–83.

income tax returns. It also decided that financial amounts should not be specified, and that, with one small exception, interests of a Member's spouse should not be registered.

9. The Willey Committee defined the purpose of the Register as being:

" to provide information of any pecuniary interest or other material benefit which a Member of Parliament may receive which might be thought to affect his conduct as a Member of Parliament or influence his actions, speeches or vote in Parliament ".

To assist Members in providing entries for the Register, the Committee set out nine specific classes of pecuniary interest to be registered, emphasising that they should be seen as " broad guidelines " within which Members should proceed with good sense and responsibility. The Committee believed that " the institution of a Register can give no guarantee against evasion. In the end, responsibility must rest on the Member himself to disclose those interests that might affect his parliamentary actions ".[1] The principle of the individual responsibility of a Member for his or her conduct and actions underlies much of the procedure and practice of the House, including the long established convention of declaration of interest in debate which the Register supplemented but did not replace. The major change was the almost equal weight given by the Willey Committee to the proper scrutiny by other Members and by the public of the manner in which Members discharged that responsibility. A complaints procedure to be administered by a Registrar and a Select Committee was devised as the machinery through which such scrutiny could take place.[2]

10. Successive Select Committees on Members' Interests have given guidance on the interpretation of the Willey Committee's " rules " and categories of registration.[3] But essentially the structure and procedures of the Register remain as they were established in 1975; and a copy of the Willey Committee's report is still the key document sent to all new Members of Parliament to assist them in understanding this part of their responsibilities.

Registers abroad

11. Since a Register of Members' Interests was established in the United Kingdom several overseas Parliaments have instituted Registers. These include not only Commonwealth Parliaments but also the German Bundestag, where a regularly updated Register of Interests appears as a part of the Official Handbook, and Norway where the Storting has recently agreed to rules for registration very similar to our own. Perhaps the most comprehensive Register is that of the House of Representatives in the Australian Federal Parliament where Members are required to disclose detailed information on their assets and liabilities. Since the Australian rules are framed in more specific terms than those of the United Kingdom they leave less scope to Members' individual discretion. We have found reference to this contrasting approach useful when considering revision of our rules.

Comparison with members of local authorities and Ministers of the Crown

12. As in 1974, our review of the Register has coincided with the preparation of measures to strengthen conflict of interest regulation in local government. In 1986 yet another Government committee was appointed to examine the conduct of local authority business.[4] In its Report the Widdicombe Committee quoted contemporary research which found that about 50 per cent of local authorities in England and Wales had already introduced some form of register of interests.[5] The Committee recommended that there should now be a statutory requirement to keep a public register of the pecuniary and non-pecuniary interests of councillors.[6] A draft circular and draft regulations were sent to local authority associations for comment at the end of May 1991. The main features of the proposals are conveniently set out in a memorandum which was provided for us by the Department of the Environment.[7]

---

[1] HC 102 (1974–75), paragraph 10.

[2] *ibid*, Annex 1, sections E and F.

[3] References to the principal decisions of this kind can be found in the footnotes to the Introduction to the latest (1992) printed edition of the Register of Members' Interests (HC 170, 1991–92).

[4] The conduct of local authority business: Report of a Committee of Enquiry under the chairmanship of Mr David Widdicombe, QC. Cmnd. 9797.

[5] " The Administration of Standards of Conduct in Local Government " by Alan Parker, Aiden Rose and John Taylor, pub. Charles Knight, 1986.

[6] Cmnd. 9797, pp 118–119.

[7] *See* Appendix 6, p 86.

13. Comparisons are often drawn between the position of Members of Parliament and that of local authority councillors. These should be treated with caution. There are significant differences of function between the two. In the words of a former Clerk of Committees who submitted evidence to us:

> "Local councillors have executive responsibilities, in awarding contracts or deciding planning applications, for example, and it is essential that they take no part in such business when they are personally financially interested. The position is totally different in the House of Commons, where Members are debating matters of public policy and holding to account those who take executive decisions. In a sense all Members have an interest, on behalf of their constituents, as well as themselves, on all questions of public policy and must be allowed to participate in their deliberation. Strictly enforced, the local government solution would bring the work of the House to a halt."[1]

14. Comparisons are also occasionally drawn between Ministers and Members generally. In evidence, we heard ingenious arguments suggesting that there was little real distinction between the duties of Ministers of the Crown and the duties of other Members and proposing that both should comply with variants of the same rules.[2] We did not find these arguments convincing. There is a world of difference between the position of Ministers, who have the responsibility for initiating policy and for taking executive decisions, and backbench Members, the powers of whom (as individuals) are confined to the exercise of influence.

15. Nevertheless, we recognise that this is not the public perception. If Parliament imposes more stringent rules relating to disclosure of interests upon local councillors, there is likely to be greater expectation that Members of Parliament should disclose more. Moreover, if the rules for local councillors are to be supported by sanctions imposed under the criminal law then, at the very least, the House is likely to be subject to increased criticism if it fails to exercise effective discipline over any of its Members who flout its rules. While we have stressed the distinction between the functions of Members on the one hand and Ministers and local councillors on the other, there is at least one important area where a valid comparison may be made: that is access to information. One of the objects of the ministerial rules is to remove the suspicion that Ministers may use the information they receive during the course of their official duties for private gain. This is also one of the purposes of the rules regulating members of local authorities. As we have pointed out in an earlier Report,[3] if some Members, such as Chairmen and members of Select Committees, acquire privileged insight into the development of policy they must expect that public opinion will eventually require that they should abide by rules which prevent them from holding particular interests or which require their withdrawal from certain proceedings. Members are similarly in a better position to become fully informed upon a variety of matters than the public; they also have much readier access to Ministers and Government Departments, and can participate in the proceedings of the House. Therefore there is ample justification for Members being required to make full and public disclosure of relevant pecuniary interests.

Should Members' interests be subject to statute law?

16. The rules relating to the registration and declaration of Members' interests derive their authority from resolutions of the House. We believe that they now have a permanent place in the procedures of the House; and the evidence which we have received confirms us in the view that the great majority of Members, whatever reservations of detail they may have, recognise that they are in the public interest and of value to the House.[4] From time to time the argument has been advanced that the rules should be enacted in statute law, as is the case for members of local authorities. Mr Enoch Powell was a notable advocate of this view, when a Member of the House; he held that the resolution establishing the Register " [is not] binding upon Members, in as much as it purports to impose obligations which can only lawfully and constitutionally be imposed upon Members by statute."[5] On these grounds Mr Powell declined to register. The House did not enforce compliance with its rules and for some years the status of the Register was diminished in consequence.

---

[1] *Public Law*, Autumn 1990, p 320; see also Appendix 2, p 78.
[2] Evidence, pages 23–45, esp Q 134–5, 152.
[3] HC 108 (1990–91).
[4] Eg Q 181, 263–5, 314–5. Appendix 5, p 85.
[5] Letter to Registrar of 1 July 1975. See also HC Deb Vol 893, col 745 (12 June 1975).

17. If there were to be any continuing and general doubts in the House about this matter, it is clear that appropriate legislation would have to be introduced. We do not believe that this is necessary. There are no current cases of Members declining to register on these grounds; and, like our predecessors in 1986,[1] we do not accept Mr Powell's arguments. The affairs of the House are frequently regulated by resolutions which have effect until rescinded. For example, one of the cornerstones of the parliamentary law on bribery is the resolution of 2 May 1695 which we quoted, together with related resolutions of the House, in our report on the interests of Members and Chairmen of Select Committees.[2] There are many other examples.[3] The Register of Members' Interests of the House of Representatives of Australia, which has a parliamentary tradition based on Westminster's, is also applied by resolution of the House.

18. Mr Tony Benn MP presented proposals to the House during the debate on 7 March 1990, which could be implemented only by statute. He subsequently enlarged upon them in evidence to the Committee.[4] Mr Benn proposes, among other things:

—that certain financial interests should be held to disqualify a person from serving in the House of Commons (in addition to the disqualifying offices already prescribed by the House of Commons Disqualification Act 1975);

—that every candidate for election to the House should submit a return of his interests to the Returning Officer when handing in his nomination papers, and that these should be circulated to each elector with the poll card;

—that consideration should be given to extending to Members the confidential rules governing the private interests of Ministers.

Such comprehensive provisions would necessarily have to be supported by legal processes of investigation and adjudication comparable (for example) with those applicable to contested elections.

19. Some comments made during the March 1990 debate, criticising the House's procedures for investigating and deciding upon complaints of failure to register or declare financial interests, might be read as similarly implying the need for the application of the criminal law to this aspect of Members' responsibilities.[5] It is certainly difficult to see how it would be possible to provide for independent investigation of complaints or for judicial processes of hearing and adjudication without crossing the dividing line between an internal and a statutory procedure.

20. A useful assessment of this issue was offered to us in evidence by Mr John Biffen MP. He agreed that, if it were judged that " the problem of corruption " was growing and was potentially serious, the present arrangements based upon the regulation by the House of its own affairs could not continue because " the House would soon perceive the profound problems of interpretation, enforcement and punishment ". However, he went on: " On the basis of my own experience between 1982–87 [as Leader of the House] I conclude that the problems of corruption are so minuscule that it would be wise to remain with the present system of self-regulation operating upon a resolution of the House."[6] He also argued, on the same basis, against· any attempt to introduce greater precision into the Register. For the reasons set out in paragraphs 24–26 below, we disagree with this part of his argument; but we accept the rest of his assessment. The present Leader of the House, Mr John MacGregor MP, supported his predecessor in arguing for a continuation of the procedures whereby the House itself regulates this aspect of its affairs.[7] We are also bound to take account of the fact that at the end of the debate of 7 March 1990 the House rejected, by a majority of 107 votes, an amendment moved by Mr Benn which incorporated his principal proposals for statutory regulation of Members' interests.

21. In deciding against any recommendation that would entail putting the Register, or any other aspect of the rules regarding Members' interests, onto a statutory footing, we do not delude ourselves that we are settling this question for all time. The issue is one which the House will doubtless need to review occasionally in the light of changing circumstances and changing ethical

---

[1] HC 110 (1986–87), p v.
[2] HC 108 (1990–91), p x.
[3] See Erskine May's Parliamentary Practice, 21st edition, p 5.
[4] Evidence, pages 23–45.
[5] Eg HC Deb, Vol 168, Cols 905–6, 934–6, 956–7.
[6] Evidence, page 15. See also Q 113.
[7] Q 340. See also Q 182, 184.

perceptions; but the intervention of the criminal law, the police and the courts of law in matters so intimately related to the proceedings of the House would be a serious and in our view regrettable development, and would have profound constitutional implications.

Complaints procedure

22. The second limb of the remit which the House gave to the Committee by its Resolution of 7 March 1990 requested us to review:—

" (ii) the procedures whereby complaints may be brought before the Select Committee and whereby the Select Committee investigates such complaints."

The Committee has discussed the House's request but for reasons similar to those adduced in the preceding paragraphs does not consider that any change is necessary. For the time being we believe that there is no compelling reason to modify the procedures laid down by the report of the Willey Committee.[1]

Scope of the Report

23. Our recommendations for change are directed almost exclusively at the form of the Register and the rules and procedures for registration: these recommendations are to be found in section 2 of the Report. In addition, in sections 3 and 4, we make some comments about the rule of the House relating to declaration of interest and about conflict of interest as it applies to Members of Parliament. With one small exception, these comments take the form of interpretation and advice rather than proposals for amendment of existing rules.

2. REGISTRATION OF INTERESTS

24. Although the opinions presented to the Committee in evidence were diverse, one point noticeably recurred more frequently than any other, and was voiced in different ways both by Members and non-Members. This was that the rules of registration required clarification.[2] The Leader of the House, among others, said that he thought there was uncertainty among many Members about exactly what should and should not be registered under different headings.[3] The Committee has therefore devoted most of its attention to the registration form and to the definitions of the categories of registrable interest set out in it. The objective of the changes we propose is two-fold: first, to make the Register a more informative, useful and respected document; and secondly, to give Members clearer and more explicit guidance on their obligations with regard to registration.

25. As to the first of these objectives, we were struck by the fact that those journalists and outside academic commentators who gave evidence all (to a greater or lesser extent) criticised the Register as "inconsistent and uninformative".[4] We do not accept all the criticisms that were made; but considering that one of the principal motives for the original introduction of the Register was to enhance public confidence in Parliament as an institution and in Members of Parliament as individual legislators, this expression of opinion from outside should be a matter of some concern to the House.

26. The second objective, to give Members clearer and more explicit guidance about the registration of their interests, is also of great importance. We agree with those who told us that " a great deal can be achieved by making the guidelines more precise " and that " detailed rules are . . . for the benefit of all honourable Members ".[5]

The definition of the Register's purpose

27. In paragraph 9 above the definition of the purpose of the Register laid down by the Willey Committee in 1974 is quoted in full. It has stood the test of time well; and we wish to propose only two significant modifications. The first is to replace the phrase " might be thought " by the phrase " might reasonably be thought by others ": the object of this change is to remove any possibility of

---

[1] HC 102 (1974–75), p xviii, sections E and F. These provisions are reproduced in Annex 3 of this Report.

[2] See Q 40, 163; Appendix 8, p 88.

[3] Q 316–7, 324, 332.

[4] Appendix 4, p 82, See also Q 2, 10, 12; Appendix 1, p 76, Appendix 3, p 81.

[5] Q 185; see also Q 7. Appendix 4, p 82.

the existing words being misinterpreted in a wholly subjective sense and this misinterpretation then being advanced as a justification for a failure to disclose relevant interests.[1] Secondly, we consider it desirable that the definition should extend to *any* action by a Member of Parliament in that capacity, and not just to " actions, speeches or votes in Parliament ". Our proposed new definition of purpose is therefore as follows:

> " The main purpose of the Register of Members' Interests is to provide information of any pecuniary interest or other material benefit which a Member receives which *might reasonably be thought by others* to influence his or her actions, speeches or votes in Parliament, *or actions taken in his or her capacity as a Member of Parliament.*"

28. If the House agrees with this Report, we intend that this definition should appear as an introduction to the revised registration form, together with appropriate supporting and explanatory material drawn both from this Report and the Report of the Willey Committee.

29. The Willey Committee emphasised that its definition of purpose was the fundamental requirement of the Register and that the specific categories of registration were intended as " broad guidelines ". In practice, however, the provision of a list of categories, divided into compartments on a form, has encouraged Members to assume that they constitute a comprehensive list of the items that need to be registered. This has had the effect of limiting the scope of the Register, because the present categories, intended mainly as a guide, are not comprehensive nor always precise. The revised categories and new style of registration form which we are now proposing will provide more detailed and explicit guidance to Members about the classes of interest which they are required to disclose. However, we do not wish this increased precision to detract from the obligation upon Members to keep the overall definition of purpose in mind when registering their interests. It is a cardinal principle that Members are responsible for making a full disclosure of their own interests in the Register; and if they have relevant interests which do not fall clearly into one or other of the specified categories, they will nonetheless be expected to register them.

Non-pecuniary interests

30. The Willey Committee was precluded by its terms of reference from considering the registration of interests other than pecuniary interests. From time to time it has been proposed that other interests, such as the membership of particular organisations, connections with charities or particular interest groups (freemasons, for example), or unremunerated positions in industry or commerce should be required to be registered. Indeed, since Members, rightly, are not prevented from registering more than is strictly required, there has been an increasing practice to register items such as unremunerated directorships. We do not consider it necessary or desirable to follow the rules of the Australian House of Representatives, which require a wide variety of unremunerated interests to be disclosed. Members inevitably have many varied interests. We believe that it would be confusing and laborious for all of them to be registered. It would also greatly increase the size of the Register, and consequently the cost (and therefore the accessibility) of the published version.

31. We have therefore retained the general principle that the requirement to register should be limited to interests entailing remuneration or other material benefit. The one minor exception that we have introduced is aimed at the problem of associated directorships, where a Member remunerated for one directorship holds other related directorships within the same group which are unremunerated. In such circumstances we believe that all subsidiary or associated directorships should be disclosed, whether remunerated directly or not. Category 1 of our proposed registration form has been worded accordingly.

Disclosure of amounts of remuneration

32. Several witnesses, mainly from outside the House, advocated the disclosure of levels of remuneration in the Register, either as precise amounts or through use of a banding structure.[2] The principal argument advanced in favour of the registration of amounts of remuneration is that it is difficult for a reader of the Register properly to assess the nature and extent of a Member's interests without knowing the amounts involved. " The bigger the reward, the more likely is a Member to be influenced in the event of a conflict of interests; publishing its size might serve to modify his vigour in furthering the interests of outside bodies."[3]

---

[1] *See* HC 135 (1989–90), paragraphs 52–4.

[2] Appendix 3, p 81; Appendix 4, p 83.

[3] Appendix 2, p 79; Q 6, 37.

33. We have reconsidered these arguments; but on balance we do not accept them. As Mr Speaker succinctly put it, "it is the nature of the interest, not the actual sum of money, that is important".[1] Nor is it necessarily the case that amounts of remuneration would be a reliable guide to the degree of influence which an interest might exert on a Member of Parliament: this could depend at least as much on the personal circumstances of the individual Member and on other, non-pecuniary, considerations. To require the disclosure of amounts would represent a significant intrusion into the privacy and personal affairs of a Member of Parliament, and we can find no substantial justification for recommending such a step.

Spouses' interests

34. The present registration form refers to spouses' interests only in relation to shareholdings (category 9). To require general disclosure of the interests of a Member's spouse would be completely contrary to the thinking which underlies such current policies as separate taxation. It would also run counter to the proposed new arrangements for local authority councillors.[2] We do not think that such a requirement would be defensible; nor is it necessary. In drawing up the new categories of registration and the associated notes of guidance, we have inserted references to spouses in the sections relating to hospitality, gifts and overseas visits, to cover those situations where a spouse is the recipent of some material benefit arising out of the Member's membership of the House. We have also retained the existing reference to spouses in the section relating to shareholdings. With those limited exceptions, we have not followed the example of Australia where the full registration of the interests of a Member's spouse is required.

The new registration form

35. A draft of the new registration form that we propose appears in Annex 1.[3] For the purposes of comparison, the current registration form is reproduced in Annex 2. In the following paragraphs we draw attention to the principal changes of substance that we are suggesting.

The nine categories of registration

36. The Willey Committee defined nine categories of registrable interests. We propose the amalgamation of category 2 (Remunerated employments or offices) and category 3 (Remunerated trades, professions and vocations), on the grounds that this distinction is now somewhat blurred and artificial. At the same time we propose the division of the present category 5 (Financial sponsorships) into two separate categories: one covering sponsorship (which we further define as meaning predictable, regular or continuing support in money or kind), and the other covering more occasional gifts, hospitality and benefits received from United Kingdom sources. The distinction between these two new categories may not always be clear cut; but we believe that the change is necessary because the present form sometimes leads Members to forget that they are required to disclose United Kingdom gifts in the same way as those from overseas sources. We explain the two new categories in more detail below. As a result of these changes, the proposed new form contains nine categorised sections, as did the old one, but the categorisation is slightly different. In addition we propose the inclusion of a Miscellaneous box at the end of the form, for the registration of interests which Members consider to be relevant and covered by the definition of the Register's purpose, but which do not obviously fall within any of the specified categories.

The use of questions

37. The categorised sections of the present form contain no more than descriptive headings of the interests to be registered in each: there is no request made nor question posed to the Member filling in the form. We consider that it will help to focus Members' minds more clearly on their obligations if each section is introduced by a question requiring a "yes" or "no" answer. This style has an additional drafting advantage, in that it makes it easier to incorporate the extra detail and guidance for Members which is the primary objective of the new format.

---

[1] Appendix 5, p 85. *See also* Appendix 4, p 83; Q 213–4, 294–5, 326; Evidence p 25.

[2] Appendix 6, p 87. *See also* Q 157–160; Appendix 5, p 85.

[3] Page xxvi.

Provision of information on the nature of businesses, etc

38. Several witnesses pointed out that entries in the present Register, under (for example) the directorships category, were often uninformative, in that only the name of the company in question was given, without any indication of the nature of the company's business.[1] This is an obvious instance where the Register is failing to fulfil its main purpose, to provide information to others on the interests which might reasonably be thought to influence a Member in his parliamentary activities. If it is necessary to contact Companies House to discover that a named firm is engaged in the provision of garage services rather than the manufacture of guided missiles, this objective is not being achieved. We have therefore included in all the relevant categories a requirement that, where a firm is named, a brief indication should be given of the nature of the firm's business.

Guidance on the interpretation of the categories

39. Although the new form is more comprehensive in its definitions and notes of guidance than the old, it would become unduly complicated and clumsy if it attempted to cover all conceivable situations and answer all conceivable questions. In the following paragraphs we provide some supplementary guidance and explanation of the different categories. Further questions of interpretation will continue to be dealt with by the Registrar, as they have in the past, with reference to the Committee in cases of particular difficulty.

Directorships (Category 1)

40. We have already mentioned the new requirement to register directorships of subsidiary and associated companies, even if not directly remunerated.[2] Several Members register other unremunerated directorships, for example of charitable trusts or learned societies. Members should feel free to register any interest of this nature if they consider it relevant to their parliamentary activities and to the purpose of the Register; but we consider that honorary and unremunerated positions of this sort should more appropriately be entered under the new Miscellaneous box (category 10).

41. It has never been the practice to require the registration, whether under this category or category 9 (shareholdings), of companies which have not begun to trade or which have ceased trading. We endorse that practice and propose that it should now be formalised. However, we wish to stress that our view of the phrase " not trading " is a stringent one; if any company covered by the rules is engaged in any transaction additional to those required by law to keep it in being, then the company should be registered.

Remunerated, employment, office, profession etc (Category 2)

42. This section of the form is the amalgamation of the existing categories 2 and 3, already mentioned in paragraph 36 above. It will be the principal catch-all category for registering outside employment and sources of remuneration not clearly covered elsewhere in the form.

43. There is at present no clear rule requiring Members to register membership of Lloyd's. Since the Register was established, Members who have consulted the Registrar on this point have consistently been advised to register an interest in Lloyd's under what is currently Category 3, and the great majority have done so. We propose a note in the new amalgamated Category 2 to make this requirement explicit. When a Member resigns from Lloyd's, the entry should remain in the Register until all the Member's outstanding obligations have been discharged and all outstanding benefits realised. We also believe that membership of individual Lloyd's syndicates can be of considerable significance. We therefore believe that members of Lloyd's should be required to disclose their syndicate numbers for the current year and their membership of any syndicates which remain unclosed.

44. Entries should be as clear and informative as possible, consistent with brevity. Many Members already provide quite sufficient information in their current entries: for example, a short description of activity as " barrister ", " author " or " occasional lecturer " seems to us to be adequate for the purpose. " Consultant ", however, is not adequately clear, and we consider that Members who have paid posts as consultants or advisers should indicate the nature of the consultancy: for example, " management consultant ", " legal adviser ", " parliamentary and

---

[1] Appendix 3, p 81; Appendix 4, pp 82–3.
[2] Paragraph 31 above.

public affairs consultant". Similarly, it is not adequate under this category simply to name a company and indicate the nature of its business without at the same time indicating the nature of the post which the Member holds in the company or the services for which the company remunerates him.

45. Several Members who have practised a profession but have ceased to practise on being elected to Parliament or taking up ministerial office continue to register the profession with a bracketed remark such as " non-practising "after it. We approve of this form of entry, particularly in the case of sleeping partnerships and where it is likely that the Member will resume the profession at a later stage.

Clients (Category 3)

46. The only substantial innovation in this section of the proposed new form is the second explanatory note.[1] Members are increasingly accepting positions which involve advice or consultancy deriving from their knowledge or expertise as parliamentarians or in other ways related to their parliamentary activities. In some cases consultancy or advice of this sort is provided to companies or partnerships which are themselves consultancies. Some of these lobby Parliament and Government on behalf of clients. It is the normal practice in such circumstances for Members to register the consultancy firm to which they provide advice or other services; but it is less normal to identify the ultimate beneficiaries of the advice or services, that is to say the clients of the consultancy firm. We accept that it is unreasonable and impracticable, especially in the case of a large consultancy firm, to require a Member to register all of the firm's clients; but we do believe it both reasonable and necessary to require that a Member should be able to identify, and should register, those of the consultancy's clients with whom he has a personal connection or who benefit, directly or indirectly, from his advice and services.

47. The types of services which are intended to be covered by this category of registration were clarified in a resolution of the House of 17 December 1985. The first explanatory note in this section of the new form is based on that resolution. A Member is exempt from the requirement to register a professional client only where it is clear beyond doubt that the services being provided to the client do not arise out of or relate in any manner to the Member's membership of the House.[2]

Sponsorship (Regular or continuing support in money or kind) (Category 4)

48. Our predecessors considered that " sponsorship is a term well understood by Members ".[3] We have not found this to be so and we have ourselves encountered difficulties in defining this category in a clear and satisfactory manner. The term " sponsorship " is commonly associated with the trade unions, because sponsorship is a traditional method used by the unions, historically part of the Labour movement, to support the political party. Members who are sponsored by a trade union tend to think of sponsorship in terms of the particular form of sponsorship used by their own union; but in fact practice varies quite widely. A common factor is that payment is made to the constituency party by an affiliated organisation on the basis of an agreement which limits the sums that may be paid.[4] In the majority of cases no personal payment is made to the Member; but the payment to the constituency party is often linked to the promotion by the affiliated organisation of a particular parliamentary candidate.

49. Where there is such a link between the promotion of a particular candidate and the payment to the constituency, we believe that the payment should be regarded as an indirect benefit to the Member and therefore covered by the definition of the Register's purpose; and we observe that it is already the practice of Labour Members to disclose such sponsorships in their Register entries. The question is how far this principle can or should be applied to other forms of support received by a Member's constituency party rather than by the Member personally. This issue was raised in the context of a recent complaint considered by the Committee, which concerned a failure to *declare* (rather than register) a trade union sponsorship. On that occasion we expressed our provisional opinion that " Members should continue to declare any sponsorship arrangement, by a trade union or otherwise, *in which they are personally involved* and irrespective of whether they

---

[1] This note is as follows: " Where you receive remuneration from a company or partnership engaged in consultancy business which itself has clients, you should list any of those clients to whom you personally provide [such] services or advice, directly or indirectly."

[2] *See* HC 677 (1974–75) paragraph 5(b).

[3] HC 102 (1974–75) paragraph 18.

[4] *See* HC 161 (1990–91), p xxvii, where the standard form of financial agreement (based on the " Hastings Agreement " of 1933) is set out.

receive personal payment.[1] We reaffirm that view, and we propose that the same principle should also apply to registration. We consider that Members should be required to register (and declare, where relevant) any substantial donations which are made by an organisation or company on a regular basis to their constituency party and which are linked directly to their own candidacy or membership of the House,[2] or where they have themselves acted as intermediary between the donor organisation and the constituency party. For this purpose we interpret "substantial" as meaning any payment (or benefit in kind of an equivalent value) of £500 or more per annum. Donations made directly to a constituency party as an expression of general political support, not linked to the Member's candidacy or membership of the House, should not be registered; and similarly it will not be necessary to register a trade union donation to a constituency party which is not linked to the promotion of a particular parliamentary candidate. Contributions to a Member's election expenses in excess of 25 per cent of the total of such expenses should continue to be registered, as is already required by the existing rules.

50. During this Parliament we have drawn attention to two examples of material or quasi-financial benefits which in our opinion should definitely be recorded in the Register of Members' Interests: the provision of the services of a research assistant or secretary whose salary, in whole or in part, is met by an external organisation;[3] and the provision of free or subsidised accommodation for the Member's use, other than accommodation provided solely by the constituency party.[4] Whether benefits of this kind should more appropriately be registered under the sponsorship category or under gifts (Category 5) is likely to depend on the individual circumstances, for instance whether the arrangement is a continuing or short-term one. The important thing is that they should be registered.

51. To improve understanding of this section of the registration form we have subdivided it into three separate sub-categories and questions: the first relating to contributions to election expenses; the second relating to other forms of sponsorship of the Member in support of his role as a Member of Parliament (including donations to the constituency party which meet the criteria outlined in paragraph 49 above); and the third relating to payments or other material benefits received personally by the Member. Experience may well demonstrate the need for further adjustments of detail. But we hope that our proposals, and the consequent redrafting of the form, will resolve some of the long-standing difficulties which have arisen over this section of the Register.

Gifts, benefits and hospitality (UK) (Category 5)

52. This category is intended for the registration of more occasional or individual benefits, not appropriate for registration under the sponsorship category, and received from sources within the United Kingdom. Gifts, hospitality or material benefits which relate in any way to a Member's membership of the House should be registered in this section. We propose, however, an exemption for benefits known to be made available without discrimination to all Members of Parliament. This is intended to exclude from registration arrangements such as the airport parking facilities kindly provided for Members by the British Airports Authority.

53. The present rules give no guidance about the financial value above which gifts and material benefits should be registered. We propose that gifts should be registered if they are of a value greater than £125,[5] and that any hospitality, service or other material benefit should be registered if its value exceeds one half of one per cent of the current salary of a Member of Parliament. In some cases the calculation of financial value will necessarily be imprecise. The general rule in all such cases of doubt is to err in favour of registration.

54. In our First Report of 1989–90, we recommended that Category 7 (Overseas benefits and gifts) should be amended so as to make it clear that the requirement to register under that category extended to benefits received by a company in which the Member has a controlling interest, and not just to benefits received by the Member personally.[6] We propose that the same provision (extended to include companies controlled jointly by Member and spouse) should also apply to United Kingdom gifts and benefits. An explanatory note has been inserted in the relevant sections of the new form accordingly.

---

[1] *ibid*, paragraph 14.
[2] *ibid*, p xix, for examples of such payments being registered in the past.
[3] HC 314 (1987–88).
[4] HC 428 (1988–89).
[5] This is the current financial limit which governs the acceptance of gifts by Ministers.
[6] HC 135 (1989–90) p xix.

Overseas visits (Category 6)

55. We propose no change of substance for this category, which is essentially intended to cover overseas visits not paid for out of United Kingdom public funds. The explanatory note in the proposed new form lists various types of visit commonly undertaken by Members but which are exempt from the requirement to register, namely visits undertaken under the auspices of the Commonwealth Parliamentary Association, the Inter-Parliamentary Union, the Council of Europe, the Western European Union and the North Atlantic Assembly. Such visits relate closely to Members' parliamentary responsibilities and are paid for directly or indirectly from United Kingdom public funds or involve reciprocity of payment between the United Kingdom Government or Parliament and the Governments or Parliaments of other countries. The CSCE Parliamentary Assembly, which is due to be inaugurated later this year, will have a similar status, and so we have added it to the list. Other visits excluded from registration by previous decisions of this Committee or its predecessors are those made to the Republic of Ireland in connection with meetings of the British-Irish Parliamentary Body and visits the costs of which are borne by any institution of the European Community. Visits of a private and personal nature, or visits of a purely business character, wholly unrelated to membership of the House, are excluded from registration at present and should remain so.

56. We propose to add to these exclusions certain other types of overseas visit which arise naturally or necessarily from a Member's parliamentary duties, namely:

(i) Visits arranged and paid for wholly by a Member's own political party.

(ii) Visits paid for wholly by a political group of the European Parliament.

(iii) Visits undertaken under the auspices of the British-American Parliamentary Group, which for the most part are financed out of the grant-in-aid which the Group receives from the Government of the United Kingdom.

(iv) Visits abroad as part of an Industry and Parliament Trust fellowship.

It would be cumbersome to list all these exclusions at length in the registration form itself. Instead we believe that this is the sort of explanatory material which would be better suited to the pamphlet of guidance which we recommend in paragraph 70 below.

57. When part of a visit is paid for by the Member or from public funds, only that part of the visit paid for from other sources is subject to registration. When an overseas visit has been arranged by an All-Party or registered backbench parliamentary group, it is not sufficient to name the group as the sponsor of the visit: the Government, organisation or person which is ultimately meeting the cost should be specified.

Visits and benefits for Members' staff

58. We are aware of a growing practice among lobbying companies of offering visits and other facilities to Members' staff; and we have considered whether these too should be entered in the Register of Members' Interests, under categories 5, 6 or 7 as appropriate. However, there are obvious difficulties in placing the onus upon Members to disclose benefits received by their staff. We therefore **recommend** that holders of permanent passes as Members' secretaries or research assistants should be required to register visits, gifts or benefits which they receive and which are covered by the definitions in categories 5, 6 or 7 of the new registration form for Members, in the same way as they are already required to register any relevant occupation which they may pursue other than that for which the pass is issued.

Overseas benefits and gifts (Category 7)

59. This category requires no additional elaboration. The remarks made about gifts and benefits from United Kingdom sources (see paragraphs 52 to 54 above) apply equally to this section of the form.

Land and property (Category 8)

60. There is considerable divergence of practice between Members when filling in this section of the present form. Some provide quite explicit details; some simply make a generic entry such as " Farm "; and some register properties which are apparently their private residences, although that is not required. We accept that it would be unduly burdensome to require Members to list all their

individual land and property holdings in minute detail. This would, moreover, breach the principle of reasonable privacy to which we attach importance. But we do consider that more uniformity of practice is desirable, and that entries should be reasonably specific as to the nature of the property and its general location. For example, " Woodland in Perthshire " or " Six lock-up rental garages in Lewisham, SE London " would be perfectly acceptable entries. The text of this section of the proposed new form is designed to produce such a result.

61. We have considered the desirability of defining the phrases "substantial value" and " substantial income ", which constitute the basic criteria for registration in this section. In the end, however, we have found it impossible to arrive at a satisfactory monetary formula and have decided to retain the terms as they are in the present form. Members who are in doubt whether property which they own is substantial enough to require registration are advised to consult the Registrar, and in any case to err on the side of registration rather than non-registration.

Shareholdings (Category 9)

62. This category of the register has been subject to much criticism and misinterpretation.[1] The Willey Committee concluded that to require Members to register all their shareholdings would " create serious administrative difficulties for the Registrar [and] would be an unnecessary burden on Members ". They also accepted the opinion of Stock Exchange witnesses that it could have undesirable consequences in other ways.[2] Believing that what was chiefly important was "the relationship between the Member's shareholding and the company", the Committee recommended that the obligation to register should be limited to holdings in excess of one per cent of the issued share capital of any company; and that is the rule which still stands. It has been criticised principally on the grounds that it catches minor shareholdings in small, even tiny, companies but does not reveal substantial shareholdings in large companies. This means, among other things, that Members known to have large personal wealth can often, with perfect propriety, make a " nil " return in the Register.

63. Nonetheless, we believe that the reasoning of the Willey Committee was fundamentally sound. It would be both impracticable and an intolerable invasion of personal privacy to require publication of share dealings made by a Member or on his behalf; and any rule requiring the disclosure of shareholdings above a certain monetary value would be open to the additional objection that market values are constantly changing. The new rule which we propose therefore represents only a modest modification of the old one. It is in essentially the same terms as the rule being proposed for the registration of shareholdings held by members of local authorities,[3] and would require the registration of shareholdings which have a *nominal* value of more than £25,000 or which constitute more than one per cent of the issued share capital of the company. This will not eliminate the need to register some shareholdings of quite small value; but it will go some way to meet the criticism that very large holdings can escape registration under the existing rule.

64. It is noticeable that some Members presently register shareholdings which do not fall within the requirements of the rule. Normally this is obvious from the terms of the entry, but occasionally real misunderstanding may result. Although in general we support the right of Members to register any interest which they consider relevant to their parliamentary activities, whether or not strictly required by the rules, this is one case where we would urge them not to do so. If any Member considers it essential to register a shareholding which does not fall within the definition laid down in category 9, we ask that it be done in the Miscellaneous box at the end of the form.

The rules of registration

65. We recommend that the House approve the proposed new registration form set out in Annex 1. The categories of registration in that form, together with the supplementary interpretation given in this section of our Report, would then constitute the House's rules of registration, replacing previous resolutions and decisions of the House and Members' Interests Committees on those matters, with the exception of the original, governing resolution of 22 May 1974. We are conscious that some Members may find the new form unduly detailed; but we regard this as an inevitable consequence of meeting the requests which we have received for clearer and more explicit directions to be given to Members about the registration of their interests.[4]

---

[1] Q 7.
[2] HC 102 (1974–75), paragraphs 23–26.
[3] Appendix 6, p 87.
[4] Paragraphs 24–26 above.

66. However, this is not to claim that the new rules will answer every question or resolve every doubt. It will still be necessary for Members from time to time to consult the Registrar on a confidential basis about the application of the rules to their particular circumstances. Where the Registrar encounters a problem of interpretation which he feels unable to resolve on his personal authority, he will lay it before the Select Committee on Members' Interests for decision. Occasionally cases of this sort may indicate a need for modifications to the wording of the form or the guidance contained in this section of our report. We **recommend** that the Committee be given authority to make such modifications, without the need for further recourse to the House, provided that the modifications are minor in character and designed to remove ambiguities or alter the financial limits (where stipulated) in line with changes in monetary values. Other changes—and particularly any which involve a major alteration of the categories or definitions of registrable interests—will of course still require approval by the House.

Registration of interests after a General Election

67. At present there is a requirement upon new Members and upon all Members elected at a General Election to return a completed registration form to the Registrar within four weeks of taking the oath. In respect of by-elections we recommend no change in the rule. But more serious problems arise after General Elections when many Members, no doubt concerned with the many other matters that need to be settled at the commencement of a Parliament, fail to meet the time limit. This is understandable; and so we **recommend** that in future three months should be fixed as the period within which Members should be required to register their interests after a General Election. Notification of changes of interest should continue to be made by the Member concerned, in writing, to the Registrar within four weeks of the change occurring.

Explanatory material

68. This inquiry has made the Committee aware of a weakness in the present administrative arrangements for registration. When a new Member first takes his seat after a by-election or General Election he is sent a registration form and copies of the relevant resolutions of the House, the text of the Willey Committee report of 1974, and the most recent published Register. The introduction to the annual published Register, which is written by the Registrar on his own authority, is a usefully succinct and accessible summary of the rules both of registration and declaration. However, none of this material (not even the registration form) is normally recirculated to Members during the lifetime of a Parliament (or, indeed, after their re-election to a new Parliament) although it may later become much more relevant to them than it was at the outset.

69. We propose two improvements to these arrangements. The first is that when the Registrar sends his annual circular letter to all Members, reminding them of the forthcoming publication of a new printed edition of the Register and enclosing a copy of each Member's current entry for checking, he should also enclose a blank registration form. This does not mean that Members will be expected to re-register all their interests afresh, or even necessarily to use the form to register alterations. But it will provide a convenient reminder to Members of the categories of registration and the questions they need to ask themselves before submitting revisions to the Registrar.

70. Our second proposal is based on a suggestion by Mr Speaker,[1] namely that a short guide or pamphlet should be produced, explaining the rules of registration in a straightforward manner, but at greater length than is possible in the rubrics and notes on the registration form. Such a guide might include examples of entries under the different registration categories; and we also agree with Mr Speaker that it should contain advice about the rules of the House on *declaration* of interest. A pamphlet of this nature would be less cumbersome to circulate than the Committee reports and other documents sent to new Members at present. It would also be easier to update and more convenient for Members to retain for reference. If the House agrees to this Report, it will be for the Registrar to produce such a pamphlet, under the supervision of our successors.

Administration of the Register

71. We have no significant changes to recommend in the administrative arrangements for the inspection of the Register or in the position and functions of the Registrar. The provisions laid down by the Willey Committee, therefore, should continue to have effect.[2] The same applies to that Committee's observations on the enforcement of the requirement to register.[3]

---

[1] Appendix 5, p 86, *See also* Q 202, 267, 272.

[2] HC 102 (1974–75), p xvii, Sections A–D. These provisions are reproduced in Annex 3 of this Report.

[3] *ibid*, p xii (paragraph 37).

3. DECLARATION OF INTERESTS

72. As has already been made clear, the Register of Members' Interests was intended to supplement and not to replace the longer-standing practice of the House that a Member should draw attention to a relevant pecuniary interest when making a speech in the House or in Standing Committee, or when examining a witness before a Select Committee. This is emphasised by the fact that on the same occasion when the House passed the resolution approving the principle of a Register, it also passed the resolution which strengthened the previous convention about declaration of interest into a rule.[1] The resolution also clarified the application of the rule to communications which a Member may have with other Members or with Ministers or servants of the Crown. In practice the introduction of the Register may well have had the unfortunate consequence of leading Members (and in particular, inexperienced Members) into the belief that registration adequately fulfils their obligations in regard to the disclosure of their financial interests. It is easy to assume that, because a relevant interest is fully noted in the Register, everyone who is concerned already knows about it and that it would therefore be otiose and tiresome to repeat the information when speaking in debate or communicating with Ministers or fellow Members.

73. We do not accept Mr Benn's sweeping judgement that the practice of declaration " has fallen into desuetude ",[2] but there are grounds for believing that some Members are less punctilious than they should be in observing the rule. We were especially struck that the Leader of the House, an experienced former departmental Minister, did not even expect that a Member should necessarily declare a relevant financial interest when seeking a ministerial favour.[3] We are anxious that this trend (if it is one) should be reversed, and that the additional precision and detail of the new registration form should not be regarded by Members as additional justification for neglect or casual observance of the declaration rule.

74. One memorandum submitted to us rightly commented that an important function of the Register is to " sensitise Members to their outside interests and how they might be perceived ";[4] but this is even more true in regard to the declaration rule. The registration rules impinge on Members' consciousnesses only occasionally, and perhaps only once a year when Members are confronted with the requirement to check or update their entries. The Register is constantly available, but of use only to those who take the trouble to consult it. By contrast the declaration rule operates in respect of particular debates, proceedings and parliamentary activities, and it requires the Member positively to draw attention to any relevant financial interest. As Mr Speaker put it " possession of a particular financial interest might be just the reason why a Member should be silent when a relevant matter is debated ".[5] Correct compliance with the declaration rule confronts the Member with this decision much more sharply than the existence of an entry in the Register. We therefore consider it important that Members individually, and the House as a whole, should continue to take the rule seriously and insist on it being properly observed. In the following paragraphs we offer guidance on the interpretation and application of the rule.

Past and potential interests

75. There is one significant difference between the declaration rule and the rules of registration. The Register records interests that are current or (in the case of visits, gifts etc) date from the recent past. The declaration rule, on the other hand, lays down:

> "That in any debate or proceeding of the House or its committees, or transactions or communications which a Member may have with other Members or with Ministers or servants of the Crown, he shall disclose any relevant pecuniary interest or benefit that *he may have had*, may have or *may be expecting to have*."

---

[1] The two Resolutions are quoted in paragraph 5 above. *See also* paragraphs 1 and 9 above.

[2] Evidence, p 24.

[3] Q 329-331. *See also* Q 297-9; Appendix 9, p 88. Since at least 1940 it has been clear that when a Member corresponds with a Minister or leads a delegation he should inform the Minister of any relevant pecuniary interest; *see* HC 5 (1940), paragraphs 48, 55-6.

[4] Appendix 4, p 81. *See also* Appendix 2, p 78.

[5] Appendix 5, p 85.

76. We see no good reason to extend the Register to cover past and potential interests. It would add to the complexity of entries and could easily cause confusion. There is also a particular difficulty in recording potential interests: whereas it is a relatively straightforward matter to explain the nuances of an expected or possible financial benefit in the context of a speech in the House, it is much more difficult to convey a fair and accurate impression of the situation in a terse Register entry which may have to remain on the record for several months. But we see no justification for changing the declaration rule either. The reference to past pecuniary interests, although on the face of it unnecessary, does not in practice give rise to problems. Such interests need be declared only when they meet the test of relevance (see paragraph 78 below); and this will be a comparatively rare occurrence. The requirement to declare potential interests raises greater problems of definition, but in our view is far too important to consider abandoning. Where, for example, a Member is debating legislation or making representations to Ministers on a matter from which he has a reasonable expectation of personal financial advantage, candour is essential.

77. The greatest problem about the rule relating to potential interests is deciding when a possible future benefit is sufficiently tangible to necessitate declaration. The key word in the declaration resolution in this respect is "expecting". Where a Member's plans or degree of involvement in a project have passed beyond vague hopes and aspirations and reached the stage where he has a reasonable or realistic expectation that in certain circumstances a financial benefit will accrue, then a declaration explaining the situation should certainly be made.[1]

The test of relevance

78. It is for a Member to judge whether a pecuniary interest is sufficiently relevant to a particular debate, proceeding, meeting or other activity to require a declaration. In the case of proceedings in the House or Committee, the advice of the Clerks or the Chair is available to any Member who needs a second opinion on the relevance of a pecuniary interest. We believe that the basic test of relevance should be the same for declaration as it is for registration of an interest,[2] namely that an interest should be declared if it "might reasonably be thought by others to influence" the speech, representations or communication in question. A Member who acts as a paid consultant to an outside firm or organisation should invariably make a declaration when speaking on a subject which affects the interests of that firm or organisation. Members who practice a profession, such as banking, medicine or the law, should declare that fact when the *pecuniary* interests of the profession are clearly and directly affected by the issue under discussion. Otherwise Members with professional interests should use their discretion and personal judgement in deciding when a declaration is appropriate. The same applies to Members sponsored by a trade union.

79. As a general rule any interest which is covered by the nine categories of registration set out in Annex 1 of this report should also be declared if it meets the criteria of relevance outlined in the preceding paragraph. There may also be occasions when it is appropriate to declare interests which are not covered by the rules of registration: for example, a relevant shareholding which falls outside the criteria laid down in category 9 of the registration form, or a spouse's or family interest.

What form should a declaration take?

80. There is considerable variety of practice among Members when declaring an interest in debate. Some say no more than " I declare an interest "; others are more specific. We consider that a declaration should be sufficiently informative to enable a listener to understand the nature of the Member's pecuniary interest without recourse to the Register or other publications.

The role of the Chair

81. Mr Speaker told us that he did not believe that it was a function of the Chair to remind an individual Member that he or she should declare an interest,[3] and we agree. It would not be feasible or desirable for the Chair to monitor Members' speeches in this way; nor could the Chair be expected to have the necessary knowledge of the pecuniary interests of individual Members. Nonetheless, declaration is a clearly stated rule of debate, and we would expect the Chair, if appealed to, to be prepared to reassert that rule.

---

[1] For a recent example of a ruling by this Committee on this matter, *see* HC 135 (1989 90), paragraph 49.

[2] *See* paragraph 29 above.

[3] Appendix 5, p 85.

82. As a consequence of the recommendations of the Willey Committee, the registration of an interest in the Register of Members' Interests is "regarded as sufficient disclosure for the purpose of taking part in any division in the House or in any of its Committees."[1] Recommendations which the same Committee made for the declaration of interests in relation to notices of Questions, Motions and Amendments by means of symbols and accompanying explanations on the Notice Paper were not implemented by the House. The then Leader of the House (Mr Edward Short) advised the House that "the printing complications of such a procedure would be considerable, particularly in cases when, for example, a considerable number of Members had appended their names to a motion or an amendment. When an interest had not already been registered, there would be the problem of agreeing with the Member, possibly at very short notice, the text of the declaration of interest."[2]

83. We have reconsidered this issue, and have sought the views of Mr Speaker and the Leader of the House. There are attractions in the idea of extending the declaration rule to Questions and thus deterring Questions asked with a view to a pecuniary interest. But we have concluded that the practical objections remain strong. Verbal declarations would take up valuable time during Question Hour; and symbols on the Order Paper could have a similar consequence, by provoking points of order.[3] Therefore we propose no change in the present practice that declaration of interest is not required in the case of parliamentary questions.

84. On the other hand we see a case for reviving the Willey Committee's recommendation in relation to Early Day Motions and amendments to them. The difficulties which Mr Speaker and the Leader of the House foresaw in the case of Questions do not apply to EDMs; and neither had any fundamental objections to the idea, although Mr MacGregor thought that a distinction should be made between the sponsor of an EDM and other Members who signed it later.[4] We accordingly **recommend** that the sponsor and first five supporters of any Early Day Motion, or amendment thereto, should be required to declare any relevant registered interest verbally or in writing to the Table Office at the time of tabling. When the motion or amendment appears on the notice paper, a symbol should be printed by the name of any Member making such a declaration, the symbol to be explained by the footnote: "Relevant registered interest declared".

4. CONFLICT OF INTEREST

85. The main motive of the House and the Government when establishing the Register and clarifying the declaration rule in 1974–75 was to reassure the public, in the aftermath of the Poulson affair, that the House of Commons was not corrupt. To the extent that the rules of registration and declaration require Members to subject their personal pecuniary interests to public scrutiny, this purpose is being achieved. It may also be the case, as we suggested in paragraph 74 above, that the obligation to register or declare an interest publicly may occasionally deter a Member from pursuing a course of action which is in conflict with his position as a Member or which is potentially corrupt. However, as the Willey Committee acknowledged, no Register can prevent a Member who is knowingly corrupt from acting corruptly; nor will it deter the Member who has a calculated determination to use his position for personal financial gain.[5]

86. Indeed, just as there is a danger that the existence of the Register may tempt Members into being casual in their observance of the declaration rule, so there is a danger that some Members may make the mistake of believing that correct registration and declaration adequately discharge their public responsibilities in respect of their private interests.[6] Such a mistake could have serious consequences both for the Member concerned and ultimately for the House. As Mr Speaker reminded us, "a Member must be vigilant that his actions do not tend to bring the House into

---

[1] HC 102 (1974–75, pp xiv–xv, paragraphs 48–9, Resolution of the House of 12 June 1975. This Resolution does not affect the right of Members to vote on matters of public policy at the beginning of a new Parliament before a new Register is published (*See* HC Deb, 1987–88, 119, cc 195–7).

[2] *ibid*, paragraphs 44–6 and Annex 4, p xxi; HC Deb (1974–75), Vol 893, col 739.

[3] Appendix 5, p 85; Q 315.

[4] Q 323.

[5] HC 102 (1974–75), p vii, paragraph 10. *See also* Q 154; Appendix 2, p 80.

[6] This danger was foreseen by one or two speakers in the debate on 22 May 1974. *See* HC Deb 1974, Vol 874, col 508, 520.

disrepute "; in particular " Members who hold consultancy and similar positions must ensure that they do not use their positions as Members improperly ".[1] A financial inducement to take a particular course of action in Parliament may constitute a bribe and thus be an offence against the law of Parliament. In the words of Erskine May:

> "the acceptance by any Member. . .of a bribe to influence him in his conduct as such Member or of any fee, compensation or reward in connection with the promotion of or opposition to any bill, resolution, matter or thing submitted or intended to be submitted to the House or any committee thereof is a breach of privilege."[2]

The power of the House to punish contempts against it is the ultimate sanction in such cases, just as it is the ultimate means of enforcing the obligation to register and declare pecuniary interests.

87. The business of the House and the duties of a Member of Parliament are so all-embracing in their scope that inevitably there are occasions when a Member's private pecuniary interests are pulling in a different direction from the policy of his party or his wider responsibilities as an elected legislator. For this reason, and others, some have advocated that Members of Parliament should be debarred from outside employment and pecuniary interests altogether.[3] Since the Register, and therefore the existence of this Committee, is based on the premise that Members should retain the freedom to undertake outside activities, we have not thought it appropriate to pursue that line of argument.

88. An alternative approach is to suggest that the long-standing practice and resolutions of the House concerning misconduct by its Members (outlined in paragraph 86 above) should be restated to apply in explicit terms to modern circumstances. The Select Committee on Members' Interests of 1969, chaired by Mr George Strauss,[4] proposed a resolution with that intention; at the same time it rejected the concept of a Register.[5] The proposed resolution was never put to the House because, as Mr William Whitelaw (then Leader of the House) told the House in 1971, it was considered that it would be too restrictive.[6] The idea of a more detailed code, defining what types of conduct and activity are unacceptable for a Member of Parliament, raises comparable difficulties. Our recommendations in relation to conflict of interest as it applies to the Chairmen and Members of Select Committees[7] represent a small step in that direction; and we await the House's reactions to those recommendations with interest. Those proposals are aimed at a specific aspect of a Member's parliamentary activities, and one which is readily amenable to control by the House, because of the House's power to nominate and replace the members of Select Committees. To attempt to define, on a much wider and hypothetical basis, the types of conduct which the House might in particular circumstances judge to be contempts, would be a far more hazardous enterprise and one doomed to almost certain failure. As we have already indicated,[8] we believe that if such a code were eventually to be considered essential, it would have to take a statutory form and that such a step would be regrettable. We hope that the measures which we have proposed in this report to make the rules of registration and declaration clearer and more explicit will sharpen Members' perceptions of these issues and make such a development still more unlikely.

5.   CONCLUSION

89. We recommend that the House give its approval to this Report as a whole. By doing so it would in particular:

(i) authorise the use of the new registration form set out in Annex 1;

(ii) approve the supplementary guidance on registration contained in section 2 of this Report as constituting (together with the rubrics and notes in the new form) the House's rules for registering financial interests;

---

[1] Appendix 5, p 86.

[2] Erskine May's Parliamentary Practice, 21st edition, pp 119–121, where the relevant cases and past resolutions of the House are set out.

[3] Eg HC Deb 1968–69, Vol 783, cols 1567–8. Appendix 1, pp 75–6.

[4] Member of Parliament for Lambeth North, 1929–31 and 1934–50, and for Vauxhall, 1950–79.

[5] HC 57 (1969–70).

[6] HC Deb 1970–71, Vol 811, col 522.

[7] HC 198 (1990–91), paragraph 17 ff.

[8] Paragraphs 20 and 21 above.

(iii) permit this Committee's successors to make minor modifications to the form and the supplementary guidance in order to remove ambiguities or alter the financial limits in line with changes in monetary values (paragraph 66);

(iv) extend the time limit for the registration of interests after a General Election from four weeks to three months (paragraph 67);

(v) approve the recommendation that holders of permanent passes as Members' secretaries or research assistants should be required to register visits, gifts or benefits which they receive and which are covered by the definitions in categories 5, 6 or 7 of the new registration form for Members (paragraph 58);

(vi) authorise the production of a short guide or pamphlet, prepared for the use of Members under the supervision of this Committee's successors, explaining the rules of registration at greater length than is possible in the rubrics and notes on the registration form. The pamphlet would also contain advice about the rules on declaration of financial interests (paragraph 70);

(vii) give its general approval to the guidance and interpretation of the rules on declaration of interest contained in section 3 of this report and to the supplementary comments on conflict of interest contained in section 4;

(viii) approve the recommendation that the sponsor and first five supporters of any Early Day Motion, or amendment thereto, should be required to declare any relevant registered pecuniary interest to the Table Office at the time of tabling; and that, when the motion or amendment appears on the notice paper, a symbol should be printed by the name of any such Member, explained by the footnote: " Relevant registered interest declared " (paragraph 84).

ANNEX 1

PROPOSED REGISTRATION FORM

Registrable Interest	Details
DIRECTORSHIPS 1. Do you have any remunerated directorships in any public or private company? **YES/NO** *(Please delete as appropriate)* If so, please list opposite (briefly stating the nature of the business of the company in each case). [Notes: (i) You should include directorships which are individually unremunerated but where remuneration is paid through another company in the same group. (ii) In this category and category 2 below, "remunerated" should be read as including taxable expenses, allowances or benefits.]	
REMUNERATED EMPLOYMENT, OFFICE, PROFESSION, ETC. 2. Do you have any employment, office, trade, profession or vocation (apart from membership of the House or ministerial office) for which you are remunerated or in which you have any pecuniary interest? **YES/NO** If so, please list opposite. Where a firm is named, please briefly indicate the nature of the firm's business. [Note: Membership of Lloyd's should be registered under this category. If you register membership of Lloyd's, you should also list your syndicate numbers for the current year and your membership of any syndicates which remain unclosed.]	
CLIENTS 3. Does any of the paid employment registered in categories 1 or 2 above entail the provision to clients of services which depend essentially upon or arise out of your position as a Member of Parliament (see Note (i) below)? **YES/NO** If so, please list opposite all clients to whom you personally provide such services. Please also state in each case the nature of the client's business. [Notes: (i) The services covered by this category include action connected with any parliamentary proceeding, sponsoring meetings or functions in the parliamentary buildings, making representations to Ministers, fellow Members or public servants, accompanying delegations to Ministers, and the provision of advice on parliamentary or public affairs. (ii) Where you receive remuneration from a company or partnership engaged in consultancy business which itself has clients, you should list any of those clients to whom you personally provide such services or advice, directly or indirectly.]	

589

Registrable Interest	Details

SPONSORSHIP (REGULAR OR CONTINUING SUPPORT IN MONEY OR KIND)
 	
4. (a) Did you benefit from any sponsorship before your election, where to your knowledge, the financial support in any case exceeded 25 per cent of your election expenses at that election?
                    YES/NO
 	
If so, please give details opposite. Where a company is named as sponsor, please indicate briefly the nature of its business.
 	
(b) Do you benefit from any other form of sponsorship or financial or material support as a Member of Parliament?   **YES/NO**
 	
If so, please give details opposite, including the name of the organisation or company providing the support. Where a company is named, please indicate briefly the nature of its business.
 	
(c) Do the arrangements registered under category 4(b) above involve any payment to you or any material benefit or advantage which you personally receive?   **YES/NO**
 	
[Notes: (i) You should register under this section any source of regular or continuing support from which you receive any financial or material benefit, directly or indirectly; for example the provision of free or subsidised accommodation, or the provision of the services of a research assistant free or at a subsidised salary rate.
      (ii) You should not register sponsorship by your constituency party. But you **should** register, under category 4(b), any regular donations made by companies or organisations to your constituency party in excess of £500 per annum which are linked directly to your candidacy in the constituency or for which you yourself acted as an intermediary between the donor and the constituency party.]	

GIFTS, BENEFITS AND HOSPITALITY (UK) **5.** Have you, or your spouse received any gift of a value greater than £125, or any material advantage of a value greater than 0·5 per cent of the current parliamentary salary, from any company, organisation or person within the United Kingdom which in any way relates to your membership of the House? **YES/NO** If so, please give the details opposite. [Notes: (i) You should include any hospitality given and services or facilities offered *gratis* or at a price below that generally available to members of the public, **except that** where the advantage is known to be available to all Members of Parliament, it need not be registered. (ii) You should include not only gifts and material advantages received personally by you and your spouse, but also those received by any company or organisation in which you (or you and your spouse jointly) have a controlling interest.]	

Registrable Interest	Details		
OVERSEAS VISITS 6. Have you or your spouse made any overseas visits relating to or in any way arising out of your membership of the House where the cost of the visit was not wholly borne by yourself or by United Kingdom public funds? **YES/NO** If so, please list opposite, in chronological order. [Note: You are not required to register visits undertaken on ·behalf of the Commonwealth Parliamentary Association, the Inter-Parliamentary Union, the Council of Europe, the Western European Union, the North Atlantic Assembly or the CSCE Parliamentary Assembly. Other categories of overseas visits which are exempt from the requirement to register are listed in the guidance pamphlet on Registration and Declaration of Members' Interests.]	**Countries Visited**	**Dates of Visit**	**Who Paid?**
OVERSEAS BENEFITS AND GIFTS 7. Have you or your spouse received any gift of a value greater than £125, or any material advantage of a value greater than 0·5 per cent of the current parliamentary salary, from or on behalf of any foreign Government, organisation or person which in any way relates to your membership of the House? **YES/NO** If so, please give the details opposite. [Note: Overseas hospitality and travel facilities should be entered under category 6. Otherwise the notes under category 5 apply here also.]			
LAND AND PROPERTY 8. Do you have any land or property, other than any home used solely for the personal residential purposes of you or your spouse, which has a substantial value or from which you derive a substantial income? **YES/NO** If so, please indicate opposite the nature of the property (eg Estate, Farm, Smallholding, Woodland, Residential rented/leasehold property, Commercial rented/leasehold property) and give the general location of the property in each case.	**Nature of Property**		**Location**
SHAREHOLDINGS 9. Do you have (either yourself or with or on behalf of your spouse or dependent children) interests in shareholdings in any public or private company or other body which have a **nominal** value (a) greater than £25,000, or (b) less than £25,000 but greater than 1 per cent of the issued share capital of the company or body? **YES/NO** If so, please list each company or body opposite, indicating in each case the nature of its business and whether your holding falls under sub-category (a) or (b) above.			

Registrable Interest	Details
MISCELLANEOUS **10.** If, bearing in mind the definition of purpose set out in the introduction to this Form[1], you have any relevant interests which you consider should be disclosed but which do not fall within the nine categories set out above, please list them opposite.	
Date:	Signature:

CURRENT REGISTRATION FORM

Registrable Interest	Details
* 1 Remunerated directorships of companies, public or private	
* 2 Remunerated employments or offices	
* 3 Remunerated trades, professions or vocations	
4 The names of clients when the interests referred to above include personal services by the Member which arise out of or are related in any manner to his membership of the House	
5 Financial sponsorships a as a Parliamentary candidate where to the knowledge of the Member the sponsorship in any case exceeds 25 per cent of the candidate's election expenses, or b as a Member of Parliament by any person or organisation, stating whether any such sponsorship includes any payment to the Member or any material benefit or advantage direct or indirect	

* In Items **1, 2** and **3** remuneration includes taxable expenses, allowances or benefits.

Registrable Interest	Details
6 Overseas visits relating to or arising out of membership of the House where the cost of any such visit has not been wholly borne by the Member or, by public funds	
7 Any payments or any material benefits or advantages received from or on behalf of foreign Governments, organisations or persons	
8 Land and property of a substantial value or from which a substantial income is derived	
9 The names of companies or other bodies in which the Member to his knowledge has, either himself or with or on behalf of his spouse and infant children, a beneficial interest in shareholdings of a nominal value greater than one-hundredth of the issued share capital	

Date

Signature

ANNEX 3

ADMINISTRATION OF REGISTER AND PROCEDURE FOR COMPLAINTS[1]

A. *Status of Register*

(1) The Registrar shall be a senior officer of the Department of the Clerk of the House, to whom he shall be directly responsible.

(2) The Registrar shall act as Clerk to the Select Committee on Members' Interests appointed for each Parliament by the House.

(3) The Registrar shall act only under the authority of the Resolutions of the House and on the instructions given to him by the Select Committee from time to time.

B. *Compilation and maintenance of Register*

(1) It shall be the duty of the Registrar at the beginning of each Parliament to send to every Member the copy of the form, agreed by the House, for the register of interests, together with a notice that the form should be completed and returned to him within *three months*[2] of the Member taking his seat.

(2) The Registrar shall thereafter compile the Register which shall be put before the Select Committee who shall direct by what date it shall be laid before the House by the Clerk of the House and ordered to be printed.

(3) The Register shall be published as a House of Commons paper by Her Majesty's Stationery Office.

(4) The form for the register of interests together with the notice about the date of completion shall similarly be sent to every Member who takes his seat following a by-election.

(5) It shall be the responsibility of Members to notify the Registrar of any changes which may occur in their registrable interests within four weeks of the changes occurring.

(6) It shall be the duty of the Registrar to keep the Register up to date on the basis of the returns from new Members together with information given to him by Members of any changes in their registrable interests. He shall arrange for a revised Register to be published from time to time.

C. *Access to Register*

(1) The Register shall initially be available for public inspection on Mondays to Fridays between the hours of 11 am and 5 pm when the House is sitting and between 11 am and 1 pm during recesses, except on public holidays, and during the month of August when it shall be available for public inspection on one day of the week. These hours may be varied from time to time by the Select Committee on the advice of the Registrar.

(2) Access to the Register by members of the general public shall not be permitted except by appointment. Any appointment made by telephone shall, save in exceptional circumstances, be confirmed in writing and at least 48 hours' notice shall be required.

(3) Before granting an appointment the Registrar shall require the applicant to furnish in writing his name and address.

(4) Members shall be able to inspect the Register without prior appointment on sitting days; during recesses an appointment shall be necessary. ·

(5) To enable Members to have access to the information contained in the Register outside the normal hours for inspection, the Registrar shall arrange for an up-to-date copy to be placed from time to time in the Library.

D. *Relationship with Members*

(1) All correspondence between Members and the Registrar relating to the entry in the Register or to any matters connected with a possible disclosure of their interests shall be treated by the Registrar as confidential, subject to the provision that he shall remind Members that such correspondence may be required by the Select Committee.

---

[1] Reproduced from the Report of the Select Committee on Members' Interests (Declaration), 1974–75 (HC 102, 1974–75, Annex 1).
[2] New time limit recommended in paragraph 67 of this Report.

(2) The Registrar shall seek to settle, so far as is possible, any difference of opinion between himself and a Member without recourse to the Select Committee, subject to the terms of the Resolutions of the House.

(3) In the event of any dispute about the inclusion of any item in the return of the interests of a Member which cannot be settled between the Member and the Registrar, it shall be the duty of the Registrar to refer the matter to the Select Committee; in such cases, however, he shall refer the question in general terms without mentioning the Member by name, except with the consent of the Member.

(4) If the Committée, after giving the Member the opportunity to be heard and after due consideration of the case, decide that the interest ought to be registered, the Registrar shall so inform the Member. If the Member is still not satisfied, the Committee shall make a Report to the House together with a recommendation as to what action should be taken; such Report shall, however, be in general terms, without reference to the Member by name.

E. *Complaints by Members*

(1) Any allegation by one Member against another Member relating to the Register or to the disclosure of interests, shall be in writing to the Registrar, who shall refer the matter to the Select Committee and shall furnish to the Member concerned details of the allegation.

(2) The Select Committee may hear both Members, together with other evidence, as they think fit and may then make a Report to the House together with a recommendation as to what action should be taken. Before making any such Report the Committee shall give the Member concerned the opportunity to make written representations and of being heard with such witnesses as he may desire to call.

F. *Complaints by the Public*

(1) If any member of the public wishes to allege that a Member is in breach of the Resolutions of the House relating to registration or disclosure of interests he must make a complaint in writing to the Registrar.

(2) The Registrar shall inform any member of the public who wishes to complain that before taking any further action he should know that any communication between them is not covered by Parliamentary privilege or privileged at law.

(3) The Registrar shall have discretion to require from any member of the public wishing to make a complaint details of his name and address together with prima facie evidence as to the accuracy of his allegation; in the event of this not being supplied, he shall have the discretion to refuse to consider the matter further.

(4) If the Registrar is satisfied that a failure to comply with the Resolutions of the House has been established, he shall report the matter to the Select Committee.

(5) The Select Committee may, if they think fit, call for an explanation from the Member, to whom the details of the case shall be communicated by the Registrar.

(6) If the Member confirms that the allegation is true, the Committee shall forthwith make a Report to the House together with a recommendation as to what action should be taken.

(7) If the Member disputes the allegation, the Committee shall take evidence from such persons including the Member and his witnesses if he so wishes, as they think fit, and shall then after due consideration make a Report to the House together with a recommendation as to what action should be taken.

VOLUME I   GOVERNMENT ETHICS

APPENDIX PART III

Government Ethics:

Secrecy, Access to Information and Privacy

APPENDIX III

12

Access to Information: the Experience of Other Countries

by Dr Rosamund M. Thomas, Director,
Centre for Business and Public Sector Ethics, Cambridge

1. What is 'Open Government'?

'Open Government' is associated frequently with a Freedom of Information or Access Act. The term assumes that greater openness by government officials in making available documents, papers and records will be achieved only if a *statute* to this effect is framed, enacted, and implemented, and proper machinery for appeal and oversight of the law is established. Yet, to equate 'open government' with a freedom of information law is to define it too narrowly. [1] In a Parliamentary democracy, such as the United Kingdom, mechanisms have been built into the system of government to check possible abuses of executive power and to obtain information (for example, the new system of Select Committees). Moreover, a freedom of information law in many instances provides a right of appeal to the courts in respect of administrative decisions to withhold official information. In Britain, which has an unwritten constitution [2] and where the judicial branch is less concerned with 'political' matters than the courts in the United States and other countries having more rigid constitutions, such a law would sit awkwardly on our framework of government. Distrust of administrative discretion and the wish to redistribute political power from the government to the public usually accompany demands for a freedom of information statute, as may the call for less secrecy by means of the repeal of any Official Secrets law. In practice, a freedom of information statute does not necessarily achieve its aims. The extent of administrative discretion remaining in decisions to release government

---

1 In 1972 the Franks Committee underlined the point that too much emphasis should not be placed on the nature of a country's laws when discussing 'openness in Government'. See *Departmental Committee on Section 2 of the Official Secrets Act 1911* (Chairman: the late Lord Franks) Vol. 1. *Report*, Cmnd. 5104 (HMSO, London 1972), Chapter 6.

2 Both the United States and Sweden have written constitutions, and a degree of separation of powers foreign to a Parliamentary system of the British type (for example, the responsibility of Ministers for the execution of policy and their accountability to Parliament is absent in Sweden). Therefore, the right of access to official documents in Sweden must be seen as one part of a system which differs in many ways from the British system, Ibid pp. 34-35.

information depends on the exemptions to the Act and whether these are couched in broad or narrow terms – and so discretion varies between countries according to the legislation, and is not eliminated. Nor is the general public always the recipient of official information made available under a Freedom of Information (or similar) Act. In the United States, for example, foreigners, criminals, business organisations seeking information about their competitors, and the press have all benefitted from the openness of government. Therefore, openness is not associated exclusively with a freedom of information statute and, in countries having enacted one, such an Act does not preclude exploitation of government openness or ensure a better informed general public. This paper examines the main differences and similarities between freedom of information, or access, legislation in various countries and also identifies some of the operational problems experienced in the implementation of such laws.

2. Some Differences and Similarities Concerning Freedom of Information Legislation

2.1 Differences

– a Freedom of Information Act or an Access Act?

Sweden and the United States were the first developed democracies to adopt a law creating the public's right of access to government information. For more than two hundred years, the Swedish constitution has provided for open access to official documents and full information to any citizen about administrative matters. This provision was established in 1766 in Sweden's old Freedom of the Press Act and, apart from a few years, [3] has continued – presently being laid down in the 1949 Freedom of the Press Act, as amended in 1976. [4] In the United States at the Federal level, the Administrative Procedure Act of 1946 attempted to require the disclosure of government information by means of free public access to administrative documents, except for certain exemptions. The 1946 Act failed for several reasons, not least because its enactment was followed fairly quickly by the Cold War in the 1950s when government officials were preoccupied with protecting national security information. [5] However, in 1966 the American Federal law on freedom of information was passed, replacing the provisions of 1946 and

---

3 The years 1772-1774 and 1792-1810 were exceptions.

4 For full details of the Swedish law, see S. Holstad 'Sweden' in D.C. Rowat (Ed.) *Administrative Secrecy in Developed Countries* (Macmillan, London, 1979).

5 Other reasons why the United States' Administrative Procedures Act of 1946 failed include (1) the vague language of the exemptions; and (2) no provision for appeal to a court was enacted. See D.C. Rowat 'The Right to Government Information in Democracies' *International Review of Administrative Sciences,* Vol. XLVIII, 1982, p. 64.

embodying the same basic principles as those in the Swedish [6] access law. The long-standing American statute has served to a large extent as a model for other countries. Interestingly, though, a waning in enthusiasm for the legislation in the United States has coincided with the introduction of information legislation in Australia, Canada and New Zealand. [7] D. C. Rowat (1982) has criticised the American term 'freedom of information' as less precise than 'access to government documents' and pointed out that the new Canadian Act and the new French law use the word 'access'. It is useful to note this distinction but, for ease of discussion, this paper will refer mainly to 'freedom of information'.

Examples of Countries having a
Freedom of Information Act or Access Act

Sweden	1949	Freedom of the Press Act (as amended last in 1976). Contained in the Swedish constitution.
Finland	1951	Publicity of Documents Act (unlike Sweden, this law is not part of the constitution).
United States	1966	Freedom of Information Act at Federal level (amended in 1974 and 1976). Also freedom of information legislation at State level.
Denmark	1970	Access of the Public to Documents in Administrative files (the Open Files Act) – electronic data banks are exempted.
Norway	1970	Act concerned with Public Access to Documents in the (Official) Administration.
France	1978	Law on the Freedom of Access to Administrative Documents.
The Netherlands	1978	Access to Official Information Act.

---

6 By 1966 the other Scandinavian countries had enacted laws on public access to official documents. Finland was part of Sweden in the nineteenth century and so inherited much of the latter's tradition of openness. In 1951 Finland's existing practices and regulations on access were consolidated into the Law on the Public Character of Official Documents; and in 1970 both Denmark and Norway adopted laws on public access to official documents, although Denmark already had a law of 1964 providing for 'a citizen's right of access to documents in his own case'. See D.C. Rowat 'The Right to Government Information in Democracies', p. 62.

7 H. N. Janisch 'The Canadian Access to Information Act' *Public Law* Vol. 27, 1982, pp. 548-49.

Australia	1982	Freedom of Information Act at Commonwealth level (amended in 1983). Freedom of Information legislation also introduced at State level (e.g. State of Victoria 1983).
Canada	1982	Access to Information Act and the Privacy Act at Federal level. Certain Canadian Provinces have passed Access laws (e.g. Nova Scotia 1977; New Brunswick approved 1978; became effective 1980; and Quebec 1982).
		See also the paper in this Volume (Part III) by Robert Gillis, Treasury Board of Canada.
New Zealand	1982	Official Information Act – came into force 1 July 1983. The Official Information Amendment Act 1983 made only a few minor technical changes to the 1982 Act – although more significant amendments are proposed.

– a Privacy Act

Another distinction between countries relates to the matter of a Privacy Act. Sweden was the first country to enact national legislation on privacy and data protection in 1973, known as the Data Act. [8] This Act gives citizens access to files in the public sector containing *data on themselves* (except where personally damaging) and also access by third parties to personal information. Sweden not only has a tradition of open government legislation but few countries collect as much information on its citizens. Swedes, therefore, have access to information and public records about themselves as well as to data about their fellow citizens. In the computer era it is relatively simple for any Swede to look up, for example, the income of a neighbour reported to the tax authorities and ascertain what taxes he or she has paid. [9] The third party access to personal information under the Data Act was considered at first unlikely to cause problems because the Swedish press adheres to a self-imposed code of conduct which precludes discussion in newspapers of the

---

8 The Swedish Government dealt with the matter of privacy largely in separate legislation, unlike the recent Canadian Act which combines access and privacy provisions in the same statute. See the paper in this Volume (Part III) pp. 230-55 by Robert Gillis, Treasury Board of Canada.

9 In Sweden 'each resident is assigned a 10-digit official number called a "person number", which not only makes access to personal data easy but makes it relatively simple to link data banks'. See *International Herald Tribune*, 13 March 1986. See also *Disclosure of Official Information: A Report on Overseas Practice* (HMSO, London, 1979), p. 12.

affairs of named individuals and also the press Ombudsman investigates complaints. However, by March 1986 an intense debate on privacy had arisen in Sweden due to the conflict between 'the official appetite for information' and the citizen's concern for privacy. By making use of the Freedom of the Press Act and the Data Act, a team of social researchers was found to have compiled over twenty years detailed profiles, by name, of nearly 15,000 Swedes – all obtained from official files! [10] The Data Inspection Board ordered the team to 'de-identify' its files so that no name could be linked to the personal information amassed. The deep anxieties being felt presently in Sweden over the issue of privacy are likely to continue for some time.

In the United States the Freedom of Information Act of 1966 was strengthened in 1974 during the Ford Administration. The same year a companion piece of legislation – a Privacy Act – was passed, providing persons with access to their own personal files held by the government and an opportunity to lodge a correcting statement. D. C. Rowat explains:

> 'The two Acts overlap, and a person requesting his own file can make the request under either or both pieces of legislation. There are advantages in making use of the Information Act, because the Privacy Act does not cover the Federal Bureau of Investigation (FBI) and the Central Intelligence Agency (CIA) and the FOI Act requires a reply within ten working days. A great many of the requests that came in after 1974 were requests for personal files, because many people knew that the FBI and the CIA were holding thousands of files on American citizens, and suspected that these agencies might be holding a file on them. The FOI Act provided access to many of these files'. [11]

Problems soon arose in the FBI and the CIA as a consequence of these two overlapping Acts. In 1979 a spokesman of the United States Department of Justice drew attention to the procedural and substantive conflicts between the FOI Act and the Privacy Act and also criticised the time, expense, and difficulty in complying with them – as well as the lack of benefit to the

---

10 The sociological study is entitled 'Project Metropolitan' and follows for twenty years the lives of all 10 year olds who lived in Stockholm in 1963. The project compiles portraits of them and their families detailing across two generations marital status, family size, the extent of welfare benefits received, incomes, school and employment records as well as police records and other information; all obtained from official files. Health and criminal files are supposed to be exempt from public access, but the authorities waived the restrictions because of a priority placed on social research. See *International Herald Tribune,* 13 March 1986.

11 D. C. Rowat 'Recent Developments on Access Laws' *Indian Journal of Public Administration,* Vol. XXVIII, 1982, pp. 251-63. The aim of the US Privacy Act 1974 is 'to safeguard individual privacy from the misuse of Federal records, to provide that individuals be granted access to records concerning them which are maintained by Federal agencies, to establish a Privacy Protection Study Commission, and for other purposes', US Code Title 5 552a.

ordinary public. [12] Other reports allege that the FBI and CIA were paralysed at the operational level because of the need to recall field agents to cope with all the requests. The FBI, for example, increased its full-time staff handling the two Acts from less than twenty people in 1974 to more than three hundred by 1979 and, during the calendar year 1978, made 19,982 final responses to requests under the FOI Act releasing two and a quarter million pages to requesters! [13] Perhaps it is not surprising that in Australia the Intelligence organisations, but not the Australian Federal Police, are among those exempted totally from the 1982 Freedom of Information Act. [14]

A further problem in the United States has been the inadvertent, or negligent, release in recent years of highly sensitive and confidential business data. Provisions for the protection of *individual* privacy were introduced into Federal law by the Privacy Act of 1974, which imposes 'certain procedural limitations on agency disclosure of individually identifiable records'. However, the 1966 Freedom of Information Act omitted to provide a comparable set of procedures to protect the privacy of *business* organisations (for example, membership lists, marketing information, business data, and other aspects of organisational privacy). High-level agency officials may apologise to submitters for releasing, for example, 'trade secret chemical formulae', but the 1984 Reform Bill [15] called for procedural changes to ensure that agencies which do not provide 'prerelease notice to submitters' should be obliged to do so. Furthermore, substantive changes may be necessary in the future to the

---

12 Q. J. Shea 'Is Openness Working? A Dissenting View' *The Federal Bar Journal,* Vol. 38, 1979, p. 109.

13 From 1974 to end 1978 the cost to the FBI of responding to requests under the FOI Act and the Privacy Act was over $28 million. See T. Breeson 'FOI and Privacy Act Implementation by the FBI', *The Federal Bar Journal,* Vol. 38, 1979, pp. 154-5.

14 See Australian Freedom of Information Act (reprinted 29 February 1984) Schedule 2 Part I p. 56 'Exempt Agencies' which covers the Australian Secret Intelligence Service and the Australian Security Intelligence Organisation. The 1983 Amendment Act introduced a new section to exempt an agency from the FOI Act in relation to documents which originated with, or were received from, any of the five Commonwealth Intelligence agencies. Anomalies had arisen under the 1982 FOI Act because, although these Intelligence agencies are exempt from the Act, their documents in the possession of other agencies were not exempt automatically prior to the Amendment Act. In all, twenty-six government agencies are exempted totally from compliance with the Australian FOI Act and nineteen other agencies are exempted as to certain classes of documents. The New Zealand Official Information Act 1982, unlike the Australian FOI Act, provides no total exemption from the Act for any specific government agencies – neither does the Canadian Access Act. Indeed, it was forecast that in Canada, as in the United States, 'controversial' departments such as the Department of Justice; the Royal Canadian Mounted Police, and the Correctional Service Canada, would receive almost all the requests. See P. Butler 'Public Access: Problems of Implementing the Access Act of 1982' in D.C. Rowat (Ed.) *Canada's New Access Laws,* (Carleton University, Ottawa, 1982), p. 13.

15 Known as the Hatch Bill (S774 98th Congress; 1st Session 130).

fourth exemption under the US Freedom of Information Act which covers confidential commercial data. The wording of this exemption has led to unsatisfactory and unpredictable case law – the current standard applied being 'substantial competitive harm' which is a nebulous one with wide variation. Reformers in the United States seek the replacement of the 'substantial competitive harm' test by new statutory law and fear that, until Congress acts, submitters, agencies, requesters, and the courts will have to continue to struggle with market and economic factors, while the real issue of the handling of information relating to both private persons and organisations receives inadequate attention. Recently the US Food and Drug Administration analysed its 30,000-40,000 annual FOI requests and found that more than 80% came from businesses seeking information about other business organisations. Some companies have stopped doing business with the government, while others have filed 'reverse freedom of information suits' to block the release of information. [16]

Australia, the first Commonwealth country to adopt a Freedom of Information Act, has no companion Privacy Act. [17] By contrast, in Canada legislation has been enacted at the Federal level which combines concerns for privacy in a comprehensive new Access Act. [18] Furthermore, the Canadian Access Act is designed to overcome the problem of 'reverse FOI cases' and hence to protect *business* privacy better. If a commercial organisation requests information from the government about another firm, the government must notify the other company (that is, third party notification). The competitive company, whose secrets are about to be freed, will then be able to argue why the information requested should not be released.[19] The French access law is not a specific new Act but takes the form of amendments to a heterogeneous law on the public service approved by Parliament in July 1978. France has a

---

16 See *Congressional Record – Senate* (daily edition 27 February 1984) S1805. See also 'Protecting Business Secrets under the FOI', *RIPA Report*, Vol. 6, No. 4, 1985, p. 6.

17 The Australian Law Reform Commissioner's Report to the Attorney-General on Privacy (1983) recommends strengthening substantially both a person's right to privacy and right to have records about him/her amended if incorrect. The proposed right of correction of personal records is wider than that contained in the 1982 Australian FOI Act. Legislative action for a Privacy Act and amendment to the FOI Act will be necessary, if the Government accepts the Commission's recommendations.

18 An Act to enact the Access to Information Act and the Privacy Act, to amend the Federal Court Act and the Canada Evidence Act, and to amend certain other Acts in consequence thereof, S.C. 1980-81-82 C.111. See also the paper in this Volume (Part III) pp. 230-55 by Robert Gillis, Treasury Board of Canada.

19 See D. C. Rowat 'Recent Developments on Access Laws'. Similar procedures exist in the Australian FOI Act. The Australian Act also incorporates 'reverse FOI proceedings', allowing the supplier to apply to the Administrative Appeals Tribunal to prevent disclosure. See Australian Freedom of Information Act 1982, s. 27.

separate Privacy law of January 1978 and, like Sweden and the United States, experiences the same problem that the two Acts are 'prey to internal contradictions – their objectives being to open wide the door of the right to information while simultaneously protecting the right to privacy.' [20]

– a Secrecy Act?

Campaigners for a freedom of information statute in the United Kingdom often called simultaneously for the repeal of section 2 of the Official Secrets Act 1911 (in fact, section 2 of the 1911 Act was repealed and replaced by the new Official Secrets Act 1989), but *without* the enactment of a Freedom of Information statute). Yet, the situation in developed democracies varies regarding official secrets legislation. In New Zealand the Official Secrets Act 1951 was repealed under the provisions of the Official Information Act 1982. [21] There is no longer any general Official Secrets Act of the British kind. Instead offences under that Act have been brought under the New Zealand Crimes Act 1961, but the scope of the criminal sanction is narrowed considerably. Australia still retains a broad Official Secrets law of the old British type, which makes it a criminal offence to disclose official information without proper authority, and it forms part of the Commonwealth Crimes Act 1914-73. [22] The Canadian Official Secrets Act 1939 is modelled closely on the British Act and, despite some attempts, it has not been repealed. Indeed, Sweden passed a new separate Secrecy Act in 1980 which was the 'special enactment' referred to in the Freedom of the Press Act. The new Secrecy Act has wider scope than the old legislation of 1937, [23] which

---

20 See D. C. Rowat 'The French Law on Access to Government Documents' *Government Publications Review,* Vol. 10, 1983, p. 37 and A. Holleaux 'The New French Laws on Freedom of Infomation' (English Summary) *International Review of Administrative Sciences,* Vol. 47, 1981. Like Australia, New Zealand has no separate Privacy Act but the NZ Labour Government is committed to a review of the Official Information Act 1982 with a view to liberalising its provisions. Indeed, a Bill of Rights is planned which also would grant privacy rights relating to the collection and storage of computerised personal information and, possibly, legal safeguards against electronic surveillance. See NZ Labour Party's *Open Government Policy 1984.* See also the Hon. Justice Michael Kirby's 'Media Law – Beyond Shangri-la' in *The Right to Know* (Granada, London, 1985), p. 61.

21 See NZ Official Information Act 1982 Public Law No. 156 (Wellington, NZ Government publication 9840A – 83 PT), s. 51. See also *Towards Open Government* (Danks Committee) *General Report* I (Government publication 591843 – 4500/1/81 PT 19, Wellington, NZ, December 1980).

22 S. 70 of the Commonwealth Crimes Act 1914-1983. A Report of 1979 of the Senate Standing Committee on Constitutional and Legal Affairs criticised s. 70, arguing that it should be narrowed. The Committee also urged that secrecy provisions in other Commonwealth legislation should be identified in a schedule to the FOI Act. These proposals were rejected and, at present, there are no plans to alter the existing secrecy laws in Australia.

23 The Act on the Right to Obtain Access to Official Documents (The Official Secrets Act) 1937.

dealt only with the secrecy of documents. The 1980 Act concerns official secrecy generally and contains prohibitions against the divulgence of information by a public servant whether orally, through delivery of official documents, or any other means. Also it places restrictions on the right of access to official documents and regulates the extent to which secrecy shall be maintained between authorities and, as such, is a comprehensive law. [24]

The United States has no Secrecy Act dealing generally with unauthorised leaks on the lines of the British legislation. Official information is 'classified' under executive orders and the US Code contains the Espionage Act, which covers spying, and other *specific* secrecy laws. [25] Leakage of official information to the press has been a problem recently in the United States which has led to two developments. First, the uncharacteristic use of the Espionage Act in order to bring a charge of leakage of information to the press. [26] Second, renewed proposals to introduce a *general* law of the British kind (that is, an Official Secrets Act) to cover unauthorised leaks of official information. [27] As the Franks Committee concluded in 1972, there is no evidence to support 'the stark contrast' drawn by a minority of people between an obsessively secret system in Britain and 'gloriously open systems in some other countries'. Most countries retain secrecy for some basic functions of government. [28]

2.2 Similarities

Three basic principles underlie similarities in freedom of information legislation. These principles will be examined in turn and, although there are some

---

24 Unlike the Freedom of the Press Act, the Swedish Secrecy Act is not a constitutional law and may be amended at short notice. The new Secrecy Act of 1980 also contains rules about secrecy in respect of court proceedings and the Code of Judicial Procedure was amended at the same time.

25 The Espionage Act (US Code Title 18 Chapter 37). See also *Departmental Committee on Section 2 of the Official Secrets Act 1911*, pp. 128-130.

26 Samuel L. Morison was charged under the US Espionage Act in 1985 for passing classified intelligence photographs to a British military magazine (*Jane's Defence Weekly*). It was only the second time that the Federal espionage laws have been used in a prosecution for disclosing classified information to a publication. See *International Herald Tribune*, 9 October 1981.

27 In 1985 the Central Intelligence Agency proposed to the White House that legislation should be sought to make it a crime for government employees, or former employees, to disclose national secrets without authorisation. See *International Herald Tribune*, 21 March 1985. Earlier proposals for British-type Official Secrets law were put forward under the Nixon Administration.

28 In France two sets of laws govern official secrecy (1) 'le statut de la fonction publique' 1983 and (2) article 378 of the Penal Code which makes it a criminal offence for professionals (for example, doctors, chemists, public servants) to disclose secrets entrusted to them in confidence.

differences in detail between countries which will be noted, the principles are the same. They are:-

— disclosure of official information as of right (subject only to exemptions)

— exemptions prohibiting the release of certain kinds of information deemed necessary to be kept secret in the nation's interests

— machinery for appeal against denials by administrators to supply information

— disclosure of official information as of right

One principle of freedom of information legislation concerns the public's right to official information (that is, 'the right to know'). Instead of relying on the judgement of civil servants to release or withhold information, a general statutory right places the onus on government authorities to justify withholding information. Accordingly, any citizen is entitled as of right to access to government documents, unless denial of access is justified by law.

Three questions need to be asked about the public's right to official information. First, who is the 'public'; second, how is the request for information made; and, third, do time limits apply to disclosure?

Question One: Who is the public?

According to the Swedish Act, the free access to official documents belongs to 'every Swedish national'. In practice, however, *foreign* citizens are treated in much the same way as other members of the public. The United States Freedom of Information Act says nothing about the citizenship of the member of the public, referring simply to 'any person'. [29] This wide access to government information in the United States has created problems. [30] Foreign nationals and governments make requests to American Federal Departments, sometimes contrary to the interest of the United States. Reforms to the American Freedom of Information Act, put forward in a Senate Bill of 1984, included an amendment to provide information only to a

---

29 The Finnish Act mentions only the country's own citizens as legitimate applicants but, as in Sweden, *foreign* citizens may be given access to a document at the discretion of the agency. The Danish and Norwegian Acts (like that of the United States) refer to 'anyone'. See B. Wennergren 'Civic Information – Administrative Publicity' *International Review of Administrative Sciences,* Vol. 36, 1970, pp. 245-46.

30 See *Congressional Record – Senate* (daily edition 27 February 1984) S1815. The earlier Administrative Procedure Act of 1946 did restrict access in respect of certain government records to 'persons properly and directly concerned'.

requester who is a 'United States person'. Recently, Congress failed to pass this Reform Bill but, in any case, it has been pointed out that it is impossible to prevent abuse by foreigners, for all that is required is for a foreigner to ask an American citizen to make a request for him or her. [31] Nonethelsss, the New Zealand Official Information Act and the Canadian Act at Federal level restrict the right of access to citizens or permanent residents of those countries[32] – although in respect of Canada a further provision was incorporated in committee to permit the Governor in Council to extend the right to others. France and Australia, like the United States, have *not* limited access to their own citizens.

Another problem in the United States concerns the use of the Freedom of Information Act by criminals and organised crime. In 1974 Congress passed several amendments to the Act, which made access by the public easier. However, the Director of the Federal Bureau of Investigation testified before Congress in 1979 that 12-16% of the Bureau's requests under the FOI Act came from prison inmates, seeking to identify informers. Also, terrorist and organised crime groups, [33] with both the motive and resources to subject the releases to detailed analysis, have been requesting government information. Another group to benefit considerably under the American Freedom of Information Act, as seen earlier, is business organisations – although they may also lose trade secrets. One of the 1974 amendments was the introduction of a 'fee waiver' clause which provides that documents shall be made available without charge, or at a reduced rate, where the agency determines that it is in the public interest to do so. As a result of the 'fee waiver' provision an increase has occurred in the use of the American Act by business enterprises. Organisations offering commercial services often make anonymous requests for disclosure of documents on behalf of unnamed clients, gaining free or subsidised search, selection, and provision of documents from Federal agencies. One such organisation, FOI Services Inc of Rockville, Md, charges 'several hundred dollars annually to each of its subscribers, who then pay $18.50 plus mailing for each document which the Service anonymously requests from the federal agencies'! [34]

---

31 See footnote 15. See also D.C. Rowat 'Recent Developments on Access Laws'.

32 The NZ Act also gives the right of access to 'a body corporate which is incorporated in New Zealand'. See NZ Official Information Act 1982 s. 12. See also H.N. Janisch 'The Canadian Access to Information Act' *Public Law,* Vol. 27, 1982, p. 540. In Australia see *Re Lordsvale Finance and the Treasurer (No.1)* (a decision of the Administrative Appeals Tribunal).

33 The Hatch Reform Bill of 1984 contained provisions to amend the FOI Act by (1) protecting more clearly 'confidential sources' and (2) proposing a new provision, exempting from disclosure all files relating to organised crime. See *Congressional Record – Senate* (daily edition 27 February 1984) S1801-5. However, Congress failed to reach a consensus on the Reform Bill. Although the Bill is dead, plans exist to revive the proposals.

34 Provisions on cost recovery were proposed in the Hatch Reform Bill of 1984 since it was considered that the subsidisation of such FOI services is not a useful expenditure of taxpayer funds. See *Congressional Record – Senate* (daily edition 27 February 1984) S1802-1809.

In response to a survey by the Department of Justice, [35] the US Customs Service observed that there has been little use of the Freedom of Information Act by the general public or the media. The main users have been 'law firms, corporations, or individuals who have some type of involvement in specific cases'. Similarly, the Environmental Protection Agency stated that 'business interest groups it regulates were "the most common beneficiaries" and that "by far the largest volume of use" was by law firms, [36] corporations, FOIA service companies, and trade associations'. [37] An expert who compared the four Scandinavian Acts and the American Freedom of Information Act, concluded that:-

> 'The wordings of the Acts give the impression that free access to agency records is meant for individual members of the public, for the man in the street. And true enough, the little man has the right to inspect and copy most records. However, such members of the public do not often inform themselves directly ... in practice, it is predominantly representatives of the news media who profit professionally by the administrative publicity ... Among the customers should also be mentioned freelance opinion makers and, last but not least, politicians and the secretariats of the political parties and interest organisations'. [38]

The initial workings of the Australian Act of 1982 are now being analysed. [39] Indeed, in 1983 a Freedom of Information Amendment Act was passed which included extending the right of access by providing that a number of exemption categories be subjected to 'an overriding public interest test in favour of disclosure'. Although Australia has no privacy act, the Freedom of

---

35 1979 survey.

36 The Hatch Reform Bill sought to amend the US FOI Act to prevent a party to a pending judicial proceeding or administrative adjudication, or any requester acting for such a party, using the Act for the purpose of 'discovery' and sometimes to harass and burden government agencies. Parties have been using the FOI Act to avoid applicable rules of discovery established, for example, under the Federal Rules of Criminal Procedure. In both criminal and civil cases, a defendant seeking discovery information normally has to demonstrate not only the relevance of the information sought but also that compliance with the request would not be unreasonably burdensome. See *Congressional Record – Senate* (daily edition 27 February 1984) S1815.

37 See J. E. Bonine 'Public Interest Fee Waivers under the Freedom of Information Act' *Duke Law Journal*, Vol. 1981, No. 2, pp. 216-17.

38 B. Wennergren 'Civil Information-Administrative Publicity' *International Review of Administrative Sciences*, Vol. 36, 1970, p. 249.

39 See Second *Annual Report* (1983-84) of the Attorney-General to the Australian Parliament on the operation of the Freedom of Information Act 1982 (Australian Government Publishing Service, Canberra, 1985).

Information Act at Commonwealth level grants four kinds of rights [40] to the public, including the right of access to personal records held by government. Of the countries which have adopted freedom of information legislation recently, the experiences of Australia and Canada show a high demand for 'personal information' rather than information relating to government performance or accountability. [41] As in the United States, this personal information includes requests by people wanting access to police records about themselves (Australian Federal Police), as well as to their medical records. Other typical applicants for personal information in Australia are recipients of welfare benefits and immigrants requesting records about deportation. [42] As in Scandinavia, journalists in Australia make full use of the Act [43] and one in particular from the *Canberra Times* has made over one hundred applications under the Freedom of Information Act and the use of the Act for investigative journalism purposes has caused some concern! [44] In common with the Scandinavian and American legislation, the Australian FOI Act also benefits business interests, lobby groups, academics, solicitors (regarding litigation in government cases) and Opposition Members of Parliament seeking background information to Questions they may lodge.

Question 2: How is a request for information made?

This second question raises numerous others – for example, what government agencies are affected by the statute; is a register of documents provided to aid identification; if a document is secret or exempted, will non-exempted

---

40 The Australian Freedom of Information Act at Commonwealth level grants to the public three other kinds of rights as follows:- (1) a right of amendment of personal records held by government agencies/departments; (2) a legally enforceable right to government documents; (3) a right (or obligation) placed on agencies/departments to *publish* documents and to make arrangements (e.g. by index) for internal rules and guidelines to be made available for inspection and purchase (e.g. rules for administering an agency scheme). See Australian Freedom of Information Act, 1982.

41 Unlike trends in Australia and Canada, the New Zealand experience of the first year of the Official Information Act 1982 showed that just over half the total requests were for *official* information as distinct from personal information. See E. Longworth 'New Zealand's Official Information Act: the First Year' *Transactional Data Report,* Vol. VII, No.7, pp. 402-03.

42 Talk by S. Zibzek at a Royal Institute of Public Administration Seminar, London 9 May 1985 on 'Australian Freedom of Information'. (NOTE: the RIPA is now extinct). See also *Australian Freedom of Information Act 1982 Annual Report 1983-84* (Australian Government Publishing Service, Canberra, 1985).

43 In Sweden, for example, the news media make more use of the legal right of access than in the United States since incoming and outgoing documents are available for inspection at public offices without the need for a special request. See *Departmental Committee on Section 2 of the Official Secrets Act 1911,* p. 34.

portions be released; and what fee, if any, has to be paid by the requester? What to charge a requester is a difficult issue. If the cost is too high, there is the danger that a right of access is created in theory but denied in practice. If the cost is too low 'fishing trips' [45] or other abuse are encouraged with the costs being borne by the taxpayer at large. Another factor is whether the fee covers reproduction costs only or includes a contribution towards search and production costs. [46]

The Swedish constitution confers a general public right to inspect and publish documents held by a government authority. The term 'authority' is not made clear in the Freedom of the Press Act. In principle, it applies to every State or Municipal body but in practice corporations under civil law, which are wholly or partially owned by the State or Municipality, are not covered by the Act. Free access does not apply to all government information in Sweden, but only to 'official documents' – with exceptions laid down in the separate Secrecy Act of 1980. An 'official document' is any document in the keeping of an authority that has been either received or drawn up by the authority (in writing, picture form, or recording). Incoming and outgoing documents may be inspected on a daily basis on their arrival to, or despatch from, government offices. One change brought about by the 1980 Swedish Secrecy Act is that official documents must now be registered – and a request can be made in writing, or in person or by telephone. The press uses government agencies to examine each day's public mail and some authorities put special rooms at their disposal. By contrast, the use by ordinary citizens of the right to see documents in Sweden is slight outside areas of personal concern. Inspection of documents is free of charge on government premises, but a small copying fee is levied if a copy is ordered. When documents contain secret or exempted material, deletions are made and the non-exempted portions released. [47] Ministries in Stockholm are small and work is often done orally, but one criticism of the Freedom of the Press

---

44 See the Hon Justice Michael Kirby's 'Media Law – Beyond Shangri-la' in *The Right to Know*, p. 50.

45 In Australia, for example, protection against 'fishing expeditions', or searches which are too time-consuming, is built into the Commonwealth FOI Act. The agency or Minister is entitled to refuse requests which 'would substantially and unreasonably divert the resources of the agency from its operation . . . having regard to the number and volume of the documents and to any difficulty that would exist in identifying, locating, or collating the documents'. This protection does not prevail at State level. See Australian Freedom of Information Act 1982, s. 24.

46 See H. N. Janisch 'The Canadian Access to Information Act' *Public Law*, Vol. 27, 1982, p. 539.

47 See S. Holstad 'Sweden' in D. C. Rowat (Ed.) *Administrative Secrecy in Developed Countries*. See also *Departmental Committee on Section 2 of the Official Secrets Act 1911*, pp. 33-35 and *Disclosure of Official Information: A Report on Overseas Practice*, pp. 9-13.

Act is that telephone calls and other oral media are used instead of written information in order to circumvent its provisions. Also, agencies 'try to get rid of hot-potato documents by destroying them, returning them to the sender, or stowing them away'! [48]

In the United States by the end of 1974, thirty-five States had freedom of information laws. The American Freedom of Information Act of 1966 (as amended) applies, therefore, to agencies of the Federal Executive. The term 'agency' is defined broadly and includes 'any executive department, military department, government corporation, government controlled corporation, or other establishment in the executive branch of the government (including the Executive Office of the President), or any independent regulatory agency'. [49] The Act requires government agencies to publish in the *Federal Register* [50] information about their organisation (for example procedures and policy decision) and it then confers a general right, subject to exemptions, on the public to see documents held by agencies. Unlike Sweden, however, incoming and outgoing documents of government agencies are not made available for inspection on a daily basis but instead requests have to be lodged [51] in the United States. Since the 1974 amendments, it is no longer necessary to request a specific document but only to 'reasonably describe' the records required. Additionally, all documents on specified matters will be made available. The only other access requirement is that requests are made in accordance with agencies' published procedural regulations. No reason has to be given for the request, as purpose or relevance do not have to be shown. [52] Any 'reasonably segregable portion of a record' is made available, after the deletion of exempt material. [53] Because of the problems to the Central Intelligence Agency of the risk to intelligence sources of releasing documents with secret information deleted, and the heavy backlog of FOI requests, Congress amended the National Security Act in 1984, exempting completely certain CIA files from the Act. This change provides a degree of relief to the CIA from the Freedom of Information Act but is less comprehensive than the proposal of some reformers who would like 'agency

---

48 B. Wennergren 'Civil Information – Administrative Publicity' *International Review of Administrative Sciences,* Vol. 36, 1970, p. 249. Also *private* letters are sent to officials in Sweden to circumvent publicity.

49 The statutory definition of 'agency' in the United States FOI Act of 1966 caused confusion. Therefore, the Act was amended to define agency as given in this text.

50 The *Federal Register* is a daily government gazette which is codified annually in the Code of Federal Regulations.

51 See *Departmental Committee on Section 2 of the Official Secrets Act 1911,* p. 33.

52 See above, footnote 36.

53 M. J. Singer 'United States' in D.C. Rowat (Ed.) *Administrative Secrecy in Developed Countries.*

immunity' to be granted to the CIA, FBI and other executive branch organisations – so excluding entire agencies possessing especially sensitive records from the provisions of the Act (as in the case of Australia's exempt agencies).

Concerning the cost to the requester, the American Freedom of Information Act allows an agency to recover only the 'direct costs' of a search together with charges for duplication. However, as noted earlier, the 1974 amendments encourage the agencies to reduce or waive fees for conducting searches and copying records when the release of information principally benefits the public interest. [54] The 1974 amendments led to a large increase in requests and the unexpected expense of processing them. Critics of the present law have observed that the 'direct costs' make up only 4% of the total cost of responding to applicants; the remaining 96% going on reviewing documents, redacting exempt material, and processing accounting. Accordingly, the Hatch Reform Bill of 1984 sought to alter the provisions relating to the collecting of fees under the Act by, first, making agency fee schedules more uniform [55] and, second, allowing agencies to recover more nearly the true costs of complying with requests (except where the public interest or the small nature of the request warrants a waiver or reduction of the fee). This amendment was designed also to encourage applicants to narrow broad requests. A related amendment in the Reform Bill intended to replace the 'direct cost fee' by a 'fair value fee' in cases of requests containing 'commercially valuable technological information' generated or procured by the government at substantial cost to the public and likely to be used for commercial gain – thereby depriving the government of its commercial value. [56]

In France the law on the Freedom of Access to Administrative Documents entitles any citizen or corporate body to government documents, providing the latter are *not* of a *personal* [57] character. In other words, the right of access concerns only administrative non-nominative (that is, not naming an individual personally) documents, since access to personal files was covered

---

54 The 1974 amendments 'also give the courts discretion to award "reasonable attorney fees and other litigation costs" to a party who "has substantially prevailed in proving his right to records under the FOIA".' Ibid, p. 340.

55 The 1974 amendments to the United States FOI Act contain a provision requiring each agency to produce regulations 'specifying a uniform schedule of fees applicable to all constituent units of such agency'. However, a lack of uniformity of fee schedule still developed at the various agencies.

56 See *Congressional Record – Senate* (daily edition 27 February 1984) S1794-1822.

57 However, the French access law contains a special provision which permits 'persons to have access to the file where a decision has gone against them, and have the right to attach statements to the file'.

already by the Privacy Act of January 1978. The French law has extensive coverage, applying to regional and local authorities, all public agencies including corporations which administer a public service (for example, the railways, airlines and broadcasting) as well as to the central administration. [58] Like the United States, France differs from Sweden, Australia and Canada where, in the latter countries, corporations operating under civil law or in a commercially-competitive environment, are not covered by the access legislation. Documents may be consulted free of charge in France but a small payment set by regulation (not exceeding the actual cost) applies to the provision of copies. This regulation may be amended in the future to include the cost of search. [59] A request for access can be made by letter or in person. A listing of all official documents is required but, in addition, 'secret law' is published in France (that is, internal guidelines for making decisions which affect the rights of individuals, such as ministerial directives, instructions and circulars). In Australia, likewise, manuals and other documents used by an agency in reaching decisions or recommendations in respect of schemes administered by the agency (for example about rights, benefit, and penalties) are listed in the *Gazette* and the manuals themselves are copied and made available for public inspection and purchase. [60]

The United States, Canada, and New Zealand take a less open approach to unpublished policy guidelines. Under the United States Freedom of Information Act, each agency is required to maintain and publish a considerable amount of descriptive and explanatory material in the *Federal Register*, including its substantive rules and general policy statements and interpretations. However, arguments have arisen about which rules are of 'general applicability' and which policies have been 'adopted', and administrative positions taken in this area of the Act have been challenged in court. [61] In Canada, a description of all agency manuals must be published. Although a provision to the Access Act was added in committee allowing 'for public inspection of manuals' it fell short of a recommendation by the Canadian Bar Association that the manuals and guidelines themselves should be published. [62] Similarly,

---

58 The French access law applies 'to all emanations of the State including territorial collectivities'. See D.C. Rowat 'The Right to Government Information in Democracies', *International Review of Administrative Sciences*, Vol. XLVIII, 1982, p. 66.

59 In 1983 the fee set by regulation was one franc per page for copying. The regulation may be amended to provide a variety of charges which depend on the cost of search and reproduction.

60 See Australian Freedom of Information Act 1982 s. 9.

61 M. J. Singer 'United States' in D.C. Rowat (Ed.) *Administrative Secrecy in Developed Countries*, pp. 314-5.

62 H. N. Janisch 'The Canadian Access to Information Act', *Public Law*, Vol. 27, 1982, p. 539.

in New Zealand, agency manuals are not required to be published, only a description of them. [63] However, 'a right of access to internal rules affecting decisions' is incorporated in the New Zealand Act so applicants are given access to manuals on request (with exceptions and portions deleted).

The Australian FOI Act applies to Departments of the Public Service and to prescribed Commonwealth Authorities and, as noted earlier, several Australian States have passed their own information Acts. Total exemption from the Commonwealth Act applies to some agencies – including national banks and the Australian National Airlines and Railways Commissions. As in the United States, a requester in Australia must provide enough information 'as is reasonably necessary' [64] for the agency to identify the document but, unlike the American FOI Act, a provision is contained in the Australian Act to discourage 'fishing expeditions'. [65] The agency *may* make a charge for a request for access or the provision of documents and an applicant has to be notified in writing to this effect, together with a statement of how the fee is calculated. [66] In the year 1983-84, there was a fourfold increase in the amount of charges collected per month and a doubling of the number of Commonwealth agencies making charges. Even so, the proportion of requests on which charges were levied in that year was less than 6%. In any case, the Australian Act permits a requester to seek total or partial remission of any charge paid or notified to him. [67] Proposals made in the August 1986 Budget papers, if implemented by legislation in Australia, would have a significant impact on the cost both of an initial request for access and of an application for review to the Administrative Appeals Tribunal (for example, the cost of an initial request would increase). In New Zealand costs have been considered restrictive. The New Zealand Official Information Act requires only that charges be fixed at a 'reasonable' rate and both labour and materials involved in a request may be included in the cost. [68] The New Zealand Act provides for no remission of charges. Regarding the Canadian Access Act, the Bill 'initially provided that an application fee not exceeding $25 would include search and production costs with additional payment levied for every hour in excess of five hours "reasonably required" for search

---

63 New Zealand Official Information Act 1982 Part III s. 20 and s. 22.

64 See Australian Freedom of Information Act 1982 s. 15.

65 See above, footnote 45.

66 See Australian Freedom of Information Act 1982 s. 29.

67 The average fee per FOI request in Australia for which a charge was notified during the year 1983-84 was $27.53 (as against $22.90 for the previous period).

68 In New Zealand the requester can be charged for the time it takes to find information (this being compulsory for any search over four hours), as well as reproduction costs. New Zealand Official Information Act 1982 s. 12.

and production'. Criticisms were expressed of this fee arrangement, but only a small change was effected in committee to exclude search and production costs from the initial application fee. The Act does contain a 'fee waiver' provision, that allows the head of a Canadian government institution to waive all or part of a fee. [69] Nevertheless, reports allege that requesters are being charged 'excessive search fees' in Canada.

Some examples of *overall* costs to governments operating a freedom of information law are as follows. In the United States, Federal agencies recorded total expenses of $47.8 million for the calendar year 1978 for administering the Freedom of Information Act. [70] This figure was believed to underestimate the real cost and a later estimate for 1980 indicated a cost of $57 million for government-wide compliance with the Act. In Australia, the Freedom of Information Act was not used greatly during the first seven months of its operation and costs incurred by agencies amounted to only $8 million. During the next twelve-month period July 1983-June 1984, more use was made of the Act and administrative costs rose to in excess of $17 million [71] – with further increases expected in the use of the Act. However, both countries recorded difficulties in measuring costs – for example, costs reported by different agencies 'are not always readily comparable'. [72]

Other points to note are that the New Zealand Act does not extend to local (Municipal) government, which is regarded by some as a flaw in the statute. In Canada, Crown corporations like the Canadian National Railways, Air Canada and others which operate in a commercially-competitive environment, are excluded from the Act. [73] In Australia, New Zealand, and Canada, portions of exempted documents are made available but not in France.

Question 3: Do Time Limits apply to disclosure?

Freedom of Information or Access legislation commonly stipulates a time limit in which a government agency or Department is obliged to respond to

---

69 See H. N. Janisch 'The Canadian Access to Information Act', *Public Law,* Vol. 27, 1982, pp. 539-40. See also (Canadian) Act to enact the Access to Information Act and Privacy Act s. 11. In Canada, similar freedom of information laws have been passed in Nova Scotia (1977 and under review for change); Newfoundland (1981); Quebec (1982 – became effective later). British Columbia, Manitoba, Ontario and Saskatchewan have considered laws. See also the paper in this Volume (Part III) pp. 230-55 by Robert Gillis, Treasury Board of Canada.

70 Department of Justice survey of 1979.

71 During the twelve-month period July 1983-June 1984, 19,227 FOI requests were received at Federal level in Australia (as opposed to only 5,669 requests during the seven-month period 1 December 1982-30 June 1983).

72 For example, see *Freedom of Information Act 1982 Annual Report 1983-84* (Australian Government publishing Service, Canberra, 1985), p. 123.

73 (Canadian) Act to enact the Access to Information Act and the Privacy Act.

a request for a document. In the United States the current time period for initial requests is within ten working days and, if disclosure is to be refused, to notify the requester why documents are exempt. With regard to an appeal by a requester to a higher authority in the agency against an adverse decision, the agency has twenty working days to determine the appeal. These time limits may be extended by ten working days in 'unusual circumstances', such as the need for additional time to search and collect the documents from distant offices. These short time limits were introduced by the 1974 amendments to the United States Freedom of Information Act and are criticised by some as being unrealistic and inadequate, leading to a hasty processing of requests with the likelihood of errors (for example, the improper release of trade secrets or other sensitive information). The Hatch Reform Bill of 1984 retained the existing requirements of ten working days for an initial request and twenty working days for the determination of an appeal, but sought both to extend the allowable time period for 'unusual circumstances' and to specify additional circumstances in which more time for completion would be allowed. [74]

In Canada, officials are permitted thirty working days to deal with requests under the Access Act. [75] The time limit has been reduced progressively in Australia by the 1983 Amendment Act from sixty days to thirty days by 1 December 1986 – bringing it in line with the Canadian legislation. [76] However, in France there is a more generous time limit of two months for response. Neither the Swedish nor New Zealand legislation gives a precise time limit. Under the Swedish Freedom of the Press Act, authorities are required to make the document available 'immediately or as soon as possible', [77] while in New Zealand the request has to be met 'as soon as reasonably practicable'. [78] However, during the first six months of the

---

74 *Congressional Record – Senate* (daily edition 27 February 1984) S1795-10.

75 The Canadian Access Act permits the head of a government institution to extend the thirty-day time limit in the following circumstances:- (1) a large number of records is requested, necessitating an extensive search; (2) consultations are required to comply with the request, which cannot reasonably be completed in the original time limits; and (3) written notice has to be given to a third party that the institution intends to disclose the record or part thereof (for example, in the case of trade secrets to a third party). See (Canadian) Act to enact the Access to Information Act and the Privacy Act s. 9.

76 The time limit is extended by fifteen days under the Australian Act in special circumstances specified in the act, s. 19(4). Another feature of the Australian Act is the distinction drawn between formal and informal requests; only the former attract time limits s. 19. See (Australian) *Freedom of Information Act, 1982 Annual Report 1983-84*, p. 2.

77 S. Holstad 'Sweden' in D.C. Rowat (Ed.) *Administrative Secrecy in Developed Countries*, p. 44.

78 A person in New Zealand may ask that his/her request be treated *urgently*, but must give the reason why and is liable to pay any costs in having the official information made available urgently. See New Zealand Official Information Act, 1982, Part II, s. 12 and s. 15.

operation of the New Zealand Act, the Chief Ombudsman of the Official Information Act received some 11% of requests for investigations relating to delays in answering requests. [79]

—exemptions prohibiting the release of certain kinds of information deemed necessary to be kept secret in the nation's interests.

Public access to government information in all countries is subject to exemptions restricting its release. How many exemptions are specified; whether or not the exemptions are mandatory or permissive are all questions which need to be addressed. Some information laws permit an official to release a document under an exemption if the release would do no harm (that is, it is a *permissive* exemption only, allowing him or her to withhold information according to his or her discretion). A mandatory, or compulsory, exemption means that the information *must* be withheld. Furthermore, exemptions couched in broad, general terms tend to lead to greater retention of documents than specific, narrow ones – although the extent of retention or release of information depends also on other provisions in the law, such as whether there is independent judicial review.

In theory, there is a choice between the general language of exemptions and the technique of enumeration. The latter in pure form would suggest that the range of non-disclosure information is listed document by document. This pure form does not exist in Sweden but, nevertheless, the enumeration technique is highly developed. An enumeration may be by categories of cases or of documents. Categories of documents is the most common technique, but Sweden uses categories of cases, in a case concerning, for example, medical treatment, it is implied that a medical certificate as well as other documents are, in principle, out of access. In a case about a driving licence, on the other hand, a medical certificate is accessible because neither that kind of case nor a medical certificate as such is contained in the catalogue. [80] This catalogue of hundreds of items to be kept secret appears in a separate statute – the Swedish Secrecy Act of 1980 – and these specific rules and regulations are based on seven grounds for exemption stated in the Freedom of the Press Act. These grounds are:- (1) national security and foreign policy; (2) the State's central financial, monetary, or currency policy; (3) the activities of public authorities for the purpose of inspection, control, or other supervision; (4) activities of public authorities for the prevention or prosecution of crime; (5) economic interests of the State or Municipalities; (6) protection of the individual's personal and economic privacy; and (7)

---

79 See *Transnational Data Report*, Vol. VII, No. 7, p. 403.

80 See B. Wennergren 'Civic Information – Administrative Publicity' *International Review of Administrative Sciences*, Vol. 36, 1970, p. 248.

protection of species of animals and plants. This list of exemptions covers all the general circumstances against public access to government information in Sweden. The detailed Secrecy Act 'closely defines' the restrictions and leaves little room for administrative discretion. A public employee in Sweden implementing the Freedom of the Press Act has to determine simply whether an access request relates to an 'official document' and, if so, whether it is exempt (i.e. listed in the Secrecy Act). [81] In practice, intricate problems have developed because the right of access applies only to 'official documents' – which are those either received by, or drawn up by, a public authority. The question arises as to whether minutes, diaries, memoranda, and drafts are 'official documents'? The general rule in Sweden is that documents are considered to be 'drawn up' when they have been despatched, or, 'if they are to be used only within the authority, when the case or matter to which the documents belong has been finally settled'. Besides this general rule, distinctions are made in the Freedom of Press Act between different classes of documents as to what constitutes 'drawn up'. 'Minutes' are deemed to be drawn up when they have been approved; 'records, registers, diaries and similar lists' are considered drawn up as soon as they are ready for use, and 'memoranda' [82] are regarded as 'official documents' only if they are filed together with the other documents in a case or matter. Despite these legislative guides, draft – or unfinished – documents have posed problems in Sweden. If, for example, an official in one authority sends a draft to an official in another authority for consultations, is this document available to the public? The new Freedom of the Press Act 1976 clarified the situation by ensuring that 'working papers' are not accessible until a decision has been reached or action completed. [83] Once a decision has been taken the working papers are available. However, there is no prohibition against releasing draft documents (unless in its completed form it would be secret), since the Secrecy Act applies only to information incorporated in an 'official' document'. [84]

---

81 A document that 'cannot be classified as belonging to any one of the categories listed in the Secrecy Act shall be deemed public'. Ibid, p. 247.

82 'Memoranda' are 'notes that have been made within an authority exclusively for the presentation or preparation of a case or matter' (Freedom of the Press Act Ch. 2 s. 9).

83 However, 'Factfinding documents prepared as part of a decision process would be open to the public, as would any document forwarded to another agency or authority of the government. But the advice tendered by one official to another within a ministry, or by an official to a Minister, would not be disclosed'. See *Disclosure of Official Information: A Report on Overseas Practice*, p. 11.

84 Nevertheless, the unwarranted release of an unfinished document in some cases may be regarded as 'a punishable service irregularity'. See S. Holstad 'Sweden' in D.C. Rowat (Ed.) *Administrative Secrecy in Developed Countries, pp. 36-39.*

In the United States nine categories of exempt information apply at the Federal level but, unlike Sweden, they are contained in the Freedom of Information Act itself.[85] Most of the exemptions are permissive, so that agencies may *choose* to release information. [86] They are:- (1) national defence and foreign policy; (2) internal personnel rules and practices; (3) other statutes (that is, this exemption applies to matters that are 'specifically exempted from disclosure by statute'. Recently, after much controversy, the Privacy Act has been declared *not* an exemption-three statute); (4) commercial and financial information (for example, commercial information obtained in confidence); (5) agency memoranda (this exemption protects the 'deliberative process' in government, including premature disclosure of an agency's position and strategy and fosters uninhibited debate within the government to the issues under consideration); (6) personnel, medical and similar files (for example, if their release would invade personal privacy); (7) investigatory records; (8) reports on financial institutions; and (9) information concerning wells (for example, protects against speculation in respect of oil wells).

Some of these exemptions have created little controversy, while others have acted as 'battlegrounds' for contests over rights of public access to government information. [87] Since the 1974 amendments, exemption-one documents relating to national security are subject to *in camera* inspection and the court has authority to determine whether they are 'properly classified'. This *de novo* review of sensitive (that is, classified) information by the Federal courts in freedom of information cases has been sharply criticised. [88] Concerning exemption four, it was noted earlier that the proposed Hatch Reform Act of 1984 recommended substantive changes to be made to the wording of this exemption to improve the protection of business privacy. Indeed, most litigation in the United States has arisen in connection with the fourth exemption and the 'reverse FOI lawsuit' was unanticipated! [89] Exemption five has been invoked frequently by agencies and has proved to be one of the most controversial. Thereunder, agencies have to make their 'final opinions' available to the public but, as was the case in Sweden, it is unclear whether an agency's pronouncement is a 'final opinion'

---

85 The United States Privacy Act has similar exemptions to the FOI Act, although they are fewer in number.

86 The US Justice Department has encouraged voluntary disclosure 'when the public interest would be better served thereby'. See M. J. Singer 'United States' in D.C. Rowat (Ed.) *Administrative Secrecy in Developed Countries,* p. 325.

87 Ibid, pp. 325-340.

88 *Congressional Record – Senate* (daily edition 27 February 1984) S1818.

89 *Disclosure of Official Information: A Report on Overseas Practice,* pp. 24-27.

or an internal memorandum subject to further review. This exemption also affects 'discovery' and persons have been obtaining information under the FOI Act contrary to other Federal rules. [90] Regarding exemption seven, the 1974 amendments altered the 'investigatory files' to 'records' (narrowing the exemption and thereby encouraging information within certain files to be released). An unintended consequence of this amendment has been the threat to informers referred to earlier. The proposed Hatch Act sought to broaden the scope of this exemption by extending it to 'records and information'. [91] Exemptions eight and nine are rarely used. The categories of exemptions in the United States' Freedom of Information Act are much broader than those in the Swedish law and leave more room for official discretion and judicial interpretation. [92]

The Canadian Access Act has fifteen exemptions in all compared with nine in the United States' law and seven in the Swedish law. Both the Canadian and New Zealand information laws have more exemptions which are compulsory than the American legislation. In other words, the Canadian Act has many general categories, or classes, of records to which a harm test does not apply (that is, 'class' exemptions) – and a public official has only to prove that a record belongs to one of these classes in order to withhold it (for example, Cabinet documents; law enforcement and investigation; safety of individuals; and third party information). Moreover, several exemptions state that documents in that class *must* be withheld (for example Cabinet and related documents – unless the Prime Minister gives permission for their release). [93] Commentators on the Canadian Act belong to two schools: one school believes that 'By and large, care has been taken to make the exceptions both limited and specific'. [94] The other criticises the fifteen exemptions as being too numerous and broader than those in the American law. For example, the exemption for Federal-State relations is worded broadly and deemed unnecessary by some – the American FOI Act has no such exception. [95] Three other exemptions in the Canadian Access Act are worthy of

---

90 See footnote 36. The courts in the United States have tended to take a restrictive judicial reading of the fifth exemption (i.e. against the agency). See M. J. Singer 'United States' in D. C. Rowat (Ed.) *Administrative Secrecy in Developed Countries*, pp. 331-2.

91 *Congressional Report – Senate* (daily edition 27 February 1984) S1796-1801.

92 See D. C. Rowat 'The Right to Government Information in Democracies' *International Review of Administrative Sciences*, Vol. XLVIII, 1982, p. 64.

93 D. C. Rowat 'Recent Developments in Access Laws'.

94 This first school is represented by, for example, M. J. Singer 'United States' in D. C. Rowat (Ed.) *Administrative Secrecy in Developed Countries*, p. 541.

95 The second school is represented by, for example, D. C. Rowat 'Recent Developments in Access Laws'. It should be noted that, although the United States FOI Act has no exemption for Federal-State relations, the Australian FOI Act incorporates such an exemption.

note. First, the law enforcement exemption is phrased more carefully than its counterpart in the United States FOI Act to avoid the American problem of criminals obtaining information about informants. Second, the exemption concerning 'policy advice' has proved contentious in Canada. Any document within this class must be withheld – without any harm test or other 'filter' applying. The Canadian Bar Association Model Bill sought to introduce further exceptions within this broad class so that 'factual' studies (for example, feasibility and cost studies) would be released and only 'opinion' withheld. This proposal was not enacted and, in any case, it is not easy to draw a line between facts and opinions. The third exemption of note relates to Cabinet documents. In earlier Canadian Access Bills, Cabinet documents were treated as a class exemption rather than being subject to a harm test. However, exceptions could be subject to review by the Federal court, which caused the Government to make a last-minute change before the Access Bill was passed. Cabinet minutes, records, agendas, policy papers and advice were given a 'special exemption category' from court review. [96] Some critics argue that, because almost the entire policy-making level of the government is excluded from public access, Ministers and officials may try to hide embarrassing documents! [97]

Like the Canadian Act, the New Zealand Official Information Act of 1982 has two kinds of exemptions. The first group concerns information to be withheld if there are *conclusive* reasons for doing so (for example if the information is likely to prejudice national security or defence). The second group contains a 'balancing test': information may not be withheld unless there are good reasons in the public interest, such as on the grounds of personal privacy or to protect the conduct of public affairs through the 'free and frank expression of opinions' by, between, or to Ministers and officials. There are seventeen exemptions in the New Zealand Act – four in the first group and the others in the second. [98] The New Zealand Act incorporates some interesting exemptions – for example, the second group involving a balancing test permits an official to withhold information on the grounds of (1) to 'maintain the principles and conventions of the constitution', such as collective or individual ministerial responsibility or to protect the confidentiality of advice tendered by Ministers and officials, and (2) to prevent

---

96 Moreover, this special exemption is not integrated into the body of the Act but is added awkwardly to the end (s. 69) (i.e. 'almost 50 sections away from the other exceptions and the statutory exemptions'). See H. N. Janisch 'The Canadian Access to Information Act' *Public Law*, Vol. 27, 1982, pp. 542-45.

97 For example, see D.C. Rowat 'Recent Developments in Access Laws'.

98 In fact, the second group of exemptions containing a balancing test is broken down into two categories having (1) *special* reasons for withholding official information and (2) *other* reasons for withholding official information.

improper disclosure or use of official information for gain or advantage![99] The two exemptions relied upon most in New Zealand for withholding official information have been to 'maintain the effective conduct of public affairs through the free and frank expression of opinions' within government administration, and 'to maintain the constitutional conventions'.[100] The Ombudsman stated publicly that there is a problem in identifying what a 'free and frank' opinion is and critics view this exemption as providing blanket protection to the bureaucracy. Indeed, the Ombudsman has referred to the exemption section of the New Zealand Act as leading 'the information gatherer by a maze of paths deeper and deeper into enemy territory where, if he has succeeded in avoiding the many pitfalls by the way, he is likely to die of exhaustion'! Others have criticised the exemptions as being too vague and broad in scope.[101]

Besides the exemption of entire agencies,[102] the basic approach to exemptions in the Australian Freedom of Information Act is that they are defined in terms of the 'public interest' and not the interest of the executive government (that is, they contain a harm or balancing test).[103] The Australian Act sets out sixteen exemptions from mandatory disclosure (that is, the exemptions are permissive and agencies or Ministers, by section 14 of the Act, are encouraged to provide access to documents where it is lawful or proper to do so notwithstanding that the document might properly be claimed to be exempt). Even the power to issue a conclusive certificate withholding information on the ground, for example, of defence may be lawfully exercised only where the Minister or official can properly form the opinion that its release 'would be contrary to the public interest as being prejudicial to defence'. There is no *explicit* reference to the public interest in some exemptions within the Australian Act, but in such instances the ground of exemption involved is 'one that is indisputably recognised as being in the public interest, or in the interests of private individuals and not of the government itself'.[104] Indeed, the courts and the Administrative Appeals

---

99 See New Zealand Official Information Act 1982 s. 9(f) and (k).

100 The section of the New Zealand Act relied upon most by officials for withholding *personal* information is s. 27(1)(c) concerning information the disclosure of which 'would breach a promise made to the person who supplied it . . . and the identity of the person who supplied it, or both . . .'

101 E. Longworth 'New Zealand's Official Information Act: The First Year' in *Transnational Data Report*, Vol. VII. No. 7.

102 In addition to certain agencies exempted entirely from the Australian FOI Act, other agencies have been granted exemption in respect to particular documents, see footnote 14. Both groups of agencies are listed in Schedule 2 (Parts I and II respectively) of the Act.

103 Two points have to be demonstrated when dealing with requests at the Federal level in Australia: first, if the information falls under an exemption and, second, if it is contrary to the public interest.

Tribunal have rejected 'class' claims in Australia in all but Cabinet documents and in other circumstances it is necessary to look at the *individual* case or document and the public interest related to it. [105]

In Australia the Amendment Act of 1983 made a number of changes to exemptions intended to facilitate greater disclosure: for example, by excluding documents containing 'purely factual material' from the scope of both Cabinet and Executive Council documents and by adding an 'overriding public interest test' to a few exemptions, such as 'relations with States' which in the 1982 Act contained no explicit public interest clause. [106] Criticisms of the Australian Act focus on the excessive number of exemptions and the lack of clear rules for performing the balancing test. The French Access Act, by contrast, contains a short list of eight exemptions which, as in the United States Freedom of Information Act, are couched in broad, general terms. All the exemptions are subject to a 'harm test' meaning that a document cannot be withheld unless the authorities can show that its release would do demonstrable harm (that is, all the exemptions are governed by the introductory words 'would adversely affect'). [107]

> *—machinery for appeal against denials by administrators to supply information*

An information law is regarded as strong or weak depending on whether there is independent judicial review of administrative decisions to withhold information. In Sweden, a decision by an authority to release a document is subject to appeal (in most cases to the Administrative Court of Appeal) with a further appeal to the Supreme Administrative Court. No leave to appeal is needed. The Swedish Ombudsman also receives some complaints about access to documents. [108]

In the United States the 1974 amendments to the Freedom of Information Act provided for disciplinary action by the Civil Service Commission (now reorganised) against officials who wrongly refuse to release information. [109]

---

104 Even where the Australian FOI Act seems to protect the interest of the government as, for example, in the exemption for Cabinet documents, it is because it is conceived that there is an interest of the public at large in providing that protection. See L. Curtis 'Who Owns Government Information?' *Australian Journal of Public Administration*, Vol. XXXVIII, 1979, pp. 40-1.

105 Talk by S. Zibzek at the Royal Institute of Public Administration Seminar, London 9 May 1985 on 'Australian Freedom of Information'.

106 *Australian Freedom of Information Act 1982 Annual Report 1983-84*, p. 36.

107 See *Disclosure of Official Information: A Report on Overseas Practice*, pp. 36-7.

108 See *Departmental Committee on Section 2 of the Official Secrets Act 1911*, p. 35.

109 See *Disclosure of Official Information: A Report on Overseas Practice*, p. 24. If the court finds the withholding of information 'may have been "arbitrary and capricious"', it may order the Civil Service Commission to investigate and require the punishment of the responsible agency officials, a power very rarely used'. (However, the responsibilities of the US Civil Service Commission were restructured in the late 1970s.)

However, a key feature of American government is the persuasive role of the courts in the economic and political life of the country and the area of freedom of information is no exception. In fact, many deplore the immense amount of freedom of information litigation with its 'huge cost in time and money'. [110] The Canadian Access Act is viewed by some as being better than the American Act regarding review, since it embodies a unique 'two-step system' which avoids immediate litigation. Instead of direct appeal to the courts as in the United States, applicants in Canada denied information or unhappy about delays to a request or fees may file a complaint, free of charge, with the independent Information Commissioner (stage 1). He or she has extensive powers to investigate complaints and, if necessary, to persuade government Departments to provide the information. The Information Commissioner is like an Ombudsman, reporting to Parliament, and assists a citizen to exercise his or her right of access. However, the Information Commissioner makes only a recommendation and cannot overturn Ministers' decisions (that is, the Minister is responsible to Parliament and so ministerial responsibility is retained). If the government Department or agency refuses the recommendation, a person can still appeal to the Federal court to obtain review of the denial (stage 2). If the court finds that the information has been denied improperly, the government agency will be *ordered* to release it.

The advantage of this two-step appeal system is that the majority of appeals or complaints will be settled informally, quickly, and cheaply by the Information Commissioner, but there is still the opportunity to go to the courts for 'a binding determination'. Despite the victory to the freedom of information campaigners in Canada of independent judicial review, it was seen earlier that there was a retreat from reliance on the courts regarding some documents. [111]

In Australia, in addition to a successful scheme of internal review within government agencies of freedom of information decisions, several other avenues for review have been established. These are:- (1) tribunal review; (2) court review; and (3) assistance from the Ombudsman. These numerous opportunities reflect recent changes in Australia in administrative law (created by the Administrative Appeals Tribunal Act 1975; the Administrative Decisions (Judicial Review) Act 1977; and the Ombudsman Act 1976), which provide other modes of review of departmental decisions, besides ministerial responsibility.

---

110 Ibid, p. 27.

111 See above, page 595. See also D.C. Rowat 'Recent Developments on Access Laws', and T. Riley 'Access to Government Information – An International Perspective' *Media Law and Practice*, May 1981, pp. 96-98. A Parliamentary committee has been created to oversee on a permanent basis the operation of the Canadian Access and Privacy Act.

The Australian Freedom of Information Act lays down a general public right to seek a review by the Administrative Appeals Tribunal of an executive decision to refuse access. [112] The scope of the review function undertaken by the Administrative Appeals Tribunal differs from that performed by the courts – the Tribunal examines the merits of the decision to claim an exemption. Judicial review by the courts has not been excluded by the Australian FOI Act, but the courts are restricted to questions of *law* (that is, to see whether the decision-maker has acted within his powers, and according to the law). [113] The advantages of review by the Administrative Appeals Tribunal are not only that it is speedier and less costly than final appeal to the ordinary courts, but also it provides more expertise of administrative matters and much wider scope for review. During the year 1983-84, the Tribunal handed down twenty-five interim and final decisions under the FOI Act. [114] Like the Canadian Access Act, then, the Australian FOI Act provides an improvement over the American FOI Act in its review system, but it goes much further than the Canadian system in that the Tribunal has power to set aside a claim of exemption. (It may not, however, order that access to an exempt document be given.) The role of the Tribunal, though, is different in the case where a conclusive certificate has been issued. In such cases the Tribunal may decide only whether there exist reasonable grounds for the claim of exemption.

One criticism has centred on such conclusive ministerial certificates. [115] Initially a right to review in such cases was conferred on the Document Review Tribunal, judicially constituted, but it was abolished by the Australian FOI Amendment Act of 1983, which introduced a number of changes affecting review under the Act. These modifications included transferring to the Administrative Appeals Tribunal, which was given an enlarged jurisdiction, the power to determine questions relating to 'the claim of exemption in respect of which a conclusive certificate is issued'. The principal use of the conclusive certificate has been in cases where the Minister certifies that it would be contrary to the public interest for access to be granted. In such cases the Administrative Appeals Tribunal is confined to deciding 'whether there exist reasonable grounds for the claim', that is to say as at the time when the matter is before the Tribunal. Since the Tribunal is able in such instances to make only a recommendation, a further provision was added by the Amendment Act requiring a Minister who does not accept the Tribunal's finding or

---

112 Australian Freedom of Information Act 1982, s. 55.

113 Talk by S. Zibzek at a Royal Institute of Public Administration Seminar, London 9 May 1985 on 'Australian Freedom of Information'.

114 *Australian Freedom of Information Act 1982 Report 1983-84,* p. 85.

115 D. C. Rowat 'Recent Developments in Access Laws'. See also T. Riley 'Access to Government Information – An International Perspective' *Media Law and Practice,* May 1981, pp. 98-99.

to lay before each House of Parliament (and to advise the applicant about) the *reason* for not revoking the certificate. [116] The first such instance occurred in August 1986 subsequent to the decision in *Re Lordsvale Finance and The Treasurer (No. 4)*.

Turning now to court review, *Harris v. Australian Broadcasting Corporation* (1983) is an example of an FOI case brought under the Administrative Decisions (Judicial Review) Act 1977. It is interesting to note that, besides exempting entire agencies, the Australian Freedom of Information Act also exempts certain other agencies in respect of particular documents. The Broadcasting Corporation is exempt in relation to its programme material, but otherwise the FOI Act applies to the Corporation (subject to the sixteen specific exemptions). The Federal Court ruled against the Corporation's decision to grant a journalist access under the FOI Act to two consultants' reports relating to its legal department. The decision revolved around the 'internal working documents' exemption (that is, the deliberative process of policy-making in the Corporation). The Court ordered access to be granted to purely factual matter in the reports but deferred access to the rest on public interest grounds. In *Harris v. ABC* on 8 February 1984, 'the Full Federal Court affirmed the first instance decision to allow disclosure of purely factual material'. [117]

The third avenue for review under the Australian FOI Act is via the Commonwealth Ombudsman. The traditional role of an Ombudsman is to be concerned with defective administration, a term preferred by the Commonwealth Ombudsman to *mal administration*. The Freedom of Information Bill of 1982 denied to the Ombudsman an extension of powers to assist applicants in the practical utilisation of the FOI Act (for example, by representing them before the Administrative Appeals Tribunal). However, in committee, the Government suffered defeats in respect of the FOI Bill and it was enacted that the Ombudsman may investigate matters associated with the FOI Act. Furthermore, the FOI Amendment Act expanded the role of the Ombudsman under the Act – who is now empowered to represent an applicant in proceedings before the Tribunal. [118] For further details of these Australian developments, see the next paper in this volume by Robert K. Todd, recently President of the Australian Capital Territory Administrative Appeals Tribunal.

The New Zealand Official Information Act has come under attack by freedom of information advocates as having been weakened by the lack of independent judicial review. In the event of an information denial, or a

---

116 *Australian Freedom of Information Act 1982 Annual Report 1983-84*, pp. 88-89.

117 Ibid, p. 91.

118 Ibid, p. 93.

request taking too long, or being too costly, an individual may appeal to the Ombudsman. However, final decisions on the release of information rest with the Minister, who holds the veto power. [119] Furthermore, if under conclusive reasons for exempting material, a denial of the existence of such information should be deemed 'prejudicial', the government official has the right neither to confirm nor deny the existence of the requested documents. [120] Also a Minister in New Zealand is able to sign a conclusive certificate preventing the Ombudsman from stating publicly his reasons for the release of information if he disagrees with the department or agency.

By contrast, the French Access law is regarded as a strong one – providing appeal to authorities independent of the government. The special independent Commission for the Access to Administrative Documents has the duty of ensuring freedom of access to administrative documents. The Commission's main job is to receive appeals against the refusal to release documents and to make recommendations to the authorities concerned and, therefore, is something like the Information Commissioner in Canada or an Ombudsman – although its powers are greater. As a further recourse to documents, an individual may proceed under the normal system of quasi-judicial review in France. Under the independent administrative court system, a citizen can turn to an administrative judge, who must answer within six months (that is, an appeal is lodged as of right on any administrative decision, not just information requests). Finally, there is an implicit right guaranteed under French law to a further appeal to a higher court. Although potentially strong, the French Access law is little known as yet and only a small number of appeals have been received by the Commission. [121]

Conclusions

Two conclusions will be examined. First, is there more openness of government in countries which have information legislation and, second, are constitutional conventions affected by this legislation in Commonwealth countries such as Australia, Canada, and New Zealand? The extent of openness depends partly on how liberal the information law is. In the United

---

119 Following the Ombudsman's investigation, the Minister has twenty-two days in which to put in writing his disagreement with the Ombudsman. If he does not do so, the information is released automatically. The ministerial veto was invoked four times within one month in late 1983 and the use and misuse of the veto power is emerging as an area of conflict. See E. Longworth 'New Zealand's Official Information Act: The First Year' *Transnational Data Report*, Vol. VII, No. 7. See also D. C. Rowat 'Recent developments in Access Laws'.

120 New Zealand Official Information Act 1982 s. 10.

121 D. C. Rowat 'Recent Developments in Access Laws', and D. C. Rowat 'The Right to Government Information in Democracies' *International Review of Administrative Sciences*, Vol. XLVIII, 1982, pp. 66-7.

States more official information has been released since the 1974 amendments (which were vetoed by President Ford) [122] but, in turn, too much openness can create problems: of damage to national security (which led Congress in 1984 to amend the National Security Act); of heavy expenditure of time and money in answering information requests; and of certain abuses which have been pinpointed in this chapter. In Australia an increased amount of official information has been made available following the Amendment Act of 1983, but it is too soon to say whether, for example, the overall cost of implementing the Freedom of Information Act of 1982 will prove unduly burdensome, although there are now signs that the Government is of the view that it will.

The extent of openness of government is subject also to the wording of the information statute. Problems of definition in connection with key terms have arisen in most countries. In practice difficulties have centred in the Swedish legislation on the meaning of 'official document' and in the United States FOI Act on what is a government 'record' and what is an 'agency'? In several countries a 'final opinion' is a matter of controversy and in the New Zealand statute what is a 'free and frank' opinion has been difficult to interpret. Openness depends also on the methods of external review of administrative decisions and the balancing tests used in both the decisions and their review – for example, whether withholding official information because it may 'harm' the nation outweighs a person's right to know? In New Zealand the exercise of the ministerial veto has caused conflict and is seen by some to reduce openness. [123] It is clear that there is no simple answer as to how much openness an information statute provides. Furthermore, experience shows that personal (not official) information is sought in most countries by ordinary citizens under such legislation.

Turning now to the second conclusion, each of the Commonwealth countries of Australia, Canada, and New Zealand attempted, in drawing up freedom of information, or access, legislation to retain to some extent the constitutional conventions associated with Cabinet government. The New Zealand Official Information Act of 1982 contains as one of the seventeen exemptions the need to 'maintain the constitutional conventions for the time being' which are listed as:- (1) the confidentiality of communications by or with the Sovereign or her representative; (2) collective and individual ministerial responsibility, (3) the political neutrality of officials; and (4) the confidentiality

---

122 See Veto of Freedom of Information Act Amendments Vol. 10 *Weekly Compilation of Presidential Documents*, p. 1318 (1974).

123 On several occasions the ministerial veto has been used in circumstances described as 'neither exceptional nor compelling'. In each case the Ombudsman recommended in favour of disclosure. See above footnote 119.

of advice tendered by Ministers of the Crown and officials. [124] It has been noted already that this exemption has been relied upon extensively by officials in New Zealand to withhold information and the Ombudsman has pointed publicly to the lack of definition concerning these conventions. [125] Ministerial responsibility is retained under the New Zealand Act by the ministerial veto which means that, after an investigation and recommendation by the Ombudsman in respect of a decision to withhold information, the final authority rests with the Minister as to whether to release it. [126] Similarly, the power to issue conclusive certificates in respect of the several types of sensitive information listed in the Act is another way of safeguarding ministerial responsibility. [127]

The Australian FOI Act at Commonwealth level established a system of independent review of administrative decisions by the Administrative Appeals Tribunal and the courts, and no minsterial veto of the New Zealand kind exists (that is, New Zealand depends on the Ombudsman for review). However, the FOI Act confers on a Minister, or his or her delegate, the right to issue a conclusive certificate in relation to particularly sensitive information (for example, in respect of defence, security, and the deliberative and policy-forming processes of government). Additionally the final decision in connection with disclosure of Cabinet or Executive Council documents is vested in the Prime Minister. [128] The Amendment Act of 1983 in Australia affected the conclusive certificate mechanism insofar as it extended the jurisdiction of the Administrative Appeals Tribunal so that now it can determine whether reasonable grounds exist for the claim. The Tribunal may not set aside a conclusive certificate: instead it falls within the discretion of the Prime Minister or relevant Minister to revoke the certificate in the light of the Tribunal's review. However, as noted earlier, if the Minister decides *not* to revoke the certificate, notice of that decision has to be given to the requester with a copy to each House of Parliament. In other words, the conclusive certificate system was not abolished by the Amendment Act, but remains controversial in Australia. [129]

---

124 New Zealand Official Information Act 1982, s. 9(f).

125 See E. Longworth 'New Zealand's Official Information Act: The First Year' *Transnational Data Report*, Vol. VII, No. 7

126 However, the Minister is obliged to give the Ombudsman (and publish in the *Gazette*) a copy of his decision and the grounds for it. The Ombudsman has the duty to inform the complainant of the result of the investigation. See New Zealand Official Information Act 1982, s. 32 and s. 33.

127 The New Zealand Official Information Act 1982 empowers the Prime Minister and the Attorney-General respectively to certify that the making available of information would be likely to prejudice defence, security, crime prevention, and other specified types of information. See s. 31 (a) and (b).

128 See *Australian Freedom of Information Act 1982 Annual Report 1983-84*, p. 76.

129 Ibid, pp. 76-8.

The confidentiality of advice tendered by Ministers and officials is protected in the New Zealand, Australian, and Canadian statutes. In the New Zealand Official Information Act this convention comes under the constitutional exemption and in the Australian FOI Act it takes the form of the 'internal working documents' exemption which safeguards from mandatory disclosure communications between Ministers and their advisers and other documents reflecting 'advice opinion recommendation or deliberation', where disclosure would be contrary to the public interest (that is, the confidentiality of the decision-making process). [130] This exemption has received much attention from the Administrative Appeals Tribunal and Federal Court since the Act came into force. The decisions have established a broad test for a document being classified as an internal working document while, at the same time, examining critically whether disclosure would be contrary to the public interest. [131] 'Operations of government' is the relevant exemption in the Canadian Access Act. It permits the head of a government institution to refuse the disclosure of any record containing 'advice or recommendations' without having to apply a harm test (that is, the use of a class of documents as the basis of exemption rather than a harm test). [132]

Protection of political neutrality as a convention is harder to identify within the freedom of information, or access, legislation in these Commonwealth countries, although it is listed in the New Zealand Act. Nonetheless the system of Cabinet government itself is afforded some protection in both the Australian and Canadian statutes. In the Australian FOI Act, Cabinet documents constitute one of the exemptions so that Cabinet deliberations and records are safeguarded from mandatory disclosure. [133] However, as was seen earlier, the Amendment Act of 1983 narrowed this exemption to exclude 'purely factual material' in certain circumstances. [134] The New Zealand Official Information Act differs because the Danks Committee (1980) reported that the Cabinet system did not need 'blanket protection as a special category of exempted information'. The committee considered the other exemptions: for example, the free and frank exchange of views between Ministers and their colleagues and officials. [135] In Canada strong second thoughts emerged about Cabinet confidences. The last minute amendments to the Access Bill announced by Prime Minister Trudeau in 1982 placed Cabinet documents and discussions in a special category not subject at all to

---

130 Australian Freedom of Information Act 1982, s. 36.

131 See *Freedom of Information Act 1982 Annual Report 1983-84*, p. 57.

132 (Canadian) Act to enact the Access to Information Act and the Privacy Act (C111), s. 21.

133 *Australian Freedom of Information Act* 1982, s. 34.

134 See *Australian Freedom of Information Act, 1982. Annual Report 1983-84*, p. 54.

court review or scrutiny by the Information Commissioner instead of keeping them, as drafted, as a class exemption (not subject to a harm test). Fears prevailed that judicial review would encroach upon Cabinet confidentiality. [136]

Despite the foregoing provisions, less reverence is being paid in countries like Australia and New Zealand today to traditional constitutional conventions like ministerial responsibility. Australia, for example, has been developing since the mid-1970s alternative modes of reviewing departmental decisions besides ministerial responsibility. And the constitutional conventions in New Zealand are retained under the Information Act only 'for the time being'.

---

135 Towards Open Government (Danks Committee) *General Report* I (Wellington, N.Z. publication 59184J – 4500/1/81 PT 19 December 1980) p. 20.

136 H. N. Janish 'The Canadian Access to Information Act' *Public Law*, Vol. 27, 1982, pp. 543-45.

13

Independent Review of Administrative Decisions on the Merits – Successes and Strains in the Australian Experience

by Robert K. Todd, recently President of the Australian Capital Territory Administrative Appeals Tribunal, and a Deputy President of the Administrative Appeals Tribunal of the Commonwealth

'True law is Reason, right and natural, commanding people to fulfil their obligations and prohibiting and deterring them from doing wrong. Its validity is universal; it is immutable and eternal. Its commands and prohibitions apply effectively to good men, and those uninfluenced by them are bad. Any attempt to supersede this law, to repeal any part of it, is sinful; to cancel it entirely is impossible. Neither the Senate nor the Assembly can exempt us from its demands; we need no interpreter or expounder of it but ourselves. There will not be one law at Rome, one at Athens, or one now and one later, but all nations will be subject all the time to this one changeless and everlasting law'.

M. Tullius Cicero *On the State* (III. 33)

Introduction

Since the mid 1970s a reformed system of administrative law has been in existence in Australia. That system is comprised of three elements:

i.   reformed judicial review under the *Administrative Decisions (Judicial Review) Act* 1977 ('the ADJR Act') which rationalised the scope of such review;

ii. an Administrative Appeals Tribunal ('AAT') created by the *Administrative Appeals Tribunal Act* 1975 ('the AAT Act'), the function of which is to review decisions on their merits. With one exception, the power of the Administrative Appeals Tribunal is not merely recommendatory, but is decisive. It has however no power to act at all unless power is specifically conferred upon it;

iii. an Ombudsman, whose office was created by the *Ombudsman Act* 1976, and whose sphere of responsibility primarily relates to defective administration. The jurisdiction of the Ombudsman is widely expressed, subject to exceptions, but the power of the Ombudsman is recommendatory only.

While it is of the Administrative Appeals Tribunal that this paper will principally speak, it is desirable to say something of each of these three elements, and to refer to the historical and constitutional reasons why each was found to be necessary in the interests of creating a cohesive system.

1. The Past

1.1 The Courts were reluctant to interfere and remedies were outmoded

Countries which, like Australia, derived their legal systems from the English common law, adopted the traditional limitations which the courts imposed upon themselves in relation to interference with governmental functions. This reluctance can be traced back at least, and perhaps primarily, to the Civil War which took place in England between the King and Parliament in the middle of the seventeenth century, and to the Revolution Settlement of 1688. For that Settlement established what came to be seen as the heart of freedom: Parliamentary democracy; the independence of the judiciary; and the subjection of the executive to the law. It was part of the price of securing the independence of the judiciary that the judges used sparingly the power to interfere with executive decisions. In fact the courts virtually ceased to create new remedies in that regard, so that the only means whereby a citizen could challenge governmental decisions came to be confined to some ancient procedures known as 'prerogative writs', principally those known as 'prohibition', 'certiorari' and 'mandamus'. It is true that in the hands of knowledgeable lawyers and judges these procedures could be used quite creatively. The courts also extended the use of the declaratory judgement. But as some of these writs were created in mediaeval times under the prerogative powers of the King of England, chiefly for the purpose of ensuring that no-one usurped the authority of the courts which he was creating and seeking to support as a centralised system of justice, it can be seen how outmoded those procedures were.

1.2 The increasing role of government led to reforms

When legislation and regulation by government played a comparatively small part in the organisation of society, the self-denying restrictions which the courts placed upon themselves were of comparatively little importance. From at least the time of the First World War, government has played an increasingly interventionist role in society. Whereas the business of the courts previously had related primarily to the resolution of disputes between citizens, or between citizens and corporations, a great wealth of decision-making by government descended on ordinary citizens. The ancient procedures to which I have referred began to be seen as unsuitable for the purpose of resolving disputes between government and citizen. Demands for reform arose from distinguished academic lawyers, and, in England, from the then Lord Chief Justice, Lord Hewart. [1] The Second World War, and the governmental intervention needed for post-war recovery, increased the demand for change.

1.3 Later spurs to reform

The principal spur to reform in Australia was the appointment of the Commonwealth Administrative Review Committee, referred to as 'the Kerr Committee' after its chairman. Another member of that Committee was Sir Anthony Mason, who is now Chief Justice of the High Court of Australia. At paragraph 58 of its Report (August 1971) that Committee, speaking of the situation which then obtained, said:

> '58. It is generally accepted that this complex pattern of rules as to appropriate courts, principles and remedies is both unwieldy and unnecessary. The pattern is not fully understood by most lawyers; the layman tends to find the technicalities not merely incomprehensible but quite absurd. A case can be lost or won on the basis of choice of remedy and the non-lawyer can never appreciate why this should be so. The basic fault of the entire structure is, however, that review cannot as a general rule, in the absence of special statutory provisions, be obtained "on the merits" – and this is usually what the aggrieved citizen is seeking.'

2. The Changes Made in Australia

The Kerr Commitee recommended four principal lines of reform:

a. the conferring of jurisdiction upon a suitable court to exercise a supervisory role in relation to administrative decisions with a reformation of procedure so that the technicalities of the prerogative writs and related procedures would no longer apply;

b. the creation of a new tribunal to review administrative decisions on the merits;

c. the establishment of a 'General Council for Grievances'; and

d. the creation of an Administrative Review Council to oversee the whole system of the review of administrative decisions and to make recommendations as to the classes of case in which jurisdiction should be conferred upon the Administrative Appeals Tribunal and other bodies.

---

1 Hewart of Bury, The Rt. Hon. Lord *The New Despotism* (London, Benn 1929).

After further consideration of these recommendations all were accepted and implemented, except that in place of the suggested 'General Council for Grievances', the Office of Ombudsman, on the Swedish model, was created as mentioned above.

An associated reform was the passing of the *Freedom of Information Act* 1982. This statute conferred a general right, subject to exemptions set out in the Act, to obtain access to documents containing information in the possession of Ministers, Departments and public authorities. Decisions about exemptions are reviewable by the Administrative Appeals Tribunal.

3. How does the System work?

The role of judicial review, and in some respects that of the Ombudsman, is supervisory. The aim is to ensure that, substantively and procedurally, the administration acts according to law, and does not exceed or abuse the proper limits of its powers, and does not deny procedural justice and fairness. But judicial review does not presume to tell the administration how to exercise its powers. Neither does the Ombudsman, who has a power of recommendation only, although those recommendations carry considerable persuasive force.

The role of the Administrative Appeals Tribunal is quite different. It has power to 'review' decisions on their merits, and to affirm or, save in one case, to vary or set aside decisions and to substitute a different decision. Thus it can, and does, intrude into general administration.

It should be noted that 'review' has a different meaning in Australian law, and accordingly in this paper, from that which it has in the French and related systems of administrative law. There, a court of review ('cassation') has no power to substitute its own decision, and 'appeal' connotes the bringing of the entire litigation before the appellate body for a new decision. [2] In Australia, the meanings are reversed.

A fundamental principle of the new Australian system is the provision of reasons for decisions made by government, for it would impede a citizen seeking to challenge a decision if its basis in law and/or fact could not be ascertained. Both under the Administrations Decisions (Judicial Review) Act and under the Administrative Appeals Tribunal Act there is provision for a general right to obtain a statement in writing setting out the findings on material questions of fact, referring to the evidence or other material on which those findings were based, and giving reasons for the decision. The Administrative Appeals Tribunal Act also provides for the making of such a statement where application is made to the Administrative Appeals Tribunal for review of a

---

2 See Jolowicz 'Appeal and Review in Comparative Law: Similarities, Differences and Purposes' [15 *Melb. Univ. Law Review* 618].

particular decision, whether or not a prior request for reasons has been made. To complete the picture the Administrative Appeals Tribunal, when giving reasons for a decision when the review has been completed, is itself placed under the same obligation as to the provision of reasons.

This paper is primarily concerned with review of decisions on their merits. That is not to deny the importance of reformed judicial review or of the role of the Ombudsman. Each of the trio of reforms is vital. But if any one of the three could be said to have a uniquely Australian flavour it would be the Administrative Appeals Tribunal, in whose hands review on the merits has been placed.

4. Essential Features of the Administrative Appeals Tribunal

The Administrative Appeals Tribunal is required in reviewing an individual decision:

- to give each party the opportunity to present its case;
- to weigh the evidence or other information placed before it;
- to construe and apply the relevant law;
- to apply that law to the facts as found by it;
- to expose its reasoning processes to the parties and, by publication of them, to expose those processes to those, whether administrators or citizens, whose rights are later affected by the same or similar legislation.

To perform this function the Administrative Appeals Tribunal, on general principle but also as required by the Administrative Appeals Tribunal Act, conducts a hearing unless a compromise has been arrived at. That hearing has varying degrees of formality/informality as dictated by the nature of the issue and the level of representation, or lack of it, of the parties. Quite extensive use of telephone hearings has been made, and although this mainly occurs in pre-hearing procedures, it sometimes includes the taking of some at least of the evidence at a hearing. Occasional complaint is made of the use of a hearing procedure, but it is a legislative requirement, and in my opinion a degree of formality serves to confer, and not to detract from, that true equality to which all parties, but in particular unrepresented applicants, are entitled.

The review is not confined to deciding whether the decision was based on legal error or on some erroneous procedural ground, nor is it confined to a review of the reasons given by the decision maker for the decision that is under review. Indeed those reasons, while properly placed before the Tribunal as required by the Administrative Appeals Tribunal Act, are essentially background information. In a leading case the Federal Court of Australia said:

'The function of the Tribunal is, as we have said, an administrative one. It is to review the administrative decision that is under attack before it. In that review, the Tribunal is not restricted to consideration of the questions which are relevant to a judicial determination of whether a discretionary power allowed by statute has been validly exercised.

The question for the determination of the Tribunal is not whether the decision which the decision maker made was the correct or preferable one on the material before him. The question for the determination of the Tribunal is whether that decision was the correct or preferable one on the material before the Tribunal. [3]

When the Federal Court referred, in the passage cited above, to the Tribunal's obligation to make the 'correct or preferable' decision, I suggest that the court was speaking, in terms of the word 'preferable', of a case where the exercise of a discretion was involved, or perhaps some value judgement. Other than in such circumstances the Administrative Appeals Tribunal does not have a choice as to which decision it should make. Its duty is to 'stand in the shoes' of the primary decision maker, and to make up its own mind what is the correct decision having regard to the facts which it has found, and to the applicable law as identified by it.

The Administrative Appeals Tribunal is thus far from being a tribunal deciding facts only. The Administrative Appeals Tribunal conducts its reviews under the law, and an important aspect of its work is the interpretation of the legislative provisions that give rise to the power of the administrative decision maker to make the decision in question. A striking feature of the institution of the Administrative Appeals Tribunal has been the creation of an opportunity to examine the meaning and effect of legislative provisions which had had little occasion to be considered by the courts. There is ample evidence that government Departments have welcomed this opportunity, not least when there have been competing interpretations within the Department. A prime example has been in relation to the law relating to the imposition of customs duties. Although revenue from customs and excise was one of the main sources of revenue granted to the Commonwealth of Australia by the Constitution of 1901, the number of cases in the courts in relation to customs duties and, in particular, the meaning and interpretation of the Customs Tariff, could just about be counted on the fingers of one hand. There have been many decisions of the Administrative Appeals Tribunal that have illuminated the meaning and application of these difficult provisions.

It has been held by the Federal Court of Australia that the Administrative Appeals Tribunal's powers extend to consideration of government policy.

---

3 *Drake v. Minister for Immigration and Ethnic Affairs* [1979 2 ALD 60].

The Administrative Appeals Tribunal is not bound by government policy unless the Act of Parliament conferring the right of appeal requires the Administrative Appeals Tribunal to apply relevant government policy. This is a very complex area and it cannot be adequately dealt with here. In fact the proportion of the work of the Administrative Appeals Tribunal that involves review of policy is quite small. It should also be said that there are different levels of policy, and that the approach by the Administrative Appeals Tribunal will be different depending upon the level at which the policy has been formed. At the highest level is a policy that has been developed by a Minister and placed before Parliament. The Administrative Appeals Tribunal is much less likely to depart from such a policy. It would be otherwise in the case of a policy formed at a comparatively lowly departmental level.

5. How has the Administrative Appeals Tribunal developed?

The Administrative Appeals Tribunal has experienced remarkable growth in the thirteen years of its existence. Jurisdiction has now been conferred upon it to review decisions under some two hundred and seventy enactments. In its earliest years the jurisdictions conferred were in areas where there had never been any form of right of review. Later, consistently with the notion that it should be a general appeals tribunal, previously existing forms of review tribunal were abolished and the jurisdiction transferred to the Administrative Appeals Tribunal. The first related to what is more generally known as workers' compensation, in this case as applied to Commonwealth public servants. The second instance was that of review of the pension rights of Defence Force veterans. In numerical terms the most significant was the abolition in 1986 of the old Taxation Boards of Review and the conferring of jurisdiction in taxation appeals upon the Administrative Appeals Tribunal. There had been concern in the Administrative Appeals Tribunal when it was discovered that the backlog of veterans' appeals at the point of the change-over was some 13,000 cases. It can be imagined how much anxiety there was when it was revealed that the acquisition of the jurisidiction in taxation appeals carried with it a backlog of some 70,000 cases, to be followed shortly afterwards by the referral to the Administrative Appeals Tribunal of another 20,000.

A feature of the Administrative Appeals Tribunal has been its determined use of pre-hearing procedures, in particular those known as preliminary conferences. These are held before a member of the Administrative Appeals Tribunal, around a conference table, in a very informal atmosphere. Something like 80 percent of all cases coming to the Administrative Appeals Tribunal are determined at or after such a conference, without the need for a hearing. By this means the so-called 'backlog' that the Administrative Appeals Tribunal acquired in taxation matters has been reduced to not much above 30,000, and it will not be long before the Administrative Appeals Tribunal can set down for prompt hearing all taxation appeals referred to it.

Another feature of the Administrative Appeals Tribunal's work, particularly apposite in relation to those areas of jurisidiction where there had never been a previous right of review, is that the number of cases coming before the Tribunal tends to peak at a fairly early stage, and then to level out and fall away as the Administrative Appeals Tribunal's consideration of the relevant legislation resolves questions both of principle and of the application of the legislation to particular facts. The conferral of new jurisdictions then permits the Administrative Appeals Tribunal to move on to start the process all over again in 'fresh fields and pastures new'. The system improves the quality of primary administration as senior administrators have come to acknowledge.

There is some inconsistency in the system in relation to the interposition of 'first tier' tribunals between the original administrative decision maker and the Administrative Appeals Tribunal. In the areas of social security and veterans' affairs, both 'high bulk' in terms of numbers of cases, such tribunals exist. Their aim is to filter out cases giving rise to less difficult issues and to do so using speedier and more informal methods than an Administrative Appeals Tribunal hearing. My own opinion is that no matter should be able to be taken to the Administrative Appeals Tribunal for review unless, in 'bulk' jurisdictions, there has been first tier review by an intermediate tribunal, or, in less frequently invoked areas, there has been reconsideration of the decision at a high level in the Department. This is a requirement in some but not all of the Administrative Appeals Tribunal's areas of review.

6. The Degree of Acceptance of the new System

It is fair to say that the Administrative Appeals Tribunal started with strong bipartisan political support, but with a substantial degree of suspicion from the bureaucracy, particularly from some older members who saw a system of independent review as an unnecessary intrusion into a system which they believed produced correct decisions in the great majority of cases.

In some ways these attitudes have now been reversed. There are grounds for thinking that some on both sides of politics may have come to regret the existence of an independent body which demands the application of Acts of Parliament according to the words in which the legislation is expressed rather than according to the government's belief as to what the legislation says or, worse, as to what it would like it to have said. There has been heavy criticism from one quarter of the 'fact', as it is put, that the Tribunal 'does not have regard to the economic consequences of its decision'. It is not however for the Administrative Appeals Tribunal to distort or to ignore the meaning of an Act of Parliament in order to avoid or to promote a particular economic result. The criticism overlooks the fact that the responsibility for the way in which the law is expressed in an Act of Parliament lies with the

641

Parliament and with the Government that has introduced the legislation into the Parliament. It also overlooks the fact that an appeal may be made to the Federal Court if the Administrative Appeals Tribunal decision is claimed to be not correct in law. It would be both undemocratic, and contrary to the rule of law, for the Tribunal to act in the manner in which it appears to be suggested that it should.

My own feeling is that some of the most understanding support of the Australian system, and of the concepts underlying it, now comes from bureaucrats, particularly from those who have appeared before the Administrative Appeals Tribunal at hearings and are conversant with the system. From early days these younger bureaucrats have indeed been very supportive of the new system. The support mentioned does not however now stop with administrators at that level. In a recent decision of the Tribunal (*Re Denison and Civil Aviation Authority*) (Decision No. 5034, 7 April 1989) a close analysis was made of the consideration to be taken into account in relation to the grant of a pilot licence to a person who did not meet the colour vision medical standard. What happened is noteworthy. The Civil Aviation Authority and its predecessors had long wrestled with the problem. It welcomed the opportunity to have the whole matter reviewed. It supported an application for the grant of legal aid to the applicant so that the case could be fully presented. The decision went in favour of the applicant, and the Civil Aviation Authority did not appeal. I understand that the decision and the reasons therefor, the transcript of the evidence, and copies of the exhibits may be sent to the ICAO in Montreal. It is considered that in the relevant area there is no other country in the world where such independent review is possible.

Support of course comes not only from those whose decisions are regularly reviewed, but also from an army of persons, often at the very disadvantaged end of society, who have not in the past had the ability to ensure that they have been treated fairly by the governmental process.

7. Pitfalls to Avoid

The Administrative Appeals Tribunal has had one area of power that is recommendatory only – the power to review deportation orders. Experience suggests strongly that such a limited power should not be conferred again. The original decision maker, the decision having been made the subject of an unfavourable recommendation by the Administrative Appeals Tribunal, has to reconsider the matter again. The applicant, apparently successful before the Tribunal, can after the lapse of much time, the incurring of much expense and the infliction of much heartache, find the case lost after all. The Administrative Appeals Tribunal's task is made difficult and unsatisfactory by the fact that it is making no decision at all, unless it be to affirm the decision under review. There is a manifest distortion of responsibility.

A body with the power and responsibility of the Administrative Appeals Tribunal needs a secure basis of funding. It needs to be made proof against cost-cutting by a Government which, fearing the independence of an Administrative Appeals Tribunal but unwilling to incur the opprobrium involved in abolishing it, seeks to reduce its power by financial starvation. An Administrative Appeals Tribunal needs to be assured of funding by the setting, by an arbiter independent of executive government, of a base overall assessment of its need; by the base being reviewable every, say, five years; by the base being adjusted when significant new areas of power are conferred; and by the Administrative Appeals Tribunal having overall control of how it spends the total fund allotted to it.

8. An Independent System

It is of the essence of an Administrative Appeals Tribunal that it be independent. That is the very purpose of its existence. This makes it uniquely vulnerable unless its members, particularly those who preside at hearings and are primarily responsible for preparing reasons for decision, are secure from political attack. First, these members need to be appointed to a normal retiring age. They should not be appointed for terms of years. Secondly, their conditions of service should be set upon appointment, and not be reduced during their term of office. In Australia, the first of these requirements was eventually satisfied, only to be eroded later. The second has, regrettably, not been satisfied at all.

9. Conclusion

Some, in the United Kingdom in particular, would still say that judicial review enlivened by modern developments is enough. The Australian experience is such that I cannot conceive that a system of administrative law can adequately cope with the need for just and cohesive review of administrative action unless somewhere in the system there is the capacity to go beyond judical review of a decision on the basis of legal error.

Between the member countries of Lawasia [4] there are no doubt great differences in the extent of judicial review. I imagine that the differences in the extent of independent review of administrative action are greater still. I hope that this paper may be of assistance by indicating one way of providing for such review. The Australian system of judicial review may be apposite to common law traditions only. I suggest however that the institution of an Ombudsman, and in particular of a general tribunal for the review of administrative decisions on their merits, can be seen to have universal values.

---

4 This paper by Robert K. Todd was presented originally at the Eleventh Lawasia Conference in Hong Kong on 18 September, 1989.

Perhaps some day, as far as the nations represented in Lawasia are concerned, there will in this area not be 'one law at Rome, one at Athens', but nations subject to 'one changeless and everlasting law', as Cicero hoped two thousand years ago.

14

Independent Review of
Administrative Decisions on the Merits
– Successes and Strains
in the Australian Experience

Commentary by Robert K. Todd, recently President of the
Australian Capital Territory Administrative Appeals Tribunal,
and a Deputy President of the Administrative
Appeals Tribunal of the Commonwealth

1. In the foregoing paper I have described how Australia has developed a system of review of administrative decisions based on –

    i.   reformed judicial review

    ii. an Administrative Appeals Tribunal ('AAT')

    iii. an Ombudsman.

2. The Courts historically had been reluctant to interfere in administrative decision-making, and the remedies available in them were outmoded. The increasing role of government had led to demands for reform.

3. The three arms of the Australian system, which began effectively in 1977, have different roles. The roles of reformed judicial review and of the Ombudsman are essentially supervisory. But the role of the Administrative Appeals Tribunal is quite different, as it has power to review a decision on its merits, and to set aside a decision and to substitute its own for it. The one exceptional area, in which the Tribunal has only a recommendatory power, has demonstrated the unsatisfactory character of such a limitation.

4. In the paper I observe that the Administrative Appeals Tribunal reviews the decision and not the reasons for it; that it conducts hearings, normally in public; that it reviews the legal grounds for the decision as well as the facts upon which it is based; and that it is obliged to review relevant Government policy, although the extent to which it will scrutinise policy will depend on the level at which that policy was evolved.

5. The Administrative Appeals Tribunal is required –

   • to give each party the opportunity to present its case;

   • to weigh the evidence or other information placed before it;

   • to construe and apply the relevant law;

   • to apply that law to the facts as found by it; and

   • to expose its reasoning processes to the parties.

6. While the Administrative Appeals Tribunal started out with bipartisan political support, and suspicion from bureaucrats, in many ways these attitudes have been reversed. The bureaucrats who work in the field have in my experience been very supportive. There is a core of politically supported bureaucratic thinking that is opposed to Administrative Appeals Tribunal review, but it is based on a lack of understanding of the law, and on a lack of concern for individual rights.

7. The Administrative Appeals Tribunal has experienced remarkable growth, as appears from the paper. I believe that the system is now too well-entrenched, and has too many supporters, for it to be seriously threatened.

8. Two very significant statements have been made in Australia since I prepared my paper.

9. The first was in the *Report of the Commission of Inquiry into Possible Illegal Activities and Associated Police Misconduct*, known better as the Fitzgerald Report. Mr Tony Fitzgerald, Q.C., was for a time a Judge of the Federal Court of Australia, and during that time he was also a Presidential Member of the Administrative Appeals Tribunal. The Report's wide-ranging analysis includes statements of great clarity in relation to the need for a proper system of determinative review of administrative decisions as part of a modern and just system of government. It is a resounding, and a positive, answer to those few who continue to complain about such review. I will read just a few passages:

   'The Judiciary are empowered to protect an individual from the abuse of governmental powers by ensuring that those powers are kept within the legal bounds imposed by Parliament, and their exercise constrained by accepted principles of natural justice.

   . . .

   Any judicial review of administrative or ministerial actions is limited to a review of the manner of the decision-making process. . . .

These deficiences in systems for review of administrative action have been tackled in other common law jurisdictions by the adoption of a general system of administrative review. There is wide agreement that this system has improved the quality of decision-making in those jurisdictions. A similar system could be adopted in this State under which:

- *the existing complicated judicial remedies are replaced by simple machinery for the making of applications for judicial review, and an array of statutorily based remedial powers;*

- *the rights of an individual to bring an application are broadened;*

- *there is a right to obtain reasons for a decision, subject only to limited exceptions; and*

- *decisions are reviewed on their merits by an external independent review body.*

This general system of effective administrative review could be accompanied by efforts to ensure that those tribunals, boards and courts which already exist are given, where possible, the authority to make. . . . determinative decisions on the matters under consideration rather than mere recommendations or reports.

The only ministerial involvement in reviews should, in the normal circumstance, be to ensure that there are proper systems and policies which are being honestly and efficiently implemented by the board, tribunal or court, and that they are properly resourced . . .'

10. The second of the two statements was a recent address by the Chief Justice of the High Court of Australia, Sir Anthony Mason. Sir Anthony was a member of the Kerr Committee, as mentioned in my paper, and is a former Solicitor-General of the Commonwealth. Delivering a paper in Canberra entitled 'Administrative Review – The Experience of the First Twelve Years', Sir Anthony canvassed a number of issues. For present purposes I simply give you the following:

'As was to be expected, the new system has generated criticism. The most fundamental criticism is the claim that it is undemocratic. Other objections are that the system is too favourable to the individual and too insensitive to policy or government interest, that it is too expensive and inefficient and that it has made administrative decision-making inefficient and more complex.

In its widest form the anti-democratic objection questions the legitimacy of any form of review of administrative action. But in its strongest form the attack of legitimacy is directed to review by the Administrative Appeals Tribunal, particularly of Ministerial decisions. The objection is important and requires an answer.

. . .

... The blunt fact is that the scale and complexity of administrative decision-making is such that Parliament simply cannot maintain a comprehensive overview of particular administrative decisions. Parliament's concentration on broad issues and political point-scoring leaves little scope for oversight of the vast field of administrative action. And in Australia the doctrine of individual Ministerial responsibility, which was once a valuable sanction compelling sound administrative action, is in decline. Inefficient, even incompetent, action or inaction by a government department or statutory authority is no longer regarded as a matter for Ministerial resignation. The decay of the doctrine of Ministerial responsibility appears to be the consequence of a perception that it is beyond the capacity of Ministers to oversee all that is done by their departments or the statutory authorities for which they are responsible. What is beyond the capacity of the Minister is certainly beyond the capacity of Parliament.

The fact that Parliament has vested the decision-making process in an administrator does not mean that review of his decision is anti-democratic. After all, Parliament has provided for review by the various means available under Federal law ... Administrative justice is now as important to the citizen as traditional justice at the hands of the orthodox court system. Viewed in this way, judicial and Tribunal review of administrative decisions is simply one of the checks and balances indispensable to our democratic constitutional structure.

It is a natural reaction on the part of the administrator and the politician to think that the new system is too favourable to the individual. They are not attuned to review of their decisions by an impartial adjudicator. They are not independent and they view a case from the perspective of government. The attraction of judicial review and of Tribunal review on the merits is that they offer justice to the individual by means of independent adjudication. Politicians and administrators profess an enthusiasm for independent adjudication – but all too often their preference is for an outward form of independent adjudication which defers to government policies and attitudes...

...

It is clear that the Administrative Appeals Tribunal is a Tribunal in the judicial mould; its independent character is reinforced by the absence of any statutory restriction on its capacity to review policy. Unquestionably there is a tension between the independent character of the Tribunal and an expectation or belief on the part of some administrators and politicians that the Tribunal should defer to government policies. This tension has been evident in deportation cases where the Tribunal and, on appeal, the Federal Court have set aside administrative decisions, including Ministerial decisions, based on government policy. As the Tribunal determines the rights of individuals, there are strong reasons for not compromising its independence.

Executive policy is enunciated in various forms and at various levels of government. It is one thing to say that the Tribunal should respect policies determined at Cabinet or Ministerial level that relate to international affairs or the national economy. It is a very different thing to say that the Tribunal should respect a policy determined at departmental level or defer to a decision which is expressed to be based on a particular policy, when the connection between the facts of the case and the stated policy is tenuous. It is difficult to devise an immunity for decisions based on government policy which would apply across the board, yet conform to an acceptable standard of justice to the individual.

...

I should make some final reference to the impact of the new system on the administrative process. Critics say that, as a result of the new system, the administrative process is more time-consuming and more costly than it was before. But it can scarcely be a legitimate point of criticism that more attention is now given to the authority of the law, to the need to give the citizen an opportunity to put his side of the case and to the statement of reasons for a decision. If these innovations have a price in time and additional cost then, within proper limits, it is a price well worth paying, so long as we obtain a greater measure of administrative justice.

11. I believe that the two important statements which I have quoted, coming from such eminent authorities, bear out the claims that I have made for the recognition of the need for a system of independent review of administrative decisions. The founder of the Christian religion said that 'A prophet is not with honour, save in his own country, and in his own house'. Notwithstanding that in Australia we have sceptics in our midst, we are fortunate to have also the kind of appreciation of the system that I have put before you. We are also gratified and encouraged by the fact that from time to time that system attracts some admiration from other countries. [1]

---

1 This Commentary accompanied the paper by Robert K. Todd presented originally at the Eleventh Lawasia Conference in Hong Kong on 18 September, 1989.

VOLUME I   GOVERNMENT ETHICS

APPENDIX PART IV

Government Ethics:

Concepts, Education and Training

15

The Public Interest

by Walter Lippman [1]

1. What Is the Public Interest?

We are examining the question of how, and by whom, the interest of an invisible community over a long span of time is represented in the practical work of governing a modern state.

In ordinary circumstances voters cannot be expected to transcend their particular, localized and self-regarding opinions. As well expect men laboring in the valley to see the land as from a mountain top. In their circumstances, which as private persons they cannot readily surmount, the voters are most likely to suppose that whatever seems obviously good to them must be good for the country, and good in the sight of God.

I am far from implying that the voters are not entitled to the representation of their particular opinions and interests. But their opinions and interests should be taken for what they are and for no more. They are not – as such – propositions in the public interest. Beyond their being, if they are genuine, a true report of what various groups of voters are thinking, they have no intrinsic authority. The Gallup polls are reports of what people are thinking. But that a plurality of the people sampled in the poll think one way has no bearing upon whether it is sound public policy. For their opportunities of judging great issues are in the very nature of things limited, and the statistical sum of their opinions is not the final verdict on an issue. It is, rather, the beginning of the argument. In that argument their opinions need to be confronted by the views of the executive, defending and promoting the public interest. In the accommodation reached between the two views lies practical public policy.

Let us ask ourselves, How is the public interest discerned and judged? From what we have been saying we know that we cannot answer the question by attempting to forecast what the invisible community, with all its unborn constituents, will, would, or might say if and when it ever had a chance to vote. There is no point in toying with any notion of an imaginary plebiscite to discover the public interest. We cannot know what we ourselves

---

1 An extract from Walter Lippman *The Public Philosophy* (USA, Little Brown and Co. 1955) Chapter IV.

will be thinking five years hence, much less what infants now in the cradle will be thinking when they go into the polling booth.

Yet their interests, as we observe them today, are within the public interest. Living adults share, we must believe, the same public interest. For them, however, the public interest is mixed with, and is often at odds with, their private and special interests. Put this way, we can say, I suggest, that the public interest may be presumed to be what men would choose if they saw clearly, thought rationally, acted disinterestedly and benevolently.

2. The Equations of Reality

A RATIONAL man acting in the real world may be defined as one who decides where he will strike a balance between what he desires and what can be done. It is only in imaginary worlds that we can do whatever we wish. In the real world there are always equations which have to be adjusted between the possible and the desired. Within limits, a man can make a free choice as to where he will strike the balance. If he makes his living by doing piecework, he can choose to work harder and to spend more. He can also choose to work less and to spend less. But he cannot spend more and work less.

Reality confronts us in practical affairs as a long and intricate series of equations. What we are likely to call 'facts of life' are the accounts, the budgets, the orders of battle, the election returns. Sometimes, but not always, the two sides of the equations can be expressed quantitatively in terms of money, as supply and demand, as income and outgo, assets and liabilities, as exports and imports. Valid choices are limited to the question of where, not whether, the opposing terms of the equation are to be brought into equilibrium. For there is always a reckoning.

In public life, for example, the budget may be balanced by reducing expenditures to the revenue from taxes; by raising taxes to meet the expenditures, or by a combination of the two, by borrowing, or by grants in aid from other governments, or by fiat credit, or by a combination of them. In one way or another the budget is in fact always balanced. The true nature of the reckoning would be clearer if, instead of talking about 'an unbalanced budget', we spoke of a budget balanced not by taxes but by borrowing, of a budget balanced by inflation, or of a budget balanced by subsidy. A government which cannot raise enough money by taxes, loans, foreign grants, or by getting its fiat money accepted, will be unable to meet its bills and to pay the salaries of its employees. In bankruptcy an involuntary balance is struck for the bankrupt. He is forced to balance his accounts by reducing his expenditures to the level of his income.

Within limits, which public men have to bear in mind, the choices as to where to balance the budget are open. In making these choices, new equations confront them. Granted that it is possible to bring the budget into balance by raising taxes, how far can taxes be raised? Somewhat but not ad infinitum. There are no fixed criteria. But though we are unable to express all the equations quantitatively, this does not relieve us of the necessity of balancing the equations. There will be a reckoning. Practical judgment requires an informed guess: what will the taxpayers accept readily, what will they accept with grumbling but with no worse, what will arouse them to resistance and to evasion? How will the taxpayers react to the different levels of taxes if it is a time of peace, a time of war, a time of cold war, a time of social and economic disturbance, and so on? Although the various propositions cannot be reduced to precise figures, prudent men make estimates as to where the equations balance.

Their decisions as to where to balance the accounts must reflect other judgments – as to what, for example, are the military requirements in relation to foreign affairs; what is the phase of the business cycle in relation to the needs for increased or decreased demand; what is the condition of the international monetary accounts; which are the necessary public works and welfare measures, and which are those that are desirable but not indispensable. Each of these judgments is itself the peak of a pyramid of equations: whether, for example, to enlarge or to reduce the national commitments at this or that point in the world – given the effect of the decision at other points in the world.

I may say, then, that public policy is made in a field of equations. The issues are the choices as to where the balance is to be struck. In the reality of things X will exact an equivalence of Y. Within the limits which the specific nature of the case permits – limits which have to be estimated – a balance has to be reached by adding to or subtracting from the terms of the equation.

Oftener than not, the two sides of the equation differ in that the one is, as compared with the other, the pleasanter, the more agreeable, the more popular. In general the softer and easier side reflects what we desire and the harder reflects what is needed in order to satisfy the desire. Now the momentous equations of war and peace, of solvency, of security and of order, always have a harder or a softer, a pleasanter or a more painful, a popular or an unpopular option. It is easier to obtain votes for appropriations than it is for taxes, to facilitate consumption than to stimulate production, to protect a market than to open it, to inflate than to deflate, to borrow than to save, to demand than to compromise, to be intransigent than to negotiate, to threaten war than to prepare for it.

Faced with these choices between the hard and the soft, the normal propensity of democratic governments is to please the largest number of voters. The pressure of the electorate is normally for the soft side of the equations. That is why governments are unable to cope with reality when elected assemblies and mass opinions become decisive in the state, when there are no statesmen to resist the inclination of the voters and there are only politicians to excite and to exploit them.

There is then a general tendency to be drawn downward, as by the force of gravity, towards insolvency, towards the insecurity of factionalism, towards the erosion of liberty, and towards hyperbolic wars.

A Plea for Applied Ethics

*by Neil Richards, Tutor, Chief Police Officers' Course,
Police Staff College, Bramshill, England*

Introduction

As the title suggests, the main object of this paper is to recommend that applied ethics be given more attention within the police service. The social sciences have an established place within police training and education, so much so that police experience is often expressed in their language. It is a language which is much taken up with accurate observation, conjectures resting upon significant correlations, and prediction. When applied to police the emphasis is typically on how officers do or will act in various situations. However, there is a tendency to set aside questions of how officers *should* act, particularly in problematic or conflicting circumstances. It is the business of ethics to consider just such questions and to provide the conceptual framework with which to do it.

I believe, however, that the promise of applied ethics goes further than this. Such an approach enhances the possibility that moral problems will be more fully understood, analysed more carefully and made more tractable. It also raises questions about the values served by an occupation and focusses upon how these ends are to be legitimately achieved. Logically, it demands, therefore, that policing's key concepts, such as 'authority', 'consent', 'impartiality', 'discretion' and 'professionalism', are unravelled carefully and defined so that value commitments and moral requirements are made explicit. The application of applied ethics to an occupation also encourages reflection on one's personal obligations, on the rights and obligations of colleagues and upon the virtues which it is appropriate to cultivate as a police officer and within society at large.

But why should applied ethics be of particular importance for the police? The police are invested with the authority, which includes a virtual monopoly of legitimate coercion, to deal with a wide range of emergencies which include relatively minor domestic disputes, criminal activities, road traffic accidents, natural disasters and public disorders. They are also granted wide discretionary powers that afford them the scope and opportunity to respond to such emergencies in a flexible and appropriate manner. In other words, public trust in, and dependence upon, the police is considerable and conditional. They are expected to justify that trust by maintaining not only commitment and capacity but also the highest standards of conduct. Applied ethics has an important part to play in securing this last condition.

This paper is divided into five sections. The first presents a review of recent policing developments with particular emphasis upon those which have been inimical to the police-public relationship together with some indications of the circumstances in which they arose. The following section seeks in simple, but I hope not too pedestrian terms, to make explicit the relationship between policing, morality and the liberal democratic State. Here the focus is upon the moral conditions of that relationship. The third section deals with the part which a concern for moral values and standards must necessarily play in the leadership and management of a public service. The next section identifies some of the moral dilemmas of police. It does not attempt solutions but seeks rather to point up the conceptual difficulties and moral choices which are centred upon their occupational functions. Finally, a section is devoted to a more detailed discussion of what a greater emphasis upon applied ethics might be expected to achieve for police together with some suggestions for its implementation.

1. Trust and Confidence

The British police service, which was diffidently introduced into a libertarian political and social climate, has, throughout the one hundred and fifty years or so of its existence, managed to combine a high order of public acceptance with the discharge of its duties. Indeed, from its beginnings, its relationship with the public, that vast and amorphous body, has been governed by the principle that only by gaining its co-operation and trust could it hope to secure the objective of helping to uphold social order. That it has generally managed, in pursuit of this objective, to police in a mild and unaggressive way says much for both police and public. However, during the past twenty years there have been considerable social changes in British society which have affected all sections of it and hence both parties to the police-public relationship. Many of these changes undoubtedly made the task of the police in seeking the support of the public more difficult.

A brief retrospective of some of the changes most affecting police will highlight the challenges they faced. The number of laws unpopular with sections of the public, such as those relating to traffic, drugs and pornography, and which police have been required to enforce, has increased. Protest marches and public demonstrations have become a regular occurrence; welfare agencies have arisen which have a social regulation function, thus reducing the number of services which used to be performed by the police. [1]

---

1 N. W. Richards 'The Concept of a Police Ethic' (unpublished paper, Police Staff College, Bramshill 1982). The term 'police' and 'police officer' in this paper covers both male and female staff.

A public has emerged which is better educated, is less ready to defer to authority without reasons and has an increased awareness of its legal rights. Demands for economic and social justice have often been expressed through political and industrial action. The changes brought about by the *Police Act,* 1964, combined with the effect of amalgamating police forces to form larger units, have weakened democratic control generally. [2] Until recently, when the trend was reversed, police strategies have tended to increase crime response efficiency at the cost of greater remoteness from the public. The growth of ethnic minorities has contributed to increasing social pluralism. The increase in pay and status has tended to distance them socially from some of the public whom they police while bringing them closer to others.

Such changes serve to emphasise that favourable public attitudes cannot be entirely earned. They are the product of complex social forces, many of which are beyond the control of the police. What they also illustrate is a period when social norms and values were being challenged, when class and status underwent a process of redefinition [3] and individuals experimented with different styles of life and demanded the freedom to do so. As upholders of the *status quo,* the police lagged behind in reflecting this process; but reflect it they eventually did. Conditions of service improved, a predominantly directive style of leadership and management became gradually more consultative and both the discipline code and informal practice allowed for a more permissive distinction between the public and private morality of police officers. In operational terms the police found themselves working to a social contract whose terms were often being re-evaluated by members of the public, when they were not being challenged and tested through action. And they found themselves, like other public institutions, subjects of the greatest critical scrutiny and controversy since that of the years of their origins in the 1820s and 1830s.

From the mid 1960s onwards incidents, investigations and inquiries cumulatively began to erode public confidence in the integrity and competence of the police service in general, and the Metropolitan Police in particular. There were remarkable achievements, such as the successful resolution of the Spaghetti House, Balcombe Street and Iranian Embassy sieges, and the impressive successes against organised crime, all of which took place against a background of unspectacular but effective daily peace keeping. Conversely, The Times inquiry, the Soho pornography scandal, Operation Countryman, the riots of Summer 1981, the Yorkshire Ripper investigaton and inquiry, Michael Fagan, Grunwick, Lewisham, Southall and Blair Peach and similar

---

2 T. A. Critchley 'The Idea of Policing in Britain: success or failure' in *The Police we Deserve* by J. C. Alderson and P. J. Stead (Wolfe Press 1973) p. 3.

3 R. Dahrendorf *B.B.C. Reith Lectures* (London, Routlege, Kegan Paul 1975).

happenings lent credibility to the growing accusations about abuse of suspects while in custody, racism, corruption, the excessive use of force in effecting public order, and scepticism about police effectiveness and efficiency in dealing with crime.

Reference has been made already to the weakening of democratic control. This could not have come at a less opportune time as the constitutional accountability of the police, with its tripartite arrangements of Chief Constable, Home Office and police authority outside London, and Home Secretary and Metropolitan Police Commissioner for London, was called into question with demands for greater accountability. The coincidence of diminished democratic control and the events inimical to the reputation of the police gave a fresh urgency too to the quest for a means of dealing with complaints against the police that were acceptable to both police and public. It is worth adding that the inquiries and measures initiated to reform police procedures, allay public disquiet and redress grievances themselves, perhaps inevitably, served to keep the informed public eye upon police short-comings. In this respect Sir Robert Mark's purge against corruption, Lord Scarman's various reports and the Royal Commission on Criminal Procedure, which was instituted to consider the vexed issue of police powers, their proper extent and the safeguards over their exercise, may be instanced. Later, the four Policy Studies Institute reports published in November, 1983, under the general title, *Police and People in London*, present a generally uncomplimentary view of police performance, behaviour, attitudes and management.

Although the circumstances which gave rise to these developments are complex, there are a number of factors which help to explain them. Three have already been mentioned. As the people within our society have become freer, better educated and informed than ever before so their expectations of public services, including the police, have risen. With regard to the police in particular they would seem to expect a heightened awareness and understanding of the dignity and rights of the individual. Overall they are more likely to criticise and complain about police behaviour which, in the recent past, would have been thought unremarkable. It is also the case that if widespread changes offer opportunities, they also create a climate of uncertainty as the *mores*, conventions, rules and usages, which pattern human relationships, are reformed, revised, developed or discarded. Within such a climate the police, in their role as upholders of law and order, can be put under considerable strain. In seeking for certainty in the face of pressing practical decisions they may assume functions which go beyond those with which they have been entrusted. They may also sometimes over-react towards those sections of society for whose causes they have little sympathy or whose motives they do not understand. Again, uncertainty about the moral basis of law, as is the case to some extent with pornography, soft drugs and some driving offences, when combined with high monetary profitability provides necessary, is not sufficient, conditions for some police corruption. In addition to those factors, prior to the Edmund Davies pay award, many police forces were under-manned and there was considerable loss, through resignation, of experienced constables. The quality of recruits was also lowered, in-service probationary training was starved of the appropriately experienced tutor-constables and the time allowed for it was often skimped. More importantly, this factor exacerbated all the pressures mentioned so far.

2. Police, Morality and the Liberal Democratic State

The circumstances, responses and explanations outlined above all serve to illustrate three fundamental points. Firstly, the truth of the often overlooked fact that policing a liberal democratic State is a demanding and delicate activity. Secondly, that there is a continuous need for police at the supervisory levels to possess high qualities of leadership and management and to seek to develop them. Lastly, that the changes and developments within the police service, which have grown symbiotically with social change, often make it difficult to get by with habitual moral practices, vague moral perspectives, and intuitively applied values. Tried, and still valid, ethical principles have to be understood and interpreted afresh, and then applied to some very problematic situations. For my purposes, it is this last point which serves to show the relationship between the first two. Ethical problems are unavoidable and pervasive and they are necessarily bound up with practice. Without a thorough grasp of the values which it serves and the means which may be legitimately employed to realise them, no public service can properly understand its role or purpose within society.

It is one of the remarkable achievements of the modern liberal democratic State that it facilitates a wide range of human goals and enterprises in a manner which satisfies, if imperfectly, the demands of morality. By morality here is meant a system of social control which is effected through principles whose main purpose is to protect the interests of other persons, as well as the individual, and which present themselves to the individual as checks on his natural inclinations or spontaneous tendencies to act, where those are purely self-interested. In Britain, there is a high degree of public order because social control is effected voluntarily by a people who generally adhere to moral principles and are prepared to make the sacrifices of personal self-interest which such adherence requires. This same people, through its democratic political arrangements, bring into existence rules which are enacted by the Queen-in-Parliament and upheld by the courts; in short, the law. Such laws are both substantive and procedural and one of their functions is to reinforce, with an elaborate battery of sanctions and penalties, some of those moral principles which are central to social control.

Under these same political arrangements the police service as a public body is entrusted, in the interests of citizens, with upholding the rule of law, preventing crime, protecting life and property and preserving public tranquility. For this purpose, individual police officers are invested with rights and duties which prescribe their role, give them authority and provide them with the necessary powers to carry out their duties. Moreover, in a liberal democratic State to say that the police enjoy the trust, confidence and respect of the public is often summed up by the notion of policing by consent. It is also to claim that the values served by both police and citizens are the same. So, in British society the police act with consent and are legitimately in authority if, and only if, the generality of citizens consent to the constitutional provisions – rules, usages, conventions – which determine the office.

As with all models, this represents an idealised abstraction which merely serves to show, in bald terms, the relationship between police, morality and the democratic State. Nonetheless, it supports the contention that, to the extent that the police service has managed to combine a high order of public acceptance with the discharge of its duties, it has enjoyed such a relationship in part because it has been recognised as pursuing worthwhile ends in a morally acceptable manner. Both the worthwhile ends and the morally acceptable manner present dilemmas for police, a line of argument I shall develop later. For the moment what this characterisation of the police-public relationship identifies is the social interface position of the police and the high expectations which their public have of them. Somehow the police have to serve the public by upholding individual rights and liberties while exercising their lawful powers for the well-being of the society. They are required to strike a balance between preserving fundamental freedoms and containing crime and disorder. When it is remembered that majorities can be tyrannous on occasions, acquiesing in questionable police practices in the interest of detection and conviction, then the moral burdens placed upon the police are readily apparent. These must surely be prominent amongst the demands which make policing a democratic society such a difficult and delicate activity.

3. Leadership and Management

That the modern police service needs effective and efficient leadership is a truisim. What is not nearly so obvious is the importance of ethical standards for the achievement of this objective. Most leadership and management models give prominence to the setting, maintaining and reassessing of those practical standards and principles which have to do with ensuring that an organisation has the capacity to fulfil its objectives. [4] But those standards which concern ethical practice often are given either cursory treatment or

---

4 J. Adair *Action Centred Leadership* (Macgraw Hill 1973) and C. Hodgkinson *The Philosophy of Leadership* (Basil Blackwell 1983).

neglected altogether. For the police service, as I have already indicated, this area is of vital importance and to view it from the leadership/management perspective should throw new light upon it.

In our society the relationship between law and morality is complicated. There are laws which refine and clarify moral precepts while others are open to ambiguous moral evaluation. Indeed, the borderline between law and morality is often blurred. For many, and this includes some police officers, being moral is simply doing that which the law requires and their sole motivation is fear of the penalties for not doing so. It is also the case that all too often the same people see obedience to the law as a kind of game, as a set of rules whose requirements the clever or cunning avoid whenever poss-ible and especially when there is no chance of a penalty being incurred. This is one of the limitations which attaches to discipline codes and other instruments of quasi-legal regulation within organisations. Were such attitudes to be pervasive in a liberal democracy or its institutions it is doubt-ful whether it would long survive as such. Freedom exercised with respon-sibility is the touchstone of such a society and laws could not be enforced unless most people believed in the moral basis of law and were committed to it. The law does not tell us what we ought to do in most situations. At most it sets a framework which determines the minimum acceptable behaviour which a society will accept. Moreover, the requirements of morality go beyond those of law. Law does not require sympathy, kindness, altruism or civility.

There is, then, vast scope for the use of moral judgement and this is nowhere more so than within the police service. This presents an organisa-tional problem for its command structure. Police officers are independent officers under the Crown, and, as such, are personally responsible for their unlawful acts. They also are entrusted with considerable discretion in the performance of their duties and much of their activity is not directly super-vised. It follows that they have considerable latitude in the way they effect their office, and how this is done will depend upon the attitudes of the individual. Of course, the setting of moral standards by police supervisors will involve reference to shared codes but what it also involves is the more complex process of fostering an atmosphere where moral dilemmas may be faced and shared and the cultivation of personal and occupational virtues is a possibility. In such a process example is as important as precept but in secur-ing practice which is informed by the appropriate principles critical attention to the moral requirements is a necessity.

There is one closely related comment to add. Many police officers, perhaps the majority, have come to see themselves as professionals offering a profes-sional service. If by 'a profession' is meant a body which provides a service deemed both essential and worthwhile by its clients, exercising skills resting upon a systematic body of knowledge and governed by concern for the principles and values which sustain both the commitment of members to each other and their clients, then the police service is clearly a good candidate for professional status. [5] However, an explicit occupational ethic, and a commitment to it, is a logical requirement of professionalism in the above sense and it is through making such a commitment that a body satisfies one of the main conditions of professional status.

4. Some Moral Dilemmas of Policing

Thus far I have been arguing that greater emphasis upon applied ethics in the training, education, leadership and management of police would be beneficial both for them, as individuals and in terms of their occupation, and for the public they serve. What I have not done is show the sorts of problem which such an emphasis might be expected to ameliorate. This I shall shortly remedy with what I believe is a representative sample of the types of moral dilemma which regularly confront police officers. Some of them highlight the difficult choices facing police and may well excite sympathy, but others focus upon those, the unsuccessful resolutions of which, are impediments to good police-public relations.

However, before proceeding further it is appropriate to consider a notion which is inseparable from any consideration of police action: discretion. Discretion, the liberty or power of deciding, or of acting according to one's own judgement or as one thinks fit, [6] used to be referred to *soto voce* by police administrators. [7] This is because of their concern with the control of the police and the recognition that impartiality as well as discretion is a condition of police action. A marriage between discretion and impartiality *is* possible, but only if there are uniformly applied rules which govern the exercise of discretion. To fulfil this requirement would tax the ingenuity of administrators to breaking point given the myriad situations for which rules would be needed. It would burden police with extra rules, when they already have enough to cope with in knowing the law and keeping abreast of developments within it and would mean getting involved in regressive procedures. This is because discretion would still be required to apply the discretionary rules. The exercise of discretion by police officers is inevitable: it is logically impossible for laws to be deductively applied without intermediate inductive judgements; the whole body of the law cannot be applied on practical grounds and the police are expected to exercise discretion in order to realise the 'spirit' rather than the letter of the law.

---

5 N. J. Greenhill 'Professionalism in the Police Service' in *Modern Policing* ed. by D. W. Pope and N. L. Weiner (Croom Helm 1981).

6 Concise Oxford English Dictionary.

7 H. Goldstein 'Police Discretion – the ideal versus the real' in *Public Order* Decision Making in Britain II ed. by R. Finnegan et al (Open University Press 1976).

Morality and discretion are intimately connected. Because police officers are expected to use discretion when making peace keeping choices the moral space, so to speak, within which they act is quite extensive. I mention this because it is contrary to first appearances. Although police officers are independent officers under the Crown they are bound by law, police discipline regulations, force orders, the Judges' Rules [8] and Administrative Directions as well as the pressures of a disciplined service. In terms of individual motivation this suggests that prudential considerations might be very much to the fore, and, no doubt, with many they are. However, this does not affect the fact that they exercise discretion in countless ways and are expected to do so. A few examples and one quotation will serve to support this contention. Discretion is used in the selection of suspects, in deciding which offences to 'notice' and which laws apply. Police must decide whether to caution or charge formally, and determine at which point, after arrest, to apply the provisions of the Judges' Rules [8] and make decisions about the extent of seizure and search and prosecution and bail. Lord Scarman wrote in his report that:

'... discretion lies at the heart of the policing function ... The good reputation of the police as a force depends upon the skill and judgement which policemen display in the particular circumstances of the case and incidents which they are required to handle. Discretion is the art of suiting action to particular circumstances. It is the policeman's daily task'. [9]

I suggested above that public acceptance of trust in the police has been continually secured because, in part, they have been recognised as pursuing worthwhile ends in a normally acceptable manner. To take worthwhile ends first, I shall assume for the sake of argument that the traditional ends of policing, upholding the rule of law, preventing crime, protecting life and property, maintaining public order and preserving public tranquility, as understood within a liberal democracy, are morally worthwhile. But even allowing for this assumption, the scene is still set for a classic conflict between *prima facie* duties. Nowhere has this been better exemplified than by Lord Scarman in his report. [10] According to him the choice for the police of Brixton on the eve of the riots was between upholding the law or preserving public tranquility. In the event they chose to uphold the law. Lord Scarman argues, according to what looks very much like utilitarian moral logic, that they were wrong to do so; that under the specific conditions which prevailed

---

8 Judges' Rules have been replaced now, see *Postscript* to this paper.

9 The Rt. Hon. Lord Scarman *The Brixton Disorders 10-12th Apr. 1 1981* (London, HMSO 1981).

10 Ibid. p. 62.

in Brixton on the eve of the riots the police had the duty to preserve public tranquility. But whether the police ranked their *prima facie* duties correctly or not on this occasion they were posed with a very tricky moral dilemma. This situation also provides a reminder that moral reasoning is dependent upon beliefs as to fact. Had the Brixton community been less tense then the actions might have been judged the right ones.

Less dramatically, and on a day-to-day basis around the country, the same dilemma is faced by police officer engaged in case conference consultations with other social agencies which have a social control aspect to their work. Police often have to decide whether to initiate judicial proceedings or to allow other agencies to effect a possible reform of criminality by extra-legal or quasi-legal methods. Another instance is that of police in pursuit of motorised criminals. Police drivers clearly run the risk of endangering life and property in the interest of law enforcement. The reader can probably think of further examples.

I now wish to look at the dilemmas which are posed by policing in a morally acceptable manner. It is both a moral and legal requirement that the police should apply the law impartially. It is also the case that some police officers allow their prejudices, interest and strong personal moral convictions to outweigh their commitment in this respect. More subtly, police interest groups also, on occasion, undermine impartiality in this way. However, although these constitute problems enough, they are not the main concern here. Put formally the principle of impartiality requires that each person should be treated equally unless there is a relevant reason for doing other- wise. This implies only that people should be treated equally with respect to something, such as goods or opportunity, but, negatively, that on occasions people should be treated differently. Now, *prima facie*, this presents no prob- lem for police officers. In their capacity as upholders of the law they are required to apply to everyone what the law allows. And there are 'legalists' within the service who try to conduct themselves strictly according to the letter of the law. But if, as many police officers believe, they are required to take account not just of the letter but also of the spirit of the law then more is demanded of them. This is certainly so if their comprehensive peace keep- ing role is stressed. In fact they exercise a judicial function. They are in the business of taking account of other considerations beside the strict prescrip- tion of laws. The main candidates here are entitlement, need, and morality. The following examples will give some idea of how these considerations find their way into practice.

The impartiality principle requires that all motorists be treated equally in respect of speed limits, but a father's plea of a special entitlement to exceed the limit on his way to a sick child would probably count as a relevant reason for unequal treatment by a police officer. Again, it is well known that the police regularly exercise discretion over the prosecution of shoplifters with social and mental needs counting as the relevant grounds for unequal treatment. Protestors who, acting in accordance with their declared moral convictions, break the law in minor ways, are sometimes treated sympathetically. Whether such reasons for unequal treatment are relevant in these sort of cases is not at issue here. What, hopefully, they show is that moral dilemmas are posed in the exercise of impartiality. Such dilemmas are complicated further by what might be called the third person problem; police are usually subject, either directly or indirectly, to public scrutiny in what they do and the need to be seen as acting impartially, and hence credibly, exerts its own pressure. This is particularly so if it is conceded that we live in a society where consensus is lacking over how different substantive concepts of impartiality and justice are to be accommodated to each other.[11]

Conceptual difficulties too lie at the root of the failure to take sufficient account of the differences between the notions of discrimination, prejudice and impartiality. Clearly if it is a case of to each what the law attributes to him then criminals have no grounds for complaint when they flout the law and are duly apprehended by the police. The police have discriminated between them and non-criminals and acted accordingly. And this too is completely unremarkable since discrimination, the making or observing of differences that are there to be made or perceived, is an essential precondition for such human action. Difficulties arise for police in this area because they have a duty to prevent crime. Whenever possible they must anticipate criminal activity and counter criminogenic situations. What then of subcultural groups who, experience shows, are regularly associated with particular sorts of crime? For police officers to engage in what might be called professional discrimination and the corresponding crime preventative measures towards such groups would seem not unreasonable and to meet the requirements of impartiality. Of course, the reality of such responses is not so straight forward. Professional discrimination all too easily can degenerate into prejudice. Criminal dispositions are conflated with other characteristics, such as those of race or dress or manner, within the habit of practice and people are treated differently solely on the basis of such differences, which is irrational, immoral and partial, that is, prejudiced. For police here is yet another moral dilemma.

When considering pre-trial procedure two dominant perspectives are discernable which, when they conflict, produce some of the most acute moral dilemmas in policing. The first perspective lays emphasis upon what is referred to as 'due process'. It gives prominence to the need to control governmental interference in people's lives. It claims that abuse is especially frequent by those who uphold the law and those who apply it. Thus, it

---

11 A. MacIntyre *After Virtue: A Study in Moral Theory* (Duckworth 1981) Chapter 17.

stresses the need for clear and narrow guidelines regulating the use of confessions, the conduct of searches and arrests, the availability of legal aid and advice to people accused of crimes and the protection of individuals against self-incrimination. It argues most strongly that it may be necessary to support these guidelines by letting guilty persons go free, as a price for upholding the principles of judicial procedure. It also supports this view by maintaining that there are values in society, such as freedom, privacy and the integrity of the law, which may rightly override the minimisation of crime. The second perspective, which has been labelled the 'crime control' perspective, [12] simply takes as its objective the streamlining of pre-trial procedure so as to facilitate a greater number of convictions and so deter crime through securing a higher conviction rate. This perspective is less sensitive to the rights of the individual in relation to the State largely because it is more trusting of governmental powers and believes them to be used, on the whole, for the general good. It is worthy of note that a recent Royal Commission on Criminal Procedure wrestled to achieve a balance between these two perspectives and clearly found the task very demanding. I should add that, although it is being eroded, the rules of the English pre-trial procedure still reflect the strong libertarian outlook which predominated for the two centuries preceding the growth of the modern welfare State.

Police officers, because of their occupational orientation, tend to have a predeliction for the crime control perspective and it, or its implications, are a recurrent feature of their justifications for nominally immoral behaviour. Here I want to concentrate upon one aspect of that behaviour: deception. Sissela Bok [13] notes that the reasons most commonly used to defend deception appeal to four principles: that of avoiding harm, that of producing benefits, that of fairness, and that of veracity. Nor is such a procedure peculiar to police officers. Within conventional morality deception, either by commission or omission, is both practiced and justified in terms of such moral principles which are seen as overriding the requirement to be non-deceptive. Four illustrations, which employ each of the four principles in turn, will serve to expand this theme.

Firstly, detective officers who practice elaborate deceptions when questioning a person suspected of sexual assault, for example, will argue that the innocent suspect suffers no harm but that to omit such 'regularly successful techniques' would be to risk the possibility of releasing the sort of offender who would be likely to repeat the offence. Secondly, the officer who perjures himself in court, because he swears to having administered a caution when he did not, might well argue both for the relative lack of significance of the

---

12 Packer, 1968.

13 S. Bok *Lying: Moral Choice in Public and Private Life* (Quartet Books, 1980) p. 76.

caution in the pre-trial procedure, and hence the triviality of the harm done, and the benefits of getting a conviction which might otherwise have been lost on a technicality. Moreover, an officer might justify including in his testimony before the court things that are 'not quite true' partly for the practical reason that otherwise it would lack coherence and credibility, but also on the grounds that the adversarial procedures of the court could not be relied upon to secure a just or fair outcome. Lastly, police are not merely regarded by those they serve as being *in* authority but as being *an* authority; as having knowledge that and knowledge how, which they are able to put at the disposal of the public in their peace keeping role. And public confidence in this capacity time and again contributes to the outcome of police interventions in a self-fulfilling way. Because people do have such confidence in the police when they are on the scene of a serious traffic accident, for instance, panic and confusion does subside, belief in some restoration of a normal state of affairs is bolstered and things tend to go better as a result. A police officer, therefore, in some situations, may pretend to knowledge he does not have and simulate confidence which he does not possess. And his justification is that the truth of police trustworthiness is preserved through his deception and that things will go better if this is so.

The dilemma posed in this last illustration is to be found writ large in the police service, largely as a result of technological and research developments, and officers are usually fully aware that they risk the accusation of being manipulative. Victorian police did not have to concern themselves much with crime statistics or clear-up rates; a very imperfect measure of police effectiveness since they reflect only a part of the police function. Moreover, it seems to me that the police have to be effective enough to support the assurance of the generality of people that an uncertain world is free enough from risks and hazards for the normal pursuits of life to be possible. So, effectiveness is relative to different conditions of, and within, society; assurance will vary with regard to both time and place within society and the different climates of opinion of society as a whole. The problem for police, and chief officers in particular, is how far they should go through their reports and publicity to foster such assurance and how far they should go in presenting the statistically based 'truth'.

Conflicts between claims to rights constitute further dilemmas for police. What follows is a familiar and fairly typical example of such a conflict. A racist organisation wants to have a march and, as it is required to do by law, it notifies its proposed march route to the police. The route would take the march through areas largely inhabited by ethnic minorities. It is also virtually certain that political groups opposed to the racist organisation will mount counter demonstrations, which will, on past experience, probably be violent. The police are aware that certain rights are at issue and in conflict and that their decision will determine which right or rights prevail. They have to take account of the right to demonstrate peacefully, the right of minorities not to have hatred preached against them and the general public's right to be protected against outbreaks of violence. There may be others.

At a more private level, police officers often find themselves in the painful position of having to choose between vocational and family commitments. Most officers develop a vocational commitment to policing; they accept the responsibility for developing their police knowledge and upholding the principles and values of their office. The police, however, provide a twenty-four hours' service which operates a demanding shift in which contingent happenings requiring immediate attention continually occur. This places considerable demands upon wives or husbands and families and the choices involved in them are often moral choices.

The dilemmas which cluster around loyalty within the police service are the subject of my final example in this section. As with any other fairly abstract concept, the notion of loyalty is not at all easy to pin down. Ordinary usage indicates that it takes its place with such notions as faith, trust, devotion and, even, reverence. In the interest of clarity, I will content myself with a stipulative definition which captures well enough the meaning in general use. A person is loyal if he has a disposition to act in such a way that the relationship into which he has willingly entered with another person or persons is upheld. Although, ideally, feelings of affection or devotion often attend such a disposition, they may not necessarily do so, even if a sense of purposiveness does. From this definition it follows that loyalty is to be valued instrumentally: it takes its value from the ends which it serves. It also admits of degree; a person may be more or less loyal.

Because comradeship and loyalty are inculcated by the service the individual often may be motivated to sacrifice his own narrow self-interest to the interests of his fellow officers and thus to the many policing situations where it is imperative that concerted action be taken. Where loyalty is absent from such collective activities hurt and failure are often the outcome. This is so with public order, kidnap and armed fugitive incidents, for example. Incidents are 'winnable' for so long as ranks are closed. This partly explains and characterises, one of the salient features of the police sub-culture. Unfortunately, loyalty is sometimes misplaced and the same disposition is tolerant of, or supports, corrupt or irregular practices. Looked at from the viewpoint of one committed to the values and ideals of the service and only concerned with strictly professional relationships, there is little problem with misplaced loyalty. His loyalty is directed towards sustaining a professional relationship and the corrupt, by abrogating the principles and rules which prescribe their office, and hence their professional relationships, forfeit their claims to his loyalty. However, because loyalty is inculcated and, consequently, directed intuitively, there tends to be a reluctance to be disloyal towards those who are undeserving of it. Indeed, where loyalty is reinforced by the

the ties of friendship and comradeship, the dilemmas are often felt even more keenly. Such dilemmas are a recurring experience for a service in which loyalty upwards, sideways and, for those with rank, downwards is given prominent emphasis and strongly influences practical expectations.

5. Applied Ethics

In my introduction I sketched out the benefits which I believe would accrue to the police service through its paying more attention to applied ethics. The implied recommendation is a response to events and circumstances and in what followed I indicated what those were, the practical demands which they make and the particular sorts of dilemmas which a concern for applied ethics might be expected to ameliorate. In this section I shall outline further what applied ethics is, what it could be expected to achieve in the policing context and some suggestions for its implementation.

It seems to me that an occupational code is a necessary, if not sufficient, practical step on the way towards the emphasis I am suggesting. The Metropolitan Police, on the initiative of the Metropolitan Police Commissioner, Sir Kenneth Newman, has promulgated a new code of police ethics. [14] But what is the practical purpose of such a code and what is the theory behind it?

Moral conduct requires the possibility of choice, that there be alternative courses of action open to the individual, but it does not require that conscious choice be made on every occasion. It may be practised habitually once acquired as a skill. The same point is made differently with the contention that we regulate our lives by the application of intuited moral principles. Principles which urge us to keep our promises, make reparation for past wrongs, care for our parents and children, act with honesty, respect the rights of others, and so on. Moral principles structure our experience: not only do they prescribe how we ought to behave but, because they have a descriptive content, they indicate what it is we should attend to. We learn of them in a complicated and largely informal way in childhood from parents, teachers and other adults, and, more often than not, in the context to which they have application. They often appear as the abstractions of practice, from such a viewpoint. Indeed, so habitual does the application of such principles become that they may be said to inform our perceptions and we are not aware of 'applying' them at all.

The British police service, with its long and creditable tradition, has evolved a body of practice, a way of going about things, which is generally responsive to the society which it serves. The individual police officer is initiated into this practice and learns much of the substance of his work

---

14 See *Police Review* 'Newman's Contract' 8 October 1982 p. 1957; R. Evens 'Newman's Code of Ethics to cement contract between police and public' *The Times* 31 October 1983, and M. Kettle and J. Shirley 'Revolution at the Yard' *The Sunday Times* 6 November 1983.

through a process of apprenticeship in which good conduct is understood as appropriate participation in the activities of policing. The rules, formal and informal, which guide his practice are gradually assimilated into his outlook and help form his actions. Many of these rules are not so much the product of design but the product of countless, long-forgotten choices which encapsulate suggestions of how to achieve practical results. Others are those which relate to the prudential arts of the job: those which embody the hints, tips and clues which prescribe the sort of officer who is acceptable to his colleagues of all ranks. There are also formal rules, embodied in the Discipline Code, the Judges' Rules and other quasi-legal instruments which, together with the law, establish a pattern of organisational accountability and requirements. The 'good conduct' referred to above, as sustained by those various rules, has generally enabled the police to satisfy the public's expectations as to their capacity, commitment and way of fulfilling their role. But, as I endeavoured to show in the first section, there has arisen a dislocation – crisis is too strong a word – in the police-public relationship and the police themselves have both recognised it and are in the process of responding to it. Part of that response is a code of police ethics. [15]

How, then, might such a code be expected to help mend the dislocation? It is suggested by G. J. Warnock [16] that the primary purpose of morality, in a world where human wants, needs and interest are likely to be frustrated by the limitations of resources, information, intelligence, rationality and sympathies, is to counteract the limitations in human sympathies. I believe that this is so, with the qualification that limitations in intelligence, rationality and information are also counteracted by morality to a more modest extent. This accepted, the purpose of morality can be extended, by analogy, to an occupational code. Such a code, when developed for police, would function to help counter those limitations to good policing which are rooted in limited sympathies, rationality, intelligence and information. Besides prescribing responses to situations and recommending dispositions, it would also identify the appropriate *loci* of attention – some of which are specified in the section on moral dilemmas above. This type of code would be made up of principles arrived at in a number of different ways. One major source would be the tradition of the police service itself. It would seek to make explicit some of the principles which have served it so well, such as those which prescribe impartiality and treating the public with civility. Another source would be the human rights provision of such bodies as the Council of Europe. [17] A

---

15 N. W. Richards 'The Concept of a Police Ethic' Unpublished paper, Police Staff College, Bramshill.

16 G. J. Warnock *The Object of Morality* (Methuen 1971) Chapter 2.

17 Declaration on the Police *Parliamentary Assembly of the Council of Europe* Resolution 190 (1979).

third way of proceeding would be to take account of those practices which tend to undermine public confidence and trust in the police and frame countervailing principles. A code of this sort should enable officers to form clearer expectations concerning ranges of permissible behaviour regarding each other and the public.

Important though such a step would be, however, something more is required: applied ethics. A police code, in terms of its possible influence upon practice, stands somewhere between applied ethics and habitual morality. It provides a set of principles which act as a reference point for guidance for a great many regularly recurring situations, and in a fairly straight forward manner. Nonetheless, they still have to be applied, and applied with understanding, sensitivity and consistency. Only thinking in general terms about priorities, as well as how to apply them, would promote such an outcome. And this links in another argument. It was indicated, in the fourth section above, that the police are expected to exercise discretion and to do so with skill and judgement which relates to the particular circumstances which they are required to handle (Scarman, 1981). One of the necessary conditions which must be fulfilled, if this demand is to be met, is that police officers act with autonomy. Put simply, they must be able to think for themselves, and think well. I have already referred to the process whereby intuitive moral principles are inculcated and one of the points that emerges is that we do not reach adult life with open minds about morality. Our responses, all too often, are simply the result of childhood conditioning and this is compounded by our unthinking acceptance of occupational *mores* and the adoption, in an unreflective manner, of views which are the products of society's whims and fashions. We advance in an autonomous direction and avoid such manipulation to the extent that we are able to subject such processes and influences to critical thinking. Applied ethics provides one of the tools for that purpose in a very important area of our lives.

Intuitive moral principles need to be considered again in order to show the part played by applied ethics in more detail. Such principles fall into four broad categories: those which require us to avoid harming others, those which prescribe sympathy and benevolence, those which require that we act honestly and avoid deception and those which prescribe fairness. [18] But, as was shown with the moral dilemmas which confront police officers, there are many situations within policing when moral principles conflict and it is difficult to decide which should guide action. When we remember that there are many such principles and they give rise to rights, duties and obligations then there is a problem of selection too. It is also the case that the principles must be simple enough to be learned and able to refer to a fairly wide number of situations. In other words, they must be general. But what is often required are principles which relate to specific situations. For example, there

---

18 G. J. Warnock *The Object of Morality* (Methuen 1971).

are certain situations where we would wish to make an exception to 'Never kill people' to allow for self-defence. What is required is the more specific principle, 'Never kill people except in self-defence'. So, although our moral practice is guided well enough by intuited principles for much of the time, we would seem to require some way of selecting between them, rendering them more specific and resolving conflicts between them on certain critical occasions. I should add that a code of police ethics is also subject to these problems.

What all this means, when translated into attitudes, is that the habitual application of intuitive moral principles often leads people to dig their heels in when convinced of what they believe to be their duty, fair, impartial, right, and this often results in disagreement, dissension and unnecessary misery. If this sort of predicament is to be avoided what is needed is a commitment to think critically. That is, a willingness on the part of people to criticise their own intuitions, as well as those of others, and a preparedness to acquire the appropriate conceptual apparatus to do so effectively. For much the same reasons, it is not enough just to be well-meaning; it is not for nothing that the old saying, 'the pathway to perdition if paved with good intentions', has a ring of truth.

For all these reasons what is required is the application of a normative ethical theory. In fact, some theoretical position is an integral part of taking a stand on issues. If I were to recommend an increase in the use of police discretion, for example, I should implicitly commit myself to some theoretical position about the benefits this would bring as well as to a view of current circumstances. It is surely far better to know what one's theoretical position is. Engaging with an ethical theory would suggest ways in which intuitive moral principles might be ranked, selected and arbitrated when moral dilemmas arise. It would also, ideally, satisfy rational criteria: it would not be arbitrary in the ultimate principle or principles which it set and the reasons given for adopting it, or them, would be, at least, plausible. It would demand clear conceptualisation; much founders on a lack of conceptual clarity in the practical domain. Earlier, when discussing dilemmas, I endeavoured to show, but in a way which was far from exhaustive, the importance of defining terms. Too often discussion and action proceeds as if it were obvious what was being talked about or what was required. Conceptions of critical notions, such as fairness or the morality-law relationship, are allowed to pass unexamined when important practical outcomes hang on a clear understanding of their meaning(s). The theory would also give an account of moral reasoning: of how moral principles and factual beliefs contribute to moral judgements and resolutions. Finally, it would require resolute critical thinking of the order which is needed if the moral dilemmas which regularly confront police officers are to be resolved satisfactorily. For this is the sort of rehearsal which makes for effective practice in this area.

The theory which I believe to be by far the most plausible, and to meet the requirements outlined above, is utilitarianism, 'the creed which accepts as the foundation of Morals, Utility or the Greatest Happiness Principle. Utilitarianism holds that actions are right in proportion as they tend to promote happiness, wrong as they tend to produce the reverse of happiness. By happiness is intended pleasure and the absence of pain, by unhappiness, pain and the privation of pleasure', [19] although not in quite this form. But it is not for this reason that I recommend it here. From the point of individuals coming to ethics for the first time, and training/education courses where topics vie with one another for time on the curriculum, this theory is readily understandable, if difficult in application. It is also probably the most influential moral theory in British society today, albeit at a subterranean level for most of the time. Probably most people would not claim to be utilitarians if asked, and yet many also behave and reason as if they were. Utilitarianism is unconsciously taken for granted. This provides the considerable advantage that, as theory, it links with intuitive convictions and makes explicit some elements of conventional moral reasoning.

For the police as a public service utilitarianism has the related advantage that whenever civil servants, those involved professionally in politics and in public administration, talk about what they do, often the underlying assumptions are utilitarian in character so that insights are incidentally gained into aspects of public life. Further, many of our social, legal and institutional arrangements presuppose utilitarianism, a fact hardly surprising given that it has been with us for one hundred and fifty years or so in one influential form or another.

Nor is utilitarianism put forward in any exclusive spirit. There is no shortage in the literature of arguments against utilitarianism. Indeed, rival theories and outlooks often use it to point up their own merits. [20] Objections are raised against the difficulties of utilitarian calculation. The problems of predicting the consequences of actions; of comparing different people's happiness, and even of measuring happiness at all. There are also moral objections which suggest that the utilitarian is prepared to sacrifice other values – honesty, fairness, mercy, beneficence – to utilitarian ends. All this has the considerable advantage of engaging individuals in the process of considering arguments for and against utilitarianism and other rival theories. From my own experience, where moral dilemmas are encounterd, or presented in the form of case studies, say, the application of utilitarianism is a reasonably direct affair which, for the non-utilitarian, acts like a catalyst in making explicit some of the thinking behind otherwise repressed intuitions. And this, after all, is certainly the beginning of what I am concerned be achieved.

---

19 J. S. Mill *Utilitarianism* ed. by Warnock (Fontana 1962).

20 D. Brown *Choices, Ethics and the Christian* (Basil Blackwell 1983).

To conclude briefly, if, as I have argued, the police, in order to enjoy the trust and confidence of the public, need to police towards worthwhile ends in a morally acceptable manner, then applied ethics, as well as such instruments as police codes, are a necessary requirement for officers. [21]

Postscript

An invitation to provide a Postscript to an article one wrote some eight years ago might be considered problematic. Should it be a recantation, a justification or an extension? There is little that I would wish to withdraw, nor do I feel that it needs further justification: the arguments are stated plainly and those that depend upon authority are supported, in the main, by philosophers whose compelling reasoning has withstood criticism.

Extension is a different matter. A spate of recently disclosed miscarriages of justice, the most notorious of which arose out of the Irish Republican Army (IRA) bombing campaign of 1974, the Guildford Four, the Birmingham Six and the Maguire Seven, inevitably raise questions about our judicial system and demand answers. These are currently in the process of being considered by the Royal Commission on Criminal Justice under the chairmanship of Lord Runciman of Doxford. It is due to report in June 1993. A Postscript is not the place for an in-depth treatment of these issues, but a few comments are probably appropriate.

Regrettably, on re-reading the article I have a deep sense of *deja vu*. When the article was written, late in 1983, the police service was the subject of considerable criticism, and the reasons for this are sketched out in the section entitled 'Trust and Confidence.' They are still the object of intense criticism,

---

21 This paper by Neil Richards was published originally in a group of Essays on the police edited by J. R. Thackrall entitled *Contemporary Policing: An examination of society in the 1980s* (Sphere Reference Books). Later, Mr Richards attended the Second Conference of the Centre for Business and Public Sector Ethics held in Cambridge on 14 May 1991, contributing to the discussions, but he did not present a Conference paper. Therefore, as Editor of *Teaching Ethics* Volume I: *Government Ethics*, I selected this earlier essay to appear here and invited Neil Richards to add a *Postscript*.

[*Editor*]: This article is extremely helpful, although I should point out that the term 'Applied Ethics' is one open to debate, as is reliance on the philosophy of Utilitarianism. For my part, I prefer *not* to use the term 'Applied Ethics' but, instead, to adopt the definitions of 'moral conduct' and 'ethical ideals' which I put forward in my book *The British Philosophy of Administration by Rosamund M. Thomas* pp. 140-42, as follows:

> *'Ethics differs from morality in that conduct may be described as "moral" when it is maintained or observed as a fact, but, conduct becomes "ethical" as it rises from fact to idea.'*

However, these points of debate do not detract from the overall importance of the article by Neil Richards: hence its inclusion in this volume. Rather, they point to the complexity of the subject of ethics in both theory and practice.

and yet during the last decade the service has been the subject of strenuous attempts at reform, notably through the *Police and Criminal Evidence Act 1984* (PACE) and the *Prosecution of Offences Act 1985*, both of which grew out of the 1981 *Report of the Royal Commission on Criminal Procedure*. Included under section 66 of PACE is an elaborate code of practice (introduced in 1986) that supersedes the Judges' Rules with more stringent arrangements that seek to provide clear and workable guidelines for the police, balanced by strengthened safeguards for the public.

The Operational Policing Review (OPR, 1990) [22] and consequent Association of Chief Police Officers Strategic Document, *'Setting Standards for Policing: Meeting Community Expectations'* (ACPO, 1990), [23] and the support for the same strategy of Her Majesty's Inspectorate of Constabulary stressing the need for quality of service, are some of the many initiatives within the service which have, and are, eliciting changes to police practice. These initiatives have happened within an environment that is placing ever greater demands upon the police and their services, as evidenced by the seemingly inexorable annual increases in levels of recorded crime. The police meet many of these demands, and are trying to satisfy the general condition, emphasised in the article, that in order to gain the consent and co-operation of the public they must strive to police towards worthwhile ends in a morally acceptable manner.

To reforms can be added other changes. It would not be an exaggeration to claim that cumulatively the service has experienced a managerial revolution during the last decade. This was heralded by the Home Office circular 114/83 issued in 1983, which stressed the need for greater efficiency and effectiveness. It was supported by the full weight of the Financial Management Initiative introduced by the then Prime Minister, Margaret Thatcher, and set in train detailed, thorough-going organisational improvements. Nonetheless, the police are dogged by failures in practice that continue to provide fresh ammunition for their critics. The Tottenham Three convictions for the murder of PC Blakelock during the Broadwater Farm riots in 1985 have been set aside recently as unsound, and the suspension of the West Midlands Police Serious Crime Squad for alleged malpractice are just two instances which have done nothing to allay public concern about police conduct.

How might ethics be expected to contribute to these measures to further improve police practice? In the article I refer to the crime control orientation of the police sub-culture and, in particular, by using the notion of

---

22 *Operational Policing Review* (1990), published by the Police Joint Consultative Committee, Surbiton, Surrey.

23 Association of Chief Officers Strategic Document (1990), printed by the Receiver of the Metropolitan Police District, New Scotland Yard, London.

deception as a vehicle, of the way in which officers responsible for crime investigation, work in an arena of moral hazard marked by critical, moral dilemmas. I refer, too, to the way in which the police have evolved a body of practice which enables them both to cope with such internal circumstances, as well as the requirements set by the nature of their role in a particular social and political order. I have some sympathy, therefore, for answers to this question which are couched in terms of the workings of the police culture, and its resistance, in common with most other cultures and subcultures, to change. [24] I want here, however, to post a number of reminders about less culture specific features of human groups, which might help to explain aspects of police conduct in general and that of officers responsible for criminal investigation in particular.

Immanuel Kant drew attention to the necessary connection between obligation and freedom. [25] Obligation implies freedom, 'I ought' implies 'I can', that is, I can obey or disobey. Although I dealt with some of the conditions influencing the exercise of authority and choice in the article, the general tenor was to assume the workings of conscious, rational activity and moral autonomy. I wrote nothing about the social psychology of those circumstances where the exercise of clear, independent judgement is most difficult. Where the freedom to exercise moral choice is circumscribed in ways that are complex and which involve little or no awareness on the part of the agent.

The sorts of miscarriages of justice mentioned above point to recurrent circumstances under which things have a strong tendency to go badly wrong with pre-trial and, indeed, with trial procedure.

Such circumstances are marked by a general and desperate concern, within a social climate of moral intensity, that the perpetrators of horrific crimes should be apprehended and brought to trial. They are characterised also by the exercise of authority through the institutions of State, including the police service and criminal justice system, to apprehend the perpetrators. This authority is effected in a hierarchical, top-down manner, which is unremarkable in itself but it constitutes the crux of a problem. Despite laments in the 1960s and 1970s about the decline of authority in society at large, within public institutions, and large parts of the private sector, it is still firmly in place. Although this is generally to the advantage of both public institutions and the public they serve, there are disadvantages. The problem is one of zeal, which over-rides procedural requirements.

---

24 M. McConville, A. Sanders and R. Leng *The Case for the Prosecution: Police Suspects and the Construction of Criminality* (London, Routledge 1991).

25 L. W. Beck Editor and Translation *Immanuel Kant: Critique of Practical Reason and Other Writings in Moral Philosophy* (Chicago, 1949).

Under the conditions outlined above, what might be called the Becket syndrome tends to come into play. Whether or not Henry II actually spoke the famous words 'Will no one rid me of this turbulent priest (Archbishop Becket)' he uttered some such words, and four knights, by all accounts loyal, practical people, acted upon them. [26] To formalise this syndrome, if an order, of the sort that is essentially what an organisation is about and which fits with its sense of loyalty, is enunciated by its leadership then the organisation goes into action to realise that order.

Most authority encounters in life result in uncomplicated compliance. Authority is not automatically resisted nor even questioned, and that is as it should be because authority-agent relations are, as Stanley Milgram [27] emphasises, the simple machinery of social routine. What Milgram's experiments have shown convincingly is that sixty-three percent of people when subject to what they take to be legitimate authority are totally conformable to it, and that moral autonomy and choice is severely blunted. This is a result that generalises across gender as well as occupation and nationality. Milgram worked with individuals not groups, but there is research to suggest similar results to the extent that a group is hierarchical, cohesive, insular and subject to legitimate authority, [28] and the police necessarily approximate to such a group. These are counter-commonsensical and uncomfortable findings.

This is not to argue that such factors are sufficient to explain illegitimate practices, but they do, ironically, make such practices more likely in an organisational sub-culture which is intensely committed to securing worthwhile outcomes – the apprehension of violent criminals and the safeguarding of their victims in particular. Because we are in possession of such knowledge about our limitations, we should be better able to understand the determining processes to which we are subject, particularly if we exercise the responsibilities of leadership.

This may enable us to ameliorate the worst effects of such processes in the future. Applied ethics will enable us more readily to identify such situations, and match our 'oughts' to our 'cans' in ways that are more sensitive to our human limitations and thus help to avoid deleterious practices.

Finally, it should be noted that in December 1992 a Code of Police Ethics was put forward (in addition to the existing published Metropolitan Police Code of Ethics to which I refer in my paper). The *'Police Statement of Ethical Principles'* was disseminated at the Quality of Service Seminar held on 8 December 1992 at the Police Staff College, Bramshill. It was disseminated by the Quality of Service Committee (Association of Chief Police Officers: Subcommittee/Working Party on 'Police Ethics').

---

26 W. L. Warren *Henry II* (Methuen 1973).

27 S. Milgram *Obedience to Authority* (New York, Harper and Row 1974).

28 R. Brown *Social Psychology* (New York, The Free Press second edition 1986).

VOLUME I   GOVERNMENT ETHICS

ADDENDUM

Presidential Documents
Executive Order 12834 of January 20, 1993

Ethics Commitments by
Executive Branch Appointees

By the authority vested in me as President of the United States by the Constitution and laws of the United States of America, including section 301 of title 3, United States Code, and sections 3301 and 7301 of title 5, United States Code, it is hereby ordered as follows:

Section 1. *Ethics Pledges.* (a) Every senior appointee in every executive agency appointed on or after January 20, 1993, shall sign, and upon signing shall be contractually committed to, the following pledge ("senior appointee pledge") upon becoming a senior appointee:

"As a condition, and in consideration, of my employment in the United States Government in a senior appointee position invested with the public trust, I commit myself to the following obligations, which I understand are binding on me and are enforceable under law:

"1. I will not, within five years after the termination of my employment as a senior appointee in any executive agency in which I am appointed to serve, lobby any officer or employee of that agency."

"2. In the event that I serve as a senior appointee in the Executive Office of the President ('EOP'), I also will not, within five years after I cease to be a senior appointee in the EOP, lobby any officer or employee of any other executive agency with respect to which I had personal and substantial responsibility as a senior appointee in the EOP."

"3. I will not, at any time after the termination of my employment in the United States Government, engage in any activity on behalf of any foreign government or foreign political party which, if undertaken on January 20, 1993, would require me to register under the Foreign Agents Registration Act of 1938, as amended."

"4. I will not, within five years after termination of my personal and substantial participation in a trade negotiation, represent, aid or advise any foreign government, foreign political party or foreign business entity with the intent to influence a decision of any officer or employee of any executive agency, in carrying out his or her official duties."

"5. I acknowledge that the Executive order entitled 'Ethics Commitments by Executive Branch Appointees', issued by the President on January 20, 1993, which I have read before signing this document, defines certain of the terms applicable to the foregoing obligations and sets forth the methods for enforcing them. I expressly accept the provisions of that Executive order as part of this agreement and as binding on me. I understand that the terms of this pledge are in addition to any statutory or other legal restrictions applicable to me by virtue of Federal Government service".

(b) Every trade negotiator who is not a senior appointee and is appointed to a position in an executive agency on or after January 20, 1993, shall (prior to personally and substantially participating in a trade negotiation) sign, and upon signing be contractually committed to, the following pledge ("trade negotiator pledge"):

"As a condition, and in consideration, of my employment in the United States Government as a trade negotiator, which is a position invested with the public trust, I commit myself to the following obligations, which I understand are binding on me and are enforceable under law:

"1. I will not, within five years after termination of my personal and substantial participation in a trade negotiation, represent, aid or advise any foreign government, foreign political party or foreign business entity with the intent to influence a decision of any officer or employee of any executive agency, in carrying out his or her official duties."

"2. I acknowledge that the Executive order entitled 'Ethics Commitments by Executive Branch Appointees' issued by the President on January 20, 1993, which I have read before signing this document, defines certain of the terms applicable to the foregoing obligations and sets forth the methods for enforcing them. I expressly accept the provisions of that Executive order as part of this agreement and as binding on me. I understand that the terms of this pledge are in addition to any statutory or other legal restrictions applicable to me by virtue of Federal Government service."

Sec. 2. *Definitions*. As used herein and in the pledges:

(a) "Senior appointee" means every full-time, non-career Presidential, Vice-presidential or agency head appointee in an executive agency whose rate of basic pay is not less than the rate for level V of the Executive Schedule (5 U.S.C. 5316) but does not include any person appointed as a member of the senior foreign service or solely as a uniformed service commissioned officer.

(b) "Trade negotiator" means a full-time, non-career Presidential, Vice-presidential or agency head appointee (whether or not a senior appointee) who personally and substantially participates in a trade negotiation as an employee of an executive agency.

(c) "Lobby" means to knowingly communicate to or appear before any officer or employee of any executive agency on behalf of another (except the United States) with the intent to influence official action, except that the term "lobby" does not include:

(1) communicating or appearing on behalf of and as an officer or employee of a State or local government or the government of the District of Columbia, a Native American tribe or a United States territory or possession;

(2) communicating or appearing with regard to a judicial proceeding, or a criminal or civil law enforcement inquiry, investigation or proceeding (but not with regard to an administrative proceeding) or with regard to an administrative proceeding to the extent that such communications or appearances are made after the commencement of and in connection with the conduct or disposition of a judicial proceeding;

(3) communicating or appearing with regard to any government grant, contract or similar benefit on behalf of and as an officer or employee of:

(A) an accredited, degree-granting institution of higher education, as defined in section 1201(a) of title 20, United States Code; or

(B) a hospital, a medical, scientific or environmental research institution; or a charitable or educational institution; provided that such entity is a not-for-profit organization exempted from Federal income taxes under sections 501(a) and 501(c)(3) of title 26, United States Code;

(4) communicating or appearing on behalf of an international organization in which the United States participates, if the Secretary of State certifies in advance that such activity is in the interest of the United States;

(5) communicating or appearing solely for the purpose of furnishing scientific or technological information, subject to the procedures and conditions applicable under section 207(j)(5) of title 18, United States Code; or

(6) giving testimony under oath, subject to the conditions applicable under section 207(j)(8) of title 18, United States Code.

(d) "On behalf of another" means on behalf of a person or entity other than the individual signing the pledge or his or her spouse, child or parent.

(e) "Administrative proceeding" means any agency process for rulemaking, adjudication or licensing, as defined in and governed by the Administrative Procedure Act, as amended (5 U.S.C. 551, *et seq.*).

(f) "Executive agency" and "agency" mean "Executive agency" as defined in section 105 or title 5, United States Code, except that the term includes the Executive Office of the President, the United States Postal Service and the Postal Rate Commission and excludes the General Accounting Office. As used in paragraph 1 of the senior appointee pledge, "executive agency" means the entire agency in which the senior appointee is appointed to serve, except that:

(1) with respect to those senior appointees to whom such designations are applicable under section 207(h) of title 18, United States Code, the term means an agency or bureau designated by the Director of the Office of Government Ethics under section 207(h) as a separate department or agency at the time the senior appointee ceased to serve in that department or agency; and

(2) a senior appointee who is detailed from one executive agency to another for more than sixty days in any calendar year shall be deemed to be an officer or employee of both agencies during the period such person is detailed.

(g) "Personal and substantial responsibility" "with respect to" an executive agency, as used in paragraph 2 of the senior appointee pledge, means ongoing oversight of, or significant ongoing decision-making involvement in, the agency's budget, major programs or personnel actions, when acting both "personally" and "substantially" (as those terms are defined for purposes of sections 207(a) and (b) of title 18, United States Code).

(h) "Personal and substantial participation" and "personally and substantially participates" mean acting both "personally" and "substantially" (as those terms are defined for purposes of sections 207(a) and (b) of title 18, United States Code) as an employee through decision, approval, disapproval, recommendation, the rendering of advice, investigation or other such action.

(i) "Trade negotiation" means a negotiation that the President determines to undertake to enter into a trade agreement with one or more foreign governments, and does not include any action taken before that determination.

(j) "Foreign Agents Registration Act of 1938, as amended" means sections 611-621 of title 22, United States Code.

(k) "Foreign government" means "the government of a foreign country", as defined in section 1(e) of the Foreign Agents Registration Act of 1938, as amended (22 U.S.C. 611(e)).

(l) "Foreign political party" has the same meaning as that term in section 1(f) of the Foreign Agents Registration Act of 1938, as amended (22 U.S.C. 811(f)).

(m) "Foreign business entity" means a partnership, association, corporation, organization or other combination of persons organized under the laws of or having its principal place of business in a foreign country.

(n) Terms that are used herein and in the pledges, and also used in section 207 of title 18, United States Code, shall be given the same meaning as they have in section 207 and any implementing regulations issued or to be issued by the Office of Government Ethics, except to the extent those terms are otherwise defined in this order.

Sec. 3. *Waiver.* (a) The President may grant to any person a waiver of any restrictions contained in the pledge signed by such person if, and to the extent that, the President certifies in writing that it is in the public interest to grant the waiver.

(b) A waiver shall take effect when the certification is signed by the President.

(c) The waiver certification shall be published in the **Federal Register**, identifying the name and executive agency position of the person covered by the waiver and the reasons for granting it.

(d) A copy of the waiver certification shall be furnished to the person covered by the waiver and filed with the head of the agency in which that person is or was appointed to serve.

Sec. 4. *Administration.* (a) The head of every executive agency shall establish for that agency such rules or procedures (conforming as nearly as practicable to the agency's general ethics rules and procedures, including those relating to designated agency ethics officers) as are necessary or appropriate:

(1) to ensure that every senior appointee in the agency signs the senior appointee pledge upon assuming the appointed office or otherwsie becoming a senior appointee;

(2) to ensure that every trade negotiator in the agency who is not a senior appointee signs the trade negotiator pledge prior to personally and substantially participating in a trade negotiation;

(3) to ensure that no senior appointee or trade negotiator in the agency personally and substantially participates in a trade negotiation prior to signing the pledge; and

(4) generally to ensure compliance with this order within the agency.

(b) With respect to the Executive Office of the President, the duties set forth in section 4(a), above, shall be the responsibility of the White House Counsel or such other official or officials to whom the President delegates those duties.

(c) The Director of the Office of Government Ethics shall:

(1) subject to the prior approval of the White House Counsel, develop a form of the pledges to be completed by senior appointees and trade negotiators and see that the pledges and a copy of this Executive order are made available for use by agencies in fulfilling their duties under section 4(a) above;

(2) in consultation with the Attorney General or White House Counsel, when appropriate, assist designated agency ethics officers in providing advice to current or former senior appointees and trade negotiators regarding the application of the pledges; and

(3) subject to the prior approval of the White House Counsel, adopt such rules or procedures (conforming as nearly as practicable to its generally applicable rules and procedures) as are necessary or appropriate to carry out the foregoing responsibilities.

(d) In order to promote clarity and fairness in the application of paragraph 3 of the senior appointee pledge:

(1) the Attorney General shall, within six months after the issuance of this order, publish in the **Federal Register** a "Statement of Covered Activities", based on the statute, applicable regulations and published guidelines, and any other materials reflecting the Attorney General's current interpretation of the law, describing in sufficient detail to provide adequate guidance the activities on behalf of a foreign government or foreign political party which, if undertaken as of January 20, 1993, would require a person to register as an agent for such foreign government or political party under the Foreign Agents Registration Act of 1938, as amended: and

(2) the Attorney General's "Statement of Covered Activities" shall be presumed to be the definitive statement of the activities in which the senior appointee agrees not to engage under paragraph 3 of the pledge.

(e) A senior appointee who has signed the senior appointee pledge is not required to sign the pledge again upon appointment to a different office, except that a person who has ceased to be a senior appointee, due to termination of employment in the executive branch or otherwise, shall sign the senior appointee pledge prior to thereafter assuming office as a senior appointee.

(f) A trade negotiator who is not also a senior appointee and who has once signed the trade negotiator pledge is not required to sign the pledge again prior to personally and substantially participating in a subsequent trade negotiation, except that a person who has ceased employment in the executive branch shall, after returning to such employment, be obligated to sign a pledge as provided herein notwithstanding the signing of any previous pledge.

(g) All pledges signed by senior appointees and trade negotiators, and all waiver certifications with respect thereto, shall be filed with the head of the appointee's agency for permanent retention in the appointee's official personnel folder or equivalent folder.

Sec. 5. *Enforcement*. (a) The contractual, fiduciary and ethical commitments in the pledges provided for herein are enforceable by any legally available means, including any or all of the following: debarment proceedings within any affected executive agency or judicial civil proceedings for declaratory, injunctive or monetary relief.

(b) Any former senior appointee or trade negotiator who is determined, after notice and hearing, by the duly designated authority within any agency, to have violated his or her pledge not to lobby any officer or employee of that agency, or not to represent, aid or advise a foreign entity specified in the pledge with the intent to influence the official decision of that agency, may be barred from lobbying any officer or employee of that agency for up to five years in addition to the five-year time period covered by the pledge.

(1) The head of every executive agency shall, in consultation with the Director of the Office of Government Ethics, establish procedures to implement the foregoing subsection, which shall conform as nearly as practicable to the procedures for debarment of former employees found to have violated section 207 of title 18, United States Code (1988 ed.), set forth in section 2637.212 of title 5, Code of Federal Regulations (revised as of January 1, 1992).

(2) Any person who is debarred from lobbying following an agency proceeding pursuant to the foregoing subsection may seek judicial review of the administrative determination, which shall be subject to established standards for judicial review of comparable agency actions.

(c) The Attorney General is authorized:

(1) upon receiving information regarding the possible breach of any commitment in a signed pledge, to request any appropriate federal investigative authority to conduct such investigations as may be appropriate: and

(2) upon determining that there is a reasonable basis to believe that a breach of a commitment has occurred or will occur or continue, if not

enjoined, to commence a civil action against the former employee in any United States District Court with jurisdiction to consider the matter.

(d) In such civil action, the Attorney General is authorized to request any and all relief authorized by law, including but not limited to:

(1) such temporary restraining orders and preliminary and permanent injunctions as may be appropriate to restrain future, recurring or continuing conduct by the former employee in breach of the commitments in the pledge he or she signed; and

(2) establishment of a constructive trust for the benefit of the United States, requiring an accounting and payment to the United States Treasury of all money and other things of value received by, or payable to, the former employee arising out of any breach or attempted breach of the pledge signed by the former employee.

Sec. 6. *General Provisions.* (a) No prior Executive orders are repealed by this order. To the extent that this order is inconsistent with any provision of any prior Executive order, this order shall control.

(b) If any provision of this order or the application of such provision is held to be invalid, the remainder of this order and other dissimilar applications of such provisior, shall not be affected.

(c) Except as expressly provided in section 5(b)(2) of this order, nothing in the pledges or in this order is intended to create any right or benefit, substantive or procedural, enforceable at law by a party against the United States, its agencies, its officers, or any person.

William J. Clinton

THE WHITE HOUSE
January 20, 1993. [1]

---

1 Reprinted in this Volume 1: *Government Ethics* from the *Federal Register* Vol. 58, No. 13, Friday, January 22, 1993.

United States
Office of Government Ethics
1201 New York Avenue, NW., Suite 500
Washington, DC 20005-3917

December 21 1992

Dr Rosamund M. Thomas
Director
Centre for Business and Public Sector Ethics
Lilac Place, Champneys Walk,
Cambridge CB3 9AW
England

Dear Dr Thomas,

This is in response to your letter of December 2,[1] 1992, in which you request information regarding a number of ethics matters. I am happy to provide you with the following information on the six areas of interest described in your letter.

The transition of President-elect Clinton has issued a "Transition Code of Ethical Conduct" that applies to any person serving as a member of the transition team. A copy of this Code is enclosed.

I am enclosing a copy of Public Law No. 101-194, the Ethics Reform Act of 1989, as originally enacted, together with a copy of Public Law No. 101-280, which made a number of technical corrections in the Ethics Reform Act of 1989. Also enclosed is a copy of section 314 of Public Law No. 102-90, which made amendments to the Ethics Reform Act of 1989, as well as the Ethics in Government Act of 1978.

The Director of OGE is nominated by the President, with the advice and consent of the Senate, and serves for a five year term. I was sworn in as the Director of OGE on August 13, 1990, and I continue to serve as the Director.

On January 25, 1989, President Bush promulgated Executive Order 12668,[2] establishing the President's Commission on Federal Ethics Law Reform. On March 9, 1989, the Commission issued its report "To Serve With Honor" which discussed ethics issues and presented certain recommendations. Contemporaneously, on February 2, 1989, a Bipartisan Task Force on

Ethics was appointed in the House of Representatives. The Task Force received input from the Commission in developing legislation that was eventually enacted as the Ethics Reform Act of 1989. Enclosed is a copy of the report of the Bipartisan Task Force on Ethics that provides background on the relationship between the Commission's report and the Ethics Reform Act of 1989.

The Commission's report made 27 principal recommendations. An excerpt from the report listing the 27 recommendations is enclosed for your reference. [3] The current status of those recommendations is as follows: recommendations implemented – 4, 12, 13, 14, 17, 18, 19, 21, 24, 25; recommendations implemented in part – 2, 3, 5, 6, 7, 8, 10, 11, 16, 20; recommendations not implemented – 1, 9, 15, 22, 23, 26, 27.

With regard to your final question, this Office is in the process of developing proposed regulations that will implement certain authorities or directives contained either in the Ethics Reform Act of 1989 or in an Executive Order [4]. These include: (1) an interpretive regulation dealing with 18 U.S.C. § 208 (conflict of interest); (2) an interpretive regulation dealing with 18 U.S.C. § 209 (private supplementation of salary); (3) a regulation providing for a general waiver of certain interests from coverage under 18 U.S.C. § 208(a) pursuant to 18 U.S.C. § 208(b) (2); and (4) a regulation providing guidance for the issuance of individual waivers of 18 U.S.C. § 208(a) pursuant to 18 U.S.C § § 208(b) (1) and 208(b) (3). It is anticipated that these proposed regulations will be published for public comment during the coming year.

I hope that this information is useful as you prepare your material for publication. If I may be of further assistance, please do not hesitate to contact my Office.

Sincerely,

Stephen D. Potts
Director

---

1 My letter of December 2, 1992 to Mr Stephen Potts enquired about the latest situation regarding ethics matters and about the relationship between the report 'To Serve with Honor' and its recommendations reprinted in this Volume 1, pp. 155-60, and the Ethics Reform Act of 1989. Extracts from Mr Potts' letter in reply are given above. [Editor]

2 Executive Order 12668 is reprinted in this Volume 1, pp. 165-66.

3 See this Volume, pp. 155-60 for the 27 recommendations.

4 See the new Executive Order 12834 of January 20, 1992 reprinted in this Volume 1, pp. 683-90.

VOLUME I   GOVERNMENT ETHICS

Bibliography

Bibliography
(Selected)

ABELSON, Raziel 'History of Ethics' *Encyclopaedia of Philosophy Vol. 3* (U.S.A., New York, MacMillan and Free Press, 1967)

ABSE, L. *Margaret, Daughter of Beatrice: A Psychobiography of Margaret Thatcher* (London, Jonathan Cape, 1989)

ADLER, Mortimer J. and CAIN, Seymore *Ethics: The Study of Moral Values* (U.S.A., Chicago, Encyclopaedia Britannica, 1962)

*ALDRIDGE [1], John H., MILLER, Gary J., OSTROM Jr, Charles W. and ROHDE, David W. *American Government* (U.S.A., Boston, Houghton, 1986)

ALI, Shaukat, 'Ethics in Administration: A Study in the Moral Side of Human Enterprise' *Pakistan Administrative Review* Vol 14, Oct-Dec 1976 (Pakistan, Lahore, 1976)

AMERICAN POLITICAL SCIENCE ASSOCIATION MEMBERSHIP DIRECTORY (U.S.A., Washington, American Political Association, 1985)

ARENDT, Hannah *On Violence* (U.S.A., New York, Harcourt Brace and World, 1969)

ARNOLD, Matthew 'Stanzas from the Grande Chartreuse' in Frost, William ed. *Romantic and Victorian Poetry* (U.S.A., Englewood Cliffs, New Jersey, 1955)

ARTHUR, P., *The Government and Politics of Northern Ireland* Second edition (London, Longman, 1984)

ASSOCIATION OF CHIEF POLICE OFFICERS' STRATEGIC DOCUMENT (London, printed by the Receiver of the Metropolitan Police District, New Scotland Yard, 1990)

BAILEY, Stephen 'Ethics and the Public Service' *Public Administration and Democracy*, MARTIN, Roscoe C. ed. (U.S.A., Syracuse, Syracuse University Press, 1965)

---

1 For the significance of the asterisk, marked against thirty American Government Text Books in this Bibliography, see Chapter 24 by Professor Leicester R. Moise, Note 2, p. 380.

BARBOUR, Richard 'Ethics and Nuclear War' *Organizational Policy and Development*, Moise, Leicester R. ed. (U.S.A., Centre for Continuing Studies, University of Louisville, 1984)

BARNES, Gerald 'Utilitarianism' *Ethics* 82, Number 1 October 1971

BECK, L. W. ed. and trans. 'Immanual Kant: Critique of Practical Reason and Other Writings in Moral Philosophy' (U.S.A., Chicago, 1949)

BECK, Robert N. ed. *Aristotle*, 'Happiness and Virtue' *Perspectives in Philosophy*, (U.S.A., New York, Holt Rinehart and Winston, 1975)

BELLAH, Robert N. 'Social Science as Practical Reason' *Ethics and the Social Sciences, and Policy Analysis*, Callahan, Daniel and Jennings, Bruce eds. (U.S.A., New York, Plenum, 1983)

BENN, A. 'Manifestos and Mandarins' in Rodgers, W. et al, *Policy and Practice: the Experience of Government* (London, Royal Institute of Public Administration, 1980)

BENN, A. *Arguments for Democracy* (London, Harmondsworth, Penguin Books, 1982)

BENYON, J. *The Police: Powers, Procedures and Proprieties* (Oxford, Pergamon, 1986)

BENYON, J. *The Roots of Urban Unrest* (Oxford, Pergamon, 1987)

BIOGRAPHICAL DIRECTORY (U.S.A., Washington, American Political Science Association, 1988)

BOWIE, Norman E. 'Preface' *Ethical Issues in Government* (U.S.A., Philadelphia, Temple University Press, 1981)

BOWMAN, James S. and ELLISTON, Frederick A. *Ethics, Government and Public Policy: a Reference Guide* (U.S.A., New York, Greenwood Press, 1988)

BRANDT, Richard B. 'The Real and Alleged Problems of Utilitarianism' *Hastings Center Report* 13, Number 2, April 1983

BROAD, C. D. *Five Types of Ethical Theory* (Routledge, 1930)

BROAD, C. D. *Religion, Philosophy and Psychical Research* (Routledge, 1953)

BROAD, C. D. 'War Thoughts in Peace Time' reprinted in Broad, C. D. *Religion, Philosophy and Psychical Research* (Routledge, 1953)

BROCK, Daniel W. 'Truth or Consequences: The Role of Philosophers in Policy-Making' *Ethics* 97, Number 4 July 1987

BROOKS, John *The Takeover Game* A Twentieth-Century Fund Book (U.S.A., New York, E. P. Dutton, 1987)

BROWN, R. *Social Psychology* Second edition (U.S.A., New York, The Free Press, 1986)

BUCHANAN, Allen 'A Critical Introduction to Rawl's Theory of Justice' *John Rawl's Theory of Social Justice: an Introduction* Blocker, H. Gene and Smith, Elizabeth H. eds. (U.S.A., Athens, Ohio University Press, 1980)

BUCHANAN, James and TULLOCK, Gordon *The Calculus of Consent* (U.S.A., Ann Arbor, University of Michigan Press, 1962)

*BURNHAM, Walter D. *Democracy in the Making* (U.S.A., Englewood Cliffs, Prentice-Hall, 1983)

*BURNS, James M., PELTASON, J. W. and CRONIN, Thomas E. *Government by the People* (U.S.A., Englewood Cliffs, Prentice-Hall, 1988)

CAIDEN, Gerald E. 'Ethics in the Public Service: Codification Misses the Real Target' *Public Personnel Management* 10, April 1981

CALLAHAN, Daniel and JENNINGS, Bruce 'Introduction' *Ethics, the Social Sciences and Policy Analysis* Callahan, Daniel and Jennings, Bruce eds. (U.S.A., New York, Plenum, 1983)

CANADA 'Diminishing Privacy is a Part of Life in Information Age' *Toronto Star* 23 November 1986

CANADA 'Gutted - FOI Bill Angers Opposition' *Ottawa Citizen* 9 June 1982

CHAPEL, Yves *The Comparative Study of Administrative Measures for the Eradication of Corruption* Research Prospectus (IIAS, Brussels, June 1972) Unpublished Report

CHAPMAN, L. *Your Disobedient Servant: the Continuing Story of Whitehall's Overspending* (London, Chatto and Windus, 1978; Harmondsworth, Penguin Books, 1979)

CHAPMAN, Richard A. *Ethics in the British Civil Service* (London, Routledge, 1988)

CHATURVEDI, T. N. 'Value-Orientation in Human Problem Solving' *Management in Government* Vol. 15 July-September 1981

Congressional Ethics (U.S.A., Washington, Congressional Quarterly Inc., 1980) 'Corruption and Reform: An Editorial Essay' *Corruption and Reform* Vol. 1 Number 1, 1986

COX, B., SHIRLEY, J., and SHORT, M. *The Fall of Scotland Yard* (London, Harmondsworth, Penguin Books, 1977)

*CUMMINGS, Milton C. and WISE, David *Democracy Under Pressure* (U.S.A., New York, Harcourt, 1989; Sixth edition pub. Brace, Jovanovich)

*CURRY, James A., RILEY, Richard B. and BATTISTONI, Richard M. *Constitutional Government* (U.S.A., New York, West, 1989)

DETTER DE LUPIS, Ingrid *The Law of War* (Cambridge University Press)

DOIG, A. *Corruption and Misconduct in Contemporary British Politics* (London, Harmondsworth, Penguin Books, 1984)

DUNSIRE, Andrew 'Bureaucratic Morality in the United Kingdom' *International Political Science Review* 9 July 1988

DUNSIRE, A. and HOOD, C. C. *Cutback Management in Public Bureaucracies* (Cambridge and New York, Cambridge University Press, 1989)

DWIVEDI, O. P. 'Conclusions: A Comparative Analysis of Ethics, Public Policy and the Public Service' *Ethics, Government and Public Policy: a Reference Guide* Bowman, James S. and Elliston, Frederick A. eds. (U.S.A., New York, Greenwood Press, 1988)

DWIVEDI, O. P. and ENGLEBERT, E. A. 'Education and Training for Values and Ethics in the Public Service: An International Perspective' *Public Personnel Management* 10 April 1981

DWIVEDI, O. P. 'Ethics and Administrative Accountability' *Indian Journal of Public Administration* 29, July-September 1983

DWIVEDI, O. P. 'Ethics and Values of Public Responsibility and Accountability' *International Review of Administrative Sciences* 51, 1985

DWIVEDI, O. P. 'Moral Dimensions of Statecraft: A Plea for Administrative Theology' *Canadian Journal of Political Science* December 1987

DWIVEDI, O. P. 'Public Service Ethics', *International Institute of Administrative Sciences* (Belgium, Brussels, June 1978)

DWIVEDI, O. P. 'Teaching Ethics in Public Administration Courses' *International Review of Administrative Sciences* 54, March 1988

DWIVEDI, O. P. 'Teaching Ethics in Public Policy and Administrative Courses' *Public Policy and Administrative Studies* Dwivedi, O. P. ed. (Canada, Guelph, University of Guelph, 1986)

DWIVEDI, O. P. ed. *The Administrative State in Canada* (Canada, Toronto, University of Toronto Press, 1982

*EBENSTEIN, William C., PRITCHETT, Herman, TURNER, Henry A. and MANN, Dean *American Democracy* (U.S.A., New York, Harper and Row, 1970)

EDEL, Abraham 'Ethics Applied or Conduct Enlightenment' *Ethical Principles and Practice* Howie, John ed. (U.S.A., Carbondale, Southern Illinois Press, 1987)

*EDWARDS, David V. *The American Political Experience* (U.S.A., Englewood Cliffs, Prentice-Hall, 1988)

EMBRY, Charles R. 'Ethics and Public Administration' *News for Teachers of Political Science* (U.S.A., American Political Science Association, Number 42, Summer 1984)

FITZWALTER, R. and TAYLOR, D. *Web of Corruption* (London, Granada, 1981)

FLEISHMAN, Joel L., LIEBMAN, Lance and MOORE Mark H. eds. *Public Duties: The Moral Obligations of Government Officials* (U.S.A., Cambridge, Harvard University Press, 1981)

FLINT, David *The Philosophy and Principles of Auditing* (London, MacMillan, 1988)

FRANKENA, William K. *Ethics* (U.S.A., Englewood Cliffs, Prentice Hall, 1963)

FRIEDRICH, C. J. *Constitutional Government and Politics* (U.S.A., New York, Harper and Brothers, 1937)

FRIEDRICH, C. J. *Secrecy Versus Privacy: Democratic Dilemma* (London, MacMillan, 1977)

FRY, G. K. *The Changing Civil Service* (London, George Allen and Unwin, 1985)

GARLAND, Michael 'Politics, Legislation and Natural Death' *Hastings Center Report* Vol. 6 Number 5 October 1976

GERTH, H. H. and MILLS, C. Wright *From Max Weber: Essays in Sociology* (U.S.A., New York, Oxford University Press, 1958)

GILCHRIST, Chris 'Getting in on this Good Thing. The Chancellor's Gift to the Small Investor' *The Daily Telegraph* 7 August 1982

*GITELON, Alan R., DUDLEY, Robert L., DUBNICK, Melvin J. *American Government* (U.S.A., Dallas, Houghton, 1988)

GOAR, Carol 'National Affairs' *Toronto Star* 5 July 1988

GOLEMBIEWSKY, Robert *Men, Management and Morality: Towards a new Organizational Ethics* (U.S.A., New York, McGraw Hill Book Co., 1965)

GOODPASTER, Kenneth E. 'Is Teaching Ethics Making or Doing' *Hastings Center Report* Vol 12 Number 1 February 1982

GRAY, A. G. and JENKINS, W. I. eds. *Policy Analysis and Evaluation in British Government* (London, Royal Institute of Public Administration, 1983)

GRAY, A. G. and JENKINS, W. I. eds. *Administrative Politics in British Government* (Brighton, Wheatsheaf Books, 1985)

HARE, R. M. *Moral Thinking it's Levels, Methods and Point* (Oxford University Press, 1981)

HECLO, H. and WILDAVSKY, A. *The Private Government of Public Money* (London, Macmillan, 1974)

HENNESSY, Peter 'Genetic Code of Conduct Inherited by Mandarins' *The Independent* 5 June 1989

HINDUSTANI TIMES NEW DELHI 'Demand to Repeal Official Secrets Act' 23 April 1989

HOSKYNS, J. 'Conservatism is not enough' *Political Quarterly* 55 3-16 1984

HOUSE OF COMMONS, Expenditure Committee 1976-77 *Eleventh Report, The Civil Service: HC 535-I* (London, HMSO, 1976)

*JANDA, Kenneth, BERRY, Jeffery M., GOLDMAN, Jerry *The Challenge of Democracy* (U.S.A., Boston, Houghton, 1989)

JENKINS, K. CAINES, K. and JACKSON, A. *Improving Management in Government: the Next Steps. Efficiency Unit: Report to the Prime Minister* London, HMSO, 1988)

JONSEN, Albert R. and BUTLER, Lewis H. 'Public Ethics and Policy Making' *Hastings Center Report* Vol. 5 Number 4 August 1975

KAPLAN, Abraham *American Ethics and Public Policy* (U.S.A., New York, Oxford University Press, 1963)

KATEB, George 'The Moral Distinctiveness of Representative Democracy' *Ethics* Vol. 91 Number 3 April 1981

*KATZNELSON, Ira and KESSELMAN, Mark *The Politics of Power* (U.S.A., New York, Harcourt, 1987)

KATZNELSON, Ira and KESSELMAN, Mark *A Critical Introduction to American Government* 2nd edition (U.S.A., New York, Harcourt, 1987)

KERNAGHAN, Kenneth *Ethical Conduct: Guidelines for Government Employees* (Canada, Toronto, Institute of Public Administration of Canada, 1975)

*LADD, Everett C. *The American Polity* (U.S.A., New York, Norton, 1987)

LEIGH, D. *The Frontiers of Secrecy: Closed Government in Britain* (London, Junction Books, 1980)

*LELOUP, Lance T. *Politics in America* (U.S.A., St Paul, West, 1989)

LEVINE, Carol 'Do Ethics Testing Get a Passing Grade' *Hastings Center Report* Vol. 13 Number 3 June 1983

LINKLATER, M. and LEIGH, D. *Not with Honour* (London, Sphere Books, 1986)

*LINEBERRY, Robert L. *Government in America* (U.S.A., Boston, Scott Foresman, 1989)

*LIPSITZ, Lewis and SPEAK, David M. *American Democracy* (U.S.A., New York, St Martins, 1969)

LOCKE, John 'A Priori-Liberalism' *Political Ideologies* Gould, James A. and Truitt, William H. eds. (U.S.A., New York, MacMillan, 1973)

LYONS, David *Ethics and the Rule of Law* (U.S.A., Cambridge, Cambridge University Press, 1984)

MACINTYRE, Alasdair 'Why is the Search for the Foundation of Ethics so Frustrating' *Hastings Center Report* Vol. 19 Number 4 August 1979

*MACKENZIE, G. Calvin *American Government* (U.S.A., New York, Random House, 1986)

MACKENZIE, W. J. M. *Politics and Social Science* (U.S.A., Baltimore, Penguin, 1967)

MACKLIN, Ruth 'Theoretical and Applied Ethics' *Applied Ethics and Ethical Theory* Rosenthal, David and Shehadi, Fadlon eds. (U.S.A., Salt Lake City, University of Utah Press, 1988)

MAHESHWARI, S. R. 'Secrecy in Government in India' *Indian Journal of Public Administration* Vol. 25 October-December 1979

MARTY, William R. 'The Search for Realism in Politics and Ethics' *The Ethical Dimension of Political Life* Canavan, Francis ed. (U.S.A., Durham, Duke University Press, 1983)

MARX, F. M. *The Administrative State: an Introduction to Bureaucracy* (U.S.A., Chicago University Press, 1957)

MASLOW, A. *Motivation and Personality* (New York, Harper and Row, 1954)

McCONVILLE, M., SANDERS A., LENG R. 'The Case for the Prosecution: Police Suspects and the Construction of Criminality' (London, Routledge, 1991)

701

McDOUGAL, William *Ethics and Some Modern World Problems* (U.S.A., New York, Putnam, 1924)

METCALFE, L. and RICHARDS, S. *Improving Public Management* (London, Sage, 1987)

MILGRAM, S. *Obedience to Authority* (U.S.A., New York, Harper and Row, 1974)

*MORLAN, Robert L. *American Government* (U.S.A., Boston, Houghton, 1975)

MOTIWAL, O. P. 'Secrecy in Government in India' *The Indian Journal of Public Administration* Vol. 25 Oct-Dec 1979

NIGRO, Felix, A. and NIGRO, Lloyd G. *The New Public Personnel Administration* (U.S.A., Ithaca, Illinois, F. E. Peacock Publishers Inc., 1976)

Operational Policing Review (Police Joint Consultative Committee, Surbiton, Surrey, 1990)

*PARENTI, Michael *Democracy for the Few* (U.S.A., New York, St Martins, 1974)

PARRIS, H. *Constitutional Bureaucracy* (London, Allen and Unwin, 1969)

*PATTERSON, Samuel C., DAVIDSON, Roger H. and RIPLEY, Randall B. *A More Perfect Union* (U.S.A., Pacific Grove, Brooks/Cole, 1989)

PENNOCK, Ronald and CHAPMAN, John W. eds. *Privacy* (U.S.A., New York, Atherton Press, 1971)

*PIOUS, Richard M. *American Politics and Government* (U.S.A., New York, McGraw-Hill, 1986)

PLANO, Jack C. and GREENBERG, Milton *The American Political Dictionary* (U.S.A., New York, Holt, 1985)

PONTING, C. *The Right to Know: the Inside Story of the Belgrano Affair* (London, Sphere Books, 1985)

*PREWITT, Kenneth, VERBA, Sidney *An Introduction to American Government* (U.S.A., Cambridge, Harper and Row, 1988)

PURTHLO, Ruth B. 'Ethics Teaching in Allied Health Fields' *Hastings Center Report* Vol. 8 Number 2 April 1978

*PYNN, Ronald E. *American Politics* (U.S.A., Monterey, Brooks Cole, 1987)

RACHELS, James 'Can Ethics Provide Answers' *Applied Ethics and Ethical Theory* Rosenthal, David M. and Shehadi, Fadlon eds. (U.S.A., Salt Lake City, University of Utah Press, 1988)

BIBLIOGRAPHY

RAU, Chalopathi M. 'Official Secrets and Freedom of Information in India' *Indian Journal of Public Administration* Vol. 25 October-December 1976

REDFORD, Emmette S. *Democracy in the Administrative State* (U.S.A., New York, Oxford University Press, 1969)

REINER, R. *The Politics of the Police* (Brighton, Wheatsheaf Books, 1985)

REINER, R. 'Dixon's Decline: Why Policing Has Become So Controversial' *Contemporary Record* Vol. 3(1), 2-6 1989

REST, James R. 'A Psychologist Looks at the Teaching of Ethics' *Hastings Center Report* Vol. 12 Number 1 February 1982

ROBITSCHER, Jonas B. 'The Right to Die' *Hastings Center Report* Vol. 2 Number 4 September 1972

ROHR, John A. *Ethics for Bureaucrats: an Essay on Law and Values* (U.S.A., New York, Marcel Dekker Inc., 1978)

ROSE, R. *Governing without Consensus: an Irish Perspective* (London, Faber and Faber, 1971)

*ROSS, Robert S. *American National Government* (U.S.A., Guildford, Duskin, 1988)

ROWAT, D. ed. *Administrative Secrecy in Developed Countries* (London, MacMillan, 1977; translated from French, 1979)

ROYAL INSTITUTE OF PUBLIC ADMINISTRATION *Top Jobs in Whitehall: Appointments & Promotions in the Senior Civil Service* (London, RIPA, 1987)

RYN, Claes G. *Democracy and the Ethical Life* (U.S.A., Baton Rouge, Louisiana State University Press, 1978)

SAMUELSON, Paul *Economics* (U.S.A., Baton Rouge, Louisiana State University Press, 1978)

*SCHMIDT, Steffen, SHELLEY, Mack C. and BARDES, Barbara A. *American Government and Politics Today* (U.S.A., New York, West, 1989)

*SHEA, John C. *American Government and Politics* (U.S.A., New York, St Martins, 1987)

SIMMEL, Arnold 'Privacy' *International Encyclopaedia of the Social Sciences* Vol. 12

*SKIDMORE, Max J. and TRIPP, Marshall C. *American Government* (U.S.A., New York, St Martins, 1989)

SLOAN, Douglas 'The Teaching of Ethics in the American Undergraduate Curriculum' *Hastings Center Report* Vol. 9 Number 6 December 1979

SMITH, R. Michael 'The Purposes of Undergraduate Curriculum Reconsidered' *News for Teachers of Political Science* American Political Science Association, Number 53 Spring 1987

SMITH, T. *British Politics in the Post-Keynesian Era* (London, The Action Society Trust, 1986)

SNYDER, David P. 'Privacy: The Right to What?' *The Bureaucrat* Vol. 5 July 1976

STAHL, O. Glenn *Public Service Administration* (U.S.A., New York, Harper & Row, 1976)

STALKER, J. *Stalker* (London, Harrap, 1987)

STEINBERGER, Peter 'Objectives of the Undergraduate Curriculum' *News for Teachers of Political Science* Americam Political Science Association, Number 46 Summer 1985

*STEPHENSON, D. Grier, BRESLER, Robert J., FRIEDRICH, Robert J. and KARLESKY, Joseph J. *American Government* (U.S.A., Cambridge, Harper and Row, 1988)

*STONE, Alan and BARKE, Richard *Governing the American Republic* (U.S.A., New York, St Martins, 1988)

TELLIER, Paul M. 'The Obligations of Public Service' (Apex Symposium, Ottawa, Canada, 21 January 1988)

THOMAS, Rosamund 'British Administrative History, Culture and Values' *Public Policy and Administrative Studies* Dwivedi, O. P. ed. (Canada, Guelph, University of Guelph, 1988)

THOMAS, Rosamund *The British Philosophy of Administration* (Cambridge, Centre for Business and Public Sector Ethics, July 1989)

THOMAS, Rosamund 'The Duties and Responsibilities of Civil Servants and Ministers: a Challenge within British Cabinet Government' *International Review of Administrative Sciences* Vol. 52 No. 4 (December 1986). Reprinted in this Volume 1: *Government Ethics,* pp. 383-408.

THOMAS, Rosamund *Espionage and Secrecy: the British Official Secrets Acts 1911-1989* (London, Routledge and New York, Routledge Chapman and Hall, 1991).

THOMAS, Rosamund 'The Politics of Efficiency and Effectiveness in the British Civil Service' *International Review of Administrative Sciences* Vol. L No. 3, Autumn 1984

THOMPSON, Dennis F. 'Moral Responsibilities of Public Officials: The Problem of Many Hands' *American Political Science Review* Vol. 74 Number 4 December 1980

THOMPSON, Dennis F. *Political Ethics and Public Office* (U.S.A., Cambridge, Harvard University Press, 1987)

THOMPSON, Dennis F. 'The Possibility of Administrative Ethics' *Public Administration Review* 45, September-October 1985

TONG, Rosemarie *Ethics in Policy Analysis* (U.S.A., Englewood Cliffs, Prentice-Hall, 1986)

TWEEDIE, David and WHITTINGTON, Geoffrey 'Financial Reporting: Current Problems and their implications for Systematic Reform' *Accounting and Business Research* Vol. 21, No. 81, 87-102 1990

WADE, H. W. R. *Administrative Law* Fifth Edition (Oxford, Clarendon Press, 1982)

WALDO, Dwight *The Administrative State* (U.S.A., New York, Ronald Press, 1948)

WALDO, Dwight and MARX, F. M. *The Administrative State: an Introduction to Bureaucracy* (U.S.A., Chicago, Chicago University Press, 1957)

WARREN, W. L. 'Henry II' (Methuen, 1973)

WARWICK, Donald P. *The Teaching of Ethics in the Social Sciences* (U.S.A., Hasting-on-Hudson, The Hastings Center, 1980)

WARWICK, Donald P. 'The Ethics of Administrative Discretion' *Public Duties: the Moral Obligations of Government Officials* Fleishman, Joel L., Libman, Lance and Moore, Mark eds. (U.S.A., Cambridge University Press, 1981)

WASS, D. *Government and the Governed* (London, George Allen & Unwin, 1984)

*WEISSBERG, Robert *Understanding American Government* (U.S.A., New York, Random House)

*WELCH, Susan, GRUHL, John, STEINMAN, Michael and COMER, John C. *American Government* (U.S.A., New York, West, 1986)

WHITTINGTON, Geoffrey *Financial Reporting: Current Problems and Future Direction* (London, Institute of Chartered Accountants in England and Wales, 1990)

WIDDICOMBE *The Conduct of Local Authority Business* Cmnd. 9797 (London, HMSO, 1986)

WILLIAMS, D. G. T. *Not in the Public Interest* (London, Hutchinson, 1965)

WILSON, D. ed. *The Secrets File: the Case for Freedom of Information in Britain Today* (London, Heineman, 1984)

WOLF, Charles Jr. 'Ethics and Policy Analysis' *Public Duties: the Moral Obligations of Government Officials* Fleishman, Joel L., Libman, Lance and Moore, Mark eds. (U.S.A., Cambridge University Press, 1981)

*WOLL, Peter *American Government* (U.S.A., New York, Random House, 1989)

WOLL, P. and ZIMMERMAN, S. E. *American Government: The Core* Second edition (U.S.A., New York, McGraw-Hill, 1992 - previous edition 1989)

WORTHLEY, J. A. 'Ethics and Public Management Education and Training' *Public Personnel Management* 10 April 1981

YOUNG, H. *One of Us: a Biography of Margaret Thatcher* (London, Croom Helm, 1989)

YOUNG, H. and SLOMAN, A. *No, Minister: an Inquiry into the Civil Service* (London, British Broadcasting Corporation, 1982)

GOVERNMENT REPORTS/LAWS

CANADA/

Access and Privacy: the Steps Ahead (Ottawa 1987)

An Act Respecting the National Archives of Canada 35-36 Elizabeth II, 1987

BILL C-15, 31 at Parliament, 28 known as the Elizabeth II *Freedom of Information Act, 1979*

BILL C-43, 29-30-31, Elizabeth II, Chapter III
An Act to enact the Access to Information Act and the Privacy Act, to amend the Federal Court Act and the Canada Evidence Act, and to amend certain other Acts in consequence thereof 1982

The Canada Elections Act

Canadian Criminal Code

Civil Service Amendment Act 1908

Civil Service Act 1918

COMMISSION OF INQUIRY CONCERNING CERTAIN ACTIVITIES OF THE ROYAL CANADIAN MOUNTED POLICE, *Second Report 'Freedom and Security under the Law'* (Ottawa, 1981)

CONSUMER AND CORPORATE AFFAIRS CANADA AND THE DEPARTMENT OF COMMUNICATIONS *From Gutenberg to Telidon: a Guide to Canada's Copyright Revisions Proposals* (Ottawa, 1984)

DEPARTMENTS OF COMMUNICATIONS AND JUSTICE *Computers and Privacy* (Ottawa, 1972)

DEPARTMENT OF THE SECRETARY OF STATE *Green Paper on Legislation on Public Access to Government Documents* (Ottawa, 1977)

DEPARTMENT OF THE SECRETARY OF STATE *Legislation on Public Access to Government Documents* (Ottawa, 1977)

HOUSE OF COMMONS, REPORT OF THE STANDING COMMITTEE ON JUSTICE AND SOLICITOR GENERAL ON THE REVIEW OF THE ACCESS TO INFORMATION ACT AND THE PRIVACY ACT *Open and Shut: enhancing the right to know and the right to privacy* (Ottawa, 1987)

INTERIM POLICY GUIDE PART II AND FEDERAL COURT, TRIAL DIVISION *Order in the Matter of Piller Sausages and Delicatessens Ltd. and the Minister of Agriculture and the Information Commissioner of Canada and Jim Romahn* (8 September 1987)

INTERIM POLICY GUIDE PART II AND FEDERAL COURT, TRIAL DIVISION *Order in the matter of Air Atonabee Ltd. and the Minister of Transport* (19 October 1988)

MINISTER OF SUPPLIES AND SERVICES *Commission of Inquiry into the facts of allegations of conflict of interest concerning the Honourable Sinclair M. Stevens* (1987). Reprinted in this Volume *Government Ethics*, pp. 479-516.

OFFICE OF THE ASSISTANT DEPUTY REGISTRAR GENERAL OF CANADA *Conflict of Interest and Post-Employment Code for Public Office Holders* (September 1985)

Order in Council R.C. 1985 - 3783 (27 December 1985)

Public Service Act 1967

Revised Statutes of Canada 1970, 1985

The Parliament of Canada Act

To Know and Be Known: the Report of the Task Force on Government Information (Ottawa, 1969)

TREASURY BOARD OF CANADA *Communications Policy of the Government of Canada, Chapter 480, Administrative Policy Manual* (Ottawa, 1988)

TREASURY BOARD OF CANADA *Conflict of Interest and Post-Employment Code for the Public Service* (October 1985)

TREASURY BOARD OF CANADA *Government Security Policy* Circular 1986-40 (Ottawa, 1986)

TREASURY BOARD OF CANADA *Index of Federal Information Banks 1979* (Ottawa, 1979)

TREASURY BOARD OF CANADA *Interim Policy Guide to the Access to Information Act and the Privacy Act, Part II* (Ottawa, 1983)

TREASURY BOARD OF CANADA *Policy on Data-Matching and Control of the Social Insurance Number* (Ottawa, TBS Circular 1989-12, 1989)

INDIA/

Indian Official Secrets Act 1889

Indian Official Secrets Act 1923

Indian Penal Code

Press (Emergency Powers) Act

MALAYSIA/

PRIME MINISTER'S OFFICE, GOVERNMENT OF MALAYSIA *Guide to Excellence in Service* (1 January 1979)

UNITED KINGDOM/

Administration of Justice (Miscellaneous Provisions) Act 1933

Army Act 1955

Air Force Act 1955

The Citizen's Charter Cm. 1599 (HMSO, 1991)

The Civil Service Report of the Committee 1966-68 Chairman: Lord Fulton (London, Cmnd. 3638)

Companies Act 1985

Courts Martial (Appeals) Act 1968

Criminal Justice Act 1987, 1988

Criminal Justice Act 1987 (Notice of Transfer) Regulations 1988

Criminal Law Act 1977

Defence (Transfer of Functions) Act 1964

Efficiency and Effectiveness in the Civil Service: Government Observations on the Third Report from the Treasury and Civil Service Committee HC 236 Cmnd. 8616 (1981-1982)

Epitome of the Public Accounts Committee Reports 1857 to 1937

Financial Services Act 1986, 1988

Geneva Conventions 1949 AND 1977

HER MAJESTY'S TREASURY *Competing for Quality* Cm. 1730 (London, HMSO, 1991)

HER MAJESTY'S TREASURY *Central Government: Financial Accounting and Reporting Framework* (London, HMSO, 1988)

HER MAJESTY'S TREASURY *Policy Evaluation: a Guide for Managers* (London, HMSO, 1988)

TREASURY AND CIVIL SERVICE COMMITTEE 1987-88 EIGHTH REPORT *Civil Service Management Reform: the Next Steps* HC 494, (London, HMSO, 1988)

Magistrates Courts Act 1980

Magistrates' Courts (Notices of Transfer) Rules 1988

NATIONAL AUDIT OFFICE *A Framework for Value for Money Audits*

NATIONAL AUDIT OFFICE *Ministry of Defence: Prices paid for Spare Parts* HC 34 (London, HMSO, 1992)

NATIONAL AUDIT OFFICE *Quality of Service: War Pensions; Mobility Allowance; Attendance Allowance; Invalid Care Allowance* HC 24 (London, HMSO, 1992)

NATIONAL AUDIT OFFICE *Review of the Operations of HM Land Registry* (London, HMSO, 1987)

NATIONAL AUDIT OFFICE *Use of Operating Theatres in the National Health Service* (London, HMSO, 1987)

Naval Discipline Act 1987

Official Secrets Act 1911, 1923, 1989

Police and Criminal Evidence Act 1984

Prevention of Fraud (Investments) Act 1958

Queen's Regulations for the Army (London, HMSO)

Sexual Offences Acts 1956 AND 1967

Status of Forces Agreement Annex A(J) to Chapter 7 of Queen's Regulations

1763 Treaty of Paris

UNITED STATES OF AMERICA/

Freedom of Information Act 1966 (at Federal level), amended in 1974 and 1976. Also Freedom of Information legislation at State level.

Ethics in Government Act of 1978 (at Federal level)

Ethics Reform Act of 1989 (at Federal level)

EXECUTIVE ORDER 11222 *United States Code Standards for Ethical Conduct* (May 8, 1965)

EXECUTIVE ORDER 12668 *President's Commission on Federal Ethics Law Reform* (January 25, 1989)

EXECUTIVE ORDER 12834 *Ethics Commitments by Executive Branch Appointees* (January 20, 1993)

VOLUME I   GOVERNMENT ETHICS

Index

Index

ACAS Code of Disciplinary Practice and Procedures in Employment 463

access, legislation (Canada) 108, 233, 252

Access Act (Canada) 230, 236, 237, 238, 240, 242, 244, 245, 246, 247, 248, 249, 250, 251, 252, 253, 254, 524, 605, 615, 616, 618, 622, 626, 627, 632

Access Acts, general 237, 601, 602

access law, France 607, 629

access laws, Canadian Provinces 602

Access of the Public to Documents in Administrative Files Act 1970 (Denmark) 601

access to information (general) 201, 251, 292, 499, 599, 601

access to information (Canada) 255

Access to Official Information Act 1978 (Netherlands) 601

accountability 231, 233, 235, 301, 302, 316, 332, 349, 385, 386, 387, 397, 405, 476

accountability, police 660, 672

Accounting Standards Board 32

Act Respecting the National Assembly (Quebec, Canada) 550

Administrative Appeals Tribunal Act 1975 (Australia) 628, 634, 637, 638

Administrative Appeals Tribunal (Australia) 634, 635, 636, 637, 638, 639, 640, 641, 642, 643, 645, 646, 647, 648, 649

Administrative Decisions (Judicial Review) Act 1977 (Australia) 626, 628, 634, 637

Administrative Procedure Act 1946 (USA) 600

Advisory Committee on Business Appointments (UK) 447

AIDS 76, 77

Air Force Act 1955 (UK) 67, 68, 69, 76, 78

Aird Report 494, 499, 502, 503, 510

Armed Forces Act 1991 69, 78

Armstrong, Sir (Lord) Robert 5, 9, 10, 58, 328, 385, 389, 390, 391, 402

Armstrong Memorandum 9, 10, 50, 58-62, 385, 386, 387, 388, 410, 441

Army Act 1955 (UK) 67, 68, 69, 76, 78, 256, 257, 258

Army General Administrative Instructions 71

Audit Manual 34

Auditing Practices Committee 34, 39

behaviour, honourable 330

behaviour, unethical 342

Benefits Agency 30

Bill C-6 (Canada) 121, 125, 126, 129, 140

Bill C-15 (Canada) 235, 236, 238

Bill C-43 (Canada) 120, 121, 147, 236, 535, 537

Bill C-46 (Canada) 120, 121, 125, 126, 127, 129, 130, 132, 134, 519, 535

Bill C-61 (Canada) 121

Bill C-62 (Canada) 105, 125, 126, 129, 140

Bill C-82 (Canada) 105

Bill C-114 (Canada) 118, 121, 125, 126, 129, 132, 134, 535

Bridges, Sir Edward (later Lord) 21, 23, 25

713

Browne, John, M.P., 559, 562-5
Bullock, Sir Christopher 24, 25, 26
Business Appointments Rules (UK) 445

censorship 305
character ethics 206
Charter of Rights and Freedoms 1985 Statute Law Amendment (Canadian) 244
Citizen's Charter (UK) 29, 279, 408
Civil Service 3, 5, 9, 14, 18, 22, 23, 24, 26, 27, 28, 48, 49, 50, 51, 53, 54, 55, 56, 57, 59, 60, 62, 63, 64, 65, 66
Civil Service, Canada 124
Civil Service, Northern Ireland 64
Civil Service Act (Nova Scotia, Canada) 553, 554
Civil Service Commission (UK) 3, 64-5
Civil Service ethic 26
Civil Service (Management Functions) Act 1992 (UK) 408
Civil Service Order in Council 1969 422
Civil Service Orders in Council 1991 49, 63, 65, 66, 392, 400, 408
Civil Service Pay and Conditions of Service Code (now superseded by the Civil Service Management Code) 49, 53, 57, 62, 410, 418, 422, 435, 436
Civil Service Reform Act 1978 (USA) 407
code(s) of conduct 24, 49, 56, 109, 115, 129, 148, 209, 343, 351, 352, 442, 486, 520
code of conduct, press 602
Code of Conduct and Ethics for the

Public Service of Alberta (Canada) 542, 543
Code of Ethical Conduct (Saskatchewan, Canada) 545
Code of Ethics, British civil servants 388
Code of Practice, Civil Service discipline 462
Code of Practice, British press 287
Codes of Practice, Police (UK) 259, 671-3, 679
Commission for Racial Equality Code of Practice: Race Relations 463
Commonwealth Crimes Act 1914-73 (Australia) 608
conduct, general principles 5
conduct, standards of 8
confidence, in government 352
confidential sources 291
confidentiality 44, 50, 61, 239, 261, 262, 263, 264, 271, 274, 275, 277, 280, 303, 337, 338, 442, 443, 630, 635
confidentiality, British Nuclear Fuels industry 270
confidentiality, Cabinet 633
conflict of interest 7, 9, 10, 25, 42, 103, 105, 106, 107, 108, 109, 110, 111, 112, 114, 117, 118, 119, 121, 122, 123, 124, 125, 126, 127, 128, 129, 130, 133, 134, 135, 136, 137, 138, 140, 141, 142, 143, 144, 145, 146, 150, 151, 152, 156, 167, 168, 174, 191, 204, 339, 341, 342, 343, 362, 394, 399, 400, 469, 471, 473, 474, 476, 478, 479, 480, 481, 482, 483, 484, 485, 486, 487, 488, 489, 491, 492, 493, 494, 495, 496, 499, 501, 503, 504, 507, 508, 509, 510, 511, 512, 517, 519, 521, 522, 523, 524, 525, 530, 531, 533, 535, 536, 537, 538, 539, 540, 541, 542, 543,

544, 546, 547, 549, 550, 551, 552, 553, 554, 555, 556, 557, 558, 566, 567, 568, 575, 576, 587, 588

conflict of interest, guidelines 110, 111, 113, 115, 143, 351, 474, 523, 529, 533

Conflict of Interest Act (New Brunswick, Canada) 552, 553

Conflict of Interest Act (Newfoundland, Canada) 556, 557

Conflict of Interest Act (Prince Edward Island, Canada) 555

Conflict of Interest and Post-Employment Code for Public Office Holders (Canada) 529, 531, 532, 533, 534, 535, 538, 539, 540, 543

Conflict of Interest and Post-Employment Code for the Public Service (Canada) 532, 534, 536

Conflict of Interest and Post-Employment Guide for Public Office Holders 115

conflict of interest code (Canada) 343, 477, 480, 482, 483, 485, 486, 488, 489, 492, 497, 498, 500, 505, 517

Conflict of Interest Directive (Canada) 541

conflict of interest guidelines, New Brunswick, Canada 553

Conflict of Interest Guidelines for Cabinet Ministers and Parliamentary Assistants 1990 (Ontario, Canada) 548

Conflict of Interest Guidelines for Ministers and Parliamentary Secretaries 522

Conflict of Interest Guidelines for Ministers of the Crown (Canada) 480, 483

Conflict of Interest (Ministers) Guidelines (Newfoundland, Canada) 556, 557

conflict of interest legislation 119, 120, 124, 127, 150, 155, 163, 511, 525

conflict of interest policy 504

conflict of interest policy, Manitoba (Canada) 545, 546, 547

Conflict of Interest (Public Employees) Regulations (Newfoundland, Canada) 556, 557

conflict of interest régimes, non-statutory 122, 123

conflict of interest régimes, statutory 122, 123, 124, 128

conflict of interest regulation, UK 572

conflict of interest regulation 131

Conflict of Interest Regulation (New Brunswick, Canada) 552

conflicts of interest statute (USA) 150

conflict of interest rules 129, 521, 526, 528

Conflict of Interest Rules (Manitoba, Canada) 545, 547

conflict of loyalties 9, 337

Constitution Act (British Columbia, Canada) 539, 541

Copyright, Designs and Patents Act 1988 (UK) 443

Copyright Act (Canada) 242

Crimes Act 1961 (New Zealand) 606

Criminal Code (Canada) 529, 530

Crown Prosecution Service (UK) 5

D Notices 99, 100, 101

Data Act 1973 (Sweden) 602, 603

Davies v. Presbyterian Church of Wales [1986] 419, 426

Department of Social Security (UK) 30

Department of Transport (UK) 27

diplomacy 2

Diplomatic Service   1, 2, 3, 4, 5, 6, 7, 8, 9, 11, 12, 15, 16, 17, 19, 64

Diplomatic Service Order in Council 1964   4

Diplomatic Service Order in Council 1991   5, 63, 65

Diplomatic Service Orders   12, 14, 18

Diplomatic Service Regulations   4, 5, 6, 7, 8, 10, 19

Directives to Members of the Executive Council concerning Conflicts of Interest (Quebec, Canada) 551, 552

drugs   77, 78

Duties and Responsibilities of United Kingdom Civil Servants (see also Armstrong Memorandum)   5

economy   21, 30, 31, 36, 37, 38, 39, 41, 44, 45, 46

Edwards v. Skyways Ltd. [1964]   419, 427

effectiveness   21, 30, 32, 36, 37, 38, 39, 41, 44, 45, 46, 318, 395

efficiency   21, 30, 31, 36, 37, 38, 39, 41, 44, 45, 46, 278, 316, 395

efficiency, police   659, 660

Efficiency and Effectiveness in the Civil Service   27

Efficiency Unit   27, 29, 55, 322

effectiveness   278

effectiveness, police   660, 669

effectiveness, public sector   348

Employment Protection Act 1975 (UK)   424

Employment Protection (Consolidation) Act 1978 (UK)   424

Equal Access to Justice Act (USA)   180

Equal Opportunities Commission Code of Practice   463

Equal Pay Act 1970 (UK)   424

espionage   212, 213, 214, 215, 242, 337

Espionage Act (USA)   607

ethic(s)   1, 26, 105, 146, 675

ethic, professional   48

ethic, public service   160, 333

ethical approach   32

ethical behaviour/conduct   32, 33, 107, 110, 175, 204, 206, 207, 355, 358, 359, 360, 361, 368, 372, 377, 475, 518, 526

ethical code   205

ethical code, Civil Servants   387

ethical considerations   365

ethical dilemmas, predicaments/ problems   72, 144, 152, 161, 243, 308, 315, 339, 341, 347, 348, 389, 407, 480, 661

ethical dimension, public management   349

ethical doubts   331

ethical guidelines   344, 352, 374

ethical issues   150, 174, 192, 365, 366, 370, 373, 525, 528

ethical lapses   525

ethical precepts   311

ethical principles   107, 173, 207, 244, 342, 357, 376, 663

ethical problems, police   663

ethical propriety   156

ethical régime   114

ethical rules/regulations   148, 154, 179, 196

ethical standard(s) 2, 3, 6, 40, 42, 72, 114, 148, 149, 154, 155, 159, 160, 168, 172, 177, 193, 197, 205, 334, 351, 369, 370, 477

ethical standards, police   657, 664, 677

ethical standards, press   287, 363

ethical technology   411

ethical theory   357, 358, 364, 367, 372, 375, 676

ethical values   355, 372, 519

ethical violations 155, 168, 177

ethics, administrative 345, 363

ethics, AIDS testing 76

ethics, applied 520, 659, 660, 666, 673, 675, 678, 681

ethics, bureaucratic 337, 362, 363

ethics, business 203, 262

ethics, Canada 519

ethics, corporate 519

ethics, education 168, 186, 188, 193, 195, 313, 347, 363, 365, 376, 653

ethics, egoism 365, 366

ethics, environmental 203, 320

ethics, governance 315, 327, 336

ethics, government/public sector 20, 103, 110, 114, 115, 121, 122, 130, 132, 146, 148, 165, 170, 172, 184, 185, 201, 203, 204, 205, 313, 316, 317, 320, 334, 337, 339, 347, 348, 350, 351, 352, 365, 366, 367, 381, 409, 471, 520, 521, 599, 653

ethics, government secrecy 209

ethics, information law 230

ethics, legal 363

ethics, marketplace 522

ethics, medical 363

ethics, military 67, 71, 79

ethics, normative 374

ethics, of stewardship 317

ethics, personal 272

ethics, physical violence 75

ethics, policy 172, 173, 178, 184, 359, 364

ethics, political 105, 106, 355, 357, 358, 360, 361, 362, 364, 365, 367, 374, 375, 376, 377, 378

ethics, professional 303

ethics, programmes 168, 170, 171, 172, 175, 177, 185, 186, 187, 188, 189, 191, 197

ethics, public 206, 218, 373

ethics, public school 332

ethics, teaching/training 57, 168, 178, 180, 186, 188, 189, 193, 194, 197, 199, 313, 347, 348, 354, 358, 359, 363, 364, 365, 376, 378, 518, 653

ethics, utilitarian 366

ethics, war 79-81

ethics agreements 181, 183, 184, 191

Ethics in Government Act 1978 (USA) 121, 130, 132, 133, 134, 158, 167, 180, 185, 189, 190, 191, 192, 193, 197, 362, 374, 474, 500, 510

Ethics Reform Act 1989 (USA) 121, 126, 130, 132, 134, 168, 169, 172, 173, 175, 176, 177, 179, 180, 181, 182

ethics legislation 150, 154, 171, 174, 186, 189, 192

ethics of responsibility 204

ethics of ultimate ends 204

ethics watchdog, Canada 524

ethos 26, 31, 48, 49, 333

ethos, government 148

ethos, military 71

ethos, professional 31

ethos, public service 57

Evidence Act (Canada) 236

Exchequeur and Audit Act 1866 (UK) 21

Executive Order 12668 (USA) 149, 165

Executive Order 12674 (USA) 168, 175, 176, 177, 179, 180, 189, 197

Executive Order 12731 (USA) 175, 189

Executive Order 12834 (USA) 683-690

Executive Power Act (Quebec, Canada) 550, 551

expense account fiddling 74

Export of Goods (Control) Order 1991 264 268

Federal Advisory Committee Act (USA)   175
Federal Court Act (Canada)   236
Financial Disclosure Act (Canada)   539, 540, 541
Financial Management Initiative (UK)   21, 28, 55
Fisher, Sir Warren   21, 23, 24, 25
Foreign and Commonwealth Office (UK)   1, 2, 3, 4, 5, 6, 8, 9, 10, 22, 100, 269, 284, 301, 446
Foreign Gifts Act (USA)   175
Forensic Science Service   27, 28
Franks Committee 1972   404, 607, 625
freedom, individual   53
freedom, press   264
Freedom of Access to Administrative Documents Law 1978 (France)   601, 614
freedom of information   210, 217, 245, 249, 326, 403
freedom of information, initiatives   233
freedom of information, reform   233
Freedom of Information Act 1966 (USA)   173, 174, 178, 180, 600, 601, 603, 606, 607, 608, 613, 614, 615, 616, 617, 618, 621, 622, 623, 625, 627, 630
Freedom of Information Act 1982 (Australia)   602, 604, 605, 610, 611, 616, 617, 618, 624, 626, 627, 628, 629, 630, 631, 632, 637
Freedom of Information Amendment Act 1983 (Australia)   612, 627, 629, 632, 634
Freedom of Information Act (Canada),   235, 601, 602, 629, 630, 632 See also Access Act (Canada)
Freedom of Information Act (India) (arguments for)   209, 218
Freedom of Information Act (UK) (arguments for)   281, 326, 403, 404, 606
freedom of information legislation   234, 245, 250, 404, 405, 601, 602, 607, 608, 617
freedom of information legislation, New Zealand (known as the NZ Official Information Act 1982)   602, 628, 629, 630, 631, 632, 633
freedom of information legislation, Scandinavia   610
freedom of information legislation, Sweden   622, 625, 630
freedom of speech   293, 303, 308
Freedom of the Press Act 1949 (Sweden)   600, 601 603, 606, 612, 619, 620
Fulton Committee Report 1968 (UK)   21, 27, 65

Geddes, Sir Eric   24, 25
genetic code of ethics   11, 26, 411
government accounting   20, 21, 23

Hague Conventions 1907   80
homosexual acts   69
homosexuality   76, 78
honesty   3
honesty, intellectual   365
House of Assembly Act (Nova Scotia, Canada)   553, 554
House of Commons Disqualification Act 1975 (UK)   461

House of Commons Trade and Industry Committee Second Report: *Exports to Iraq: Project Babylon and Long Range Guns* 264, 268, 269

Human Rights Act (Canada) 232, 250

Ibbs Report 'Improving Management in Government: the Next Steps' 28

Import, Export and Customs (Defence) Act 1939 (UK) 268

Indian Civil Service 2, 24; *see also* this *Volume 1*, Chapter 10, pp. 203-18

Industrial Relations Act 1971 (UK) 424

information law (Canada) 230, 231, 234, 235, 236, 237, 253; *see also* freedom of information

Inland Revenue Commissioners v. Hambrook [1956] 419, 423, 427

Inquiry Commission Act (India) 217

irreproachable conduct 8

John Browne M.P. Case 562-5

Kerr Committee (Australia) 636, 647

Kodeeswaran v. Attorney-General of Ceylon [1970] 419, 420, 423, 427

Lam Yuk-ming v. Attorney-General [1980] 419, 425, 427

Leech v. Deputy Governor of Parkhurst Prison [1988] 431

Legislative Assembly Act (Yukon, Canada) 536

Legislative Assembly and Executive Council Act (North West Territories, Canada) 537, 538, 539

Legislative Assembly and Executive Council Act (Saskatchewan, Canada) 544, 545

Legislative Assembly and Executive Council Conflict of Interest Act (Manitoba, Canada) 545, 546

Legislative Disabilities Act (Newfoundland, Canada) 556, 557

lobbyists 105, 106, 133

loyalty 2, 9, 49, 56, 317, 327, 328, 342, 385, 386

loyalty, police 670, 671

loyalty, professional 329

Machine Tools Saga; 264 *see also* Scott, L.J.; *see also Matrix Churchill* trial

Maclaren v. The Home Office [1990] 419, 424, 430, 432, 433, 438, 439

Management Information Systems for Ministers (MINIS) 27

Manual of Military Law 79, 85

Matrix Churchill trial 264

Members and Public Employees Disclosure Act (Nova Scotia, Canada) 553, 554

Members' Conflict of Interest Act 1988 (Ontario, Canada) 547, 548, 549, 550

Members of Parliament and Conflict of Interest (Green Paper, Canada) 110, 121, 125, 126, 140

Members of the Legislative Assembly Conflict of Interests Act (Saskatchewan, Canada) 544, 545

military law (UK) 256; *see also* Military Ethics, this *Volume 1* Chapter 4, pp. 67-100

moral attitudes 74

moral code 203, 208

moral behaviour/conduct 355, 671

moral considerations 365

moral dilemmas 517, 663, 672, 673, 674, 675, 678

moral dilemmas, police 658, 664, 666, 667
moral expectations 316, 325
moral government 345, 352, 353
moral judgements 350
moral principles 204, 207, 304, 342, 345, 373, 376, 668, 671, 673, 674
moral problems 144
moral practices/standards 133, 149, 344, 661, 665
moral theory 675
moral thinking 21
moral values 11, 203, 206, 356, 364, 658
morality 2, 9, 204, 210, 340, 345, 350, 351, 372, 374, 663, 668, 672, 673,674
morality, of drug taking 77
morality, police 661, 665, 666
morality, public office 339, 352
morals, and law 303, 304, 306

National Archives of Canada Act 242
National Audit Act 1983 (UK) 22, 30, 38
National Audit Office (UK) 20, 22, 30, 31, 32, 34, 36, 37, 39, 40, 42, 43, 45, 47, 262, 309, 322
National Defence Act (Canada) 530
National Security Act 1984 (USA) 613
Naval Discipline Act 1957 67
'Next Steps' agencies 28, 51, 54, 55, 302, 415
'Next Steps' Initiative 21, 28, 54, 65, 279, 408
Northcote-Trevelyan Report 1854 2, 64, 392, 409

Office of Government Ethics (USA) 129, 132, 135, 150, 151, 153, 154, 155, 158, 159, 162, 163, 164, 165, 167, 168, 169, 170, 171, 172, 174, 175, 177, 178, 179, 180, 181, 182, 183, 184, 185, 187, 188, 189, 190, 191, 192, 193, 194, 195, 196, 197, 199, 510
Office of Program Assistance and Review (USA) 185
official information 442, 443
Official Information Act 1982 (New Zealand) 404, 606, 609, 616, 617, 618, 619, 623, 628, 631, 632, 633; see also Freedom of Information
official secrets 78
Official Secrets Act 1911 (UK) 212, 256, 295, 311, 326, 328, 329, 383, 404, 440, 606
Official Secrets Act 1920 (UK) 256
Official Secrets Act 1939 (UK) 256
Official Secrets Act 1989 (UK) 212, 256, 278, 279, 295, 326, 383, 404, 466, 606
Official Secrets Acts 1911-1989 (UK) 4, 9, 19, 44, 52, 61, 78, 87, 93, 100, 256, 257, 258, 263, 274, 311, 328, 329, 442, 599
Official Secrets Act 1939 (Canada) 606
Official Secrets Act 1889 (India) 212, 214, 215, 217, 218
Official Secrets Act 1923 (India) 212, 213, 216, 217, 219, 221
Official Secrets Act 1951 (New Zealand) 606
Official Secrets Act 1937 (Sweden) 606
official secrets law, Australia 606
official secrets legislation 277
official secrets legislation,USA 607
Ombudsman Act 1976 (Australia) 626, 634
O'Reilly v. Mackman 439-40

Parker Enquiry (Canada) 118

Parliament of Canada Act 107, 120, 147, 530, 531, 535

Parliamentary Oaths Act 1886 (UK) 294

Parliamentary Papers Act 1840 (UK) 294

period of 'calculation' 21, 27

period of 'ethos and tradition' 21, 23, 27

period of 'rules' 21, 22

Police 318, 321, 330-1, 657-79

Police and Criminal Evidence Act 1984 (UK) 258, 259, 677

political activities 6

Ponting case 383, 384, 402, 415

post-employment 131, 132, 168, 193, 540, 541

post-employment advice 176

post-employment code (Canada) 105, 115, 116, 475, 478, 480, 481, 483, 484, 521, 527, 529, 535, 538, 539, 545; *see also* Conflict of Interest and Post Employment Code

post-employment culpability 134

post-employment guidelines 114, 115

post-employment legislation 135

post-employment obligations 112, 534

post-employment practices 119

post-employment principles 111

post-employment provisions 130, 133, 134, 136, 548

post-employment questions 122

post-employment régime 126, 131, 132, 145, 476

post-employment restrictions 134, 150, 152, 158, 160, 167, 169, 175, 180, 554

post-employment strictures 123, 127, 132

post-employment training 186

Premier's Guidelines on Conflict of Interest 1990 (Ontario, Canada) 547

President of the Methodist Conference v. Parfitt 419, 426

Press (Emergency Powers) Act (India) 215

Prevention of Corruption Act 1906, 1916 (UK) 446

privacy 201, 210, 211, 217, 232, 237, 240, 241, 243, 246, 247, 255, 270, 272, 288, 509, 582, 597, 603, 606, 668

privacy, Australia 605

privacy, business 604, 605

privacy, Canada 499, 605

privacy, legislation 233, 237, 252

Privacy Act 1978 (France) 615

Privacy Act (Canada) 230, 236, 240, 241, 242, 244, 245, 250, 252, 602

Privacy Act (USA) 173, 174, 178, 180, 197, 603, 604, 621

privilege, Parliamentary 292, 293, 294, 295, 296

probity 2, 8, 11, 26, 316, 411, 413, 571

Prosecution of Offences Act 1985 (UK) 677

Public Access to Documents in the (Official) Administration 1970 (Norway) 601

Public Government Act (Yukon, Canada) 536, 537

Public Inquiries Act (Canada) 543

Public Inquiries Act (Ontario, Canada) 548

Public Service Act (North West Territories Canada) 537, 538

Public Service Act (Ontario, Canada) 550

Public Service Act (Quebec, Canada) 550, 551

Public Service Act (Saskatchewan, Canada) 544, 545

Public Service Employment Act (Canada) 535
Public Services Act (British Columbia, Canada) 541
Publicity of Documents Act 1951 (Finland) 601

Queens Regulations 71, 72, 73, 78, 82, 85, 89, 93

R. v. Lord Chancellor's Department ex parte Nangle [1991] 49
R v. Civil Service Appeal Board ex parte Bruce [1988] 417, 419, 420, 423, 424, 428, 429, 431, 434, 435, 436, 437, 439
R v. Derbyshire County Council ex parte Noble [1990] 419, 429, 439
R v. East Berkshire Health Authority ex parte Walsh [1984] 419, 420, 429, 435, 436, 439, 440
R v. Panel on Takeovers and Mergers ex parte Datafin plc [1987] 419, 428
R v. Secretary of State for Foreign and Commonwealth Affairs ex parte Council of Civil Service Unions [1985] 419, 431
R v. Secretary of State for the Home Department ex parte Attard [1990] 419, 431, 432, 433
R v. Secretary of State for the Home Department ex parte Benwell [1985] 419, 431, 432, 433
Rayner Scrutinies 27, 322
recruitment 3, 63
Recruitment and Assessment Services (UK) 3, 65, 66, 392
Regulation 881 (1989), see Public Service Act (Ontario, Canada) 550
Reilly v. The King [1934] 419, 423, 424
reliability 2, 144

right of access 232
rights, individual 53
Rogers v. Booth [1937] 419, 426
Rose and Frank Co v. J. R. Crompton and Bros Ltd. [1923] 426
Royal Canadian Mounted Police Act (Canada) 530
rules of conduct 3, 203
Saskatchewan (Canada) Public Employees Conflict of Interest Guidelines 544, 545
Scott L.J., Inquiry under (November 1992) 264
secrecy 53, 201, 210, 211, 212, 213, 214, 245, 250, 251, 271, 277, 279, 280, 326, 338, 599, 606
secrecy, and the press 215
secrecy, government 203, 209, 211, 219, 237, 597
secrecy, official 211
Secrecy Act 1980 (Sweden) 606, 607, 612, 619, 620
secrecy legislation, USA 607
secret information 298
secrets, trade 456, 457
Servants of the Crown (Parliamentary, European Assembly and Northern Ireland Assembly Candidature) Order 1987 461
Service Acts (UK) 67, 71, 74, 78, 85
Service Discipline Acts (UK) 257, 258
Sex Discrimination Act 1975 (UK) 424
Sexual Offences Acts 1956, 1967 69, 78
Sharp, Mitchell 114, 131, 133, 134, 143, 474, 476
Sharp-Starr Report (Canada) see Starr-Sharp Report
Social Security Benefits Agency 28, 55
Social Security Pensions Act 1975 (UK) 466

St Petersburg Convention 1868 80

Standard of Conduct for Public Service Employees (Canada) 474

standards, professional 40, 42

standards of conduct 1, 57, 69, 72, 106, 115, 148, 160, 167, 168, 177, 179, 181, 188, 189, 193, 197, 208, 330, 349; *see also* conduct

standards of conduct, Civil Service 441

Standards of Conduct Guidelines for Public Servants (British Columbia Canada) 539, 541

standards of propriety 445

Starr, Michael 114, 131, 133, 134, 143, 472, 474

Starr-Sharp Report 115, 132, 143, 472, 474, 494, 501, 502, 506, 510

Status of Forces Agreement 68

statutory provisions 4

Stevens, Sinclair M. (Canada) 117, 343, 479, 480, 481, 482, 483, 484, 485, 486, 487, 489, 490, 491, 492, 493, 497, 498, 502, 515

Street v. Mountford [1985] 419, 426

Super Gun affair 264, 265, 268

Theft Act (UK) 295

Trade Union and Labour Relations Act 1974 (UK) 424

Treasury and Civil Service Committee (Westminster) 28

trust 75, 105, 106, 144, 335, 336, 342

trust, in government/public service 352, 475, 534, 541

trust, in police 657, 658, 662, 665, 670, 673, 676

trust, in public officials 344, 353

truthfulness 2, 3

United States' Code 474; *see also* end of index

Unemployment Benefit Offices 27

unethical activities 344

unethical activity 340, 351

unethical behaviour 207

unethical conduct 205, 207, 208, 338, 339, 341, 342

Value for Money (VFM) Audit 45, 322

Value for Money (VFM) Investigations 7

Watergate affair 110, 121, 122, 233, 394

Westland affair 301, 328, 383, 384, 385, 386, 387, 388, 393, 400, 402, 405, 406, 415

White Paper, 'Competing for Quality' (UK) 29

2 U.S.C. 701 (USA) 500

5 U.S.C. App. 180

5 U.S.C. App. 402 197

5 U.S.C. section 7351 169

5 U.S.C. section 7353 169

18 U.S.C. section 202-209 (USA) 175

18 U.S.C. section 203 (USA) 162

18 U.S.C. section 204 (USA) 163, 164

18 U.S.C. section 205 (USA) 162, 163

18 U.S.C. section 207 (USA) 160, 163, 169, 175, 176, 180

18 U.S.C. section 208 (USA) 127, 155, 156, 157, 162, 163, 168, 169, 175, 180, 181, 183, 189, 191, 192

18 U.S.C. section 209 (USA) 143, 163, 168, 180

28 U.S.C. section 535 (USA) 197

31 U.S.C. section 1353 169, 190

5 C.F.R. Part 2634   179, 183
5 C.F.R. Part 2635   175, 179
5 C.F.R. Part 2636   179
5 C.F.R. Part 2637   180
5 C.F.R. Part 2638   179, 180, 185, 193, 197
5 C.F.R. Part 2600   180
5 C.F.R. Part 2641   180
5 C.F.R. Part 735   175 (replaced in 1992 by Part 2635)
41 C.F.R. Part 301-1   180
48 C.F.R. Part 3   180

1975 Premier's Statement re: Senior Public Officials – Public Disclosure of Interest (Alberta, Canada) 542-3